Principles of Engineering St

1. Stories enable people to share an understanding of user needs.
2. Stories help people to focus on user benefits, instead of on technical solutions.
3. Stories help to protect requirements from deletion or well-meaning editing.
4. More generally, stories provide a pattern for new requirements (probably related to existing ones) to follow.
5. Stories help people to identify and resolve feature interactions.
6. Stories help to justify proposed features and requirements.
7. Stories help to elicit requirements (that may have been assumed to be obvious).
8. Stories can index features and requirements.
9. Stories provide engineers with an overview of stakeholder needs.
10. Stories describe wanted behaviour.
11. Stories, being end-to-end descriptions at user level, are the right kind of structure to prioritise (all the requirements needed in a story must have at least that story's priority).
12. Stories are conveniently stable units of specification reuse, whereas individual (atomic) requirements are vulnerable to technological change.
13. If requirements are carefully (accurately and completely) traced back to stories, those stories form a means of recycling requirements in subsequent products.
14. Stories can serve as a 'corporate memory' for design decisions.
15. Stories help to explore side effects, consequences, and easily forgotten situations that need to be designed for.

from Chapter 16, Story Use and Reuse in Automotive Systems

Principles of Storyboarding

- Scan adds milk to database of historical purchases
- Ambiguous brands and amounts are resolved from the history
- History started by scanning in old receipts
- Each bar code scan = one amount of that size

Bad Milk

recycle

swipe barcode

Trash

Collect together actual sequences (scenarios) with similar primary intents into consolidated as-is sequences.

Lay out the detailed steps of the redesigned work—guided by the consolidated sequences—showing Process, User Interface, and System steps. Draw a storyboard cell for each step.

Explore the implications of the storyboards to guide User Environment Design (system modelling).

(This is an example *System* step, as users are not involved.)

based on Chapter 10, The Role of Scenarios in Contextual Design

SCENARIOS, STORIES, USE CASES

Through the Systems Development Life-Cycle

Edited by

IAN ALEXANDER AND NEIL MAIDEN

John Wiley & Sons, Ltd

CONTENTS

PREFACE

A quoi ça sert?
What's it for?

President Chirac of France,
on being shown a famous white elephant,
the Millennium Dome, Greenwich

Communicating Needs

Much of the recent history of large engineering projects—software or systems—has been a tale of waste, error, mismanagement, over-optimism, and lack of proper planning for likely costs and risks. Projects come in late, over budget, and with miserably reduced functionality. Systems sometimes never work, fail on their first period of operational stress, or are permanently unreliable and costly to maintain. We will not name names, as it is fruitless to play the blame game; indeed, engineering systems badly and passing blame are two sides of the same coin. In any case, it is all too easy to find examples in news reports of the demise of famous projects.

By the way, we do not think this is a software issue: it seems to affect complex systems of diverse kinds. The solution cannot therefore be a matter of finding better software-specific tools and techniques; it must be something that helps master complexity.

People have suggested many possible cures for this disease. Most come down to two things:

- the needs that systems are supposed to fulfil ought to be defined much earlier and far more carefully;
- people on projects ought to be made aware of and become skilled in techniques to define needs adequately.

We think that a critical element that is therefore lacking is communication and, in particular, skill in techniques for communicating needs. With the other authors of this book, we believe that the scenario is one of the most powerful techniques for discovering and communicating requirements and often the first choice for organising them.

On a lighter note, scenarios pass the party test, where the requirements engineer has to explain what he or she does for a living to a stranger in 15 seconds. Where

> "I'm a systems, errm, a requirements engineer, and I help to specify complex systems..."

gets a glazed look every time; the description

> "I get people to tell the stories of what their systems are meant to do, so they build the right thing"

always seems to work (and even arouse interest). Story telling is so obviously sensible that it seems surprising that it has taken so long to become a mainstream engineering activity.

Scenarios and Requirements

If you are wondering whether we recommend replacing requirements entirely with scenarios in all circumstances, we can at once tell you that we think that distinctly unwise, for several reasons:

- The main strength of scenarios is in telling the story of functional behaviour; it is possible to cover various non-functional aspects with stories, but it is doubtful whether such coverage could ever be comprehensive—even if that were desirable.
- Many engineers, organisations, and standards bodies are strongly attached to traditional requirement forms (like 'The system shall ... '), and if those forms work for those people, they should continue using them—anyway, they may have little choice if they have to comply with standards. People work better with familiar artefacts and work processes, even if these sometimes seem to outsiders to be sub-optimal.
- Making a scenario approach work well often requires flair, experimentation, and the courage to take risks, for example, running active workshops rather than writing up requirements in a back room. The implied style of engineering simply does not suit everybody.
- the needs governing large projects are complex and require a range of information structures including stakeholder and goal models, business rules, algorithms and formal specifications of behaviour, interface definitions (protocols, data structures, hardware connections), and commercial and physical constraints (like cost, size, and weight), many of which cannot be framed as scenarios.

Other vital ingredients of a successful project include

- realistic and supportive managers, including one who champions the project;
- effective training for engineers, that is, practical knowledge that changes their behaviour;
- sufficient contact with stakeholders, whether through traditional meetings and reviews, or through some form of participatory design or inquiry cycle, to ensure that the project is working from valid requirements;
- sufficient openness within teams to enable people to speak out when absurd plans are placed on the table ("test and debug a million lines of safety-critical air traffic control software in three months").

But these are not all within our scope; scenarios don't do everything. However, much of the book is in one way or another about helping to ensure sufficient contact with stakeholders, and the book will, we hope, help to inform engineers in a practical way about using scenarios.

Scope: A Wealth of Purposes and Techniques

In this book, we present a range of scenario techniques from light, sketchy, and agile to careful and systematic. There is no single 'right way' to use scenarios; we celebrate diversity in requirements discovery and modelling. There is supposedly a saying among French cooks that the English have only two sauces: brown Windsor soup (salted gravy thickened with flour) and custard (sweetened milk thickened with corn flour). Obviously, if such a thing were true, the English diet would be somewhat monotonous. Happily, there are as many ways of using scenarios as there are French sauces—for every palate, season, and occasion, and like sauces, each basic scenario technique has any number of variations.

It would have been possible while editing to impose a uniform style and 'voice' on all the contributed chapters, but while we have arranged for a common chapter structure and cross-references, we have chosen to encourage authors to speak in their own way. This may help readers to see that people—engineers and researchers—come to technical issues from different directions, with their own backgrounds and preconceptions, just as project stakeholders do. No one on a project has a monopoly on truth; a major strength of scenario approaches is that they allow stakeholders to share and own a description of what they want. Indeed, each step of an operational scenario may be the responsibility of a different player.

Equally, there are many kinds of scenario structures, and these may well be applicable in projects of different types. The question of which approach is best for a given type of project is open, and in the final part of this book, we sketch some preliminary answers to it.

What all the scenario techniques described here have in common is the motivation to improve industrial practice, a clearly defined approach which has been applied to projects and has a grounding in theory.

We have taken care to ensure a consistent framework for each contribution. There are no tall claims here for commercial tools; equally, there are no chapters asserting elegant but untried academic hypotheses.

Structure of This Book

The book is structured as a whole to put across the message that scenarios work and are good for your projects,

> **Part I** provides an Overview of the nature and use of Scenarios.

> **Part II** looks at how to apply Scenarios through the System Life cycle. It is introduced by an overview of the chapter structure used in this part of the book, and then by two chapters that review what scenarios are and how they are used. Then the chapter authors describe their techniques in their own words, but in a fixed structure, which we hope makes the different approaches easy to compare and contrast. Each chapter includes a Comparisons section to guide the reader to related chapters and to help weave the book into a unified whole. The chapters are supported not only by references to the literature but also by recommendations for further reading.

Part III presents industrial experiences of Scenarios in Action: Case Studies. It begins with an overview of the chapter structure used in this part of the book. Then the chapter authors tell their stories in their own words, but again in a structure that we hope will help you to select the experiences most relevant to your projects. Where appropriate, the text is cross-referenced to the techniques described in other chapters.

Part IV reasons and speculates a little about the future of Scenarios in The Way Ahead. Chapter 22, Putting Scenarios into Practice, reflects on the lessons learnt from the techniques and case studies in Parts II and III—the book itself serving as the basis for some very preliminary research. Part of the Way Ahead lies in the dissemination of what we already know and in the education of tomorrow's engineers; this challenge is discussed in Chapter 23, Teaching Computer Scientists to Make Use.

The Appendices are designed to help make this a practical guide by explaining the terms used and by providing a set of scenario-based engineering templates to get you started, with simple exercises in their use—and providing answers to the exercises.

BIOGRAPHIES AND PHOTOGRAPHS

Ian Alexander

Ian Alexander is an independent consultant specialising in requirements engineering. He is an experienced instructor and has written training courses for a range of organisations. He is the author of the Scenario Plus toolkits for the DOORS requirements tool. His principal research interest is in improving the requirements engineering process by modelling business goals, processes, constraints, and scenarios. He is currently exploring whether Use Cases can assist reuse of specifications for automobile control systems. He was lead author of *Writing Better Requirements* published by Addison-Wesley, 2002. He helps to run the BCS Requirements Engineering Specialist Group and the IEE Professional Network for Systems Engineering. He is a Chartered Engineer.

Kent Beck

Kent Beck is the founder and director of TRI. He has pioneered patterns for software development, the xUnit family of testing frameworks, the Hot-Draw drawing editor framework, CRC cards, re-factoring, and most recently Extreme Programming. He is the author of *Extreme Programming Explained*, *Planning Extreme Programming*, and *The Smalltalk Best Practice Patterns*. He lives on 20 acres in rural southern Oregon with his wife, five children (one sadly now gone to college), four dogs, two sheep, and a variable number of domestic fowl.

David Benyon

David Benyon has held the post of Professor of Human–Computer Systems at Napier University, Edinburgh, since 1996. He obtained his MSc at Leicester Polytechnic and his PhD at the Open University, where he designed and implemented courses in human–computer interaction. He contributed to the 1994 book *Human-Computer Interaction* by Preece, J. et al. His research focus is to shift HCI to the idea of navigation of information space. He is working to replace the 1994 book *Designing Interactive Systems* and is conference co-chair for the ACM conference of the same name, DIS2004. He has attracted well over €1 m of funding to support his research and published over 100 conference and journal papers.

David Bush

David is completing an engineering doctorate at University College London, as a mature student, examining the application of Goal Based Requirements approaches to large-scale industrial projects. He has significant experience in systems engineering and project Management in IT, aerospace, and defence projects and is currently a Principal Engineer in the UK National Air Traffic Services Ltd, working in the development of systems, software, and safety engineering techniques. He is Secretary to the British Computer Societies Requirements Engineering Special Interest Group, a member of the Management Committee of the UCL Centre for Systems Engineering, a Chartered Engineer, and a member of the Chartered Management Institute.

John Carroll

John M. Carroll is the Edward Frymoyer Chair Professor of Information Sciences and Technology at the Pennsylvania State University. His research interests include methods and theory in human–computer interaction, particularly as applied to networking tools for collaborative learning and problem solving. He has written or edited 14 books, including *Making Use* (MIT Press, 2000), *HCI in the New Millennium* (Addison-Wesley, 2001), *Usability Engineering* (Morgan-Kaufmann, 2002, with M.B. Rosson), and *HCI Models, Theories, and Frameworks* (Morgan-Kaufmann, 2003). He serves on nine editorial boards for journals, handbooks, and series; he is a member of the US National Research Council's Committee on Human Factors and editor-in-chief of the *ACM Transactions on Computer-Human Interactions*. He received the Rigo Career Achievement Award, from ACM (SIGDOC), and the Silver Core Award from IFIP and was elected to the CHI Academy. In 2003, he received the CHI Lifetime Achievement Award from ACM.

Andrew Farncombe

Andrew Farncombe has a first class honours degree and spent his early career in the software industry. He subsequently moved into the defence and aerospace sector where he held a number of senior technical and management positions including that of technical director and where he led the codification of systems engineering knowledge and experience for one of the groups as a whole. At John Boardman Associates, he has applied systems engineering to the aerospace and transportation industries. Andrew is Visiting Professor of Systems Engineering at Cranfield University.

Chris Fowler

Chris Fowler has a degree in psychology and sociology and a Ph.D in cognitive psychology. From 1977 to 1990, he worked in various HE Institutes, undertaking teaching and research into cross-cultural psychology, research methods, human–computer interaction, and the use of computers in education. In 1990, he joined the Human Factors Division of BT Labs. Whilst at BT, he worked on introducing human factors into various software design methodologies, created and managed the Education & Training Research Group, and set up BT's Asian Research Centre in Malaysia. In April 2002, he became Professor and Director of Chimera, a new institute of sociotechnical innovation and research set up at the University of Essex with support from BT.

Ellen Gottesdiener

Ellen Gottesdiener is Principal Consultant of EBG Consulting, Inc. She works with project teams to help them explore requirements, shape their development processes, and collaboratively plan their work. Before becoming a consultant, Ellen had a 13-year career with CIGNA Corp. as a developer, analyst, trainer, and project manager. She is a Certified Professional Facilitator and an expert in using facilitated workshops in software development projects for developing project charters, defining requirements, and conducting retrospectives. She also presents seminars and advises on industry conferences. Ellen has written numerous articles on requirements, facilitated workshops, methods, and modelling. She is the author of *Requirements by Collaboration: Workshops for Defining Needs* (Addison-Wesley, 2002).

Peter Haumer

Dr. Peter Haumer is a content developer for the IBM Rational Unified Process product platform. Currently, he is working as the content architect for the future generations of IBM's integrated process architecture. Before joining the RUP team, he worked as a Senior Professional Services Consultant for IBM's Rational Software Brand. He assisted and coached customers on how to be successful with the Rational Unified Process platform and Rational tools, performing on-site consulting and providing training courses. His areas of work include requirements management, object-oriented analysis, and design for enterprise application architectures, as well as Software process implementation. He is also a member of Rational's steering committees for Model-Driven Development, Software Process Adoption, as well as Business Modelling, Requirements Management, and Rational XDE education. Before joining Rational, he worked in basic research in the areas of requirements engineering and flexible CASE tool architectures.

Karen Holtzblatt

Dr. Karen Holtzblatt, President and CEO of InContext Enterprises, is the co-developer of the customer-centred process Contextual Design. She originated this approach to field data collection and pioneered its introduction into working product design and engineering teams. In 1992, Karen Holtzblatt and Hugh Beyer founded InContext to provide design and consulting services to clients backed by the Contextual Design method. Their book *Contextual Design: Defining Customer Centered Systems*, published by Morgan Kaufmann, is a key reference for anyone doing or teaching customer-centred design. InContext works with leaders in the technology industry, including SAP, Microsoft, Hewlett-Packard, IBM, Novell, Motorola, Nokia, Thomson Corporation, and others.

Frank Houdek

Frank Houdek is a senior researcher and project leader at the DaimlerChrysler research centre in Ulm, Germany. After finishing his Ph.D. in the field of systematic process improvement and empirical software engineering, he worked in different requirements engineering research projects, and he is involved in technology transfer activities in passenger car and commercial vehicles development. His research interests are requirements engineering processes and requirements recycling. He is an IEEE CS member and part of the steering group of the Requirements Engineering Group of the German Computer Science Society.

Pericles Loucopoulos

Pericles Loucopoulos holds the chair of Information Systems Engineering at the University of Manchester Institute of Science & Technology (UMIST), in Manchester, UK, where he has worked since January 1984, following a period of many years in industry. His research interests focus on the provision of information processing systems that support large, complex, and dynamic organisational systems. To this end, his research addresses both systems engineering issues and issues relating to organisational objectives, strategy, and business processes. He is co-editor-in-chief of the *Journal of Requirements Engineering* and also serves on editorial boards of four other international journals. He is the co-author of five books, the co-editor of one book, and the author or co-author of over 100 journal and conference papers.

Catriona Macaulay

Dr Catriona Macaulay's two sons sometimes let her go for long enough to allow her to play at being Programme Leader of the new BSc honours programme in Interactive Media Design at Dundee University/Duncan of Jordanstone College of Art and Design. Her research interests are in the areas of experience design/human–computer interaction, design ethnography, and interactive soundscape design. She also works as a user experience design consultant in industry. Mostly, though she builds pirate ships out of Lego, many of which have met tragic ends because of the large number of crocodiles, witches, and dragons they encounter.

Neil Maiden

Neil Maiden is Professor of Systems Engineering and Head of the Centre for Human–Computer Interface Design, an independent research department in City University's School of Informatics. He has been directing interdisciplinary research in requirements engineering for 15 years and has worked on numerous EPSRC- and EU-funded research projects. He has over 100 refereed academic publications in journals, conferences and workshops.

Alistair Mavin

Alistair Mavin is a requirements engineer with Praxis Critical Systems Limited, a UK-based company specialising in requirements, systems, software, and safety engineering. He has undertaken requirements engineering projects in a range of industries including defence, aerospace, rail, automotive, and local government. He has been involved in a number of capability enhancement projects, which have the aim of improving engineering capability within the client organisation. He previously worked in the Centre for HCI Design at City University in London, where he was involved in research and consultancy in requirements engineering.

Suzanne Robertson

Suzanne Robertson is a principal and founder of the Atlantic Systems Guild. Suzanne is co-author of *Mastering the Requirements Process* (Addison-Wesley 1999). Current work includes research and consulting on stakeholders and all aspects of requirements. The product of this research is *Volere*, a complete requirements process and template for assessing requirements quality and for specifying requirements. She is editor of the requirements column in IEEE Software magazine.

Con Rodi

Con Rodi retired from the United States Air Force after a 30-year career as a fighter pilot and communications officer. He is now a graduate student at Virginia Tech pursuing a doctorate in Computer Science. He has bachelor's and master's degrees in computer science from the University of Utah and Stanford University respectively. Con's research interests include collaborative systems, case studies supporting scenario-based design, and weblogs as they relate to community computing.

Perminder Sahota

Parm is a systems engineer with Praxis Critical Systems. He has experience with carrying out requirements engineering work in the transport and aerospace domain. He has specific skills in requirements elicitation, analysis and management, use case and scenario modelling, and dependency modelling and object oriented analysis and design. Parm holds a degree in computer science from City University, where he specialised in requirements engineering and object-oriented analysis and design.

Mary Beth Rosson

Mary Beth Rosson is Professor of Information Sciences and Technology at Pennsylvania State University. Her research interests include scenario-based design and evaluation; the use of network technology to support collaboration, especially in learning contexts; and the psychological issues associated with the use of high-level programming languages and tools. She is co-author of *Usability Engineering: Scenario-Based Development of Human-Computer Interaction* (Morgan Kaufmann, 2002) and author of *Instructor's Guide to Object-Oriented Analysis and Design with Application* (Benjamin Cummings, 1994), as well as numerous articles, book chapters, and tutorials. Dr. Rosson is active in both ACM SIGCHI and ACM SIGPLAN, serving in numerous technical programs as well as in conference organisation roles for the CHI and OOPSLA annual conferences.

Camille Salinesi

Dr. Camille Salinesi is a senior lecturer of computer science in the Department of Mathematics and Informatics at the University of Paris 1 Panthéon—Sorbonne. He does research in information systems engineering, process engineering, and requirements engineering and has published more than 20 referred papers on use case & scenario elicitation and authoring, and on information system evolution. Dr Salinesi is an active animator for the RE community: he was involved in fundamental research projects such as NATURE and CREWS; he has organised a number of conferences and has been guest editor for several journals. He belongs to the RE discussion group of AFIS (French Association of Systems Engineering). He used to be a project leader and RE consultant in projects with French companies.

Juha Savolainen

Juha Savolainen is a researcher and project manager at the Nokia Research Center (NRC) in Helsinki, Finland. He assists Nokia's business units to create innovative products and solutions for complex problems. His current work involves research and consulting in requirements engineering, product line development, and software architecture. He loves cooking, inventing new mobile applications while traveling, and watching Finnish ice hockey.

Ramin Tavakoli

Ramin Tavakoli Kolagari is writing his PhD thesis on requirements engineering and product lines at the DaimlerChrysler Research Centre in Ulm, Germany. In addition, he is engaged in requirements engineering projects and in technology transfer activities for commercial vehicles development. His research interests are—in addition to the topics covered by his PhD—software engineering for embedded systems, agile software development, and category theory.

Joy Van Helvert

Joy van Helvert joined BT in 1995 after an IT career in government, and in the last seven years, has worked at a senior professional level in a socio-technical research group specialising in E-learning. In April 2002, the research group transferred to the University of Essex to become Chimera—Institute for socio-technical innovation and research. Her work within the group has included formal and organisational learning research and the development of scenario-based methodologies that have been used successfully as a consultancy product and on European collaborative projects (5th Framework and EURESCOM). She is an experienced facilitator and is currently researching cross-cultural communication using ICT.

David West

David West is a Professor at New Mexico Highlands University (Ph.D., University of Wisconsin, 1988). He teaches systems analysis and design, introduction to business and informational systems, informational modelling and databases, website authoring and management, and enterprise information modelling and databases. He has had more than 23 refereed articles and/or invited appearances at academic and professional conferences, and multiple presentations at national and international conferences. West has worked as a consultant to more than 50 corporate clients (many of them Fortune 100 companies), as well as international clients in India.

Thomas Zink

Thomas Zink was with DaimlerChrysler research for two years helping in projects applying new requirements engineering approaches. His research focus was on use cases and stories for requirements recycling in a product family context. Thomas recently joined Nokia at the product creation site in Ulm/Germany.

OVERVIEW

INTRODUCTION: SCENARIOS IN SYSTEM DEVELOPMENT

Ian Alexander
Scenario Plus, London, UK

SCENARIOS ARE a powerful antidote to the complexity of systems and analysis. Telling stories about systems helps ensure that people—stakeholders—share a sufficiently wide view to avoid missing vital aspects of problems. Scenarios vary from brief stories to richly structured analyses, but are almost always based on the idea of a sequence of actions carried out by intelligent agents. People are very good at reasoning from even quite terse stories, for example detecting inconsistencies, omissions, and threats with little effort. These innate human capabilities give scenarios their power. Scenarios are applicable to systems of all types, and may be used at any stage of the development life cycle for different purposes.

CONTEXT

Scenarios are simple, human things. This book reveals that there are many possible variations on the theme, and the Scope section below introduces some of the concepts; but the basic idea is just a story: someone does this, someone else does that:

> *The driver walks towards the car and presses his key.*
> *The car recognises the driver, unlocks the doors, and adjusts the driving seat, steering wheel, radio, and mirrors to the driver's preferred settings.*

"Scenarios are arguably the starting point for all modelling and design" (Sutcliffe 2003). Since systems either do something that somebody wants, or are shelfware, and scenarios describe how to do things, it seems hard to disagree with the idea that scenarios are the way to begin a development—if not also to continue, as several authors in this book argue.

More and more modelling notations are being invented—I saw one in a new gadget being shown off at a trade fair, and it had no fewer than 26 symbols that somebody believed

Scenarios, Stories, Use Cases: Through the Systems Development Life-Cycle. Edited by Ian F Alexander and Neil Maiden
© 2004 John Wiley & Sons, Ltd. ISBN: 0-470-86194-0

were necessary for requirements analysis—and no end to the madness is in sight. I have no idea how the developers of such things imagine that ordinary people are going to use anything so intricate, and so far removed from life. I do have a lively idea of the blank looks I'd get from practical engineers if I tried to pull any such trick on them.

The use of the narrative scenario in engineering seems in one way to be a kind of reaction against too much technology, too fast. There is no need to be a Luddite to wonder what is being missed in the race to construct ever more complex, formal, and unfamiliar models for ever more risky projects.

Scenarios allow us to take a backward glance. They use a simple, traditional activity—storytelling—to provide a vital missing element, namely a view of the whole of a situation. And they do this at low cost, at least once people are trained in their use (Sommerville and Sawyer 1997).

The scenario perspective looks at what people do and how people use systems in their work, with concrete instead of abstract descriptions, focus on particular instances rather than generic types, being work- and not technology-driven, open-ended and fragmentary rather than complete and exhaustive, informal, rough, and colloquial instead of formal and rigorous, and with envisioned rather than specified outcomes (Carroll 1995).

Analysis means 'dissolving [into component particles]', which is fine and very necessary; but it also means looking at details, which as everyone knows is a way of not seeing the wood for the trees. Engineers love analysis and design: our profession's occupational hazard is diving into detail, ignoring the people involved, and what they may want.

Using scenarios in analysis is thus paradoxical. Analysis is about refinement, precision, and completeness with respect to the parts of a problem. But scenarios are basically holistic. Whether in terse and summary form, or written out at length in a carefully studied sequence—or even in a complex analytical framework with multiple paths ingeniously fitted together—the scenario is in essence, a single thing that conveys a human meaning. And that meaning is enhanced by the reader from her own experience; the story told in the written scenario slips effortlessly into the context of the network of meaning in the reader's mind.

> "What are you doing?" sobbed the Djinni.
> "I'm throwing you back into the sea", said the Fisherman.
> "Let me out of this bottle" wailed the desperate Djinni, "and I'll make you richer than King Solomon".
> "You are a tricky Djinni", answered the Fisherman. "You deserve the same fate as the King in the story of The King and the Doctor."
> "What story is that?" inquired the Djinni.
> *The Djinni and the Fisherman*, in *The Thousand and One Nights* (850 AD onwards)

Stories are quite insistent on one point: a tale is not over until it's finished in every detail. The Djinni is not just playing for time by exploring side issues: he's thinking out other options and tricks that might result in a better outcome—from his dark and devious point of view. It goes without saying that the exploration is by storytelling, and the Fisherman has to use all his cunning to outwit his immensely powerful opponent. Scenario-based techniques such as searching for Exceptions, Functional Hazard Analysis, and Misuse Cases (*see* Chapter 7) make use of the power of storytelling to explore likely weaknesses, and thus to make systems more reliable, safer, and more secure in the face of active and intelligent opposition.

Sven Birkerts, in his richly reflective *Gutenberg Elegies* (Birkerts 1994), states that humanistic knowledge is unlike instrumental knowledge, since it aims to fashion a comprehensible narrative. His thesis is essentially that the Internet and electronic media detract from the ability to concentrate in the way that a printed book encourages; that the private world that a good book lets you into is a doorway into civilisation, as it fosters just that depth of thought that the instant availability of colourful hypertext banishes. He would argue that narrative is extremely important, and for quite different reasons than those I have set out above.

Well, we believe that at least one kind of instrumental knowledge, that needed to serve system designers, testers, safety engineers, and others in their work by giving them a mental picture of how the system-to-be is going to be used, also needs to be fashioned into a 'comprehensible narrative'. Our goal is not, indeed, anything as grand as enabling humanity to grow emotionally or spiritually, as Birkerts believes literature may do; but more humbly, we hope that scenarios may help engineers to make systems that serve humanity a little better.

Narrative can fulfil these diverse purposes because sequences of events in time are at the heart of our ability to construct meaning.

In David Attenborough's wonderful television series, *The Life of Mammals*, one story shows a group of monkeys of different species feeding on the ground (Attenborough 2003). Suddenly one spots a snake. At once, all the members of the group shout out the 'Snake' call of their own species. Everyone looks about for the snake. The youngest realise the danger, learn the calls, and live to watch out for snakes another day.

> The story:
> "A snake slithers silently up to our group and grabs one of us."
> could hardly be more elemental. The variation:
> "but someone sees it, gives the 'Snake' alarm call, and we all escape."

could hardly carry a clearer survival message. And this tale of communication in the face of danger is part of our shared primate heritage. Actually there is a further twist: some monkeys give not only the basic call, but accompany it with a modifier, which seems to mean something like 'serious', 'intense'—the monkeys have not only nouns but adjectives to convey their meaning.

Human language is a far richer medium for sharing meanings than even the most sophisticated calls of our primate relatives, but Stephen Pinker is surely right when he writes in *The Language Instinct* that it grew out of the need to share knowledge with similar survival value (Pinker 1994). He quotes a conversation, imagined by the evolutionary biologist George Williams, between a mother and a child along the lines of, "Don't play with that, dear, that's a Sabre-Toothed Tiger and it wants to eat you" (page 289). The rest of the scenario hardly needs to be told; the child that understood grew up safe and well, and the one that didn't, didn't.

Every parent of young children has made the same striking observation as I have: even very little ones instantly appreciate being shown different kinds of beast, and never tire of hearing about the noises they make, or of seeing how the crocodile snaps his jaws. These things are important to know if you're inexperienced and want to live.

It's no exaggeration, then, to suggest that spoken language, and with it the human mind, evolved precisely because planning—constructing and evaluating scenarios—is a survival skill.

Planning becomes important when resources are short, when outcomes are uncertain, and especially when intelligent opponents are making their own plans that contradict our own. That's pretty much all the time. We are social animals; gangs and tribes and shifting alliances and treachery are a permanent feature of our existence. Our social brain—the one that enjoys watching the scheming complexities of Shakespearean tragedies and soap operas—is adapted precisely to understand stories. It is adept at filling in details from scant evidence; at guessing and reasoning about people's intentions; at predicting how people would respond if we chose a certain course of action.

The scenario exploits exactly these mental abilities. It uses narrative—a time-threaded sequence of actions. It focuses on agents and their (inter)actions. It is at root brief and abstract, but highly suggestive of context. It is helpful for predicting outcomes. It is all about courses of action.

In a nutshell, scenario approaches allow projects to benefit from the inherent strengths of narrative, and from the excellent match of the story form to the story-processing capabilities of the human brain—whether trained or not. We predict that scenarios will always be useful in engineering.

Scope — What Does Scenario Mean, and What Does it Cover?

Like other important concept terms in systems engineering, Scenario has multiple connotations, all subtly different. Fortunately, these form quite a coherent set of meanings, which we'll explore below to set out the scope of the book.

One other concept intimately connected with scenarios is that of the Stakeholder. Scenarios are all about communicating with people. One of the main reasons why traditional development approaches failed was precisely that they excluded non-engineers—and quite often the kinds of models used were not too helpful for communicating with other engineers. So we'll start by defining what we mean by Stakeholder, and then look at what Scenarios can offer.

Stakeholders

Scenarios are for people: a way to explain what they want, and to check that what is being asked for is correct. People with a legitimate interest in a System are its Stakeholders, and they are the people we have in mind throughout this book. Who are they? At the least, they represent diverse groups.

Incidentally, scenario techniques such as role-play (*see* Suzanne Robertson's account in Chapter 3) can be used to document stakeholders' viewpoints: they can tell the story of how people behave and to paint a picture of their "motivations, expectations, and attitudes." (Kuniavsky 2003). Such an ethnographic perspective—getting a user experience point of view—is valuable, as it gives engineers the chance of

"putting on the shoes of the people you've created, and looking at their problems and your solutions through their eyes." (Kuniavsky 2003, page 149)

While this may seem a surprising application of scenarios, making a user profile is common practice in the worlds of user-interface design, marketing, and product management: perhaps it should be more widely used in system design also.

Figure 1.1 shows an 'onion' model of a system's stakeholders (Alexander 2003, Alexander and Robertson 2004). Since the concepts of both 'system' and 'stakeholder' are slippery, let us take a moment to define what we mean. The central circle, labelled 'The Kit or Product' denotes whatever it is that we are making—the hardware and software, the equipment, machinery, and installations of any kind that we are specifying and designing. If we were making something for a market, we would call it our Product. That is often called a *system*, but we'll choose to call 'Our System' the next circle out. 'Our System' consists not only of kit, but also of the people who are actually operating that kit. Consider an aircraft: it's clearly a system, as it consists of a set of connected parts that together produce the behaviour of controlled flight. Those 'parts' include engines, airframe, controls, electronics, and the aircrew. From this point of view, therefore, any Stakeholder who is directly involved in operating the Kit or Product is part of Our System, the one that produces the results we are describing with our Scenarios.

The onion model provides generalised 'slots' such as 'Normal Operator' and 'Maintenance Operator', which need to be filled with specific stakeholder roles for a particular project. For instance, the Normal Operator slot in an aircraft contains roles such as the Pilot, the Navigator, and arguably the whole of the rest of the aircrew. The Maintenance Operator slot for an aircraft includes the first-line daily maintenance crew—the refuelling

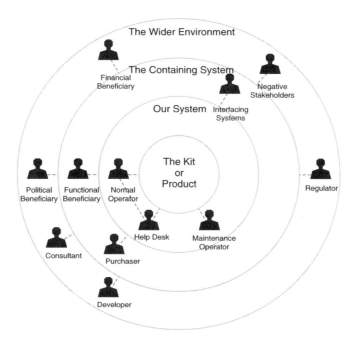

FIGURE 1.1 Onion model of system stakeholder roles

team, the cleaners, and so on, as well as second- and third-line roles like radar fitter, engine fitter, and so on. All such 'direct' (Kotonya and Sommerville 1997) Roles, those that belong in 'Our System' slots on the onion model, can play Operational Roles in Scenarios, and can serve as 'Actors' in Use Cases.

All other Stakeholder Roles, those outside the 'Our System' circle, are 'indirect' or non-operational; these terms have some value, but as Figure 1.1 shows, they cover many different kinds of roles. For example, the Aviation Authorities who certify that an aircraft is safe to fly belong in the 'Regulator' slot in the 'Wider Environment' circle. Regulators don't pilot planes; they don't even work for airlines that operate those planes; but although they are outside those 'system' circles, they are among the most important stakeholders in an aircraft development project.

Finally, notice that the owners of Interfacing Systems are also Stakeholders in our system: they are part of the 'Containing System' that includes our system. In the case of an aircraft, that Containing System consists of the airports and air traffic control that the aircraft operates with. For example, the towbar that connects a tractor to an aircraft's nose-wheel is an interface: both tractor and aircraft have to comply with a standardised design so that they can be sure to be compatible. Interfacing Systems (like tractors) can appear in scenarios and can serve as Actors in Use Cases, even though they are not human. But while the company managing the towing of an aircraft is potentially a Stakeholder, tractors, and towbars are not.

Story

The story form is, as has been argued above, as old as language. It seems simple, but is hard to describe. A story is essentially a narrated description of a causally connected sequence of events in some domain, or more usually of actions taken by a small number of interacting protagonists:

> *A poor woodcutter had two children. There was little to eat, so to keep them safe he decided to send them to his brother, who lived deep in the forest...*
> *The pilot has no stick or rudder pedals. Instead, a small joystick mounted in the armrest allows the pilot to control the craft with one hand. With the joystick in the neutral, vertical, position, the craft remains stationary. When the pilot tilts the joystick to the left, the craft turns, banking according to the joystick's left–right angle to the vertical. When the pilot pushes the joystick forward, the craft accelerates smoothly...*

Even the simplest story has the power to create in our minds an image of a world—maybe magical, maybe technical—so that we almost feel we are there. Questions and guesses arise unbidden. Will the children meet a witch, or an ogre? Can the craft fly or hover? If it does, can it climb or descend vertically, and if so how would you control that with a little joystick?

The most basic form of story is a spoken or written narrative, but stories can also be told more visually. Indeed, story underlies nearly every kind of scenario. For example, an organisation could make a film of people actually using a legacy system, set in context by shots of customers phoning up, asking for a service, and so on. More simply, a story can be told by acting out a scene, live in a workshop or recorded on video. For instance, a sub-group of workshop participants can pretend to interact with a future device, to illustrate a desired capability or to bring to life a possible problem that ought to be handled.

Stories bring with them a wealth of context, mostly unwritten, from our shared culture. As long as this is what the story's author intended, it is useful, as it provides a frame of reference in which the reader can evaluate the story as a whole, and make sense of its individual statements—which can therefore individually be short.

Stories provide an internal logic—of a sequence of events in time; of causality—which is valuable to engineering as it permits, indeed encourages validation. Questions like

Are these steps in the right order?
Has a step been omitted?
What could go wrong here?
Is this story complete?
Would doing this achieve the goal?
Can this actor carry out this action?
Is this a safe approach?

spring naturally to mind, and stakeholders—people with a legitimate interest in a system—in practice correct stories rapidly and deftly, in marked contrast to their behaviour when asked to review a list of requirements.

Stories are coming into favour in various branches of engineering, notably in human–computer interaction and in 'agile' (or 'extreme') methods of software development.

Kent Beck and David West propose in Chapter 13 that some kinds of software should be written on the basis of brief 'User Stories' and tests devised from them (Beck 2000).

Thomas Zink and Frank Houdek write about Story Use & Reuse in Automotive Systems in Chapter 16. Here the stories are seen not as system specifications, but as ways of carrying the gist or essence of the system's purpose from one project to another—for after all, despite all the differences, one car remains much like another. But recycling and reuse of requirements are harder than they look.

Roger Schank, a pioneer of artificial intelligence and much else, has almost cornered the market in arguing the value of stories in engineering. He and his colleagues invented the script in the 1970s, basically a simple sequential scenario describing a stereotypical interaction—famously, when a hungry customer walks into a restaurant, is shown to a table by a waitress, hangs up his coat, and so on. In his *Tell Me A Story* (Schank 1990) he goes further, and argues that knowledge is stories, and that everything we know is embodied in stories. It seems clear that he would include scripts and sequence scenarios (*see* below) as stories.

A story, like any scenario, is inherently episodic, "an illustrative instance of a set of behaviours, not a definition of the set"[1]. The more structured kinds of scenario and use case (*see* below) go some way to mitigating this 'for instance'-ness, but arguably they never throw it off altogether.

Development based on stories alone, is possible only if you are not too concerned with perfection (at least at the start). If you want a system to be as safe as possible, you

---

[1] Michael Jackson, personal communication.

will specify and analyse its every behaviour, and use formal logic to prove that its code is logically equivalent to its specification. If, frankly, you don't care but you have a few situations in mind that describe what you'd broadly like the system to do, then telling a few stories may well be quite adequate—the team can make the system converge with stakeholders' intentions by iteration (rapid prototyping, agile methods, etc.). These mindsets are poles apart, and it is easy for engineers with such different backgrounds to talk past each other. However, there are more structured forms of scenario that many engineers may find more comfortable.

Situation, Alternative World

To the businessman or politician, a scenario means a projected future situation or snap-shot. Typically, either a team brainstorms a few possible scenarios, or more scientifically, a simulation is run say, 15 years into the future to project a set of variables.

For instance, in an approach pioneered by Shell, an oil company might look at a moment in the future where the oil price is $100 per barrel, alternative sources of electricity are cheap at just 10¢ per Kilowatt hour, and fuel cells are available for 50% of all cars. The values of these variables suggest a pattern of energy use very different from what would happen if electricity cost $1 per Kilowatt hour, and so on; and that pattern can be convincingly modelled using suitable mathematical models and simulation tools.

This usage of 'scenario', as an instantaneous snapshot that illustrates the outcome of a set of trends, is plainly helpful in long-term business planning. In a world where politicians had any foresight, it would undoubtedly be useful in long-term government planning also. But on the whole it seems to be rare in systems engineering. When engineers need to refer to a specific outcome they tend to use other words, such as system state or failure mode.

Happily, David Bush (Chapter 6) gives a concrete example of its usefulness in assessing requirement stability by looking ahead to whether goals are relevant in various imagined alternative worlds.

Simulation

Simulations can, as we've just explained, be used to model more-or-less static situations, but they are also ideally suited for exploring dynamic, story-like aspects of scenarios.

Any story that has a direct concrete interpretation can be modelled, animated, and simulated. If stakeholders say they want to run trains with more passengers on board, and that the trains must stop for half the time at each station to improve speed and punctuality, then engineers can model how long it would take to get so many passengers onto and off the trains given different door sizes and carriage layouts. Consider the following scenario:

> *A train crush-loaded with 2000 passengers pulls into Central Station in rush hour. There are 1000 people waiting on the platform. Seven hundred passengers leave the train and 700 join it. The driver closes the doors and the train moves off 30 seconds after it halted.*

Simulation can give precise answers about whether such a scenario could be realised with any plausible design, given the existing constraints on train length, platform width, and so on. Simulation can also be used to evaluate the implications of alternative possible worlds or situations (*see* above). Used for that purpose, simulation is interesting not so much for its ability to step through a story as for the results that it generates (e.g. did the passengers manage to leave the train within 30 seconds?).

A simulator with visual output enables scenarios to be replayed directly to stakeholders, in much the same way as a prototype system can allow users to see the effect of their requirements. David Harel and Rami Marelly's recent book, *Come, Let's Play* (Harel and Marelly 2003) presents Live Sequence Charts—extended Message Sequence Charts—with supplied "non-commercial" software, to enable readers to try capturing and executing user-interface scenarios for themselves; underneath are formally defined model semantics. You could justifiably say that such a simulator is a prototype system; the fact that it is executable and behaves like the real thing effectively overcomes the difficulty of presenting formal specifications to stakeholders. An effective commercial implementation would continue the trend seen in "fourth-generation" programming languages and visual program design environments like those for Visual Basic and Visual C++, moving specification away from code towards the user interface. This is not simply a matter of graphical user interface (GUI) design, nor even of the use of an editing tool's GUI, but of specifying system behaviour by means of the system-under-design's own GUI. Since that is something that system operators need to understand, it is—at least from a system point of view!—the logical place to define what behaviour the system operators want. However, not all stakeholders are operators, and not all requirements are conveniently stated in terms of an operator's interface.

The sorts of comments and suggestions that stakeholders typically make when they first see a running system or animated simulation are 'But what if ...' or 'And then I'd like to be able to...'. These illustrate why scenarios are so valuable: once the implications of a set of choices are displayed, everyone can see if the result is right or needs improving.

In Chapter 21, Evaluating Scenarios by Simulation, Pericles Loucopoulos shows how the negotiations over the requirements for Olympic stadiums were informed by simulation. A simulation model can show stakeholders the likely effects of their requirements when implemented as design parameters. We may be interested in the dynamic results, as when people queue for admission to a stadium and its facilities at peak times, or in a more static conclusion that option A is more cost-effective than option B. Either way, appropriate use of simulation—possibly involving many runs—can explore scenarios that might be too slow, too costly, or too dangerous to try out for real. Simulation also answers questions (as the Olympic stadium example demonstrates) too difficult to visualise and to make decisions on without the kind of quantitative evidence that simulation can provide.

There is a close connection between scenario, simulation, and prototyping: all explore ways a system would work when in service, and all imply the need for an iterative and participative development life-cycle (*see* the section below, 'Through the Life-Cycle', and Andrew Farncombe's discussion of life-cycles in Chapter 15).

Storyboard

A variation on the story is the storyboard, invented in Hollywood in the 1920s and still in wide use on film shoots of all types today. Anyone who has tried to understand a play by reading its script knows the problem: the words as they lie there on the page just fail to conjure up a visual impression of the action. The scripted dialogue is a kind of scenario, but while it is essential for telling the actors what to say, it is not sufficient for organising shoots. If the heroine walks out of one shot in a blue skirt and a red top, and into the next in a red skirt and a blue top, the continuity of the story is badly damaged. The team producing the shot needs quite detailed information to set everything up correctly, to ensure continuity among other things. Each frame of the storyboard gives just the right amount of detail for that shot (Figure 1.2); the storyboard as a whole tells the story of the film.

Unsurprisingly, storyboards find their main engineering use in human–computer interaction (HCI) (e.g. Eberts 1994). HCI designers may sketch all or some of the desired screens in the user interface. These screen concepts can serve as prototypes: they are effectively software-free implementations of the system in various states. A user-interface prototype acts as a window into the (future) system, allowing stakeholders to reason about its behaviour. David Benyon and Catriona Macaulay discuss Scenario-Based Design of HCI in Chapter 11. Joy Van Helvert and Chris Fowler explain their approach to Scenario-Based User Needs Analysis in Chapter 4.

On one project, when the user-interface requirements were extremely uncertain, I made a set of storyboard sketches in ink and watercolour, before going on to use a sophisticated GUI design tool. Colleagues later joked about my Early Watercolour Phase, but at least a dialogue on the required functionality and design had been started. The design tool, incidentally, did a beautiful job of setting up a possible graphical design, but it was a dangerous journey down a 'rabbit hole', as it focused my attention too sharply on the implementation of the interface—when what the interface ought to have been showing was anything but decided.

Sequence

A straight-line sequence of (possibly numbered, typically interactive) steps taken by independently-acting (presumably intelligent) agents playing (system) roles is roughly

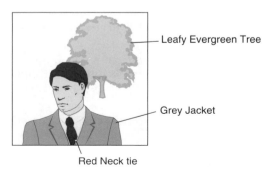

FIGURE 1.2 Storyboard frame

what most people mean by Scenario in engineering today—but note all the caveats. Synonyms or partial synonyms for this include Operational Scenario—itself part of a Concept of Operations, (Test) Case or Script, Path, and Course (of actions or events). It is evident that the terminology is slippery. We'll try to define Scenario a little better below.

Given that systems are by definition, complex structures made up of interacting components, there are usually many possible interaction sequences for any system. For instance, if a tool offers only 10 menu options that may be chosen in any order, then a sequence of just three commands can be constructed in 1000 ways, or 720 if repeat commands are not allowed. When a tool has over a hundred menu options, as does Microsoft Word, and many of those allow numerous choices and sequences are typically many commands long, the number of scenarios that could be generated quickly runs into the billions.

This is at the heart of the twin problems of specification and verification: it is impossible to test everything, as Edsger Dijkstra long ago argued so eloquently (Dijkstra 1972). There are simply too many possible test scenarios (*see* Chapter 14 by Ian Alexander). But by the same token, it is impossible to specify everything either, if we attempt to do it with scenarios alone. Surely it would be better to rely on analytic, program-like structures that can in the twirl of a *while* loop or a *case* statement take care of many possible scenarios?

Well, it would be much better, save for one crucial fact: humans are not at all good at expressing themselves in precise, systematic, logically complete, and consistent form—or in understanding such things either. Even professional programmers make frequent mistakes when encoding system behaviour in software. It is said that carefully debugged code still contains 1 error per 1000 lines. We should expect specifications written like code to be just as error-prone—otherwise, we could solve all the problems of software just by compiling code from our specification languages.

Since requirements come ultimately from people, we have a problem: we need precision in requirements, but we need people to express and understand and agree the same requirements. Precision means analysis and formalisation by engineers. But requirements elicitation and validation must be from and by stakeholders—people whose expertise is not in stating requirements. Therefore an altogether softer approach is mandatory.

Scenarios offer some hope of bridging this particular gap, as they are good raw material for analysis, but are close enough to ordinary stories for people to understand without effort. There are many possible ways in which straight-line time-sequence scenarios might be applied in engineering. Notably, they could be either inputs received from stakeholders, or 'people-friendly' outputs generated by a specification engine (presumably one that contains a database). Neil Maiden explains how to use Systematic Scenario Walkthroughs to validate complex requirements in Chapter 9.

Any bridge between the ordinary world and the domain of systems analysis is subject to enormous tension. Research engineers of different kinds constantly come up with ways of 'improving' the languages and notations used to express requirements and specify systems. The naivety of a simple scenario is a red rag to a bull to people thinking about how to make better specifications. Obviously you can just add a branch here and an exception mechanism there and a looping construct down here, and in no time at all you'll have a fully capable specification language! Ah yes, but you'll also have left your stakeholders stranded on the far side.

Numerous researchers of undoubted intelligence claim that they have successfully demonstrated that a group of normal 'users' readily understood some (usually graphical) notation or other. Well, maybe they did; but the users were buoyed up by the excitement of being pioneers; they were probably self-selected as being the most adventurous people in their company—since they'd agreed to work with a researcher!—and not least, they had the pioneering researcher playing the role of the humble systems analyst. It isn't surprising that these approaches often don't work in less rarefied atmospheres.

The plain old list-of-steps scenario is not a perfect medium for specification. But it is a workable medium for the purpose of getting started on the task of writing requirements, and providing grist for the analyst's mill. Suzanne Robertson explains in a simple and practical way in Chapter 3 how you can use Scenarios in Requirements Discovery. If you follow some of the authors in this book, you may find that the scenario is capable of much more than that; for example, Karen Holtzblatt explains in Chapter 10 how they use scenarios in system design. What is incontrovertible is that scenarios can be understood by ordinary people and engineers alike.

Structure

The further you go into analysis and specification, the greater is the pressure to impose structure on scenarios. Several ways to structure scenarios are described in this book. Ian Alexander takes a sideways look at use cases by examining Negative Scenarios and Misuse Cases in Chapter 7. Camille Salinesi describes how to author Use Cases in Chapter 8.

There are some longstanding techniques for defining the order of steps in a business process or program.

- The flowchart, despised by analysts but beloved of businessmen, is alive and well even in the UML as the Activity Diagram (Fowler 1999). Flowcharts give a good impression of what has to be done when, including places where decisions are required and the outcomes of those decisions. What flowcharts on their own don't do is to show who is responsible for each action. This is quite a serious weakness, given how central stakeholders are to requirements. Happily, UML has also adopted the swimlanes diagram, which has been in use since the 1920s. Each role (or 'actor', to use Jacobson's term[2], adopted for UML) has a lane. Roles carry out actions by swimming down the page. Combining an Activity Diagram with a background of swimlanes allows the humble flowchart to show clearly who does what.

---

[2] Apparently based on Swedish 'Aktör' which can mean both 'Role' and 'Actor'. The word is borrowed from French 'Acteur', and as is usual with borrowings, the meaning tends to become abstract. The usual and concrete Swedish word for Actor is quite different—'Skådespelare'; so the abstract meaning of 'Aktör'—'Role'—is presumably what was intended, as engineers would expect.

The common English connotations of the word 'Actor'—an individual human playing a part in a performance—are misleading, as Roles can be played by machines, subsystems, and software objects; and these are typically described generically, without reference to individual instances. The use of the human-seeming stickman symbol for 'Actor' does not reduce the confusion.

- Another notation that can be used to analyse scenarios is the (message) Sequence Chart, which is found in the UML and the ITU frameworks. This provides a timeline for each object or role down the page, with messages between roles shown as labelled horizontal arrows. Various different symbols can be used to annotate the sequence to define more elaborate behaviours, for example, an hourglass to denote a timer for time-triggered events. It seems clear that such notations are suitable for analysts rather than for scenario-like communication with other stakeholders. A yet more sophisticated notation, the Live Sequence Chart invented by David Harel and Werner Damm (Harel and Marelly 2003) takes sequence charts even further into the analyst's world, but see the discussion of simulation above.

Activity Diagrams and Sequence Charts may be fine as representations, but they do not solve the problem of identifying all the if..then..else.. branches—all the exceptional business events that have to be handled. There are usually far more of these than anyone thinks of initially. Programmers are all too familiar with filling in all the missing elses by experience and guesswork.

UML's answer to this problem is the Use Case[3], which has evolved far beyond what Jacobson originally proposed (Jacobson et al. 1992). The Use Case began life as not much more than a Story or Sequence: it had a name, an actor, and some text.

> "A use case is just what it sounds like: it is a way to use the system. Users interact with a system by interacting with its use cases." (Jacobson 1995, page 310.)

Unfortunately, several tool vendors eagerly jumped on to the bandwagon and created tools that concentrate on drawing Use Case diagrams (Figure 1.3), leaving aside the much duller work of dealing with what the Use Cases contain—scenarios. This would be funny if it had not misled so many people. It is a necessary step to identify the various ways that people and systems may interact, but the scenarios give much more information.

Erring the other way from such a diagrammatic over-simplification, several authors have suggested ways of adding more structure to the contents of each use case, and to the relationships between them; and this trend is continuing.

Alistair Cockburn has been one of the most successful, as his *Writing Effective Use Cases* is based on practical experience, and he emphasises simplicity (Cockburn 2001). A Cockburn Use Case has a Goal—its title: a very sensible minimalist choice; a Main Success Scenario composed of about three to nine steps; and usually several Extension Scenarios to describe other things (such as failures) that can happen, and must be handled. In addition, Cockburn provides slots for a range of other requirement-like things including Preconditions, Stakeholders and Interests (i.e. Viewpoints); Minimal (i.e. failure) and Success Guarantees; Scope and Level. To fill in all of this is a substantial piece of work, but in return you communicate much more of the stakeholders' intentions with far less ambiguity than you would with just a single scenario.

---

[3] A somewhat clunky term. With its emphasis on usage, it tends to imply that the product or system is the centre and stakeholders are peripheral: the system comes first, and we are just users of it (as Julian Hilton asked, "Is the human a computer peripheral?"). However, the term is firmly established, and since the concept has certainly done more than anything else to popularise scenarios, we must be grateful.

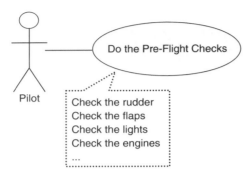

FIGURE 1.3   A use case diagram is only a summary

A closer look at Cockburn's approach will help us towards an understanding of what scenario means. Notice that the term 'scenario' in Cockburn's usage has subtly shifted its meaning. Consider what happens if you start executing a Use Case and a failure occurs. You execute part of the main success 'scenario' and then the appropriate failure 'scenario'—but the entire sequence of activities you've just executed is what we'd call a scenario: *a particular complete path in time through the options available when interacting with a system*. The Main Success Scenario, which at first sight matches our initial idea of a scenario, turns out to be just a tree-trunk, with several branches documented elsewhere. A Use Case changes from being pretty much 'a named scenario', to an analytic description of what happens when one or several actors try to achieve a goal with the system.

Now analysis is necessary for system specification, but a key question is whether it should take place in a scenario / Use Case framework, or somewhere else, with reference to scenarios which themselves can remain simple and comprehensible. I'll call these the Modernist and Traditionalist positions, respectively (Figure 1.4).

The Modernist view is broadly that if you know what your stakeholders want as a set of Use Cases, you can build your software straight from that: Scenarios are Specifications; the Pattern of the Problem corresponds to the Process of Design (to paraphrase Alexander 1964).

For example, to develop an order processing system, you identify Use Cases such as Place Order, Make Payment, Deliver Goods and so on. You then detail what is meant to happen in each case, identify what can go wrong and work out what should happen in each of those extension cases. You add any other details such as guaranteed performance and availability, and you are ready to start designing the software.

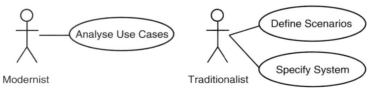

FIGURE 1.4   Modernist versus traditionalist views on scenarios

The Traditionalist view is roughly that scenarios are fine for describing how your system may be pressed into service, and that they may well suggest a range of functions and quality requirements, but that they in no way express all the requirements, let alone specify the system.

For instance, if your tanks are going to have to drive across the desert, they must not sink into soft sand, and the engine and other parts must not get damaged by ingesting sand. These needs may translate into qualities such as low ground pressure (below so many KiloPascals) and functions such as the ability to filter sand-laden air. But whatever the ultimate analysis of requirements, these are entirely separate from the scenarios. It would be quite inappropriate to expect the soldier who describes what he wants to do with the vehicle in the desert to know about KiloPascals—indeed, if he is only describing desired actions, he knows neither the area of the tracks nor the weight of the vehicle, and sand mechanics isn't his forte either. The scenarios are insufficient as system specifications. But the scenarios remain valuable for discovering requirements, for acceptance testing, and as something to validate the requirements against—so traceability becomes essential.

It isn't an accident that these examples imagine very different environments: one may suspect that much of the confusion about scenarios stems from people with different viewpoints talking past each other, using disjoint languages. The rather small number of books on scenario-based development (as opposed to books on specific tools and techniques, such as UML and Use Cases) illustrates this quite neatly: see the 'Recommended Reading' section at the end of this chapter.

This book represents a wide range of viewpoints, but our chapter authors have been specifically invited to comment on each others' work. The result may not be consensus, but we hope it is a step towards greater mutual understanding, an appreciation that many different traditions of scenario use exist, and the realisation that there is already a great deal of practical knowledge of scenarios in system development.

THROUGH THE LIFE CYCLE

If people give different meanings to scenario, we also think that scenarios help with quite different tasks in the system life cycle. We have used an intentionally simple 'Waterfall' list of system development activities to indicate how widely each technique described in this book applies during development. This appears to assert that each activity is necessary, happens in the order shown, and happens only once. In this simplistic view of development, the obvious place for scenarios is up front in Requirements Elicitation. Ellen Gottesdiener describes how to run a successful use case workshop to elicit and structure requirements at the start of a project in Chapter 5. There is plainly something in common between this modern logic and the Traditionalist view of scenarios. However, scenarios are also very useful at the end of the Waterfall life cycle for testing. A Test Case is in essence, a sequence of activities, just like the steps of a scenario. Ian Alexander explains the relationship of use cases and test cases in Chapter 14.

Andrew Farncombe explicitly critiques the naïve 'Waterfall' life-cycle model. He unpacks the telling of development project stories in his reflective Chapter 15, Stories and Life-Cycle Process Models, based on his experience both as a developer and as a consultant. He shows that successful projects must not only tell the stories of the products they set out to create; they must also select the right story to describe their own development process—and follow it.

A key point that Andrew Farncombe makes is that the development life cycle is often evolutionary or iterative. Kent Beck and David West describe their pioneering and highly iterative approach employing User Stories in Agile Software Development in Chapter 13. Contextual Design, the method underlying Karen Holtzblatt's account of Scenario-Based System Design in Chapter 10, is an excellent example of a participative, evolutionary approach. Peter Haumer explains how Software Development can be based on Use Cases in Chapter 12.

TYPES OF SYSTEM

It is practically a hopeless task to describe the types of system where scenarios may be used. There are no obvious limits to the applicability of scenarios. This is not to say that every development will find scenarios useful, but simply that there is no a priori reason to believe that scenarios are inappropriate to whole classes of development project. Our position is, therefore, that projects should consider writing scenarios as a matter of course. Once they have decided on that, the question of *how* arises, and that is the subject matter of this book.

Thomas Zink and Frank Houdek describe Story Use & Reuse in Automotive System Engineering in Chapter 16. Ian Alexander and Andrew Farncombe describe some applications of use cases in railway systems in Chapter 17. Perminder Sahota of Praxis describes the use of scenarios in Air Traffic Control in Chapter 18. Juha Savolainen of Nokia illustrates scenarios in Telecommunications in Chapter 19. Alistair Mavin describes a use of scenarios for rail rolling stock with the safety-related REVEAL method in Chapter 20. Pericles Loucopoulos describes the power of working out precise scenarios with simulations of Olympic stadiums in Chapter 21.

Development projects are those that are doing something new, and therefore something risky and uncertain. This is the natural home of the scenario, as discussed earlier in this chapter. It matters little whether the project concerns hardware or software, structures in concrete or structures in silicon, complex business interactions or home entertainment, deep space exploration or easier-to-use video recording.

Projects that are essentially routine—doing yet another inspection of a civil engineering structure like a bridge, installing yet another virtually identical computer network—are not developments in this sense. Scenarios will only be useful to such projects individually when there are local conditions that have not been encountered before; then, there may be value in examining threats to the project, and planning suitable mitigations. On the other hand, there may be a powerful case for preparing a set of generic scenarios to be applied to all bridge inspections or all network installations.

This book is about the use of scenarios in engineering of all kinds, not only software. Obviously software is today extremely pervasive. It is finding its way into many structures and devices that were formerly completely passive—bridges have inbuilt monitoring systems; binoculars have image stabilisation; keys and credit cards authenticate themselves using strong encryption.

Much of the complexity of systems now goes into control software—in aircraft and luxury cars, software is already the single most costly constituent. DaimlerChrysler predicts that by 2010, 45% of the cost of a Mercedes will be in electronics—what in aerospace is called avionics, combining both hardware and software (Weber 2003). This has profound effects, some beneficial, some not. The complexity, size, and weight of hardware components is falling, and the chance of hardware failure is therefore falling with it, so we can build systems that are smaller, more efficient, and more reliable than ever before. But taking onboard software into account, we are also building systems that are growing rapidly in complexity, and we are in danger of introducing a multitude of unwanted interactions and failure modes. Overall reliability and safety are not guaranteed to improve in this situation. They will only do so if we keep control of system behaviour. Scenarios are valuable tools in this struggle, because they contribute in several ways to our understanding of wanted behaviour, and to our ability to prevent unwanted effects. This is the reason why DaimlerChrysler (for instance) is looking at stories and use cases, as Thomas Zink and Frank Houdek explain in Chapter 16. Obviously, many other tools are needed to maintain control throughout the system development life cycle, as requirements are passed to subcontractors, and design choices introduce additional interfaces and risks.

SCENARIOS FOR SYSTEMS – NOT NECESSARILY SOFTWARE

Both because software is almost ubiquitous in systems, and because it carries an increasing share of system complexity, it is right that scenarios should often be intended for software. But what we absolutely deny is that there is anything inherently software-oriented about the idea of using scenarios. Indeed, the most accessible examples of scenario use are Hollywood storyboards and military planning (*see* below), which both existed long before computers became available. Businesses also constitute systems that are governed by carefully thought out scenarios—business processes. Let us take a brief look at all three of these examples.

Military Operations

Military plans take the form of orders that necessarily share the same hierarchical structure as the units (of infantry, armour, and so on) to which they apply. At each level in the hierarchy, a Schedule of Manoeuvre tells the story of what is to be done, not only by the forces on the friendly or 'blue' side, but also what actions or counter-measures might be taken by the enemy or 'red' side (*see also* Ian Alexander's account of Misuse Cases in Chapter 7). A military operation is of course conducted by people and machines playing many roles. The actions of those roles have to be coordinated. This is achieved by breaking down the story into the military equivalent of a UML swimlanes chart, a Synchronisation Matrix. This is a table that shows at each time stage (column) what each unit (row) within the blue forces is to do. A map is drawn for each time-step showing the position and movements of each unit at that time. The commander of the blue forces uses this to derive the orders for each such unit—which in turn consists of a (lower-level) Schedule of Manoeuvre and (if applicable) a Synchronisation Matrix showing the further breakdown of tasks to lower-level roles. In other words, orders have a similar structure at every level in the hierarchy, and they always tell a story, using a combination of text, tables, and graphics.

Film-Making

The system that makes a film is another instructive example, because through most of the history of film, hardly any of the process was automated. The credits that roll at the end of a movie reveal job titles whose function most of us can barely guess at—best boy? key grip? gaffer?—yet they form precise and necessary parts of an intricate and highly polished system for rolling out enormously complex products (measured in data terms, a 90-minute film is some Terabytes of uncompressed images and sound). That system contained for decades very little hardware—hand-controlled cameras, hand-controlled editing tools, and hand-controlled lamps were about the sum of it, if you don't count the trucks and catering equipment. Nowadays, animations and computer-generated imagery find their way into many films, but these are to be understood as particular implementation mechanisms among a wide choice of techniques. However a film is made, the chosen techniques have to be applied to create the desired effects. Those effects themselves tell a story to viewers, so it is not surprising that a storyboard (*see* above) is needed to define them. The storyboard scenario gives the right amount of information (in graphics and text) to support the planning and preparation of each shot independently—for it is a rare film that is shot in real time, or in the order in which it will be shown—and also of the subsequent editing and assembly of all the shots into a viewable sequence.

Business 'Systems' and Processes

A system is a set of interconnected components that work together to produce an effect that none of them could produce alone. Business systems generally contain people, procedures, and supporting equipment (telephones, fax machines, computers, etc.), organised into departments that play different business roles (marketing, sales, design, production, etc.).

Therefore, from a purely logical point of view, it ought to be easy to justify the consideration of business scenarios or use cases—scenarios are good for exploring how systems do or ought to work; businesses are systems; ergo, scenarios are good for business analysis (Alexander 2000). But in practice there are sizable cultural obstacles in the way—business analysts are wary of software and technology. Given the history of how businesses have jumped to conclusions (and expensively inappropriate software and solutions) they have cause to be. Scenarios and especially use cases are seen as coming from software engineering. Even systems thinking (e.g. Simon 1996) has been opposed, sometimes quite rightly, on the grounds that 'hard' engineering thinking is not appropriate in a 'soft systems' world—where 'soft' means dealing sensitively with the social and political dimensions of work, and 'hard' means focussing excessively narrowly on the technical and hence computerisable aspects (e.g. Checkland and Scholes 1999).

So, analysts should not imagine business systems as some distorted form of software without code, and business use cases as a bizarre mutant form of software specifications! It is quite sufficient to examine what a business wants to achieve, who is involved in it, what these people—the stakeholders—do, and what their viewpoints are (Alexander and Robertson 2004); and then to construct scenarios in one of the ways described in this volume. Thoughts of automation can come later. Indeed, a key strength of the scenario approach is the way that it encourages us to look at the whole problem before diving into possible solutions.

Systems, then, are not necessarily software, nor even hardware: people and procedures are and will remain important. Scenarios are ideal for exploring and defining the behaviour of systems involving people (socio-technical systems) in complex business procedures—indeed, every written procedure is scenario-like, however poorly expressed it may be.

THE WAY AHEAD

The last part of the book looks at the way ahead for systems development with scenarios. Ian Alexander and Ramin Tavakoli look at how to put scenarios into practice in Chapter 22. Mary Beth Rosson, John Carroll, and Con Rodi present their method of teaching computer scientists enough scenario-based design to make software 'with use in mind' in Chapter 23—involving teaching students both human–computer interaction and usability engineering. We reflect on what scenarios are not good for in Chapter 24, and finally we assess the future of scenarios in Chapter 25.

KEYWORDS

Scenario	Narrative	Exception	Role
Story	Life-Cycle	Misuse Case	Stakeholder
Storyboard	Planning	Test Case	
User Story	System	Situation	
Use Case	Simulation	Alternative World	

REFERENCES

Alexander, C., *Notes on the Synthesis of Form*, Harvard University Press, 1964.

Alexander, I., Introduction to scenarios, a range of techniques for engineering better systems, *Proceedings of IEE Informatics Division Seminar 'Scenarios through the Life Cycle'*, London, December 7, 2000.

Alexander, I., Stakeholders—Who is your system for? *Computing and Control Engineering*, **14**(1), 22–26, 2003.

Alexander, I. and Robertson, S., Understanding project sociology by modeling stakeholders, *IEEE Software*, **21**, 23–27, 2004.

Attenborough, D., *The Life of Mammals*, 2003, http://www.bbcshop.com/

Beck, K., *Extreme Programming Explained: Embrace Change*, Addison-Wesley, 2000.

Birkerts, S., *The Gutenberg Elegies, The Fate of Reading in an Electronic Age*, Faber & Faber, 1994.

Carroll, J., *Scenario-Based Design, Envisioning Work and Technology in System Development*, John Wiley, 1995.

Checkland, P. and Scholes, J., *Soft Systems Methodology in Action*, John Wiley, 1999. (This book is an extended version of the first edition (1990), with a useful '30-year retrospective' of Checkland's thinking.)

Cockburn, A., *Writing Effective Use Cases*, Addison-Wesley, 2001.

Dijkstra, E., Notes on structured programming, in O.-J. Dahl, E.W. Dijkstra, and C.A.R. Hoare (Eds.), *Structured Programming*, Academic Press, 1972.

Eberts, R., *User Interface Design*, Prentice Hall, 1994.

Fowler, M., with Scott, K., *UML Distilled: A Brief Guide to the Standard Object Modeling Language*, Addison-Wesley, 1999.

Harel, D. and Marelly, R., *Come, Let's Play: Scenario-Based Programming Using LSCs and the Play-Engine*, Springer-Verlag, 2003

Jacobson, I., *The* use-case construct in object-oriented software engineering, *Scenario-Based Design, Envisioning Work and Technology in System Development*, John Wiley, 1995, pp. 309–336.

Jacobson, I., Magnus, C., Patrik, J., and Övergaard, G., *Object-Oriented Software Engineering: A Use Case Driven Approach*, Addison-Wesley, 1992.

Kotonya, G. and Sommerville, I., *Requirements Engineering, Processes and Techniques*, John Wiley, 1997.

Kuniavsky, M., *Observing the User Experience, A Practitioner's Guide to Research*, Morgan Kaufmann, 2003.

McGraw, K. and Harbison, K., *User-Centered Requirements, The Scenario-Based Engineering Process*, Lawrence Erlbaum Associates, 1997.

Pinker, S., *The Language Instinct*, Penguin Books, 1994.

Schank, R., *Tell Me a Story: Narrative and Intelligence*, Northwestern University Press, 1995 (first published by Charles Scribner's Sons, 1990).

Simon, H., *The Sciences of the Artificial*, 3rd ed., The MIT Press, 1996.

Sommerville, I. and Sawyer, P., *Requirements Engineering, A Good Practice Guide*, John Wiley, 1997.

Sutcliffe, A., Scenario-based requirements engineering, mini-tutorial, 11th *IEEE International Requirements Engineering Conference*, Monterey Bay, CA, September 8–12 2003, pp. 320–329.

Weber, M. and Weisbrod, J., Requirements engineering in automotive development: experiences and challenges, *IEEE Software*, **20**, 2003, 16–24.

RECOMMENDED READING

John Carroll's excellent *Scenario-Based Design* (Carroll 1995) is a useful book, the product of a meeting of industrial and academic researchers. It is unfortunately out of print, and becoming dated—a lot has happened in the requirements field in the decade since it was written. These facts form part of the reason for writing this volume now. Carroll himself has an HCI background, and his book looks at using scenarios to help design systems (mainly software), often from the point of view of usability. For example, Jakob Nielsen writes a fine chapter on usability engineering; Morten Kyng writes about creating contexts for design, which he rightly states is based on earlier movements such as user-centred design and participatory design; while Ivar Jacobson makes a cameo appearance in a chapter on use cases in object-oriented software engineering—it's doubtful if even he would say that that was all use cases were good for today. We are privileged to have a contribution from Carroll in the form of Chapter 23, Teaching Computer Scientists to Make Use.

Karen McGraw and Karan Harbison's *User-Centered Requirements: The Scenario-Based Engineering Process* (McGraw and Harbison 1997) is another good book whose title firmly places it in the usability tradition. It is also sadly out of print—let us hope that 'third time lucky' applies to the present volume. Its coverage is again excellent but its language is that of knowledge acquisition for expert systems, and to a lesser extent that of HCI. Hardly any requirements books or papers appear in the quite extensive list of references.

The process described in the book consists of first planning the requirements project, then selecting techniques, creating scenarios, interactive observation (aka Contextual Inquiry, *see* Chapter 10), interviewing, work process analysis, defining domain concepts, analysing decision-making, group sessions (aka Workshops), and finally evaluating and refining requirements. It's practical and soundly based on theory and experience, but it doesn't mention UML or Use Cases.

Alistair Cockburn's *Writing Effective Use Cases* (Cockburn 2001) focuses as you'd expect on the Use Case construct; but the advice on writing textual scenarios within this framework is more widely applicable, and the emphasis on getting an external, stakeholders' view of what a system should be doing—and expressing that in 'prose' (narrative text) is exactly right. The book's frame of reference is object-oriented software development using UML, but behind that mask is an approach that can be applied to systems of many kinds. It is a well-written and practical book, which presents and discusses many real examples in full.

Alistair Sutcliffe's *User-Centred Requirements Engineering, Theory and Practice* (Sutcliffe 2002) covers a lot of ground in its 200 pages, but includes a useful chapter on Scenario-Based Requirements Engineering (SCRAM), "a practical method of scenario-based RE". This is a prototyping approach involving cycles of preparing storyboards, scenarios, and so on; walking users through them; and redesigning the prototypes collaboratively. The book describes three techniques:

- Storyboards/concept demonstrators/prototypes: "to provide a designed, interactive artefact that users can react to";
- Scenarios: "the designed artefact is situated in a context of use, thereby helping users relate the design to their work/task context"; and
- Design rationale: "the designers' reasoning is deliberately exposed to the user to encourage user participation in the decision process".

The book has a researchy flavour, but the techniques have all been tried out in practice, and the use of each type of model and technique is exceptionally clearly explained.

David Harel and Rami Marelly's *Come, Let's Play: Scenario-Based Programming Using LSCs and the Play-Engine* (Harel and Marelly 2003) provides a completely different take on scenario use, based on playing scenarios into the computer so that it can both make executable models and play them back, through the system-under-design's user interface. The lavishly illustrated book comes with a CD of software so that the reader (or should that be 'operator'?) can try out the ideas directly.

Roger Schank's *Tell Me a Story: Narrative and Intelligence* (Schank 1990) is a charming and inspiring book by a pioneer of computing, artificial intelligence, and scenario use—he is famous for his work on scripts, for example. The book scarcely mentions computers at all: instead, it is a deeply thought out essay on story. Schank comes up with sayings like "People think in terms of stories. They understand the world in terms of stories that they have already understood." You can perhaps guess from that, that Schank has come to believe that a rule-based approach (if X then do Y else do Z) to specification doesn't work too well; a case-based approach using stories/scenarios might be better. The book gives a fascinating insight into another way of thinking about knowledge, about human reasoning, and about how we perhaps ought to be specifying business processes and systems—with stories.

CHAPTER 2

SCENARIO-BASED APPROACHES

Neil Maiden[1] and Ian Alexander[2]

[1] *Centre for HCI Design, City University, London, UK*
[2] *Scenario Plus, London, UK*

THE CREWS project created a framework to classify scenario approaches by their form, contents, purpose, and life cycle. It was developed to inform further research and development work in scenario-based systems development, and as such provides a useful framework for classifying and reviewing the many pieces of work reported in the chapters in this book. This chapter explains what that framework is, and applies it to highlight distinctive features and trends in the various scenario approaches described in Part II of the current volume.

OVERVIEW: THE CREWS SCENARIO FRAMEWORK

The CREWS scenario framework is described in (Rolland et al. 1998). Readers are referred to that report for a full description of the framework, with detailed examples. The framework considers different scenario approaches from research or industrial practice along four different axes or views, each capturing an aspect of the scenarios:

— *The form view* deals with the expression mode of a scenario. Are scenarios formally or informally described, in a static, animated or interactive form?—are the kinds of questions that this view deals with. Scenario form can include text, tables, and so on.

— *The contents view* concerns the kind of knowledge that is expressed in a scenario. Scenarios can, for instance, focus on the description of system functionality or they can describe a broader view in which the functionality is embedded in a larger business process with various stakeholders and resources bound to it.

— *The purpose view* is used to capture the role that a scenario is aiming to play in the requirements-engineering process. Describing the functionality of a system, exploring design alternatives or explaining drawbacks or inefficiencies of a system are examples of roles that can be assigned to a scenario.

Scenarios, Stories, Use Cases: Through the Systems Development Life-Cycle. Edited by Ian F Alexander and Neil Maiden
© 2004 John Wiley & Sons, Ltd. ISBN: 0-470-86194-0

— *The life-cycle view* considers scenarios as artefacts that evolve in time through operations carried out in the requirements-engineering process. Creation, refinement, or deletion are examples of such operations. The question of persistency versus transience is also addressed.

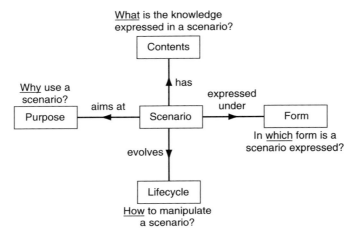

FIGURE 2.1   The four views of scenarios in the crews framework

These facets and a summary of their meanings are depicted in Figure 2.1.

The framework uses a faceted classification method for classifying reusable components. Each view has a set of *facets*, which are viewpoints or dimensions for characterising and classifying scenarios. For example, the *description* facet in the *form* view helps to classify scenarios according to the medium and the language that they use. Each facet has a metric and is measured by a set of attributes. For instance, the *description* facet is measured with two attributes, namely *medium* and *notation*. Attribute values are defined within a domain such as Integer, Boolean, Enumeration, Set, or Tuple.

In this chapter, the framework is outlined and then used to introduce the scenario approaches described in Part II of this volume.

THE FRAMEWORK

The framework consists of four views (Form, Contents, Purpose, and Life cycle), each with several facets. Each facet is defined in several attributes, whose types are listed, and illustrated with examples from some popular approaches. The framework uses three example approaches (Rolland et al. 1998) chosen to illustrate the spectrum of scenario usage. Readers are referred to that paper for further details and original references:

- *Jacobson's use-case approach* (1992) illustrates the use of scenarios in the form of use cases for software engineering, and is now very widespread in the form of UML, as popularised by Alistair Cockburn and others (Cockburn 2001).

- *Kyng's prototyping approach* (1995) tries to show that mock-ups, prototypes, and scenarios can support all steps of the design process enhancing creative end-user participation. The six artefacts (summaries, work situation descriptions, use scenarios, mock-ups and prototypes, exploration/requirement scenarios, and explanation scenarios) used during Kyng's design process can be viewed as kinds of scenarios.

- *Potts' inquiry cycle approach* (1994) is representative of scenario-based approaches, involving a detailed requirements analysis model supporting documentation, discussion, and evolution of requirements.

The form view has two facets with relevant attributes. The description facet has two attributes—notation, which is enumerated with the values {formal, semi-formal, informal} and medium, which is enumerated with the values from the set {text, graphics, image, video, software prototype}. The presentation facet also specifies two attributes—animation, which has the Boolean value (equating to Static or Animated) and interactivity, which can have the values {None, hypertext-like, advanced}. For example, Table 2.1 summarises the position of three published scenario approaches according to the Form view by providing values for the Description and Presentation facet attributes.

The contents view has four facets, each with specified attributes. The facets are coverage: (i.e. what sets of things does the scenario cover?), context: (i.e. what level is this scenario at?), argumentation (i.e. does the scenario support different types of argumentation and justification?), and abstraction (i.e. does the scenario describe agents and events at the type or instance levels?). Some of the attributes for each of these facets, for three published scenario approaches, are shown in Table 2.2. The value True value indicates whether each approach supports the facet's attribute, whereas the False value indicates that the approach does not.

The purpose view has only one facet—role—with three attributes defining whether or not the scenario fulfils a descriptive role, an exploratory role, or an explanatory role. For example, Table 2.3 shows how some published scenario approaches differ in the purpose view.

The life-cycle view has two facets and attributes—lifespan (i.e. whether the scenario is transient or persistent in the life cycle). The lifespan facet has one attribute, which is enumerated to 2 values {Transient, Persistent}. The capture facet is more complex and has five facets—capture, integration, refinement, expansion, and deletion—each of which has a Boolean value indicating whether each approach supports the different

TABLE 2.1 Classification of three approaches according to the form view (from Requirements Engineering Journal, Rolland et al. 1998)

		Jacobson	**Potts**	**Kyng**
Description	Medium	{Text}	{Text}	{Text, Prototype}
	Notation	Informal	Semi-formal	Informal
Presentation	Animation	False	False	True
	Interactivity	None	Hypertext-like	Hypertext-like

TABLE 2.2   Scenario-based approaches classification according to the contents view (from Requirements Engineering Journal, Rolland et al. 1998)

		Jacobson	**Potts**	**Kyng**
Abstraction	Instance	True (scenario)	True	True
	Type	True (use-case)	True	True
	Mixed	False	True	True
Context	System_Internal	False	True	True
	System_Interaction	True	True	True
	Org.Context	False	True	True
	Org.Environment	False	False	False
Argumentation	Position	False	False	True
	Arguments	False	False	True
	Issues	False	False	True
	Decision	False	False	False
Coverage	Functional	{S, F, B}*	{S, F, B}	{S, F, B}
	Intentional	{}	{}	{Goal, responsibility}
	Non-functional	{}	{}	{User support, security, performance, design constraints}

*{Structure, Function, Behaviour}

TABLE 2.3   Scenario-based approaches classification according to the purpose view (from Requirements Engineering Journal, Rolland et al. 1998)

		Jacobson	**Potts**	**Kyng**
Role	Descriptive	True	True	True
	Exploratory	False	False	True
	Explanatory	False	False	False

operations in the software development life cycle. For example, Table 2.4 demonstrates how some published scenario approaches differ by the life-cycle view.

THE SCENARIO APPROACHES DESCRIBED IN THIS BOOK

We applied the CREWS classification scheme to review the 14 approaches reported in the second section of this book. Table 2.5 summarises the results of the review. The

TABLE 2.4   Scenario-based approaches classification according to the life-cycle view (from Requirements Engineering Journal, Rolland et al. 1998)

		Jacobson	**Potts**	**Kyng**
Lifespan		Persistent	Persistent	Persistent
Operation	Capture	from_scratch	from_scratch	from_scratch
	Integration	False	True	False
	Refinement	True	False	False
	Expansion	False	False	True
	Deletion	False	True	False

classification highlights some interesting commonalities and differences between the approaches. Let us examine the approaches facet by facet.

Most approaches use text and graphics to represent scenarios rather than images and prototypes: for example, the use of scenarios reported by Suzanne Robertson in Chapter 3. This result is surprising given findings that have been reported elsewhere. For example, Weidenhaupt et al. (1998) report a Europe-wide survey of scenario use in software development that revealed that two-thirds of all projects enhanced the use of scenarios with prototypes. The results of our review of the approaches do not necessarily argue that prototypes are not used, but the results do suggest that the reported approaches do not explicitly mandate or depend upon the use of prototypes, although they may encourage it. Another finding is that other scenario representations exist, even if only in the background. For example, Suzanne Robertson also reports the use of scenes that are acted out by stakeholders as an innovative form of scenario, similar to the use of role-played reported elsewhere, for example in (Graham 1998).

A less surprising result is that only one approach, the use of imagined future world scenarios reported by David Bush in Chapter 6, uses formal representation of scenario parameters—the 13 other approaches all use informal and semi-formal scenario representations. David Bush describes how he creates snapshot scenarios of imagined future worlds to evaluate the stability of goals. It is one of the few approaches of non-narrative scenarios—static, rather than sequences of steps—and also one of the few that capture non-functional aspects.

The trend towards the use of simple scenario representations of software tools continues with the presentation facet. None of the approaches explicitly use scenario animations, even in simple form, and few approaches support interactive exploration of the scenarios. Instead, scenarios are used as artefacts that can be changed during systems development, but they tend to be static rather than dynamic artefacts, in spite of exceptions such as the ART-SCENE approach reported in Chapter 9.

The abstraction facet revealed greater variations across the 14 approaches. Some use scenarios to describe instances of agents, objects and their behaviour, while other approaches use scenarios that express type-level constructs. To our surprise, given the informality of most scenario representations, few of the approaches appear to mix instance and type-level representations in the same scenario.

TABLE 2.5 Classification of Scenario Approaches Presented in this Book

		Robertson	Van Helvert & Fowler	Gottesdiener	Bush	Alexander (Misuse Cases)	Sutliff	Maiden	Holtzblatt	Benyon & Macaulay	Haumer	Beck & West	Alexander (Test Cases)	Farncombe
Descri-ption	Medium (1)	{T, G}	{T}	Any	{T}	{T, G}	{T}	{T}	{T, I, P}	{T}	{T, G}	{T}	{T}	{T}
	Notation (2)	I	I	Any	F Parameters	S-F	I Natural Language	S-F	Any	I, S-F	S-F	I	S-F	I
Presen-tation	Animation (3)	F	F	F	F	Any	F	F	F	F	F	F	Any	F
	Interactivity	F	F	F	F	F	F	F	F	F	F	None	F	F
Abstra-ction	Instance	Any	T	Any	T	Any	F	T	T	T	F	T	T	T
	Type	Any	F	Any	F	Any	T	T	T	T	T	?	F	F
	Mixed	F	T?	F	F	F	F	F	F	F	F	?	T	F
Context	System internal	T	F	T	T	T	T	T	T	T	T	F?	T	T
	System interaction	T	T	T	T	T	T	T	T	T	T	T	T	T
	Org. context	T	T	T	T	T	T	T	T	F	T	F	T	F
	Org. environment	?	?	F	T	?	F	F	T	F	?	F	T	F
Argu-mentation	Position	F	F	T	F	T	F	F	T	F	F	F	F	F
	Arguments	F	F	F	T	T	F	F	T	F	F	F	F	F
	Issues	T	T	T	F	T	F	F	T	F	F	F	F	F
	Decisions	F	F	T	F	T	F	F	T	F	F	F	F	T
Coverage	Functional (4)	{F, B}	{B}	{F, B}	{}	{F, B}	{F, B}	{F, B}	{S, F, B}	{F, B}	{F, B}	{B}	{F, B}	{F}
	Intentional (5)	{G}	{O}	{G, GD}	{}	{G, GD}	{G, GD}	{G}	{G, GD, R, O}	{G}	{G, GD}	{G}	{G}	{}
	Non-funct (6)	{}	{}	via misuse cases	{Stability}	{Safety, Security, etc}	{}	{}	{} captured in UED	{}	{}	{}	{}	{}
Role	Descriptive	T	T	T	F	T	T	T	T	T	T	T	T	T
	Exploratory	T	T	T	T	T	F	F	T	T	F	F	F	F
	Explanatory	?	F	F	T	T	F	F	T	T	F	F	F	F
LifeSpan (8)		Persist	Persist?	Persist	Transient	Any	Persist	Persist	Persist	Persist	Persist	Persist	Persist	Persist
Operation	Capture	T	T	T	T	Scratch	Scratch	T	T	T	T	Scratch	T	T
	Integration	T	F	T	F	F	F	?	T	T	T	F	F	F
	Refinement	T	T	T	F	T	F	T	T	T	T	T	T	T
	Expansion	?	F	T	F	T	F	T	T	T	T	T	F	F
	Deletion	F	F	F	F	F	F	F	F	T	F	F	F	F

(1) T: Text, I: Image, G: Graphics, P: Prototype.

(2) Any: any accepted value, I: Informal, S-F: Semi-Formal, F: Formal.

(3) T: True, F: False.

(4) S: Structure, F: Function, B: Behaviour.

(5) G: Goal, GD: Goal decomposition, R: Responsibilities, O: Opportunity.

(6) TC: Time Constraints.

(7) (Performance, Time/Cost Constraints, User Support, Flexibility, Error Handling.)

(8) "?" is used for indeterminable values.

The context facet examines what is described in a scenario in each approach—whether it describes the internal system behaviour, the wider organisational environment, or system-level interactions and the context of use that we would characterise as linking internal system behaviour to the wider organisation context. All but two of the approaches describe internal system behaviour and interaction between the system and external agents such as people and other systems, indicating the continuing focus on systems development, and is consistent with the use of scenarios and use cases in the Rational Unified Process (RUP). For example, in Chapter 5, Ellen Gottesdiener holds participative workshops to define system requirements that are mainly for system function, but she also mentions the use of misuse cases to capture non-functional requirements, something covered in more depth in Chapter 7 by Ian Alexander but with more of a focus on safety and security requirements. Likewise, in Chapter 11 David Benyon and Catriona Macaulay apply user stories, conceptual scenarios, concrete scenarios, and use cases to define system interactions. What is more surprising is the focus in most of the approaches on also describing the context and organisational environment in which the systems will be developed. All but two of the reported approaches cover at least one of the contextual aspects. For example, Peter Haumer in Chapter 12 reports the transformation of use cases and goals into analysis and design models to define business processes and system behaviour.

Scenarios in six of the 14 approaches do not support any of the four argumentation and rationale facets, in contrast to Karen Holtzblatt's use of storyboards, use cases, and object models throughout implementation and testing that can effectively describe positions, arguments, issues, and decisions, as reported in Chapter 10. The remaining approaches offer scenarios that describe some but not all of these facets, but without any discernible pattern.

The framework enables us to describe the coverage of each approach using the intentional, functional, and non-functional facets. Scenarios in most approaches are behavioural and functional—again only Holtzblatt's use of scenarios (Chapter 10) goes further by additionally enabling developers to handle the more structural elements of process, work, and organisation. Likewise, most approaches support goal modelling and goal decomposition. In contrast, only the two approaches reported in Chapters 4 and 10 support opportunities, and only the Holtzblatt approach also explicitly supports the expression of actor responsibilities. In Chapter 4, Joy van Helvert and Chris Fowler report the use of 'a day in the life of' scenarios mined in a workshop to identify user needs. These are evaluated to create a service specification.

Many of the results reported from the review depend on the role for which the scenarios are being used in each approach. In most approaches, scenarios are persistent and last throughout the life cycle of the system's development. The framework identifies three facets—or roles—for scenarios: descriptive, exploratory, and explanatory. All but one of the 14 approaches use scenarios of descriptions of some current or future system or environmental situation. Not surprisingly, the approaches intended to be used towards the beginning of the life cycle—in particular, during requirements and system specification—support exploratory behaviour with scenarios to discover and surface issues, whereas approaches used in the later implementation and testing stages do not. For example, in Chapter 13, Kent Beck and David West use stories to capture users' requirements, and these stories have different roles—they can be interrogatory, support delegation, composite, collaborative, or fuzzy. Only one approach—misuse cases in Chapter 7—uses scenarios to explain as well as to describe and explore. Likewise, facets that describe operations that developers are expected to undertake with scenarios reveal that most approaches use scenarios to capture, acquire, surface, and discover, and to refine what has been discovered. One exception to this is Andrew Farncombe's treatment (Chapter 15) of the basic life cycles as stories, combining these stories to create tailored life cycles for specific projects.

CONCLUSION

In this book, we have sought to bring together reports of many of the leading scenario-based approaches currently available to researchers and practitioners. As such, we believe that the 14 approaches are representative of scenario approaches that have been successfully applied in practice or have emerged from research and have significant potential of being successfully applied in the future. The gaps that the classification based on the CREWS framework identifies indicate both potential limits for the applicability of scenario-based approaches and areas for future research and development challenges.

Section 2 reports these 14 approaches in more detail. Read on and enjoy them.

KEYWORDS

Scenario Approaches   Framework   Attributes
Classification   Facets

REFERENCES

Beck, K., *Extreme Programming Explained, Embrace Change*, Addison-Wesley, 2000.

Cockburn, A., *Writing Effective Use Cases*, Addison-Wesley, 2001.

Graham, I., *Requirements Engineering and Rapid Development: An Object-Oriented Approach*, Addison-Wesley, 1998.

Rolland, C., Ben Achour, C., Cauvet, C., Ralyté, J., Sutcliffe, A., Maiden, N.A.M., Jarke, M., Haumer, P., Pohl, K., Dubois, E., and

Heymans, P., A proposal for a scenario classification framework, *Requirements Engineering Journal*, **3** (1) 23–47, 1998.

Weidenhaupt, K., Pohl K., Jarke M., and Haumer P., Scenario usage in system development: a report on current practice, *IEEE Software*, **15**, 1998. Also available as CREWS Report Series No. 97–16 from sunsite.informatik.rwth-aachen.de/pub/CREWS/CREWS-97-16.ps.gz

PART II

SCENARIOS THROUGH THE SYSTEM LIFE-CYCLE: TECHNIQUES

OVERVIEW OF PART 2—TECHNIQUES

INTRODUCTION

This part of the book consists of a set of chapters written by authors with expertise in different scenario-based techniques. Each chapter can stand alone as an introduction to a technique; but the chapters follow a common framework, explained below, and authors have where appropriate, drawn comparisons between their own and other techniques, especially those described in other chapters. Therefore, there are several ways of using this part of the book, other than simply reading it from start to end,

- find the chapters that describe the techniques you are most interested in, and study those in detail;
- read the Summaries of all the chapters to get an idea of the range of techniques;
- skim through the chapters, especially the Strengths and Weaknesses and Comparisons sections, to get an appreciation of the relative merits of the techniques.

STRUCTURE OF THE PART 2 CHAPTERS

Each chapter has the following framework:

Summary

A few paragraphs telling the message of the chapter.

Applicability

A brief factual statement of the types of project for which the described approach is suitable—for example: information systems, distributed systems, control and embedded systems, safety-critical systems.

Position in the Life Cycle

A diagram like the one below, showing the parts of the life cycle covered by the described approach.

Requirements Discovery	Requirements Validation	System Specification	**System Design**	Coding, First of Class	Integration & Testing	Operations & Maintenance

Key Features

A short factual description of the distinguishing marks of the approach.

Strengths

A brief statement of the key benefits of the approach.

Weaknesses

The principal areas that the approach does not address.

Technique

A detailed description of the methods, techniques and conceptual tools involved in the approach.

Worked Example

A detailed stepwise illustration telling the story of how the technique works.

Comparisons

A few pages reviewing how the approach works compared to other approaches, what it doesn't do, what else needs to be evaluated, and what other techniques would be beneficial.

Keywords

A list of terms for the main concepts in the chapter.

Recommended Reading

Recommendations and gentle critiques of the readily available books that chapter authors consider the most suitable for engineers in industry to read to learn more about the topic of their chapters.

TOPICS COVERED

The techniques are organised broadly by the parts of the system development life cycle that they address, namely,

- Discovery and Validation
- Collaborative Approaches (focusing mainly on the early parts of the life cycle)
- Design and Implementation (extending more into the later parts of the life cycle)

- Testing
- Management

This classification is of course, only approximate, and each chapter gives more detailed guidance on the applicability of the techniques it describes.

CHAPTER 3

SCENARIOS IN REQUIREMENTS DISCOVERY

Suzanne Robertson

The Atlantic Systems Guild Ltd, London, UK

EXPERIENCED requirements engineers know the truth—most people do not know what their requirements are. When you ask the question, "What are your requirements?" you usually get a response that is in some form of a solution. Or the respondent admits he does not know precisely what he wants but will know it when he sees it—usually in the form of the finished product when it is difficult, if not impossible, to make changes. Why does this happen? Because requirements come from people, and people are influenced and constrained by their own knowledge, experience, imagination, and attitudes. Regardless of whether you are specifying requirements for a banking system, a control system for a pacemaker, a nuclear submarine, a vacuum cleaner or a teddy bear, the requirements must come from people. But each person's requirements will be influenced by his own experience of the world and, someone else might not even consider something that is vital to one person. Given these variations between people, it is not enough to just ask people what they want. We need a variety of different techniques for discovering requirements and we need to choose the technique that best fits each situation.

Scenarios are a technique that is being increasingly used as a requirements discovery tool because a scenario helps people to think past the obvious, to discover the real requirements, and to come up with creative and inventive ideas. Scenarios provide a vehicle for involving people in telling a story by exploring a scene and thereby discovering the requirements.

APPLICABILITY

Projects in many different domains have used the approach described in this chapter. These include: stock control for an office products manufacturer, development of motor vehicle electrical components, a television scheduling system, a computer operating system, redesign of the structure of a medical insurance company, calibration and measurement

---

Scenarios, Stories, Use Cases: Through the Systems Development Life-Cycle. Edited by Ian F Alexander and Neil Maiden
© 2004 John Wiley & Sons, Ltd. ISBN: 0-470-86194-0

tools for automotive engineers, billing system for mobile phone company, implementation of enterprise resource software, financial management and banking, and tracking shipments.

POSITION IN THE LIFE CYCLE

Requirements Discovery	Requirements Validation	System Specification	System Design	Coding	Integration and Testing	Operations and Maintenance

Building requirements scenarios encourages imagination and exploration and sets the stage for discovering unconscious and undreamed of requirements. Informal sketches (described in this chapter) are especially helpful in requirements discovery.

You can play through a scenario with a number of different stakeholder groups to discover discrepancies and conflicts. The scenarios help you discover the atomic requirements. These requirements—and all their attributes—can be individually validated. If you are using this discipline you can ask testers to help validate the requirements. Each requirement is formally linked to all the scenarios it applies to. So groups of requirements can be validated as a functional group.

You also use the requirements scenarios as input to system specification decisions. The more you explore the scenarios, the more you learn about the subject matter and the better you are able to make decisions about allocation. Which parts of the scenario are inside the system you plan to build and which parts are outside.

The scenario-related groups of atomic requirements are input to designing tests. This provides a feedback loop between the testers, the developers, and the business or subject matter experts.

KEY FEATURES

This approach uses scenarios as a tool for discovering requirements and linking the business investigation to the building of a product. A variety of scenario-building techniques provide options for differing degrees of formality. The requirements knowledge model—illustrated in this chapter—provides a common language for grouping and linking requirements. Business events, business use cases, and product use cases work in conjunction with scenarios to discover and organise the requirements.

STRENGTHS

This is a way to discover requirements that can be used and followed by business people, requirements analysts, and developers. Business events are a consistent stepping-stone for exploring scenarios, leading to product use cases, and for functionally linking requirements. Flexible techniques are underpinned by a formal structure for organising and communicating requirements knowledge.

WEAKNESSES

There is a danger of building too many scenarios and being overcome by "analysis paralysis". We need to develop more guidelines on recognising which business events will benefit from additional scenarios. Sometimes the whole point of building a scenario is to explore and discover requirements that might otherwise be missed. However, once a scenario is built, I have noticed that people are reluctant to throw it away and this can result in yet more deliverables to maintain. Without the guidance of an experienced requirements engineer, there is a danger of requirements discovery scenarios losing the business focus, turning into product designs, and never discovering the real requirements.

WHAT IS A REQUIREMENTS SCENARIO?

The Shorter Oxford Dictionary defines a scenario as

> "Scenario 1880 from the Italian scena meaning scene. **a.** A sketch of the plot of a play giving particulars of the scenes, situation etc. **b.** The detailed directions for a cinema film."

A scene in a play or a film tells a story with a beginning, middle, and end. Each scene involves specific actors, props, direction, and dialogue. To explore alternatives, the early versions of the scene (scenarios) are rough sketches of the idea. As the live performance draws closer, the details of the scenario become more precise. Let's consider the parallels with requirements discovery.

Suppose that your client is Handsome Cabs, a taxi company in London. This client wants you to build a product to help them deal with the taxi bookings from their customers. They also want help in allocating the jobs to the taxi drivers. In order to discover the requirements, you need to study a system that involves taxi drivers, passengers' booking habits, the rules for allocating jobs, the traffic patterns, new ideas for improving the customer service, and so on. The list goes on and the context of your study is potentially huge, clearly too big to study as one big scenario without missing pieces or wasting time. However, if you can break your context of study into a number of linked scenes then you could explore each scene individually by building a number of scenarios.

For example, one scene tells the story of what happens when the customer decides to book a taxi. You can build a scenario that captures the story of what normally happens in this scene. You can also build some exception case scenarios to discover the requirements that people often forget to mention.

A requirements scenario is a simulation of what happens within the boundaries of a specific scene for the purpose of discovering the business requirements. You will discover more business requirements if your scenario has a business boundary as opposed to a product boundary. Let's have a look at some examples.

A Business Event

When a customer wants to book a taxi, he asks Handsome Cabs to provide a taxi at a specified time to take him to a specified destination. The taxi company responds by carrying out procedures that are based on their pre-planned business policy.

As defined by Steve McMenamin and John Palmer (1984), a business event is something that happens, within the boundary of your investigation, to which there is a pre-planned business response. The response to the business event is a business use case (Figure 3.1), and that business use case contains all the related business requirements (bear in mind that the business can be related to any kind of domain: management information, electrical engineering, medicine, defence, consumer products, and so on. I am using the taxi system as an example because it is less specialised and hence more likely to be familiar).

Regardless of the domain in which you are working, you can discover requirements by building scenarios for the business event response, commonly referred to as the business use case. In the course of this chapter, I will build up a picture of how all these components are related to each other.

We can apply the business event, business use case pattern to one of the business events for the taxi company. For example, take the business event: *Customer wants to book taxi*. This event takes place when a Customer makes up his mind that he needs a taxi. The event causes a *Taxi Booking Request* to be communicated by the customer to the taxi company. When the taxi company receives the Taxi Booking Request it triggers a business use case (*Make Taxi Booking*) that satisfies all the business requirements that respond to the event.

As we can see in Figure 3.2, one of the requirements is to communicate the *Taxi Booking Confirmation* to the customer. But what is a taxi booking confirmation, under what circumstances is a confirmation produced, and what are all the other requirements that are related to this business use case? The business event has set the scene, now we can build some scenarios to help discover the detailed requirements.

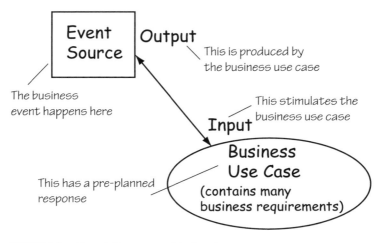

FIGURE 3.1   Event Response Abstract

FIGURE 3.2   Event Response Specific

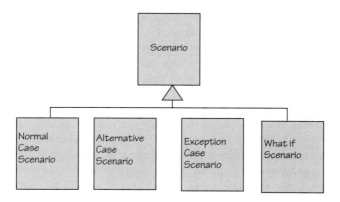

FIGURE 3.3   Scenario Types

Normal Case Scenario

You can build a variety of scenarios for the response to a business event. The four main types are the normal case, the alternative cases, the exceptions, and the what-ifs.

You do not necessarily need to build scenarios for each of these viewpoints (Figure 3.3). The most effective approach is, rather than get diverted by alternatives, exceptions and what-ifs, to start with the normal case, and then you will be in a better position to assess how much effort you need to put into the other views.

Later in this chapter I will talk about a number of techniques for building scenarios. For now, let's look at an example of building a normal case scenario using a text-based approach. Here is a guide on what you need to consider when building a scenario. You do not necessarily have to do all of these things; neither do you have to do them in any precise order. But it will help your scenario-building skills if you understand the thinking behind the following points:

a. Identify a business event

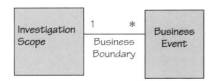

FIGURE 3.4   Scope Event: This model illustrates how your scope of investigation identifies the business boundary for a number of business events (the * indicates many)

b. Identify the business use case

c. Identify the stakeholders

d. Write an informal sketch of the scene of the business use case

e. Formalise the sketch to identify scenario steps

Identify a business event   The process of discovering requirements involves the study and investigation of many interconnected rules and policies that are specific to your scope of investigation. As this diagram illustrates, your investigation will involve a number of business events. And these business events identify the boundary of the business that will lead you to your requirements. For the moment we will focus on one business event.

The business event provides a way of logically partitioning your investigation and a focus for building a relevant scenario (Figure 3.4). A business event has the following attributes:

— Business Event Name: *A name to help understand what the business needs to respond to*

— Business Event Number: *Unique number for tracing the event and connecting it to the business use cases and atomic requirements*

— Input Data: *Input data caused by the business event*

— Output Data: *Output data produced in response to the business event.*

For example, the event we have identified from the taxi company project has the following attributes:

— Business Event Name: *Customer Wants to Book Taxi*

— Business Event Number: 1

— Input Data: *Taxi Booking Request*

— Output Data: *Taxi Booking Confirmation*

Identify the business use case   Once you find a business event it leads you to the business use case; this is because the event is the reason for the business use case. When a business event happens, it triggers the business use case to respond to the business event.

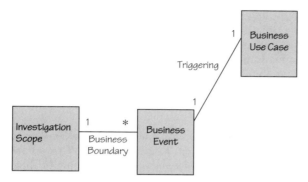

FIGURE 3.5   B Event B Use Case: When a business event happens, it triggers a business use case

To identify the business use case for the business event, *Customer Wants to Book Taxi*, we ask what does the business have to do in order to respond to the business event. Well, the business has to do lots of things, but they are all related to making a taxi booking. So we can name this business use case *Make Taxi Booking*. The business use case (*Make Taxi Booking*) does not exist unless there is a business event (in this case *Customer Wants to Book Taxi*) to which the use case must respond (Figure 3.5). A business use case has the following attributes:

— Business Use Case Name: *A name to help understand the business functionality*
— Business Use Case Number: *Unique number for tracing the use case and connecting it to business events and atomic requirements*
— Input Data: *Input data to which the business use case must respond*
— Output data: *Output data produced by the business use case*

In our example, the business use case attributes are

— Business Use Case Name: *Make Taxi Booking*
— Business Use Case Number: 1
— Input Data: *Taxi Booking Request*
— Output Data: *Taxi Booking Confirmation*

The boundary for the scenario is everything that normally happens (remember we are starting with the normal case) during the time between the customer deciding to make a taxi booking request and the taxi company producing a taxi booking confirmation.

Identify the stakeholders   Given what you know about the business event and business use case, who are the stakeholders who can provide input for the scenario? Of course, the answer to this question depends on the sociology of the particular project that you are doing. It makes sense to do a project sociology analysis at the start of a project (Robertson 2000, Robertson and Suzanne 1999), to discover the people who are the best sources of requirements knowledge. In a very simple world, there would be one person who knows all the requirements but in practice that rarely happens. Instead, you have a number of people in different parts of the organisation and in other organisations, who have some business understanding of the requirements.

To deal with this fragmentation, it is a good strategy to agree on a business owner for each event. The responsibility of the business owner is to help find all the requirements for that business use case. Bear in mind that the business owner will not necessarily know all the requirements but will guide the requirements analysts to the other stakeholders who are the sources of answers.

Let's suppose in the Handsome Cabs example that Erika, the chief despatcher, has agreed to be the owner for the business event *Customer Wants to Book Taxi*. Erika has agreed to do her best to help you discover the requirements for the business use case *Make Taxi Booking* (Figure 3.6). She has also suggested some other stakeholders who have some understanding of that part of the business and are likely to be able to answer questions to which she does not know the answers. The result of your identification of the stakeholders for this event is as follows:

— Business Event: *Customer Wants to Book a Taxi*
— Business Use Case: *Make Taxi Booking*
— Owner: *Erika, the chief despatcher*
— Other Stakeholders: *Accounting department for details of customer accounts, Customers who use the taxi company's services, Other despatchers who work for the taxi company, Public Carriage Office who are responsible for setting the tariff for taxis.*

Now you can start to build your scenario.

Write an informal sketch of the scene   You can start to get to grips with the scenario by writing an informal sketch of the scene of the business use case. If you already have a good understanding of the business use case, then you can choose to skip

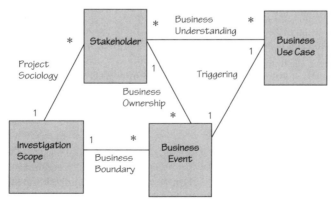

FIGURE 3.6   B Event Stakeholder: There are lots of stakeholders who are within the scope of the investigation. You usually need a different subset of stakeholders to help you understand each business use case

this step and go straight to writing a more formal scenario. However, do not underestimate the power of doing a relaxed investigation before you impose structure and maybe miss asking valuable questions.

In this example, let's suppose that you do not know much about the business use case. You can learn more about it by asking Erika to have a coffee with you, tell her you need 15 minutes of her time and ask her to talk to you about what normally happens when a *Customer Wants to Book a Taxi*. Tell her that you want to stick to this particular business event and not get sidetracked by anything else. Say that you will help her to concentrate on this use case. Tell her that you have ways of making sure that you cover all the business use cases and the connections between them. Ask her to tell you a story.

> *"Well, our customers are from all over London and the vast majority of them are account customers. They communicate with us by phone, some of the bookings are for as soon as possible and others might be up to a couple of weeks in the future. We use our computer system to make sure that the account number is valid and that the account payments are up to date. We have to know when the customer wants the taxi and where he wants to go. The customer also needs to tell us the pickup address, often that is the account address. Given the experience of all our despatchers with London traffic, we can tell the customer the best pickup time for getting to his destination in time. We give the booking a job number and we record all the details on a job docket. We file the job dockets in pickup time order in those trays over there. Then we give the customer a booking confirmation that includes the job number."*

It's likely at this point that Erika will start to veer off into another use case, probably the one that is activated when it is time to allocate a taxi for a job. Tell her that you will deal with that as a separate use case but that, with her help, you will establish formal connections between all related use cases.

Keep track of what she tells you in your requirements notebook using whatever mixture of words, pictures, and models that works for you. Try using a mind map as described by Tony Buzan (1997) to help you to recall all of the details.

If you can get Erika to agree to you, recording what she says will help you trap details that might otherwise be missed. By this I mean voice or video recording. The ideal is a small video camera that also captures sound. However, people are often very wary about being recorded; you need to be very formal and agree on precisely how the recording is to be used and who will have access to it. If you do not feel comfortable using this sort of technology, then ask if you can take a photo of her workplace. Tell her that you want to use it to help recall what she has told you, to trigger questions, and to help you remember and show your colleagues how her organisation works. I carry a small digital camera around with me and use it as a note-taking device. I always ask permission and also send a copy of the photo to the stakeholders concerned.

Formalise the sketch and identify scenario steps   Now you think you know enough to write a more structured scenario. Your input is the analysis that you have done on the stakeholders, the business event and the business use case together with the informal sketch of the normal use case and any other notes, samples or photographs that you have collected (Figure 3.7). First use the sketch to help you to identify the scenario steps according to your understanding so far.

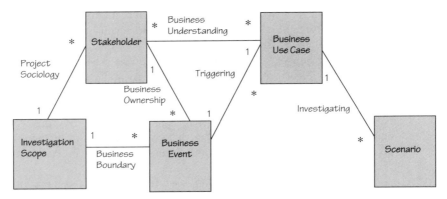

FIGURE 3.7 B Use Case Scenario: Now you have a rough sketch of the normal case scenario. This model indicates that you might build more than one scenario for the same business case; we will look at that later

"Well, our customers are from all over London and the vast majority of them are account customers. They communicate with us by phone, some of the bookings are for as soon as possible and others might be up to a couple of weeks in the future.

1. The first step is that the customer tells us he wants to book a taxi

2. The despatcher needs to get the account number from the customer? Does the despatcher also need the name of the account? Does the despatcher also ask for the name of the passenger?

We use our computer system to make sure that the account number is valid and that the account payments are up to date.

3. The despatcher verifies the account number and payments? Does the despatcher also verify the account name?

We have to know when the customer wants the taxi and where he wants to go. The customer also needs to tell us the pickup address, often that is the account address.

4. The despatcher asks the customer for the pickup date, pickup time, pickup address, and destination.

Given the experience of all our despatchers with London traffic, we can tell the customer the best pickup time for getting to his destination in time.

5. The despatcher tells the customer the optimum pickup time.

We give the booking a job number

6. The despatcher allocates a job number to the booking? Where does the job number come from?

and we record all the details on a job docket. We file the job dockets in pickup time order in those trays over there.

7. The despatcher records the job booking details

Then we give the customer a booking confirmation that includes the job number."

8. The despatcher confirms the booking details to the customer

Your scenario model now looks like this

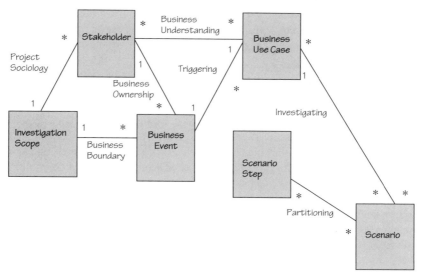

FIGURE 3.8   Scenario, Scenario Step: You have partitioned your normal case scenario into a number of steps. The steps reflect your current understanding of the business use case

Normal Case Scenario for Business Use Case 1: Make a Taxi Booking

1.1 A Customer phones us and tells us he wants to book a taxi
1.2 The taxi despatcher asks the customer for his account number and account name and passenger name
1.3 The taxi despatcher verifies the customer's account details and payments
1.4 The despatcher asks for the pickup address the desired pickup time and the destination
1.5 The despatcher tells the customer the optimum pickup time
1.6 The despatcher allocates a job number to the booking
1.7 The despatcher records the booking details
1.8 The despatcher confirms the booking details to the customer

Bear in mind that a scenario is not a use case; however, it does provide content for the use case. Later you can combine the normal, alternative, and exception scenarios to produce the complete use case as per commonly used structures. You will find that Ian Alexander (2003) and Alistair Cockburn (2001) give practical guidance on the contents and structure of a use case. For now, let's have a look at how the normal case scenario provides a starting point for finding the alternative paths and exceptions and hence discovering the requirements that might otherwise be missed (Figure 3.8).

Identifying Alternative Cases

An alternative case is one that indicates a legitimate business choice that significantly alters the normal case. A way to find alternatives is by taking each step in your normal case scenario and questioning it by using a checklist:

— Does this step always happen precisely as stated?

— Do we know the precise meaning of each noun?
— Do we know the precise meaning of each verb?
— Is there any missing data?
— Are there any subjective judgements?
— Am I making any assumptions?
— Does this make sense to me?

Here is an example of looking for alternatives by asking some of the questions in the exception checklist:

1.1 A Customer phones us and tells us he wants to book a taxi

Is a customer always an individual or could it be an organisation?
Does the customer always communicate with us by phone?
Do customers always want to book one taxi or could there be a booking for several taxis?

1.2 The taxi despatcher asks the customer for his account number and account name and passenger name

Is it always the taxi despatcher who asks the customer or is anyone else involved?
Does the customer always have an account?
Could there be more than one passenger name?
Suppose that you ask these questions and you discover that sometimes (around 25% of the time) the customer does not have an account. Then you could build an alternative case scenario for this situation.

Alternative Case Scenario for Business Use Case 1: Make a Taxi Booking

Customer does not have an account   The taxi despatcher asks the customer for the passenger name and a credit card number
The taxi despatcher verifies the customer's credit card details
The taxi despatcher adds "Non Account" to the recorded booking details

Note that I have not written down the steps that are identical to those in the normal case scenario. I have limited the alternative case scenario to just those steps that are different from the normal case.

Identifying Exception Cases

An exception case is one where an error or an unwanted processing condition arises. You can discover exception cases by taking each step in your normal case and asking:

— What data conditions could make the step unable to proceed?
— What historical conditions could make the step unable to proceed?
— What human behaviour could make the step unable to proceed?

For example, one of the steps in the normal case is

The taxi despatcher verifies the customer's account details and payments

What happens if the taxi despatcher discovers that the customer has provided incorrect account details?

What about if the customer's account has not been paid within the agreed period?

What happens if the customer is impolite to the despatcher?

The answers to these questions might indicate exceptions that might be worth working into a separate scenario.

What-If Scenarios

People usually ask for what they think is possible or what they already have. When you deliver the finished product it often inspires them to ask for something else. Or maybe there is an unexpected change in the world that creates new requirements for you product. You cannot anticipate every change in the world, but a little creative thinking can help you discover requirements that might otherwise be missed. Here is how you can use scenarios to help.

Take your normal case scenario as a starting point and for each step identify the constraints and say: what would happen if this constraint did not exist? For example, the first step in your normal case is

1.1 A Customer phones us and tells us he wants to book a taxi

One of the constraints is that the customer contacts you by phone. If you remove that constraint how else could the customer contact you. An obvious answer is the Internet. But maybe you could have bookings made by travel agents as part of a package deal. Or you could include taxi vouchers as part of tube tickets for the parts of the journey that are not serviced by tube. Or you could issue people with special ultrasonic devices that would pick up the nearest taxi in the area, and so on. Once you remove the constraints and you are in brainstorming mode, the possibilities are endless. By doing this, you uncover business ideas that will not otherwise occur as most of the time we are imprisoned by the present.

While this is a very powerful technique for encouraging creativity and invention, you also have to be careful to review each of the requirements ideas and formally grade them as being inside or outside your business scope. Otherwise you can derail your project by never making any decisions.

FROM SCENARIOS TO ATOMIC REQUIREMENTS

Scenarios are a vehicle for discovering the atomic business requirements (Figure 3.9). Another advantage is that scenarios that are derived from business events provide a logical business grouping for individual requirements. And that business grouping in turn connects to a product grouping and to the resulting system requirements. In other words, you are laying the foundations for traceability.

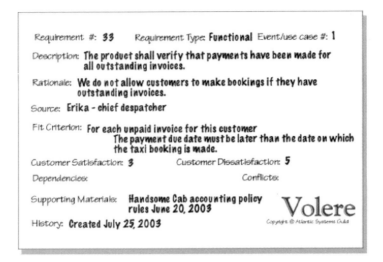

Requirement #: **33**   Requirement Type: **Functional** Event/use case #: **1**

Description: **The product shall verify that payments have been made for all outstanding invoices.**

Rationale: **We do not allow customers to make bookings if they have outstanding invoices.**

Source: **Erika - chief despatcher**

Fit Criterion: **For each unpaid invoice for this customer The payment due date must be later than the date on which the taxi booking is made.**

Customer Satisfaction: **3**   Customer Dissatisfaction: **5**

Dependencies: Conflicts:

Supporting Materials: **Handsome Cab accounting policy rules June 20, 2003**

History: **Created July 25, 2003**

Volere
Copyright © Atlantic Systems Guild

FIGURE 3.9   Atomic Requirement in the Volere Template

Before we talk about how to derive the requirements from the steps, it is worth pointing out that an atomic requirement has a number of attributes. The following is an atomic requirement that I have derived from the scenario step:

1.2 The taxi despatcher verifies the customer's account details and payments

The requirement's attributes are as follows:

— A Unique Requirement Number
— The requirement type (Functional, Non-Functional (there are many subtypes of non-functional requirements (Robertson 2000) or Constraint)
— The Business Event Number
— The Product Use Case Number
— Requirement Description
— The Rationale for why we have this requirement
— Source of this requirement
— Fit Criterion, specifies how we will know whether the requirement has been met. This is the input to writing tests.
— Customer Satisfaction/Dissatisfaction. On a scale from 1 to 5, how satisfied will the customer be if we meet this requirement and how dissatisfied will the customer be if we do not meet this requirement. This is the first informal thinking about prioritising the requirements.
— Dependencies, other requirements that depend on the implementation of this one
— Conflicts, other requirements that are in conflict with this one

— Supporting materials, support for the fit criterion and for further understanding of the requirement.

— History, keeping track of creation, reviews, disputes, and decisions.

These attributes combine to specify the requirement so that there is a common understanding between all the relevant stakeholders. In other words, if you have stakeholders who are working very closely together then your requirements definition procedures (and the attributes you define) can afford to be less formal than if you have stakeholders who are separated in terms of geography, time, and experience. Some organisations, especially large ones who want to reuse requirements, choose to record many more attributes of a requirement. Other organisations make do with fewer attributes, especially when the stakeholders have a lot of experience in working together.

I discovered the atomic requirement in the example by examining a step in the scenario. You will find that, because each of your steps will be at a different level of abstraction, some of the steps will result in one requirement and others will result in a number (Figure 3.10). In the case of this step:

1.3 The taxi despatcher verifies the customer's account details and payments

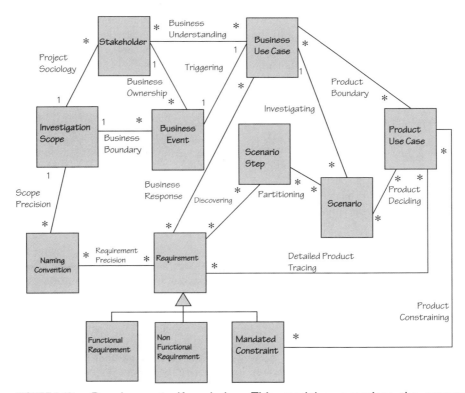

FIGURE 3.10   Requirements Knowledge: This model summarises the connections between atomic requirements and other requirements-related knowledge

We would have one requirement, as per the example, which is concerned with verifying the payments have been made for outstanding invoices and another requirement that specifies the verification of the customer's account details. If the customer's account details are made up of a number of disparate parts, then there might be a case for having more than one requirement. When you write the fit criterion it helps you to decide whether you really have one atomic requirement or whether you need to divide it.

As you can see, there is a great deal of detail necessary to define an atomic requirement. So do you need to define all of the atomic requirements for all of the steps of every scenario? The answer depends on who needs to know about each requirement and how many translations the requirement will go through.

Here is a real example from one of my client's projects. The requirements are being specified by a group of business people and requirements analysts. Then the requirements will be sent to a group of implementers in another country. The people in the two countries do not know each other. Clearly, in a case like this the risk of misinterpretation is high and the investment in precise requirements will pay off.

Another question to help you decide which atomic requirements should be specified in detail is: for each step, do I know whether the requirements related to this step will be included within the scope of the product or not?

If you are sure that the answer is no, then it is likely that you do not need to define each of the atomic requirements for the step. If the answer is partly, then you need to define some of the atomic requirements for the step—those that will be included in the product. If the answer is don't know or maybe, then you should define the atomic requirements for the step.

KEEPING TRACK OF THE INVESTIGATION

As you see in the knowledge model, the investigation scope is concerned with a number of business events and their resulting business use cases. We have focused on one business event in order to explore how to use scenarios to discover requirements. The Handsome cabs project would have a number of business events as summarised in this context diagram (Figure 3.11).

WHO PRODUCES THE SCENARIOS?

Who should be involved in writing the scenario? My ideal is to have a small group (up to six) of representative stakeholders do it together in a workshop session. For more on how to run requirements workshops see (Gottesdiener 2002). However, it is not always possible to get the necessary stakeholders together at the same time. Often, the requirements analyst has to gather input from a number of different stakeholders, derive the scenario, and then help individual stakeholders review it.

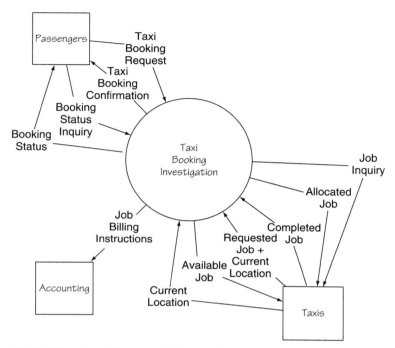

FIGURE 3.11 Taxi Context: This model summarises the business events that are part of the taxi booking investigation. In our exploration of scenarios we have focused on just one business event and its related business use case

TECHNIQUES FOR BUILDING SCENARIOS

We identified the business use case *Make a Booking*, as the response to the business event *Customer Wants to Book Taxi*. As already discussed we can build a number of different scenario views (normal, alternative, exception) for the business use case. We can also use a variety of techniques for building the scenarios. I have had most success with techniques that we refer to as *Low-Fidelity* techniques. In other words techniques that do not require a lot of technical equipment and props, but rely on using tools that people are used to. Like paper, pencils, coloured markers, post it notes, white boards, and flip charts. To start with, a new tool like a digital camera is a High-Fidelity tool. People are not used to it and have to concentrate on learning how it works rather than using it to help build a scenario. When the tool becomes more of an everyday fixture then it becomes a tool that you can use to build low-fi scenarios.

Text Scenarios

In this chapter, I have focused on building scenarios using text. As illustrated with the Handsome Cabs example, text scenarios range from very informal stories to very structured steps. We have seen that an informal story is a very good way of getting started. Then as you get a better understanding you can derive a more structured scenario by identifying scenario steps and eventually deriving atomic requirements.

Story Boards

Anyone who has seen a cartoon strip is familiar with the concept of storyboards. They are widely used by the film industry to plan a scene in a movie. Instead of writing the scenario steps in plain English, you draw a picture of each step (Figure 3.12). You use a combination of drawing and words to explore a scenario. This works well as a technique for exploring the "what-if" scenarios mentioned earlier in this chapter.

As Neil Maiden (2001) illustrated during our creative design workshops with Eurocontrol, people find it easier to build storyboards if you give them a starting point. Instead of a blank sheet of paper we started with an A3 piece of paper marked like this (Figure 3.13).

When we provided this starting point people immediately got involved in the building of a storyboard without having any delays. People who believed that they could not draw just went ahead and drew their own representations of the story. We also provided room for writing comments to expand on each frame of the story.

FIGURE 3.12 Storyboard: This storyboard explores a scenario where there is an emergency and no taxis are available

Storyboard for: Business Use Case...

What if scenario...

- - - - - - - - - - - - -	- - - - - - - - - - - - -	- - - - - - - - - - - - -	- - - - - - - - - - - - -
- - - - - - - - - - - - -	- - - - - - - - - - - - -	- - - - - - - - - - - - -	- - - - - - - - - - - - -
- - - - - - - - - - - - -	- - - - - - - - - - - - -	- - - - - - - - - - - - -	- - - - - - - - - - - - -
- - - - - - - - - - - - -	- - - - - - - - - - - - -	- - - - - - - - - - - - -	- - - - - - - - - - - - -
- - - - - - - - - - - - -	- - - - - - - - - - - - -	- - - - - - - - - - - - -	- - - - - - - - - - - - -

FIGURE 3.13 Storyboard Form

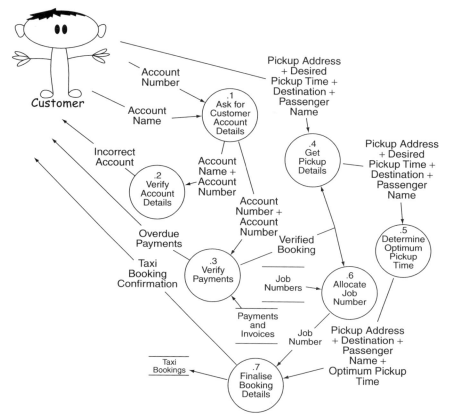

FIGURE 3.14 Process Model Scenario: This scenario process model is a picture of the business use case that responds to the event: customer wants to book taxi

Scenario Process Models

A scenario process model is a picture of the fragments of process together with the dependencies between them (Figure 3.14).

Building a scenario process model is rather like doing a jigsaw puzzle. You are trying to find all the processes that are part of the response to the business event (the business use case). You are also looking for the data that connects those processes: data that is flowing is indicated by an arrow, data that is stored is indicated by two horizontal parallel lines.

The advantages of a scenario process model are as follows:

— You are not forced to write things in a sequential order, so you can identify the true dependencies between processes.

— The medium helps you to expose missing data and raise questions.

— You verify your investigation context by identifying necessary connections with other business use cases. For example, this model is looking at Payments and Invoices, so there must be another use case that is creating this data.

Disadvantages of a scenario process model are as follows:

— You need to be a skilled modeller to be able to build one of these models (or any other analytical model), especially if you are doing it while asking questions and getting input.
— The model exposes details that can lead you away from the normal case before you really understand it.
— Sometimes people are not used to working with models and are more responsive if you show them text.

Scenario Playthroughs

Rob Austin and Lee Devin (2002) draw parallels between the activities involved in producing a play and the activities involved in discovering requirements. We can make use of some of the ideas developed in the theatre to discover requirements. A scenario playthrough brings a scenario to life by acting out a specific scene.

In the Handsome Cabs example, someone plays the part of a customer wanting to book a taxi. The customer asks the despatcher for a taxi at a particular time on a particular day. The despatcher responds accordingly. Then maybe the customer changes his mind, or asks for two taxis instead of one or elects to pay by credit card rather than account. This prompts the despatcher to remember facts he has not yet mentioned or to realise that there are other business possibilities that nobody has yet thought of.

To be effective, a playthrough has to have an element of fun or silliness. Maybe the customer can have a silly name or have an address like Fawlty Towers. Or the customer could talk with a strong accent or have a very long-winded way of explaining what he wants. This makes people more relaxed and relaxation prompts questions and ideas that otherwise do not occur.

WHEN TO USE SCENARIOS

There are a number of situations when scenarios are the best tool for requirements discovery: when you do not know where to start, when you have difficulty involving a stakeholder, when you want to encourage invention and creativity, when you want to establish relevant boundaries.

Suppose that you want to talk to the Erika, the chief despatcher at the taxi company, about what happens when a passenger wants to book a taxi on his account. Erika does not seem keen to talk to you. Maybe, like almost everybody these days, she is very busy. Or maybe she can't see the relevance of talking to you. Or maybe she is afraid. Afraid that you will ask her questions she cannot answer or make her feel confused or inadequate by talking to her in technospeak. A scenario can help you to overcome these obstacles because you can use the technique to ground the questions in terms of Erika's world.

Scenarios do not work well if people use them as an excuse for not exploring and defining the detailed requirements. If you hear comments like, "Well this seems clear enough, let's go ahead and build the product without bothering about details," it is likely that you will miss requirements.

This chapter has focused on using scenarios to discover business requirements by exploring the investigation scope for each business event. As illustrated in the knowledge model, you can also use scenarios to help you explore alternative product use cases for each of the business use cases. In other words, you can focus on a scenario that helps you understand the business and you can also focus on a scenario that helps you decide which parts of the business will be implemented by the eventual product.

KEYWORDS

Business Event	Requirements	Scenario
Business Use Case	Product Use Case	Stakeholders

REFERENCES

Alexander, I., *Scenario Plus*, 2003, http://www.scenarioplus.org.uk
On this website you can find downloadable templates for structuring use cases and including relevant content.

Austin, R. and Devin, L., Beyond requirements: software making as art, *IEEE Software*, **19** 2002.
The authors draw many parallels between the work of collaborative artists in the theatre and the work of systems developers. In particular they draw attention to the iterative nature of the work and the use of play to discover unknown requirements.

Buzan, T., *The Mindmap Book*, BBC Books, London, 1997.
Mindmaps are a creative tool for taking notes so that you can easily recall the details. This books teaches you how to combine colours, shapes, keywords to capture understanding and ideas. The skill of building mindmaps is invaluable for anyone who is trying to capture complex parallel details.

Cockburn, Alistair, *Writing Effective Use Cases*, Addison-Wesley, NJ, 2001.
Read this for practical guidance on how to write use cases and what to include in their content. Useful way of identifying use cases at different levels of detail but would benefit from a formal classification system.

Gottesdiener, E., *Requirements by Collaboration: Workshops for Defining Needs*, Addison-Wesley, 2002.
A valuable source of advice on techniques for planning and running requirements workshops.

Maiden, N. and Gizikis, A., Where do requirements come from? *IEEE Software*, **18** 2001.

McMenamin, S. and Palmer, J., *Essential Systems Analysis*, Yourdon Press, New York, 1984.
Definitive work on identifying business investigation scope and how to partition it into business events.

Robertson, S., *Project Sociology: Identifying and Involving the Stakeholders*, The Atlantic Systems Guild Ltd, 2000, http://www.systemsguild.com
An overview of how to find the right stakeholders for your project and how to involve them in requirements discovery and specification.

Robertson, James and Suzanne, *Mastering the Requirements Process*, Addison-Wesley, 1999.
A process for gathering and specifying requirements that is based on producing the relevant deliverables for each project. The Volere requirements template provides a structure for identifying stakeholders and gathering requirements.

CHAPTER 4

SCENARIOS FOR INNOVATION: DEVELOPING SCENARIO-BASED USER NEEDS ANALYSIS (SUNA)

Joy van Helvert and Christopher Fowler

Chimera, University of Essex, UK

SCENARIO-BASED USER Needs Analysis (SUNA) is a method for envisioning innovative, user-centred software products and services for future markets, six months to two years ahead. The approach is multi-disciplinary and based around the creation of a number of 'day in the life of' (DILO) scenarios in a series of workshop settings. As a research organisation, we have found it particularly effective as a precursor to formal requirements activity and to inform the build of concept demonstrators. Overall, SUNA functions to create explicit space for the exploration of innovative ideas informed by social research and the possibilities offered by new and emerging technologies. Its outputs are designed to interface with conventional 'use case' oriented development methodologies.

APPLICABILITY

So far SUNA has only been used and evaluated in a limited context. It began as a by-product of British Telecom's (BT) collaborative research efforts involving researchers from a number of different European organisations. The teams combined expertise from business, software development, and the social sciences in a mutual effort to generate innovative web-based products and services. Typical real life examples are a web-based Community Learning Service, a Device Unifying Service and a Distributed Working Environment Service. Furthermore, all applications of SUNA have involved product or service concepts with significant levels of human activity, normally with high communication content, and with limited pre-conditions or constraints. It has not been used for more traditional bespoke system development, and is unlikely to be of value to highly technical and automated systems that have limited human involvement. It is equally

---

Scenarios, Stories, Use Cases: Through the Systems Development Life-Cycle.   Edited by Ian F Alexander and Neil Maiden
© 2004 John Wiley & Sons, Ltd.   ISBN: 0-470-86194-0

unsuitable for very futuristic envisioning work (i.e. 10 to 20 years out) or to inform policy or strategy, which is normally in the realm of Scenario Planning techniques.

Despite the caveats, it is a very straightforward approach that could potentially be applied beyond its original context to any situation that requires innovative thinking and is not limited by a large number of legacy constraints. It can be used to generate an initial set of requirements as a precursor to more detailed requirements work or as a guide to the development of a demonstrator or prototype.

POSITION IN THE LIFE CYCLE

Requirements Discovery	Requirements Validation	System Specification	System Design	Coding First of Class	Integration and Testing	Operations and Maintenance

KEY FEATURES

With respect to SUNA, we define a scenario as a concrete description of an activity that the users engage in when performing specific tasks, a description that is sufficiently detailed so that design implications can be inferred or reasoned about. The key features of SUNA are

1. Innovation—We are all creative thinkers but often we operate within regimens or social structures that inhibit our creative potential. Sometimes this is necessary; unbridled creativity at the micro level can equal spiralling costs and overly complex products. However, creating a specific space and time to think holistically and creatively about an issue can result in a solution that takes a radically different path than would otherwise have happened.

2. Narrative— Story telling is a natural human activity that does not require the learning of new conventions, builds trust, and is non-hierarchical. It contains both content (the story), structure (the conditions of telling) and can exist in a variety of contexts

3. Collaboration—Complex System Design is a collaborative activity—best undertaken by a team involving people with the right mix of competences and skills.

4. Dialogue— Good communication is the 'glue' that holds together the team. Through dialogue, the team can create a shared understanding or common vocabulary, reconcile multiple perspectives and explore alternative realities.

5. Flexibility—Its processes are flexible and not prescriptive—it provides a structure rather than a recipe.

6. User focused—Social research and user experience help the team to concentrate on the users, their needs and desires, and thus helps to keep the design activity focused and to minimise requirements 'drift'.

7. Compatibility with existing design methods (e.g. Universal Process by the generation of Use Cases from the Needs Hierarchy).

None of the elements of SUNA are original, they are a collection of well-used tools and techniques that we combined together to form a valuable logical process that continues to evolve as we learn from each application.

STRENGTHS AND WEAKNESSES

The specific strengths and weakness of SUNA can be best described by our 'Four Ps'

1. Processes inherent in the SUNA technique
2. Product and Service concepts being exposed to the SUNA method
3. People who facilitate and participate
4. Places where SUNA is used.

The strength of the SUNA process undoubtedly lies in its simple and non-prescriptive structure. However, consideration should be given to the product or service concepts it will be applied to, the team makeup, the place chosen for workshops and timing in accordance with the flow of the method.

A specific process weakness is uncertainty about where the scenarios come from. Our early SUNA examples were in the e-learning domain, an area in which we had considerable expertise. On reflection, the key success factor in the earlier cases was the notion of focusing around the everyday lives of prospective users to both scope and define the starting point for each scenario. The weakness may become apparent when the SUNA facilitators lack the domain knowledge, and SUNA provides minimal support for the creative process of generating scenarios.

A final process issue is the fact that SUNA is premised on workshops, and these can be expensive in terms of time and money, and are seen as less acceptable at the earliest stages of the development life cycle (*compare* the Rapid Application Development (RAD) approach). Consequently, there is pressure to look for ways in which the method can be 'discounted' to improve efficiency without loss of effectiveness. One step taken to partially meet this need is to collect and archive scenarios that could be re-used. These are not just SUNA-generated scenarios. We have also been trawling through other projects that have created scenarios, and after a vetting procedure, including them in the archive.

SUNA does not directly address issues of requirements/needs management or tracking. Future versions are likely to be able to assess the impact of late design decisions on user acceptability. Doing this requires prioritisation based on value. Our embryonic value attribution process addresses this and also importantly provides a direct link back into the business model or business case—high-value solutions should meet high-value needs.

The section on applicability above, described the situations where we think SUNA can be used. However, each application of SUNA is never identical, and we need more case studies to provide heuristics to support the less experienced user of the method.

A further concern about SUNA is whether it's the 'singer or the song'. It's been mainly the same team that has used and developed SUNA. To be confident about the generalisability of the method requires new teams using it on new service concepts.

Finally, there has been the issue of 'place'. SUNA workshops are best undertaken away from the work place and all of its distraction, as this encourages a commitment to the task in hand. However, it does not require specialised 'innovation laboratories'. Such facilities are useful but not essential.

TECHNIQUE

Traditional requirements capture, particularly for the development of bespoke systems, has relied on 'information gathering' mainly through the use of interviews or workshops (e.g. Joint Application Development) to build a picture of the extant system. The results are described abstractly through the use of diagrams and models. This approach provides a technical description of the movement and behaviour of system objects, often with scant regard for the user issues, and this can result in the development of unusable or unacceptable solutions. For proprietary software development, the problem was similar. The customer's needs or requirements were supposedly 'captured' in the Market Definition documents, validated by market research, and defined in Service Definition documents. However, the main thrust of marketing is to identify an opportunity, not to generate a valid and completed set of user needs.

There is a 'gap' between what the requirements analysis and marketing tools and approaches could provide and what the designer actually needed. In terms of usability engineering, people attempted to fill that gap by incorporating Human Factors tools and techniques (e.g. Task analysis) into existing and structured design methods such as SSADM v6, USTM (see e.g., Hutt et al. 1988) or by developing new 'user-centred' methodologies (e.g. HUFIT see Taylor 1990). 'Human Factors by stealth' has certainly helped improve the usability of services, but has been less effective in ensuring that there was a real user need for the service (i.e. utility not just usability is important).

A further difficulty with the traditional life-cycle approach (including more user-centred and iterative design methods) is the emphasis on *system requirements* at the expense of *user needs*. Although both, if employed properly, should be technology independent, one is a description of what developers are required to build, and the other a description of the user's expectations, motivations and actions (*see* Carroll 1995). In a user-centred design philosophy, the scenario can both encapsulate the needs and be used to derive the requirements. But there is a particular problem with discovering user needs when you are looking to innovate. This falls in the realm of consumer prediction—until a market need has emerged and awareness has propagated through the marketplace, locating new ideas and needs by relying solely on asking mainstream customers what they want is likely to be ineffective. Mainstream users will only be able to articulate their needs in terms of enhancements to existing products and services. They are less aware of the possibilities offered by new developments in technology or embryonic social, economic, environmental, or political trends (Haywood 2003, Goldenberg and Mazursky 2002).

The SUNA method we describe in this chapter was designed to fit more within an innovation process rather than the traditional life-cycle approach. Indeed, it could be considered as a bridge between ideation and design—it begins before the traditional 'requirements capture or discovery' activities. The scenario at this level is not trying to enrich traditional descriptions (e.g. data flow diagrams—*see* Harker and Eason 1999) or support the description of specific user–computer behaviors (e.g. use cases). It is more about the use of narrative or story telling to understand the relationships or connections between actors and events (*compare* Denning 2000) and to elicit new thinking. As such, narrative is replacing or at least preceding the analytical and descriptive tools of traditional methods (e.g. data flow diagrams, entity models, etc.) with a more Tolstoyan approach or 'ecological' thinking that enables us to imagine and describe new perspectives and new realities. Description of existing or future services initially through the use of scenarios involves conventions of story telling that are known and understood by users thus improving communication and validation. With scenarios, users have a language and convention that makes true participation in design more likely—scenarios should be engaging, comprehensible, and critically, should build trust and understanding.

Throughout the following description of the method, we use the term 'service' for describing the software system that is intended as the end result of the requirements capture, design, development, and testing life cycle; however, other terms such as 'system', 'product', 'bespoke development', and so on, could equally be substituted.

Method Outline

The basic framework (see Figure 4.1) is made up of some preparatory work to gather all artifacts that are relevant to the task and to set up the team, ensuring that everybody is

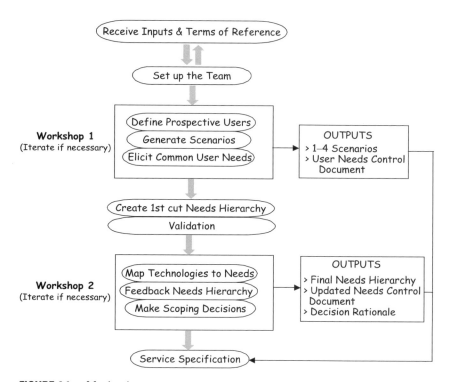

FIGURE 4.1   Method map

fully briefed. This is followed by a first workshop to generate and analyse the scenarios. The outputs of the first workshop are a number of DILO style scenarios and a list of user needs (extracted from the scenarios), which make up the Needs Control Document. Once the workshop is over, a nominated individual further analyses and organises the outputs to a form of hierarchy, termed a 'Needs Hierarchy', that provides a conceptual structure for the service. A final workshop is used to evaluate the hierarchy and decide on the scope of the development work. The outputs are a final Needs Hierarchy, an updated Needs Control Document, and documentation of the decision-making rationale. Collectively, the outputs form a high-level Service Specification document.

The Team

SUNA is based around a team and workshop model. The teams typically bring together business people, social scientists, and requirements analysts with designers, developers, and technologists. Each person brings with them the expert knowledge of their domain allowing new thinking to form at the nexus of these different disciplines. Of course, as in any real world situation, it is not always possible to select the people who you want to join in the team. However, there is an underlying philosophy that diversity is good; it helps promote the possibility of creativity, provided the environment is non-threatening and any conflict is managed effectively.

Team numbers can be critical. We found that five to seven works best although, once again, it is not always possible to control the numbers. Large numbers can slow things down, and it may be necessary to split into sub-groups to avoid total inertia.

To support the core team we also use people that can act as consultants, stand-ins, or 'sanity checkers'. We make sure that we keep the wider circle up to date with progress, but in most cases we choose not to include them in workshops unless the numbers are short.

Inputs

At the start of any software development endeavor, there is an initial brief of some kind defining the purpose of the project. These can vary from well-defined terms of reference or a statement of collaboration goals, market propositions or statements through to vague verbal instructions. Where there is a vagary, it is useful to clarify, agree, and document the overall objectives of the task. This provides a reference point for all further discussions. In our use of SUNA, the task instructions have generally been in the form of research proposals that contain an outline description of the expected research deliverables and details of both funding and manpower, which form the constraints of the task.

Once this initial statement of the problem has been received, the team can then start collecting supplementary input that can inform the envisioning process. This is gathered and circulated prior to the first workshop to ensure that all the members of the team are fully informed. Examples are as follows:

- Future trend reports (social, technical, environmental, economic, and political)
- Social Science research
- Technical research/data

- Market reports/research/propositions
- Reports on problems existing within the domain
- Vision statements
- Feature lists
- Minutes of meetings, and so on
- Details of legacy systems that will form constrains on the new development
- Details of funding and any other constraints not in the task instructions.

Knowledge of the problem domain is also key. This can be gathered by identifying domain experts, for example, technical specialists or users of existing services, and by conducting interviews and by observations, which are transcribed to become inputs to the project. Alternatively, the experts can be brought into the workshop when relevant subject matter is being discussed.

Workshop 1

The workshops are the key face-to-face meetings of the process and each has a specific set of aims. We found that one-and-a-half to two consecutive days for each workshop is generally sufficient; however, if the problem is complex or the team is large then additional sessions might be needed. The aims of workshop 1 are to gain a common understanding of the problem area and to generate a number of scenarios and an agreed document that contains a common set of user needs extracted from the scenarios

Typically, the workshop can be broken into three parts. The first part is concerned with creating scenarios by considering who are the main 'actors', the prospective users of the service, and what type of service will they interact with. The second part is generating or refining the scenarios, and the third part is extracting the user needs and considering appropriate technologies to deliver the solution. If the end result is not a bespoke development, then we also try and match prospective Commercial Off The Shelf (COTS) products to the different needs to gain a first cut idea about 'buy or build' decisions.

Setting the Scene

At this point, we generally assume that all the members of the team have read the supporting documentation and are well versed in the background material to discuss different scenario possibilities. The scenario-building process starts with a discussion about the 'actors' whose needs the service must satisfy. In this context, an actor is taken to mean any person (or device) who either interacts directly with the proposed development or has an indirect requirement for the outputs. Key actors are those who interact directly and are the most likely candidates to form the basis of a scenario. An alternative approach, which is most useful when there are no legacy constraints and there is flexibility about the type of service, is to prepare a number of 'personas' prior to the workshop. These are a selection of fictional characters complete with 'lifestyle' details that are based on a mixture 'lifestyle research' and personal knowledge about real people. One or more of these can be used to form the basis of a scenario (Cooper 1999). The details of the service, described in the scenario, are borne out of discussion and creative thinking that can marry the technical possibilities with the actor's lifestyle.

The objective is to write each scenario from a different actor or persona perspective. Scenarios can feature more than one actor or 'persona'; however, there is no need for continuity between the different scenarios, each should be written as a separate entity. The vision for the software development is formed at the intersection of the different scenarios, that is, when a set of common 'user needs' is extracted across all the scenarios

Writing Scenarios

The purpose of writing scenarios is to describe a context and an inter-relationship between the actor and an idealised service that meets the actors needs. As our concern is the fit of the service into the everyday life of the actor, we write scenarios as short DILO vignettes that provide a rich picture of the users needs and how they are met by the service. The act of creating the story organises our thoughts and enables the needs and the potential technical solutions to be considered simultaneously. In a group setting, creating narrative helps people to think 'out of the box' (i.e. beyond any preconceived constraints) and to synthesise their inspiration and experience into a logical whole. At the point of scenario generation, we do not consider potential constraints such as the development budget as this can limit creative thinking. Constraints are applied to the service outline at a later stage in the process. However, it may be appropriate to consider legacy systems from the start where they impact the potential development.

The following is an extract from a scenario written for a European research project concerned with services to help develop formal and informal learning relationships.

> John, George and Paul are 16-year-olds who are studying Geography 'A' level at the same school. They have been friends since joining the school at the age of 11. They meet quite regularly outside of schools and share many interests (e.g. supporting the local football club). They all have Internet access from home, and frequently communicate with each other over the 'phone. John's grandfather, who lives in the next town, is a retired Geography Professor, and he and John have a close and strong relationship. . . Paul has an older cousin in America who is in regular e-mail contact. His cousin is very knowledgeable about the Internet and can usually find a URL for anything!. . . . . .
>
> *George suggests to Paul and John that they use the CL (Community Learning) service that evening to discuss this matter further, and they agree to be online at 19.00. George logs in first. The system asks him what CL group he wishes to connect to and what level of service he requires. George chooses 'friends' and the audio graphic service (audio conferencing, shared white board, URL push), he also chooses to make an audio recording of the meeting. . . . .*

Having decided the rough outlines of the scenarios, we use one of two different approaches to getting the scenarios written. On the majority of projects we have nominated one or more team members, usually willing volunteers, to write a scenario each, generally at the end of a full day workshop discussion. The individual is responsible for distilling the key discussion points into the text but also has the opportunity to input her or his own creative thinking. On occasion we have chosen to break the team into small groups each collaborating to produce a single scenario text. In our experience, good teams usually have people with different but complimentary strengths and, therefore, some people find it easier than others to produce the kind of descriptive narrative that the scenarios require. Consequently, the former approach is more popular.

Extracting User Needs

Once the scenarios are complete, they are analysed and the user needs are highlighted and listed. A 'user need' should indicate one or more broad functional or non-functional requirements of the prospective service. They are drawn from the text of the scenarios by reading through the text and identifying verbs and/or active software system related phrases. The implications for the service can be either explicit or implied by the user interactions. For example,

Scenario Text:

> *While they are in discussion, Paul receives an alert that his cousin in the States is trying to ring him. He tells the others, and they suggest that he should join them as he always has interesting ideas.*

The user needs might be

1. Users shall be alerted to incoming calls and whom these are from.
2. Users shall be able to join callers into an already established audio conference.

The needs are generally couched in definite terms, that is, the use of the words 'shall' and 'will' rather than 'should' and 'may' and recorded in table with a unique number for each item. Definite terminology helps to challenge people's thinking and draw out issues and alternative solutions.

The needs from each scenario are merged. The group then checks through the list of needs removing duplications, particularly those arising from the same needs being described in different ways. The final list of needs is recorded in the Needs Control Document.

Mapping Technologies to Needs

In the telecommunications industry, few new services are bespoke developments. More often than not, they are developed from existing COTS software packages that are specifically designed to be customised and integrated with other packages. Mapping technologies to user needs at this early stage provides an initial guide to the types of software product, platform or technology that could be integrated to deliver the overall service. It also highlights user needs that will require bespoke software development and the scope of the integration work that will be required. Table 4.1 illustrates some specific needs to technology mappings taken from a Needs Control Document for a learning system.

Between the Workshops

Validation

An important advantage of narrative scenarios is that both technical and non-technical people can understand them. In between the workshops, therefore, scenarios can be

TABLE 4.1 Mapping needs to technologies

	User Need	Technology
1	Ability to submit work to Tutor for assessment (need to distinguish from other types of correspondence from students to tutors)	Learning Management System (LMS)
2	Summary table giving details of the files relating to the conference event: • File name • Where stored • Who requires a copy	LMS
3	One click to e-mail conference files (as above) to people who require a copy (recipients must be specified when files are generated or use rules yet to be identified)	E-mail
4	On tool bar—show clocks for countries where students and tutors are based, that is, Malaysia and UK	Portal

checked with prospective users and other interested parties to see if they are reasonable, viable, desirable and so on. They can also be modified or elaborated on the basis of the feedback that is given. Normally the scenario is simply presented to the individual and comments noted, but in one case the scenarios were transformed into animated PowerPoint presentations and presented to a large group of potential users. The latter not only was a very efficient way of presenting the scenarios to large groups, but it also ensured greater validity as the responses of more than one individual were considered.

Needs hierarchy

At the end of the first workshop one of the team is nominated to produce a 'Needs Hierarchy' from the Needs Control Document. Constructing a hierarchy is a way of rationalizing and organizing the user needs. It helps to complete the picture of the embryonic service by creating a structure, highlighting missing needs, and refining existing ones. The end result is a conceptual overview in a format that can easily be discussed and agreed by the group and that provides an interface to structured design and development methods. One of its key roles is to inform the process of scoping the service boundaries, that is, what will and will not be built. This takes place in the second workshop.

The needs are organised into logical groups. The approach we have used is to scan through for high-level needs that can be decomposed and/or logical groups of needs that could be collected under a single higher-level heading. Headings are decomposed to single system tasks or to a level that is judged to be valuable and which captures the original thinking of the group. How far each element is broken down is a matter of

TABLE 4.2 User needs Table

No.	User Need
1.	It shall be possible to create new Learning contracts
2.	It shall be possible to base the Learning Contract on a generic course profile
3.	It shall be possible to tailor the course profile to the students requirements
4.	Learning Contracts must be authorised
5.	It shall be possible to amend and re-authorise existing Learning Contracts
6.	It shall be possible for students to request the Tutor of their choice
7.	The Learning Account Manager shall conduct online meetings with the student and the students line manager to agree the Learning Contract.

choice, it is a not a precise science. However, it's important to ensure that the highest-level headings represent the total scope of the concept, including service support needs such as billing and maintenance.

The following example is a set of User Needs (Table 4.2) and the resulting hierarchy (Figure 4.2) taken from project work to define a distance learning service. The User Needs were generated in the workshop, but once organised into a hierarchy, missing elements were identified and added to complete the concept. The diagram only shows the decomposition of one level, Manage Learning Contract; the full Needs Hierarchy would also show the other higher levels decomposed in a similar fashion.

Workshop 2

The second workshop builds on the work done in the intervening period and it is the point where constraints are considered. The draft Needs Hierarchy provides an overall picture of the problem space and the objective of the workshop is to review, agree, and document the scope of the software development or detailed requirements capture exercise. The hierarchy is generally presented to the team in PowerPoint form or similar, and is talked through level by level. Some of the questions that we consider when reviewing the Needs Hierarchy are

- Where is the boundary of the software development, that is, what is in and what is out?
- or, What is the boundary of the detailed requirements capture exercise?
- Is this an appropriate/logical grouping of functions/needs?
- Are there any missing levels?

Scoping decisions are usually made on the basis of one or more of the following criteria:

- Available funding and resources
- Consistency with the original task description

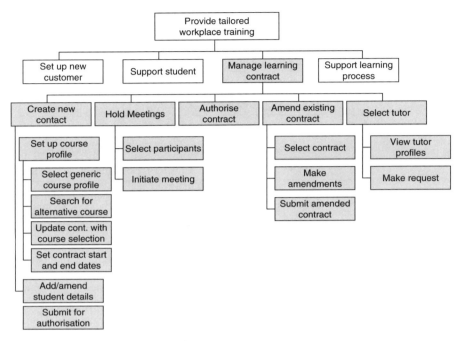

FIGURE 4.2 User needs hierarchy

- Cost benefit ratio of certain needs as opposed to others
- Requirements to focus on certain technologies
- Requirements to focus on certain markets

In a few cases, the workshop output may require changes to the Hierarchy. These are reflected back in the Needs Control document. Most of the outputs, however, consist of high-level design decisions and their rationale that makes clear the scope of the proposed system and a final list of user needs. This output becomes a section of the Service Definition document.

Use Cases

If the objective of the project is to produce a prototype or demonstrator then the Needs Hierarchy provides a good starting point from which to produce Use Cases (*see* Chapter 12, *Use Case-Based Software Development* by Peter Haumer). A team member who will also be involved with the software design and development is usually the best person to do this.

We would generally define a Use Case as "a concrete description of activity that the user engages in when performing a specific task, description sufficiently detailed so that design implications can be inferred and reasoned about" (Carroll 1995). It should describe a single activity from beginning to end including all possible alternative actions. For example, a use case title might be 'Withdraw Cash from ATM'.

Identifying the different use cases from the Needs Hierarchy is a similar activity to generating the hierarchy itself. Sometimes it requires further decomposition of the elements of the hierarchy, other times it requires aggregation, frequently elements will already be at the right level. The task is to look at the lowest-level elements of the hierarchy, ask what constitutes a single user interaction with the system and encapsulate the essence of the interaction in a succinct title.

Service Definition

At the close of the second workshop, a team member is nominated to produce the Service Definition document. This is the final deliverable from the SUNA process. It contains all the outputs from the previous stages plus details of the project background, team members, and any other relevant information to create a complete and accurate record of the exercise. The target audience is either the software development team who will design and build the required software based on the contents of the document, or Requirements Analysts who will use the document as the basis for detailed requirements capture work.

WORKED EXAMPLE

We first started using a SUNA approach in 1998 and it has now been used extensively on small collaborative research projects in, primarily, commercial and some academic environments. It has been applied in fields ranging from learning and education to the technicalities of multiple device management and overall has been found to help promote clarity, innovation and good relationships. When considering which case to use as an illustration of the method, we decided it would be most engaging to select one where adaptations had to be made along the way and that was ultimately a learning experience.

Device Unifying Service

The Device Unifying Service (DUS) project resulted from a short research proposal submitted to a European collaborative research organisation by a technologist from a Norwegian telecommunications company. The proposal outlined his ideas about the technical feasibility of unifying certain aspects of personal devices, such as a mobile phone, personal digital assistant (PDA) or laptop computer. He also implied that users would 'need' this type of integration as the number of devices owned by any one individual is predicted to proliferate and currently each has it's own user interface, options, preferences and peripheral devices. He envisaged the unification as a 'single virtual terminal' allowing the user, among other things, to unify certain elements of the user interface and to transfer voice sessions from one device to another. It would also allow users to split data streams which would, for instance, allow sound to come out of one device synchronised with vision from another.

We responded to the initial proposal, along with others from Greece, Germany, Iceland, and the Czech Republic and together we formed the DUS project team. It was agreed that BT should lead the initial requirements stage, using SUNA to inform the development of a functional concept demonstrator that could be used to conduct user trials.

Inputs

Aside from the research proposal, which contained a high-level description of the concept, plus details of the financial and resource constraints, the minutes of the introductory meeting were a valuable input. In particular, a list of other known research projects that were in a similar vein conceptually or were experimenting with the relevant technologies, provided a starting point for further investigation.

Workshop 1 Preparation

The first SUNA workshop, held in Berlin, had the objective of defining a common view of a DUS and a high-level set of requirements. In planning for the workshop, we considered how to apply the SUNA process to the specifics of the DUS project. The first stage of the SUNA process concerns the selection and set up of the project team. In this instance, the team was self-selecting on the basis of the response to the initial research proposal, however, we were fortunate by default to have a good mixture of different backgrounds and skills on the team. Guidelines such as keeping the team size within the range of five to seven people and ensuring the team contains a cross-section of view points (technical, business and social) and people with the appropriate level of authority were beyond the control of the SUNA facilitators. Also, the DUS concept was not a straightforward evolution of an existing service with a well-defined market. It was, therefore, not possible to include formal user representation, however, as the proposed service was based on the use of everyday personal devices, members of the project team could easily empathise with future users.

The first task of the workshop was to get to know the participants, understand how they had interpreted the proposal and what each imagined a DUS might comprise in terms of functionality. The next would be to identify the commonality, consider the possible business models and then generate a set of DILO scenarios looking from different business and user perspectives.

Workshop 1 — Day 1

Altogether there were 10 participants at the workshop, three from Norway, two from the UK, one from Greece, one from Czech Republic, two from Germany and one from Iceland. In a social/collaborative context, each had their own particular interests in the project and each brought with them their own cultural and organisational perspective, influencing their interpretation of the proposal and shaping their participatory role in defining the service.

As would be expected, the initial workshop discussion revealed a very sketchy understanding of the DUS concept and little commonality in the interpretation of the proposal between the different participants. The initiator of the proposal presented a more detailed technical description of the development possibilities. Participants from other partners asked questions and registered their expectations and concerns and gradually a feeling for the mental models that each participant had built began to emerge. Up to this point the discussion had been largely technical and centred on establishing common ground. It had not yet attempted to drawn on the creative potential of the participants. The SUNA facilitators initiated a discussion about who would use the service, that is, the target market and how the service would be delivered to the users. This resulted in the participants collaborating to define a number of alternative business models.

The next step was to write the scenarios. The general approach is to consider the key actors and select three to five, one to form the central character of each scenario. However, as there was no firm consensus within the group on the target market and business model, it was also decided to write the scenarios from the different business model perspectives. Each scenario would, therefore, centre on characters in a different target market. This meant that the scenarios would be more diverse than is suggested by the method, depicting different systems rather than different aspects of the same system. As it was clear that there were diverse opinions within the group, it had the advantage of encouraging participants to explore, in more detail, a range of possibilities for the implementation of DUS. Commonality was emerging on the technical front so it was hoped that the approach would clarify the target market for the service demonstrator and at the same time help generate a common framework that would support a range of different business models in the future.

The group was split down into four sub-groups each to adopt a different business model to base a scenario on. Examples were presented and discussed so that everybody was clear about the form of a DILO type of scenario. The sub-groups then split into syndicate rooms or areas to produce their material.

The four scenarios that emerged from the exercise were

- ***Business to Business***
- ***Fireman/Paramedic***
- ***Corporate Intranet***
- ***Home/Family***

Here is a short excerpt from the ***Corporate Intranet*** scenario:

Before he leaves his house he switches at his mobile phone his profile to 'travel' that means all messages reach him at his mobile phone or PDA.

He goes to the office by underground. It takes him 40 minutes. In the underground, he uses the time to prepare the draft for to days conference on his PDA.

After finishing the draft, he calls his boss Paul to ask him for comments on the draft and tells him that he will send the document to him by e-mail within 5 minutes. The configured output device beside the boss' PC is his printer, so the document comes additional directly out of the printer.

Paul, the head of department, looks through the document of Peter and makes some important remarks and adds some very confidential figures.

In between Peter has arrived in the office. At 10 minutes to 10:00, from the PC in his office, he switches on the necessary equipment in the conference room like beamer and so on. He configures the profile to indicate that incoming e-mails and messages will be redirected to the secretary except for urgent e-mails and calls via voice mail from his boss Paul.

Workshop 1 — Day 2

The first task of the second day was to review the scenarios and extract the user needs. This was done in accordance with the method. The Home/Family was selected as the base scenario; the user needs were extracted into a table of unambiguous statements alluding to system requirements. The other scenarios were analysed in the same way and any new user needs were added to the table. When the list was complete the group went through again marking each user need with a priority from 1 to 3 relating to proposed development phases (1 first phase, highest priority and 3 last phase, lowest priority). This gave a first cut indication of the core functionality of DUS as agreed by the group.

Finally, discussions about the most appropriate target market and business model to base a service demonstrator on culminated in a decision to conduct an investigation of existing offerings with elements of similarity to DUS such as Unified Messaging services. The objective of the exercise would be to confirm the unique selling points of the DUS concept and help determine the finer points of the service demonstrator.

Between the Workshops

The SUNA facilitators reviewed the user needs and constructed a Needs Hierarchy. At this point the mode of thinking was still 'in an ideal world', that is no constraints, such as available budget, were applied. Several additional aspects of the conceptual service were identified such as the ability to produce bills and a user interface for third party service developers. No validation was done in this case.

Workshop 2

The funding and the dispersed nature of the DUS project meant that it was not possible to meet face-to-face for the second workshop. This presented a fundamental difficulty for the SUNA facilitators who were reliant on the thorough discussion of the hierarchy leading to collaboratively agreed decisions about the scope of the service demonstrator. Decisions about how to split the development between the partners would also be required. The only available option was to circulate the documents and generate an e-mail discussion prior to a final teleconference. To add to the difficulties, the teleconference had to be scheduled during the summer holidays and therefore not all the partners could attend.

Comments on the hierarchy were received by e-mail and two attempts were made at the final teleconference. The technical conditions of the audio conference were poor both times, making it difficult for some participants to hear the proceedings. Finally, however, the service demonstrator was roughly scoped and the development work was divided up between the partners in a logical manner.

Post suna

The participants from Germany led the following phase of the project and were able to produce a full set of Use Cases for the demonstrator based on the Needs Hierarchy supported by the other outputs from the SUNA process. There was some 'requirements drift' in the subsequent phases but the service demonstrator was completed and user tested. Along the way, the work produced at least two applications for patents on behalf of BT and a second project has recently started to look at developing some of the functionality that was defined in the original SUNA-generated concept.

Scenarios based on different business models worked well for the particular circumstances of the DUS project and helped generate a framework concept that could be delivered to multiple markets. Also encouraging the participants to write their own scenarios contributed to the cohesion of the group. Some participants found it difficult to write in the DILO format but still managed to produce viable scenarios that contributed to the vision of the service. However, conducting Workshop 2 by audio conference did not work well and resulted in a loss of focus on the final stage of the SUNA process. Commitment and collaboration remained good throughout the following phases of the project, although rigorous critique of the hierarchy in a face-to-face situation may have improved the outline of the service demonstrator and prevented requirements drift in the final stages.

Informal discussions with participants about the value of the SUNA process were positive. The consensus seemed to be that it had been key in helping to create an unified vision for DUS from a diverse set of initial understandings.

COMPARISONS

SUNA to date has been mainly used for developing relatively small-scale non-bespoke products and services for the Telecommunication's sector. The development of larger scale generic products demands stronger needs management (particularly tracking and auditing changes) and a more 'business' orientated interface. Recent developments of SUNA have been addressing the business interface through a proposition validation technique and a value attribution process.

Like many commercial organisations, BT generates 'propositions'; documents outlining new product or service opportunities. These propositions are often created in workshops or are the inspiration of an individual or marketing team. Currently propositions can be checked or validated through market research, but this is expensive and too often the service description is still poorly defined and difficult for users to understand. A process called Lifestyle Due Diligence (LDD) is being developed as an alternative to market research for validating propositions. It is purely analytical and based on SUNA principles, particularly that services must be based on sound and grounded understanding of user needs. The LDD team takes the proposition description and using their knowledge of customer behavior and user needs are able to create scenarios. The assumptions underpinning the scenarios can be mapped against those underpinning the proposition. According to the type and level of mismatch, the LDD team can make certain recommendations (e.g. to add, modify or remove some of the proposed service attributes). Naturally if the proposition is to be further developed, then SUNA can be quickly and easily applied.

A Value Attribution Process (VAP) is also evolving, which attempts to help prioritise user needs based on what users or customers value. Most value attribution models are marketing tools designed to determine the overall value of a product to inform pricing decisions or indicate levels of customer satisfaction (see Woodruff and Gardial 1996). VAP determines the value of individual needs (determined by a selected level within the needs hierarchy) and can therefore help make decisions about inclusion, costs (i.e. to buy or build) and presentation (e.g. what to present when promoting the service). A draft version VAP has been developed and tested on the DUS outputs.

The reader should also compare this chapter with others in this volume. In particular, there are many similarities as well as key differences between the SUNA method and the approach described by Ellen Gottesdiener in Chapter 5 (*Running a Use Case Workshop*). Both are workshop-based and recognise the importance of collaboration for increasing understanding and building trust. They also highlight the same strengths and weaknesses of workshops, particularly in persuading the uninitiated to invest valuable time before, after and during the event. That is, a position that still reflects the doubts about the benefits of early investment in such 'soft' areas like user needs. However, Gottesdiener's approach begins with creating the Use Cases or at least the Use Case list, whereas the Use Cases are very much the end point for SUNA. The SUNA Scenarios are broad and rich, often containing many possible Use Cases, some of which have to be discarded in the scoping process. The value lies not just in producing a starting point for the development of use cases to satisfy an immediate objective, but also in the creative consideration of the backdrop, the context, the bigger picture in which they sit.

The use of scenarios in contextual design (Karen Holtzblatt, Chapter 10) and Human-Centred Interaction (HCI) design (David Benyon & Catriona Macaulay, Chapter 11) highlights what could be considered as a weakness of the SUNA process.—where do the scenarios come from? In SUNA's case, the scenarios are not directly based on empirical data but on expert knowledge and extant social research. The reason for this is that it is not always desirable to shape products and services for future markets around existing practices and lifestyles. If innovation is required, some element of envisioning is necessary; an imaginary leap into the future has to be taken. The process becomes grounded again by conducting thorough concept acceptance trials with prospective users. On the other hand, where there is a lack of expert or domain knowledge, ethnographic techniques as are described by Karen Holtzblatt and Benyon and Macaulay become essential. The use of such techniques, however, can be time consuming and expensive, and may be hard to justify in a commercial environment.

At least two questions come to mind:

1. Are SUNA, and other front-end loaded methods, over-indulgent, wasting valuable time generating scenarios to drive Use Cases which could be elicited more quickly and simply without additional effort and cost? The answer to this question requires a deeper analysis and comparison of the approaches than can be done here, although it is not dissimilar to the argument that has raged for years more generally about the value of user-centred or usability engineering methods in software design.

2. Secondly, are these methods complementary in that they reflect on different parts of the development life cycle? We would argue that the question of position in a traditional life-cycle model may not be relevant to SUNA. SUNA is more akin to an ideation rather than requirements capture and analysis process and bridges

marketing with design. We expect, in the final analysis, that methods like SUNA will have their place in software development, particularly for the design of highly user-centric and market driven services.

KEYWORDS

Scenario	Envisioning	Software	Vignette
Workshop	Product	SUNA	
Innovation	Service	DILO (day in the life of)	

REFERENCES

Carroll, J.M, Introduction: the scenario perspective on system development, in J.M. Carroll (Ed.), *Scenario-Based Design: Envisioning Work and Technology in System Development*, Wiley, New York, 1995.

Cooper, A., *The Inmates are Running the Asylum*, SAMS, USA, 1999.

Denning, S., *The Springboard: How Story telling Ignites Action in Knowledge-Era Organisations*, Butterworth-Heinemann, Boston, MA, 2000.

Goldenberg, J. and Mazursky, D., *Creativity in Product Innovation*, Cambridge University Press, Cambridge, UK, 2002.

Harker, S.D and Eason, K.D, The use of scenarios for organisational requirements generation, *Proceedings of the 32nd Hawaii International Conference on System Sciences*, Hawaii, Vol 3, 1999. Available from http://www.computer.org/proceedings/hicss/0001/00013/00013054.PDF

Haywood, A *The Conceptual Approach Report*. An Essex University internal report, 2003. Available from the chapter authors.

Hutt, A.T.H., Donnelly, N., Macaulay, L.A., Fowler, C.J.H., and Twigger, D., Describing a product opportunity : a method for understanding the users' environment, in D. Diaper and R. Winder (Eds.), *People & Computers III*, Cambridge University Press, Cambridge, UK, 1988.

Taylor, B. The HUFIT planning, analysis and specification toolset, in D. Diaper, G. Cockton, D. Gilmore, and B. Shackel (Eds.), *Human-Computer Interaction—INTERACT '90 Conference Proceedings*, North Holland, Amsterdam, ISBN 0-444-88817-9, 1990, pp. 371–376.

Woodruff, R.B and Gardial, S.F., *Know Your Customer: New Approach to Understanding Customer Value and Satisfaction*, Blackwell, Oxford, 1996.

RECOMMENDED READINGS

Jack Carroll's (1995) book of readings on using scenarios in design, although now becoming dated, is still one of the best introductions to the practical uses of scenarios. It is, however, written for an academic audience, and the techniques described often lack 'real world' testing.

Stephen Denning's (2000) book is an excellent read if you are interested in a discussion about the use of narrative (or scenarios) generally, and more specifically their uses with organisation settings. His discussion about engineering versus ecological viewpoints and their role in designs is particularly interesting.

CHAPTER 5

RUNNING A USE CASE/SCENARIO WORKSHOP

Ellen Gottesdiener
EBG Consulting Inc., Indiana, USA

WRITING REQUIREMENTS is a crucial early step in software development, and use cases and scenarios are a natural way to discover and describe requirements in many domains. But how exactly do you elicit them? That's where *collaborative* (or *facilitated*) requirements workshops come in. They give project teams a structure and techniques to guide creation of use cases and scenarios.

Requirements workshops are the best way to ensure timely collaboration between businesspeople, technical people, and customers. These workshops focus participants' actions on generating work products based on proven models. The workshops use an iterative approach: Participants build the documents step by step, periodically reviewing their work.

Workshops generate requirements documents of the highest quality and also build trust and enhance communication among team members.

Workshops have their drawbacks. Key stakeholders must spend chunks of time. Some cultures may not like empowering participants to make binding requirements decisions. To be effective, you need a neutral facilitator.

Collaborative workshops call on the use of learnable, repeatable techniques. One is careful preparation, including draft work products and decisions on how closure will be achieved. Others include guided activities, such as small-group work, the use of templates and models, and tests of the work products. Guided retrospectives help teams review their deliverables and process.

As you'll see in the detailed example here, people can use collaborative requirements workshops to get a great deal of high-quality work done in a short time.

APPLICABILITY

Many kinds of projects can use facilitated requirements workshops, although these sessions are used most often for business systems. They also work well for other applications where technical people are trying to implement the requirements of subject matter experts

Scenarios, Stories, Use Cases: Through the Systems Development Life-Cycle. Edited by Ian F Alexander and Neil Maiden
© 2004 John Wiley & Sons, Ltd. ISBN: 0-470-86194-0

(SMEs). These applications include financial, accounting, logistical, human resources, and similar infrastructure applications. Additionally, products involving both hardware and software components such as lab automation systems, workflow, device management, manufacturing tracking and controlling, stock trading, gaming systems, and so on can benefit from this technique.

Workshops are not applicable in organizations that do not value strengthening the relationship and communication among business and technical people. Nor are they an advisable technique when the requirements can be wholly and correctly derived from technical staff or when management is unwilling to bear the expense of having subject matter experts gather in the same place at the same time for hours or days.

In organizations where certain individuals or groups direct the requirements toward a single, predetermined point of view, workshops likely will not be successful. The goal of workshops is true collaboration. They deliver justifiable decisions about requirements to meet end-user and customer goals, while at the same time balancing technical considerations.

Requirements workshops are less applicable in the following situations:

- The participants don't share a common goal.
- You don't have an experienced, neutral facilitator.
- Your facilitator is a key stakeholder in the outcome and thus has difficulty being neutral and focusing on the group process.
- Project or company politics hamper the players' ability to collaborate.
- Management has no intention of using or acknowledging the deliverables created in the workshop.

POSITION IN THE LIFE CYCLE

Requirements workshops employing use cases and scenarios are most applicable in the early phases of the life cycle. They excel as a technique for requirements discovery and validation and are a useful technique during design. In sum, workshops excel when life-cycle products are best derived by human collaboration and invention.

Requirements Discovery	Requirements Validation	System Specification	System Design	Coding, First of Class	Integration & Testing	Operations & Maintenance

KEY FEATURES

The key features of workshops are customer collaboration, neutral process leadership, the use of multiple requirements models, and a process of iterating through the requirements process in a short period of time.

Customer Collaboration

Customer collaboration is at the heart of the workshop process. Direct end users (or appropriate surrogates) and business experts are essential participants. Workshops go beyond classic customer meetings or interviews, which focus on one-way information exchange. In workshops, all the participants—customer and technical—share a common goal and agree to join together to create the work products (such as use cases and scenarios) in the pursuit of that shared goal. Workshops rely on customer and technical people interacting, challenging, questioning, clarifying, specifying, prioritizing, and finally reaching closure on the requirements. Workshop participants are productive because collectively they have the right mix of skills and knowledge to create the work products. They act interdependently; relying on one another's knowledge, experience, skills, and perspectives.

To ensure that the workshop includes the right participants, you need both technical and business sponsorship. Management assists by kicking off or being part of the workshop closing activities (in the form of a participants' "show-and-tell" for the sponsor). In some cases, managers may even be full-fledged participants.

In a workshop, a neutral facilitator and a recorder act as process leads to ensure that everyone participates and that all points of view are understood and resolved. To maintain energy, creativity, and motivation, the facilitator uses interactive as well as parallel group activities. For example, subgroups may be formed to work on portions of a single deliverable, such as scenarios for a set of use cases. Or subgroups might be assigned to work on related work products. One group might work on use cases while another drafts prototype screens and yet another creates a high-level domain model. The subgroups then reconvene in a plenary (whole group) activity to share and critique their work.

Multiple Requirements Models

Several types of requirements models can be used during a workshop, depending on the problem domain. Many problem domains benefit from using use cases and scenarios as the hub for related requirements representations, including a list of actors, a glossary, domain models, business rules, and state charts. Of course, the use cases and scenarios elicited in workshops evolve through the life cycle into test cases.

The Iteration Process

In agile development projects, workshops are conducted early in each iteration to quickly identify high-priority use cases (or stories) before testing and coding begin. Depending on customer availability, one or more workshop events are held over a short period. Each workshop is well planned and builds on the prior session.

Between sessions, participants often work on refining the requirements by creating additional scenarios, atomic-level business rules associated with use cases, or other requirements deliverables such as nonfunctional requirements or documentation (particularly in regulated or high-process project environments). In other cases, prototypes are built directly from the workshop deliverables.

STRENGTHS

Direct, face-to-face collaboration in a structured, productive environment builds trust, enhances communication, and ensures quality requirements. This sets the tone for productive relationships among project stakeholders, customer and technical alike. The workshop process can be adapted to a wide variety of development styles and cultures, from agile development to highly process-oriented cultures.

Combining effective collaboration techniques with scenarios and use cases enables the requirements to "come to life" quickly. All the key stakeholders are together at the same time and place, so real needs (versus wants or "nice to haves") surface quickly. The stakeholders are led to assign priorities based on business value and to reach closure following an agreed-upon decision rule and decision-making process. Compared with traditional approaches, such as interviews, observation, or multiple rounds of customer reviews of lengthy, tedious requirements documentation, these workshop techniques create a leaner, more agile requirements process.

Iterating through multiple models using subject matter experts accelerates the requirements process. Participates verify each other's work directly in the session, often using mini-walkthroughs and reviews. This approach reduces the risk of requirements errors and increases not only throughput during the workshop but also project community understanding of the requirements.

Decisions are made in real time using an agreed-upon decision-making process, reducing typical delays in reaching closure. In requirements workshops, project stakeholders learn from one another, enriching their experience and leading to more constructive team relationships.

WEAKNESSES

Facilitated use case and scenario workshops require involvement of project subject matter experts for blocks of time ranging from three hours to three days, an investment that may be problematic for some organizations. Additionally, some cultures eschew what they see as "too much" end-user or customer involvement. The need to agree on a process for making requirements decisions during the workshop is threatening to some cultures, in which either the IT group or the business group wishes to control decisions without exposure in a group setting.

If an organization typically holds a great many unproductive meetings, participants may overbook themselves, expecting to come and go during the workshop or even work on other activities. Because a requirements workshop is an intense, ongoing elicitation process, inattention or inconsistent attendance will hamper or prevent trust from being built in the workshop session.

Workshops rely on one or more skilled and neutral facilitators to guide the process, not only during the session but also beforehand during planning. Some organizations do not train people to develop these skills nor reward skilled facilitation, making it difficult to find in-house facilitators. Other groups are resistant to getting outside help by hiring an external facilitator, particularly when the political issues are painful or shameful. In other organizations, there is an over-reliance on using project members who have difficulty staying neutral rather than use facilitators from outside the project or organization.

TECHNIQUE

A collaborative (or facilitated) requirements workshop is a structured event in which a carefully selected group of stakeholders and content experts works together to create, correct, and document a predefined set of deliverables, or work products. (This technique is similar to an approach called JAD™, which stands for Joint Application Design or Joint Application Development.) The participants agree ahead of time on what the deliverables will be, and they often produce some of them before the workshop. In use case or scenario workshops, business and technology people assume the roles of various users of the system. Guided by use cases, scenarios, or both, the workshop participants act out examples of the system in use.

Workshops reflect the simple fact that the process of building software and defining its requirements depends on the collaborative brainpower of project stakeholders. Workshops provide a means for harvesting the collective knowledge, experience, and points of view of an often diverse set of project stakeholders.

Workshops rely on the following techniques:

- You follow a framework to plan and run a successful workshop. I refer to this structure as "the six P's": purpose, participants, principles, products, place, and process.
- You have the right people in the room at the same time.
- Before the workshop, you create a starting point for project requirements. For example, you write a project vision or charter with a statement of scope, and you generate a draft list of use cases, scenarios, and actors, a context diagram, or some combination of these.
- You design a workshop process and write an agenda that consists of a series of logically related activities to create the requirements. In each activity, participants will use existing or newly created models or portions of models to generate the overall deliverables.
- Before the workshop, you define prioritization schemes and a decision rule for workshop decisions (including assigning priorities to the use cases or scenarios). You use this agreed-upon decision-making process throughout the workshop.
- You obtain senior stakeholder sponsorship of both the workshop and the decision-making processes.
- You elicit the scenarios or use cases in logical groups, progressing from small groups into multiple concurrent groups. In this way, you maximize the session's throughput.
- You use elicitation techniques such as role-playing use cases, modeling use case steps on a wall, or completing a scenario template.
- You integrate *collaboration patterns,* which are pre-tested, step-by-step instructions for groups who are working together on complex tasks.

- You clarify how the project team can declare that requirements are sufficiently complete to move onto prototyping, test, design, and build activities; this *doneness test* lets you plan the workshop deliverables and test for closure.
- You test the generated requirements for correctness and completeness by using mini-walkthroughs and reviews.
- You design a strategy to navigate through the requirements during the workshop.
- You iterate through the requirements using multiple, intertwined models.

A Word about Scenarios

Scenarios are used in many requirements workshops even when use cases aren't the best way to express requirements. For example, some business problem domains—such as reporting, rule-based decision-making, and data analysis—are less behavioral, so use cases aren't an appropriate way to represent the requirements.

Scenarios are always helpful for uncovering or testing requirements in the workshop. For example, in a series of workshops for a disability claim adjudication application (a rule-based problem domain), the participants used scenarios to test the correctness and completeness of business rules they had generated during the workshop.

Workshop Framework

Planning is essential. The planning framework—purpose, participants, principles, products, place, and process—helps the facilitator and planning team to design and run a successful workshop. They answer the questions why, who, how, what, where, and when, as shown in Table 5.1.

Purpose: The statement of the workshop's purpose outlines the reason and justification for the workshop. It explains why you're conducting the workshop and serves as a frame of reference. Because the workshop's context is the project itself, the workshop's purpose is linked to the project's purpose, which describes the business reason for undertaking the project. The statement of the project's purpose usually references the current business situation, the desired situation, the obstacles to achieving the desired situation, and the changes that are desired. Similarly, the workshop's purpose describes the business reason for gathering the players together. The link must be evident to all project and workshop stakeholders.

Participants: The people involved in a facilitated workshop are the workshop sponsor, the subject matter experts (business and IT), a facilitator, a recorder, observers, and on-call subject matter experts. When you explicitly define the individuals who are to play each of these roles, the group can better plan the session, the participants are better prepared, and the event is more likely to succeed.

Not all of these roles are necessarily present during a given workshop. For example, the workshop sponsor may be present only at the beginning and end of the session.

Principles: Also called *ground rules,* principles are guidelines for participation, working agreements, or the codes of conduct that participants agree to follow. Groups need these precepts to maintain socially acceptable behavior and to promote

TABLE 5.1   Framework for designing a collaborative workshop: "The six P's"

Focus	Purpose	Participants	Principles	Products	Place	Process
Questions	Why are we doing the workshop?	Who is involved?	How should we function as a group?	What should the workshop produce?	Where should we gather and share space?	When should things happen, and in what order?
Concerns	• Goals • Need • Motivation	• Roles • Stakeholder • Experts	• Guidelines for participation • Working agreements • Ground rules • Group norms	• Work products • Dependencies • Models • Decisions • Next steps • Issues for resolution	• Location • Time	• Steps • Activities • Order • Concurrency

the goals of the workshop: delivering the appropriate work products in the allotted time. The principles serve as a process guide for the facilitator as well as the participants. The facilitator and participants are responsible for monitoring the adherence to the principles.

Products: The work products, or deliverables, of a workshop take the form of text or diagrams. For user requirements workshops, they are lists of use cases, scenarios, business rules, use case maps (use case dependencies), domain models, and the like. These workshop deliverables, in turn, serve as input to project activities, including test cases, design, code, or additional workshops. To accelerate the delivery of workshop products, the participants need certain input products such as draft models, text, and documentation. These materials may already exist or may need to be created before the workshop.

Place: The location of a workshop can influence the outcome. If you're using a technique that requires the use of giant pieces of paper mounted on the walls, for example, the room needs plenty of wall space. If the room is crowded, small-group activities might be impossible. It's also important that the room have the space and amenities you need to serve refreshments. In evaluating the best place to hold the workshop, consider room size, wall space, support for refreshments, seating (a U-shape arrangement is best), availability of outlets, access to on-call subject matter experts (via physical proximity or phones), and access to phones during breaks and lunch.

Process: Activities in a workshop should follow a logical flow whereby the outputs from one activity are used in another activity in the session or in a post-workshop task. An activity may consist of several steps in which members work individually, in small teams (subteams), or as a whole group.

Role Playing

One sample technique that is useful for modeling use cases in workshops is to role-play them. In general, you can specify a use case using a sequential, stepwise description or using a left-side, right-side conversational approach originated by Rebecca Wirfs-Brock (Wirfs-Brock 1993). Using the latter approach, the "left side" represents what the actor does, and the "right side" represents what the system does in response. The use case describes the interaction between the two.

When workshop participants are creating this format for use cases, the facilitator can use a role-playing approach in which multiple people play various roles. A subject matter expert will likely be assigned the role of one actor. Another participant will act out the system role. Using scenarios invented in a prior workshop activity or as part of the workshop pre-work, the two people act out the scenarios. They may toss a Koosh ball (a soft or string ball) or some other item back and forth as the scenario proceeds. During the role-play, other support roles are necessary. The facilitator monitors the interaction while the recorder captures the conversation on a laptop, often projected on the wall for all to see so that the steps are captured correctly. This way of interacting in a workshop is not only productive but also fun.

Other roles are assigned to project team members responsible for specifying related requirements models such as the data or class model, business rules, and prototypes. For example, a data analyst's role is to listen to the interaction, record notes, and ask questions surrounding data elements. This same person may also be responsible for writing the business rules that are enforced in the use cases. Another person, often a developer, may begin to make sketches or dialogs to help envision the prototype to be built after the workshop.

Wall Modeling Use Cases: Storyboarding

Another way to elicit use cases using the sequential use case format is to capture them on the wall using a storyboarding approach. A *storyboard* is a series of continuing panels, sketches, or scenes depicting a plot or sequence of actions. In business, storyboards are popular for solving problems and creating collaborative plans. In a storyboard, the group uses text or diagrams to build a deliverable or set of deliverables by successively using individual, subgroup, and whole group activities. I like to call this technique the Wall of Wonder, an approach based on a storyboarding approach taught by the Institute of Cultural Affairs (Spencer 1989).

To model use cases on a wall as a storyboard, you might start with a well-named use case and a scenario. The facilitator asks participants a focus question such as, "What task, actions, or steps are needed to <goal or use case name, such as 'sell ticket package'>? Please write down one per card or sticky note." Next, participants take their cards to the wall and arrange them in sequence. Eventually, subgroups are formed in which team members work on different use cases at the same time.

For each set of steps arrayed on the wall, the facilitator asks questions to test the appropriateness of the sequence and may also elicit business rules and data elements. These are captured in a separate location, such as another wall or flipcharts nearby. The group then focuses on additional scenarios, adjusting the steps on the wall as needed.

Scenario Walkthroughs: Testing Use Cases

Scenarios are one of the most productive ways to test use cases. In workshops, one group might generate a set of scenarios, perhaps using a template as shown in Table 5.2. The values generated for the scenarios are used to create test cases and scripts, adding to the benefit of capturing the information.

Participants work in subgroups to generate details to complete a template for a set of use cases. If other models are employed, the template may be used for capturing business questions or information domains. To accelerate documentation delivery and reduce variability across subgroups, each subgroup might be supplied with a laptop in which the recorder enters the scenario details.

After scenarios have been generated, the subgroups test each other's requirements. For example, one subgroup might use scenarios to walk through use cases that another subgroup generated in a prior workshop activity (using a role-playing or storyboard technique) or even in a prior use case workshop. They might use a template, such as the one shown in Table 5.3, to find errors in each other's use cases. The entire group reviews the walkthrough findings, and then each subgroup returns to its set of use cases to correct or clarify the defects detected.

TABLE 5.2 Scenario template

Project:

Feature Area:

Author(s):

Date:

_____

Scenario Number: _____

Scenario Name: _____

Related use case(s):   _____   _____

Actor(s):   _____   _____

Brief goal description for this scenario:

_____

Scenario Information	Values Provided

Collaboration Patterns

As mentioned earlier, collaboration patterns are high-level blueprints for the behavior adopted by successful groups to accomplish results together. When groups collaborate in a facilitated workshop setting, the facilitator often establishes the collaboration patterns. With experience, the group learns to incorporate these patterns, reducing the need for the third-party facilitator.

For example, "Divide, Conquer, Correct, Collect" is one pattern that groups can use to elicit and test a requirements deliverable. Suppose the workshop wants to deliver a complete set of scenarios for a software product that has four or five feature sets. In the first step—Divide—the team is separated into subgroups, and each subgroup is given responsibility for generating scenarios for one of the feature sets. (The use cases will already have been written, either before the workshop or in an earlier activity.) In the Conquer step, the subgroups focus on creating detailed scenarios for each use case in their assigned feature set. They might use a template to ensure that they capture the

TABLE 5.3 Scenario walkthrough template

Scenario Tests of Use Case

Use Case # _____ Use Case Name _____   Workshop Date: _____ Page _____ of _____

Participant Authors:

Scenario Name	Scenario Number	This scenario tests the use case for: Normal Case (N), Error (E), or Exception (Ex)	Additional/ corrected business rules	Additional/ corrected use case steps	Additional/ corrected data needed	Comments

desired level of detail. For example, the template might call for the scenario description, sample data, an assigned priority, and a specified degree of complexity.

In the Correct part of the collaboration pattern, the group tests the completeness of the scenarios in each feature set by using a different requirements model, a quality assurance (QA) checklist, or another requirements discovery tool. Examples of these models include a model called *The Voice of the Customer* (Pardee 1996) in which the participants identify so-called spokens, unspokens, expectors, and delighters. In this way, the group uncovers any missing scenarios.

In the Collect step, the group collects all the scenarios, maps them to use cases, and perhaps trims the use case list.

This final list of use cases—revised after scenarios have been generated for them—can then be tested. One example of a testing mechanism is to create a use case map or workflow diagram (a visual diagram showing the relationships among all the use cases) and then compare it to a business flow diagram.

Doneness Testing

Doneness tests are used to ensure that the requirements—use cases, scenarios, and related requirements appropriate for the domain—are captured to the predetermined degree of precision and correctness. Walkthroughs are one kind of doneness test. Another is to use quality assurance questions. Here are some examples:

- Do all the use cases fall within the scope we have defined for this project?
- Does each actor initiate at least one use case?
- Is each in-scope use case necessary to fulfill the project's goals and objectives?
- Does each scenario have one or more use cases that define it?
- Have we defined the business rules necessary to handle each scenario and associated them with it (or with the scenario's associated use case)?

Using a checklist of QA questions has additional benefits. The very process of creating and agreeing on the checklist helps business and technical people to clarify and define expectations for each deliverable clearly and precisely. Like walkthroughs, checklists also push participants to create high-quality requirements in the first place, or to clarify what constitutes "good enough" requirements.

Checklists can be used in the 'Correct' phase of "Divide, Conquer, Correct, Collect." In that case, participants compare each requirement to the checklist questions and discuss and correct any discrepancies—right away if feasible.

Iterating Through the Requirements

In a workshop, the participants work on one model, such as use cases, and then shift to scenarios, the domain model, and business rules. Then they test the doneness of the requirements models. You might do all this in one workshop over one to three days, or you might spread these tasks over one or more weeks.

In the example shown in Figure 5.1, a set of four workshops is used to iteratively produce use cases, scenarios, business rules, prototypes, some nonfunctional requirements, prioritized use case packages, and a release strategy. These sessions might be held over a week or two and might take three to six hours each, depending on the scope of the project.

Often, participants work on requirements in preparation for the next workshop. For example, a developer or data analyst would likely create a draft domain model in conjunction with the prototype to be used as input to workshop 4.

In one series of workshops, each afternoon the developer drafted prototype screens to show participants during the next morning's workshop. Meanwhile, that same afternoon, the data analyst also added more details to the domain model, and the subject matter experts completed scenario templates for the use cases to be worked on in the next workshop gathering. They continued this process over the course of five days to complete the majority of their requirements during the week—half in the workshop setting, and half alone at their desks.

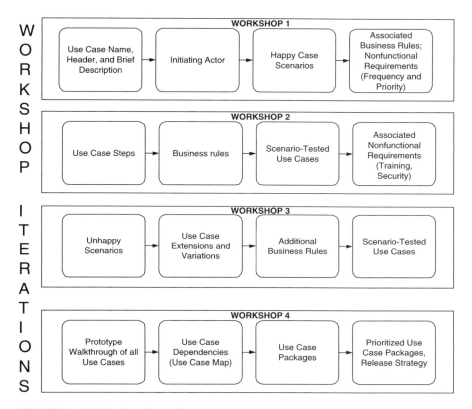

FIGURE 5.1   Workshop iterations

WORKED EXAMPLE

eTikets is an 18-month-old seller of online tickets. With decent profit margins on tickets, its niche is selling ticket packages for large parties of well-to-do people attending sporting events, auto races, theater shows, and concerts. The eTikets strategy includes moving into the European market, so it recently acquired a UK-based start-up in the same market space.

"We need to clarify and finalize the requirements for the first release of the next generation of the eTikets application," said Leslie, the project leader for GobSmack, the code name for the project. "Let's do a requirements workshop to gather and prioritize our use cases. I think it will save time and help us collaborate on the release."

The project team members faced several obstacles to solidifying their requirements and building their next release. They were adding new functionality and integrating US and European staff and infrastructure. They had a history of outsourcing requirements gathering, with resulting poorly defined requirements and disastrous outcomes in time and money. Key stakeholders were already disagreeing on how to approach the next release and what features should be included and why.

Leslie knew that defining and documenting crisp requirements, along with creating working prototypes, would alleviate many of the political, logistical, and technical issues the team faced with the GobSmack release. She was determined to get a good set of working requirements and somehow get everyone to collaborate effectively early in the project. Gaining the support of Jason, the VP of Product Development, she proceeded to make arrangements to conduct a series of requirements workshops.

Leslie decided to contract with Eli, an experienced requirements workshop facilitator. Using an outside facilitator was necessary because the passions and political issues around the release made it a problem for eTikets' own staff to be neutral. Jody, the business analyst, had a keen interest in facilitating in the future, so Leslie arranged for Eli to simultaneously mentor Jody in workshop design and facilitation.

Workshop Pre-Work

With Leslie as workshop sponsor and Justin as project sponsor, Eli began by asking Leslie to form a planning team of at least one technical person and one business person. Leslie's counterpart, Marc, a product marketing director reporting to Justin, agreed to help plan the requirements session. Because Marc had worked on the first release and had been charged with the market analysis for the GobSmack release, he would also be a participant in the workshop.

As facilitator, Eli knew he needed to get multiple perspectives on the needs of the project's stakeholders. He interviewed a number of the management stakeholders and a half-dozen members of the project community, including the lead architect as well as the UK-based product manager, a lead designer, the testing and QA lead, and three of the developers assigned to GobSmack. Eli also reviewed existing requirements and project documentation, run through a demo of the product, and reviewed the company strategy.

The workshop participants agreed to gather over four part-day sessions to allow them to do some requirements and prototyping work in between. Figure 5.2 shows the overall strategy for each day.

To maximize the use of time, the planning team asked Justin to document a product vision for GobSmack and write a two-page business case with goals, objectives, a next-generation Web site feature list, and the project sponsors. With these materials in hand, the planning team then drafted a few scope-level requirements to help jump-start the workshop: a categorized list of stakeholders, an actor table and a glossary.

The planners created a starting list of stakeholders: package sellers, customer service reps, ticket buyers, ticket brokers, shippers, credit card companies, internal travel agents, search engines, and so on. Their list of actors, drawn from the stakeholders, included customer service reps, an inventory manager, a marketing manager, ticket buyers, and ticket brokers. They used this list to draft an actor table that included a brief description of each actor. Their draft glossary included essential business terms such as *ticket, inventory, event, package, global inventory, virtual order, created order,* and a few other terms they were stumbling over and knew they needed agreement on.

Now the participants were ready for the first workshop.

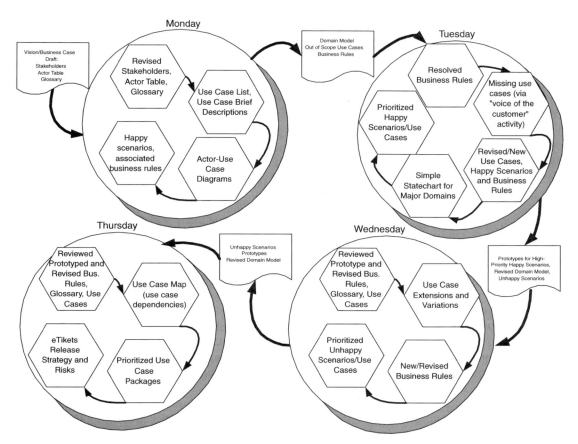

FIGURE 5.2   eTikets workshops strategy

Workshop 1: Monday

Monday's first workshop was kicked off by Justin and several other key stakeholders. They took some questions and then left the room. Next, Eli reviewed the workshop process, including the agenda and decision-making rules.

The team members then reviewed the pre-work material, beginning with the list of stakeholders and actors. Their recorder, a QA specialist, displayed the documentation on the wall using a laptop and data projector. After some energetic discussion about the actors, numerous changes were made directly in the document. Unfortunately, some of the participants wanted to begin debating the importance of some features related to certain actors, but it was too soon for that kind of discussion. To head this off, Eli pointed out that the goal of these early sessions was to take a "mile wide, inch deep" view of release.

Eli next asked the 12 participants to form subgroups of three people each to review and revise the names and descriptions of the actors they were most familiar with. Eli was careful to give them a time limit of 25 minutes for this work to ensure that they moved along and didn't spend too much time debating small issues. After all the groups had completed work on their assigned actors, they reconvened as a whole group and shared the results.

The whole group reached closure on the relevant actors in GobSmack and then moved on to the glossary. Mutual understanding of some terms required structured discussion, largely because of the differences between the US and UK products and market approaches. For example, the terms *package* and *order* were revised and broken into several new terms and definitions. Again, the recorder updated these on the wall for everyone to see.

The participants continued by meeting in their initial subgroups to generate a list of well-named use cases. To help them, Eli handed out a "cheat sheet" for naming use cases. Each use case was written on an oval-shaped sticky note. There were 35 in all. After each subgroup exhausted its ideas, the participants placed all the use cases on a wall for viewing.

Now everyone discussed the use cases to uncover overlaps, duplicates, and out-of-scope use cases. For example, use cases such as "sell package," "monitor events," "monitor market value," "transmit inventory to global inventory," and others were agreed upon as being in scope. This winnowing process yielded a net list of 22 use cases.

Next, the same subgroups wrote brief use case descriptions based on the set of actors. They also used actor sticky notes to create actor-use case diagrams on a wall. One person in each subgroup was assigned to be the recorder for the group, and another was the timekeeper. Each recorder used a laptop to enter the use case descriptions into a simple use case template so that the documentation would be readily available. Using a portable printer in the room, the subgroups printed copies of the use case descriptions and made sure to display use case ovals on the wall with actor icons next to them.

After the whole group reviewed and revised the entire set of use case descriptions and diagrams, the participants then worked on *happy scenarios* (ones in which no errors, exceptions, or variations occur). Again they worked in subgroups, using laptops to enter scenario details into a scenario template.

In addition to the subgroup roles of recorder and timekeeper, Eli asked the third person to act as the "quality keeper." This person's role was to ensure that all the elements in the scenario template were documented.

The participants had lunch together and took care of phone calls. After a brief break, they resumed their work.

The next task for the subgroups was to write business rules associated with the scenarios they had drafted before lunch. They wrote one business rule per index card. For this task, they did not use a template but instead used free-form business rules text. After they had worked on the business rule cards for 35 minutes, the cards were placed on another wall for everyone to see, discuss, and clarify.

The team members discovered some patterns among the business rules. Eli moved the cards into groups and labeled each group. The group names included "reservations," "order shipment," "seat assignment," "discounting tickets or packages," and "ticket liquidation."

Some of the rules, such as rules concerning discounting, were controversial. As per the agreed-upon decision rule and decision-making process (Gottesdiener 2001c) regarding eTikets business rules, these controversies would need to be resolved in consultation with the project sponsors. Each disputed business rule was placed as an item on the "Parking Lot" poster, where the team put things that could not be resolved (or did not need to be resolved) immediately in the workshop.

To conclude their first workshop, the participants reviewed the Parking Lot items and discovered that some of the issues were no longer of concern, having been addressed during the session. Open issues were assigned to specific participants to resolve for the next day.

The workshop ended in the early afternoon with a *workshop retrospective*. In this structured analysis of their work products as well as the process, the participants decided that they wanted to do the following: continue with subgroups as much as possible the next day and make speakers get to the point more quickly by flashing red index cards when they felt they were off-track. (Eli had suggested this in the beginning of the workshop, but only a few of them had used it.) They also agreed to continue with frequent short breaks and to refer to and revise their glossary during the workshop so that they would stay in sync on new or revised terms.

Several participants took on assignments for the next day. Justin's task was to research some of the controversial business rules, and Tina, a developer and data analyst needed to revise the domain model based on the new understanding of terms. Leslie was to review the list of use cases that were out of scope, along with certain troublesome business rules, with the project sponsors to get their concurrence (and to ask them to return in the morning to share their decisions). The rest of the group needed to generate additional scenarios for some of the use cases that had only a few scenarios defined. All in all, the group members agreed that it had been a productive first workshop.

Workshop 2: Tuesday

Tuesday's workshop was aimed at ensuring that the group had a complete set of use cases and that each use case had enough detail that the developers would be able to build draft prototypes. The plan was to have them create a subset of the most important and riskiest scenarios. The other goal for Tuesday was to resolve business rule issues.

The workshop began with a visit from the sponsors to explain their decisions on the business rules regarding discounting, reservations, and shipment orders. Then the participants, led by Eli, used a Voice of the Customer activity to rethink the customer needs for the GobSmack release. This activity yielded four new use cases, including "prepare inventory info for accounting" and "set prices."

The team formed four new subgroups, assigned one of these new use cases to each group, and took 15 minutes to draft use case descriptions. For this, they used the use case document on the laptop. Then they created the associated scenarios (using the template on the laptop) and business rules (one per card). Creating a simple state chart of the domains "ticket" and "package" proved most useful in generating new business rules and finding domain values that Tina needed to add to the domain model.

Next, the workshop participants generated a list of objective criteria for defining risk as well as customer priorities for the first 30-day iteration of the GobSmack release. Applying these criteria to assign priorities was surprisingly simple and uncontroversial. By creating their own criteria, the group was able to reach closure on the four most important use cases and related happy case scenarios.

This part of the workshop took only three hours, leaving them time during the rest of the day to do their post-workshop assignments. The developers set to work on a first-cut prototype of the prioritized use cases and scenarios. Marc updated the domain model, and the rest of the group worked on unhappy case scenarios (also known as negative scenarios) for the use cases.

Workshop 3: Wednesday

On Wednesday, workshop 3 began with a prototype walkthrough using the happy scenarios the participants had generated earlier. As the participants walked through the prototype, discussions broke out about the look and feel of the user interface. Eli knew that project members tended to have religious issues about the system's look and feel—issues that would be difficult to resolve and, in any case, weren't relevant at this point. So he interrupted the discussion, asking whether the points being made were related to requirements. With this reminder, the group regained its focus: using the prototype to verify the requirements. They discovered some subtle gaps in their business rules, along with additional data values related to differences between the UK and US implementations of the scenarios.

Now it was time to review the unhappy scenarios. As a result of this review, the team added more unhappy scenarios (mostly business rule violations) and drafted business rules for handling them. The group also added one- or two-sentence use case extensions to describe how to handle each unhappy scenario. Again, they reviewed the scenarios and used the criteria developed earlier to add six more high-priority unhappy scenarios to the prototype.

In post-work on Wednesday afternoon, the participants revised the prototype based on the day's work and revised the domain model. That evening, they enjoyed a nice dinner, relaxing and enjoying each other's company. By now, they had their own "in" jokes and were teasing each other, showing genuine appreciation of their various personalities and backgrounds.

Workshop 4: Thursday

Thursday started with another prototype review and walkthrough of the additional unhappy scenarios. Several more business rules were clarified.

Now it was time to step back and gain some perspective on where the project stood. Guided by Eli, the participants modeled the entire set of use cases (not just the first 30-day cycle, the topic of their prototype) as a workflow. Using the last available wall space, they arranged each use case post in predecessor/successor order.

When they finished, they had five sets of use cases grouped together. They tested the correctness and completeness of the order using some of their scenarios and then tweaked the flow. They then grouped the use cases into packages. Using arrows, they drew dependencies between the packages. Next, they prioritized the packages and arrived at a recommended release strategy, and this four-hour session drew to a close.

After lunch, the senior sponsors rejoined the session for the show-and-tell. They were impressed by the volume and quality of the work. They asked how long it would have taken if the team had not used a workshop approach, and the participants laughed. "Months!" said one. "Even if it took us weeks, we never would have really agreed like we were able to do here," said another.

After the sponsors left the room, the team members reviewed and cleaned up their Parking Lot list. Then they conducted their final workshop retrospective.

COMPARISONS

Collaborative workshops are a flexible approach for discovering requirements. In addition to use cases and scenarios, these workshops can employ a variety of tools, including requirements walkthroughs, prototypes, contextual design, unhappy scenarios, and misuse cases. They are a natural fit with the low-fidelity and storyboarding techniques described by Suzanne Robertson in this volume, Chapter 3 for defining events, stakeholders, scenarios, use cases and a context diagram. Likewise, they can be adapted to elicit and verify work models and storyboards produced in several phases in Contextual Design (*see* Karen Holtzblatt, this volume, Chapter 10). The workshop-based approach described as scenario-based user needs analysis (*see* Joy Van Helvert and Chris Fowler, this volume, Chapter 4) while more prescriptive is similar to the framework and techniques described in this chapter.

Requirements workshops are perhaps the original agile requirements development approach. They are adopted by agile projects as an efficient means of capturing lightweight requirements, such as stories (*see* Kent Beck and David West, this volume, Chapter 13), or any requirements representations, such as use cases and scenarios, that strive toward minimal requirements documentation and reduced formalism in customer sign-off.

Walkthroughs of use case text (see Chapter 9 of this volume, Systematic Scenario Walkthroughs, by Neil Maiden) or a prototype are especially popular. To check for requirements errors or omissions, scenarios or a QA checklist (or both) can be used as the driving tool. A workshop is a good place for constructing low-fidelity prototypes (whiteboard sketches, flipcharts, or color posts), which in turn can be used to build high-fidelity prototypes outside the workshop. Then the high-fidelity prototypes can be used in a subsequent requirements workshop to verify and validate the requirements. In some cases when the technical staff is unfamiliar with the domain, they are encouraged to observe users interacting with the current product, if possible. This is akin to observations, a central component of the contextual design approach to requirements and design.

Requirements workshops also use unhappy scenarios as a matter of course. They are extremely useful in uncovering business rules, writing extensions to use cases, and planning releases or iterations.

Generating *misuse cases,* or the negative form of use cases in which the actor has some hostile or harmful intent (as Ian Alexander explains in this volume, Chapter 7), has also proven useful in requirements workshops. Some requirements workshops focus on authentication, authorization, and administration use cases, which are useful for helping the team to thoroughly understand the requirements. If you're specifying nonfunctional requirements, it's a good idea to create misuse cases, doing most of that work outside the workshop setting.

Requirements workshops must be tailored to deliver the requirements that are appropriate to the project, application, and culture. If your aim is to write lightweight requirements, such as simple use cases, business rules, or a domain model, workshops are an effective way to gather the requirements, prioritize them, and reach closure quickly and with customers entirely engaged.

A workshop approach can be adapted to result in well-run and efficient story-elicitation sessions (*see* Kent Beck and David West, this volume, Chapter 13) when more than two people are needed. This may be the case in projects whose scope is large or whose requirements are complex.

KEYWORDS

Facilitated Workshop
Collaborative Workshop
Requirements Workshop
Customer Collaboration

JAD
Joint Requirements
  Workshop
Use Case Workshop

Happy Case Scenario
Unhappy Case Scenario
Collaboration Pattern
Use Case Extension

Misuse Case
Workshop Retrospective

REFERENCES

Bens, I., *Facilitating with Ease: A Step-by-Step Guidebook with Customizable Worksheets on CD-ROM*, Jossey-Bass, 2000.

Doyle, M. and Strauss, D., *How to Make Meetings Work*, Berkeley Books, 1976.

Gause, D.C. and Weinberg, G.M., *Exploring Requirements: Quality Before Design*, Dorset House, 1989.

Gottesdiener, E., *Specifying Requirements with a Wall of Wonder*, The Rational Edge, November 2001a, http://www.therationaledge.com/content/nov_01/t_wallOfWonder_eg.html

Gottesdiener, E., Collaborate for quality: using collaborative workshops to determine requirements, *Software Testing and Quality Engineering*, **3**(2), 51–59, 2001b.

Gottesdiener, E., Decide how to decide: a collaboration pattern, *Software Development*, **9**(1), 65–70, 2001c.

Gottesdiener, E., *Requirements by Collaboration: Workshops for Defining Needs*, Addison-Wesley, 2002.

Gottesdiener, E., Requirements by collaboration: getting it right the first time, *IEEE Software*, **20**(2), 52–55, 2003.

Kaner, S., with Lind, L., Toldi, C., Fisk, S., and Berger, D., *Facilitator's Guide to Participatory Decision-Making*, New Society Publishers, 1996.

Pardee, W.J., *To Satisfy & Delight Your Customer: How to Manage for Customer Value*, Dorset House, 1996.

Spencer, L.J., *Winning Through Participation: Meeting the Challenge of Corporate Change with the Technology of Participation*, Kendell/Hunt Publishing Company, 1989.

Wirfs-Brock, R., Designing, Scenarios: making the case for a use case framework, *The Smalltalk Report*, **3**(3), 7–10, 1993.

Wood, J. and Silver, D., *Joint Application Development*, 2nd ed., John Wiley & Sons, 1995.

RECOMMENDED READING

Ingrid Bens (2000) is a facilitator's guide loaded with generic techniques, tips, and tools. Although they are not described in a software setting, these tools can be adapted to chartering and requirements workshops.

Michael Doyle and David Strauss (1976) describe the basic elements of successful meetings in several chapters on how to be a good facilitator, recorder, and group member.

Don Gause and Jerry Weinberg (1989) provide a fun and straightforward look at the human side of requirements, with several pithy chapters devoted to workshop-like meetings.

Ellen Gottesdiener (2001) describes blow-by-blow examples in these three articles. One article (The Rational Edge) explains in detail how to use the room's walls in workshops and how to use focus questions to deliver use cases and actors. Another provides details on how to reach closure in workshops (Software Development). The other (STQE) focuses on how to integrate walkthroughs, reviews, and role-playing into requirements workshops.

Ellen Gottesdiener (2002) is a "how to" requirements workshop handbook useful to workshop sponsors, facilitators, and participants.

Ellen Gottesdiener (2003) outlines the value of requirements workshops, highlighting the roles played by various stakeholders.

Sam Kaner et al. (1996) provides practical, high-level guidance to new and experienced facilitators. The book includes a framework for participatory decision-making.

Jane Wood and Denise Silver (1995) update their classic 1989 on JAD, describing the phases and related participatory approaches. They also give an overview of tools and techniques as well as group dynamics.

CHAPTER 6

ALTERNATIVE WORLD SCENARIOS TO ASSESS REQUIREMENT STABILITY

David Bush
UK National Air Traffic Services Ltd, London, UK

ALL SYSTEMS change over their lifetimes. Unless you are fortunate enough to be responsible for delivering a very small system, with a limited life expectancy, people will want to change your system. This will almost certainly happen while you are developing and delivering the system, and it will definitely happen when you are operating it—unless it is one of the significant numbers of systems that are delivered and never used—which is hardly a consolation.

There are really only two things you can do about this: you can ignore it and hope that you are moved onto another system before anyone thinks too much about changing the system; or you can specify and build your system so that it is robust in the face of the changes it faces, that is, so that change is not needed, so that it is easy to achieve, and so that it does not detract from the operation of your system.

If you are bold enough to take the responsible approach to this problem, this chapter offers you a mechanism for identifying what changes might occur over your systems life cycle. Armed with that knowledge, you have chance of future-proofing your system, and probably getting a promotion for your successor.

APPLICABILITY

Using scenarios of the system environment to identify possible requirement changes requires an investment of time, both to establish the scenarios and to carry out the assessment. As change is an effect that accrues over time, it is not worthwhile carrying the overhead for a small project with a short expected lifetime. Where it is worthwhile is in

- Security- or Safety-related systems, where changes to the system are likely to seriously jeopardise the effectiveness of the system, and where redesign and revalidation of the system is inevitably expensive.
- Architecturally complex systems, where in-service changes will rapidly compromise the architecture and impair system performance.

Scenarios, Stories, Use Cases: Through the Systems Development Life-Cycle.   Edited by Ian F Alexander and Neil Maiden
© 2004 John Wiley & Sons, Ltd.   ISBN: 0-470-86194-0

- Long lifetime systems, where the long term changes that the system will face are difficult to predict by extrapolating current trends.
- Business critical systems that are highly sensitive to external factors, such as international agreements, government policy and regulation, and/or public attitudes and opinions.

POSITION IN THE LIFE CYCLE

The approach applies across the life cycle, but is most relevant in the darker box, and somewhat relevant in the lighter ones.

Requirements Discovery	Requirements Validation	System Specification	System Design	Coding, First of Class	Integration & Testing	Operations & Maintenance

KEY FEATURES

Strategic planners in business and government settings have long acknowledged the benefit of exploring possible future environments. Scenarios are developed describing a number of possible future worlds in which the business might exist, and using these to create robust plans, structures for the business in the future. Similar environmental scenarios can be used to describe the environment surrounding a planned future system. Emerging requirements are then analysed in each of those possible future worlds to identify which requirements are likely to change. Requirements Engineers and System Architects can then use these evaluations to make judgements about what requirements should be specified, and how they might be fulfilled within an architecture that can accommodate the possible changes identified.

STRENGTHS

This approach has a number of benefits over other approaches in identifying requirements changes. Firstly, it is proactive and seeks to predict possible future change, rather than simply measure the change that has taken place through change metrics. Secondly, it addresses change as a system life-cycle issue, unlike risk management based approaches—which tend to concentrate only on project risk. Finally, it provides a more creative approach to identifying possible risks to stability, and so overcomes some of the decision-making biases (concentrating on the familiar, anchoring on a single idea etc.) that hamper many approaches in identifying future problems.

WEAKNESSES

It is important to acknowledge that this approach only addresses the identification of possible future change. Its output is a list of potentially unstable requirements, and the way in which they might be unstable. Requirements Engineers and System Architects will then have to start earning their money by deciding how concerned they are about each possible change (–is it likely, would it have a big impact), and then deciding what to do about it (architect in a way that accommodates the change, design the change in from the start, etc.). A project without a strong systems engineering approach may well find such activities daunting. Even well-engineered projects, which would be carrying out such activities anyway, will find that the scale and scope of the work have increased.

Indeed, a general increase in the amount of work conducted is one effect of this approach. (As Ada programmers say, 'Slow is good'.) Time needs to be spent in investigating and developing the alternative world scenarios, and then in evaluating the requirements against each of them. While an accurate traceability structure in the requirements will limit the amount of assessment that needs to be carried out, nonetheless this is additional work, which the project must fund.

This is not an approach suitable for all projects; but on the sort of projects identified above, it has the capacity for identifying significant potential requirement changes, and giving developers a chance to address them while it is still cheap to do so.

TECHNIQUE

Change in Systems

Experience, and the extensive work of Manny Lehman, has taught us of the troubles that afflict large-scale, user-involved systems in respect of change. For our purposes, it is driven by external factors in two key ways (Lehman and Belady 1985):

- *Continuing change:* In regard to the assumptions made about the performance of systems external to the system under discussion, even if these are entirely correct at the time, they eventually become compromised as the environment of the system changes.
- *Continuing growth:* In regard to the functional capability of systems, it must be continually increased to maintain user satisfaction over the system lifetime, and so there are continually emerging new and changed requirements.

In other words, change can occur both in our assumptions about the world in which our system will exist and in the requirements the system is expected to fulfil.

Requirements and Assumptions

Jackson (1995) shows that requirements and assumptions are essentially related in the construction of any system—that it is the combination of specified behaviour of the machine and the assumptions about the world, taken together, that guarantee the achievement of the requirements.

In the normal course of system development then, we may record the requirements and the assumptions we expect to depend on, but this is always a view *at a point in time*. We usually choose this point in time to be the moment at which the system is to enter service: at that time each requirement can be shown to be met by a combination of machine behaviour and assumptions about the environment.

The Effect of Time

But as time moves on, requirements and assumptions change. As they do so, our system must respond, either by changing the specification—and hence the design, or by accepting a compromise in the functionality of the system (existing requirements can no longer be met, new requirements are ignored). At some future moment, then, requirements and assumptions may no longer be valid. This is a framework for assessing the risk that requirements will become invalid, and so for forming a view on the stability of requirements.

Assessing Requirements Stability

There are two prerequisites for such an assessment,

- the set of requirements and assumptions (at whatever stage of refinement—business, user, system); and
- scenarios—static, snapshot descriptions of the alternative future worlds.

I assume that readers are familiar with developing and documenting requirements and assumptions (if not, see the recommended books at the end of this chapter). The alternative world may, however, be a less familiar example of the myriad types of scenario used in systems development—and deserves some explanation.

Alternative World Scenarios

The use of what I call here Alternative World Scenarios seems to trace to military planning carried out at the RAND Corporation after WW2. They were used to analyse decisions against alternative enemy courses of action. Herman Kahn was influential in popularising this concept and migrated it into the business world. Perhaps the best-known user of this type of scenario was Royal Dutch/Shell.

It is accurate to call these 'World' scenarios because they describe the environment that surrounds the system under examination, in our case a software intensive system. It is also appropriate to call them 'Scenarios' as they are creative prose descriptions of possible future environments (Bush et al. 2001).

Generating Scenarios

Space precludes a full and detailed description of the mechanism for generating these scenarios (see the recommended reading section for more detailed coverage). However, an outline of the approach is worthwhile to familiarise readers with a perhaps unfamiliar style of scenario. Figure 6.1 shows the key stages.

- Firstly, a set of knowledgeable stakeholders needs to be identified who have some knowledge of aspects of the domain in question.
- Secondly, by interview or group work these stakeholders are used to identify a set of uncertain factors likely to affect the system in question.

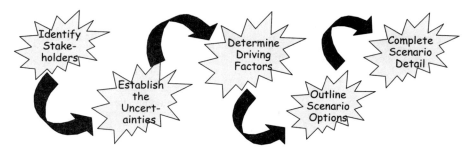

FIGURE 6.1   Key stages in generating scenarios

- Thirdly, prioritisation techniques are used to identify the most influential and important of these factors.
- Fourthly, the most important factors are used to identify a small number (2–4) of different possible world states.
- Finally, these outline world states are described in as vivid a detail as possible, and fleshed out with creative prose descriptions (based on the uncertain factors identified) into narrative descriptions of the Alternative Future Worlds.

The result of this activity is a set of prose descriptions of alternative future worlds. By asking the requirements analysts and/or stakeholders to read, and immerse themselves in, these worlds, we can get them to creatively assess the stability of their requirements.

Requirements

To effectively assess the stability of the requirements in the long term, I have argued above that it is essential to consider both requirements and assumptions. At a minimum these must be recorded in the requirements documentation in order to individually assess their stability. Preferably, these need to be recorded in such a way that their relationships are explicitly described—in order to understand the effects of changes in requirements or assumptions, one must know how they are related.

It is my opinion that a goal-based model of requirements is the best way to record them, and their interdependencies, and that is the basis of this description and the worked example that follows. However, it is possible—by using satisfaction arguments (for more detail on these, see Alistair Mavin's Chapter 20 on REVEAL) or rich traceability—to document requirements, assumptions and their interdependence in a traditional document hierarchy model, therefore, wherever appropriate I will illustrate the equivalent (document hierarchical) approach. Whichever approach is chosen, suitably documented requirements can be assessed for stability using scenarios generated from them.

Assessing Stability

Assessing the stability of the requirements is a relatively mechanical process, where each scenario is taken in turn, read through, and internalised so that the assessors can begin to feel what it would be like to be in that sort of world. Then each of the requirements is

TABLE 6.1 Assessing stability

Requirement/assumption that prompted the instability.
The likelihood of the requirement/assumption being unstable.
The type of instability suggested.
A brief description of, and rationale for, the assessment

TABLE 6.2 Types of instability

Goals	Assumptions
Goal removal	Remove assumption
Goal performance level changes	Add new assumption
Goal functionality changes	Change level of assumption
Remove goal refinement	
Add goal refinement	
Goal addition	
Change allocation	
None	

considered in turn in the light of that scenario, and in each case an assessment is made of the likely stability. The following information is usefully recorded (Table 6.1):

The types of instability referred to (for a goal-based model) could be as shown in Table 6.2.

This process is repeated for each requirement and assumption in each scenario, until all are completed.

In systems of a significant size, it is useful to carry out this process at a reasonable level of abstraction. For goal-based models this means the highest level of goal, while for a document hierarchy-based system, it means the business or user requirements, initially at least. This helps to prevent the task of assessment from growing excessively.

Reviewing Requirement Stability

With each requirement/assumption assessed in each of the scenarios, they can be viewed in order of criticality, with the requirements obtaining the highest aggregate score appearing as the most likely to be unstable. It is useful to base this classification on two aspects of the assessment,

- The aggregate score for each requirement assumption
- The number of scenarios in which the requirement/assumption was likely to be unstable.

TABLE 6.3 Severity index

	Very Low Aggregate Score	Moderate Aggregate Score	High Aggregate Score	Very High Aggregate Score
One scenario	1	1	2	3
Two scenarios	1	2	2	3
Three scenarios	2	3	3	4
Four scenarios	2	4	5	5

This classification scheme means that adequate emphasis is given to requirements that are slightly unstable in many future worlds, as well as those that are very unstable in one or two. A matrix such as that shown in Table 6.3 can be used to make such a classification.

This provides a severity index for each requirement, which can be used to prioritise the consideration of the potentially unstable requirements and assumptions.

So far the assessment has made a single pass through the set of requirements and assumptions. Sometimes this will be enough, but it must be recognised that this has only contributed a local view of instability. A more thorough view is possible, if the situation warrants it, by investigating whether the instabilities identified so far, suggest or require instabilities elsewhere.

Instability Propagation

Instability propagation allows us to overcome the purely local view we took initially, and establish whether there are any second-order effects that should be addressed. Before considering whether to include this step in a stability assessment activity, the following factors should be taken into account:

How confident are you in the assessments you made with regard to

- The consistency of your scoring;
- The consistency of your assessment of instability between related requirements and assumptions;
- The scope of your instability assessment (was it over all requirements, or just a high-level subset?);

as well as the time and resources available and the severity of the consequences of having only a partial assessment.

Including a propagation stage adds time and effort, but often improves the scoring. If the scope of assessment (limiting to high-level requirements/goals) was limited; and the whole assessment is not going to be repeated at a later requirements stage, propagation is the only mechanism for driving the assessments down to assumptions and goals that can be made operational.

Instability propagation involves the use of propagation heuristics to question, for each goal, if there are other goals that are similarly affected—for example, the deletion of a goal or requirement might suggest the deletion of all the child goals, or derived requirements. The propagation heuristics describe, for each instability type, the likely areas where related goals could be unstable.

When propagating instability, a scoring system identical to that for the original assessment is used, so that at the end of this process each requirement/assumption has both an initial and a propagated assessment. A similar coding scheme to that identified above can then be applied, in order to identify the most critically unstable requirements/assumptions.

Using the Stability Assessment Results

Stability assessment results are useful in two aspects of the system development life cycle.

Firstly, they are useful *within* the requirements development activity in order to assist analysts in selecting between alternative requirements, and in examining any 'obstacles' (Potts 1995) or threats to the achievement of requirements or assumptions (e.g. 'Obstacle Analysis' (van Lamsweerde 2000); Misuse Cases (Sindre and Opdahl 2000; *see also* Chapter 7 in this volume by Ian Alexander). In this form, the assessment would normally exclude the propagation stage, and make a contribution to the development of better and more robust requirements and assumptions.

Secondly, they are useful at the end of the requirements definition activities. Here propagation activity would normally be useful. In this form, the results of the assessment would be used to inform architectural choices and design constraints. (c.f. Architecture Based Analysis (Kazman 1996, 1998).

WORKED EXAMPLE

As I described, the prerequisites of this approach are the requirements, and the scenarios. This worked example will not cover how these are derived, but the next sections introduce them to provide a comprehensive background.

Goals/Requirements for MSAW

This worked example is based on the goals for a Minimum Safe Altitude Warning (MSAW) system. An MSAW system is intended to reduce the number of occurrences of Controlled Flight into Terrain (CFIT) by providing a ground-based early warning of pilots who are flying below the mandated minimum safe altitude.

In essence, the system uses existing external data sources such as radar returns and terrain and obstacle databases as the raw data feed for proximity detection and prediction algorithms. These algorithms then provide warnings to air traffic controllers about potentially hazardous situations, who in turn can warn the pilot.

The goal-based model of these requirements is structured like a tree (although technically it should be described as a graph) with the most general and abstract requirements at the top, and the most detailed, operationisable ones at the bottom.

Each goal is related to one or more parents, which explain 'Why' it is there, and one or more children, which explain 'How' it will be achieved.

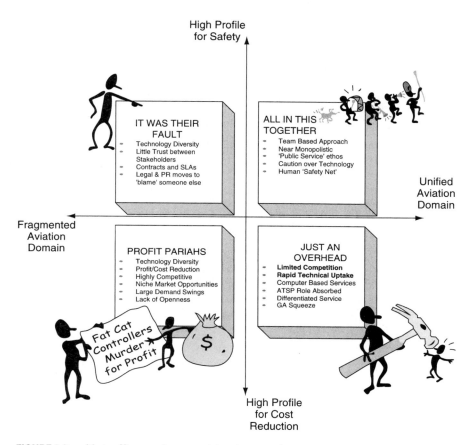

FIGURE 6.2   Air traffic service providers' scenario

In this example, we use a total of four scenarios of the environment surrounding Air Traffic Service Providers. These are the basis on which we can examine the stability of the Goals. These are depicted in Figure 6.2.

Figure 6.3 illustrates one of these scenarios in detail.

Initial Assessment

In the initial assessment stage we examine all the goals, scenario by scenario, scoring each one for its likely stability and instability category, and making any relevant notes, as shown on the screen shot of the assessment tool in Figure 6.4.

For example, in the case of the 'All in this Together' scenario, we note that

Goal 1—Achieve: Controller Alerted to proximity.
(The controller is alerted to the proximity of an aircraft to the ground. This is currently possible by identifying that an aircraft has hit the ground and/or by predicting that it will hit, and then informing the controller.)

> **"All in this Together"**
> **A 'Consumerism' Scenario for Air Traffic Service Providers in Europe.**
>
> As the state has stepped back, airline consolidation has occurred, reducing excess capacity and increasing flexibility through global alliances. Air Traffic Service Provision (ATSP) is a minority player and is heavily influenced by the airlines. The amount of co-ordination required to introduce new technologies is greatly reduced as there are only three global airline alliance and national concerns play little part in decisions. There are strong incentives to implement technical and procedural changes and once an objective has been agreed, although a strong safety emphasis means that these are not always implemented immediately. This sometimes results in a small disparity between demand and capacity, but the resulting delays are generally accepted as the price to be paid for safety.
>
> Competition among the alliances is somewhat limited, although airlines continuously review their choice of airport hubs and try to be ahead of competitors in creating a small number of new hubs. National boundaries are barely an issue in such decisions, ATSPs are extensions of the alliances, and a single unified face presented to the world.
>
> The domain is be quasi-monopolistic and Air Traffic Management (ATM) planning and provision is a team-based activity within the alliances. Where competition exists it does not affect inter-alliance co-operation in ATSP strategy (which is an exception to monopoly rules). There is also common emphasis on public safety, which arises from airlines' desire to avoid damage to their reputation. ATSPs enjoy benefits of scale and cost through co-operating technical systems in all parts of the value chain. It may be either private or publicly owned, but global airlines and strong consumers are the dominating influence.
>
> Nonetheless, for image sake the alliances ensure that General Aviation continues to have access to the airspace. If national planning systems decide to take on the airlines, traffic goes elsewhere so the nation loses economic standing. The role of ATSPs (although invisible to the ultimate customer) changes, although not too quickly because of the cautious approach to introducing technology. Regard for safety means an enduring respect for ATSPs, and they retain a valued and differentiated role in providing a 'safety net' service in case of problems or dangers arising in the system.

FIGURE 6.3   A scenario

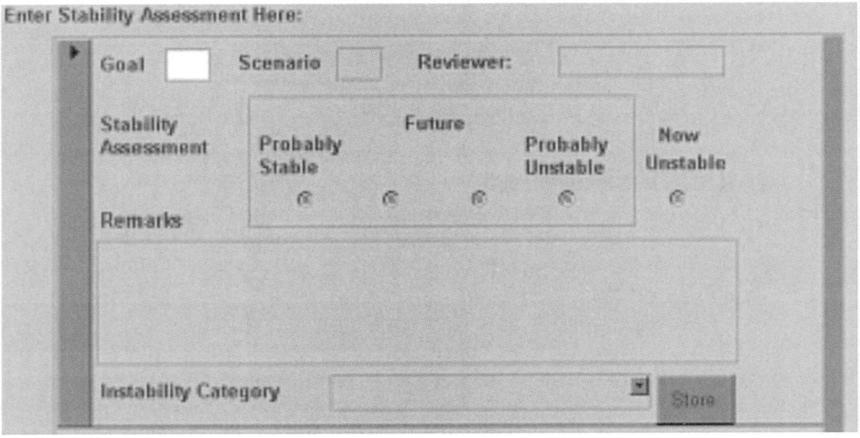

FIGURE 6.4   Stability assessment tool

could well be unstable in this scenario. This is because in this scenario technological advance happens fairly easily, and is fairly rapidly introduced, and this coupled with an emphasis on safety means that is possible that warnings would not longer be passed through the controller, but could be sent by data-link directly to the pilot. We can therefore note that in the assessment.

> Assessment Score: '2' Instability Category: *'Goal Functionality Changes'*
> Remarks: *'Likely that this would be removed altogether and replaced with direct alerting.'*

Once this process is completed for each goal, in each of the four scenarios, we have a set of instability ratings for each goal.

Results Presentation

Prioritising and colour-coding the goals allows us to take an overview of the most and least stable. Figure 6.5 illustrates how this overview can be used to quickly pinpoint the goals of most concern.

In this picture the red goals are the most unstable, and the green ones most stable. We can therefore concentrate our minds first, on those of greatest concern.

If we then drill down into one of these goals, we can examine the detailed assessments we made in order to make a more considered decision of our assessment. An example of this detail view is shown in Figure 6.6.

On the basis of this information we are in a much better position to decide what we want to do about what we have discovered, for example, can we safely ignore these possibilities? Perhaps we feel that we should make certain architectural or design decisions in order to protect ourselves against this possibility? Perhaps we can use this information to change our requirements.

A final possibility is that we decide we want to examine in some detail, the effects of this particular instability on other parts of our requirements. In that case, we would carry out the propagation activity.

Propagation

Propagation is the activity in which we attempt to overcome the limitations of the local assessments we made earlier. We choose particular Goals, or possibly all the Goals, and use change heuristics to assess what the effects of that instability might be when we traverse the trace links between Goals or Requirements.

In our example, we might decide that we wish to examine the propagation of a particular goal instability. The screenshot in Figure 6.7 shows the goal we have selected, and the original assessment we made in the 'Consumerism' Scenario. Using the Propagation Heuristic shown at the bottom for this instability type, we can identify any parent or child Goals that might be affected. If we find such a Goal we can then edit its original assessment, to provide a propagated instability type and description.

Once we have completed this we have an augmented set of assessments, which we can view in the same way as before—selecting the most critical for overview, and possible resolution action.

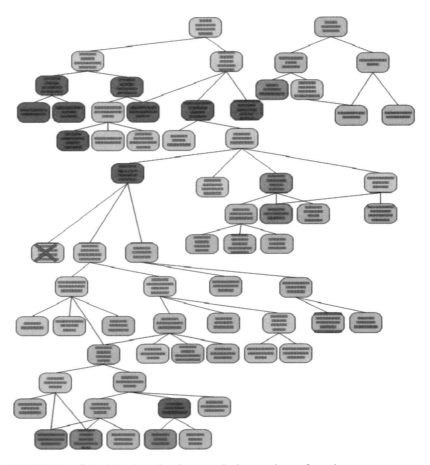

FIGURE 6.5 Prioritised and colour-coded overview of goals

Stability Display Form					
Goal **30** Heading **Achieve: Controller notifies pilot**				Stability Rating **1**	

	Scenario	Score	Instability Type	Propagated?	Comment	Propagate
1	Consumerism	1	Goal Performance Level Changes	☐	Takes on a relatively more impotant role as ATC is a 'Safety Net'. Performance Level in question is timeliness and reliability.	▸
2	Affluent Nationalism	1	Goal Removal	☐	May not be requirec for liability reasons.	▸
3	Controlled Development	0	None	☐		▸
4	Survival of Fittest	0	None	☐		▸

FIGURE 6.6 Stability display form — detail of one goal

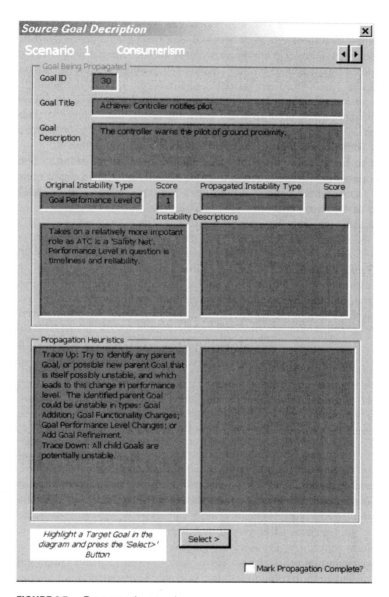

FIGURE 6.7   Propagation tool

COMPARISONS

Besides the very close comparison we can make between this approach and the classical use of such scenarios in business to assess and select appropriate business decisions, there are a number of close parallels in the systems engineering domain.

Classical requirement stability assessment, for example is an approach to identifying requirement stability, it measures the amount of change in requirements during their development, or over a number of releases of the system to obtain a measure of change. This tends to be a historical approach though, and does not provide much in the way of prediction.

In contrast, Risk Assessment Methods do tend to predict possible problems in the future, but their time horizon is rather different—being focused largely on the project timescale, rather than the system lifetime timescale.

We have already seen the close relationship between the output of this approach and the input to scenario-based assessment techniques such as Obstacle Analysis and Architecture Based Assessment. It could also be used as a creative thinking technique preceding a 'Misuse Cases' approach (*see* Ian Alexander's account in Chapter 7)—helping to elicit knowledge of possible future threats (and therefore likely instabilities when these are designed against).

Most recently, the work of Peri Loucopoulos (*see* Chapter 21) in using systems dynamic models as 'design' tools to explore requirements (no I didn't get my waterfall stages mixed up!) is a most promising-looking partner for this work. The alternative scenarios/dynamic model approach is well established in the business management domain, and may yet prove to be a fruitful technique for system engineers.

KEYWORDS

Scenario	Requirements	Goals
Scenario Planning	Assumptions	Requirement Stability

REFERENCES

Bush, D., Durand, H., Ellison, D., Rhodes-James, C., and Tulloch, A., *Alternative Futures for Air Traffic Service Provision in Europe*, LBS Project Report, 2001.

Jackson, M., *Software Requirements and Specifications*, Addison-Wesley, 1995.

van Lamsweerde, A. and Letier, E., Handling obstacles in goal-oriented requirements engineering, *IEEE Transactions on Software Engineering*, **26**(10), 978–1005 2000.

Kazman, R., Abowd, G., Bass, L., and Clements, P., Scenario-based analysis of software architecture, *IEEE Software*, **13**(6), 47–55 1996.

Kazman, R., Klein, M., Barbacci, M., Lipson, H., Longstaff, T., and Carrière, S., The architec-ture tradeoff analysis method, *Proceedings of ICECCS*, Monterey, CA, August 1998.

Lehman, M.M. and Belady, L.A., *Program Evolution—Processes of Software Change*, Academic Press, London, 1985.

Potts, C., Using schematic scenarios to understand user needs, *Proceedings of DIS '95—ACM Symposium on Designing Inter-ActiveSystems: Processes, Practices and Techniques*, University of Michigan, 1995.

Sindre, G and Opdahl, A, Eliciting security requirements by misuse cases, *Proceedings of TOOLS Pacific 2000*, November 2000, pp. 20–23, 120–131.

RECOMMENDED READING

On 'Alternative World' Scenarios

De Gues, A., *The Living Company*, Nicholas Brearly, 1999 is an excellent and highly readable introduction to the reasons for the use of scenarios in business planning.

Galt, M., Chicoine-Piper, G., Chicoine-Piper, N., and Hodgson, A., *Idon Scenario Thinking*, IDON Ltd, 1997 provides a straightforward step-by-step guide to creating scenarios, and the mechanism for using these in decision making. It includes a worked example, and is probably the best text I have seen as a simple introduction. Those weaknesses that there are in this book (it is a little too regimented, and is weak on actually writing engaging scenario descriptions), are addressed in

Schwartz, P., *The Art of the Long View*, Wiley, 1998 which is, in my opinion, unbeatable for the more confident builder of scenarios. It has excellent examples of scenario use, and a strong section (although less of a step-by-step process) on the stages, activities and tools needed for developing scenarios.

On Requirements Engineering

Robertson, S. and J., *Mastering the Requirements Process*, Addison-Wesley, 1999 is the best 'take it off the shelf and do it' guide to requirements that I have found.

CHAPTER 7

NEGATIVE SCENARIOS AND MISUSE CASES

Ian Alexander
Scenario Plus, London, UK

AMISUSE Case is the negative form of a Use Case. It documents a negative scenario. Its Actor is a hostile agent, typically but not always a human with hostile intent towards the system under design. The relationships between Use and Misuse Cases document threats and their mitigations. Use/Misuse Case diagrams are therefore valuable in security threat and safety hazard analyses. Mitigation often involves new subsystems, so Misuse Cases also have a role in system design.

Misuse Cases can help elicit requirements for systems, especially where exception cases might otherwise be missed. Their immediate applications are for security and safety requirements—in that order, but they can be useful for other types of requirement, for identifying missing functions, and for generating test cases.

APPLICABILITY

- Systems in which security is a major concern, for example, distributed and web-based systems, financial systems, government systems.
- Safety-related systems using new technologies, in which knowledge of hazards in earlier systems may be an insufficient guide to hazards introduced by new system functions and their interactions, for example, control systems in automotive, railway, and aerospace.
- Systems in which stakeholders may hold conflicting viewpoints that would threaten the project if not addressed, for example, multi-national government projects.
- More generally, any system in which threats and exceptions are not fully defined.

ROLES IN THE LIFE CYCLE

Requirements Discovery	Requirements Validation	System Specification	System Design	Coding, First of Class	Integration & Testing	Operations & Maintenance

Scenarios, Stories, Use Cases: Through the Systems Development Life-Cycle. Edited by Ian F Alexander and Neil Maiden
© 2004 John Wiley & Sons, Ltd. ISBN: 0-470-86194-0

KEY FEATURES

Negative Actors are identified. The security and other threats they pose to the system are described as goals that they desire, drawn as Misuse Case bubbles on a Use Case diagram, and if need be analysed as Negative Scenarios. The threats are then mitigated by suitable Use Cases, often representing new subsystem functions.

STRENGTHS

The Negative Scenario is essentially a conceptual tool to help people apply their experience, intelligence, and social skill to identify the following:

- threats and mitigations
- security requirements
- safety requirements
- exceptions that could cause system failure
- test cases.

The strength of this kind of approach lies in its combination of a well-structured system-facing starting point, and its human-facing open-endedness. This makes it almost uniquely suited to probing the new, unknown, and unexpected.

WEAKNESSES

The approach is essentially human and qualitative. As such, it cannot guarantee discovering all threats. It does not assure correct prioritisation of threats, though it can be combined with any suitable prioritisation mechanism, for example, card sorting, laddering, or voting. Nor does it guarantee that the response to threats will be effective in mitigating them, but then no method does that for new threats.

It does not replace quantitative methods used in Safety and Reliability analysis (e.g. Bayesian computation of risk), or Monte Carlo simulation of outcomes, though it may be a useful precursor to any of these. It helps to identify the threats, hazards, and candidate mitigations that these other techniques can explore.

It tends to focus attention on one threat at a time. However, major failures of well-engineered systems, especially when they are safety-critical, tend to be the result of multiple faults and errors. Misuse Cases help identify the individual causes but do not offer a calculus for combining them—though nor does any other technique in common use.

TECHNIQUE

Nel mezzo del cammin di nostra vita
mi ritrovai per una selva oscura
ché la diritta via era smarrita.

In the middle of my life's journey
I found myself in a dark forest,
as I had lost the straight path. . .
Dante Alighieri, *Inferno*, Canto I, 1-3.

FIGURE 7.1 Misuse case

Dante begins his *Inferno* by telling his readers about a threatening situation he once found himself in, 'in a dark forest'. The rest of the Canto expands on that dramatic theme—we know immediately that the story will be dark, the journey difficult and dangerous. The rest of this book looks at the value of telling stories—scenarios and use cases—to define what systems ought to do when things go well. This chapter looks at the other side, when things threaten to go wrong.

Guttorm Sindre and Andreas Opdahl extended the expressive power of Use Case modelling (Jacobson et al. 1992) by introducing the Misuse Case to document negative scenarios, Use Cases with hostile intent (Sindre and Opdahl 2000, 2001). They inverted the colours[1] of the Use Case to indicate the intentions of an opponent (Figure 7.1).

A Misuse Case documents conscious and active opposition in the form of a goal that a hostile agent intends to achieve, but which the organisation perceives as detrimental to some of its goals (Alexander 2003).

The first step in Use / Misuse Case analysis is to make a first-cut Use Case model (Kulak and Guiney 2000, Cockburn 2001, Gottesdiener 2002). This identifies the essential goals of the system, and documents what the system is to do in normal circumstances.

The next two steps can be seen as an adjunct to the hunt for Exceptions and the definition of Exception-handling scenarios (or separate Use Cases). These are to identify hostile agent roles, and the Misuse Case goals that such people may desire. These may be elicited in either order, or simultaneously.

Eliciting Hostile Roles

Hostile roles might want either

- to harm the system, its stakeholders, or their resources intentionally, or
- to achieve goals that are incompatible with the system's goals.

For example, if your business is fur farming, an animal rights protester might wish to damage you, your property, or your farms directly. On the other hand, a rival farmer might wish to corner the fur market, against your interests but not necessarily with any implication of criminality or malice.

Hostile roles are documented as UML 'actors', with a role name and a brief statement of their Viewpoint, for example

---

[1] In monochrome, this inevitably makes the background black. In colour presentations, it is suggested to use red as in 'red team review' for Misuse Cases. In any event, requirements engineers should not use the word black as a synonym for negative.

Role / Actor	Viewpoint
Protester	wishes to abolish fur farming (by direct action)
Rival	wishes to increase market share (at our expense)

FIGURE 7.2   Making a table of roles and viewpoints

ID	Actors and their Viewpoints	Actor Type	Acts in the Following Use Cases
2	**1.1 Actors** This section lists human and other actors with roles in the use cases.	---	
3	**1.1.1 Fur Farmer** wants to make money farming furs	Human	11 Operate Fur Farms
28	**1.1.2 Rival** wishes to increase market share (at our expense)	Human	37 Corner the Market
29	**1.1.3 Protester** wishes to abolish fur farming (by direct action)	Human	31 Damage the Business
30	**1.1.4 Weather** wishes to damage the farm / business physically	External	34 Damage the Buildings

FIGURE 7.3   Hostile roles documented as actors in Scenario Plus

Roles can readily be elicited in a workshop setting. The simplest way is to use a tabular list like this one on a flipchart (Figure 7.2). Or, you can display and edit a table in a general-purpose tool such as a Spreadsheet or a special-to-purpose tool like Scenario Plus (Scenario Plus 2003), projected onto a screen (Figure 7.3).

Eliciting Misuse Cases

A workshop is also a good place to 'brainstorm' a list of Misuse Cases. These can be gathered by the facilitator straight on to a Use Case context diagram, sketched or using a tool; or can simply be listed on a flipchart. At this stage, the Misuse Cases consist simply of the names of their (hostile) goals. Later, it may be helpful to document some of their Negative Scenarios in at least outline detail. As with Use Cases, there is a helpful ambiguity between Misuse Case as goal-in-a-bubble and as scenario—sometimes a bit of detail is helpful; sometimes it really isn't needed.

The Misuse Cases can then be drawn out neatly on a Use Case context diagram—with, for instance, cases grouped under their roles.

At this point it makes sense to indicate which Use Cases are actually affected by the newly discovered Misuse Cases. I have suggested two new relationships, *threatens* and *mitigates* (Alexander 2002b, 2002c), to describe the effect of a Misuse Case on a Use Case, and *vice versa*.

It might also be worth following (Sindre and Opdahl 2000, 2001) and defining *prevents* as a relationship, as prevention is important in safety-related domains such as air traffic control. However, they seem to have intended it to mean 'mitigates', as they

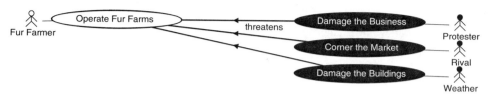

FIGURE 7.4 Documenting threats with use and misuse cases

suggest that the use case 'Enforce password regime' **prevents** a Crook from 'obtaining (a) password'—which it doesn't: it just makes doing so more difficult. So, being a bit more careful, *prevents* should only be used when a use case goal actually makes a misuse case goal impossible to achieve, certain to fail. They also use *detects*, as when a monitoring use case contributes to mitigating a misuse case by noticing when it is occurring.

If you are being really careful, you might want to distinguish between two shades of meaning of *mitigates*: *makes less serious*, and *makes less likely*. For example, making the workers in your gunpowder factory use copper instead of steel shovels prevents a spark from their shovels setting off an explosion, which makes explosion less likely. Conversely, ensuring that only one barrel of gunpowder is in the factory at a time makes any explosion less serious if it happens. If you are preparing a safety case, such distinctions are important.

Formally, these relationships are UML stereotypes that can lawfully be drawn on a Use Case diagram; in practice, they show visually which goals are threatened, and what might be done to mitigate the threats. With a tool like Scenario Plus, it is sufficient to indicate the logical links between cases, and the diagram will then show the direction and nature of the relationships (Figure 7.4). If drawn by hand, coloured arrows (I use black for *threatens*, green for *mitigates*) can be sketched in on whiteboard or flipchart.

Eliciting Exception Scenarios, Requirements, and Further Use Cases

At this point, the workshop can start to ask what to do to neutralise the Misuse Cases. From this point of view, the Misuse Cases effectively describe (and help discover) Exception Events that the hostile agents possibly intend to bring about. The project must decide if indeed the Exception Events matter enough to be worth dealing with: like all requirements, when discovered they are only candidates; prioritisation must come later.

Not everyone likes to call undesired events 'Exceptions'. A workshop participant once told me that it was too confrontational a term; he preferred something like 'unexpected situation' or 'unplanned event'. It doesn't matter what you choose to call these things: the world is full of possibilities that your system—including you—will not like. You have the choice of discovering them in advance and planning for them—or not.

Logically you could try to define an elicitation method based on Misuse Cases: you would create a named Exception (in the threatened Use Case) for each threat, for example

Operate Fur Farms
Exceptions
Business Damaged:
Market Cornered by Rival:

. . .

You would then try to elicit a procedure for handling each exception. Sometimes this is the right approach—misuse cases can identify important exceptions. But since an ounce of prevention is worth a pound of cure, the better approach is first to see if requirements can be found to prevent the identified threats from materialising—many exceptions are irrecoverable.

There are essentially two options for documenting how you are going to deal with Exceptions,

- Single actions can be documented directly in the threatened Use Case as exception-handling or exception-preventing requirements. Such requirements often do not directly call for system functions, but specify desired qualities of the system, such as its safety, reliability, or security. These 'non-functional requirements' can be justified by reference to the Misuse Case that called them into being. In a requirements tool, such a reference is simply a traceability link. A non-functional requirement for security, for instance, may be implemented in the design by adding subsystems such as alarms, cameras, and locks, or in the socio-technical system that contains the designed equipment by appropriate security procedures and training to achieve the specified quality. These components (assets and people) of course perform various functions within the socio-technical system; those functions respond to the non-functional requirements discovered by Misuse Case and other forms of analysis.

- More complex situations can be described and gradually analysed by identifying exception-handling Use Cases that could possibly mitigate the threats posed by the Misuse Cases. The mitigating actions can logically be described in the Primary (not Exception) Scenarios of these Use Cases, and *mitigates* relationships can be drawn to the Misuse Cases that are being neutralised. To complete the picture, *has exception* relationships can be made from the threatened ('parent') Use Cases to the exception-handling/threat-mitigating Use Cases (Figure 7.5).

Logically, every Use Case created to mitigate a threat ought to be considered to be an exception case—it wouldn't exist but for the undesired situation or event that it is meant to handle. However, inevitably we become familiar with old threats. With time, it seems entirely natural that we should have to lock our cars or install alarms. As these things become accepted as normal behaviour, the '*has exception*' relationship tends to give way to an everyday '*includes*'. Does 'Drive the Car' have 'Lock the Car' as an exception or simply as an included case? Once the need for locking is accepted as a requirement, it doesn't matter much

FIGURE 7.5   Documenting exceptions

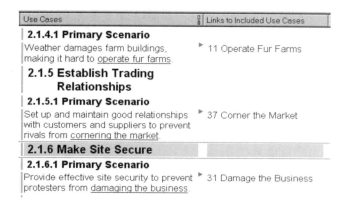

FIGURE 7.6   Use case text implicitly specifying links to misuse cases

Driving Design

The resulting new requirements (or Use Cases) may well call for new subsystems. These may have to be designed from the ground up, or they may already be available as Commercial Off-The-Shelf (COTS) products, only requiring integration with other design elements. The nature of that integration can itself be defined in subsystem-level Use Cases, in which the different subsystems play most of the roles: hence, the Use Case interactions define the functions required across subsystem interfaces.

For example, security requirements may demand new authentication, encryption, locking, surveillance, alarm, logging, and other mechanisms to be incorporated into the design. Knowledge of the existence of these mechanisms may in turn cause would-be intruders to devise new and more complex attacks: the arms race between thieves and locksmiths is never-ending.

Automatic Analysis of Use/Misuse Case Relationships

With tool support, links between Use and related Use or Misuse Cases can be created automatically by analysing their texts, as shown in the illustrations of Scenario Plus below (Figures 7.6 and 7.7), ensuring that text and diagrams stay in synch.

When Use and Misuse Cases interplay, there are four combinations to consider, namely relationships to and from each kind of case (Table 7.1):

This table can be interpreted as a four-part rule governing the automatic creation of relationship types according to the sources and targets of relationships between Use and Misuse Cases.

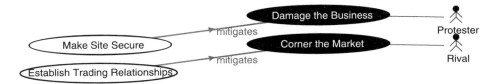

FIGURE 7.7 Diagram drawn automatically from the analysed use case model

TABLE 7.1 Rule governing creation of relationships between use and misuse cases

		Source Case	
Target Case	**Case Type**	**Use**	**Misuse**
	Use	*Includes*	*Threatens*
	Misuse	*Mitigates*	*Includes*

For example, a link from a Use Case to a Misuse Case can be assumed to be a threat, and be labelled *mitigates*. So, when a tool like the Scenario Plus analyser comes across a piece of scenario text like "... damaging the business." in a Use Case, it searches for a match to the underscored text in the names of the Use and Misuse Cases. In this instance, it finds a Misuse Case named 'Damage the Business'—the matching mechanism tolerates slight inexactitude with names, which allows scenarios to be written in a more fluid style—and creates a link to it. The type of that link—*mitigates*—is determined from the rule defined in the table.

The relationships created by the analyser are usually the correct ones, as the relationships shown in the rule are the basic ones for Misuse Case analysis. The rule breaks down in those rarer cases in which the relation between two Use Cases is in fact *conflicts with*, or in which a Use Case actually *aggravates* a Misuse Case instead of mitigating it. These relationships are important in **Trade-off and Conflict Analyses** (see below); the Scenario Plus analyser requires them to be specified explicitly in the Use Case text.

Design Trade-off and Conflict Analyses

The Misuse Case approach is also suitable for reasoning in design space for trade-off and conflict analyses (Alexander 2002a). Conflicts can arise in many ways, but a design conflict is essentially the product of uncertainty about how best to meet requirements, combined sometimes with incompatibilities between some design elements (shown as *conflicts with* relationships), and sometimes with negative effects (shown as *aggravates* relationships) on problems identified in Misuse Cases.

An interesting example from my experience of a design trade-off analysis, which illustrates this approach, is described in Chapter 17, Use Cases in Railway Systems.

Generating Acceptance Test Cases

Since Misuse Cases (and responses to them) often form strong stories at user level, one technique for generating user-level acceptance test cases is to look through the Misuse

Cases and write at least one test case to handle each threat. Of course, if a systematic list of prioritised Exception Scenarios has been prepared for each Use Case (possibly elicited partly with Misuse Cases) then that list subsumes the Misuse Case list.

Metaphorical Roles

Taken literally, the Misuse Case approach is ideal for exploring security threats, and perhaps also safety hazards (*see* **Comparisons** below).

Other challenges that might help elicit different kinds of non-functional requirement can be identified by deliberately treating inanimate things as hostile agents. In other words, we can make use of our ability to reason about people's intentions to help identify requirements by creating metaphors of intent (Potts 2001).

For example, we could say that the weather "intends" to damage the fur farming business (Figure 7.8):

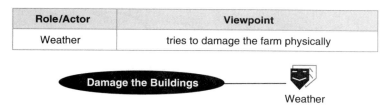

Role/Actor	Viewpoint
Weather	tries to damage the farm physically

FIGURE 7.8   Metaphorical hostile role

This example leads to requirements for weather resistance and lifetime of buildings; the same approach can yield reliability, maintainability, and other "-ility" (quality) requirements.

> **Simpler Diagrams with UML Stereotypes** Some practitioners only ever use UML's Use Case and other diagrams with exactly the symbols that come out of the shrink-wrapped box. This is fine, but needlessly restrictive. Tool designers and other UML users are perfectly allowed to define stereotypes such as new relationships and roles, and to define icons for them (e.g. Fowler 1999). The Misuse Case bubble with its inverted colours, and the Role icon that makes clear it is a generic thing rather than a particular human being (for instance), are examples of stereotype icons. They should be used when they make models easier to understand. Non-software people are quite likely to be misled by terms such as 'actor' and the use of a stick-man icon to denote a role—let alone a non-human role. It is possible and fortunately quite permissible to do better.
>
>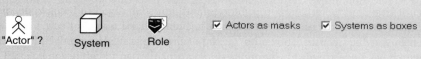

Experienced practitioners may argue that they already know about quality requirements, and have effective templates to discover them. However, novel systems are becoming increasingly complex, and it may well be worth applying a little creativity to help ensure that important requirements are not missed: quality requirements are very difficult to inject into a system after it has been designed.

Less experienced practitioners may instead welcome a simple technique that gives them an independent way of finding and filling gaps in their specifications.

WORKED EXAMPLE

Suppose that we are gathering requirements on behalf of a company that sells a burglar alarm service, including installation, monitoring, and maintenance.

The basic operational objective is to reduce the risk of burglary in households protected by the company.

The core of the design approach to achieve this is to install an alarm, consisting of a set of sensors connected to a control box, which in turn is connected to some actuators whose task is to notify the Control Centre when a possible intrusion is detected, and also when faults occur in the alarm itself.

> Notice, incidentally, that Use and Misuse Cases often quite naturally operate in the world of design (the solution space) rather than in some academically pure 'problem space' free of all design considerations.

The Control Centre analyses messages received from household alarms, and follows a procedure to determine whether to send a guard.

It is at once clear in this case that there is one kind of hostile agent for which the system is in fact designed—the burglar. Indeed, you could argue (rather theoretically) that the alarm itself, indeed the entire security system, is a response to the discovery that burglars threaten unprotected properties. The top-level misuse case is thus the obvious 'Burgle the House', threatening the fanciful (excessively high-level) use case 'Live in the House', and the response to that is the more realistic 'Protect the House'.

The analysis becomes more interesting, however, when we consider the next step in the arms race between the burglar and the alarm company. The alarm company's strategy is to detect intrusion, and to handle the detected intrusions. If the burglar can defeat either of these two steps, the property is unprotected.

Defeating Detection

How can the burglar hope to escape detection? This question is a specialised form of the more general search for exceptions: 'What can go wrong here?'. It is specialised in two ways: it is specific to the problem; and there is a hostile intelligence that we must assume is actively searching for weaknesses in our system.

There are several possible answers, including strategies such as stealth, deception, and force (not to mention the application of inside knowledge). A stealthy strategy is to burgle a house when it is seen to be occupied (references to threatened Use Cases are underlined):

> *Burglar selects a house where activity is visible upstairs, and quietly breaks in while the alarm is off, so it does not <u>detect the intrusion</u>.*

A deceptive strategy is to impersonate a maintenance engineer:

> *Burglar dresses as a Maintenance Engineer and arrives at the Protected House with forged identification.*
>
> *Burglar convinces the Householder that he is a legitimate Maintenance Engineer and gains access to the house, thus defeating the alarm's ability to detect intrusion.*
>
> *Burglar says he is testing the alarm and not to worry if it rings, he's just getting some spares from his van. He then steals some valuables and leaves.*
>
> *Householder is convinced, and waits some time before contacting the Control Centre.*

A forceful strategy is to disable the household alarm:

> *Burglar attacks the Alarm system to prevent it from <u>detecting the intrusion.</u>*

This is a strikingly diverse set of strategies, and they suggest radically different kinds of candidate requirement, such as:

> ®*The household alarm can be set up to protect unoccupied zones in the house.*
> *(mitigates Burgle Occupied House)*
>
> ®*Householders are instructed to check the identity cards of Maintenance Engineers.*
> *(mitigates Impersonate Engineer)*
>
> ®*Householders are instructed only to admit Maintenance Engineers by prior appointment.*
> *(mitigates Impersonate Engineer)*
>
> ®*The alarm notifies a possible intrusion when any sensor, actuator or power connection is lost.*
> *(mitigates Disable the Alarm)*

In general (and certainly on a more complex system than this), negative scenarios can help discover requirements that are both important and easy to miss.

Defeating the Handling of Intrusion

Similarly, there are many possible strategies for defeating the alarm company's intention to handle intrusion effectively.

A deceptive strategy is to set an alarm off repeatedly:

> *The burglar repeatedly sets off the alarm in the house he intends to burgle. The guard and call centre decide the alarm is faulty or being set off by an inanimate agent, and ignore it, thus failing to <u>handle the intrusion.</u>*

A forceful strategy is to kidnap the guard:

> *The burglar sets off the alarm without breaking in, and waits near the house for the guard to arrive. As soon as the guard gets out of his van, the burglar and his accomplice capture the guard, blindfold him, and tie him up, taking his radio and telephone. The accomplice drives the guard a few miles away in the guard's own van, and leaves him, still tied up. The burglar works undisturbed by any further attempt at <u>handling the intrusion.</u>*

A strategy based on knowledge is to burgle quickly at a time when rapid response is unlikely:

> *The burglar knows that it takes 25 minutes for the guard to get through the traffic, so he burgles the house in the rush hour and is gone within a few minutes, long before the guard can* handle the intrusion *effectively.*

Quite a different kind of strategy is to subvert the system. The Control Centre depends on human employees for much of its effectiveness. One strategy is:

> *The burglar and an associate conspire. The associate gets a job in the Control Centre and arranges to ignore or destroy alarm messages from the houses to be burgled, so the system fails to* handle the intrusions.

If anything, these strategies are even more diverse than the threats to detection, and they lead to some quite complex security requirements on the human/procedural parts of the system, far removed from the obvious functionality of the electronics of the Control Centre (let alone of the household alarm, which is where people first start looking for security requirements). Indeed, one lesson is that systems never consist solely of engineered devices; another is that end-to-end scenarios are essential.

Here are some candidate requirements suggested by the misuse cases:

®*Control Centre staff are vetted for criminal associations before starting employment.* (mitigates *Plant a Corrupt Employee*)

®*Messages to the Control Centre are logged securely.* (mitigates *Plant a Corrupt Employee*)

®*Control Centre logs are analysed regularly by a trusted employee.* (mitigates *Plant a Corrupt Employee*)

®*Patterns of repeated alarm activation are searched for continuously.* (mitigates *Set off Alarm Repeatedly*)

®*Identified patterns suggesting deception or fraud are reported immediately to the Control Centre Manager.* (mitigates *Set off Alarm Repeatedly*)

®*Patterns of burglar activity are analysed by both geographical area and time of day.* (mitigates *Set off Alarm Repeatedly*)

®*Identified patterns of burglar activity are reported daily to the Control Centre Manager.* (mitigates *Set off Alarm Repeatedly*)

®*Guards are pre-positioned at peak times close to zones of high burglar activity.* (mitigates *Set off Alarm Repeatedly* and *Burgle Very Quickly*)

®*The location of the guard is tracked continuously during call-out.* (mitigates *Kidnap the Guard*)

®*The Control Centre checks the status of the guard with an authentication challenge at 5-minute intervals during call-out.* (mitigates Kidnap the Guard)

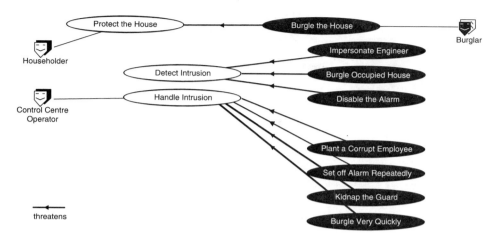

Use & Misuse Cases for 'Protect the House from Burglary'

FIGURE 7.9   Misuse cases justifying requirements

As shown, all of these requirements trace directly (in a many-to-many pattern) to the misuse cases threatening the handling of intrusions (Figure 7.9). None of them, interestingly, traces directly to any step in 'Handle Intrusion' itself—in this sense they are non-obvious, and the misuse cases (or their equivalents in negative scenarios) are necessary to show why the requirements are needed.

The use case diagram illustrates these misuse cases and their '*threatens*' relationships to the two use cases discussed. All other relationships (such as '*includes*', '*mitigates*') have been suppressed for clarity (Scenario Plus 2003). All the discussed misuse cases can be included in the top-level misuse case 'Burgle the House'—they are effectively contributory strategies or mechanisms to help achieve that case's goal.

COMPARISONS

Failure Cases

Related to Misuse Cases are Failure Cases—undesirable and possibly dangerous situations, events, or (perhaps) sequences of events that lead to system failure. Karen Allenby and Tim Kelly discuss ways of applying 'Use Cases' to model failure cases that threaten the safety of aircraft (Allenby and Kelly 2001). I'll call these 'Failure Cases' to avoid confusion.

Allenby and Kelly present a wonderful example that would certainly horrify the public if word got around. Jet engines not only power aircraft when they take off and fly; they are also used to decelerate aircraft once they have landed. This is achieved by a mechanism that basically consists of a pair of gates that shut off the backwards-directed flow of gas from the engine, and deflect the flow more or less forwards. The mechanism

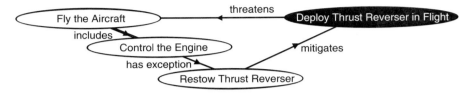

FIGURE 7.10   A failure case described as a misuse case

is called a thrust reverser, and it works splendidly—all passengers notice is that the plane slows down quickly, with slightly more noise than usual.

The situation would be very different if a thrust reverser were to be deployed in flight. That side of the plane would decelerate rapidly, while the other side continued at its previous speed: the plane would turn violently, and would either break up in the air or fly into the ground—as happened to a civil airliner over Thailand. Clearly 'Deploy Thrust Reverser in Flight' constitutes an important Failure Case (Figure 7.10), even if its negative agent (if anyone wants to identify it—Allenby and Kelly don't) is the uninteresting 'Software Bug' or 'Mechanical Fault'.

What is more interesting is to think out mitigations. In the case of the accidentally deployed thrust reverser, the mitigating Use Case is 'Restow Thrust Reverser'. This is remarkable as it is an existing function in commercial jet engine control software, whose only purpose is to correct a problem that should never occur if the engine, including its control software, is working correctly.

This particular threat / mitigation pair was thus discovered retrospectively by Failure Case analysis. Jet engines are complex machines, and are vulnerable to many less obvious functional hazards (those resulting from the way that the engine itself works). It will be interesting to see whether detailed Failure Case analysis discovers threats that engine makers are unaware of, and thus helps to predict failures before they occur. It has been well said that safety and security engineers always counter the previous generation of safety hazards and security threats[2], just as generals are said to plan how to win the last war that they fought. It would certainly be a major milestone in the progress of requirements engineering if it became a predictive discipline.

FMEA, FTA, Functional Hazard Analysis, HazOp, and so on

The work of Allenby and Kelly makes clear that Misuse Cases have a place in the armoury of safety engineering techniques. Perhaps there may be some value in taking an outsider's look at the relationship between misuse cases and safety engineering.

Traditionally, the list of hazards facing, say, a train or an aircraft was very well known and essentially static. New hazards were discovered from time to time, by investigating the wreckage after an accident, and literally piecing together the causes. The authorities then issued new standards to prevent the freshly understood hazard from causing any more accidents. For example, *EN 50126* (1999) is the European Norm for *Railway applications - The specification and demonstration of Reliability, Availability, Maintainability and Safety* (*RAMS*), while *Engineering Safety Management*, better known

---

[2] Anthony Hall, Praxis, personal communication, 2002.

as the *Yellow Book* (2000), defines best practice for the British rail industry. There are plenty of similar things in other industries.

Given a list of hazards that might be expected, safety engineers then applied a set of techniques to establish the safety of the system under design, documenting the resulting argument that the system was acceptably safe in a safety case presented to the industry regulator—such as Her Majesty's Railway Inspectorate (now subsumed in the Health & Safety Executive) or the relevant Aviation Authorities.

The techniques for establishing system safety traditionally included Failure Mode Effects Analysis (FMEA—sometimes known as FMECA with an extra 'and Criticality' for good measure) and Fault Tree Analysis (FTA). These are covered by international standards *IEC 60812* for FMEA and *IEC 61025* for FTA, among others. These techniques are quantitative and yield the best available predictions of reliability and safety. However, you can only build fault trees and calculate on the basis of the faults and failure modes that you have thought of. The fact that one crash after another has caused the discovery of new failure modes is sufficient proof of this.

Misuse Case analysis is an entirely independent technique, so it at least offers the possibility of discovering ways in which systems might fail. Allenby and Kelly elaborate the basic idea into a fully worked out technique, Functional Hazard Analysis (FHA). This will certainly not predict every possible hazard, but it can look at the way a system—such as a jet engine—works, and from scenarios involving the known functions, ask what could go wrong. This is clearly the same concept as scenario-directed search for Exceptions (see the discussion of 'Exceptions' below). From there, safety engineers can analyse the expected effects, and then work out mitigating actions.

Another traditional technique, Hazard and Operability analysis (HazOp), borrowed from chemical engineering (e.g. Gossman 1998), is traditionally applied to discover functional hazards, but since this looks at functional requirements (or indeed at design elements such as valves and pumps), it does not benefit from the context around each activity—the story around each functional step—that a scenario inherently provides. Doing a HazOp is certainly better than not doing one at all, but scenario-based techniques such as Misuse Case / Functional Hazard analysis offer a significantly different perspective that may sometimes catch hazards that HazOp would have missed.

What is new in Functional Hazard Analysis is that the stream of safety engineering activities is seen to be not merely parallel to the system engineering stream, but interacting with it. Traditional safety engineering was—to parody it gently—almost done in isolation; some domain knowledge was applied; some intensive analysis and mathematics was done; and out popped a safety case. Given the pace of change—for example, the tremendous rise in complexity and the role of software in control systems—this is no longer adequate. Hazards now arise not only from the world outside but also crucially from the design approach, and hence the system and subsystem functions. Therefore, there must be inputs not only at the start of the life cycle but also from each stage of system and subsystem specification to the safety stream.

No Crystal Ball

Misuse Case Analysis cannot in itself predict complex failure modes where multiple factors combine to cause an accident, or complex security threats devised by ingenious opponents to make use of a combination of perhaps apparently minor weaknesses.

Air Traffic Control authorities, for instance, are well aware of the kinds of hazards that might endanger air traffic, and these are carefully mitigated. The remaining risk comes from situations in which perhaps five or more causes combine to overcome all the carefully crafted safety nets built into modern air traffic systems. In a recent accident, some or all of the following events (in no particular order) reportedly[3] occurred:

1. A controller left his desk for a break during the night shift, so the single remaining controller was unsupervised and unable to obtain help if overloaded.
2. The radar was imprecisely calibrated and reported aircraft positions wrongly.
3. Maintenance work was under way on the main radar system to release new software, so the radar was in fallback mode on the standby system.
4. The short-term conflict alert (STCA) system did not alert the controller (the standby radar did not have a visual conflict alert).
5. Two planes flying in different directions were told to fly at the same height.
6. The collision warning system (TCAS) onboard an aircraft was ignored.
7. The controller noticed impending collision and gave orders ('Climb!') that were contradicted by the collision warning system ('Descend!').
8. The pilot of one of the planes was away from the cockpit (in the toilet).
9. The co-pilot took ineffective action.

Few if any of these hazards have not been considered and mitigated by air traffic authorities. What nobody expected was that they might occur simultaneously—the a priori probability for that would have been considered unimaginably small. No current technique appears to be able to gaze that far into the crystal ball, and Misuse Cases don't claim to do so either. Nor do they claim to provide a calculus for detecting ways of combining numerous security weaknesses of, say, a software system into an ingenious but obscure attack route for hackers[4].

Abuse Cases

John McDermott and Chris Fox invented the 'Abuse Case' as a way of eliciting security requirements (McDermott and Fox 1999), though the term may have been used informally by others before then. They say that an Abuse Case defines an interaction between an actor and a system that results in harm to the system, the stakeholders, or their resources. This is not quite the whole story, as the interaction between the hostile actor and the system is not just something that happens, like bumping into a lamppost and getting a bruise as a result, but intentional and indeed often malicious—the harm is intentionally caused. In the same sort of contorted dictionary-speak style, we might say that a misuse case defines a hostile goal, which if achieved would result in harm to the system, stakeholders, or their resources.

---

[3] http://news.bbc.co.uk/hi/english/world/europe/newsid_2125000/2125838.stm;
http://www.ifatca.org/locked/mid_air.ppt
[4] Dr Jonathan Moffett, University of York: personal communication.

However, there is no obvious need to restrict 'Abuse Case' to security requirements; and if we put down McDermott & Fox's soft expressions like 'interaction' and 'results in harm' (instead of 'threatened attack' and 'intentionally harms') to academic caution, essentially Abuse Case seems to be a straight synonym of Misuse Case.

> It is worth noting that the merging of misuse and failure cases suggests that safety, security, and incidentally also survivability requirements all follow a common pattern. Donald Firesmith argues that they, and the types of analysis that are used on them, should be unified under a heading such as 'Defensibility' (Firesmith 2004; *see also* Appendix 1.4, Non-Functional Requirements Template, in this volume). This brings out their essential similarities: systems are threatened intentionally by hostile agencies; threats can be analysed hierarchically and their probabilities combined mathematically; mitigations can be identified and prioritised. A Google search revealed uses of defensibility to include defence against lawsuits and wildfires—which seem entirely appropriate candidates for Misuse Case treatment.

Negative Scenarios

Misuse Cases, Abuse Cases, and Failure Cases are thus all more or less the same thing. They are forms of the centuries-old planning or game-playing technique of putting yourself in your enemy's shoes and thinking out what he would do if he did his worst: Negative Scenarios.

The traditional nursery rhyme *'London Bridge is broken down'* has for centuries[5] amused children and their parents in a game of 'what if..', exploring one Negative Scenario after another (Figure 7.11):

> *Build it up with silver and gold, my fair lady.*
> *Silver and gold will be stolen away, my fair lady.*
> *Set a man to watch all night, my fair lady.*
> *Suppose the man should fall asleep, my fair lady.*
> *Give him a pipe to smoke all night, my fair lady.*

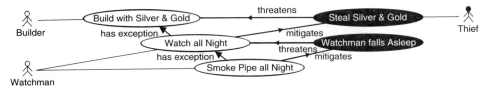

Use Cases for 'London Bridge'

FIGURE 7.11   London Bridge misuse cases

---

[5] Mentioned in *Namby Pamby or a Panegyric on the New Versification*, Henry Carey, 1725.

The idea of the Negative Scenario is not only not new; it is an essential concomitant of plan formation, namely looking for what rival intelligences, enemies, or prey would do if the plan were to be put into effect. Clearly this applies to any situation in which an agent who does not wish your plan to succeed may take actions specifically designed to defeat your plan.

Obstacles

This sense of active, intelligent, and creative opposition sharply distinguishes Negative Scenarios from passive Obstacles (van Lamsweerde and Letier 1998). An Obstacle is indeed in a limited sense something between you and your Goal(s), but it is not the opposite of a Goal. The goal of your enemy, though, really is in opposition to your goal; it is only not 'the opposite' because there can be many hostile goals, and indeed many hostile agents.

Goal-Obstacle analysis is a simple and practical way of noting unfortunate things that might happen. It is not a way of thinking that encourages awareness of the likely behaviour of hostile agents, who may intelligently but perversely modify their actions in the light of what they know of your intentions and actions.

Anti-Scenarios

In *Come, Let's Play*, David Harel and Rami Marelly define the term 'anti-scenarios' to mean

> 'ones that are forbidden, in the sense that if they occur there is something very wrong: either something in the specification is not as we wanted, or else the implementation does not correctly satisfy the specification'. (Harel and Marelly 2003, page 5)

This clearly covers a lot of ground, including mistakes in design and coding, failure to understand or follow the requirements, and things that 'we' (presumably stakeholders) do not want. Anti-scenario is thus much more general than negative scenario or misuse case. As a term it makes sense in the context of running a simulation—do you want to allow that sequence of output events or not?—as instanced by Harel's wonderfully innovative use of scenarios and Live Sequence Charts with his Play Engine. But since it covers issues both of verification (did we meet the requirements?) and of validation (were the requirements right?), it is too broad a term for use in other contexts.

i* and GRL

A radically different take on goals and non-functional requirements is to model the intentions of system stakeholders and the expectations that they place on each other as various kinds of goals: We rely on you to perform this function, you rely on him to ensure safety, and so on. This kind of approach was pioneered by E. Yu and J. Mylopoulos at Toronto in their work first on the i* notation and then on GRL (Chung et al. 2000). It is then possible to mark up both positive and negative interactions—this goal makes achieving that goal easier or more difficult. A model of this kind can certainly document some non-functional requirements, and it can indicate conflicts between goals. Much the same applies to this as to Obstacles (see above): it doesn't really capture hostile intention, but it could in principle be a useful approach. That said, it seems to be still essentially an academic matter, and it is being taken up very slowly by industry. In contrast, Use Cases have popularised the application of scenarios, and the Misuse Case approach is essentially an easy further step towards the effective handling of a wider range of requirements.

Exceptions

Negative Scenarios or Misuse Cases are not an alternative to the basic search for Exceptions that should take place in any system (Cockburn 2001, Alexander and Zink 2002). If you have a scenario, you should analyse what can go wrong at each step; most of the exceptions will not be intentionally caused, and there is no need to invent or imagine hostile agents to find ordinary exceptions. But Misuse Cases do offer an additional, independent method for finding Exceptions.

The Place of the Negative Scenario or Misuse Case

On the other hand, the metaphor of an enemy is a powerful one, and metaphors of intent are useful because humanity has evolved in a social context (Potts 2001, Pinker 1994). If thinking about hostile agents and threats helps people to find exceptions with their 'soap opera brains'—their highly specialised social interaction analysers, then the technique is worthwhile, even when the supposedly hostile agents are in fact mere passive obstacles. This may help elicit exceptions that would otherwise be missed.

Projects that are already being conducted participatively, as with Suzanne Robertson's use of scenarios for requirements discovery (Chapter 3 of this volume), Ellen Gottesdiener's workshop techniques (Chapter 5), Neil Maiden's structured scenario walkthroughs (Chapter 9) or Karen Holtzblatt's Contextual Design (Chapter 10) can consider spending a session on negative scenarios. Used informally, the technique might also be valuable in agile projects as described by Kent Beck and David West (Chapter 13) given participation from usually very small groups of stakeholders.

Pinker argues convincingly that the ability to plan and evaluate 'what-if' scenarios is close to the root of language, and indeed of human reasoning itself (Pinker 1994). Thinking out around the campfire with your fellow stone-age hunters what you would do if the Woolly Rhinoceros you are going to hunt tomorrow turns and charges you, instead of falling into the pit you have dug for it, might save your life. Having your crazy plans laughed at the night before is embarrassing, but a lot better than discovering the unhandled exceptions the hard way.

The Negative Scenario is clearly secondary to the ordinary Scenario as a requirement elicitation technique. It comes into its own where security is vital; and it may have an important role in safety, where it can contribute to functional hazard analysis (Allenby and Kelly 2001) (see the discussion of 'Failure Cases' above). Scenarios typically elicit functional requirements; Negative Scenarios help elicit exceptions (which in turn call for the functions inherent in exception-handling scenarios) and some kinds of non-functional requirements.

The Negative Scenario also has a role in documenting and justifying functions put in place for security, safety, and sometimes other reasons. When a requirement has been created in response to a threat, then continuing knowledge of that threat (through traceability) protects that requirement from deletion when budgets and timescales come under pressure.

KEYWORDS

Negative Scenario	Security	"-ility" (Quality	Failure Case
Misuse Case	Requirement	Requirement)	Trade-Offs
Requirements	Threat	Function	Conflict Identification
Elicitation	Identification	Non-Functional	
Exception	Mitigation	Requirement	

REFERENCES

Alexander, I., Initial industrial experience of misuse cases in trade-off analysis, *Proceedings of IEEE Joint International Requirements Engineering Conference (RE '02)*, September 9–13 2002a, Essen, Germany, pp. 61–68

Alexander, I., Towards automatic traceability in industrial practice, *Proceedings of the First International Workshop on Traceability*, Edinburgh, Germany, September 28, 2002b, pp. 26–31, in conjunction with the 17th IEEE International Conference on Automated Software Engineering

Alexander, I., Modelling the interplay of conflicting goals with use and misuse cases, *Proceedings of the Eighth International Workshop on Requirements Engineering: Foundation for Software Quality (REFSQ '02)*, Essen, Germany, September 9–10, 2002c, pp. 145–152.

Alexander, I., Use/misuse case analysis elicits non-functional requirements, *Computing and Control Engineering*, **14**(1), 40–45, 2003.

Alexander, I. and Zink, T., Systems engineering with use cases, *Computing and Control Engineering Journal*, **13**(6), 289–297, 2002.

Allenby, K. and Kelly, T., Deriving safety requirements using scenarios, *Proceeding of the 5th International Symposium on Requirements Engineering (RE '01)*, Toronto, Canada, pp. 228–235.

Chung, L., Nixon, B.A., Yu, E., and Mylopoulos, J., *Non-Functional Requirements in Software Engineering*, Kluwer, 2000.

Cockburn, A., *Writing Effective Use Cases*, Addison-Wesley, 2001.

EN 50126:1999, *Railway Applications—The Specification and Demonstration of Reliability, Availability, Maintainability and Safety (RAMS)*, CENELEC, Rue de Stassart, 36, B-1050 Brussels; English language version BS EN 50126:1999, British Standards Institution, 389 Chiswick High Road, London W4 4AL.

Firesmith, D., *Common Concepts Underlying Safety, Security, and Survivability Engineering*, Software Engineering Institute, Carnegie Mellon University, Technical Note CMU/SEI-2003-TN-033, January 2004, available from http://www.sei.cmu.edu

Fowler, M. with Scott, K., *UML Distilled, A Brief Guide to the Standard Object Modeling Language*, Addison-Wesley, 1999.

Gossman, D., *HazOp Reviews*, **4**(8), 1998, http://gcisolutions.com/GCINOTES898.htm

Gottesdiener, E., *Requirements by Collaboration, Workshops for Defining Needs*, Addison-Wesley, 2002.

Harel, D. and Marelly, R., *Come, Let's Play: Scenario-Based Programming Using LSCs and the Play-Engine*, Springer-Verlag, 2003.

Jacobson, I., Christerson, M., Jonsson, P. and Overgaard, G., *Object-Oriented Software Engineering: A Use Case Driven Approach*, Addison-Wesley, 1992.

Kulak, D. and Guiney, E., *Use Cases: Requirements in Context*, Addison-Wesley, 2000.

McDermott, J. and Fox, C., Using abuse case models for security requirements analysis, *15th Annual Computer Security Applications Conference, IEEE*, Phoenix, Arizona, 1999, pp. 55–66.

Pinker, S., *The Language Instinct*, Penguin Books, 1994 (and see discussion in Chapter 1: Introduction of this volume).

Potts, C., Metaphors of intent, *Proceedings of the 5ᵗʰ International Symposium on Requirements Engineering (RE '01)*, 2001, pp. 31–38.

Scenario Plus, website (free Use/Misuse Case toolkit for the DOORS requirements management system), http://www.scenarioplus.org.uk, 2003.

Sindre, G. and Opdahl, A.L., Eliciting security requirements by misuse cases, *Proceedings of the TOOLS Pacific 2000*, November 2000, pp. 120–131, 20–23.

Sindre, G. and Opdahl, A.L., Templates for misuse case description, *Proceedings of the 7ᵗʰ International Workshop on Requirements Engineering, Foundation for Software Quality (REFSQ 2001)*, Interlaken, Switzerland, June 4–5, 2001.

van Lamsweerde, A. and Letier, E., Integrating obstacles in goal-driven requirements engineering, *Proceedings of the ICSE '98—20th International Conference on Software Engineering*, IEEE-ACM, 1998.

Yellow Book, Engineering safety management, distributed by Praxis Critical Systems Ltd, Railtrack PLC, 2000, http://www.praxis-cs.co.uk

Wiley, B., *Essential System Requirements*, Addison-Wesley, 2000.

RECOMMENDED READING

I wrote what I hope is an easily approachable account of Misuse Cases in an article, Misuse cases: use cases with hostile intent, *IEEE Software*, 58–66, **20**(1), 2003.

CHAPTER 8

AUTHORING USE CASES

Camille Salinesi
Université Paris 1 Panthéon, Sorbonne, France

USE CASES are useful for representing a wide range of requirements, especially for nonspecialists. More than with any other kind of requirements, it is preferable to have well-written Use Cases (UC) rather than taking the risk of interfering with the rest of the software process with misinterpretations, missing information, inadequacy of content, and so on. But how do you write a good Use Case or scenario? This chapter puts together our experience in this domain with a set of guidelines that go beyond the simple templates that can be selected from tools and over the web.

APPLICABILITY

The proposed guidelines were developed in a tool named *L'Ecritoire*, which was implemented during the European-funded CREWS project on Co-operative Requirements Engineering With Scenarios. Theoretically grounded on a Fillmorian approach of natural language, they were empirically validated through a number of scientific experiments, and were used to good effect in projects with Europe-wide companies such as Alcatel, Eurocontrol, and Renault.

Experience shows that their main flaw is that they can hinder creativity when beginners try to apply them. However, once acquired by the authors, it is most often found that these guidelines may become extremely efficient. In particular, they reveal the importance of having an explicit view of the UC meta-model even when writing in natural language. Besides, they can easily be adapted, for instance to different languages, corporate or project policies, methodological and project constraints, and so on.

POSITION IN THE LIFE CYCLE

Let us take the example of a financial company that has decided to replace its old credit management system. A number of stakeholders are immediately involved in the project.

Scenarios, Stories, Use Cases: Through the Systems Development Life-Cycle.   Edited by Ian F Alexander and Neil Maiden
© 2004 John Wiley & Sons, Ltd.   ISBN: 0-470-86194-0

As usual, they not only have different backgrounds, skills, culture, and so on, but also different expectations from each other.

- Salesmen want to sell the products they create without being restricted by other users or by the system itself.
- Risk managers want to reduce the risk presented by the contracts made by the salesmen with customers.
- Customers want to get credits that match their financial situation and their expectations.
- Developers need good requirements specifications, system analysts expect that a good system is produced, and so on.

If Use Cases are used as a common language between all these stakeholders, then it is crucial that they meet all these expectations at the same time. With respect to the form, this means that Use Cases can be as different as completely unstructured rich stories about the system usage, or fully structured texts supported with diagrams and statements in a specification language.

This is the same phenomenon from the project life-cycle point of view: different kinds of Use Cases can be authored and used throughout the life cycle. Indeed, once a Use Case is identified, its scenarios written, completed, corrected, discussed, and revised, and if necessary split into or merged from other Use Cases, they can still be formalized, transformed, transmitted to other stakeholders, matched with other kinds of models, analyzed to elicit new requirements, to produce specifications, to inform system design coding and testing, and more generally to support any other purpose in each activity of the life cycle.

Given this diversity, answering the question how to author a good Use Case is a difficult one, if a specific context has not been chosen. Rather than trying to deal with all possible contexts in which Use Cases might be authored, we have tried in the remainder of this chapter to focus on the authoring of Use Cases in the context of initial requirements discovery. We hope that this chapter answers most of the questions you may have, and that the techniques proposed can easily be applied to your own project situation.

Requirements Discovery	Requirements Validation	System Specification	System Design	Coding, First of Class	Integration & Testing	Operations & Maintenance

KEY FEATURES

- Any Use Case should be written with a goal in mind.
- A Use Case is always composed of several scenarios that describe alternative ways to try and achieve the goal.
- All scenarios of a Use Case should be written in a consistent manner; this holds good not only for the style used in the scenarios but also for the scenario content.
- Style guidelines and content guidelines can be used as a rule to guide scenario writing as well as to check their validity.
- Once validated, scenarios can be analyzed to look for other Use Cases and scenarios.

STRENGTHS

It is easy to take a sheet of paper and draw a Use Case model, and then write a story for each bubble in the model. It is also easy to ask stakeholders to fill in a scenario form, such as the ones you will find all over the web. But, it is less easy to author Use Cases and write scenarios that are useful for dialogue with other stakeholders, or that match their goals. It is even less easy to foresee what you will get when you ask a stakeholder to author a Use Case. We believe the best way to author Use Cases is to decide first exactly what a Use Cases should look like, and then to create them by applying *guidelines* that apply the chosen definition, and that are well-understood and accepted by all.

The main strength of such an approach is of course that it is systematic. Besides, once defined and agreed, guidelines can also easily be understood and adopted by new-comers. It is a set of easy-to-use guidelines (as long as they are understood), as it does not require any complex or costly tool, and is nonintrusive as—apart from initially getting familiar with them—it does not require any supplementary activity. Lastly, Use Case authoring guidelines can be used to document the project, and can be adapted and reused from one project to another.

WEAKNESSES

The main weakness of the guidelines approach is that there are few automated facilities available on the market to systematize their application. As a result, it is hard to ensure that Use Cases are actually authored productively. Therefore, Use Case quality is a function of people's ability to apply the guidelines. This ability depends on the Use Case author's understanding the guidelines, and on the guidelines' correctness, clarity and ease of use. Tools (such as Scenario Plus 2003) can be used to retrospectively check that a number of Use Case features are correctly implemented. However, the facilities provided by scenario authoring tools are still relatively limited.

Another important weakness of guidelines is that people have to learn them before becoming fully productive with them. Of course, this learning phase is not instantaneous. As long as authors are not fully familiar with the guidelines, the general quality of Use Cases will remain low (in particular on the creative aspect). This weakness can be dealt with in three different ways,

- By training Use Case authors and testing their authoring skills;
- By introducing Use Case authoring guidelines in stages; and
- By complementing the guidelines with other techniques, for example verification tools to check correctness, or workshops to enhance creativity.

TECHNIQUE

Why Do We Need Guidance on Authoring Use Cases?

Authoring a Use Case is not just a matter of writing its main scenario. The author-ing activity also covers the identification of the Use Case, its completion, verification, correction, and sometimes transformation from one notation to another (generally more formal) notation. So, authoring a Use Case is not a task as simple and easy as it might look at a first glance.

There are several questions that authors should attend to. For instance,

- What is the Use Case boundary?
- Is there a better name for this Use Case?
- How many scenarios should we have per Use Case?
- Which scenario should we start with?
- How detailed should the description be?
- Is this a whole Use Case or just a scenario?
- Is it normal that this scenario excerpt appears in several Use Cases?
- Is it OK to put the alternative here?
- How do I deal with events that can occur anytime?
- Is this Use Case sufficiently clear, complete, well structured, and well presented?
- What misinterpretations could there be?, and so on.

If you are able to handle these questions, your approach to Use Case authoring is probably mature. But what about the other stakeholders? Can they provide the same answer as yours? Can they even answer these questions? The purpose of these guidelines is to help people learn what good Use Cases are like, by indicating how they should be authored. Authoring guidelines, in other words, also help people learn what Use Cases are. The better stakeholders know the guidelines, the better they are at analyzing them, transforming them for different purposes, and communicating them to other stakeholders.

In contrast, if stakeholders have no idea how to avoid ambiguous Use Case names, poor style in scenario descriptions, inconsistent use of terminology, inadequate structuring, or mix up levels of details, it is very likely that their Use Cases will lead to poor communication, confusions, misinterpretation, inconsistencies, inappropriate design decisions, more time spent in revising models, incomplete system validation, late correction of scenarios and costly backtracking on design decisions, and so on.

Therefore, the most important prerequisite when authoring Use Cases is certainly to be aware of Use Case style and contents. This chapter shows how to make explicit the style and the content expected in a Use Case, and indicates some of the most typical errors of Use Case authoring. The reader is free to select, transform, complete, re-present, and restructure these guidelines according to the particular needs of projects. Figure 8.1 summarizes the most commonly used contents of Use Cases.

Use Case Attributes

The main attribute of a Use Case is its name

Use Cases and scenarios are generally at user-system interaction level, that is, they describe how a user interacts with the system to get something done. At this level, Use Cases and scenarios emerge by focusing on the services provided by the system. From the system point of view, such Use Cases are described by the actions needed to provide services to the user. Conversely, from the user point of view, Use Cases describe how

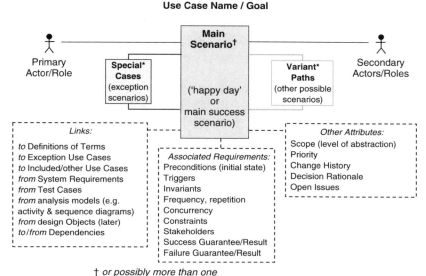

Use Case Name / Goal

† or possibly more than one
* both of these are often called 'alternative' courses/scenarios/paths

FIGURE 8.1   Structure of a use case
Many variations on this theme exist. Note that the only items normally shown on a
Use Case diagram are Actors (named icons) and Use Case Names (in bubbles). All
the remaining structures are documented in text (or database fields of various types).
© Ian Alexander/JBA Ltd 2003.

system services can be used to achieve a goal (Rolland et al 1998). All in all, a Use Case
is thus a goal that the user shares with the system. The most appropriate name for a Use
Case is thus the goal that the system and its user share. Business analysts also employ
Use Cases to define business processes, in which case the 'system' is generally socio-
technical and may not involve any particular product or equipment (such as computers
and software).

Goals are the most important attribute associated with Use Cases and scenarios,
as they identify their content, delineate their scope, and identify in a simple way what
the system should do. Any goal identifies some objective. Such objectives can be at
the service level, but can also be at the business level, or more specifically at system
function level. Besides, a goal statement can express the objectives that the system's user
has in mind, but it can also identify the objective of a company and therefore identify
the working context of the system, or more specifically identify things that a component
of the system should do. There are therefore, at least three levels at which goals can
be stated: the context level, the service level, and the physical level. At the context
level, business goals define what an organization wants to achieve with the system, at
the service level every goal identifies a service that can be obtained from the system
by interacting with it, and at the system level system functions are operationalized and
affected to system components.

In order to better understand the scope of a given scenario or Use Case, one must
first ask the question: 'what is the goal which is illustrated?' Identifying whether we are

dealing with a scenario, with a Use Case, or whether several scenarios and Use Cases have been mixed up is then a straightforward process, which immediately results from the following definitions:

> **Definition:** A *scenario* (or *course of events*) describes the system's behavior as a unique flow of interactions taking place under given conditions with its users who try to achieve their goal. Alternative scenarios describe different ways to achieve the same goal. Whether with a normal ending or exceptional, alternative scenarios should be described separately.
>
> **Definition:** A *Use Case* is composed of a collection of scenarios describing: (i) alternative ways of achieving a goal, (ii) unwanted endings, and (iii) the reaction to potential exceptions that could arise at different times during otherwise normal scenarios.

In order to define the scope of a scenario or a Use Case, it is thus necessary to

- Delineate the main goal that the scenario or Use Case should describe;
- Identify the different ways to achieve this goal (normal ways, unwanted endings, as well as those taking place when exceptions occur); and
- Associate a scenario with each way to achieve the Use Case goal.

Other Attributes

It is clear that Use Cases are more than just a collection of scenarios describing normal and exceptional interactions between a system and its users: Use Cases have numerous Attributes (GG2). For example, a Use Case can also carry information about:

- The scope, the level of abstraction/detail at which the Use Case is described;
- A list of terms (e.g. agents or objects), links to a project glossary and some of their properties;
- Preconditions, triggering event, frequency, initial situation, invariant properties;
- Success conditions, possible events, repetitions, concurrency, failure conditions, final situation;
- A description of the primary and secondary actors, of the objects involved in the Use Case;
- Dependency links, extensions and relationships to other Use Cases, scenarios or actions;
- An activity diagram for each actor;
- A sequence diagram that formalizes the message passing between the Use Case actors;
- System requirements attached to the Use Case;
- Priority, change history, decision rationales, open issues, etc.

The Use Case templates available on the web show that the list of attributes varies from one project to another. It is easy to develop your own template as a model file using any word processor. Default templates are also made available by Alistair Cockburn at URL http://members.aol.com/acockburn/papers/usecase.htm. The information developed using such a template can be managed manually, or using tools such as the Select Enterprise Case tool or Rationale's Requisite Pro.

Guidelines for Authoring Use Cases

There are different ways to provide guidance on a given activity. This goes from enforcing the achievement of a predefined sequence of actions with tools (as in wizards) up to adaptive situational advisors that suggest undertaking different kinds of actions in different contexts (as in assistants). The guideline approach is in-between as (i) it does not enforce a way of working, (ii) the way of working proposed in the guidelines can be adapted in advance as well as on the fly (e.g. the most adequate guidelines can simply be selected depending on the context), and (iii) it is a nonintrusive approach as long as the guidelines user is able to learn the guidelines rather than go forth and back between the guidelines and the Use Case authoring tools.

There are three important aspects in Use Cases: their general structure, their contents, and the style that can be used to present them. Therefore, we propose to assist Use Case authors with three series of guidelines,

- *general Use Case guidelines,*
- *scenario contents guidelines,* and
- *scenario style guidelines.*

Each series of guidelines is presented under the form of a list of suggestions that indicates what to put in a Use Case, what to write in scenarios, and which style to adopt while writing them.

Scenario content guidelines advise the author on the expected content of his/her text. Informally speaking, they indicate the *'what'* of the scenarios in Use Cases.

Scenario style guidelines provide recommendations on the style of the expected prose. They address the *'how'* of the scenarios. Scenario style guidelines aim to help scenario authors to adopt a good style, in conformity with the expected textual structure of scenarios.

Linguistic theories suggest a dependency between the two kinds of guidelines. This implies that style guidelines should not be applied without taking care about content as well. Conversely, content guidelines cannot improve scenarios without appropriate style. Therefore, the scenario style and content guidelines are *complementary*; they were developed to tackle both the surface and the deep aspects of the scenario language (i.e. the language used in textual scenario descriptions), as the linguistic theories suggest. A scenario can be written in a correct style but have the wrong content. For example, it could be out of the frame of the problem domain. Conversely, a scenario with valid content can be written in a bad style, and for example lead to an erroneous interpretation.

The guidelines proposed here were defined to help authoring Use Cases as defined in the CREWS-*L'Ecritoire* approach, but they can easily be adapted for other purposes, your own definition of Use Cases, the level of formality and structure you aim at, and so on.

For example, other guidelines exist on structuring Use Cases and scenarios, making them more complete, precise, and consistent in terminological use (see e.g. the Rational Unified Process, or Cockburn's *Writing Effective Use Cases*). Integrating these guidelines in your methodological environment is then a matter of defining the specific details of your Use Cases and scenarios, identifying the contexts in which the Use Cases will be authored, adapting the guidelines to these contexts of use, and training the Use Case authors to read, learn, and apply the guidelines.

It is crucial that authors see application of the guidelines as *mandatory*. The purpose of Use Case authoring guidelines is to avoid requirements issues caused by poor Use Case descriptions. It is now well documented that too often, such issues lead projects to overrun their schedules and budgets.

The reason for having informal guidelines lies in the human-centered nature of scenario writing and Use Case authoring activities. It is not possible, or even desirable, to control such activity completely. In fact, experiments have shown that applying more control makes Use Cases less creative and less complete. It is thus the responsibility of Use Case authors to apply the guidelines. If necessary, authors can use the guidelines as a checklist to verify the quality of their Use Cases (GG5).

General Use Case Guidelines

Authors should first make sure that the system goal that is going to be illustrated is clear. The initial goal will not only identify the individual Use Case for the rest of its lifespan, but it also provides the first input for describing its content. Our approach to state goals (and hence to name Use Cases) is to write a predicate composed of a verb and several complements. A quick look at the other chapters in this book (e.g. Chapters 12 and 17) will show you that this approach is the most widely used. Other Use Case attributes can also be used for a more accurate identification. For instance, the RUP recommends identifying the actors involved in the Use Case before entering into the detailed description of each scenario in the Use Case.

A very common approach to Use Case authoring is to describe each Use Case scenario by scenario (GG3). Most often, authors start by thinking of the most probable or common sense Use Case output. This is documented as a *normal* scenario, that is, a scenario that results in reaching the Use Case goal (so in this approach there can be *several* normal scenarios in a Use Case).

Other scenarios, such as alternative scenarios, scenarios describing exception handling, or less frequent scenarios are usually identified from the first one, then authored in turn to complete the Use Case description. This way of working has the advantage of being stepwise: the Use Case description does not have to be complete to provide a good idea of its content. Besides, elements of the initial scenario can be reused in alternative ones, which tends to increase consistency of the descriptions (GG4). However, a systematic application of this way of working requires authors to be aware that one scenario describes one path through the different possibilities, and that all the alternative scenarios should be described separately to preserve consistency.

GG₁: Identify every Use Case by a goal statement structured as a predicate composed of a verb and complements.

GG₂: Use Cases are not just composed of scenarios; employ the Use Case template that is given to you to characterize your Use Cases with all the Use Case attributes.

GG₃: A Use Case is always composed of several scenarios that describe alternative ways to try to achieve the goal. Describe each scenario separately.

GG₄: Write all the scenarios of a Use Case in a consistent way; this holds for terminology, for the style used in the scenarios, but also for their contents.

GG₅: Validate your Use Cases with a checklist (if necessary using the guidelines), and then analyze them to discover other Use Cases and scenarios.

Scenario/Use Case Style Guidelines

The different style guidelines proposed below deal respectively with: (i) the style to be used to describe scenario *interactions*, (ii) the style to be used to express *flows of actions*, (iii) the style of *initial states* and of *final states*, and (iv) the *terminology* to be used in scenarios.

Style of scenario interactions

The style guidelines SG_1, SG_2, and SG_3 deal with the style to be used for describing correct interactions.

SG_1 aims at helping the scenario author in writing *complete* interactions. On the other hand, SG_2 and SG_3 deal respectively with the *relevance* of the elements described in interactions and with the *adequacy* of the interactions described.

SG₁: Scenario interactions are described by action clauses. Write each individual interaction in an explicit and complete way. In order to avoid forgetting elements, use the present tense and the active voice when describing an interaction.

SG₂: Be careful that scenario models do not include circumstances. Thus, do not use adverbial complements or adverbs expressing time, duration, location, manner, etc. in the interaction descriptions.

SG₃: Describe interactions that should occur, not the actions that are not expected, impossible, or not relevant with regard to the problem domain. Therefore, avoid negation (e.g. 'not', 'never', etc.) and modal verbs (e.g. 'could', 'can', 'may', etc.).

Style of scenario flows of actions

The content guidelines CG_3, CG_4, CG_5, and CG_6 define the content of the scenario flows of actions. The style guidelines SG_4, SG_5, and SG_6 complement them by advising on the *difficulties* and *errors* due to inappropriate style in the description of sequences, repetitions, concurrency, and constraints in the flow of actions of scenarios.

> SG_4: Your scenario should describe sequences of interactions. Respect the ordering of the story you are describing, avoid flashbacks, forward references, and entering into action details. Separate each interaction description, even if they occur on the same object. For instance, write each interaction on a new line.
>
> SG_5: Do not factorize the description of an interaction occurring twice with different objects. Instead, make explicit the sequences, repetitions, and concurrency.
>
> SG_6: In scenarios, interactions can be constrained, but may not be alternatives of one another. Therefore, avoid using the term 'else' in constraint, and avoid conditions corresponding to alternatives in the same scenario (alternative flows are described in separate scenarios).

Style of scenario initial states and final states

Each scenario begins with an initial situation, and terminates with a characteristic final situation. The purpose of the style guideline SG_7 is to advise the scenario author on how to describe the initial and final states of scenarios.

> SG_7: Do not describe states within scenarios, but in separate sections before and after the scenario description. Describe each state in a verb clause. The main verb of a clause describing a state should be of static nature.

Describing states within the scenario flow of actions presents several difficulties: it makes implicit the role of the states with respect to the scenario, and it hinders the correct differentiation between states and flow conditions. The description of the various situations met during scenarios, and in particular of the initial situation and of the final one, should be put outside the description of the scenario flow of actions.

Style of scenario terminology

The terminology is as important in scenarios as in other kinds of requirements-engineering model. The style guidelines SG_8, SG_9, and SG_{10} advise scenario authors to use terminology that is *consistent*, and *non-ambiguous*. They also explain that the terms used to define Use Cases and scenarios (including the terms 'Use Case' and 'scenario' themselves) should *not* be used *in* scenarios.

> SG_8: Be consistent in the scenario terminology. Therefore, avoid the use of synonyms (one object with two different names) and homonyms (two different objects with the same name). The same object or action should be named identically throughout all the scenario text. If you want to refer to two different agents of the

same family (e.g. two 'customers'), then, be careful to distinguish the two agents (e.g., use the names 'customer C1' and 'customer C2').

SG9: Avoid the use of ambiguous terms such as pronouns 'he', 'she', 'it' or 'him' (use nouns or noun groups rather than pronouns), imprecise adjectives, or fuzzy adverbs.

SG10: Avoid making explicit reference to Use Case and scenario meta-models.

Scenarios/Use Case Content Guidelines

The purpose of the content guidelines is to point out to scenario authors the different information elements provided by these scenario definitions. Each guideline tells the scenario author something about the required content of his/her scenario. The content guidelines deal respectively with

- The *general definition* of scenarios as 'description of a single flow of interactions';
- The content of the different kinds of *interactions* that can be described in scenarios;
- The different kinds of *flows of actions* used to express the organization of inter-actions in scenarios;
- The *initial states* and the *final states* of scenarios;
- The content of scenarios with respect to the *goals* they are coupled to; and
- The content of scenarios with respect to their *level of context*.

The six following subsections present the content guidelines CG_1 to CG_9 dealing respectively with these key points.

Scenario general content: single flow of interactions

The content guideline CG_1 tells the scenario author that every scenario illustrates *one possible manner* to achieve a goal.

CG1: Each scenario describes a single flow of interactions illustrating one possible achievement of an agent's goal. Alternative scenarios, whether normal or exceptional, should be described separately.

The guideline emphasizes that several scenarios can illustrate the same goal in different manners. These scenarios correspond to alternative ways to achieve the goal. Such an alternative can be normal (the goal is achieved in the final state) or exceptional (the goal is not achieved). They can contain similar flows of actions, as well as variations in the actions they contain, alternative constraints, different initial states, or even events that appear in different places of the alternative scenarios.

This guideline leads the scenario author to

- Consider the goals his/her scenarios should describe;
- Separate the different ways to achieve these goals;
- Associate ways to achieve a goal to a different scenario; and thus,
- Describe each scenario as a single flow of interactions.

This guideline helps to remove several typical errors and difficulties. For example, it eliminates the merging of different behaviors in the same scenario. The separation of two behaviors into different scenarios results in easier scenario writing, better organization of the scenario collection, and easier reading of each individual scenario. Furthermore, it becomes easier to track the system features among Use Cases when each scenario that composes them describes a specific flow.

Using the content guideline CG_1, the scenario author may ask himself several questions: What is a goal? What are interactions? What are flows of interactions? What difference is there between a normal and an exceptional scenario? Content guidelines CG_2 to CG_9 assist the scenario author in answering these questions.

Scenario interaction contents

The content guideline CG_2 tells the scenario author that every interaction description includes an *interaction name*, *two agents* and *one object*.

CG_2: Interactions have a name. They are directed from one agent to another agent, and apply to an object parameter. So as to avoid forgetting elements, use one of the following templates:

- <Agent><'take'   Interaction><Object> from   <Agent>
- <Agent><'give'   Interaction><Object> to   <Agent>
- <Agent><'move'   Interaction><Object> from   <Agent> to <Agent>
- <Agent><'internal' Interaction><Object>
- <Agent>   <Interaction>   <Agent>

The templates proposed in CG_2 identify what to put in a complete interaction description. These templates correspond to common linguistic structures of scenarios.

Using the content guideline CG_2 for each of the interactions described in scenarios, the scenario author is made to identify

- The name of the interaction description,
- The parameter of the interaction,
- Whether the agents appear explicitly in the interaction description or not, and
- The direction of the interaction by distinguishing the 'from' agent and the 'to' agent.

These guidelines can be proposed to the scenario authors under the textual form proposed here. However, templates can also be easily implemented in a tool forcing the user to use the templates in a systematic way. Although this guiding strategy has the advantage of concentrating the task on the correct interaction templates, the other guidelines must also be recalled to the author to ensure that the way he/she fills-in the template entries still fits to the expected style and content.

Content of scenario flows of actions

The content guidelines CG$_3$ to CG$_6$ tell the scenario author the precise meaning of the four kinds of flows that can be met in a scenario.

CG$_3$: A scenario describes mainly sequentially ordered interactions (in other words, a story). Every sequence should fit one of the two following templates:

<Interaction 1> / * end of sentence and new line * / *<Interaction 2>*

<Interaction 1> Then *<Interaction 2>*

CG$_4$: Scenarios can contain repetitions. Every repetition is restricted by a condition that defines a finite number of occurrences of the repeated actions. Use the following template:

Repeat *<Interactions>* Until *<Condition>*

CG$_5$: State explicitly your constraints. Constraints express conditions (i.e. assumptions) differentiating your scenario from another one. A condition constrains the following flow of interactions of the scenario. Use the following template:

If *<Condition>* Then *<Interactions>*

CG$_6$: Interactions can be concurrent. Use the following template:

<Interaction> Meanwhile *<Interaction>*

The four guidelines emphasize the relationships between scenario interactions defined by the conceptual scenario model. Their templates define the content of correct descriptions of the scenario flows of actions.

In applying the content guidelines CG$_3$ to CG$_6$ the scenario author has to

- Identify in which kind of flow an interaction is involved,
- If the flow of actions is a constraint or a repetition, identify its conditions,
- Identify how the flow of actions relates an interaction to the remaining flow of actions of the scenario, and
- Express explicitly the flow of actions using one of the proposed templates.

The same remark made on CG_2 applies here. These content guidelines being presented under the form of template, their implementation in a tool is easy, and might exempt the scenario author from referring back constantly to an excessive number of guidelines. However, the other style and content guidelines still have to be applied systematically, and must thus be recalled to the scenario author in a complementary way.

Scenario initial and final states

The purpose of the content guideline CG_7 is to tell the scenario author that his/her scenarios should describe initial and final states, as defined earlier in the general guidelines.

> CG_7: Your scenario should satisfy initial states and end in final states. The initial states describe the preconditions for the scenario to be triggered. The final states describe the situation to which the scenario leads.

Content guidelines CG_1 to CG_7 deal with the content of scenarios, as defined by the scenario model presented through the general guidelines. In contrast, CG_8 and CG_9 help the scenario author to deal with the external properties of scenarios. These two guidelines are dealt with in the following two subsections.

Scenario content with respect to goals

The purpose of guideline CG_8 is to tell the scenario author that scenarios are related to the goals they are coupled to.

> CG_8: Your scenario illustrates the achievement of a goal. If the scenario is normal, the flow of interactions describes a way to succeed, that is, to achieve the goal. If the scenario is exceptional, its description should concretize a failure in the goal achievement.

Using the content guideline CG_8, the scenario author has to

- Identify the goal related to the scenario,
- Identify whether the scenario is normal or exceptional,
- Determine the scenario interactions that participate in the description of success and failure in goal achievement respectively.

Scenario content with respect to level of context

The content guideline CG_9 brings to the attention of the scenario author the precise meaning that is given by the conceptual scenario model to the level of context of scenarios.

> CG_9: Any scenario must be described at one level of context only.
>
> At the contextual level, scenarios describe flows of services among agents.
>
> At the functional level, scenarios describe the interactions with the system that are necessary to obtain its services.
>
> At the physical level, scenarios describe the interactions between the system components that are necessary to support the interactions described in scenarios of the system interaction level.

Using CG_9, the scenario author has to identify

- The context level of the scenario
- Whether the scenario interactions are homogeneously described at this level of context or not.

A scenario that does not respect CG_9 mixes up levels of context.

Short Example

Let's go back to the example of the credit management system project. A group of salesmen of the company that owns the system was asked to participate in a half-day workshop in which they would elicit their initial requirements with Use Case models. As they were asked to, the salesmen brainstormed, generated creative ideas, discussed them, and produced a large list of Use Cases. The guidelines they received were rather about creativity than on Use Case naming conventions. Therefore, they defined the Use Case names their own way.

The Use Cases resulting from the creativity workshop had names such as "marketing", "offer", "contract", or "signature". The CRUD (Create-Read-Update-Delete) pattern had been avoided (Lilly 2000), but it was very unlikely that stakeholders other than the salesmen themselves would know what "offer" meant, that the "contract" Use Case was in fact the one by which they meant that they expected the system to help them to "Define a contract proposal by amending a contract model according to an offer", and that the "signature" Use Case name meant that the system should be able to "Define a contract from a contract proposal at the moment of its signature". In fact, it was even very probable that these names were so ambiguous that different salesmen would themselves have put different scenarios under the same Use Case.

At this point in the Use Case authoring activity, the name being the first (and only) attribute defined by stakeholders, it is important that a good understanding of the rest of the Use Case can be easily intuited from it. The adequate guideline is the general guideline GG_1. The guideline shows that the initial Use Case names are not adequately stated, as they are just composed of single names or single verbs. On the contrary, Use Case names such as "Prepare an offer" or "Define a contract from a contract proposal at the moment of its signature" are complex predicates structured with a verb and one or several complements. These statements are much less ambiguous and can be further completed with additional complements.

Let us now have a look on the main scenario initially written for the "Prepare an offer" Use Case (the one initially named "Offer"). The triggering event is the arrival of credit request from a customer to a salesman. In the initial situation of this Use Case, the customer and a salesman have already discussed and the salesman has checked informally that the credit request is founded (it corresponds to the acquisition of a vehicle). The customer can be new or he could have had a credit in the past. Customers are also legally entitled to request a credit even if they already have one (in France, the legal constraint relates to a maximum debt rate). An initial draft of the scenario body was written as follows:

> *The salesman enters the customer information in the system by typing the correspond-ing data as well as the required amount with the "contract proposal" form. The system checks if there is already an account that corresponds to the entered information. If not, it can be created. The salesman complements the client's request with information about his provision, the chosen insurances, and the number of monthly installments. If there is already an account, the system can validate the customer information, and it integrates the preliminary contract offer to the collection of other customer contracts. The risk administrator uses the result of its enquiry at the bank consortium to complete the system's risk evaluation. If the risk can be accepted the administrator terminates the scenario by transforming the offer into a contract proposal. Otherwise a counter offer is made and the scenario starts again.*

However, this scenario violates several guidelines. It contains ambiguities, terminological inconsistencies, over and under specifications, it mixes up multiple levels of abstractions, multiple-paths hiding other scenarios, descriptions of actions that do not contribute to the design or evaluation of the system, ambiguities about the role of the system, and so on. Therefore, it was decided to train the salesmen in scenario authoring, and to provide them with authoring guidelines as presented above.

The first sentence in the scenario

> *The salesman enters the customer information in the system by typing the correspond-ing data as well as the required amount with the "contract proposal" form.*

is a typical case of over-specification in which the author enters into the details of how an action is performed. The problem is threefold: first, the mix up in levels of abstractions makes the reading of the scenario more complicated; this is against guideline SG9. Second, by trying to write how the system interaction is performed, the author makes a hidden design decision (the action shall be implemented using a form). Last, the author enters into one detail of the interaction, but doesn't describe it completely. These issues raise a number of questions: What is the "contract proposal" form composed of? What are the fields used? Are there different interactions or just an "OK" button? and so on. The scenario we are dealing with is an interaction scenario. It is not the place for answering these questions. On the contrary, the guidelines SG2, SG4, and CG2 suggest to write the interaction as simply as possible, for example in the form "The salesman enters the customer information in the system". This interaction can be further refined in the form of a lower level Use Case that can be authored and analyzed later, on which design decisions can explicitly be made, and which can be completely materialized with a concrete scenario.

In addition to this, the sentence also shows a case of terminology inconsistency in which the "corresponding data" becomes just another name for the "customer information". In the rest of the scenario, the "customer information" becomes the "entered information", and the "customer" becomes the "client".

The inconsistent use of terminology clearly shows that the style guideline SG8 was not applied. The guideline makes explicit that there should be no synonyms and no homonyms in scenarios. This, of course raises the question whether "contracts" and "customer contracts" are the same (or are customer contracts one specific kind of contract?). Similarly, what is a "preliminary contract offer" with respect to a "contract proposal"? Maybe the ambiguity was not embarrassing, if the salesmen perfectly knew their terminology and agreed on it when they wrote the scenario. However, once the team became heterogeneous with people from different origins (e.g. salesmen from different countries, and from different subsidiaries of the company), the difficulty became much more present, and even raised important discussions before arriving to a compromise on which term to use for which kind of business object. In this kind of situation, it is recommended to build and assess a dictionary of the business domain before even authoring the Use Cases. The terms used in the Use Cases can then refer to it, and be changed according to the evolution of this dictionary.

Later in the scenario, the constraint

If not, it can be created

shows a typical case of ambiguous statement due to the use of pronouns combined with a negation, an incomplete action description, and an implicit constraint. This is respectively against guidelines SG9 (no ambiguous terms!), SG1 (write complete actions at the active voice, present tense) SG3 (no modal verb such as "can", no negation!), and CG5 (explicit constraints!). A better application of the guidelines would have lead to a less ambiguous sentence such as "if there is no account for the customer, then the system creates a new customer account".

The fifth sentence in the scenario

The risk administrator uses the result of its enquiry at the bank consortium to complete the system's risk evaluation

is again a case of over-specification due to a complete mix-up in the levels of details. The action achieved by the risk administrator is in fact to "complete the risk evaluation in the system". This is how the action should be described at the interaction level, as required by the guidelines. How this is done, and with what information, is a concern of importance, but it should be described in a more detailed scenario. The other way round, where the risk administrator gets his/her information about customers is information that does not involve any interaction with the system. Therefore, the clause "uses the result of its enquiry at the bank consortium" should be removed from the sentence. The corresponding activity can be defined as part of the role of the risk administrator on the business level.

This sentence poses another issue as it mentions the "system's risk evaluation" as an object whereas the scenario doesn't tell when the system evaluates risk, or even if it performs this activity at all. The role of the system is ambiguous and should be clarified, either by renaming the object, or by showing where this object comes from, how the system creates it, and so on.

The scenario ends with two sentences that show a complete mix up of multiple variations of a Use Case in a single scenario.

> *If the risk can be accepted the administrator terminates the scenario by transforming the offer into a contract proposal. Otherwise a counter offer is made and the scenario starts again.*

First, the Use Case model makes it clear that each scenario in a Use Case corresponds to a unique flow of actions. This is materialized by guidelines GG_4, SG_6, CG_1, and CG_5 that require avoiding the "IF-THEN-ELSE" pattern, which is typical of this error. The error can easily be detected in the scenario through the use of the term "Otherwise". This part of the sentence should be removed from the scenario; an alternative scenario can be identified in the Use Case.

These two sentences also violate the guideline SG_{10} according to which the terms used to define the Use Case and scenario meta model shouldn't be used in scenarios themselves. This guideline is violated twice through the two occurrences of the term "scenario". In the first sentence, the impact is low as it just adds unnecessary information to the scenario. In the second sentence ". . . and the scenario starts again", the impact is more important as it hides the fact that there are several situations in which offers can be prepared: for the first time, and based on a counter proposal. The scenario that corresponds to the first case is the one at hand. The scenario that corresponds to the second case should be written separately with its specific initial states, final states, and flows of actions.

COMPARISONS

The Use Case authoring guidelines presented in this chapter aim only to improve your Use Case-based Requirements-Engineering processes. Of course, better guidelines could be created; such better guidelines could be more synthetic, more adapted to your stakeholders' skills, or even more efficient with respect to your purpose and project context. We encourage you to write down your own guidelines; not only to teach your colleagues how you expect Use Cases to be authored, but also to show that you have yourself adopted a documented, repeatable, and optimized way of working.

Several empirical experiments have been undertaken with various kinds of stakeholders to evaluate the effectiveness of Use Case authoring guidelines under different conditions (see for example Achour-Salinesi et al 1999, Cox and Phalp 2000). The results of these experiments indicate that: (i) if only suggested to the authors, the authoring guidelines improve slightly the overall quality of the Use Case prose, (ii) the different guidelines work differently and with different levels of efficiency, and (iii) Use Cases and scenarios are *never* entirely correctly written. A major lesson is therefore that

- Use Cases should *always* be checked and corrected after they have been written,
- Each guideline has a specific impact on Use Case quality, and
- Applying Use Case authoring guidelines is a learning process rather than an activity of going forth and back from the guidelines to the Use Cases.

Since the improvements due to guidelines are most often specific, it is necessary to combine guidelines (e.g. Firesmith 2002, Wirfs-Brock and Schwartz 2002) to obtain a general improvement of the overall Use Case quality. However, experience and experiments also showed that having too many guidelines increases the complexity of the authoring activity, and finally decreases their effectiveness. The number and quality of Use Case authoring guidelines can be considered correct when their application has become transparent to the Use Case authors.

Other Use Case authoring guidelines can be found in the literature. For example, Cox and Phalp (2001) propose simplified guidelines that they compare to some of the guidelines proposed here. There is also an enormous quantity of guidelines available on the web. They go from commented templates (Wiegers 2003), to complete descriptions of Use Case authoring processes (Cockburn 2001), including lists of pitfalls that should be avoided when authoring Use Cases (Lilly 2000).

KEYWORDS

Use Cases	*L'Ecritoire*	Use Case Templates	Scenarios
CREWS	Use Case Authoring	Writing Guidelines	

REFERENCES

Ben Achour-Salinesi, C., Rolland, C., Maiden, N., and Souveyet, C., Guiding use case authoring: results of an empirical study, *Proceedings of RE '99, International Conference on Requirements Engineering*, Limerick Ireland, June 1999.

Cockburn, A., *Writing Effective Use Cases*, Addison-Wesley, 2001.

Cox, K. and Phalp, K., Replicating the CREWS use case authoring guidelines experiment, *Journal of Empirical Software Engineering*, **5**(3), 245–267, 2000.

Firesmith, D., Use Case Modeling Guidelines, August 2002, http://www.donald-firesmith.com/

Lilly, S., How to avoid use-case pitfalls, *Software Development Magazine*, 40–44, 2000.

Rolland, C., Souveyet, C., and Ben Achour-Salinesi, C., Guiding goal modelling using

scenarios, *IEEE Transactions on Software Engineering*, Special Issue on Scenario Management, **24**(12), 1055–1071, 1998.

Wiegers, K.E., *Software Requirements*, 3rd ed., Microsoft Press, 2003. The Use Case template is available at http://www.processimpact.com/process_assets/use_case_template.doc

Wirfs-Brock, R.J. and Schwartz, J.A., The art of writing use cases, Tutorial Presented at *OOPSLA'02: The ACM SIGPLAN Conference on Object-Oriented Programming, Systems, Languages, and Applications*, Seattle WA, November 2002.

Scenario Plus, http://www.scenarioplus.org.uk, website providing use case editing, metrics, and Cockburn-based guidelines tools, 1997–2003.

RECOMMENDED READING

(Self-reference) the guidelines presented in this chapter were developed in the context of the ESPRIT fundamental research project CREWS. The initial purpose of the guidelines was to obtain Use Cases and scenarios that could be analyzed by automated support, so as to discover new goals in a goal model. Other papers on this topic and others by the CREWS team can be downloaded from URL http://sunsite.informatik.rwth-aachen.de/CREWS/

(Lilly 2000) gives a brief report of her experience of bad Use Case authoring and its impact on IT projects.

(Cockburn 2002) provides a complete book about Use Case authoring. Cockburn's vision of what Use Cases are, how to use them in Requirements Engineering and how they complements other models such as goal models has been determining in the Use Case community. His process description and Use Case authoring guidelines will provide you with a more detailed discussion than is possible here.

CHAPTER 9

SYSTEMATIC SCENARIO WALKTHROUGHS WITH ART-SCENE

Neil Maiden
Centre for HCI Design, City University, London, UK

THIS CHAPTER reports the research and development work on ART-SCENE, a process and environment for using scenarios to discover stakeholder requirements for a new system in a systematic manner. It describes ART-SCENE's major elements: (i) the ART-SCENE scenario; (ii) software tools for generating and walking through these scenarios; (iii) process guidance for scenario walkthroughs, and; (iv) the scenario workshop environment. Each element is demonstrated with features of the processes, tools and scenarios, supported by a running example that is also available on the ART-SCENE web site.

POSITION IN THE LIFE CYCLE

Requirements Discovery	Requirements Validation	System Specification	System Design	Coding, First of Class	Integration & Testing	Operations & Maintenance

APPLICABILITY

ART-SCENE can be applied to discover requirements for a wide range of systems. The main application so far has been to specify three air traffic management systems—ART-SCENE's automatic generation of alternative courses can complement hazard analysis work that underpins the development of safety cases. Given its roots in use case–driven approaches, ART-SCENE can also support the specification of information systems, while its use of web technologies can support distributed requirements engineering processes.

Scenarios, Stories, Use Cases: Through the Systems Development Life-Cycle. Edited by Ian F Alexander and Neil Maiden
© 2004 John Wiley & Sons, Ltd. ISBN: 0-470-86194-0

KEY FEATURES

ART-SCENE incorporates innovative software tools for generating scenarios from use case specifications and guiding the walkthrough of these scenarios during walkthroughs with stakeholders.

STRENGTHS

Scenario walkthroughs are a powerful technique for discovering stakeholder and system requirements and defining them more precisely. Scenarios provide an effective communication device for stakeholders in a walkthrough, and the structure of a scenario provides an effective structure for a walkthrough. Likewise, scenario alternative courses are needed to discover the 20% of requirements not associated with the normal and expected behaviour of the future system. Scenarios also provide a powerful technique for reviewing the intended meaning of discovered requirements. In ART-SCENE, automatic scenario generation can provide productivity benefits for scenario walkthroughs while novel web-enabled and PDA-enabled walkthrough tools support distributed scenario walkthroughs and context-specific walkthroughs in the workplace.

WEAKNESSES

ART-SCENE depends on bespoke software tools based on recent research developments; hence there are some set-up costs and concerns currently over the reliability of the more innovative software tools. The current ART-SCENE implementations rely on centralised scenario generation by the ART-SCENE support team, although we are developing new tools to make the entire process self-supporting.

THE ART-SCENE PROCESS AND ENVIRONMENT

ART-SCENE (Analysing Requirements Trade-offs: Scenario Evaluations) is a research-based approach for using scenarios to discover, acquire, and analyse stakeholder requirements during the earlier stages of the software development process. It integrates results from basic and applied research with software engineering best practice practices to deliver a complete approach that development teams can use to produce requirements and system specifications.

The kernel of ART-SCENE is an innovative software environment that delivers two important capabilities to software developers. The first capability is automatic scenario generation. In simple terms, ART-SCENE automatically generates one or more scenarios with different normal course event orderings and alternative courses from a use case specification with different parameter value settings that are produced by a developer. This enables a development team to overcome the scenario generation bottleneck, and generate and revise the scenarios quickly.

The second capability is guided walkthroughs of these generated scenarios. The big idea behind these walkthroughs is very simple—that people are better at identifying errors of commission rather than omission (Baddeley 1990). From this general trend in human cognition for recall to be weaker than recognition, ART-SCENE scenario walkthroughs offer stakeholders recognition cues in the form of generated alternative courses. If the alternative course is relevant to the system being specified but not yet handled in the specification, then a potential omission has been identified, and ART-SCENE guides the developers to acquire and document the relevant requirements.

On top of this capability we have developed layers of process guidance and support: additional software features; guidelines about who should attend scenario workshops; design of a scenario workshop; workshop facilitation processes; and profiles to tailor the generated scenarios to the relevant attendees.

We are now applying the ART-SCENE process as part of the wider RESCUE process (Jones et al. 2004), a user-centric requirements and design process in which stakeholders are encouraged to *own* the scenarios (Carroll 2002). This can be difficult when the scenarios are generated automatically, albeit from use case specifications that are produced by the development team and other stakeholders. Therefore, to give stakeholders greater ownership of ART-SCENE scenarios, we have implemented new ART-SCENE functions that offer more control over the scenario content and presentation.

ART-SCENE'S RESEARCH PROVENANCE

The ART-SCENE process and environment has been developed from research that has been funded from different sources since 1995. The original scenario generation and walkthrough environment was developed as part of the EU-funded Framework IV CREWS (Cooperative Requirements Engineering With Scenarios) long-term research project. The result—CREWS-SAVRE—was a prototype research tool for automatically generating scenarios and walking through them systematically to discover stakeholder and system requirements (Maiden et al. 1998). The CREWS-SAVRE prototype was a cornerstone of the ART-SCENE environment developed as part of the UK EPSRC-funded SIMP (Systems Integration for Major Projects) project that was completed at the end of 2003. ART-SCENE extended the CREWS-SAVRE prototype with software tools for simulating systems architectural models with scenario inputs (Zhu et al. 2003), and exploring the emergent properties of a system through visual simulation tools. It also led to the development of better use case authoring tools, an innovative web-based scenario walkthrough tool, a version of which has been developed for Personal Digital Assistants (PDAs), so that scenario walkthroughs can be done in the work context, thereby linking contextual inquiry and structured walkthrough techniques for requirements discovery.

ART-SCENE's development has been strongly influenced by its use in several large-scale applications. During the CREWS project, Marconi Naval Systems (later BAE SYSTEMS) funded SERPS, a bilateral project to specialise CREWS-SAVRE to the naval warfare domain (Maiden and Corrall 2000). In the GOMOSCE project funded by Dstl, ART-SCENE is being extended to generate scenarios to explore complex trade-offs that arise at the beginning of system specification. However, the largest application of

ART-SCENE has been in the air traffic management domain. Eurocontrol has funded the adoption and use of ART-SCENE to develop operational requirements for three major air traffic management systems. The first, for the CORA-2 project, is reported partially in (Mavin and Maiden 2003), and partially in Chapter 18 of this book. At the time of writing, ART-SCENE is being applied to discover requirements for DMAN, a NATS-managed Eurocontrol-owned Departure Manager system for major airports, and will soon be used to discover requirements for Eurocontrol's future Multi-Sector Planning system.

THE ART-SCENE APPROACH

ART-SCENE provides a four-layered environment for discovering requirements with scenarios. The four layers, and the relationships between them, are depicted graphically in Figure 9.1.

The innermost layer is how to represent and structure a scenario in ART-SCENE. ART-SCENE's scenario generation and walkthrough tools manipulate these scenario structures and representations. The features of the walkthrough tool are used during the scenario walkthrough process with stakeholders to discover, acquire, and analyse their requirements. Scenario walkthroughs take place in structured workshops.

THE STRUCTURE AND REPRESENTATION OF AN ART-SCENE SCENARIO

An ART-SCENE scenario is composed of two parts—the normal course event sequence for the scenario, and the alternative courses that have been generated for each normal course event. The normal course event sequence for a simple example scenario—describing how a bus passenger using an information system to catch the right bus at a bus stop—is shown in Figure 9.2. The ART-SCENE environment generates zero, one or many possible alternative courses for each normal course event. Example alternatives for 1 of the normal course start events—the passenger looks at the Countdown display—are also shown in Figure 9.2. Generated alternative courses include what if this event does not occur in the scenario (i.e. the passenger does not look at the display), what if this event occurs earlier in time than expected in the scenario (i.e. looking before the passenger gets to the bus stop), and what if the passenger is unusually young or old.

The ART-SCENE tool maintains all scenarios in a scenarios database that implements and instantiates the scenario meta-model described using UML notation in Figure 9.3. An Event is a point in time when an Action either starts or ends. An Action is a description of

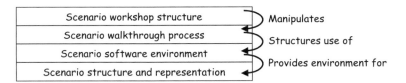

FIGURE 9.1   The four layers of the art-scene approach, and their interactions

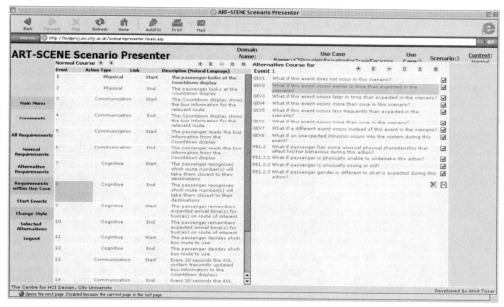

FIGURE 9.2 art-scene's main scenario walkthrough window, showing a simple scenario related to the London Bus Countdown system—a computerised system that provides passengers with information about buses at bus stops

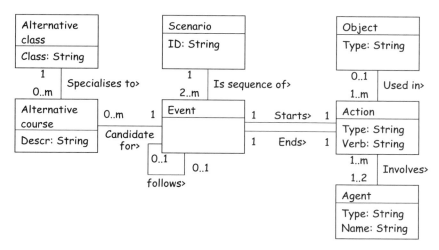

FIGURE 9.3 The art-scene scenario meta-model

some behaviour that involves one or more Agents, and has the attributes Type and Verb. One or more Agents can be involved in an Action. Each Agent has the attributes Name and Type. An Action can also manipulate one or more Objects. Distinguishing between Events that represent the times when an Action starts and ends enables ART-SCENE to represent concurrent Actions in a sequential list.

For example, if Actions A and B occur concurrently, then this concurrency might be represented in the following sequential list: start-A, start-B, end-A, end-B.

Each normal course event is also associated with one or more alternative courses that are generated by the ART-SCENE tool. Different alternative courses are generated for events that start an action and for events that end an action. Each alternative course is an instantiation of a class of abnormal behaviour or state that can occur. As the section titled 'The ART-SCENE Approach' describes in more detail, the association of an alternative course and an alternative class to a normal course event is a parameter of the type and verb of the action linked to that event, the type and name of the agents involved in the action, the class of alternative, and the parameters set at scenario generation time.

The principal advantages of this simple meta-model are its robustness and applicability. The meta-model has remained stable for six years (first reported in Maiden 1998), having been evaluated using the applications outlined in the section titled 'Position in the Life Cycle; Applicability. Furthermore these applications are diverse, demonstrating how the meta-model can be used to represent scenarios for different types of systems. The meta-model has been instantiated to represent scenarios for applications ranging from air traffic management and warfare scenarios to business processes and simple interactive applications such as bank automatic teller machines. Figure 9.2 demonstrates its application to the Countdown example. The normal course is a sequence of events that start actions of different types, for example, physical actions (the passenger looks at the Countdown display), human–computer interactions (the Countdown display shows the bus information for the relevant route) and cognitive actions (the passenger decides which bus route to use).

THE ART-SCENE SOFTWARE ENVIRONMENT

ART-SCENE scenarios are manipulated within the ART-SCENE software environment, which is composed of three basic components:

- The use case specification component. Use cases are inputs into the scenario generation process—this component enables developers to write and specify use cases, then export them to the use case database;
- The scenario generation component, which generates one or more scenarios from a use case specification in the use case database;
- The scenario presenter component, which presents the generated scenarios to stakeholders during a walkthrough in order to discover, acquire, and describe requirements.

The use case specification and scenario generation components run on a Windows 2000 platform supporting Access 2002 to maintain use cases and scenarios in the environment, and MS-Word extended with tailored macros and supporting Visual Basic applications to edit use case specifications. Three versions of the scenario presenter component have been developed to enable the walkthrough of scenarios maintained on the scenarios database:

1. A web-enabled tool developed using Microsoft Visual InterDev supporting dynamic ASP pages on top of the Microsoft Access database, and running on IE5.0 and above—the version described in this chapter;

2. A web-enabled tool for Personal Digital Assistants (PDAs) built with Microsoft's ASP.NET technology, a presentation layer consisting of a set of ASP.NET web pages, and the business logic realised by a set of components implemented in C# that interact with the database;

3. A tailored MS-Excel tool that enables the developers to download the scenario information into the workbook so that it can be transported to the walkthrough location.

The use case specification component: A development team uses the Use Case Specification component to write and import use cases into the tool. Firstly, it writes use case descriptions using a structured Microsoft Word template, and style and content guidelines from the CREWS-L'ECRITOIRE method (Rolland et al. 1998), enhanced with temporal action-ordering rules. The team then imports the use case into ART-SCENE, either manually or automatically. In the manual approach, the user uses a simple Visual Basic application to copy each use case action into the tool and define its attributes. The automated version uses macros implemented in the Microsoft Word template to import the normal course description of the use case directly into the use case database, setting attributes according to the domain lexicon defined for that project. The user then parameterises these attributes.

The scenario generation component: This component implements a two-step scenario generation algorithm to generate one or more scenarios. In the first step, the algorithm uses the use case specification to generate normal course scenarios from the action ordering rules and generation parameters in the use case specification. Each different possible ordering of normal course events is a different scenario. In the second step, the algorithm generates candidate alternative courses, which are expressed as 'what-if' questions for each normal course event, by querying a database that implements a simple model of abnormal behaviour and state in socio-technical systems. The model specifies 54 classes of abnormal behaviour and state using the structure shown in Figure 9.4. Some class hierarchies were derived from definitions of scenario concepts such as events and actions. Others were derived from error taxonomies in the cognitive science, human–computer interaction and safety-critical disciplines, and are reported at length in (Sutcliffe et al. 1998). For example, the algorithm generates alternative courses about events not occurring and actions not completed by instantiating the EC-coded classes in Figure 9.2, and about human agent mistakes, machine failures and interaction failures by instantiating the PE1-coded sub-classes in Figure 9.2.

ART-SCENE generates such domain-independent alternative courses using domain-independent type for each concept in the meta-model shown in Figure 9.3. Each normal

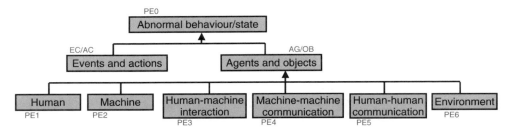

FIGURE 9.4 Hierarchical classes of the alternative courses in the original crews-savre database

course event describes either the start or the end of an action that is typed as cognitive, physical, communication, system-internal or composite, and involves agents of different types, for example human, machine and composite. For each generated normal course event, the algorithm applies 17 domain-independent rules that link the action and agent types involved in the event with the 54 abnormal behaviour and state classes to generate candidate alternative courses that instantiate these classes. For example, if the event starts a cognitive-type action involving a human-type agent, the algorithm generates alternative courses that instantiate the cognitive-error classes that specialise PE1 (e.g. what if the passenger makes a slip?). If the event starts a communication-type action involving two machine-type agents, then the algorithm generates alternative courses that instantiate the PE4 machine-communication classes (e.g. what if communication between the machines is slow?).

The tool enables the development team to generate scenarios that fit a specific walkthrough and workshop participants. An ART-SCENE scenario is a dynamic artefact that can be changed and even re-generated at run-time. Therefore, ART-SCENE recommends that the team generates scenarios for the stakeholders who are anticipated to be at a specific walkthrough. This is achieved by setting different generation parameter values for a use case, so that the Scenario Generator generates two different scenarios for the same use case according to the stakeholders present. For example, in the air traffic management domain, air traffic controllers, and maintenance engineers are likely to have different requirements, often triggered during the walkthrough by different events of the same scenario. ART-SCENE can support this variability by generating two scenarios with different alternative courses, one describing abnormal traffic and human behaviours, the other describing abnormal system and communication behaviours and states. It supports this with scenario generation profiles that contain pre-defined parameters for generating different classes of alternative courses that can be reused at the click of a button during scenario generation.

The scenario presenter component: The third component is the Scenario Presenter. This chapter describes the web-enabled version, the main version used for scenario walkthroughs in ART-SCENE. The Scenario Presenter is implemented using Microsoft Visual InterDev, and supports usage with IE browser version 5.0 and above. Guest access to the Scenario Presenter is available from www.soi.city.ac.uk/artscene.

Providing web-enabled scenario walkthrough capabilities offers three advantages to stakeholders,

- Stakeholders often work in distributed environments—web-enabled access to a central server that stores the generated scenarios in a single database can increase stakeholder access to the scenarios and communication between stakeholders;
- Bringing stakeholders together in the same place at the same time is both difficult and expensive—web-enabled access offers possibilities for distributed and asynchronous scenario walkthroughs when linked with video-conferencing facilities;
- Stakeholders can review and even comment on scenarios that have been posted on the server prior to the face-to-face walkthrough, thus allowing the scenario to be revised beforehand in order to make best use of the face-to-face walkthrough time.

The Scenario Presenter satisfies different sets of requirements that we identified in order to improve walkthrough capabilities and features,

- Improved features that overcome limitations with the earlier MS-Excel tailored scenarios. Examples include improved look-and-feel, scrolling to read long alternative course descriptions, and displaying relevant normal and alternative course information in the same window (Mavin and Maiden 2003);
- New features that enable stakeholders to view scenarios from different perspectives. Examples include displaying normal course events that describe the start of actions only (thus removing analysis of concurrent actions), and viewing new requirements in a separate list or embedded in the normal course event sequence for the scenario. To manage these features, each Scenario Presenter user is allocated one of five access levels that correspond to five different scenario walkthrough roles—systems administrator, walkthrough facilitator, requirements engineer, stakeholder, and guest;
- New features that give stakeholders greater ownership and control over the scenarios (Carroll 2002). Examples include features to add, edit and delete scenario normal course events, remove generated alternative courses from view, and incorporate additional alternative courses not generated by the Scenario Generation component.

The most important window during a walkthrough is the scenario window shown in Figure 9.2, which presents a scenario in 4 parts. The left-side menu provides different functions for viewing the scenario and the requirements generated for it. The top-line buttons offer walkthrough functions (e.g. next or previous event) and functions to add, edit or delete events, comments and requirements. The left-hand main section describes the normal course event sequence for the scenario. Each event describes the start or end of an action, thus enabling a scenario to describe concurrent actions in this text-list form. The right-hand main section describes generated alternative courses for each

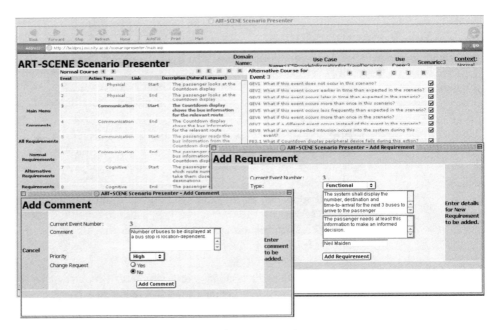

FIGURE 9.5 Adding requirements and comments in art-scene

normal course event, presented in the form of 'what-if' questions. Different alternative courses are presented for different normal course events.

Some of the most important features are accessed using the top-line buttons. Each major feature is available either for the selected event in the normal course (accessible above the normal course event sequence) or the selected alternative course (accessible above the alternative course list). The most important features are the *add comment* [C] and *add requirement* [R] features shown in Figure 9.5. A user can enter a requirement or comment associated with any normal or alternative course event at any time during a walkthrough. To add a requirement, the Scenario Presenter allows the user to specify the type, description, rationale, and source of the requirement. These attributes are a subset of the VOLERE requirements shell attributes (Robertson and Robertson 1999) that are used to describe requirements in the RESCUE process. We chose the type, description, rationale, and source attributes to be completed during a walkthrough as each attribute can be specified during a walkthrough independently of other (unknown) requirements such as conflicts and customisation satisfaction rating. Likewise, a user can add one or more comments to any event and define its level of importance and whether it requires a change to the scenario.

The left-side menu provides different functions for viewing the scenario and the requirements generated for it. The user can view all of the requirements generated using the scenario, all requirements generated for the selected normal course or requirements generated for a selected alternative course event in list form. Alternatively, the user can view the requirements inserted into the scenario normal course event sequence underneath the associated event. The user can also choose to restrict the amount of

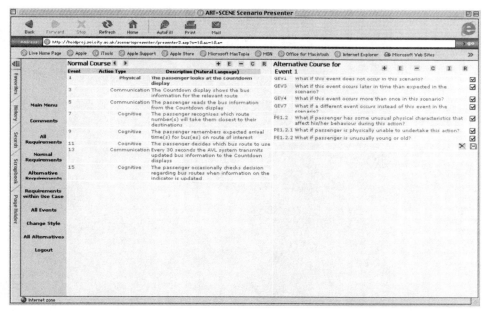

FIGURE 9.6 The same Countdown scenario in art-scene, after tailoring it for a scenario walkthrough

information presented on the scenario. Figure 9.6 shows the same Countdown scenario as in Figure 9.2. However, the end-action events are hidden and unwanted alternative courses are deselected using the tick boxes, so that these are not shown during the walkthrough.

All users, from guests to facilitators, are given a unique ID and password that provides them access to the scenarios made available to them at different access levels by the system administrator. At any time the user can produce a report in an MS-Word report structure on the status, requirements and comments for any scenario.

FACILITATING SCENARIO WALKTHROUGHS

The Scenario Presenter provides features that are needed to undertake systematic scenario walkthroughs. In ART-SCENE, we integrate these features with facilitation and process guidelines for conducting a walkthrough (see Figure 9.7). To ensure cost-effective stakeholder involvement, we normally schedule a walkthrough to last for half a day. For most applications, this enables the walkthrough of one scenario and possible variation scenarios (generated from variations in the original use case). During an ART-SCENE walkthrough we recommend that each stakeholder has access to documents containing the use case specification, existing stakeholder requirements, and related background documents such as the Human Activity Models and *i** system models recommended in the RESCUE process (Jones and Maiden 2003).

FIGURE 9.7 An art-scene scenario walkthrough, demonstrating the actions of the facilitator, scribe, and stakeholders

A scenario walkthrough with ART-SCENE can be busy, so we recommend that two people who fulfil different roles manage a walkthrough. The first, the facilitator, controls the walkthrough process, and in particular, the communication with and between stakeholders that discover and acquire new requirements, comments and changes to the scenario. The second person, the scribe, controls the use of the Scenario Presenter tool and enters information about the requirements, comments and changes.

The facilitator guides the walkthrough of the scenario using a simple two-stage process. In the first stage, the facilitator leads the walkthrough of the normal course events. In the second stage, the facilitator leads the walkthrough of the alternative courses for each normal course event.

For each normal and alternative course event, the facilitator asks the stakeholders to recognise whether

a. This event might occur;
b. This event is relevant to the future system;
c. Does the future system, as currently specified in the requirement document, handle the event?

If the answer to the first question is NO, then stakeholders can propose changes to the scenarios such as edits to the normal course event sequence or removal of candidate alternative courses.

If the answer to the first question is YES but the answer to the second question is NO, then the walkthrough discovers events that are outside of the scope of the design of the socio-technical system and can be marked, using comments, as such.

If the answer to the first two questions is YES but the answer to the third question is NO, then omissions have been discovered and more new requirements for the socio-technical system can be specified. Furthermore, if the answer to the third question is also YES, then the scribe can use the comment feature to link the event to existing requirements via the requirement ID, thus improving the traceability links between scenario events and system requirements.

THE SCENARIO WORKSHOP ENVIRONMENT

ART-SCENE also recommends a workshop structure (*see* e.g. Chapter 18, Figure 9.6) for holding scenario walkthroughs. The walkthrough room should be structured according to RAD and JAD guidelines. Stakeholders sit around a U-shaped table with copies of documentation relevant to the scenario to be walked through. The facilitator stands inside this U-shaped table at the focal point of the interaction in the walkthrough. The ART-SCENE scenario is permanently visible using a LCD projector onto the screen. The screen is surrounded by prompts that encourage requirements discovery and creative thinking, and by a simple visual reminder of the process described in the previous section. The scribe sits next to the facilitator and manages information being stored into the Scenario Presenter tool.

WORKED EXAMPLE

In this section, I demonstrate the ART-SCENE environment using the Countdown system already presented. The example describes the generation of a scenario from a use case specified by a developer, and a walkthrough of this scenario to discover requirements.

Firstly, the software developers produce a use case model and description according to the Rational Unified Process and UML. The developers work with other stakeholders to produce the use case description implemented in Microsoft Word shown in Figure 9.8. The template captures important use case attributes as well as the normal course description. The developers then revise the normal course description to produce a more structured use case specification that is the input into other ART-SCENE software components. The template implements macros that check the correctness of simple action descriptions in the normal course description, and parse checked action descriptions to derive the agent, object, and verb table for each action in the normal course. The parsing mechanism is very simple. It relies on prior knowledge of use case agents and objects (entered by the developers in one of the specification tables) and a domain lexicon that restricts the developers in the verbs and agent and object names that can be used in the normal course description.

The developers also add parameter values to the use case specification to constrain scenario generation. These parameters are shown in the scenario generation component

Use Case ID	UC5: Provide information for travel decisions
Author	A. Developer
Date	3rd November 2003
Source	Creativity Workshop, 30th October 2003
Actors	Passenger, Countdown display, AVL system
Problem statement (now)	Arrival information is only available at bus stops, which means that some travel decisions can only be made at that time.
Precis	The passengers will be able to use various different types of Countdown displays to find out the arrival times of buses
Added Value	Passengers will be able to access bus arrival times from various locations, not just at bus stops.
Justification	Passengers will be more likely to use buses if they are able to access bus arrival information from a range of locations.
Triggering event	The passenger seeks bus information from the Countdown display
Preconditions	The Countdown display is functioning correctly
Assumptions	Passenger has normal eyesight
Successful end states	The use case is successful if the passenger receives the required bus information.
Unsuccessful end states	The use case is unsuccessful if the passenger does not receive the required bus information.
Different walkthrough contexts	Passenger has poor eyesight; the scenario shall take place during daytime; the scenario shall take place during night time; the scenario shall take place during bad weather that gives rise to bad visibility.
Normal Course	1. The passenger looks at the Countdown display.
	2. The Countdown display shows the bus information for the relevant route.
	3. The passenger reads the bus information from the Countdown display.
	4. The passenger recognises which route number(s) will take them closest to their destinations.
	4. The passenger remembers expected arrival time(s) for bus(es) on route of interest.
	5. The passenger decides which bus route to use.
	6. Every 30 seconds the AVL system transmits updated bus information to the Countdown displays.
	7. The passenger occasionally checks decision regarding bus routes when information on the indicator is updated.

FIGURE 9.8   One use case specification for the Countdown example

in Figure 9.8. The developers can define which classes of abnormal behaviour and state the algorithm will use to generate scenario alternative courses. Likewise, the developers can specify how general or specific the alternative courses should be by defining the levels in each class hierarchy that the alternative courses should be generated from.

In this example, the Scenario Generation component uses the use case specification to generate scenarios for the use case. As the specification does not define possible concurrent behaviour between actions, only the scenario with the normal course event sequence shown in Figure 9.2 is generated. The current version of the Scenario Generation component has been designed for maintainability and modifiability rather than performance. Scenario generation rules are maintained in relational database tables, and the algorithm retrieves each rule from the relevant database table when considering each candidate alternative course for each normal course event. On the current ART-SCENE hardware set-up, generating this Countdown scenario takes 40 minutes long for a computer-based process but still much quicker than human scenario development.

During a scenario walkthrough with bus passenger representatives, a facilitator and scribe use the Scenario Presenter component to discover, acquire and describe requirements for the Countdown system. Consider event 1 — the passenger looks at the Countdown display—shown in Figure 9.1. The facilitator questions the stake-holders using the 3-question process, leading to the following candidate requirements for Countdown:

- A passenger shall be able to locate the Countdown display without difficulties;
- A passenger shall be able to read the Countdown display before reaching the bus stop;
- The Countdown display will always be available to a passenger.

Later, the facilitator leads the stakeholders to consider possible alternative courses for event-1, again using the three-question process. Table 9.1 identifies some possible requirements that can be discovered or acquired from the scenario. Abnormal event timings lead to requirements about accessibility to bus information before arriving at and at the bus stop. Abnormal characteristics of human actors lead to requirements about the usability and accessibility of the system.

TABLE 9.1 Possible requirements and their sources for the Countdown example

Code	Alternative	Relevance	Requirement
GEv2	What if the event occurs earlier in time than was expected in the scenario?	The passenger might want to check bus times before reaching the bus stop	The passenger shall access to bus information before the passenger travels to the bus stop.
GEv3	What if the event occurs later in time than was expected in the scenario?	The passenger might not see the Countdown display when arriving at the bus stop	The Countdown system shall provide cues for the passenger to look at the Countdown display.
GEv5	What if the event occurs less frequently than was expected in the scenario?	The passenger might not see the Countdown display when arriving at the bus stop	The Countdown system shall provide cues for the passenger to look at the Countdown display.
PE1.2	What if passenger has some unusual physical characteristics that affect behaviour during this action?	The passenger might be disabled (e.g. blind).	The Countdown system shall make bus information accessible to all types of passenger including disabled passengers.
PE1.2.2	What if passenger is unusually young or old?	The passenger is a child who is unable to interpret the bus information	The Countdown system shall enable children 5 years old and over to make decisions about which bus to take.

COMPARISONS

Other workshop approaches can also be used to explore and validate scenarios and use cases, as for example some of Ellen Gottesdiener's techniques—see Chapter 5 in this volume.

One objective for ART-SCENE is that it should be compatible with and complementary to commercial uses of scenarios and use cases in the development life cycle. The most immediate comparison, therefore, is with the UML and software environments that support UML-based development. Some of the most sophisticated tools offer model-checking features and support limited model simulation, primarily using UML message sequence charts. Whilst such simulations are useful for exploring model completeness and correctness (e.g. Haumer et al. 1999), they depend on existing UML models for normal courses of use cases. ART-SCENE is different in two important ways. Firstly, it supports requirements discovery earlier in the life cycle, before most UML modelling of the software system starts. Secondly, one of its main advantages is automatic generation of scenario alternative courses to explore requirements completeness prior to UML modelling. As such, we see ART-SCENE as supporting rather than competing with UML-based specification processes that adopt the Rational Unified Process (Jacobson et al. 2000).

Requirements engineering research has seen a focus on scenarios in the last decade. ART-SCENE and its contributing projects, CREWS and SIMP, have been influenced by research developments. This chapter cannot completely review this work; however, comparisons with other leading-edge research in scenarios are worth making. CREWS-SAVRE was developed as part of the CREWS project that also led to other processes and software tools. The CREWS-L'ECRITOIRE approach integrates goal and scenario analyses (Rolland et al. 1998). Goals are decomposed using scenarios that describe future system behaviour that, in turn, can enable the discovery of new goals. Unlike CREWS-SAVRE, the emphasis is on exploring different means of achieving goals rather than exploring possible alternative courses.

CREWS-EVE uses multi-media representations of scenarios (e.g. with video clips) to provide more contextual data about a current system's usage and environment to inform requirements acquisition and traceability (Haumer et al. 1999). It offers strong traceability capabilities but little of the process guidance walking through requirements and discovering requirements. To remedy this, we are currently extending the Scenario Presenter with multi-media scenario capabilities that can inform systematic scenario walkthroughs.

Other work in the SIMP project has used scenarios to explore the likelihood of human error in the use of future socio-technical systems (Sutcliffe and Gregoriades 2002). It relies on computational models of human error from psychology that have been implemented using Bayesian Belief Networks (BBNs). These models are used to predict on the basis of network computations the probability of an alternative course arising and the presentation of complex data using visualisations, rather than rely on human expertise and recognition. As such, they rely heavily on accurate data input and tuning of the network's probabilities to a specific domain, in sharp contrast to ART-SCENE's approach to aid facilitators and stakeholders during walkthroughs.

KEYWORDS

Use Cases	Requirements Discovery	Scenario Workshops
Scenarios	Systematic Walkthroughs	Integrated Approach

REFERENCES

Baddeley, A.D., *Human Memory: Theory and Practice*, Lawrence Erlbaum Associates, Hove, UK, 1990.

Carroll, J.M., Scenarios and design cognition, *Proceedings of IEEE Joint International Conference on Requirements Engineering*, IEEE Computer Society Press, 2002, pp. 3–5.

Haumer, P., Heymans, P., Jarke, M., and Pohl, K., Bridging the gap between past and future in RE: a scenario-based approach, *Proceedings of the 4th IEEE International Symposium on Requirements Engineering*, IEEE Computer Society Press, 1999, pp. 66–73.

Jacobson, I., Booch, G., and Rumbaugh, J., *The Unified Software Development Process*, Addison-Wesley-Longman, 2000.

Jones, S., Maiden, N.A.M., Manning, S., and Greenwood, J., Activity Modelling in the Specification of Operational Requirements: Work in Progress', *Proceedings Bridging the Gaps II: Bridging the Gaps Between Software Engineering and Human-Computer Interaction, ICSE 2004 Workshop*, IEE Press, 2004, 1–8.

Maiden, N.A.M., SAVRE: Scenarios for acquiring and validating requirements, *Journal of Automated Software Engineering*, **5**, 419–446, 1998.

Maiden, N.A.M. and Corrall, D., Scenario-driven systems engineering, *Proceedings of IEEE Informatics Division Seminar 'Scenarios Through the Life Cycle'*, London, December 7, 2000.

Mavin, A. and Maiden, N.A.M., Determining socio-technical systems requirements: experiences with generating and walking through scenarios, *Proceedings of the 11th International Conference on Requirements Engineering*, IEEE Computer Society Press, 2003, pp. 213–222.

Maiden, N.A.M., Minocha, S., Manning, K., and Ryan, M., CREWS-SAVRE: Scenarios for acquiring and validating requirements, *Proceedings of the 3rd International Conference on Requirements Engineering (ICRE '98)*, IEEE Computer Society Press, 1998, pp. 148–155.

Robertson, S. and Robertson, J., *Mastering the Requirements Process*, Addison-Wesley, 1999.

Rolland, C., Souveyet, C., and Ben Achour, C., 1998, Guiding goal modelling using scenarios, *IEEE Transactions on Software Engineering*, **24**(12), 1055–1071.

Sutcliffe, A.G. and Gregoriades, A., Validating functional requirements with scenarios, *Proceedings of IEEE Joint International Conference on Requirements Engineering*, IEEE Computer Society Press, 2002, pp. 181–188.

Sutcliffe, A.G., Maiden, N.A.M., Minocha, S., and Manuel, D., Supporting scenario-based requirements engineering, *IEEE Transactions on Software Engineering*, **24**(12), 1072–1088, 1998.

Zhu X., Maiden, N.A.M., and Pavan, P., Scenarios: bringing requirements and architectures together, *Proceedings SCESM 2003, 2nd International Workshop on Scenarios and State Machines: Models, Algorithms, and Tools, held at ICSE 2003*, Portland, Oregon, USA, May 2003.

RECOMMENDED READING

Most information about ART-SCENE is available through the ART-SCENE website at www.soi.city.ac.uk/artscene, and in academic papers available from the author or off the author's website.

CHAPTER 10

THE ROLE OF SCENARIOS IN CONTEXTUAL DESIGN: FROM USER OBSERVATIONS TO WORK REDESIGN TO USE CASES

Karen Holtzblatt

InContext Enterprises Inc., Maryland, USA

CONTEXTUAL DESIGN (CD) is a full customer-centered design process for system and product design, providing explicit steps and deliverables from initial discovery through system specification. Contextual Design is used to characterize a market or population, identify product and system concepts, and work out the details of the specific system definition. Contextual Design uses customer data throughout the process to drive design decisions. User scenarios and scenario-based reasoning is central to the CD process. But for good design, scenario-based reasoning must be alternated with model-based reasoning. In this chapter we talk about how customer data, scenarios, and models are used within the CD process to produce designs that work for people.

At its core, a scenario is a sequence of steps that defines a task performed to achieve an intent. Life is lived in a sequence, one moment at a time. When a person performs a task we observe sequential action. Although a person might consider multiple options before choosing, "consideration" is a step in a sequence. When we collect task data from multiple people, or even multiple instances of a task from the same person, we start to identify choice points or strategies. But we will only see this structure in the work[1] when we step back from the actual activities observed and model the work. Model-based reasoning reveals structure. It lets us step outside the details of a particular instance and identify the structural dimensions of the work as it is revealed across multiple cases. Branching in a sequence of steps can be identified when we create a model of the work practice; it is not present in real life.

User tasks are one form of the sequential representations, or scenarios, necessary for good design. Redesigned work practices when represented as future scenarios are another. Even implementation design is dependent on sequential representation in the form of use case scenarios.

---

[1] I use the word "work" and "work practice" to denote any form of life activity: business tasks, consumer tasks, and leisure tasks.

Scenarios, Stories, Use Cases: Through the Systems Development Life-Cycle.   Edited by Ian F Alexander and Neil Maiden
© 2004 John Wiley & Sons, Ltd.   ISBN: 0-470-86194-0

Good systems design, work redesign, and market or population characterization is dependent on an alternation between sequential or scenario-based reasoning and model-based reasoning. Sequential reasoning alone will not allow a team to step outside the "weeds" of the individual steps of a person or a system and see where restructuring can improve the work practice or system design. Models in the form of diagrams that represent the structure of the work, the work redesign, and the system give teams the big-picture view necessary to allow them to restructure the system and the work to best support the user population. A task focus alone will optimize redesign at the level of the task and the step. Model-based reasoning supported by an appropriate diagram gives teams the larger structural perspective they need to reinvent the work, both through process changes and by applying technology.

But a structural view alone will not deal with the real details necessary to get the work and the system definition right. Alternation between these two types of reasoning provides the necessary perspectives on the design activities to ensure a high-quality result. Contextual Design builds this alternation into a customer-centered design process.

APPLICABILITY

Because CD deals with the front end of design—from finding out who your customers are through testing a specific solution for them—it is equally applicable for commercial products sold into a market or business systems built by IT departments. Contextual Design has been successfully used to design business applications, consumer applications, enterprise software, products of all sorts for sale to a market, web pages and portals, wireless applications, and manufacturing applications. Contextual Design is appropriate for any size project; the method scales up and down to accommodate the scope of the problem.

Contextual Design is often described as excellent scaffolding because it works like a backbone into which other tools and techniques can be easily added. CD provides a series of techniques that can be incorporated into a company's standard methodology; among other things it produces artifacts and data that can feed existing requirements specification formats. CD works well for organizations putting ISO 9000 or SEI-compliant processes in place: well-defined steps and measurable deliverables support the requirements of those standards for defined, repeatable processes. For companies using the Rational Unified Process, CD supports and extends the business modeling and solution design disciplines during the Inception and Elaboration phases of any project following RUP.

POSITION IN THE LIFE CYCLE

Requirements Discovery	Work Practice Design	Requirements Validation	System Specification	System Design	Coding, First of Class	Integration & Testing	Operations & Maintenance

Contextual Design maps to several components of the traditional life cycle approach. Importantly, it creates a new component—work practice redesign. Work practice redesign is a critical bridge between requirements discovery and requirements validation. Work redesign is an explicit step changing organizational and individual processes and the supporting systems. Systems often fail because there is not a clean separation between the design of the practice and the design of the system.

See Table 10.1, which defines the features of CD to see how it maps into the system life cycle. CD is not a clean waterfall process since validation, testing, and iteration with users occur throughout the process—when storyboards can be shared with stakeholders, during multiple rounds of mock-up interviews, and finally after running prototypes or beta versions are used to gather data on running systems.

KEY FEATURES

Contextual Design consists of the following key steps:

STRENGTHS

- Contextual Design ensures that real customer data drives every step of the design process
- Contextual Design is a scaffolding, easily supporting and integrating UML, use cases, personas, lab-based usability testing, X-programming, and other methodologies
- Contextual Design is a fully integrated step-by-step process that helps teams know exactly what to do so they move smoothly through the design process—from customer data to specific interaction design and to code
- Visual representations or diagrams that people can discuss, review, map, and eventually test with customers are provided.
- Contextual Design supports both large-scale and focused projects. The process can be tailored by altering project scope, number of users, number of models, and number of people needed to do the work.
- The User Environment Design supports prioritization for a coherent series of releases or for distributing coherent work to a team
- Contextual Design helps facilitate change management within businesses when they are rolling out new systems to their internal users. Because users are involved throughout the process, they start to buy in through their own participation.
- Contextual Design mitigates risk. CD encourages decision-making based on clear customer data and a tested design. Managers and developers know what to implement and what design will work for the real users. Software evaluation and platform decisions can be based on clearly defined system needs.
- Contextual Design recommends using a cross-functional team to do the design. Clear team processes foster creating a shared understanding of the customer and what to build—and a clear method for working successfully with each other.

TABLE 10.1   Contextual design steps mapped to the life cycle

Life Cycle	Step	Description	Purpose
Requirements Discovery and Population Characterization	Contextual Inquiry	Collect data using ethnographic techniques observing and questioning customers while they work	• Get reliable knowledge about what people do and what they care about • Get as-is scenarios of how people work tied to actual cases
	Interpretation Session	Capture the key issues of one individual's work practice and key work models with a cross-functional project team	• Ensure a shared and deep understanding of customer needs • Foster a structured way for cross-functions to share their perspectives
	Work Modeling	Represent the structure of work using the five work models, each capturing a different dimension of work practice	• Provide a clear way of capturing complex qualitative data • Help the team see work structure by representing it in physical diagrams
	Affinity Diagramming and Work Model Consolidation	Consolidate the individual work models and issues to reveal the structure of the work across a population without losing individual variation	• Provide a clear process for bringing data from multiple users together to reveal patterns and strategies in the work process that a system must support • Create a set of models each revealing a different aspect of the population to focus requirements and design conversations • Create coherent reusable data about a customer population

TABLE 10.1 (*continued*)

Life Cycle	Step	Description	Purpose
Work Practice Redesign	Visioning	Create a high-level story of how new technology and changed work processes will address the customer issues	• Ensure that the technology will fit into the overall work of the user • Guide invention with customer data to avoid breaking the work • Foster the creation of a shared direction by the team • Separate invention from evaluation to encourage creativity
	Storyboarding	Work out the details of this high-level story at the level of the task through drawings of each step in a new process	• Provide a clear process for mapping the change in the current, as-is task to the to-be, future scenario • Map a wider systemic vision to detailed task redesign, fostering innovation beyond a stepwise improvement • Serve as the basis for the creation of high-level use cases • Shareable with users for validation and buy in
	User Environment Design	Represent the structure, function, and flow of a system independent from the UI and implementation through a clear diagramming formalism	• Provide a clear mapping from multiple storyboards into an overall system structure ensuring coherence • Help designers separate conversations about system structure, function, and flow from UI and implementation

(*continued overleaf*)

TABLE 10.1 (*continued*)

Life Cycle	Step	Description	Purpose
Requirements Specification and Validation			• Create a system representation to support planning that is useful for any organizational methodology • Identify needed function and its context of use to drive low-level use cases
	Paper Prototyping and UI design	Test and modify the new system design in partnership with customers as they perform real work tasks with paper mock-ups of the user interface	• Provide a reliable way of talking with users about the proposed system • Create buy-in through codesign with users • Deepen the requirements of the system • Verify the design before committing ideas to code • Begin visual design with a tested interaction design and layout
System Specification	Use Case Definition and Object Modeling	Build the implementation design using a preferred methodology	• Provide a clear mapping from the User Environment Design and storyboards to use case identification and object modeling • Create validated requirements, thereby allowing developers to focus on optimizing the implementation
Integration and Testing	Implementation Testing	Use Contextual Inquiry techniques with running prototypes or beta versions	• Ensure that low-level usability issues and bugs are captured • Anticipate what users might want to do with the technology given the new function and plan for the next version

WEAKNESSES

- Task analysis alone is not recommended for larger and more innovative projects. This means more modeling and data synthesis than some teams are accustomed to doing.

- Some organizations and teams think that a well-defined process slows down the work. Organizations that measure progress by lines of code may feel slowed down. CD deliberately holds off coding until the design, or a coherent part of the design is stabilized and tested—facilitating fast, focused development.

- Contextual Design relies on paper. Tracking and saving all the data, models, and other deliverables generated by CD can be an administrative burden. We have developed our CD Tools application to address this.

- Contextual Design requires some form of training and redefinition of roles, responsibilities, and processes. As such, it requires organizational change in companies that are currently engineering driven.

- Inexperienced people can have trouble recognizing when they've reached the point of diminishing returns. They may collect more data or go to deeper levels of detail than they need.

- People can get stuck in the system definition phase and lose sight of the importance of quickly getting back to the customer with a paper prototype.

- Contextual Design is a qualitative process. Although we can collect quantitative data as well (e.g., timing metrics and cost savings estimates), some people are not comfortable with a primarily qualitative process.

- Contextual Design is a team-based process. People and management are not always accustomed to allowing such explicit teamwork. Finding the space for a team room in traditional organizations can be challenging.

TECHNIQUE

Contextual Design is a customer-centered front-end design process that supports teams in using customer data to define products and systems for any technology platform. User scenarios derived from real customer data and scenario-based reasoning are central to the CD process. Scenario-based reasoning ensures that the details of the design are worked out. But scenario-based reasoning is balanced with model-based reasoning, which reveals the structure of the work, the redesign, and the system. It is the structural view and the model-based reasoning that drives innovative design and process solutions.

The CD process has been well described in our book *Contextual Design: Defining Customer-Centered Systems* (Beyer and Holtzblatt 1997); there is a shorter account in Holtzblatt (2002). Here each technique is briefly described in conjunction with the worked example to illustrate the way scenario-based reasoning and model-based reasoning are used with customer data throughout the design process. Table 10.2 summarizes the alternation of these processes.

TABLE 10.2 Contextual design steps alternate between scenario and model-based reasoning

CD Steps	Scenario-Based	Model-Based
Contextual Inquiry and Interpretation Sessions	Observe tasks live in the field and capture them in steps in sequence models during interpretation sessions	Capture data in the flow, cultural, and physical models showing work structure
Model Consolidation		Model the structure of the work by consolidating the work models captured during individual interpretation sessions
Visioning		Draw a high-level work redesign story representing multiple people doing multiple tasks using multiple technologies
Storyboarding	Lay out the detailed steps of the redesigned work—guided by the consolidated sequences—showing process, user interface, and system steps	
User Environment Design (UED)		Abstract out the system structure from storyboards and create the UED diagram showing the places in the system, function, objects, and links
Paper Mock-Up Interviews	Test the design by having users do their real work tasks (scenarios) in a paper system	Define a rough user interface representing this system and function that maps to the UED
Functional Use Cases	Create a functional use case for each function specified in the UED	
Object Modeling		Create an object model to optimize the implementation from the use cases

TECHNIQUES AND WORKED EXAMPLE

For the purpose of illustrating the techniques, we use a design problem that we developed for training purposes: grocery shopping (InContext Enterprises 2003). This example is based on real customer data and produced an example design. We choose this design problem because it is easy for people to understand.

Shopping Design Problem: Our design team works for a company that wants to use technology to support families doing grocery shopping. We have lots of technology available to us, anything a consumer might use or access. We may think about combining technology with traditional or manual steps. Our charge is to develop an innovative new design.

Contextual Inquiry

To design a product or system that meets customers' real needs, the team must understand their customers and their work practice (see Terwilliger and Polson 1997 for related research). Work becomes so habitual to the people who do it that they often have difficulty articulating exactly what they do and why they do it (Goguen and Linde 1993). In a traditional interview when we ask people to tell us how they do an activity, they give us a summary story of what they *believe* they do or what they think they should do. These kinds of customer scenarios or typifications do not provide the detailed reliable customer data needed for design. Through Contextual Inquiry we conduct field interviews to collect real moment-by-moment sequences of activity.

A Contextual Inquiry interview is a one-on-one field data gathering technique. Team members observe people as they work and inquire into actions as they unfold to understand motivations and strategy. If designers watch people while they work, people do not have to articulate their own work practice. Field data overcomes the difficulties of discovering tacit information. Through observation, discussion, and retrospective accounts, Contextual Inquiry collects the real cases of work that a system has to support.

For the online grocery shopping design, our team conducted Contextual Inquiry interviews with customers who represent the target market. We observed them in their homes prior to shopping and at the grocery store (physical or online) while they did shopping to discover:

- How they prepare before going to shop
- How do they decide what to buy
- Where they go and what they do once at the grocery store

After each customer interview the data was heard and analyzed by the team in an interpretations session.

Interpretation Sessions

Contextual Interviews produce large amounts of customer data, all of which must be captured and shared with the team: user interface designers, engineers, documentation writers, usability specialists, internal business users, marketers, and business analysts. Traditional methods of sharing by presentations, in reports, or by email do not allow people to truly process the information or bring their perspectives to bear on the data. These summary reports also fail to capture the low-level of detail of work.

Interpretation sessions bring the cross-functional design team together to hear the whole story of each interview and capture the insights and data relevant to the design problem. Three to four people are needed to run an interpretation session. The team captures key issues that will be used to build the affinity diagram, draws work models, and develops a shared understanding of the customer's needs. It is in this context that the actual sequence models are captured.

For the shopping example, the team interpreted each customer interview, capturing the data by recording the key issues and all five work models for that user.

Work Modeling

Work models capture the work of individuals and organizations in diagrams. Work models are captured by modelers during the interpretation session: relevant data is recorded in each diagram as it is revealed during the retelling of the interviewing story.

The following five models provide different perspectives on how work is done. Because work itself is complex, no one model can capture all the dimensions of the work practice that a system must address. Each model represents a different "face" of the practice and reveals a different aspect of the structure of the work and its associated issues.

- The **flow model** depicts people's responsibilities and the communication and coordination required to support the work. The flow model reveals the actual human process used by a work-group or organization. The flow model is model-based because it shows how the players in the target population interact to get the work done irrespective of time or order. When consolidated, the flow model is the key model for driving the definition of the market or user population and for redesigning overall organizational and group process. The consolidated flow model describes and identifies the people who will be players in the future scenarios and the actors or role players in the use cases.
- The **cultural model** reveals the influences on a person, a group, or an organization, whether external to the company (such as the law) or internal company policies (standards). It reveals the cultural milieu in which the system will have to succeed. The cultural model supports a systemic view of work and so is also model-based. When consolidated the cultural model is the key model for identifying the value proposition for the system and for redesigning the values and forces within a work-group or organization.
- The **physical model** shows the physical layout of the work environment and the constraints it imposes on the design. The physical model captures the footsteps between places, the role of distance, and the usage of space. It shows the way people physically structure their work environment and workspace. Because the physical model captures the structure and flow of work as it is manifest in space, it also supports a systemic view of the work. When consolidated the physical model is the key model used to redesign the way distributed groups work, how space is used, how footsteps can be reduced, and how work can be segmented conceptually within the system.
- The **sequence model** is equivalent to a task analysis. It shows each step required to perform a task in order. A sequence model represents the activities of one player who will use the system. Along with the other models the sequence model also shows the breakdowns in the work. The consolidated sequence models become the basis for scenario-based reasoning and redesign at the level of the task itself.

- The **artifact model** shows how artifacts are structured and used during the performance of tasks. The artifact is another detailed model necessary to understand how to design or redesign online artifacts to better support the work. Analysis of existing artifacts identifies their intent, usage, structure, and information. The consolidated artifact model brings all the variations across users into one model so that they can be considered together for the redesign.

When planning a CD project, the team defines the models needed to address the scope of their project. Any project that plans to produce a user interface should use sequence models to provide the detailed cases that the system and the UI must support. The "actual" sequence model represents the real work practice of one user. It is a live "scenario of use."

Figure 10.1 shows a sequence model for one customer, designated as U2. The **steps** U2 took to make her shopping list are on the left side of the model. At the top is the **trigger**, the stimulus or condition that caused the user to start this task. Sequence models supply the low-level, step-by-step details on how the work is accomplished. Any **breakdowns** or problems in doing the steps are also captured. Last, the sequence model captures the overall **intent** of the task and the intent of key steps. Since the purpose of user data is ultimately to redesign the work, capturing the steps and breakdowns is necessary but not sufficient. Why did the user even carry out this overall task? To do the task, why did she take a certain step or series of steps?

The "whys" are the customer intents. Work redesign is the result of changing the steps of the work to better achieve the intent through technology or work process simplification. We can modify, remove, and create new steps as long as the users can

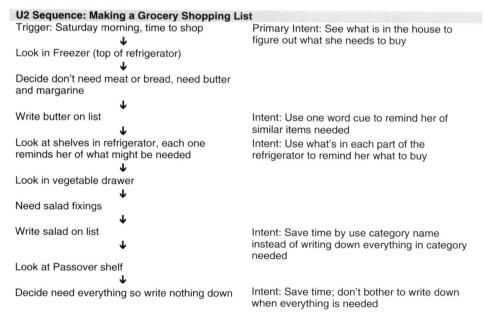

FIGURE 10.1   Sequence model for making a grocery shopping list

still achieve their fundamental intents and the business can accomplish its goals. The value of technology ultimately is to achieve the intent of our activities faster, cheaper, easier, and with more delight. The sequence model, by capturing the actual steps of a task, allows us to identify the intents and thus to redesign the work.

Use case modelers should recognize similarities between the use case artifact and the CD sequence model (e.g., triggers, event flows, etc). From the perspective of a structured design artifact, it is helpful to think of the CD sequence model as a stereotyped use case, extended to include things like event flow activity intents and breakdowns. Further, it is useful to recognize that CD sequences are really instances of use cases, achieving a traditional, generalized use case representation following the consolidation of each individually captured instance.

Consolidation

Consolidation brings data from individual customer interviews together so that the team can see common pattern and structure without losing individual variation. Consolidation of the work models is the process of stepping out of the details of an individual case to see the larger pattern of work as revealed across cases and people. Consolidated work models bring together each different type of work model separately, revealing common strategies and intents while retaining and organizing individual differences. The **affinity diagram** brings together the issues and insights captured in the interpretations sessions into a wall-sized, hierarchical diagram to reveal the scope of the problem.

Work model consolidation results in a set of diagrams that when taken together support model-based reasoning about the work practice itself. Because consolidated models segment work practice into coherent and meaningful chunks, the team is able to see, capture, and think about very complex and rich information. This clear organization of information about the practice and needs of the customer population supports and structures the team's redesign conversations. Team members can discuss changes in the model of work through the introduction of technology, redesigned tasks, roles, responsibilities, cultural values, and space as appropriate to the project scope and business goals.

Figure 10.2 shows a consolidated sequence model representing all users who made a shopping list as part of grocery shopping. There is a separate consolidated sequence model for each task in our grocery shopping design project, that is, making a shopping list, doing the shopping, and so on. Once the grocery shopping customer interviews and interpretations sessions were completed, the affinity diagram was built and all the work models were consolidated. To see an online view of the affinity diagram and other consolidated work models you can go to the team's Shopping Design Album at: http://www.incent.com/insite/shop/index.htm.

Sequences are consolidated by collecting together actual sequences with similar primary intents. Steps are grouped into chunks that represent activities. Steps within each activity are consolidated into abstract steps representing the detailed individual steps in each actual sequence model. Intents and breakdowns at the level of the task and the steps are also consolidated. The result is a single definition of the intents, steps, branches, strategies, and breakdowns for each task.

Work redesign is ultimately about redesigning the consolidated sequences. Whether the redesign eliminates or changes the steps or eliminates the entire sequence, knowing

Making a List
Activity 1: Using the House as a List

Triggers	Primary Intents
1. Regular planned time to shop	◆ Fit shopping into a planned time slot so it fits the whole life pattern
2. Decide there's "nothing" in the house, so it's time to shop	◆ Keep the house stocked
	◆ Keep it possible to have informal meal or snack at any time
	◆ Spend no time tracking what's in the house
3. Have specific need, so decide to do a big shop	◆ Consolidate shopping trips to save time
4. Have to shop for upcoming holiday event	◆ Get the majority of things needed for the holiday in one trip
5. Settle into a new place	◆ Supplement list of basics with items needed for special reasons
	◆ Get the majority of needs in one trip

Abstract Step	Intent
1. Decide to write down the list	
2. Collect list-making tools (pen and paper)	
3. Breakdown: Hard to find pen and paper–wander around a lot	
4. Systematically walk through the house looking in each place to see what you need	◆ Use the household as the list—places are the reminders
5. At each place:	
a. Decide what you need to get	◆ Don't run out of favorite things
1. Missing items we should have	
2. Items we don't have enough of	
3. Items that may have spoiled	
- Decide if an item can be rescued	
- Throw out old food	
b. Write each needed on the list as you go	
1. If you can't get the item at the store you're going to:	
- Write it on a side list	
2. If you need everything in a category	
- Write the name of the category and decide exactly what to buy at the store	◆ Save time and trouble: Depend on memory and the store to settle on items to buy
3. If you decide you're out of "everything" Abandon the list and shop by walking through the store and getting whatever it reminds you of	◆ Save time and trouble: Let the store remind you of what you need

FIGURE 10.2   Portion of consolidated sequence model for making a grocery shopping list. The full consolidated list-making sequence consists of several activities and associated abstracted steps, representing all users the team interviewed. Here you see a portion of the consolidated sequence model showing one of its activities: Using the House as a List. Each abstract step you see is a consolidation that represents a step that at least one user performed

the steps and intents keeps the team honest. Redesign will better support the work if it "accounts for" each intent, trigger, and step. This does not mean leaving the work as it is; it means that the team has seen the current activity and has completely considered what will happen to it in the new work redesign. The consolidated sequence represents the as-is state of the process. It is critical as a guide for storyboarding, the to-be redesigned task.

Visioning

Central to CD is the idea that system design is really work practice redesign. New products and system concepts; requirements for enterprise and business systems; and the identification of new features for existing systems, best emerge from a focus on redesigning the work given technological and organizational possibilities. Visioning is a high-level story of the "new world" of your customer population, achieving the task intents of the sequence model; using redesigned artifacts from the artifact model; playing the redesigned roles in the flow model; transforming the cultural forces within the cultural model; within the constraints of the physical model in order to overcome the issues identified in the affinity diagram. In other words, the vision synthesizes the findings and implications of the customer data into a productive business response.

Visioning focuses the team on inventing how technology can help people get their jobs done, rather than on what could be done with technology without considering the impact on people's real lives. Design of technology is first design of the "big picture" story of the future showing how manual practices, human interactions, and other tools come together within the planned system or product to better support the whole practice.

During a visioning session, the cross-functional team tells the story of how work will be done in the future. This is a group story-telling activity where team members build on and add to each other's ideas much like friends around a camp fire constructing ghost stories. One team member captures the team's ideas on a flip chart page using pictures to illustrate the concepts and synthesize ideas. During a visioning session, the team moves through the story of different role players in different contexts doing different tasks. Evaluation of ideas is put off until after several visions are generated.

During a vision, the individual story threads are synthesized in real time onto a page visible to all. Although the individual team members are speaking and thinking the redesign sequentially, the vision diagram allows the team to see the new work practice and associated technology from a model-based perspective. This model-based view evolves visually during the vision session and encourages the team to see and reuse emerging system and organizational concepts. The vision is a story generated from scenario-based reasoning, but its ultimate representation, the vision drawing, is a model-based view of the new work practice synthesizing changes in the work structure and the technology into one high-level picture.

Our shopping team started by walking their consolidated data, discussing their design ideas informally, and identifying the issues they wanted to address. The team then generated multiple visions. Some dealt with how the shopping list was made, others focused on shopping itself, and others brought in support of other errand running tasks associated with grocery shopping. Some visions imagined in-store solutions; others imagined web-based solutions in the home. The team then evaluated the visions, explicitly identifying each one's strengths and weaknesses in light of the customer data, business goals, and technological ease. Weaknesses were overcome. The best parts of each vision were synthesized in the consolidated vision you see in Figure 10.3. This consolidated vision simultaneously represents a very high-level future scenario *and* when viewed on a single page a systemic model-based view of the new socio-technical system.

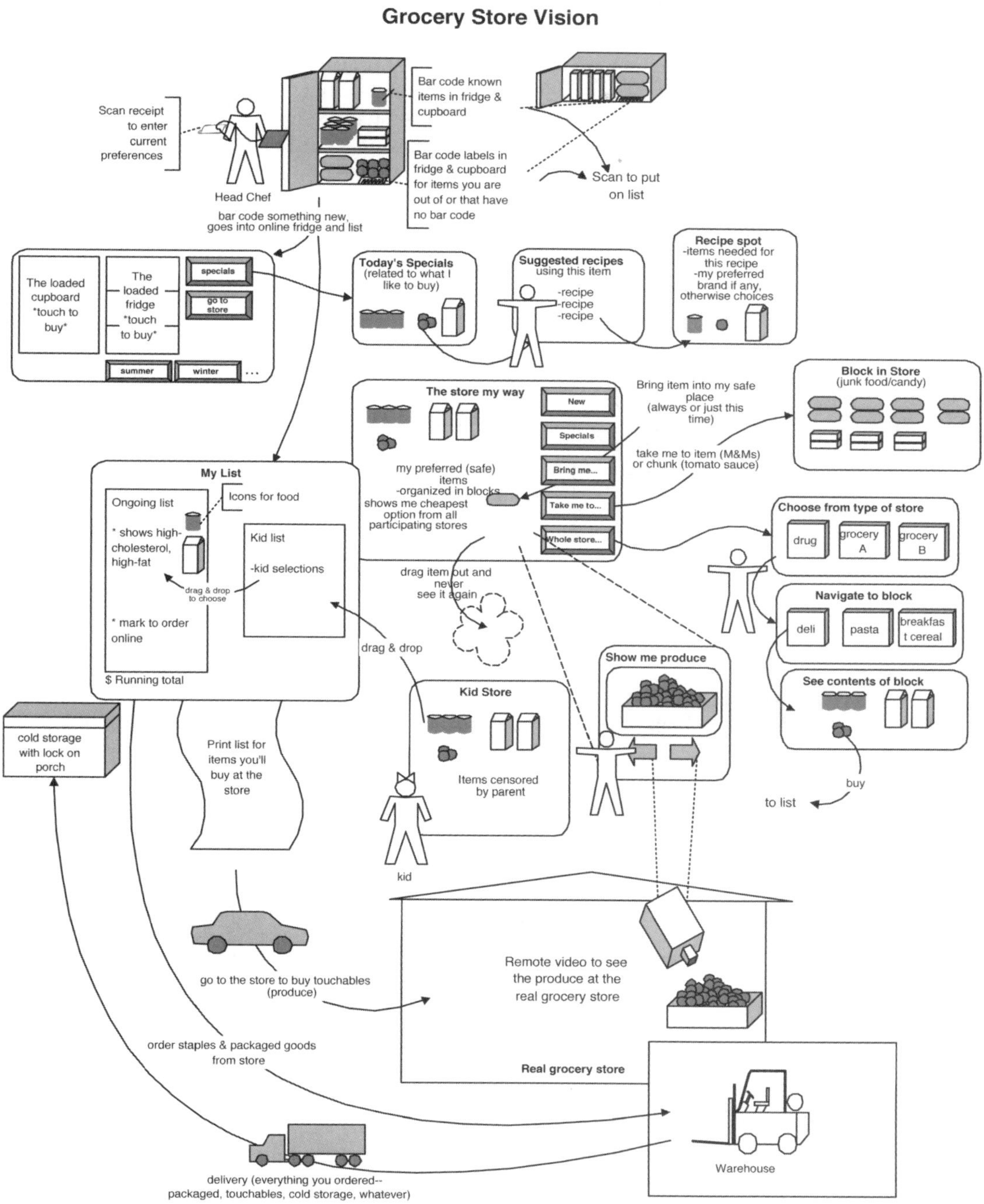

Grocery Store Vision

FIGURE 10.3   Complete, synthesized vision for online grocery shopping product

Storyboarding

The vision does not work out the details of each case or task. Nor does it clearly sort out what is technically doable or define the function that must appear in a user interface or the function to be performed by the system. Storyboarding works out the details of the vision, guided principally by the consolidated sequences representing the key tasks that the system has to support.

Storyboards are equivalent to future scenarios (Rheinfrank and Evenson 1996) or high-level use case instances and may be represented in standard use case document structure and Unified Modeling Language notation. (See Figure 10.4 for an example of a storyboard cell and its UML equivalent.) But we choose to represent the redesigned work

Making a List	
Activity 1: Using the House as a List	
Triggers	**Primary Intents**
1. ✓ Regular planned time to shop	◆ Fit shopping into a planned time slot so it fits the whole life pattern
2. ✓ Decide there's "nothing" in the house, so it's time to shop	◆ Keep the house stocked
	◆ Keep it possible to have informal meal or snack at any time
3. ✓ Have specific need, so decide to do a big shop	◆ Spend no time tracking what's in the house
	◆ Consolidate shopping trips to save time
4. Have to shop for upcoming holiday event	◆ Get the majority of things needed for the holiday in one trip
5. Settle into a new place	◆ Supplement list of basics with items needed for special reasons
	◆ Get the majority of needs in one trip
Abstract Step	**Intent**
1. Decide to write down the list	
2. ✓ Collect list-making tools (pen and paper)	

FIGURE 10.4   Storyboard cell 1. Four of the five triggers are accounted for in this storyboard. The case of the fifth trigger, ''Settle into a new place,'' is too different from the others, and needs to be worked out in its own storyboard. The customer in this case is playing the role of the household's ''head chef'' — the person who decides what meals will be prepared. This is a process step; it shows that the context of the work will not change, but the tools to respond to the work (getting the bar code pen) will be different

in frame-by-frame drawings. They include manual steps, rough user interface components showing function, system activity and automation, and even documentation use.

By working with multiple teams, we have learned that the best system design comes from this type of visual representation of the to-be models of work. Text versions of a scenario or simple user interface drawings alone fail to consider all the dimensions of the new work practice. Use case and object modelers are trained to use the text-intensive use case characterization of the redesigned work. We find that this ultimately focuses them too much on system activities and business rules and not enough on necessary human processes and user interface function. But user interface designers who are concerned primarily with the interaction design tend to overlook the system steps and over-focus on UI detail. They get stuck prematurely in detailed discussions of layout that will become irrelevant when the implications of multiple scenarios of use are worked through.

One key principle of CD is to use the right representational form for the design conversation the team is trying to have. Even though it might be possible to represent the storyboard concepts with UML models, use cases and instances, a series of UI drawings or even a high-level business process drawing—none of these individual representations encourages the team to think about all these factors simultaneously. Storyboards by their

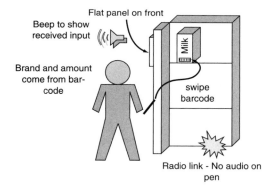

1. ✓ Systematically walk through the house looking in each place to see what you need
2. At each place:
   a. Decide what you need to get
     1. Missing items we should have
     2. ✓ Items we don't have enough of
     3. Items that may have spoiled
     - Decide if an item can be rescued
     - Throw out old food

♦ Use the household as the list—places are the reminders

♦ Don't run out of favourite things

FIGURE 10.5 Storyboard cell 2. This cell traces back to the step for adding items to the list when we are running low on them, showing how the work will be redesigned. The swipe will enter the milk brand on the list. The system design creates a problem — paper gives feedback that the item is recorded. The new system must account for that implied function or break the work. As such, the team invented the "beep" to show that the item has been received. But the team also anticipates the potential breakdown when the user moves away from the flat panel and can't hear the beep

1. ✓ Systematically walk through the house looking in each place to see what you need
2. At each place:
   a. Decide what you need to get
      1. Missing items we should have
      2. Items we don't have enough of
      3. ✓ Items that may have spoiled
      - ✓ Decide if an item can be rescued
      - ✓ Throw out old food

◆ Use the household as the list—places are the reminders

◆ Don't run out of favorite things

FIGURE 10.6 Storyboard cell 3. Storyboard cells also account for system steps as well as user steps. Notice what the system is doing automatically for the user. It is tracking historical purchases, recording and reconciling brands, and recording how much of each item to add to the list. This system step replaces what people are currently doing manually through personal memory and walking through the house. However, it improves the current process. For example, human memory no longer has to be relied upon, it takes care of household members adding to the list who don't know what should be in the house and don't recognize what's missing, and no one needs to walk around if they don't want to

very nature ensure synthetic sequential thinking and thereby a more complete design for the user, especially when guided both by the vision and the consolidated sequences. Storyboards also provide a conceptual common denominator for design discussions with users; it is much more likely that a user will grasp the metaphor of a storyboard (e.g., as used in the creation of animations, comic books and movies) over more abstract modeling symbologies or unfamiliar web design artifacts. UI screen mock-ups encourage users to focus the conversation on UI aesthetics (color palettes, widget choice and placement, etc.) rather than work practice redesign.

Driving scenarios from consolidated data ensures that different strategies for doing a task will be considered and that the design will support the different routes that real people use to achieve their intent. Figure 10.4 through Figure 10.7 show four cells of one storyboard for our online grocery shopping vision. This storyboard, usually hand drawn, works out the portion of the vision where we redesign how the customer makes the grocery shopping list. We've placed next to each storyboard frame an excerpt of the consolidated sequence that it supports, with a checkmark (√) for each trigger and step

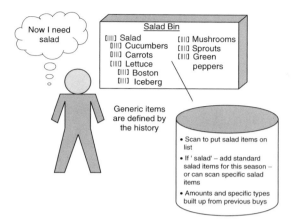

1. ✓ Systematically walk through the house looking in each place to see what you need
2. At each place:
   a. ✓ Write each needed on the list as you go
   b. ✓ If you need everything in category and decide exactly what to buy at the store

◆ Use the household as the list – places are the reminders

◆ Save time and trouble: Depend on memory and the store to settle on items to buy

FIGURE 10.7   Storyboard cell 4. The consolidated sequence model shows that users think of some food items as part of a large category. For example, individual produce items can be in the category of "salad." The user's redesigned work will let him pick an item or a category and the system will know what he likes and what is in season

that is being accounted for. Our design must ultimately account for each step, trigger, and intent in the set of consolidated sequences that represent the task within the project scope. For any system, multiple storyboards will be generated to cover the various cases. Box 1 shows the same storyboard using UML.

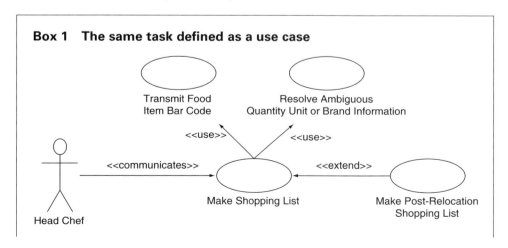

Box 1   The same task defined as a use case

Use Case Name: Make Shopping List

Use Case ID: UC14

Actors

- Head Chef

Preconditions

- Use case "Set up On-Line Grocery Shopping System" (UC01) has been completed successfully

Triggers

- Regular shopping time is approaching
- Current Food Item supply is running low
- A specific, required Food Item is missing
- A period of high Food Item demand (e.g., a holiday) is approaching

Primary Flow of Events

1. The use case begins when the Head Chef decides to generate a Shopping List.
2. The Head Chef locates the Bar Code Pen.
3. The Head Chef walks to a House Location.
4. If the House Location stimulates recognition of need for a Food Item (e.g., Food Items in short supply, spoiled Items, etc.), the Head Chef swipes the Bar Code Pen across the Food Item package's Bar Code.
5. The Bar Code Pen transmits the Food Item's Bar Code to the System (use use case "Transmit Food Item Bar Code" [UC23]).
6. The system adds the Food Item Bar Code to the Historical Purchases database for a single Quantity Unit.
7. The system confirms successful Bar Code transmission via the Audio Confirmation Signal.
8. The system displays the new Food Item on the Flat Panel Screen and the use case ends.

Postconditions

- A new Shopping List Food Item is displayed on the Flat Panel Screen
- The Food Item entry is persisted in the Historical Purchases database

Alternate Flow of Events

1. If The Head Chef has relocated and is stocking Food Items for the first time, use use case "Make Post-Relocation Shopping List" (UC15)
2. At the end of Step 8, if there are more House Locations left to explore, the Head Chef iterates Steps 3 through 8.

3. In Step 7, if the Quantity Unit or Brand Information is ambiguous, use use case "Resolve Ambiguous Quantity Unit or Brand Information" (UC34).

4. After Step 7, if the Head Chef desires a Quantity Unit greater than one, she may scan the Food Item Bar Code multiple times to appropriately increment the Quantity Unit.

5. If there are no Food Item entries in the Historical Purchase Database, the Head Chef may provide entries via old Purchase Receipts.

Issues

1. In Step 6, the use case model must account for the possibility of the Head Chef being out of auditory range for the Auditory Confirmation Signal.

User Environment Design

A good product, system, or web page must have the appropriate function and structure to support a natural workflow within it. System design really has three layers. The user interface accesses the function, structure, and flow necessary to support the user's redesigned work. The implementation (object model) makes that function, structure, and flow happen. But the core of a product is that middle layer: the explicit work the system is performing. Just as architects draw floor plans to see the structure and flow of a house, designers need to see the "floor plan" of their new system. Hidden within the storyboards are the implications for the system floor plan—the User Environment Design (UED).

The UED formalism represents a set of "focus areas" or places in the system that provide support for coherent activities. A place might be a window, web page, dialog box, or pane. The UED shows each part of the system, how it supports the customer's work, exactly what function is available in that part, and how the customer gets to and from other parts of the system—without tying this structure to any particular user interface or implementation design. The function in the UED drives functional specification and implementation level use cases. The UED supports model-based reasoning about the system structure and function.

Figure 10.8 shows the main parts of the UED formalism. Each focus area is a place that defines the purpose, functions, and work objects to be accessed from that place. Links from one focus area to another define the flow within the system that the user can traverse. Double links mean that the user needs to be able to work in one focus area in the context of another. Hidden focus areas call out new automatic system function and business rules that now support work that was previously manual.

Any vision implies multiple scenarios to fulfill the vision. Customer data shows us that multiple roles doing multiple tasks will use the system. No system should be built around one storyboard or one future scenario. Just as a kitchen supports multiple scenarios of cooking (the quick pizza, the holiday dinner, the summer barbeque), a system supports multiple scenarios of use. In our homes, we naturally "move things around" and "learn from experience" as we design and redesign our spaces implicitly and explicitly. A good kitchen has all the functions, objects, and flow needed to support any cooking scenario. Similarly, a good system defines places where all the function, objects, and flow is present to support scenarios of use.

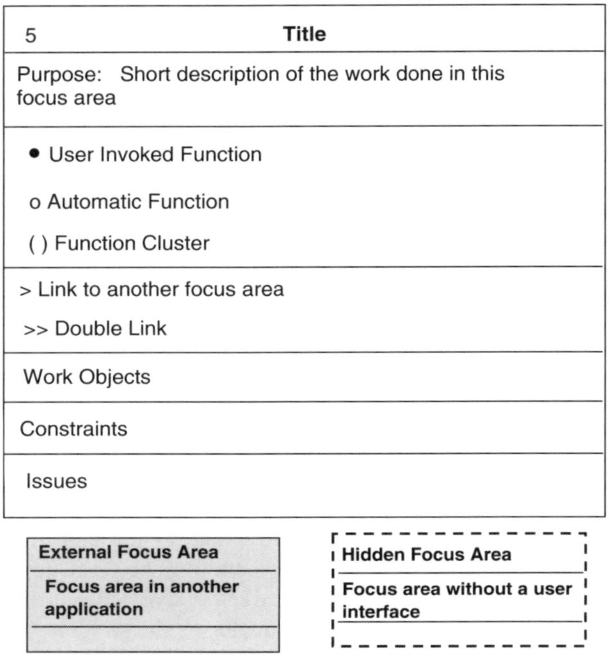

5	Title
Purpose: Short description of the work done in this focus area	
• User Invoked Function o Automatic Function ( ) Function Cluster	
> Link to another focus area >> Double Link	
Work Objects	
Constraints	
Issues	

External Focus Area
Focus area in another application

Hidden Focus Area
Focus area without a user interface

FIGURE 10.8   Formalism for user environment design focus areas

In creating a UED, the team uses the anticipated scenarios of use: the future scenarios or storyboards. They walk the storyboards and abstract out the implications of what the system needs to provide. As the implications of storyboard after storyboard are rolled into the UED creating focus areas, function, and links the team starts to see the best way to structure the system. The result is not a wizard-like, lock-step design but rather the definition of coherent places within which functions and objects may be accessed in any order. The sequential thinking of storyboarding drives the model-based thinking of the UED and results in a useful model of the system to support planning.

The UED is both the system work model and a simple definition of the functional system requirements. Because teams can simultaneously see all the parts of the system and how they relate, they can distribute work to individuals without fear of stovepipe design. And they have a big system picture from which to plan the rollout by carving up the focus areas into coherent releases.

Here's how the online grocery shopping team began to walk their storyboard cells. You'll see a portion of their completed UED in Figure 10.12. This example is for a new product. If you already have an existing product or system, you can first build a reverse UED to see how your existing system is structured. From there you can decide whether to use the reverse UED as the base of the new system, building on it and changing it in response to the storyboards. Or you can start a new UED and reuse function as it is called for by your storyboards.

Storyboard cell 1 (Figure 10.9) situates the story about making the grocery shopping list. Because our system is a mixture of hardware and software, some focus areas

FIGURE 10.9   Storyboard cell 1

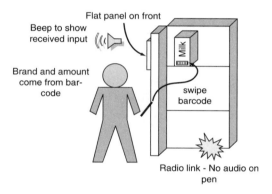

FIGURE 10.10   Storyboard cell 2

in the UED will represent physical hardware places as well as software screens. At this first cell the team is beginning to think about how work will play out, but is not ready yet to create a focus area.

In storyboard cell 2 (Figure 10.10) the user swipes the milk's barcode with the barcode reading pen. In response, he hears an auditory beep. The brand of the milk and the quantity come from the bar code. Clearly, the function needs to be documented in the UED. The team created a hardware focus area called Bar Code Scan with a user-invoked function to scan a bar code. They also created a software focus area called Manage Shopping Order and gave it an automatic function of emitting an auditory signal when the scan is successful. The system structure calls for these two focus areas to be linked to one another.

Storyboard cell 3 (Figure 10.11) has multiple functions, all automatically performed by the system. This cell leads the team to create a system focus area called Household Historian. System focus areas are not used by the user; all of the functions there are automatic and take place behind the scenes. The Household Historian focus area is linked to the Manage Shopping Order focus area.

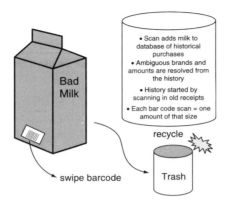

FIGURE 10.11 Storyboard cell 3

The process for generating the UED continues in this manner, using the discussion of each cell in the storyboard to identify and capture new focus areas and add to existing focus areas.

Paper Prototyping, Mock-Up Interviews and Initial User Interface Design

The initial UED is the team's working hypothesis of how the system should support and extend the customers' work. But they need to stabilize the design, fill out its function, and be sure that what they are proposing will really work for customers. To do this we need a way to extend and test the proposed system with users in their real work situations. Paper prototyping allows us to do this.

Paper mock-ups and paper mock-up interviews are now used everywhere for user interface development, although this was not so when we first developed CD (Kyng's article (1998) is the classic on this topic. Snyder's book (2003) is a more recent resource). Paper mock-up interviews work because users understand user interfaces. They do not understand models like the UED or OO (Ehn 1988). Nor can they easily imagine a new work practice from storyboard review. After all, if the customers' awareness of their work is tacit, if they don't have a systemic view of how their work fits into the larger work of the work group or organization, they are not going to be able to articulate what might work and might not work within a meeting setting.

In Contextual Design we bring low-fidelity, hand-drawn paper prototypes out into the field and engage customers in "using" the new system by walking through real cases of their work. They walk through tasks that they have to do that day or that they have recently completed, inputting and viewing information, clicking on buttons and generally moving through the paper system while they perform a necessary task. Again, we use live scenarios collected within the real work context to test our system design.

The team brings additional mock-up parts so that in the moment they can add function, move around the focus areas, rename buttons, and codesign the system with the user. Needed change and function emerge as the user tries to use the new system to accomplish real tasks. The low-fidelity representation makes it clear that icons, layouts,

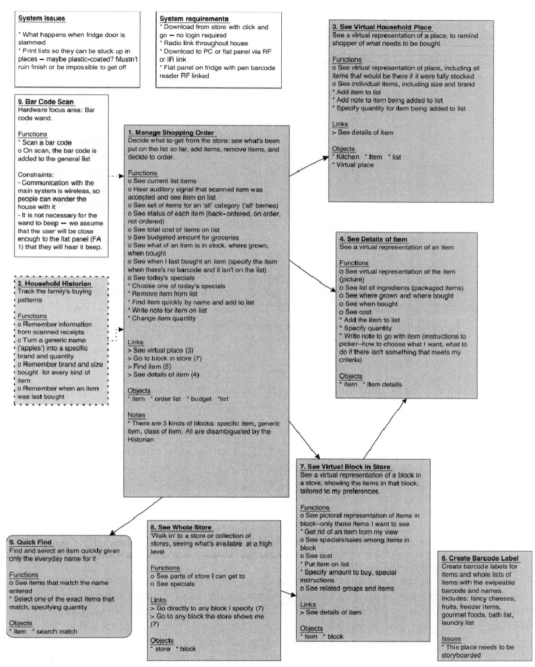

System Issues

* What happens when fridge door is slammed
* Print lists so they can be stuck up in places — maybe plastic-coated? Mustn't ruin finish or be impossible to get off

System requirements
* Download from store with click and go — no login required
* Radio link throughout house
* Download to PC or flat panel via RF or IR link
* Flat panel on fridge with pen barcode reader RF linked

9. Bar Code Scan
Hardware focus area: Bar code wand.

Functions
* Scan a bar code
o On scan, the bar code is added to the general list

Constraints:
- Communication with the main system is wireless, so people can wander the house with it
- It is not necessary for the wand to beep — we assume that the user will be close enough to the flat panel (FA 1) that they will hear it beep.

2. Household Historian
Track the family's buying patterns

Functions
o Remember information from scanned receipts
o Turn a generic name ('apples') into a specific brand and quantity
o Remember brand and size bought for every kind of item
o Remember when an item was last bought

1. Manage Shopping Order
Decide what to get from the store: see what's been put on the list so far, add items, remove items, and decide to order.

Functions
o See current list items
o Hear auditory signal that scanned item was accepted and see item on list
o See set of items for an 'all' category ('all' berries)
o See status of each item (back-ordered, on order, not ordered)
o See total cost of items on list
o See budgeted amount for groceries
o See what of an item is in stock, where grown, when bought
o See when I last bought an item (specify the item when there's no barcode and it isn't on the list)
o See today's specials
* Choose one of today's specials
* Remove item from list
* Find item quickly by name and add to list
* Write note for item on list
* Change item quantity

Links
> See virtual place (3)
> Go to block in store (7)
> Find item (5)
> See details of item (4)

Objects
* item * order list * budget *list

Notes
* There are 3 kinds of blocks: specific item, generic item, class of item. All are disambiguated by the Historian

3. See Virtual Household Place
See a virtual representation of a place, to remind shopper of what needs to be bought

Functions
o See virtual representation of place, including all items that would be there if it were fully stocked
o See individual items, including size and brand
* Add item to list
* Add note to item being added to list
* Specify quantity for item being added to list

Links
> See details of item

Objects
* Kitchen * Item * list
* Virtual place

4. See Details of Item
See a virtual representation of an item

Functions
o See virtual representation of the item (picture)
o See list of ingredients (packaged items)
o See where grown and where bought
o See when bought
o See cost
* Add the item to list
* Specify quantity
* Write note to go with item (instructions to picker--how to choose what I want, what to do if there isn't something that meets my criteria)

Objects
* Item * Item details

7. See Virtual Block in Store
See a virtual representation of a block in a store, showing the items in that block, tailored to my preferences.

Functions
o See pictoral representation of items in block--only those items I want to see
* Get rid of an item from my view
o See specials/sales among items in block
o See cost
* Put item on list
* Specify amount to buy, special instructions
o See related groups and items

Links
> See details of item

Objects
* item * block

5. Quick Find
Find and select an item quickly given only the everyday name for it

Functions
o See items that match the name entered
* Select one of the exact items that match, specifying quantity

Objects
* item * search match

8. See Whole Store
'Walk in' to a store or collection of stores, seeing what's available at a high level

Functions
o See parts of store I can get to
o See specials

Links
> Go directly to any block I specify (7)
> Go to any block the store shows me (7)

Objects
* store * block

6. Create Barcode Label
Create barcode labels for items and whole lists of items with the swipeable barcode and names. Includes: fancy cheeses, fruits, freezer items, gourmet foods, bath list, laundry list

Issues
* This place needs to be storyboarded

FIGURE 10.12 Portion of user environment design for the online grocery shopping product

and other interface details are not the central purpose of the interviews. This invites codesign and keeps the user focused on testing structure and function.

After the design has been tested with three to four users, the team redesigns to reflect the feedback. The UED is updated, restructured as necessary, and functions are described in increasingly more details. After three rounds of mock-up interviews, the UED stabilizes and the interaction design layout and basic usability have been tested and validated. Multiple rounds of interviews and iterations drive testing at increasing levels of detail: structural issues to user interface layout to detailed user interaction.

After this process, the shopping team knew that they had a system structure that worked for their customers. They were ready for final interaction design, real visual design, and object modeling.

Using Contextual Design Deliverables to Generate Use Cases and Implementation Models

Once our online grocery shopping team finished the rounds of prototype interviews, their UED is also the foundation of their functional specification. It defines exactly what functions the system will provide and how they will behave. Paper prototype iterations ensure that the function definitions are complete and correct for the users. The UED shows the structural organization of the system from the user's point of view. Nonfunctional requirements driven by the users (speed, platform, compatibility with other systems, and so forth) are captured as constraints on the UED. Nonfunctional requirements driven by the business are added to the UED for a complete specification of the system.

The UED is also the source document for the next step in systems design, usually accomplished by writing use cases. Regardless of which formalism you follow for writing use cases (Cockburn 2001, Constantine and Lockwood 2001, and Peter Haumer in Chapter 12, Use Case-Based Software Development) offer useful examples), the UED provides the information you need. System function and behavior has already been defined, so these use cases can focus on showing how the system will provide the behavior specified in the UED. Each use case can be focused on a single system task (e.g. scan an item into our grocery system) because the coherence of the whole user task (shop for groceries) is guaranteed by the storyboard and UED.

Use cases are built using scenario-based reasoning. They drive the development of the object model representing the implementation of the system through an analysis that uses model-based reasoning. Just as the structure of the system as experienced by the user needs to be driven by the vision, the implementation object model must be driven by the UED if it is to be implemented correctly. Storyboards "stitch together" the vision and UED, showing how each element of the vision is implemented by a system component that keeps the work practice coherent. In the same way use cases show how implementation components deliver the behavior defined in the UED, which keeps the system coherent. The design thinking process and alternation between scenario and model-based reasoning is parallel.

A use case's preconditions are derived from the function definition and from the scenario that the use case implements. Business rules are defined by hidden focus areas in the UED, and by the automatic function it provides. The design team can check for completeness of the use cases against the UED and storyboards: every function in the

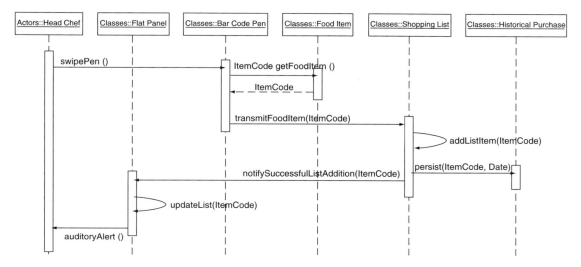

FIGURE 10.13   A UML sequence diagram derived from objects as specified in the UED

UED and every situation covered by the storyboards should be reflected in one of the use cases.

Proceeding to implementation in this way ensures that the customer-centered focus of the design is maintained as the team moves to implementation. The functions in each case can be tracked back to the user data, helping to ensure that the team does not manufacture functionality irrelevant to the customer's work practice. Being tied to customer data allows the team to invent and redesign work practice, but keeps them honest and focused.

Figure 10.13 shows a UML sequence showing the implementation enabling the use case *Make Shopping List* as detailed above. Note that class, collaboration and activity diagrams may also be created using the sequential and structural modeling provided by storyboards and the UED. By using the CD models for work redesign, the transition into industry standard modeling notations (UML) and process frameworks (Rational Unified Process) is a natural one. Standard RUP artifacts—driven by designs based on user data—bridge the communication gap between standard system architecture and model-driven software engineers and user-centered designers. As the (scenario-based) sequence diagram above shows, implementation design simply continues the alternation of scenario and model-based reasoning that started during requirements analysis.

LESSONS LEARNT

We like to say that Contextual Design has been designed with Contextual Design. We are always in a state of continuous improvement. Much of how we run meetings, consolidate customer data, and even model the work and system has been generated over the years in response to the needs of teams and their projects. We started the development of our CD Tools application because teams were losing their paper data and were collecting the same data over and over instead of reusing it. We started defining shorter, more-focused variants of the full CD process to help teams accommodate differences in project scope and organizational constraints like time and human resources. We worked out ways to support small, two-person teams with adjunct resources and very large teams that need to communicate and build buy-in with many stakeholders. We integrated metrics and timing data to help teams anticipate and show productivity gains. And we help teams integrate the techniques of CD into their existing life cycle and corporate software processes.

But our biggest lesson learned is that customer field data can't be traded off. Many of the CD techniques for modeling, representing the system, and working out design concepts and future scenarios can lend structure to the design process. But through painful experience we have learned that without real user data collected through a well-defined process teams argue about who is right and what is needed. Without data, teams and decision makers have no basis for choosing one product, feature, or rollout plan over another. And without data companies fail to see and agree upon their opportunities for new product concepts and business solutions. Contextual Design is a powerful and reliable process because it is grounded in the detailed customer data that designers really need. The most important thing a team can do is to go to the field, collect those real scenarios of use, and build their design upon them.

COMPARISONS

We are often asked to compare Contextual Design to other methods categorized as Participatory Design, particularly Extreme Programming (Xprogramming 2003) and other Agile Software Development methods (Manifesto for Agile Software, 2001) (*see* Chapter 13, *User Stories in Agile Software Development*, by Kent Beck and David West). Agile methods focus on improving the development process once the system's requirements have been defined. Contextual Design focuses on defining those requirements—so the two approaches dovetail very neatly. And they each seek to make the customer the center of the design instead of the developers or the implementation. However, how we achieve this value is markedly different.

Agile methods involve the customer by putting one or more users on the team full-time. The customer is then on-site with the developers throughout development. The customer is a representative of the business client, serving as an active, ongoing resource, telling stories of use and helping to prioritize work. But Agile teams recognize that customers are not designers, and that they need to add additional people with user interface, graphics, and user experience design skill.

Contextual Design teams can also have customers on the team, and this can be effective. However, the customer data that informs the design is collected through the Contextual Inquiry interviews. Only by seeing the true context and details of use can the stories of use be derived.

Because Agile methods are focused on fixing the development practice through rapid iterations, they don't attempt to find common patterns or structural variations in work practice. This limits the scope of the resulting solution. Basing the design on the stories of one, two, or even three customers will likely not account for all the variations that matter.

Some proponents of Agile methods (www.xprogramming.com is a good source for information) recognize that the role of the customer in XP is to be the voice of the business—not the voice of requirements or design. As such, the customer's role is to make the business decisions about what features to implement when and to track user response to implemented features. XP is defining a software development process not a software requirements and user experience design process. When we work with our clients using Agile methods we include working with field data, which then drives storyboarding of the new system, or parts of the new system. It is these storyboard stories that are being implemented within each round of XP. Continuing in the spirit of the XP process, we recommend scoping the data collected and simplifying the design steps when working with a company implementing an XP process to stay one step ahead of the programming team.

There is more commonality in another shared value of Contextual Design and XP/Agile: the belief in the value of teamwork and self-directed teams (www.xprogramming.com and www.agilemanifesto.org both describe guiding principles). Both methods emphasize that being on a team does not mean that you work by yourself and periodically come together with other team members. Rather, work is done in pairs or subteams. Both methods also have the team reflecting at regular intervals on how to be more effective, immediately followed by it tuning and adjusting its behavior.

Contextual Design differs from other Participatory Design methods by introducing more formality into the process of defining what the system is to do. Many methods exist for working with users at different points in the design process; for example Ellen Gottesdiener's workshop facilitation techniques—see Chapter 5 in this volume. In contrast to some approaches that cover only part of the life cycle, Contextual Design provides a sequence of well-defined methods for working with users and user data to produce a result that is documented in a formalism that can drive the rest of the software engineering process. As such, it provides structure to a heretofore unstructured piece of the process—structure that can be used as is, modeled in the RUP or adapted to the software engineering method of choice.

KEYWORDS

Contextual Design	Contextual Inquiry	Storyboards	Requirements Analysis
Customer-Centered Design	Work Models	User Environment Design	Requirements Definition

REFERENCES

Beyer, H. and Holtzblatt, K., *Contextual Design: Defining Customer-Centered Systems*, Morgan Kaufmann Publishers, 1997.

Cockburn, A., *Writing Effective Use Cases*, Addison-Wesley, 2001.

Constantine, L. and Lockwood, L., Structure and style in use cases for user interface design, in M. van Harmelen (Ed.), *Object-Modeling and User Interface Design*, Addison-Wesley, 2001.

Ehn, P., *Work-Oriented Design of Computer Artifacts*, Gummessons, Falkoping, Sweden, 1988, international distribution by Almqvist & Wiksell International, also Coronet Books, Philadelphia, PA.

Goguen, J. and Linde, C., Techniques for requirements elicitation, *Proceedings of the 1993 IEEE International Symposium on Requirements Engineering*, San Diego, CA, January 4–6, 1993, p. 152; IEEE Computer Society Press, Los Alamitos, CA.

Holtzblatt, K., Contextual design, in J. Jacko and A. Sears (Eds.), *The Human–Computer Interaction Handbook: Fundamentals, Evolving Technologies and Emerging Applications* (Human Factors and Ergonomics), Lawrence Erlbaum Associates, 2002.

InContext Enterprises, Shopping Design Album, 2003, http://www.incent.com/insite/shop/index.htm

Kyng, M., Designing for a dollar a day, *Proceedings of the Conference on Computer-Supported Cooperative Work*, Portland, OR, September 26–28, 1988, p. 178.

Manifesto for Agile Software, 2001, http://www.agilesoftware.org

Rheinfrank, J. and Evenson, S., Design languages, in T. Winograd (Ed.), *Bringing Design to Software*, ACM Press, New York, 1996, p. 77.

Snyder, C., *Paper Prototyping: The Fast and Easy Way to Design and Refine User Interfaces*, Morgan Kaufmann Publishers, 2003.

Terwilliger, R. and Polson, P., Relationships between users' and interfaces' task representations, in *CHI '97 Conference Proceedings*, Atlanta, GA, March 22–27, 1997, p. 99; ACM, New York.

Xprogramming.com an Extreme Programming Resource, 2003, http://www.xprogramming.com

RECOMMENDED READINGS

Beyer, H., Calling down the lightning, *IEEE Software*, **11**(5), 106, 1994. This column discusses the nature of creativity, what drives creativity, and what gets in the way. It uses the development of the spreadsheet as an example, showing that close knowledge of the customer is critical to making invention happen.

Beyer, H., Where do the objects come from?, *Software Development '93 Fall Proceedings*, Boston MA, August 1993. This paper dissects the process of going from object-oriented analysis to object-oriented design to show why it is difficult. The design of the overall system is identified as a missing step, and ways to re-introduce that step are discussed.

Beyer, H. and Holtzblatt, K., Apprenticing with the customer: a collaborative approach to requirements definition, *Communications of the ACM*, **38** (5), 45–52, 1995. This article discusses how to gather data from customers in one-on-one interviews through Contextual Inquiry. It is one of the two primary discussions of how to do Contextual Inquiry (the other is "Contextual Inquiry: A Participatory Technique for System Design," by K. Holtzblatt and S. Jones).

Beyer, H. and Holtzblatt, K. *Contextual Design: Defining Customer-Centered Systems*, Morgan Kaufmann Publishers, 1997. This is the basic book describing the full Contextual Design process.

Beyer, H. and Holtzblatt, K. Contextual design, *Interactions*, **6**(1), 32, 1999. This is an overview of Contextual Design with a focus on how to scale the process to fit the design process.

Holtzblatt, K., If we're a team, why don't we act like one?, *Interactions*, **1**(3), 17, 1994. This column describes some of the problems of working in teams, showing why they arise and why working in teams is hard. It describes some of the interpersonal problems that cause teams to break down, and suggests strategies for handling them.

Holtzblatt, K., Contextual design, in J., Jacko and A. Sears (Eds.), *The Human-Computer Interaction Handbook: Fundamentals, Evolving Technologies and Emerging Applications (Human Factors and Ergonomics)*, Lawrence Erlbaum Associates, 2002. This chapter provides an overview of the Contextual Design process along with key issues and answers to questions that are often asked about the practicalities of using the method within organisations.

Holtzblatt, K. and Beyer, H., Making customer-centered design work for teams, *Communications of the ACM*, **36** (10), 92103, 1993. This was the first article on Contextual Design published. It's a good and reasonably concise description of the process.

Holtzblatt, K. and Jones, S., Contextual inquiry: a participatory technique for system design, in A. Namioka and D. Schuler (Eds.), *Participatory Design: Principles and Practice*, Lawrence Earlbaum Publishers, Hillsdale, NJ, 1993. This article is the first published description of Contextual Inquiry. It describes the process, including three of the four interviewing principles, the interpretation session, and affinity diagrams.

Wixon, D. and Ramey, J (Eds.), *Field Methods for Software and Systems Design*, John Wiley & Sons, New York, 1996. This book describes the experience of several different practitioners using field methods. Several people who have used Contextual Inquiry and Contextual Design have written chapters describing their experiences. This is a good resource for anyone wanting to adopt customer-centred methods in their own organisation.

CHAPTER 11

A SCENARIO-BASED DESIGN METHOD FOR HUMAN-CENTRED INTERACTION DESIGN

David Benyon[1] and Catriona Macaulay[2]

[1] *Napier University, Edinburgh, UK*
[2] *Duncan of Jordanstone College of Art and Design, Dundee University, UK*

OVERVIEW

We describe a method for the design of interactive systems. The aim of the method is to ensure that the interactive systems that we design are usable, useful, and engaging. The method is scenario-based and uses four different types of scenario: user stories, conceptual scenarios, concrete scenarios and use cases. We also include a method for arriving at a conceptual system design from a 'corpus' (i.e. a logically coherent and complete set) of scenarios using and object/action analysis.

APPLICABILITY

The method was developed while working on a European research and development project to produce a new device—a home information centre (the HIC). One key feature of this setting was the large cross-disciplinary and multi-lingual project team. There were also several people working in parallel on different applications for the device. Scenarios proved very effective at providing a 'lingua franca' for the project (Erickson 2000) allowing different people to focus on concrete settings and characters in order to express their concerns and design ideas. The method also proved useful in arriving at appropriate functionality for the applications through undertaking an object/action analysis of the scenarios. Since then it has been used on another similar large European funded research and development grant to develop an online partner searching system known as OPaL (Davenport 2003). Overall the method may be most applicable for the development of more 'blue sky' products where conceptualisation of future use is key. However,

Scenarios, Stories, Use Cases: Through the Systems Development Life-Cycle. Edited by Ian F Alexander and Neil Maiden
© 2004 John Wiley & Sons, Ltd. ISBN: 0-470-86194-0

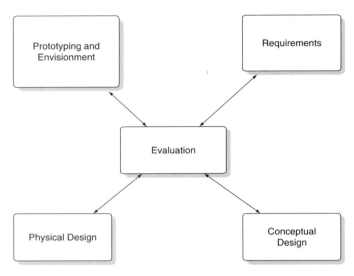

FIGURE 11.1 The star life cycle *(Adapted from Hix and Hartson 1991)*

because the method is inherently object-oriented, it fits well with many mainstream software development approaches.

POSITION IN THE LIFE CYCLE

Requirements Discovery	**Requirements Validation**	System Specification	System Design	Coding, First of Class	**Integration & Testing**	Operations & Maintenance

The method is inherently associated with a star life cycle (Hix and Hartson 1993) or with a spiral approach (Boehm 1988) to development. In the star model (see Figure 11.1), evaluation is central; everything gets evaluated as the design moves from one phase to the next. Our method starts from the user stories that have been gathered during requirements generation exercises such as observations or workshops. It finishes with a specification of a system in terms of its functionality (specified as use cases), structure (specified as a conceptual object or data model) and look and feel (specified as a design language, including interaction patterns). The amount of formality in this approach is appropriate for a wide range of systems. We do not think that the specification could simply be handed to a programmer without further elaboration, discussion, and involvement with the design team. However, we do think that the specification captures enough of the essential aspects of a design to be used for developing prototypes.

KEY FEATURES

The different types of scenario and the ways that they are used are key features of the method. The scenarios become more formalised as the design process progresses. Thus, the transition from one representation to another is also important. Another key feature is the way that claims and requirements are captured and cross-referenced through the structured representation of a scenario. Finally, we would draw attention to the way that the scenarios fit into an object-oriented analysis and design (OOAD) approach.

STRENGTHS

As with any scenario-based design method, it is thoroughly human-centred. Stories come from the future users themselves, and can be elicited using participatory methods such as workshops, focus groups and brainstorming sessions. It provides a useful 'lingua franca' for such broad-based design teams. In practice, people have rapidly begun talking in terms of specific scenarios and characters (or 'personas').

WEAKNESSES

The method appears most suitable for envisioning and designing novel systems rather than more traditional information processing applications. However, this may turn out to be a strength as increasingly we see information technology being applied to areas in which 'soft knowledge' is key. We are not as interested in the simple retrieval of hard facts as we are in the more subtle 'qualia' of information. Davenport (2003) comments that in the case of Knowledge Management software '[scenarios] must yield or deliver insights pertinent to judgements about behaviour that involve soft insights about tacit knowledge: trust, rapport, social capital, and social networks'.

THE METHOD

An overview of the method is shown in Figure 11.2. The clouds represent activities carried out during system or product development. The boxes represent artefacts. It creates a system specification in the form of a set of use cases, a conceptual object model and a design language, though all the documentation contributes to the full specification. The process is highly iterative.

> *Scenarios are used throughout. A scenario is a short story about people, their activities and the contexts in which those activities take place that are relevant to the technology in question. At different stages of the design process, scenarios are helpful in understanding current practice and any problems or difficulties that people may be having, in generating and testing ideas, in documenting and communicating ideas to others and in evaluating designs.*

Scenarios in the Method

The method employs four different types of scenario used for different purposes during design,

- user stories,
- conceptual scenarios,

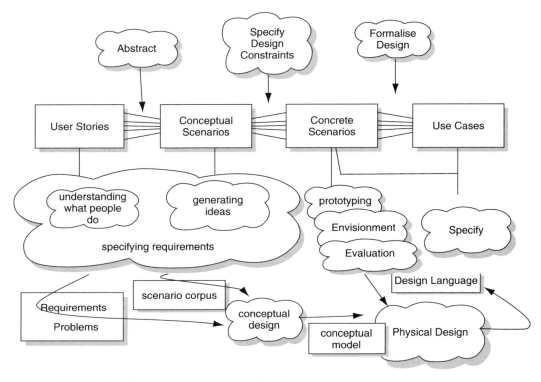

FIGURE 11.2 Scenarios throughout the life-cycle

- concrete scenarios, and
- use cases.

Figure 11.2 illustrates the relationship between the different types of scenario. The lines indicate that many user stories will be represented as a single conceptual scenario, which in turn may generate many concrete scenarios. Several concrete scenarios will be represented by a single use case. The difference between these types is elaborated below.

User Stories

User stories are the real world experiences, ideas, anecdotes, and knowledge of people. These may be captured in any form and comprise small snippets of activities and the contexts in which they occur. This could include video of people engaged in an activity, diary entries, photographs, documents, the results of observations and interviews, and so on. User stories are rich in context. They often capture the intentions of the users, leading to a more goal-centred design (Cooper 1999). That is, rather than focusing on the tasks that people perform, the aim is to understand, and design for, their personal and practical goals. User Stories also capture many seemingly trivial details usually left out of more formal representations.

Conceptual Scenarios

Conceptual scenarios are more abstract than user stories. Much of the context is stripped away during the process of abstraction (see below), and similar stories are combined together. The designer begins to design possible implementation objects from a blend of the physical objects described in the stories (Imaz and Benyon 1999). Conceptual scenarios are particularly useful for generating design ideas and for understanding the requirements of the system.

Scenarios can become messy, so in order to control the scenarios a structure is needed. We use a framework known as PACT (People, Activities, Contexts, Technologies) to critique scenarios and to encourage designers to get a good description of the domain (Benyon et al. 2004). For each scenario the designer lists the different people who are involved, the activities they are undertaking, the contexts of those activities and the technologies that are being used.

We also try to structure scenario descriptions. Each scenario should be given an introduction. The history and authorship should be recorded, along with a description of how the scenario generalises (across which domains) and the rationale for the scenario. A PACT analysis should be provided. Each paragraph of each scenario should be numbered for ease of reference and endnotes included where particular design issues are raised. Endnotes are particularly useful in documenting issues raised during the development of the scenario. They are a way of capturing the claims being made about the scenarios (Rosson and Carroll 2002). Examples of relevant data and media should be collected. Figure 11.3 provides an example scenario in this format. It was one of the conceptual scenarios developed for a project exploring designs for an HIC and looked at a particular application of a more generic scenario 'what shall we do now' (discussed below).

When working in a large design team, it is useful to accompany scenarios by real data. This means that different team members can share concrete examples and use these as a focus of discussion. Another key feature of writing scenarios is to think hard about the assumptions that are being made: to make assumptions explicit or deliberately avoid making things explicit in order to provoke debate. In the scenario sample shown in Figure 11.3, for example, the couple are deliberately kept gender neutral; so discussions about gender issues can either be avoided or can be confronted. In another scenario, an elderly woman with arthritis might be one of the characters, thus bringing to the foreground issues of access and how the physically impaired interact with technology.

Finally, with these scenarios it is important to provide a very rich context—hence the details such as food on the table, or where they had been holidaying. As already mentioned, the guiding principles for scenario writing are people, activities, contexts and technologies. A simple web-based hypertext system can be developed to help with the organisation of the scenarios, linking the user stories that led to the conceptual scenarios (Figure 11.4).

Concrete Scenarios

When people are working on a particular problem, or an issue raised by one of the endnotes or other part of the scenario, they will often identify some feature that applies only under certain circumstances. At this point they may specify a more specific elaboration of

Example

Scenario Title

What shall we do now?

Scenario History

Version	Date	Author	Description
1	20 April 2003	D. Benyon	Discussed at design meeting
1.1	4 May, 2003	D. Benyon	Modified following discussions

Scenario Type

Activity Scenario

Rationale

This scenario has been developed as part of the first prototype. It is intended to provide a rich description of a general context of use of the Home Information Centre (HIC). The scenario is deliberately vague with respect to a number of features such as input and output media and modalities, how the content is provided, and so on in order to stimulate discussion about such things.

PACT analysis

People — A couple in their mid-30s, well-educated, relatively well-off, able-bodied.

Activities - Using the HIC to find out what entertainment is available at the Edinburgh Arts festival.

Context — Living area at home. Information searching only (no communication in this version).

Technology — A Home Information Centre envisaged as a multi-modal device, something of a cross between a personal computer and a television, stylish, internet-enabled.

Scenario

Jan and Pat are a couple in their mid-30s. Pat is a university lecturer in Cultural Studies and Jan is an accounts manager at Standard Life insurance. They live in the Stockbridge area of Edinburgh, Scotland in a two-bedroom flat overlooking the river. It is 12.00 noon on August 15th . Jan and Pat are sitting in their large, airy kitchen/dining room. The remains of pizza and mixed salad mingles with a pile of newspapers on the kitchen table. Jan and Pat have recently returned from a holiday on the island of Zante and, apart from checking their e-mail, have not gone back to work. They decide that they would like to go to see one of the events that is happening as part of the Edinburgh Arts festival.

Jan activates the HIC[1] and chooses 'Edinburgh Festival[2]. The HIC connects to the different content providers who are registered as providing content about the festival. The display shows five categories of information: Times of Events, Specific Artists, Specific Events, Specific Venues, Types of Events, a catalogue and, a query facility[3].

End notes

1. How the HIC is activated is not considered here. Different methods may lead to different versions of the scenario.

2. So, Edinburgh Festival is a thing in, or accessed by, the HIC. It could be some sort of plug-in provided by a third-party content provider. For example, the Guardian Newspaper might provide a free CD-ROM for its readership, Jan and Pat may have downloaded the data from a web site, the data may be physically resident on some remote machine, or on Pat and Jan's computer.

3. Again the modality of these are not specified. The query facility could be spoken, typed on a remote keyboard or an on-screen keyboard, written by hand or take some other form such as a query agent. The catalogue facility could be represented in a number of different ways.

FIGURE 11.3 Example scenario fragment

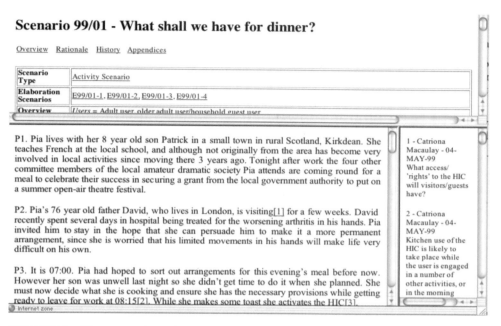

FIGURE 11.4 The scenario web

the scenario and link it to the original. Thus one reasonably abstract scenario may spawn several more concrete elaborations, which are useful for exploring particular issues.

Concrete scenarios also begin to dictate a particular interface design and a particular allocation of functions between people and devices. Concrete scenarios are particularly useful for prototyping and envisioning design ideas and for evaluation because they are more prescriptive about some aspects of the technology. For example, the scenario in Figure 11.3 has an endnote stating that how the HIC is activated is not considered. Different possible designs—an 'off/on' switch, voice activation, touching the screen and so on—result in different concrete scenarios.

For example, if the designer considers touch screen technology and works with a concrete version of the scenario 'Jan touched the screen to activate the HIC', someone might point out that with all this food lying about perhaps the screen would get very dirty. Two observations about this are worth noting. Firstly, it is only by including the rich contextual descriptions that such issues will arise. If the scenario did not mention food, people are less likely to think about the results of having food lying around. Second, notice that the concrete scenarios do not have to be implemented to prove useful in prototyping and envisioning ideas. Just working through a concrete scenario with a colleague can throw up many important design issues.

When planning more formal evaluation, the concrete scenario chosen needs to be considered very carefully. For a more formal evaluation a running prototype is often required, so design decisions about colour and screen layout and dialogue structure and so on all need to have been decided upon. This leads finally (after much evaluation) to the design language (see below).

Use Cases

A use case describes the interaction between people and devices. Each use case therefore covers many slight variations in circumstances—many concrete scenarios. The lines in Figure 11.2 indicate how many concrete scenarios result, after the process of specification and coding, in a few use cases. The line looping back illustrates that each use case will have many (concrete) scenarios associated with it.

Before use cases can be specified, tasks and functions have to be allocated to human or to the device. The specification of use cases both informs and is informed by the task/function allocation process (see below).

OTHER ARTIFACTS IN THE METHOD

Besides the four different types of scenario, four other artefacts are produced during the design process: requirements/problems, scenario corpus, conceptual model and design language. These are represented as boxes in Figure 11.2 and are explained further below.

Requirements and Problems

In the gathering of user stories and during the analysis and abstraction process, various issues and difficulties will come to light. These help the analyst/designer to establish a list of requirements—qualities or functions that any new product or system should have. For example in the HIC example, the device has to be used by the elderly and short-sighted. Another requirement was that it should look good in a living room and should not look or behave like a personal computer running Windows. The format of the requirements and problems is a prioritised list of issues.

Scenario Corpus

In our approach we seek to develop a representative and carefully thought through set, or corpus, of conceptual scenarios. Having undertaken some analysis activities, the designers will have gathered a wide range of user stories. Some of these will be very general and some will be quite specific. Some will be fairly simple, straightforward tasks and others will be more vague. It is important at some point for the designer to pull these disparate experiences together in order to get a high level, abstract view of the main activities that the product is to support. These conceptual scenarios will often still be grounded in a real example; the trick is to find an example that shares characteristics with a number of other activities.

The rationale for the development of a corpus of scenarios is to uncover the 'dimensions' of the design situation and to demonstrate different aspects of those dimensions. Dimensions include characteristics of the various domains within which the product will operate (e.g. large and small domains, volatile or static domains, etc.), the various media and data types that need to be accommodated and the characteristics of the people who will be using the system. The corpus of scenarios needs to cover all the main functions of the system and the events that trigger the functions. Different types of interaction need to be present along with any key usability issues. The dimensions include different types of content and how that can be structured, issues of style, and aesthetics.

A corpus of scenarios might consist of 10 to 12 scenarios depending on the complexity of the domain. For example, in the HIC study we had 11, and for an MP3 application (which of course is much more specific—just playing, sorting and organising MP3 files) we had six and for the OPaL partnership building system (see case study below), we had nine. The aim is to specify the scenarios at a level of abstraction that captures an appropriate level of generality that will be useful across the range of characteristics that is demonstrated within a domain.

Object Model

The object model results from the process of conceptual modelling including developing the scenarios and undertaking an object/action analysis (see below) of the scenario corpus. This will be a conceptual object model, rather than the object model that will be used to implement the system. The object model shows the main objects in the system, their attributes and the relationships that exist between them.

Design Language

The design language produced consists of a set of standard interaction patterns and all the physical attributes of a design—the colours, shapes, icons, and so on. These are brought together with the conceptual actions and objects and the 'look and feel' of the design is completed. A design language consists of a set of *design elements* such as the use of colour, style and types of buttons, sliders and other widgets and some *principles of composition* (i.e. the rules for putting them together). A consistent design language means that users need only learn a limited number of design elements and then they can cope with a large variety of different situations. A design language is how designers build meaning into objects enabling users to understand what things do and to make distinctions between different types of objects (Rheinfrank and Evenson 1996)

Any language provides a way of expressing things and design languages are ways of expressing design concepts. Languages are useful for particular purposes if they have appropriate elements, appropriate organising principles and use an appropriate medium for both expression and transmission. Design languages help ensure transparency, helping people to understand what is going on inside a device. They also afford transferability of knowledge from one device to another. The user of one Nokia phone can generally expect to find similar design elements and principles of composition on another phone. Rheinfrank and Evenson developed their ideas while working on the Xerox photocopiers using colours and symbols to provide a consistent design across a range of products. Design languages also encourage people to more readily see opportunities to use a device or function and will expect certain behaviours, structure, or functions. Finally, people will identify with a style, which helps to define their identity; they act through the design language.

A part of the design language will be a set of interaction patterns. The idea of patterns—'regularities of usage'—was originally developed in architecture (Alexander et al. 1977) and was later enthusiastically adopted by the object-oriented design community.

This idea has now arrived in the design of interactive systems as *interaction patterns*. For example, on a normal PC if you double click on something it opens it, while if you right click on it, it displays a menu of operations you can perform. Macintosh computers have only a single mouse button, so the 'right click' pattern is unknown to Macintosh users. (Interestingly though various work-arounds have now been introduced with different mice and software controls to provide the functionality of a right click pattern.) Most playing devices—VCRs, DVDs, cassette tapes, MP3 players on a computer, and so on—will have a play, stop, fast forward and rewind interaction pattern (and associated design language of single and double headed arrows). Patterns build up into the complex interactions that we are familiar with of menus and mice; patterns of layout of menus, of the highlighting when the mouse rolls over an item, flashing when it is selected and so on.

Patterns are usually described in some standard format so that they can build up into a pattern 'book', referring to one another to provide a rich guide to designs. The key elements for a pattern are to have a clear statement of the design problem, a discussion of the issues surrounding the problem and hence a solution for the problem. There are many examples of patterns for good HCI design in general and for more specific design situations. A good example is the web usability pattern language 'wu' (Graham 2003).

PROCESSES OF THE METHOD

The clouds in Figure 11.5 indicate the activities or processes that have to be undertaken. There is no prescribed order for undertaking these activities and, indeed, considerable iteration around them is inevitable as in the star life cycle (Figure 11.1). They are described in this section.

Abstraction

The process of abstraction is one of classification and aggregation: moving from the details of specific people undertaking specific activities in a specific context using a particular piece of technology to a more general description that still manages to catch the essence of the activity.

Aggregation is the process of treating a whole thing as a single entity rather than looking at the components of something. In most domains, for example, one would aggregate a screen, processor, disc drive, keyboard, and mouse and treat this as a single thing—a computer—rather than focusing on the components. However, in another situation one of the components—processor speed, or disc size, say—may prove to be critical and so it would be better to have two aggregations: fast computers and slow computers, say.

Classification is the process of recognising that things can be collected together and so dealing with the class of things is simpler (more abstract) than dealing with the individual things. There are no set ways to classify things and so the analyst has to work with the stories that have been gathered and with the users themselves to decide which things belong together and why.

Between them, aggregation and classification produce abstractions. Of course there are different degrees of abstraction and it is one of the skills of a designer to settle upon an appropriate level. The most abstract level is to treat everything simply as a 'thing' and every activity as 'doing something', but such an abstract representation is not usually very useful. Rosson and Carroll (2002) discuss abstract scenarios such as a 'browsing' scenario or an 'authoring' scenario. We would consider these to be rather too abstract for the design process and would like to take one step further towards the concrete, whilst still keeping the conceptual scenarios quite abstract. For example, we had a general 'information searching' scenario in the HIC project that we felt was too abstract. It became the slightly less abstract scenario below, which helps to focus attention on some important details of the system, before finishing up as the conceptual scenario in Figure 11.3.

> **Scenario 'What shall we do now?'** *A group (not necessarily co-located) of people are trying to decide what to do with some spare time, they want to find out what options for activities are open to them, how much they would cost, whether they can get there in time, and so on. A number of versions of this scenario can be developed, which stay within this broad framework—for example, we want to go skiing this weekend, is there anything on at a local pub tonight, what's on at that children's festival and what kind of reviews have the various events had, and so on?*

Design Constraints

As the design process continues, certain design decisions will be made. These decisions will result in design constraints—features of the technology or its usage that impose a certain way of working. Given these constraints, each conceptual scenario will generate many slight variations and concrete scenarios. The distinction between conceptual and concrete scenarios is not absolute. It depends how abstract the designer wants to be for a particular reason and how detailed the design constraints are. And of course there will be considerable iteration between these different representations.

Formalise Design

Finally, after much iteration the design is completed and so all the specific interactions with a particular system or device can be specified in terms of the use cases. The design is also formalised through providing a model of the system structure in terms of an (conceptual) object or data model and through the provision of a consistent design language that specifies the look and feel of the system. The design can only be formalised once the task, or function, allocation process has been completed (see below). Formalised design is dependent on a particular device and on how that device has been designed to function. Use cases can then be written.

Specifying Requirements

This is the process of understanding what happens now, what people would want to happen and what problems there are with existing systems or products. The use of user stories and the process of abstraction will help generate requirements, which can gradually be collected together into a prioritised list of both functional and non-functional requirements.

Conceptual Design

Conceptual Design CD involves moving from the requirements and problems that have been uncovered from the user stories and the conceptual scenarios that have been generated to an abstract model of the objects and actions that the new system should provide. A good way of doing CD is to undertake an object/action analysis of the scenario corpus. For each of the scenarios in the corpus, the analyst works through the scenario description identifying the various objects that are mentioned and the various actions that are performed. Objects are often indicated by nouns or noun phrases and activities; actions are indicated by verbs.

Working with a corpus of scenarios in this way requires four stages.

1. Analyse individual scenarios, distinguishing between specific actions and more general, higher-level activities.
2. Summarise objects and actions from each scenario, merging similar or identical actions where necessary.
3. Bring together the analyses from the individual scenarios, collating them into summarised objects, actions and more generic activities.
4. Merge actions and objects where they are identical and give them a single name.

For example in an MP3 music playing scenario a paragraph might read:

> . . . *She selects the 'play' function, which takes her down one level in the interface, to where she can see 'MP3 search'. She selects this. . .*

Analysing this produces the actions 'select' and 'search' and the object 'play function'. In undertaking this type of analysis, verbs often indicate actions and nouns often indicate objects.

Actions that could be thought of as generically similar can now be grouped together, prior to the final distillation stage. For example, 'select' might be called 'specify' in a different part of the scenario. This requires careful attention, to avoid mistakenly merging together slightly different actions. The guiding principle is to look for conceptual or functional parallels among the actions, indicating likely candidates for grouping. The process continues until an object model can be produced.

Prototyping, Envisionment and Evaluation

Designs need to be visualised both to help designers clarify their own ideas and to enable people to evaluate them. Prototyping and envisionment is concerned with finding appropriate media in which to render to design ideas. The medium needs to be appropriate for the stage of the process, the audience, the resources available and the questions that the prototype is helping to answer. Techniques for prototyping and envisionment include any way in which abstract ideas can be brought to life. Sketches 'on the back of an envelope', fully functioning prototypes, cardboard mock-ups are just some of the methods used.

Evaluation is tightly coupled with envisionment because the nature of the representation used will affect what can be evaluated. The evaluation criteria will also depend on who is able to use the representation. Any of the other design activities will be followed by an evaluation. Sometimes this is simply the designer checking through to make sure something is complete and correct. It could be a list of requirements or a high-level design brief that is sent to a client, an abstract conceptual model that is discussed with a colleague, or it may be a formal evaluation of a functional prototype by future system users.

Techniques for evaluation are various depending once again on the circumstances. The important thing to keep in mind is that the technique used must be appropriate for the nature of the representation, the questions being asked and the people involved in the evaluation.

Physical Design

Physical design is concerned with how things are going to work and with detailing the look and feel of the product. Physical design is about structuring interactions into logical sequences and about clarifying and presenting the allocation of functions and knowledge between people and devices. The distinction between conceptual and physical design is very important. The conceptual design relates to the overall purpose of the whole human-computer system. Between the people and the technologies, there has to be enough knowledge and ability to achieve the purpose. Physical design is concerned with taking this abstract representation and translating it into concrete designs. The functionality is expressed as a set of use cases, and the look and feel as a design language. There are three components to physical design.

Operational design is concerned with specifying how everything works and how content is structured and stored. Representational design is concerned with fixing on colours, shapes, sizes, and information layout. It is concerned with style and aesthetics and is particularly important not only for issues such as the attitudes and feelings of people but also for the efficient retrieval of information. Interaction design is concerned with the allocation of functions to human or to technology and with the structuring and sequencing of the interactions.

SUMMARY

The method for scenario-based design described here identifies four types of scenario

- *User stories:* are gathered from people and are effective at understanding what they do now (with the existing technologies), what problems people have and what they want to do in the future
- *Conceptual scenarios:* are generated by the analysts and designers (which may of course be a single person), with participation from the users, from the user stories. They are useful for generating ideas and for scoping the extent of the proposed system.
- *Concrete scenarios:* are generated by the analysts and designers, with participation from the users, by introducing design constraints and specific interaction methods to the abstract scenarios. They are useful for evaluating alternative physical and logical designs.

- *Use cases:* are generated by the analyst/designer as part of the formal specification of the designed system. They gather together a number of concrete scenarios into more generic interaction episodes.

The key activities involved in the method include

- ***Requirements specification by gathering and understanding user stories:*** through interviews, ethnographic methods and the use of various probes such as getting them to keep diaries, giving people disposable cameras to photograph situations, and so on.
- ***Abstraction:*** looking for regularities in the stories, grouping them into meaningful conceptual scenarios, scoping the dimensions of the domain and providing the basic 'lingua franca'—the shared language that designers, developers and users need to establish
- ***Interaction design:*** deciding how the logical processes and data that are needed from some activity are distributed between devices and people.
- ***Establish design constraints:*** this also includes establishing design opportunities. It is not all negative. This process will result in the look and feel of the system, the design language that embodies a consistent, recognisable and understandable set of actions and objects.
- ***Object/action analysis:*** for establishing a conceptual object model from the scenario corpus. The extent to which this is a rigorous process or not depends on the analyst's skills.

There is always a debate in interaction design circles as to the extent to which a method can compensate for a bad analyst/designer against whether a good analyst/designer needs a method at all. Our experience of using the method is that the different types of scenario and the clear steps that transform one into another do indeed provide analysts with a good structure that helps them go into a new domain and explore the design space.

WORKED EXAMPLE

OPaL was a European Union research and development grant concerned with developing a new system to assist people in forming partnerships without having to make physical contact. OPaL stands for 'online partner lens'. The aim was to build a system for small and medium enterprises that could represent partners in ways that allow them to be sampled as 'experiential' goods (as opposed to just seeing a bland description of a company), and to assess each other's suitability in online interactions. Such a 'rich' representation was challenging in terms of knowledge elicitation—it must capture and accommodate characteristics that are difficult to model formally, such as trust, compatibility, and confidence. It was also challenging in terms of interaction design: it must accommodate potential partners' evaluations of each other and represent them effectively. OPaL would provide users with the ability to explore the influence of 'social attributes' in contingent partnerships by building a system that assesses the strength of partnerships based on 1) matched competences, 2) compatibility and 3) perceived confidence, both separately and in combination.

The project consisted of three development partners and three user partners. The countries involved were Germany, the UK, and Spain, each of which had a user and development partner. In each country, the user partners were encouraged to produce user stories and from these develop abstract scenarios. Some partners used very participative methods to gather the stories, others used more observational methods and in other circumstances the partners came up with the stories themselves with little input from the analysts.

The documentation of the outputs was slightly different than presented earlier—but the key thing to observe is the concepts that are employed rather than the exact representation. Although representation can be important to the usability of a method, it is the key constructs that are critical. In the example below, the looser form of the scenario suited the context better, but perhaps lost some of the clearer understanding that is provided by the suggested structure and method described in the previous section.

The On-Line Partner Lens (OPaL)

The overall aim of OPaL is to provide a software facility that enables the formation of partnerships between geographically remote small to medium sized organisations. To some extent it is like a computer dating service, or a brokering service: it is a software environment that brings together organisations allowing dynamic configuration of teams. An innovative feature of OPaL is the idea that it would have three 'layers'; the first would deal with general competences, the second with compatibility issues and the third with confidence and trust.

The following sections show the original user story and how it was used to generate a specific part of the overall design. This is only a small portion of OPaL, which in fact included nine such stories. The scenario that was generated from this and similar stories is included in detail, so that the range of design decisions—and how the scenario helps generate them—are exposed. The story concerns a small IT consultancy firm, DCA.

USER STORY

For a number of years, DCA had been involved in the collection of learning opportunity data. More recently, the company had begun to get involved in software development, primarily to facilitate its data collection and aggregation activities across Scotland. It was part of the company's strategy to safeguard and expand its data collection activities and also to seek opportunities to explore further software development opportunities.

DCA collected learning opportunity data for an increasing number of areas within Scotland for the purposes of producing a Scottish database of learning opportunity information. In England, such data collection activities were carried out by around 80 individual organisations each covering a specific geographic location (known as Training and Enterprise Councils). Some of these TECs collected their own data while others contracted with third parties to collect the data. Although some TECs shared data with each other, there was no national database covering England as there was in Scotland. The Employment department in England was keen to put this situation right and in addition to ensuring there was a national database it was also intending to launch a national helpline that would provide information on education and training to callers across the country.

Not all TECs in England used the same software to store learning opportunity data and this made it difficult to aggregate data into a single database. At the same time DCA was keen to win a contract with the Employment Department to develop a version of its Scotia software for the English Market.

The Employment Department issued a contract notice that combined a number of elements including a range of Call Centre software applications that would allow for data to be imported irrespective of the original format of the data. It was the software development activities, which appealed to DCA and initiated the process outlined in the scenario below.

Although DCA had some contact with many of the agencies doing similar work in England via a number of networks that looked at software and standards issues there was a much limited number who played a significant role. The organisation, referred to as Company B below, had been active in this field for a number of years and already held contracts with the Employment Department to carry out research and promote national co-ordination in the area of data collection. It therefore seemed most appropriate that DCA initially made contact with this organisation.

Conceptual Scenario

This story and others like it were finally grouped together into the 'invitation to tender' scenario. It is reproduced here in its entirety, complete with the footnotes illustrating how the scenario helped to raise design issues.

1. **Scenario Type**
2. Invitation to tender
3. **Rationale**
4. The invitation to tender is a familiar activity for many SMEs. Tenders are issued by government agencies and are posted to a web site and published in a paper journal. Typically, any single SME will not have the full range of expertise needed to fulfil the tender so they will have to find willing and able partners. These partners must also be compatible in their ways of working and there must be confidence that the collaboration will be successful.
5. **People**—Hugo of DCA.
6. **Activities**—Finding partners and evaluating them in terms of working relationships for a particular tender.
7. **Context**—In the DCA office with all associated support.
8. **Technologies**—The proposed OPaL system, full Internet access, etc.

Scenario description

P1   Hugo browses through the OJEC (Official Journal of the European Commission) one morning and identifies an invitation to tender that would suit DCA. He requests the tender specification from the OJEC and begins working through it to identify what needs to be done for the bid.

P2 First, he notes that the closing date for tenders is less than two weeks away and so he needs to move quickly. The proposed system is divided into two sub-systems, a network system and a client-record database system. The description of requirements suggests that some legacy equipment exists, requiring integration into the new work system.

P3 At this point Hugo begins to recognise the need to form a partnership with a Network consultancy although he has no one in mind as yet. Page 13 of the tender specification, a rough floor plan, further emphasises this need. The invitation to tender suggests that some history of developing similar systems inclusive of cost-breakdown indications are considered as bonuses by the clients and so Hugo intends to refer to his 'history record' on the OPaL site. Furthermore, whilst it is suggested that tenders to supply one of the two required sub-systems will be considered, it is favourable towards tenders offering the whole system. This makes Hugo committed to finding a partner who can enable DCA to bid for the whole project.

P4 A 'pulling' factor of this bid is that there is the prospect of further work. The proposed system is to act as a pilot scheme from which it could be tailored to a further 80 sites across Scotland. Additionally, each of these sites would need integrating and so a successful bid could be very lucrative to DCA. Hugo begins to build an outline for a bid and decides that he now needs to find a partner with the additional skills set to complete his bid.

P5 Having identified the skills that DCA requires (ability to network, membership of CIPFA, ability to complete tasks on time, etc.), Hugo logs on to OPaL and inputs his search criteria. Just to make sure, Hugo checks his 'hits' for possible advances being made to him ,but at this point there do not appear to be any.

P6 The browser recognises five possible companies. The first company that Hugo contacts via e-mail is busy for the unforeseen future. The second company Hugo recognises as having a bad reputation (from personal past experience) for meeting deadlines and so chooses to ignore this company. He is now left with three companies.

P7 He needs to find out more about the remaining three companies and so explores their profiles that are posted on OPaL . None of these companies X, Y, and Z is perfect but they all seem interesting. Hugo intends to trade off against suitable shared work practices and other bonuses, and so on and play for the most appropriate, for DCA and the project tender. He decides to make contact via email. He invites them individually to layer two of OPaL.

P8 Company X and Y both respond within 4 hours and company Z does not respond for another 48 hours. Hugo takes this to be a bad sign in terms of work practices and meeting deadlines and so writes off company Z. Two companies remain, X and Y.

P9 *In layer two*, Hugo opens up the online messaging component and initiates communication with each company individually. First of all he contacts company X.

Hugo does this right away. After the initial correspondence Company X checks DCA out on the OPaL system and finds that they would seem to be a good company to enter into a partnership with. They flick through the tender specification and decide that they are keen to be involved with this partnership.

P10 Hugo and company X re-enter the online messaging function for some question and answer communication. This interaction will indirectly identify things like shared practice, shared understanding of the tender specification, approaches to be taken, and so on. Examples of questions asked are, when did you last do a costing of this kind? Do you think this is feasible or should we question the specification? What about page 3? Both companies DCA and company X later go to check the interaction patterns that have emerged from the online messaging task and find that they seem compatible.

P11 Hugo now contacts company Y. After a similar interaction with company Y, they take the initiative and invite Hugo to move to layer 3 for some 'gaming'. Hugo decides that this is not the way in which he would like to progress and considers this a bad sign. They are likely to have conflicting ways of working. He is fortunate, as Company X is looking very promising. Hugo responds to company Y's request thanking them kindly for their interest, but feel that for this project they would not be suitable.

P12 Hugo now feels that he would like to invite company X to layer three. Company X agrees and they decide to undertake a structured interaction. During this task, they open a shared document space through which they can both up-load and work on documents. They undertake a conference call in which the sharing out of tasks and responsibilities for writing the bid are negotiated. Disagreements are resolved and time scales are met for the preliminary drafts.

P13 The partnership looks as if it may work well. Having drafted out a plan of action, the intended outcome of the task, they agree to meet again (conference call) the following morning and discuss the next stage and the results of the confidence analysis. The analysis shows that there are some delicate areas that may require discussing at this point, for example, contested roles. At this point, further discussion is required to avoid further breakdowns and to ensure that they consider some repair mechanisms.

Using the Scenario in requirements

It is difficult to capture all the issues that this scenario raises and how it is used in requirements work. Of course many of the ideas raised in the footnotes were discussed in the project team. The notes included in the section illustrate some further thoughts and issues that arose.

Further notes

Time: Six weeks—Company A works frequently on a basis of 'fast track' bids with a six-week preparation time. So this is 'swift' partnership.

The approaches to other partners were made on the basis of tacit knowledge—who is good at what—in a relatively small professional network. Third-party recommendations come into play—there is a 'chain' of recommendation or a 'snowball' effect. Social capital may be a factor here.

The negotiations for the partnership were handled at Director level; the colleagues who would have to work together did not meet each other.

The face-to-face meetings between A and B, and A, B, and C were considered 'successful'; 'rapport' was good. The attributes of rapport need to be explored. These meetings were very task focused, and any underlying cultural factors were not considered.

It would be useful to know what was in the contract.

OPaL issues

Broaden the field of candidates—use of the personal network left potential possibilities unexplored—premature closure? Need to consider what attributes the candidates should have.

OPaL should be linked to tracking services for example OJEC/CORDIS calls.

The OPaL tool should allow a company to direct potential partners to OJEC notices or even allow access to a space where OJEC notices can be 'pasted' for view/comment by others.

The discussions with the companies could be held on the conference layer.

Leadership issue: OPaL might help identify/explore leadership styles. It could assist the potential partners in producing leadership criteria for a particular project in order that rational decisions can be taken.

OPaL needs to capture generic information about projects—financial structures, cash flow, deadlines—as patterns of use are likely to vary according to the project/team/partner situation and type.

'Games' need to be designed to capture situational features and reveal attributes.

Need for a sub-layer of recruitment that allows 'lower' people in the project to explore each other's working styles.

Need to have some information that allows partners motives to be assessed—need to recognise that motives vary across the team. Would standard competitive intelligence reveal anything?

Conceptual Design

The scenarios were examined for objects and actions, and these were aggregated across the nine scenarios. Individual diagrams were produced where relevant, and were finally compiled into the overall diagram of system functionality (Figure 11.5).

Use Cases

Following the process of task/function allocation, it becomes possible to specify the use cases for the system. The following table presents a first draft of Use Cases and the functions contained within each Use Case.

Figure 11.6 provides the more detailed specification of UC03.2 setting privacy levels.

Design Language

At the time of writing, little work has been done on the final design language for OPaL, certainly not much at the detailed level. A number of possibilities for the OPaL interface were discussed at a design meeting focusing on the interface design.

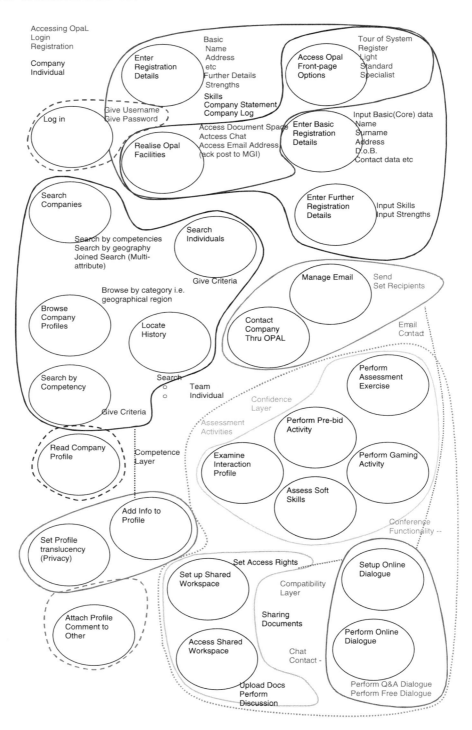

FIGURE 11.5 Systems functionality

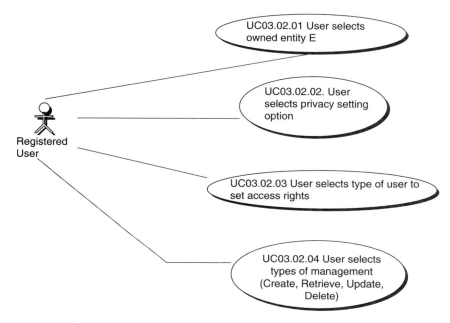

FIGURE 11.6   Use case diagram for specifying privacy

A prototype environment was developed as indicated in Figure 11.7. OPaL could be a multi-paned website which allows navigation, connections, diaries and personal organisers, and project schedules. Computer games environments, where users adopt characters and interact with other characters would be included perhaps as 3D environments. The design in Figure 11.7 shows a multi-paned window with different tabs that the user clicks to open up the screens for Profile, Competence, Conference, Confidence, and Review levels.

The language for OPaL could be seen to be developing. Different sections of the environment were represented by tabs at the top of the main pane. E-mail and other functions were enclosed in separate panes at the top level. The usual web-based interaction patterns—click to bring to front, use of 'Back' button, scrolling text in panes and so on would be adopted so that new users (of which there could potentially be many) would feel the interface to be quite intuitive. The colours and use of logo would help create an OPaL identity.

Conclusion

The OPaL case study illustrates the method in operation. It was adapted to meet the particular circumstances; the scenarios were not as strongly structured as had been the case in the HIC. We feel that this is not a good thing and that the lack of rigour may have led to misunderstandings; something that can easily happen in scenario-based design, but something that the structured scenario can avoid (Benyon and Macaulay 2002). The scenarios in this case study did help in identifying the major functions and objects that would be needed and they certainly offered a good way of dealing with the gathering of requirements across different sites.

TABLE 11.1 Use case diagram for specifying privacy

Use Case	Functions
UC01—Pre-registration	1.1 Public
	1.2 Enter as member
	1.3 Register
UC02—Registration	2.1 Enter Basic Requirements
	2.2 Approve Requirements
UC03—Profile management	3.1 Enter further details
	3.2 Privacy settings
	3.3 Specific relationships
UC04—Search partner profile	4.1 Search profile
	4.2 Browse capability
UC05—Assessment management	5.1 Add assessment to Profile
	5.2 Examine interchange
	5.3 Review assessment
UC06—Interaction component	6.1 Email
	6.2 A/V Content
	6.3 Shared workspace
	6.4 Online dialogue
	6.5 Confidence assessment activity
	6.5.1 Perform assessment
UC07—Administration	
UC08—Partnership management	8.1 New Partnerships
	8.2 View Partnerships
	8.2.1 View as owner
	8.2.2 View as member

COMPARISONS

The method is most closely related to the one provided in (Rosson and Carroll 2002) and indeed was certainly influenced by their previous writings. Their approach to capturing claims and the trade-offs that are inherent in design is more formal than the footnote method used in our method, but they do not specifically identify the differences between user stories, conceptual and concrete scenarios that we have found particularly useful. However,

FIGURE 11.7 Possible mock up for OPaL showing beginnings of a design language

their problem scenarios are similar to user stories and their future activity scenarios are clearly close to our conceptual and concrete scenarios.

Cooper (1999) also recommends a scenario-based approach, but he emphasises the development of personas—fictionalised descriptions of typical systems users containing lots of personal and contextual details first. This leads to considering the goals that people have. The personas are used to walk through different scenarios ('a scenario is a. . . . persona using a software-based product to achieve a goal', p. 179) so that designs can be evaluated. Cooper argues that the design should focus on the 'daily use' scenario—the actions that people perform with the greatest frequency—and on 'necessary use' scenarios that focus on the actions that must be performed, but are not performed frequently. He also notes the existence of 'edge case' scenarios that concern unusual conditions.

ACKNOWLEDGEMENTS

Members of the FLEX project working at Napier University, Edinburgh helped to prototype and revise the approach presented here. Thanks to members of the OPaL team for allowing the case study to be used and particular thanks to Liisa Dawson who undertook this work. Also, thanks to Martin Graham for drawing the functional diagrams and use case diagrams.

KEYWORDS

User Stories	Concrete Scenario	Design Method	Human-Centred Interaction
Conceptual Scenario	Use Case		Design

REFERENCES

Alexander, C., Ishikawa, S., and Silverstein, M., *A Pattern Language: Towns, Buildings, Construction*, Oxford University Press, New York, 1977.

Benyon, D.R. and Macaulay, C., Scenarios and the HCI-SE design problem, *Interacting with Computers*, **14**(4), 397–405 2002.

Benyon, D.R., Turner, P., and Turner, S., *Designing Interactive Systems*, Addison-Wesley, 2004.

Boehm, B., The spiral model of software development and enhancement, *IEEE Computer*, **21**(5), 61–72, 1988.

Cooper, A., *The Inmates are Running the Asylum: Why High-Tech Products Drive us Crazy and How to Restore the Sanity Sams*, Macmillan, Indiana, IN, 1999.

Davenport, E. (2003) *Interpersonal Knowledge and Organisational Foresight: The Case of Online Partnership in Micro-Organisations*, in K. Srikantaiah and M. Koenig (Eds.) *Knowledge Management; Lessons Learned.* Learned Information, 379–397, 2004.

Erickson, T., Supporting interdisciplinary design: toward pattern languages for workplaces, in P. Luff, J. Hindmarsh, and C. Heath (Eds.), *Workplace Studies: Recovering Work Practice and Informing System Design*, Cambridge University Press, Cambridge, UK, 2000, pp. 357–368.

Graham, I., *A Pattern Language for Web Usability*, Addison-Wesley, 2003.

Hix, D. and Hartson, D., *Developing User Interfaces: Ensuring Usability through Product and Process*, Wiley, 1993.

Imaz, M. and Benyon, D.R., How stories capture interactions, in C. Johnson and A. Sasse (Eds.), *Proceedings of Interact '99*, North Holland, 1999.

Rheinfrank, J. and Evenson, P., Design languages, in T. Winograd (Ed.), *Bringing Design to Software*, ACM Press, 1996.

Rosson, M.-B. and Carroll, J., *Usability Engineering*, Morgan Kaufman, 2002.

RECOMMENDED READING

Rosson, M.-B. and Carroll, J. (2002) *Usability Engineering*, Morgan Kaufman. This book provides a good method for undertaking scenario-based design. Many of the concepts discussed here appear in their book, though often under a slightly different name. Rosson and Carroll do distinguish different types of scenario, but tend to focus on different types of activity rather than where they are used in the life cycle.

Cooper, A. (1999) *The Inmates are Running the Asylum: Why High-Tech Products Drive us Crazy and How to Restore the Sanity Sams*, Macmillan, Indiana, IN. This is a very entertaining and informative book with excellent advice on design and suggestions for taking a goal-centred approach. Cooper emphasises the importance of scenarios and, importantly, the need to develop rich and meaningful descriptions of people.

Benyon, D. R., Turner, P., and Turner, S. (2004) *Designing interactive Systems*, Addison-Wesley. This new text book covering the whole life cycle of human–computer interaction and the design of interactive systems describes the method used here in defile and includes other examples of this scenario-based design approach.

Carroll, J. (2000) *Making Use*, MIT Press is a thoughtful book about scenarios in general, where they can be used and where they are most effective.

CHAPTER 12

USE CASE-BASED SOFTWARE DEVELOPMENT

Peter Haumer

IBM Rational Software, Schipol-Rijk, Netherlands

USE CASE authors have the difficult task of writing specifications for many different audiences. They have to balance the language, content, and style of their use cases for the needs of both non-technical and technical stakeholders. While most chapters in this book focus on non-technical stakeholders such as customers and users, this chapter discusses the developer as another important audience of use cases. To write use cases that are also useful to developers, analysts have to understand what developers will use them for. The difficulty is, of course, to keep the balance for the other audiences without negating the main benefit of use cases: facilitating interdisciplinary communication of requirements.

I will outline in this chapter the role Use Cases play for Object-Oriented Analysis and Design (OOAD) as described in the Rational Unified Process (RUP 2003). I will begin by discussing the particular properties use cases possess that make them such a good tool for requirements management as well as for guiding software design. I will define additional concepts required for these tasks. Finally, I will walk you through a core set of analysis and design activities, examining the role use cases play for these activities, using examples from a web-based e-commerce application.

APPLICABILITY

- Projects with interdisciplinary team communication.
- Projects utilising object technology and software design frameworks (e.g. J2EE, .NET).
- Wide range of software and systems-engineering projects in terms of scale from small web-based e-business applications via business process engineering projects to large-scale systems-engineering projects (the latter two applying a use case flow-down between systems and sub-systems not discussed in this chapter; see Cantor 2003, RUP SE 2003 for more details).

Scenarios, Stories, Use Cases: Through the Systems Development Life-Cycle. Edited by Ian F Alexander and Neil Maiden
© 2004 John Wiley & Sons, Ltd. ISBN: 0-470-86194-0

POSITION IN THE LIFE CYCLE

Requirements Discovery	Requirements Validation	**System Specification**	**System Design**	Coding, First of Class	**Integration & Testing**	Operations & Maintenance

KEY FEATURES

- Industry leading software development process.
- Iterative, risk- and use case-driven analysis and design methodology.
- Full traceability from requirements to analysis to design to code.
- Augments requirements with user experience modelling to improve communication on requirements and designs.
- Facilitates predictable and repeatable iterative development through analysis and design mechanism and trace-based impact assessment.
- Extensive tool support available (not discussed here).

STRENGTHS

- Use cases present requirements in context improving communication within interdisciplinary teams by focusing on delivering actor value and not technical detail.
- Use cases relate to stakeholder goals, which facilitate prioritisation and planning of iterative development (implementing high priority and risky requirements first).
- RUP OOAD defines well-understood and scalable process of transforming requirements into software solutions.
- RUP OOAD systematically established traceability as part of the primary activities to support iterative development as well as change impact-assessment and management.

WEAKNESSES

- Reading and understanding use cases should be easy for any stakeholder. However, modelling and writing use cases that they are easily understood as well as successfully used for analysis and design requires a well-trained system analyst and designer.
- As a result, experience is required to avoid typical pitfalls when adopting use cases and OOAD. Pitfalls include functional decomposition of use cases, over-analysis of use cases and analysis models, giving too much or too little detail

in use cases, mixing requirements and design, not using the right amount of analysis and modelling to abstract from design decisions in the right places, not enforcing design mechanisms in the teams to incorporate design decisions systematically, etc.

- RUP OOAD also requires an architect with solid methodological as well as technical understanding leading the design with experience, vision, and creativity.

TECHNIQUE AND WORKED EXAMPLE

The Use Case — Centred Requirements Framework

I will start this chapter by listing and defining the key elements a designer needs to be provided with to do OOAD, that is, the inputs to this discipline of software engineering.

Goals and Requirements

First off, let's talk about requirements and goals in general (just to avoid any misunderstandings with other sources and definitions of these terms):

> *A requirement specifies a solution in terms of behaviour (e.g. input–output interactions), structure (e.g. exchanged and stored information, business rules), and quality (e.g. usability, performance) from a black box perspective.*

A solution addresses goals stakeholders[1] have in respect to their environment, for example, the goal to achieve or to improve something.

> *A goal describes a solution-independent measurable desired state for a stakeholder's environment.*

The goal allows stakeholders to express their needs for their world or application domain (e.g. their business, their automation environment, etc.) for which a solution or an improvement to an existing solution can be defined with requirements. Requirements address or realise the solution-independent goals with concrete solution specifications. An example goal:

> "Provide automated order handling."

An example of one of the requirements addressing this goal:

> "The sales system displays the types of available order transactions. The customer selects a transaction type. The sales web displays the list of books that the customer currently has pending."

You can see that many different solutions for a given goal can be found: this example goal could have also been addressed with a phone line utilising touch-tone codes or

---

[1] An individual who is affected by the outcome of the project.

speech recognition requiring quite different set of input-output interactions. The mapping of goals to high-level requirements that have been scoped to be part of a project, which is establishing the solution, is documented in what the RUP calls a *Vision Document* (RUP 2003).

System Boundaries

On the basis of these definitions, it is not possible to write requirements without exactly knowing what the system boundary is going to be. Certainly, in early phases of a project when the boundary of the system is not clearly defined, yet, all kinds of information will be gathered from stakeholders about what needs to be achieved and done by a potential solution. However, until the boundary is defined, we will call these *stakeholder requests*. Once, the boundary is defined one can then map stakeholder requests to goals, requirements, or statements about the design.

The notion of system boundary plays an important role for organising our specifications especially in the case of projects in which a system is going to be established that is actually decomposed into more than one sub-system. The (RUP SE 2003) defines a system as follows:

> *A system, which may contain hardware (computational and non-computational), software and human workers, delivers some needed operational capability to its users. A system is composed of sub-systems, which collaborate to yield the behaviour and characteristics of the system.*

Therefore, to scale systems development you need a separate requirements specification for every sub-system, because it could be outsourced to another development team, might involve teams with completely different skill sets, and must be tested separately. If you regard every system as a box for which you produce a black-box requirements specification, you could depict a decomposed system as in Figure 12.1 below.

This simple example shows three levels of decomposed systems of three different kinds:

- A *business system*, that is, a business environment for business workers, for which the black box perspective comprises the services that the business has to offer to its customers (also often referred to as *Business Processes*).
- A *software system* that is installed and operated by business workers as well as other systems as part of the business realisation.
- A composition of the software system in *software sub-systems* (the realisations of which are also often referred to as *Software Components*).

Again, for all of these levels you specify requirements in terms of the functionality provided by the system's interfaces as well as qualities (also often referred to as *Non-Functional Requirements*) such as usability, reliability, performance, and so on. Needless to say that a real system (think of a whole financial institution) might involve many more levels including hardware with embedded software, business units or departments as sub-systems of the business.

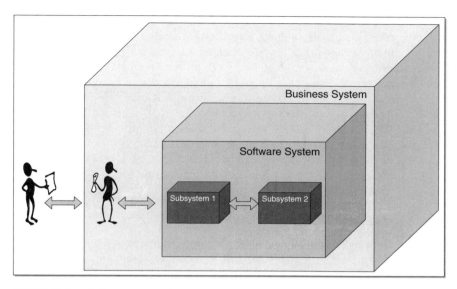

FIGURE 12.1   A decomposed system

Use Cases

Now, we are finally ready to talk about how the interfaces between the boxes and their users (called *Actors*) of Figure 12.1 should be specified, which leads us to the definition of, in respect to this book, the most import concept:

> *A use case defines a sequence of actions a system performs that yields an observable result of value to a particular actor.*

In other words, a use case describes primarily functional but also non-functional requirements from the perspective of an actor achieving particular goals. In contrast to more classical styles of specifying requirements, use cases define clusters of requirements based on goals; that is, a use case groups together all requirements for a solution to achieve one or more particular stakeholder goals.

Because there is always a many-to-many relationship between goals and requirements, you as System Analysts have to decide which goals of the overall goal set defined for a project you are going to use to derive the use cases from. Your general guideline would be to check if your use cases communicate the most important actor goals that will be addressed by the system, that is, the goals you can use to "sell" your system to stakeholders. The trick that makes use cases such a successful interdisciplinary requirements elicitation and validation technique, is the idea of present stakeholders what they are primarily interested in: their customers' or their own goals, rather than grouping and presenting requirements based on some technical criteria or the solution's components or structure. As expressed in Beyer et al. 1997, in contrast to technology experts who know and "like" technology, stakeholders tend to merely want to get their jobs done, and accordingly want computers to be as invisible as a pen's ballpoint so they can focus on their tasks.

As such, use cases cannot be decomposed into sub-units. They represent one unit of addressing needs or goals. Functional decomposition is a matter of Analysis that I describe in the section titled 'Object-Oriented Analysis with Use Cases', using completely different concepts. Always remember, working with use cases is synthesis, not analysis. You do not break a use case apart like problems that are decomposed into smaller problems following a divide and conquer strategy. A use case describes a solution, synthesising all the interactions necessary to achieve the goal expressed in its name. Bittner and Spence (2003) convey this by saying that a use case provides you with a complete experience that result in real value for at least one actor. If you need to link use cases together in order to provide value, your use cases degrade into hard to validate context-free functions and those high-level use cases you use to link them together degrade into empty shells.

Use Case Diagrams

Use case specifications are made up of graphical and textual parts. Let's have a look at an example of a graphical UML use case representation.

Figure 12.2 depicts use cases, in a UML use case diagram, for an online sales software system from the actor Buyer's perspective. Typical goals of buyers for online shopping are to browse a catalogue, maintain their shopping cart, check out their orders, review past orders, and so on. As you can see in Figure 12.2 use case names are chosen to exactly express these goals. You can also see that use cases can depend on each other as the Check Out use case depends on the Authenticate use case. Modelling these dependencies smells of functional decomposition, so use case relationships should be used only when absolutely necessary. Using them heavily makes specifications confusing and hard to read. In Figure 12.2, the ≪include≫-dependency addresses two issues,

Beech Avenue Online Sales (BAOS) Use Case Model

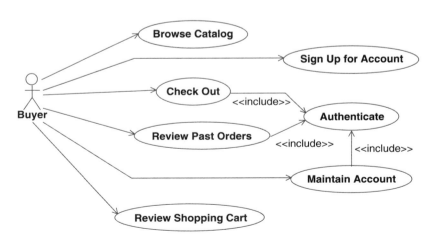

FIGURE 12.2   A use case diagram

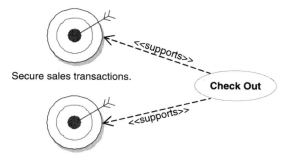

Secure sales transactions.

Provide automated order handling.

FIGURE 12.3   Goals addressed by "Check Out" use case

(a) you want to communicate the authentication goal to stakeholders saying that certain activities are only allowed to be performed after[2] the actor has been properly authenticated and

(b) you want to reduce complexity in the textual part of the use case specifications by avoiding that authentication activities have to be described three times, that is, in the specification of "Check Out", "View Last Orders", and "Maintain Account".

Let's take one more paragraph to clarify the difference between goals and use cases. A use case is solution/system boundary specific. Its name is derived from a related goal. The use case's textual representation shows the concrete requirements necessary to achieve the goal the use case name relates to. A use case can be related to many other goals identified for a particular development project. Figure 12.3 shows an example of use case "Check Out" addressing or supporting different other goals[3] especially goals of a more non-functional or quality character that are sometimes also called *softgoals* (Yu 1997).

Use Case Specifications

The graphical use case representation only presents an overview to your requirements. You always have to combine it with the textual representation of use cases that describes input–output scenarios with all their possible variants and exceptions, as well possible structural requirements (i.e. data), business rules, and non-functional requirements that directly apply to the use case. In cases where the non-functional requirements, rules, and data are of a more general nature and/or apply to more than one use case, these requirements are then typically factored into separate *supplementary specifications* (RUP 2003) and are not part of a use case specification.

---

[2] When Authentication exactly happens in the flow of events is not expressed in the diagram, but the textual use case specification. However, using the includes-dependency in the diagram sensitises the audience for this fact and is used for communication about it.

[3] This UML representation of a goal as a stereotyped class with the target icon as well as respective relationship stereotypes has been recently introduced in (RUP 2003).

Figure 12.4 is an example use case specification for "Browse Catalog" from Figure 12.2. It had to be simplified for space reasons, but it contains the most salient aspects of a use case spec. Surely, there will be many more alternatives and special requirements you can think of, which have to be added. Also, the alternatives should be structured using numbers for each step.

However, this small example already shows key features of use cases. First off, the use case presents requirements in context. Instead of listing isolated statements of system requirements, the use cases package requirements in stories, so-called Flows, which make up the Flow of Events.

A Flow is a description of a partial path through the use case description. The Flow of Events describes the entire set of use case flows.

The Basic Flow describes the simplest and most straightforward way possible to achieve the use case's observable value. An Alternative Flow, as the name suggests, relates an alternative flow to the basic flow. They should always be written in a style that indicates

(a) to what step in the basic or any other alternative flow they relate to,
(b) under what condition or based on what event this alternative would be chosen,
(c) enumerating the steps that are different from the basic or other alternative flow they relate to, and
(d) where in the basic or other alternative flow the events would resume afterwards.

The flow of events makes up the complete picture of all possible behaviour the system supports. Particular flows can then be combined into scenarios that represent exactly one path through the flows, helping to explore one concrete case covered by the use case at a time. Scenarios are not explicitly represented in a use case spec, but can be derived from it.

A Scenario is a specific instance or occurrence of a use case flow of events.

Applying Use Cases

In conclusion, you can say that use cases group together all possible stories that put system requirements in logical sequences describing how to achieve (and even not achieve) a goal. As you will partly see in subsequent sections, this is not only important for requirements elicitation and validation—to set focus and to establish a context enabling stakeholders to understand the requirements better—but also for many other disciplines of software engineering (*see also* Kruchten 2000, Kroll and Kruchten 2003).

- *Project planning and management:* Use cases help you to scope your project, that is, deciding on priorities of requirements and change requests, by discussing values and goals addressed by the use cases. You also use the priorities to plan and assess iterative development activities of the flows of your use cases (*see* Royce 1998). Realising use case flows as milestones of iterations ensures that at any time all milestones result into a system that delivers value to stakeholders for their review.

Browse Catalog

Brief Description

The <Buyer> browses through the complete list of offered BAOS publications, can search and display a sub-set of this list by keywords, and display product details of each publication. The user can select publications to be placed in a "shopping basket" for later order.

Flow of Events

Basic Flow

The use case starts when the <Buyer> selects the BAOS catalog.
1. The system displays all *publications* available. It displays for each *publication* a *unique identifier*, its *title*, and *price*.
2. The <Buyer> enters and submits a *search text* to filter the displayed list of publications.
3. The system displays a filtered list of *publications* that only show entries that have the *search keyword* as a substring in the *title field*.
4. The <Buyer> selects one *publication* to review its details.
5. The system displays the details of the *publication*. It displays the *unique identifier*, the first *author*, the *title*, the *publisher*, and the *type* of the publication, and the *price*.
The use case ends.

Alternative Flows

<Buyer> adds publication to shopping basket

After Step 5, the <Buyer> selects the displayed publication to be placed into the shopping basket. The system adds the publication to the shopping basket.
The use case resumes in Step 3.

<Buyer> sets a new filter

After Step 3, the <Buyer> can set a new filter. The system displays the newly filtered list.
The use case ends or resumes in Step 4.

<Buyer> requests to see the complete *publications* list again

After Step 5, the <Buyer> requests to display the whole paged list of publications again.
The use case resumes in Step 1.

Special Requirements

Performance

The system response in Step 3 must not take longer than 5 seconds.

Business Rules

The shopping basket cannot contain more than 10 items or items with a total value of more than 500 Euro.

Preconditions

None: The use case can be performed any time.

Postconditions

Publications list displayed
Publications details displayed

FIGURE 12.4   Use case specification for "Browse Catalog"

- *Analysis and design:* Will be discussed in the next sections.
- *Testing:* Use cases allow you to systematically derive test cases from the requirements by means of analysing use case scenarios and finding representative sets of input values for the conditions of alternative flows (*see* Heumann 2001 *and* Chapter 14, Use Cases, Test Cases by Ian Alexander).
- *Documentation:* If you look at how today's manuals and online help are organised, you see that they are structured based on what a user wants to achieve with the software. If I look, for instance, at the online help of the text processor I used to write this chapter, I see sections such as "Creating a document", "Moving around in documents", "Automatically correct text as you type", and so on. I am not saying that you should copy-and-paste your use cases to get to your online documentation, but that use cases serve as an excellent starting point for the organisational structure of your documentation. Moreover, if you see other forms of documentation delivered for software these days: a tutorial is a collection of use case scenarios demonstrating the key values of the software to the user.

A more complete introduction to use cases for requirements management and especially use case writing would be out of the scope of this chapter. However, I will get back to the use case of Figure 12.4 discussing its structure and contents in the context of performing its analysis and design in subsequent sections. See Bittner and Spence (2003) for an excellent textbook on use case modelling and writing.

Object-Oriented Analysis with Use Cases

In this section, I describe the activities to systematically create software system analysis and design models from a use case specification. As described above, we take prioritised flows of use cases as separate units of analysis, design, and implementation in iterative development to ensure that the system we construct iteratively provides the important goals first—especially when they are associated with technical risks—before we deal with the less important ones (Kruchten 2000, Kroll and Kruchten 2003). You will see that certain use case characteristics and styles directly support analysis and design. The focus for the following sections is to look at the role use cases play for analysis and design. This chapter cannot provide a detailed introduction into object-oriented analysis and design; see instead Jacobson et al. (1998), Conallen (2002), Eeles et al. (2002), RUP (2003). For recent developments in Jacobson's thinking on Use Cases, see Jacobson (2003a) and Jacobson (2003b).

The goal of object-oriented use case analysis and design is to transform the "black box" use case specifications into a "white box" use case realisations.

> *A use case realisation describes how a particular use case is realised within the analysis and/or design model, in terms of classes and collaborations between these classes that exactly support the behaviour specified in the use cases.*

Whereas an analysis model represents essential and technology-independent abstractions of the solution focusing on concepts of the business domain and the behaviour specified in the use cases, the design model includes concrete technology and design decisions representing an abstraction of the implementation. Its models comprise abstraction of concrete technology such as a J2EE session bean components or .NET Active Server pages. Whereas working on the analysis model has an emphasis on functional requirements ("getting the behaviour right"), the design model also systematically deals with non-functional requirements ("getting the quality right"[4]) on top of the functional requirements.

UML Representation of Use Case Interactions

So, how would you get started transforming our use case from Figure 12.4 into a use case realisation? A common starting point is to systematically explore the information contained in the use case and to project this information onto conceptual representations.

You can see an example of such a representation in Figure 12.5. It shows a UML sequence diagram for our use case's black box interactions between actor and system. Each pair of messages represents one round trip of events in which the actor provides a stimulus or input and gets a response or output back from the system. The use case text has been used to annotate these round trips, which makes the diagram a so-called scripted sequence diagram. Because these round trips of events denoted in the diagram play an important role for many design decisions later on, use case authors often write their flow of events with such a diagram in mind. You see from the diagram's script that every numbered step in my use case also maps to such a round trip in Figure 12.5.

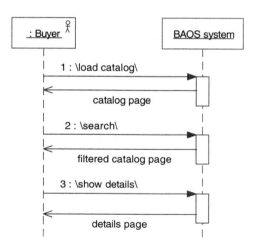

FIGURE 12.5   Scripted sequence diagram showing black box specification of "Browse Catalog" use case

---

[4] Which is in most cases dependent on the technology you apply: For example, you tweak performance by choosing for specific component types and configuration settings for your middle tier server, or reliability with replication and redundancy features supported by certain server technologies, usability by applying certain styles and UI paradigms of a specific UI technology (standardised design principles and guidelines for Windows forms are quite different than for web forms), and so on

User Experience Modelling

Just to provide you with one example of how this structure supports design decisions, let's have a look at the user experience model in Figure 12.6, also directly derived from the use case's flow of events. This type of model is particularly popular in web development projects.

> *The User-Experience (UX) Model describes the user-experience elements of the system (the screens and input forms), the dynamic content that appears on the elements, and how the user navigates through the elements to execute the system functionality.*

For a detailed introduction to UX Modelling see (Conallen 2002, RUP 2003).
How concrete should use cases be? There is a dilemma here,

- Many development teams decide that their use cases have to be kept general enough to be realised with different UI design paradigms;
- but also concrete enough to provide all essential requirements (e.g. inputs, outputs, business rules, and quality) for the application design.

Teams often create and maintain a separate user experience model in conjunction with use cases as well as screen mock-ups. Such a model is (still) a black box representation of the system helping to improve

(a) stakeholders' understanding of requirements, making the system specification more tangible with a concrete flow of screens and

(b) the conceptual design of consistent screen and navigation flows for the application's user interface (UI).

The idea here is to separate UI design from requirements, but also to use these in synergy to improve requirements and UI design as well as consistency.

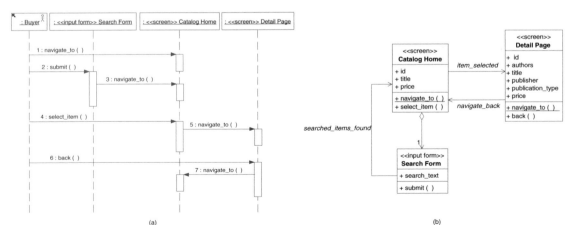

FIGURE 12.6 A user experience model. a. Use case storyboard and b. Resulting navigation map

The UX model represents the concrete UI design that is sometimes necessary to communicate how the system is really going to look like. It is owned by a special group of creative designers who are generally responsible for creating the look-and-feel of the application, and the navigation routes and contents of the pages. The UX model is used as a conceptual, UML-based plan to design concrete forms and screens, which in turn are used like storyboards to validate the requirements with stakeholders.

Figure 12.6 shows the UML representation that is then normally related to physical screen designs or mock-ups. As in most UML models the UX model also consists of a dynamic (Figure 12.6a) as well as a static model (Figure 12.6b). The diagram on the left depicts a use case storyboard that again could have been scripted with the use case flows. You could say that it details the system object of Figure 12.5 with the flow of concrete screens and forms to be used to realise the use case. The class diagram on the right represents the so-called navigation map that is produced for each individual use case, but also continuously integrated with the global navigation maps representing the combination of all use cases. Classes represent Screens and Forms in a navigation map. Screens present system outputs and Forms are reusable parts of this output, which in turn accept input from users. Associations represent paths to navigate from on screen to the next. You can see that for the "Browse Catalog" use case I decided to use two screens: one showing the unfiltered and filtered catalog information and the other for the details of a particular publication. The form capturing search input from the user has been aggregated to the catalog screen (to be designed as a search-text field and submit action perhaps somewhere on the side or top of the catalog list). A stakeholder review of this model and use case could now result in a decision that searching should also be possible from the detail screen. This decision would lead to an additional alternative flow in the use case, as well as an additional aggregation association between "Detail Screen" and "Search Form".

You can see from this last example that systematic walkthroughs of use cases with UX models can be used not only to validate, but also to refine use case specifications by eliciting new requirements such as by defining and exploring alternative flows. An interdisciplinary team can quickly relate to a story-bound application, can identify missing steps in the use case specification, and can validate inputs and outputs for completeness and consistency with the desired workflow. The team can equally well exploit the use case to help verify that the screens and forms of the UX model cover all flows by checking input and outputs (class attributes) and interactions (class operations and associations).

Use Case Analysis Overview

Moving on in the use case analysis, utilising the use case specification, scripted sequence diagrams, and the UX model (or a subset of these), the designer can now systematically map the use case to a set of standard abstractions representing system internal white box objects, and distribute the behaviour described in the use case's flow of events to collaborations between these objects.

The RUP defines three commonly used[5] class stereotypes to use for this mapping always resulting to a variation of the so-called "Duck on Skis"-diagram for use cases as depicted in Figure 12.7:

---

[5] For example, see the UML specification 1.5 (OMG and IBM Rational 2003) which defines these stereotypes in the example UML profile for software development.

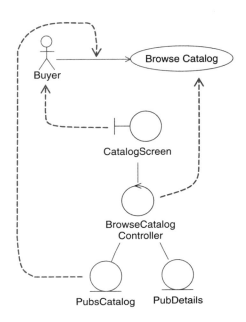

FIGURE 12.7 Use case analysis — mapping use case elements to standard abstractions

- ≪*Boundary*≫ *classes:* representing the interfaces to the outside world (either to a human actor's interfaces derived from the screens of the UX model or interfaces/APIs to actors representing external systems). Figure 12.7 shows the "CatalogScreen" as an example for a boundary analysis class.
- ≪*Controller*≫ *class:* representing the use case's actual flow of events, that is, the functional behaviour expressed by a set of operations mapping the use case's input/output round trips. It is a recommended practice of use case-based analysis and design to identify one main controller per use case. Figure 12.7 shows "BrowseCatalogController" as an example for a controller analysis class.
- ≪*Entity*≫ *classes:* representing the inputs and outputs of the use case, that is, the data flowing into the system and out of the system. Figure 12.7 depicts "PubsCatalog" and "PubDetails" as examples for entity analysis classes.

As indicated above, controllers represent use case-specific behaviour aiming to provide an overview of the system responsibilities or services that need to be realised or made available for the use case. Boundaries and especially entities are modelled with the perspective to use them in more then one use case realisations. For example, it is likely that the data abstraction "PubDetails" will also be used in the realisation for the "Checkout" and "Maintain Shopping Cart" use cases.

Use Case Analysis Dynamic View: Distribute Use Case Behaviour

Thus, after this first step of identifying these static abstractions, your second step of the analysis is walking through the use case specification round trips and distributing the use case behaviour to the classes by assigning responsibilities. Behaviour is best represented with the UML's interaction diagrams such as sequence or collaboration diagrams. As you saw in Figure 12.5 there are three round trips in the use case's basic flow: "load the catalog", "search", and "show details". The procedure for distributing responsibilities for these three round trips is determined by following the stereotypes:

- Boundaries take commands and input from actors and forward them to the controller for processing.
- The controller uses entities to persist and/or retrieve data to deliver output to a boundary for display to an actor.

Figure 12.8 shows the resulting sequence diagram after distributing the three round trips for the "Browse Catalog" basic flow to the abstractions of Figure 12.7 (plus another boundary added for the publication details transforming our duck into a duck with two heads).

For example, the use case's first round trip describes how a catalog page is retrieved, labelled as a "load()" command issued by the actor through the user interface (probably by typing the URL of our sales webpage). That is delegated by the boundary "CatalogScreen" representing this page to the controller via the "getCatalog()" responsibility. That in turn retrieves the requested information from the entity "PubsCatalog".

The result is then displayed in the same boundary from which the initial request came, via the "displayTitles()" responsibility. As you can see, all three round trips of our case study use case describe simple, technology-independent data retrieval operations, and thus all look very similar in their realisation.

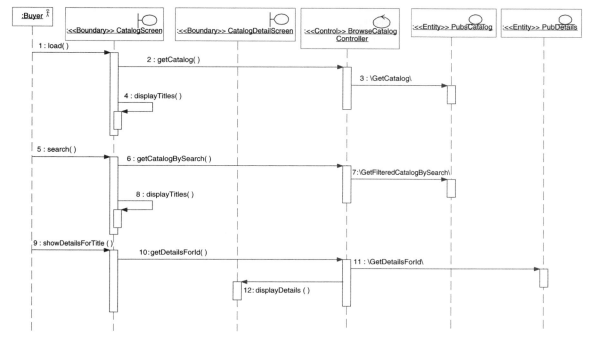

FIGURE 12.8 Allocating use case behaviour to analysis class responsibilities in sequence diagrams

Use Case Analysis Static View: Describe Relationships, Responsibilities, Attributes

The third step in use case analysis is to update your classes as depicted in Figure 12.9, with the responsibilities and relationships identified in the sequence diagram.

As a result, responsibilities are added as operations. When one class calls another class's responsibility, a relationship between the two classes is added. Between classes with different stereotypes it does not really matter at this point if you use associations (expressing a structural relationship) or dependencies (expressing local-variable or parameter-usage relationships). This will change during design anyway depending on the technology and design mechanisms used to realise these abstractions. Nevertheless, it is important to capture that these classes need to know each other to design their relationship appropriately. On the other hand, relationships between classes of the same stereotype, especially for the entity classes, represent important analysis results (as you will see in Figure 12.10). Figure 12.9 shows the extended "duck-on-skis" resulting after this step, which actually many UML design tools generate automatically or semi-automatically from the sequence or collaboration diagrams.

Looking at this diagram and comparing it against the use case text from Figure 12.4, you can see that you so far mapped the dynamics, but not all the static requirements expressed in the use case to your classes. For example, for "Step 1", we realised the *"The system displays the first page of all publications available."* part with the association between the "CatalogScreen" and the "BrowseCatalogController" and a dependency to "PubsCatalog" representing the data retrieved and presented, as well as the operations "CatalogScreen::load()", "BrowseCatalogController::getCatalogPage()", and "CatalogScreen::displayTitle()".

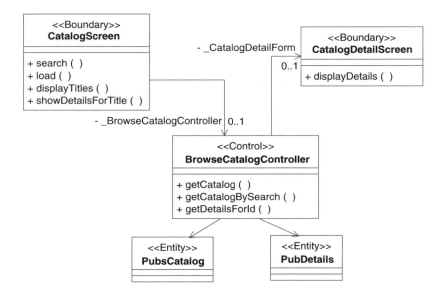

FIGURE 12.9   Analysis class diagram derived from sequence diagram in Figure 12.8

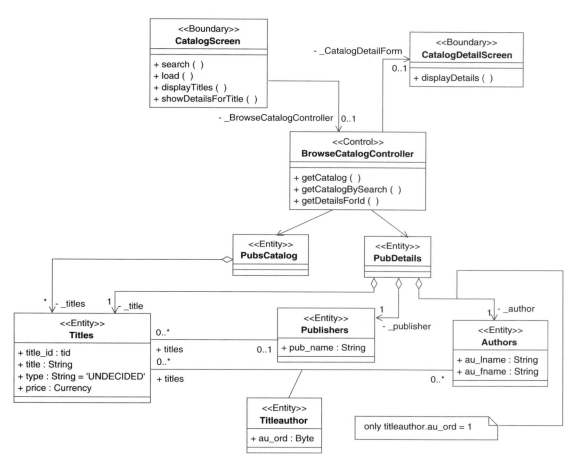

FIGURE 12.10 The completed participants class diagram after analysing "Browse Catalog"'s Basic Flow

The second sentence of "Step 1": "*It displays for each publication a unique identifier, its title, and price.*" is not yet mapped into the model. First, you might want to argue if this information is actually to be found in the use case specification or not. Clearly, different use case writing styles might factor these requirements into a separate section (data requirements) or completely different supplementary specification documents; or keep this information just as part of the User Experience model[6]. Nevertheless, although it is not important where we get this information from, detailed data specifications are

---

[6] Another style I discovered in the field with more classical Structured Analysis educated system analysts is to only capture data requirements in the analysis model itself. However, my experience shows that it is advantageous to capture data in the requirements specification or at least the user experience model, because these representations are much easier to understand for stakeholders who have to review, validate, and decide on these requirements.

essential for analysis. Therefore, you work with these requirements in the fourth step of analysis by refining the model to include an actual structure (in terms of associations and attributes) of how publications need to be represented in the system. This is the really creative part of the analysis. Whereas before, we performed a standard mapping from the use case to classes, we now need to make decisions on how to represent the data, that is, organise our entities. You cannot make good decisions based on one flow of one use case, because you want to structure the data to fit the requirements of all use cases that make use of it. However, you need to start somewhere, and other steps of the analysis deal with the integration of different use case results. Further, during design you will make more changes to these structures to meet non-functional requirements and technology-specific constraints. Thus, Figure 12.10 shows my initial decisions applying perhaps also a bit of foresight on what else will have to be realised with these entities.

This lower part of the model in Figure 12.10 comprising of new entities will evolve, in comparison to more classical data modelling techniques, into the so-called logical data model which is the basis for data-related modelling in design. Your ultimate verification step (especially after making changes while integrating with other use case analysis results) is to walk through the use cases to verify that the classes indeed support the specified behaviour.

As a result, what you see in Figure 12.10 is the UML class diagram representing the static structures needed to support the use case "Browse Catalog". Such a use case–specific diagram is also called the *Participants* diagram.

Your fifth step in the analysis is to integrate this participants diagram with the other participants' diagrams in so-called Analysis Elements diagrams. However, because we only have space to work on one use case in this chapter, refer to RUP (2003), Eeles et al. (2002) for examples on this step.

Managing and Tracing Analysis Results

As you can see from this small example, you will generate quite a few diagrams showing your analysis results from different viewpoints (such as dynamic and static). You will do this for every use case you analyse. To control complexity and to maintain traceability to your use cases, you should set up a canonical model structure for your diagrams and model elements. The UML supports this with the concepts of Package and Collaboration. Good design tools support hierarchical displays, allowing you to set up such data structures, as shown in Figure 12.11.

As you can see in Figure 12.11 the analysis model is structured into two main packages,

- *Analysis elements package:* Representing the integrated static structure view on our analysis results. Although Figure 12.11 only shows the results after analysis of "Browse Catalog", this package will always contain the continuously integrated results after merging all the use cases analysis results currently available. This ensures that analysis of the next use case will reuse and update the existing classes, and avoid reinventing abstractions already present.
- *Analysis use case realisations package:* Representing a view of each use case including the use case-specific static participants diagrams as well as dynamic interaction diagrams. These diagrams refer to model elements maintained in

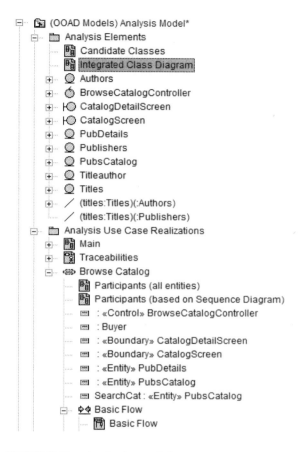

FIGURE 12.11   Analysis model structure

the Analysis Elements package, which has the advantage that when classes are updated based on the analysis of other use cases, the updates are reflected in classes participating in the use cases already analysed. The results of every use case analysis are organised as part of a use case realisation that has the same name as the use case for traceability reasons. As you can see in Figure 12.11, the "Browse Catalog" use case realisation (modelled as an UML collaboration instance) consists of its participant diagrams (shown in Figures 12.9 and 12.10) as well as an Interaction Instance for the use case's basic flow, and a sequence diagram as well as the objects being presented in the sequence diagram.

It is important that a project-wide model structure guideline exists, to provide a well-defined way of organising the 'electronic filing cabinet' of UML diagrams. I have seen many projects where the lack of such a uniform guideline has not only led to the loss of traceability, but also to the loss of analysis or design results, because they were hidden somewhere deep down in an undocumented package hierarchy.

Object-Oriented Design with Use Cases

Let's move on a step further in software development, and discuss how to design our use case "Browse Catalog" based on the analysis results presented in the last section. The objective is to map the analysis results to a concrete technology-specific realisation, covering both functional and non-functional requirements, and design constraints. To save space, I will only describe the mapping of the functional requirements into technology. I have chosen to use the .NET framework, with ASP .NET as the solution technology for our sales web application.

Software Architecture and Use Cases

To cover the mapping of non-functional requirements and to truly understand the decision-making activities conducted during software design, we would have to define Software Architecture first.

> *Software Architecture encompasses the set of significant decisions about the organisation of a software system.*

Unfortunately, architecture is beyond the scope of this chapter. Again, see RUP (2003), Eeles et al. (2002), Conallen (2002).

However, because architecture is seen as a non-trivial task, one can find many *OOAD stakeholders* offering ways of reusing architecture in specific domains and technologies. These reuse strategies are normally described as architectural frameworks and design patterns. They are often delivered by technology providers to help make their technologies successful[7]. See for example the J2EE technology in Alur et al. (2003); .NET technology at Microsoft (2003), Fowler (2002) covering both.

Typical enterprise application architectures are very often organised in layers of concern, for example, separating presentation from business logic from data storage and access. The question of interest in this section is: How do we map use cases into such a solution structure? In Figure 12.12 we see that all parts of the use case can have an influence on all parts of the architecture. This also means that a change in a use case (e.g. a new field to be shown in the details screen) will trigger changes in all these levels in all possible packages. Therefore, we need to find a way to organise our Design Use Case Realisations to keep trace of what part exactly is being designed for what use case requirement. Of course, we are going to do this via the Analysis Use Case Realisations: Tracing to the use case from the analysis model from the design model.

Use Case Design Overview

In use case design, we systematically transform and refine the analysis classes captured in our analysis use case realisation to technology-specific design classes. Looking at our analysis model results of Figure 12.10 and the layers of Figure 12.12 you might think the mapping is obvious: let's put the boundaries into the presentation tier, controller into the business layer, and entities in the data access layer. Unfortunately, it is not

---

[7] Successful in respect to concerns such as resilience of the application, cost of change and extensions, facilitation of reuse, realisation of a large set of *standard* non-functional requirements, and many, many more.

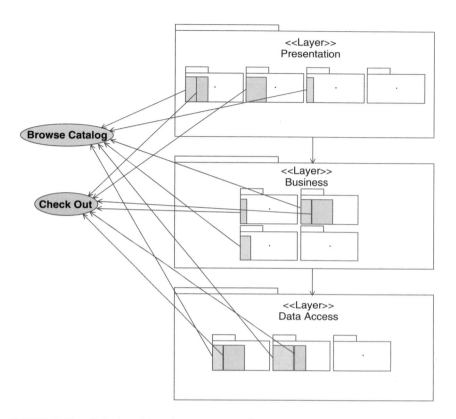

FIGURE 12.12   Relationship of use cases to layered architecture

that straightforward. As with the use cases, can all parts of the analysis model have an influence on all parts of the architecture? Consider for example entities: They have an influence on the design of all layers and the interactions between them. Publication catalog data (Entity "PubCatalog") is needed in the presentation tier, because it has to be displayed on the screens. It is processed in the business layer (e.g. if you would extend your use case to calculate rebates on the prices for a particular category of customers). It is accessed in the database and defines the structure of the database schema (not represented in Figure 12.12). Also, to be able to send the data from the database over the internet to the COM+ MTS application server executing the business logic and from there to the IIS web server using .NET Remoting, another representation of the "PubsCatalog" entity is needed to support this.

To clarify this point I already present in Figure 12.13 some final design results. This traceability diagram shows how your analysis classes have been mapped to respective design classes. Here you see the mapping of "PubsCatalog" to database tables, an ASP .NET Server Page (containing controls to present the data; not shown), as well as a class Common::PubsCatalog that represents an ADO .NET dataset for transfer between servers utilising XML. The "BrowseCatalogController" also has been *split* into three classes covering two different concerns: presentation specific logic and business specific

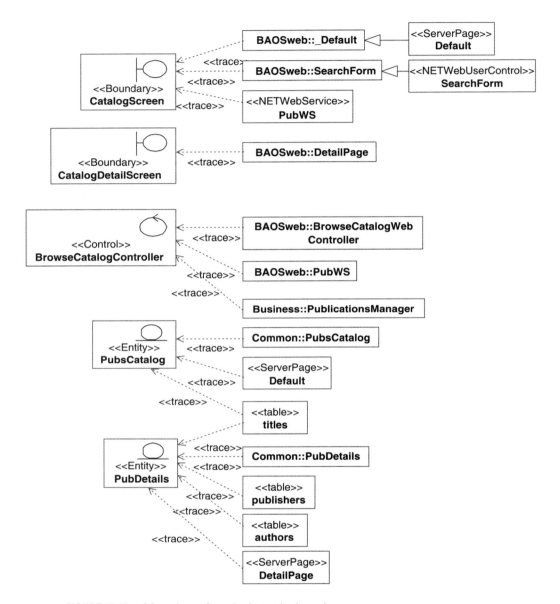

FIGURE 12.13 Mapping of analysis to design classes

logic. The "BrowseCatalogWebContoller" represents the logic realising the navigation flow in the web application, for example, which screen to use for which presentation in which particular order, which business component to contact to get business logic processed, and so on. A windows forms user interface would do things quite different. Thus, you would like to separate presentation from business logic to increase reusability of the business part. This type of presentation logic is also completely different for an application interface providing web services, which also has been model in Figure 12.13 with the "PubWS" class. Web services are intended not to provide a user interface, but an application interface for catalog functionality over an HTTP protocol[8]. The other concern of representing the pure business logic for browsing the catalog independent of the presentation form is realised with the "PublicationsManager" component that we design in the next section. Finally, if you remember that boundaries do not only represent UI responsibilities, but are also used to model APIs to access external systems (not the case for "Browse Catalog"), you can also see that these sometimes need to be mapped to design on different levels of the architecture than the presentation tier.

To design a use case realisation, you start by identifying design elements as we just discussed and presented in Figure 12.13 and then continue to systematically transform analysis elements of your analysis use case realisation with these design elements. You will do this now for "Browse Catalog" bottom-up, that is, specify and refine a design element representing a business component[9] in the next section and then in the following section replace elements of our analysis model with this component and other design elements. Surely, this could also be done the other way round: top-down. This is merely a matter of preference (as well as availability of already designed model elements) and normally performed in a more intertwined way.

Component Design

Components represent the realisation of sub-systems for software applying the principles of encapsulation to minimise dependencies between different parts of the application to achieve more resilience; for example in respect to change impact. Therefore, software components constitute black boxes providing realisations for functions and non-functions. As for all systems, we produce specification and realisation documentation for components. Hence, we could actually draw a use case diagram for our component "PublicationsManager" and describe in a use case specification round trips of an actor (in this case a class from the ASP .NET user interface) calling the component. A more popular, but less goal-oriented way as use cases, for representing component specifications, is depicted in Figure 12.14.

Figure 12.14 presents the black box specification of our component defining its interface "IPublicationsManager", which as for every system interface describes input-output transformations, is this case using UML operation declarations. The "PublicationsManager" sub-system is represented as a package realising the interface that contains the white box model elements doing the actual work of providing catalog data in a paged and searchable manner. These elements are developed with analysis and design activities in a very similar way as we discussed throughout this and the last section for the overall "Browse Catalog" use case and omitted for space reasons. See (Cheesman and Daniels 2001) for an excellent discussion on software components, their specification, and realisation with UML.

---

[8] You see two classes called PubWS, one representing the web service controller (would be realised with a .NET asmx.cs file), the other the application interface mapped to the boundary (would be realised with an .asmx file).

[9] To save space, we start in the middle layer and omit the data access layer.

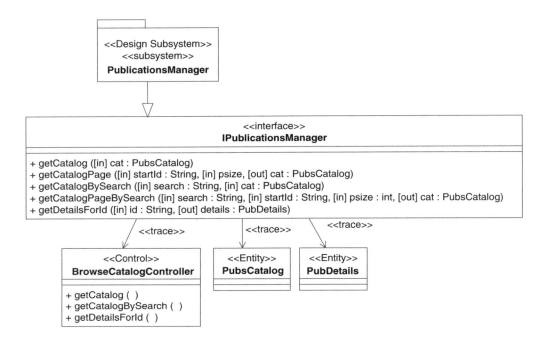

FIGURE 12.14 A component specification

UI Design and Completing the Design Use Case Realisation

In this final section, you will now put a user interface on top of the "PublicationsManager" component. We do this by taking the analysis model elements and transforming them to the design elements of Figure 12.13 resulting in updated interaction and participants diagrams. The way the design elements in Figure 12.13 had been actually identified was by applying several design patterns from (Microsoft 2003) ["Model-View-Controller with ASP .NET" and "Data Transfer Object"] and (Fowler 2002) ["Application Controller"]. An architect's responsibility is to select the appropriate set of patterns to be used for use case design in a repeatable and predictable fashion and documenting them as so-called *Design Mechanisms* (RUP 2003). Using the same mechanisms for similar design tasks in every use case ensures maintainability of the design as well as centralises architectural decision-making ensuring that not every designer invents his own solutions.

Figure 12.15 depicts the updated sequence diagram after incorporating the design elements and patterns. Our actor Buyer interacts with classes representing ASP .NET code-behind pages classes[10], which in turn interact with the "BrowseCatalogWebController" class. The web controller class uses the "PublicationsManager" to interface with the business component discussed in the last section.

---

[10] ASP .NET defines for a server page two classes: one class for the HTML presentation content as well as a second class, called code-behind class the first one derives from through specialisation, for event-handling and dynamic presentation generation.

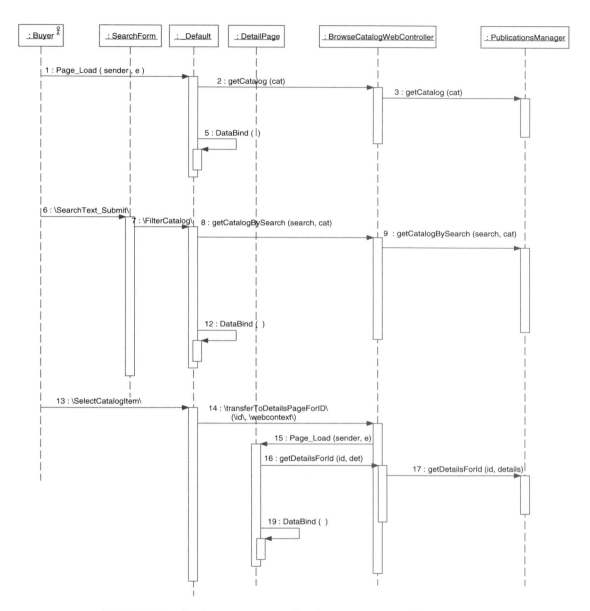

FIGURE 12.15   Design use case realisation — sequence diagram

Figure 12.16 shows the updated participants diagram. It presents the classes from Figure 12.13 as well as resulting relationships from the sequence diagram. For example, we see that relationships had to be added in our design such as associations of the ASP .NET pages' code-behind classes to the dataset classes "PubsCatalog" and "PubsDetails". These classes contain the data the "PublicationsManager" component retrieved from the

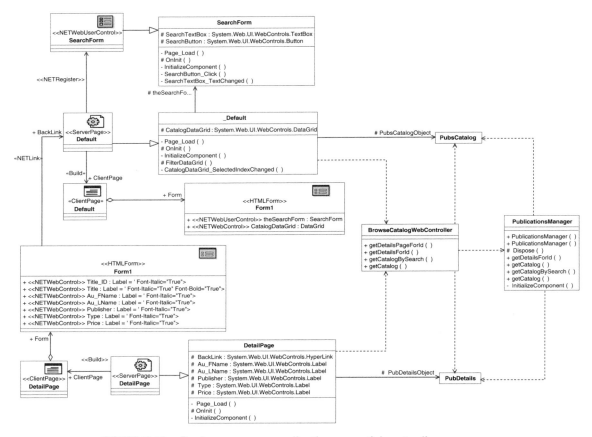

FIGURE 12.16 Design use case realisation — participants diagram

database that has to be displayed in our pages and therefore have to be accessible in the code-behind classes for presentation generation and event-handling operations.

To cut this technical discussion short, we see in these two diagrams that the essential analysis model has been transformed and extended for the concrete technical platform they are supporting. It is now imperative to verify that the "Browse Catalog" use case is still fully supported as specified after all these changes by reviewing sequence and class diagrams against the use case specification with a walkthrough. Finally, the implementation derived from this design will be tested against scenarios of the use case as well.

SUMMARY AND COMPARISONS

This concludes this chapter in which I walked you through analysis and design with use cases. My intention was to provide system analysts with a basic understanding of what designers actually do with their use case artefacts to improve their ability to include them as an intended audience for their use case writing.

In contrast to many of the scenario and storytelling techniques presented in other chapters of this book, use cases represent a compromise between formality and natural language expressiveness. Kent Beck's use of stories in Extreme Programming (Beck 2000, and *see* Chapter 13 of this volume) is a more informal and more 'agile' approach. This compromise is between facilitating interdisciplinary communication on the one hand, and providing enough structure to drive software development activities (such as user-experience modelling, analysis, and design) systematically on the other.

In addition, unlike scenarios and stories, use cases focus on actor values and are therefore not decomposed into smaller parts that would not have that focus, and which would be hard to understand, to see the rationale for, to verify, and to validate. Consequently, analysts—not users or customers themselves—need to write the use cases, but users must still be able to relate to them and perhaps claim intellectual ownership of them. To encourage such an understanding within the interdisciplinary development team, a use case writing style guide should be established formalising the way use cases steps are written, flows are structured, glossary terms are referenced, and so on.

Several of the elicitation techniques described in other chapters of this book can and should be applied to get to the actual use cases and to improve them. For example, Ellen Gottesdiener's use case workshops (Chapter 5), Karen Holtzblatt's contextual inquiry (Chapter 10), and Neil Maiden's scenario walkthroughs (Chapter 9) are all valuable techniques.

KEYWORDS

Use Cases	Object-Orientation	Design	Model-Driven Development
Requirements	Analysis	UML	Rational Unified Process

REFERENCES

Alur, D., Crupi, J., and Malks, D., *Core J2EE Patterns*, 2nd ed., Sun Microsystems Press, Prentice Hall, 2003.

Beck, K., *Extreme Programming Explained*, Addison-Wesley, 2000.

Beyer, H. and Holtzblatt, K., *Contextual Design: Defining Customer-Centered Systems*, Morgan Kaufmann Publishers, 1997.

Bittner, K. and Spence, I., *Use Case Modeling*, Addison-Wesley, 2003.

Cantor, M., *Rational Unified Process for Systems Engineering*, The Rational Edge, August–October 2003, www.therationaledge.com

Cheesman, J. and Daniels, J., *UML Components: A Simple Process for Specifying Component-Based Software*, Addison-Wesley Longman, 2001.

Conallen, J., *Building Web Applications with UML*, 2nd ed., Addison-Wesley, 2002.

Eeles, P., Houston, K., and Kozaczynski, W., *Building J2EE Applications with the Rational Unified Process*, Addison-Wesley, 2002.

Fowler, M., *Patterns of Enterprise Application Architecture*, Addison-Wesley, 2002.

Heumann, J., *Generating Test Cases From Use Cases*, The Rational Edge, June 2001, www.therationaledge.com

Jacobson, I., *Use Cases—Yesterday, Today, and Tomorrow*, The Rational Edge, March 2003a, www.therationaledge.com

Jacobson, I., Use cases and aspects—working seamlessly together, *Journal of Object Technology*, **2**(2), 7–28, 2003b, http://www.jot.fm/issues/issue_2003_07/column1

Jacobson, I., Booch, G., and Rumbaugh, J., *The Unified Software Development Process*, Addison-Wesley Longman, 1998.

Kruchten, P., *The Rational Unified Process: An Introduction*, Addison-Wesley, 2000

Kroll, P. and Kruchten, P., *The Rational Unified Process Made Easy: A Practitioner's Guide to Rational Unified Process*, Addison-Wesley, 2003.

Microsoft, *Enterprise Solution Patterns Using Microsoft.NET*, 2003, http://msdn.microsoft.com/practices/type/Patterns/Enterprise/

OMG and IBM Rational, *Unified Modeling Language Specification*, Version 1.5, 2003, http://www.rational.com/uml

Royce, W., *Software Project Management: A Unified Framework*, Addison-Wesley Longman, 1998.

RUP 2003.06, *Rational Unified Process*, IBM Rational Software, 2003.

RUP SE v2.0 2003.06, *Rational Unified Process for Systems Engineering Plug-In*, Rational Developer Network (www.rational.net), IBM Rational Software, 2003.

Yu, E., Towards modelling and reasoning support for early-phase requirements engineering, *Proceedings of the 3rd IEEE International Symposium on Requirements Engineering (RE '97)*, Washington, DC, January 6–8, 1997, pp. 226–235

RECOMMENDED READING

(*Self-Reference*) The diagrams in this chapter were created with IBM Rational XDE Developer for Visual Studio .NET 2003.06. These models and the executable code in C# as well as VB .NET code for this example can be downloaded from http://haumer.net/rational/BAOS/

(Bittner and Spence 2003) A comprehensive coverage of use case techniques and practices for requirements management, including useful examples showing how use case specifications evolve over time.

(Eeles et al. 2002) An example-based introduction to RUP and in particular OOAD for designing J2EE applications.

(Conallen 2002) An excellent introduction to the basics of web application development in the context of the RUP. This book also shows how to use the UML and RUP's OOAD workflow to model web applications, introduces the Web Application Extension to the UML used in the design diagrams of this chapter, as well as user experience modelling.

(Jacobson 2003) describes how use cases naturally support Aspect-Oriented Programming (AOP). He explains how use cases represent the "crosscutting concerns" of aspect-orientation, because they will be realised throughout the solution. Thus, a use case realisation represents one "aspect" of the architecture, that is, a modular unit of crosscutting implementation. Download this paper to learn how the things you learned here fit with this new trend in software engineering.

CHAPTER 13

USER STORIES IN AGILE SOFTWARE DEVELOPMENT

Kent Beck[1] and David West[2]

[1] *Three Rivers Institute, Oregon, USA*
[2] *New Mexico Highlands University, New Mexico, USA*

A **STORY** is just a story, but a *user* story is key for extreme programming (and agile software development). A user story is distinct from similar techniques (scenarios and use cases) because it is always told from the point of view of the user, not the developer.

A user story begins as text-on-a-card but its life extends throughout development as the on-site customer and the developers engage in dialog that confirms, evaluates, expands, and modifies the original story premise. Users can become more proficient at telling stories, and developers in listening to stories, by recognizing some basic story categories.

APPLICABILITY

User stories are appropriate, applicable and essential to every type of software application—from embedded safety critical systems to prosaic back office accounting systems. Despite the doubts advanced by traditional software engineers, user stories (and XP and Agile methods in general) are appropriate for projects at any level of scale.

While it may appear that the assertions in the previous paragraph are a bit extreme or extravagant, a bit of reflection brings the recognition: if a system has users, those users must communicate their expectations and needs and they will do so by telling you stories. Even if a user handed you a nonstory based document like a flow chart, data flow diagram, or entity relation diagram and said, "build this," it is unlikely that such a document would be sufficient specification. They would also proceed to tell you stories about what the document really means to them and how they want you to interpret the document.

All software development is a human activity (as yet) and is therefore dependent on individuals and small groups. The organization of those groups and techniques to facilitate communication among members of those groups is paramount to the success

Scenarios, Stories, Use Cases: Through the Systems Development Life-Cycle. Edited by Ian F Alexander and Neil Maiden
© 2004 John Wiley & Sons, Ltd. ISBN: 0-470-86194-0

of the project. Agile methods, and XP in particular, provide tools and techniques for maximizing individual and small-group success—and user stories are an integral part of those tools and techniques. The fact that very large projects, with geographically dispersed teams, might need additional support mechanisms is a red herring—it does not obviate the need for agility and for communication tools like user stories.

If the term 'applicability' is substituting for the term 'sufficiency'—that is, for what types of applications are user stories sufficient?—a slightly different response is required. User stories are not sufficient in any organization in which management style and culture mandates more formal documentation or any organization that believes itself[1] to be subject to externally imposed documentation standards.

Note that it is not the application type that is an issue; it is the culture and belief system of the organization in which development takes place that questions the sufficiency of user stories. If you can develop a system that has no users or in which user input is considered irrelevant, you have no need for user stories. This is not a facetious statement. There was a time when our profession developed systems for customers (those paying the bills) and actual users (seldom the customer) were not consulted, simply told, "do it—this way."

APPLICABILITY II — WHY USER STORIES?

Once upon a time (actually just a couple of decades ago) computers were wondrous and wondrously expensive things. The individuals charged with operating these behemoths were akin to priests in a glass walled temple housing "the mainframe." Business people were but humble petitioners, thankful for anything the technicians deigned to give them.

But resentment set in—the technicians "knew nothing of business" and since business was paying for systems the business people had to tell the technicians what to do instead of the other way round. The revolt of the users was successful, but only for a time because it seemed that they did not know enough about technical matters to make their desires known. An uneasy truce ensued, characterized by a strong emphasis on contracts—rigid and precisely defined requirements strictly adhered to that essentially provide little more than a means for pointing fingers when the development project inevitably failed. This unhappy state persisted "unhappily ever after."

Power—especially the imbalance of power is one of the root causes of development failure. If business folk have the upper hand, they demand unreasonable timelines and they don't eliminate scope, even less important scope, which would enable the whole team to reach those deadlines with quality. If the technical folk get the upper hand, they insist on lengthy processes focused on technical ingenuity instead of business value. What is necessary is a common currency that tends to keep both parties honest and on their toes. Enter the user story.

---

[1] Each of the XP/Agile conferences attended by the authors the past two years has featured at least one session dealing with mandated process and documentation issues (e.g. military or FDA requirements). In each case, the experts from the mandating agencies indicated that the process and documentation generated in an XP/Agile process can satisfy their agency's requirements. And yet, compliance officers in companies continue to express contrary beliefs.

User stories provide a format that is approachable for business folk while simultaneously containing enough of a reality check to keep client aspirations from spiraling off into the ether.

By starting with a low-tech format (words and sketches on index cards), we lower the barriers for business ownership of the stories. By rapidly estimating the stories and continually refining those estimates, we allow technical feedback to inform and enrich the envisioning process. Physical manipulation and public display of the stories to track progress keeps everyone on the team engaged with the stories.

User stories result in a simple, but not simplistic, meeting ground of *"desire and possibility"* in Ward Cunningham's notable phrase.

POSITION IN LIFE CYCLE

User stories are employed ***throughout*** the life cycle. That this might not be the case is because of a misunderstanding of user stories as nothing more than the index card containing a short prose paragraph. We will seek to dispel this notion in the main body of the chapter. It must also be remembered that XP/Agile are highly iterative, short cycle, practices that obscure or eliminate the kind of "discrete phases" implied for traditional development life cycles.

However, in some cases the user story takes the form of a metaphor (applied to issues of system specification and system design) or a user test (applied to integration and testing activities). Because metaphors and tests merit their own distinct label in XP/Agile, and only for this reason, we can allow that user stories are more critical in the life cycle segments indicated in boldface in the following table.

Requirements Discovery	**Requirements Validation**	System Specification	System Design	**Coding, First of Class**	Integration & Testing	**Operations & Maintenance**

KEY FEATURES

The key feature of user stories is the ***User***.

Unlike use cases and scenarios, user stories are intended to capture the voice and perspective of the user of the application or system.

User stories are expressed and documented using natural language prose: on the story card, in response to questions, and as part of the ongoing dialog with developers. Use cases and scenarios are expressed using a constrained (semi-formal) syntax. User stories are descriptive and expressive of human desires. Scenarios and use cases are specifications of object interactions. User stories contain "what" and "why;" use cases and scenarios contain "how." The key feature of user stories is the ***User***.

Typical development techniques involve the user but twice—once at project inception and again at project delivery. Project development is based only on what could be extracted from the user during the brief "requirements gathering" window—a window severely restricted in terms of time and tools[2] available. Whatever "story" the user might have told at that point in time is all you have.

XP/Agile require an on-site customer, a user, functioning as an active story-teller throughout project development. Stories are elaborated and extended and modified on the basis of the increasing sophistication and understanding of the user. Oversights and omissions are caught and corrected and the quality of requirements increases dramatically.

STRENGTHS

User stories, and the context (XP/Agile) in which they are deployed, eliminate the typical, adversarial, relationship between users and developers. The stories are a source of constant feedback and guidance from the people that will pass ultimate judgment on the success or failure of the project.

Making storytelling "official" allows both the teller and the listener to focus on developing skills in the use of stories. This is important because stories are the primary (perhaps only) means of communicating needs and desires, and providing critical feedback, to developers.

Increasing your story skills makes you a better developer—the real strength of the user story practice is the improvement in the people using the technique rather than something intrinsic to a practice, model, or tool.

WEAKNESSES

"*Tell me a story.*[3]" It seems too simple to be the basis for software development—especially since we have been telling ourselves, the past 30 years, how hard, complicated, and formalized software development "must" be.

If the two greatest strengths gained from the practice of user stories derive from giving stories official status and allowing developers to develop their human skills, the two most prominent weaknesses derive from negation of the strengths.

Stories are perceived to be too simple and too vague (they use imprecise user vernacular and ambiguous natural language). So even when they are used, there is a tendency to turn them into something they were not intended to be—a "requirement specification"—something more "software engineering-like." Storytelling is an art. Software development (traditionally) has no room for art.

---

[2] One of the best tools available for requirements gathering (both direct and indirect) is an ethnography—a period of participant observation. This tool is seldom used because it takes "too much time" and because most requirements gatherers lack adequate observation skills.

[3] Roger C. Schank wrote a wonderful book with this title—*Tell Me a Story: Narrative and Intelligence*, Northwestern University Press, 1995. The topic of that book was artificial intelligence and modeling that intelligence with hierarchically nested stories and their variants. The power of stories to capture arbitrarily complex specifications is evident in his treatment.

Storytelling relies on people. Software engineering, as a philosophy and method, seems determined to eliminate both art and people in favor of formalized (ideally automated) process and tools.

In short, the greatest weakness of user stories as a practice is its requirement for managers, users, and developers to exhibit faith in simple things, art, and people to the degree necessary for the practice to prove its effectiveness.

TECHNIQUE

Story: *"One thing that the customer wants the system to do."*

This definition (Beck 2000) is but a starting point. Once imagined, a story must be recorded, clarified, sometimes factored, developed and extended, and utilized in a series of other activities.

The user story technique is straightforward:

- The customer (user) thinks of something she wants the system to do.
- The desire is written down on an index card; given a name and a number.
- An estimate is made of how long it will take to realize the story in fully functional and releasable form.
- Stories are factored—split into smaller stories—if it appears they will take too long to implement as written.
- Stories are factored if one aspect of the story is more important than others.
- Stories are factored if they are long and rambling or overly general.
- Stories are prioritized.
- Stories are aggregated into collections, each collection defining the scope of work to be undertaken by the team this period.
- Work products are validated. Their ability to satisfy the original story is confirmed.
- The customer uses the developed system and new stories are conceived.
- Iterate.

Even the simplest technique has nuances that must be recognized, if one is to master that technique. By exploring the activities in the preceding bullet list, some heuristics can be provided that will enhance everyone's use of stories.

Users: Tellers of Stories

Users tell ALL stories. Developers may ask for a story if they think they have an idea about something the system might do or if they need clarification of some aspect of the system—but a user must actually write the story.

Stories are told (written) using natural language. The only vernacular or specialized vocabulary allowed in a story is "business" language. Almost every domain of human activity develops its own specialized linguistic extensions: special terms, acronyms, even colloquialisms and redefinitions of common words; and all of these may be employed in a story. Software developers have their own specialized jargon and, unfortunately, we have coerced users into using some of that jargon in their communications with us. But no more! Developer jargon is not to be used in stories. This means that a story, "the system will adjust COLA rates for all exempt employees," is OK; but, a story, "the UI will include a check box for COLA Y/N and a widget showing new COLA value if checked," is not OK.

A story card—a simple index card—is used to record the story. Using an index card is a heuristic that leads to good story telling. There are fairly obvious limits to the amount of prose that can fit on an index card, which encourages brevity and clarity of expression.

Story cards typically include a title for the story and a number. The title provides a handy reference label for the story and the numbers can be used to aggregate stories, for example, stories factored from the same general story.

Stories begin, but do not end with, the story card. A story card

> "... is nothing more than an agreement that the customer and the developers will talk together about a feature." (Beck and Fowler 2001)

The XP practice—on-site customer—might very well be renamed on-site storyteller. Developers engage in a continuing dialog with the customer; asking questions, restating their understanding to gain verification, and listening as the customer elaborates the original story. Elaboration may take the form of added detail or it may reveal additional stories that must be captured on a story card of their own.

Developers are not totally passive. Although they are not allowed to write stories they can suggest new stories to the customer who may find the idea worthwhile and write an appropriate story. Developers are also providing constant feedback to the customer.

Feedback definitely involves estimates—the developer telling the customer that this story will take X amount of time to complete—which the customer can use to judge whether his stories are appropriately sized. Developers also provide feedback about the "quality" of the stories, how easy or difficult they are to listen to and understand. This kind of feedback improves the customer's ability as a storyteller.

> "Don't be too impressed with your stories. Writing the stories is not the point. Communicating is the point." (Beck and Fowler 2001)

A story is the entire conversation that takes place among customers, developers, and even managers.

A story includes the contributions of all parties—not just the customer and not just that which is written down on the story card. Keith Basso is an anthropologist who studied Native American stories. He noted that published transcriptions of stories included only the narrative of the "storyteller," ignoring the responses and comments made by the audience. This omission inevitably distorted the story, sometimes inverting the actual point and meaning of the story.

If you want to be successful with user stories you must constantly remind yourself—until it is unspoken second nature—that the story card is not the story. The story is the entire conversation, only parts of which are recorded. And the recorded parts might be distributed in code, in comments, on story cards, in diagrams on a white board, or in informal notes. In fact, the only real persistent "documentation" of a story (the cards themselves can be discarded when completed) is in the code and the acceptance tests.

Story Characteristics and Typography

Telling stories is an art. People can develop their art and become better storytellers. It is also possible to become a better listener or participant in the conversation that is the true story. It is not possible to write a cookbook like

"Great User Stories in Just 30 Minutes." (Beck and Fowler 2001)

Instead, feedback and practice are required to develop your story telling (and story writing) skills. It is also possible to provide some heuristic guidance about stories that help get you started.

All stories must be:

- *Discrete:* They describe a single bit of functionality, a single feature, or an expectation the customer has of the system[4]. Discrete does not mean precise, a story can be general in nature (at least for a while), for example, "calculate the Payroll." The more general a story is, the more likely it will be factored into numerous stories with narrower scope. But do not hesitate to start with a general—yet discrete—story, they make excellent starting points.
- *Estimable:* The development team must be able to read the story and estimate the amount of time required to realize that story in production quality software. How the developers make those estimates is not of major concern here. That they provide feedback to the customer (storyteller) as to what those estimates are and how uncertainties in the story or the scope of the story contributed to the estimate's value (duration) is critical.
- *Testable:* How do you know that, "they lived happily ever after?" How long is 'ever after?' What constitutes happiness? Where they happy 24/7 or just most of the time? Defining tests is a joint responsibility, shared by the customer and the developers. Developers must define the more technical tests and can provide feedback to the customer that will enable her to define acceptance and usability tests.
- *Prioritized:* The customer, and only the customer, must be able to determine which stories are more important, more likely to generate an immediate business benefit, or otherwise more valuable to the customer (business). Story cards record the priority and developers work on the pending stories with the highest priority.

"Tell me story about what you want the system to do," asks the developer, totally intimidating the customer. There are few things as frightening in life as a blank sheet of paper

---

[4] When writing about objects, Cunningham and Beck used the term "behavior" to describe a discrete unit of object functionality. Stories and behaviors are almost synonymous, and anyone wanting to master story writing would be well served by investigating what Beck and Cunningham had to say about objects.

and the request to fill that paper with some meaningful communication. We can help our customer get started by suggesting some categories or types of story and providing some examples. We cannot write the story, he must do that, but we can suggest story topics or types. Examples of such types include: interrogatory, delegation, composite, collaborative, and fuzzy.

"Are there questions you would like the system to answer?" A lot of stories reflect the result of an implicitly asked question. The heuristic to the customer is: "think of a question (an **interrogatory**) you would like the system to answer and then describe that answer." Examples might include: (Story in plain type, implicit question in *italics*.)

> Sound an alert if a "near miss" is detected. (*Are any planes in imminent danger of collision?*)
>
> Disable any bin containing product that has exceeded its expiration date. (*Is that candy bar edible?*)
>
> Provide a count of all employees in each salary category. (*What happens if we give everyone a sliding percentage raise, greatest percent to the lowest salary categories?*)

Sometimes a customer just wants the system to perform some specific piece of work that is too tedious, complicated, or slow if assigned to a human being. **Delegation** stories tend to be fairly terse but they also tend to hide some interesting complication. Examples might include: Assign the customer a credit limit. Calculate and print an amortization schedule.

Composite stories are general stories, "calculate this week's payroll," that we are fairly certain will be broken up into smaller stories but we record as starting points for our thinking about the system. An example:

> Fill in and validate the form. (*The "and" clause is a dead giveaway that this story is composite in nature—at least one story to fill in the form and another for performing the validation.*)

In some cases, the customer can visualize an interaction with the system focused on accomplishing a specific task. (Filling in a form might require a collaborative effort, the system asking for content, the user providing the same, and the system providing a dialog for correction if the content is unsatisfactory.) An example of this type of **collaborative** story might be:

> Allow a reservation to be made from a list of available rooms based on the selection criteria entered. (*Story requires a dialog in which options are presented, selections are made, information is sorted and sifted and then presented, another selection made, and reservation completed.*)

Both composite and collaborative stories are subject to factoring—being split into simpler stories. The original composite and collaborative story card might actually be discarded once the team (customer and developers) is satisfied that they have identified all the subsidiary stories required to realize the original.

A final type, **fuzzy**, of story captures a customer desire that will not be fully explicable without a lot of dialog and probably a lot of development and feedback. It is important to capture this type of story as a reminder of important functionality even though everyone concerned knows the full parameters of the story will not be worked out for several development iteration cycles. An example of a fuzzy story:

Provide context sensitive help. *(But not that &*%$# paperclip!)*

Story characteristics and story types help the customer get started. Skill in story telling must be acquired through experience. Developers provide the feedback necessary for the customer to improve her story art. Stories should therefore be developed in small batches, perhaps focused on a single aspect of the system, so that effort is not wasted creating poorly conceived story cards.

Splitting Stories

There are numerous reasons for breaking a story up into smaller and more focused stories. Sometimes the story was intentionally general or intentionally composite in nature, just to get a starting point. Sometimes a story takes too long to implement (at least it is estimated that it will take too long). Sometimes the telling of a story—the dialog that occurs between developers and customers as tests and code are being written—reveals an unforeseen complexity that needs to be "spun off" into a separate story.

Talking about a story might reveal an exception and exception-handling requires a different story.

Stories might be split as a result of the assignment of all or part of the story to specific objects for implementation. Splitting stories for this reason requires a bit of background—XP/Agile assumes you are going to be doing object-oriented design and object-oriented programming. Stories that are specific enough in nature will become methods assigned to a particular class. Other stories might be implemented as a set of methods given to a single class. More likely, the individual tasks implied by a single story will be assigned to several classes, instances of which will collectively implement the story. This kind of story splitting may not be documented with a story card—merely as a test or a bit of code or a comment attached to code.

Ordering and Completing Stories

Stories are used as a unit-of-work, that is, the team plans their work activity based on completing a story and completing a set of stories in a specified calendar interval. The Planning Game (XP) is focused on deciding which stories the development team will complete during this time interval. If the Planning Game is to succeed, the time and resources required to complete a story must be estimated and attached to the story. The developers provide this estimate. The customer(s) must provide a priority for each story.

The customer-supplied priority must reflect business priority—it must be on the basis of business value added and nothing else. Deciding on a schedule and a set of deliverables is as simple as arranging the cards in priority order and, using the estimates, select story cards until the estimates fill the time interval available.

Of course, it is not quite this simple—there will be ties in priority, actual time may not equal estimate time, there may be more #1 priorities than can be accommodated in the given interval, etc. Negotiations take place among the team and the customers, and conflicts are resolved. Like everything else in XP/Agile, planning is an iterative process that improves with experience.

Stories continue to be told during planning. When a customer explains why she is rating this story card number one she will be elaborating the text that appears on the story card, elaborations that might merit a quick Post-It note attached to the card to further guide the developers. A story that has borderline priority might be split into parts—one with higher priority—to assure that some aspect of the story is developed this interval. A meta-story (a story about how the stories on cards are related or interact) might be told as a foundation for aggregating stories that are not, strictly speaking, highest priority but nevertheless need to be developed in concert.

The plan itself is a story. A story that captures the collective understanding of what we are trying to accomplish as a team (the team is inclusive of customers, managers, and developers). It probably includes our understanding of how we will react when things do not go exactly as planned. It is a story that captures our sense of self and of community.

Planning documents are evocative symbols of this story—not documentation or representations of it.

Confirming Stories

A test is a story recorded in a different format. Both novels and poems tell stories, but the format is quite different—so too with story cards and tests. Story cards and tests share a sequential relationship—the story card is the first chapter and the test is the final chapter[5]. The story card says, "this is what I want," and the test says, "this is how I know I got what I wanted." Tests can confirm the original story or they can reveal its shortcomings. King Midas wanted everything he touched turned to gold. The test cases - bricks, apples, and his beloved daughter—revealed a flaw in the story, not in the implementation of the story.

Similar things will happen with software development stories and their test cases.

Humans cannot seem to tell stories without embellishment. Anyone that has played the game in which a short story is passed from person to person around a circle knows how changed the story becomes by the time it returns to its origin. Development necessarily involves passing a story from person to person within the development team. Tests help assure story consistency by providing an objective (it is hard to think of automated test suites as being anything other than objective since they are implemented on machines) check on story consistency.

Hierarchical organization of test suites (unit tests done by programmers to acceptance and usability tests created by customers) also provides a means for keeping independent story lines in concert.

---

[5] There is an epilogue, a chapter after the final one, which covers the dialog that ensues once the new system is deployed. The epilogue is highly reflective and focused on lessons learned, lessons that will become the initial stories for the next system to be developed.

Communication — the Never Ending Story

Descriptions of the user story technique are inevitably misleading. The easiest things to talk about are the least important aspects of the technique. Story cards, tests, priorities, and estimates are but artifacts that arise from story telling.

An archeologist investigating a prehistoric culture finds artifacts (potsherds, arrowheads, bones, and other items) that are evidence of human existence. The artifacts themselves are trivial. The archeologist and other anthropologists can use those artifacts to reconstruct what life and culture were like at the time the artifacts were created and used.

It is the culture, the living interaction of human beings in a community, that is critical—both for those living it at that time, and for our understanding of our own culture.

User stories, story cards, estimates, priorities, tests are byproducts of a culture of communication. They provide some evidence that communication is taking place but do not in and of themselves assure that communication (or enough communication) is taking place. It is possible to generate every artifact discussed in this chapter and still fail to successfully implement the user story technique.

There is but one story—it begins the moment someone with authority says, "let's do X," and ends only when the project has been abandoned and *everyone*[6] involved has moved on to other things. Everyone contributes to the story. There is a narrator, the customer, who outlines the plot and limns the action scenes but she is not the sole speaker. The story exists in the memories of those involved in its telling. The artifacts generated by the occasional reduction to paper (or binary integers) of parts of the story serve as reminders, evoking the memories, refreshing the story.

WORKED EXAMPLE

Arriving at work one morning you are called to a meeting. Margaret, the CEO of the company, tells you that Bob, the other person in the meeting, is heading up a new division charged with designing, building, and deploying a new line of superior vending machines—the Extreme Performance Vending Machine or XPVM. You will be expected to write the software for this new line of vending machines and Bob will be your on-site customer.

You sit down with Bob and give him a quick briefing on user stories and the XP/Agile process and ask him to write the first set of stories that will get the team thinking about the project.

"I guess we already have our first story, build a better vending machine," you suggest to Bob who likes the idea and writes on the first index card: 0.0—Mission-*XPVM will outperform all other vending machines*. You have your first story.

"Can you give me a story that tells me why the XPVM is better," you ask? Bob quickly writes down some additional stories. (Bob has done this before so he is not a total novice at story telling.)

---

[6]6XP/Agile practitioners believe that a project continues as long as someone is still using the system and someone is still "maintaining" it. Deployment and maintenance are not outside the project, merely a different aspect of the project.

1.0—Payment. *XPVM will accept any kind of payment including cell phone trans-actions via the Web.*

2.0—Freshness. *XPVM will sell no merchandise that is stale or outdated.*

3.0—Restocking. *XPVM will automatically request restocking with the best selling items in its area.*

4.0—Communication. *XPVM will communicate with the customer to prevent trans-action errors.*

You have five stories, enough to get started. Unfortunately, you cannot see any way to estimate the time required to realize any of these stories. Splitting is required and probably of only one of these stories. So you ask,

"Which of these stories is most important to you, Bob?"

"Well, Margaret just came back from Scandinavia and was very impressed when her friends bought sodas from a vending machine using their cell phone. She thinks, and I agree, that the single biggest problem with vending machines is having the right change to make your purchase. So . . . the *accept all forms of payment* story is most important."

"OK, so how would you split up that story?"

Bob grabs some more cards and records the following:

1.1—Accept coins.

1.2—Accept currency.

1.3—Accept debit card.

1.4—Accept credit card.

1.5—Accept debit or credit card via a Web transaction.

1.6—Accept foreign coins and currency, at least Euros since we want to sell the XPVM in Europe.

1.7—Convert currencies appropriately.

1.8—Make sure the payment meets or exceeds the cost of the product selected.

1.9—Make change.

All of these stories are discrete, estimable and testable—except, the ones about accepting and converting foreign money, those you are not sure about. Stories 1.6, 1.7, and 1.8 are estimated to take a lot of time, perhaps exceeding the four-week cap on story implementation. (four weeks is an arbitrary (mostly) shop standard used for work planning purposes.) 1.8 will take longer because it involves an interface with other parts of the vending machine system and you are not sure what those parts look like as yet.

The developers suggest that Stories 1.1 and 1.2 might be combined as they seem to be essentially identical. The customer accepts their suggestion and throws out 1.2 and changes 1.1 to, Accept U.S. legal tender.

A planning session convenes and the customer gives 1.5 and 1.6 the highest priority followed by 1.8 and 1.7, the other stories have the same priority. Discussion ensues. Bob indicates his highest priority selections reflect the CEO's excitement when she was able to use her cell phone to buy products from vending machines in Sweden. He wants to keep her happy and feed on her enthusiasm. The developers point out that the highest priority stories presume the existence of the lowest priorities—you can't do any kind of transaction unless you can accept money and make change. The developers also have a vague sense of unease about the possible complexities involved in debit and credit card transactions.

It is decided to take one day to "spike"[7] stories 1.3, 1.4, and 1.5; to rough out some tests and some code to see if they understand the problem and understand the dependencies on the stories about accepting payment and making change. This way they will be addressing the customer's highest priorities and their own concerns simultaneously.

The next morning the planning session resumes. Developers' report:

- It appears that some debit cards can be read directly and others require a query to the issuing bank to ascertain funds available.
- Credit cards usually, but not always, depending on the amount, require an authorization transaction.
- For debit cards and credit cards, identity of the user needs to be confirmed.
- Web transactions are really just a sequence of the other transactions but the sequence needs to be maintained.
- For Web transactions, it is probably a good idea to confirm that the user is talking with the vending machine in front of him and not one across town.
- Talking about debit and credit cards made them realize that currency transaction requires an accumulator of some sort—some way to get total amount of money available instead of coin by coin.
- On the basis of their improved understanding of the stories the developers have some tests that they can offer programmers working on the accept money and make change stories reflect assumptions they are making as they develop their own stories. Those tests can be appended to the story card as annotations for teams working on them.

Bob, listening to the developers quickly writes some additional stories:

1.10—Confirm Customer Identity,

1.11—Report Available Money,

1.3.1—Authorize Debit Transaction,

1.4.1—Authorize Credit Transaction,

1.5.1—Confirm Web Conversation, and

1.5.2 Execute Web Transaction.

Programming teams select cards and development commences. Iteration follows.

---

[7] The term spike comes from XP and merely means a short intense period of exploration using test and code tools. The objective is to ask better questions, confirm understanding, and outline a framework for future story implementation.

COMPARISONS

Most readers will discern a strong similarity between XP story cards and the CRC (Class-Responsibility-Collaborator) cards invented by Ward Cunningham and Kent Beck. Both are simple index cards with simple entries. Most importantly, on both types of card, the entries are intended to describe expected behavior, something(s) that is expected of the software artifact to be constructed. Behavior is defined in terms of the domain and of the inhabitants of a domain—the users. There are also similarities between planning and card modeling sessions with clients, and some of Ellen Gottesdiener's workshops—see Chapter 5 of this volume.

This emphasis on behavior—domain-centric behavior—is a primary difference between user stories and use cases or scenarios as discussed by Camille Salinesi (Chapter 8), Neil Maiden (Chapter 9), and Karen Holtzblatt (Chapter 10) earlier in this volume.

Although nothing mandates this to be so, both use cases and scenarios tend to be used to describe the solution space (implementation space, i.e. the software) rather than the problem space (user domain). Use cases were invented by Ivar Jacobson and reflect his experience and understanding of software engineering. Scenarios have a more varied history but they too reflect their invention by software professionals. Both tools reflect the software professional's desire to have user requirements stated in a more formal manner. To participate in the construction of use cases and scenarios, users must adopt, or adapt to, the mindset of the developer, to think in terms of formal interactions, messages, and objects—all artifacts of the technical implementation. Perhaps this narrowness of vision is gradually being replaced by a wider use of scenarios: for instance, Joy Van Helvert and Chris Fowler describe using scenarios for innovation (Chapter 4), while Thomas Zink and Frank Houdek illustrate a wide range of uses of stories (Chapter 16).

User stories are deliberately intended to provide more of a metaphor than of a specification. Use cases and scenarios are generally intended to provide specification and therefore must be more formal in nature than a story. A specification is something to be satisfied—it is a contract. A metaphor is a framework for exploration, discovery, and conversation. XP in general is more concerned with iterative exploration and the use of metaphor as a framework for that exploration—a reflection of the values underpinning XP. User stories are valued as metaphors. Specifications of the sort arising from use cases and scenarios are suspect, not because they are "bad" or "wrong" but simply because they are subject to abuse. They lead too easily towards an assumption of need for upfront design or overemphasis of the intrinsic value of documentation.

As noted earlier in this chapter, (Applicability II—Why User Stories) there is a delicate balance of power that needs to be maintained between customers and developers. Both use cases and scenarios tend to tip this balance of power towards the developers.

(Although I must stress again this is not intrinsic to either tool, just to the way they are generally used.) User stories allow the customer to articulate their concerns and desires in their language—natural language, business language.

As markers or checkpoints used for common and consistent reference as the conversation between customer and developer continues, user stories allow both sides to do a better job of translating from "what" is wanted to "how" it will be delivered.

KEYWORDS

XP	Story Card	Collaborative Story	System Requirements
User Story	Discrete Story	Dialogue	
Developer Story	Composite Story	Agile	

REFERENCES

The entire XP Series published by Addison-Wesley with Kent Beck as series editor provides valuable background on what user stories are and how they are used. Of special note in this series:

Beck, K., *Extreme Programming Explained: Embrace Change*, Addison-Wesley Longman, Reading, MA, 2000.

RECOMMENDED READING

Lakoff, G. and Johnson, M., *Philosophy in the Flesh: The Embodied Mind and Its Challenge to Western Thought*, Basic Books, 1998. (For ideas on the power of metaphor and story telling to guide thinking.)

Weinberg, G., *The Psychology of Computer Programming*, Dorsett House, 1998. (For ideas on how stories are used in human interactions endemic to software development.)

Wood, J. and Silver, D., *Joint Application Development*, 2nd ed. John Wiley & Sons, 1995. (For ideas on story telling in a group context and the use of stories when development and design responsibilities are shared with all stakeholders.)

CHAPTER 14

USE CASES, TEST CASES

Ian Alexander
Scenario Plus, London, UK

USE CASES define the expected behaviours of systems in a branching structure consisting of the primary and alternative/exception scenarios. To generate deterministic, straight-line Test Cases, it is necessary to find a suitable set of paths—Test Scenarios—through each branched Use Case, at least covering all the branches and often also meeting more stringent criteria. Therefore, one Use Case can generate and trace several Test Cases. In addition, test conditions may need to be varied to take account of different operating environments. So, each Test Scenario discovered from the Use Cases may need to be executed in not one but a whole Class of Test Cases, whose members differ according to the environmental conditions in force.

APPLICABILITY

In principle, Use Cases can guide the design of tests for any type of system. In practice, this is most important for complex novel systems whose patterns of use are not predictable from previous experience.

Scenario-based testing is most clearly appropriate for user-level acceptance testing, in which the test cases should resemble the scenarios originally elicited from system stakeholders. It may also be useful for testing sub-system behaviour, and for tests of those system qualities such as maintainability in which a scenario approach makes sense.

POSITION IN THE LIFE CYCLE

Requirements Discovery	**Requirements Validation**	System Specification	System Design	Coding, First of Class	**Integration & Testing**	Operations & Maintenance

---

Scenarios, Stories, Use Cases: Through the Systems Development Life-Cycle. Edited by Ian F Alexander and Neil Maiden
© 2004 John Wiley & Sons, Ltd. ISBN: 0-470-86194-0

KEY FEATURES

- Use Case paths are traversed to generate Classes of Test Cases (abstract Scenarios)
- These are combined with environmental conditions to generate concrete Test Cases
- The approach can be automated, at least partially
- The approach is especially suitable for end-to-end, black-box testing
- It directly contributes to product quality as it demonstrates that systems are fit for the purposes for which they were designed.

STRENGTHS

Scenarios, especially when they also define the handling of exceptions—as is canonical for Use Cases—are ideal for defining functional tests, as there is a natural correspondence between saying what a system is expected to do, and testing that it does those things.

Use Cases define the goals of system use, and these correspond directly to Classes of related Test Cases.

Primary scenarios in Use Cases correspond directly to 'happy day' tests of normal operations.

Where stakeholders have personally contributed stories or scenarios describing desired system usage, user-level Acceptance Test Cases can be made to correspond directly to such stories. This gives confidence that the system is fit for purpose, at a level above detailed testing of system functions and qualities. Such stories can be encapsulated in either Normal or Exception sequences of Use Cases, depending on their nature.

Exception courses (branches) in Use Cases correspond to simple tests of exception-handling, though the exception-handling branches usually need to be combined with (parts of) primary scenarios to yield complete Test Case Scenarios.

WEAKNESSES

Domain knowledge is needed to identify the range of environmental conditions important to the tests, and in what combination. It is impractical to run separate tests for each combination of environmental conditions for each test scenario.

Use Cases do not always stand alone. Where a Use Case includes others, complete test scenarios may straddle several Use Cases. If the relationships between Use Cases are complex, it is better to make a complete behavioural model (e.g. in Flowchart/Swimlanes or Message Sequence Chart form) to define clearly the network of scenario paths to be tested.

Skill is needed to decide how many tests to run. It is impractical to run all possible test scenarios as there is generally a combinatorial explosion of different branches; when there is explicit or implicit looping the number of possible scenarios is of course infinite.

However, simple rules can be applied to generate much more limited sets of test cases if assumptions are made, for example on branch coverage.

Testing (or more generally, verification) cannot be based solely on functional requirements, that is, what a system has to do. It must also consider qualities (often known as 'ility' requirements) such as reliability, scalability, performance, maintainability, safety, electromagnetic compatibility, security, manufacturability, and so on. Of course it is possible to define scenarios to cover many of these requirements, but this is not always done, and scenario definition is not necessarily appropriate for them anyway. In general, the verification of non-functional requirements requires as much attention as the verification of system behaviour, and is often difficult to achieve by testing. For example, reliability can be demonstrated by testing, but only after a long period of time (possibly years). In practice it is often predicted by analysis, and partially confirmed by building up a history of actually attained reliability of components and whole systems.

Scenario-based testing does not claim to do everything. It is a close match for behaviour desired by specific stakeholders, such as maintenance operators; it is less likely to be the ideal technique for white-box tests, such as whether the desired voltages are available at certain points in a circuit, or whether software objects (or procedures, functions, etc.) work correctly when supplied with a selection of correct and incorrect parameters.

BACKGROUND: THE V-MODEL

A simple model of system development considers that project activities occur not so much in a straight-line story (like the 'Position in the Life Cycle' diagram that introduces each chapter of this book) as in two stories, with a relationship between them. These are often represented as the two limbs of a V (Figure 14.1). (For a more thorough look at system development life cycles, see Chapter 15 by Andrew Farncombe in this volume, which explains how the cycle of specification, design, and testing described here fits into a bigger picture.)

The traditional V-Model emphasises that the testing and integration story is rather different from the specification and design story, and indeed the two stories match like mirror images. If you create a system by specifying the whole, then sub-systems, then assemblies and finally components and modules, it follows that you verify it by testing first the lowest-level components, and if these integrate satisfactorily, then by integrating successively more parts of the system until a single working whole emerges.

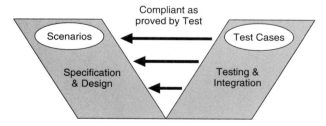

FIGURE 14.1   The V-model

In this picture, it is at once evident that if you place scenarios at the start on the left-hand side, then you should get something equivalent to them on the right. One conclusion is that scenarios or Use Cases have considerable value as test cases: if you know what the stakeholders want the system to do, what better way of verifying the system than by making it do that?

TECHNIQUE

A Use Case model is constructed, with Alternative and Exception Scenarios documented to cover all the variant courses of action and Exception Events considered to require handling (Cockburn 2001).

Each Use Case is a unit of behaviour in the special sense that it is a complete story, possibly spanning contributions from all parts of the system. The availability and correct functioning of everything that contributes to that story can, therefore, be demonstrated by a test that runs through the whole story.

Obviously, this approach will not work if Use Cases are poorly constructed—for instance, if they are made from the point of view of the system and essentially document the separate behaviours of sub-systems or components (such as software modules). Models with this orientation are often called 'inside-out' for this reason.

For instance, in the hackneyed but frequently bungled customer-gets-cash-from-teller-machine example, the customer is not talking to the ATM[1] device: he/she is talking to the bank. Ultimately the cash comes not from the hole in the wall but from the customer's account, however much the customer might wish otherwise. It is all too easy for analysts to see the world or 'problem domain' as a set of sub-systems, but this is as wrong for acceptance testing as it is for stating stakeholder requirements. We don't want to start with inside-out ATM cases; we want clean get-cash-from-bank cases.

Given a starting point of a well-founded set of Use Cases, test engineers already have the basis for first-cut test design: The functional requirements are segmented into more or less directly testable chunks of behaviour. The first task should naturally be to check that the Use Cases are indeed of this quality. If they are not, the alternatives are to improve and perhaps supplement them, or to find another basis for testing.

The second task is disarmingly but perhaps deceptively simple: to create a Test Case by copying (and linking back to, if you have tool support) each Scenario (Ahlowalia 2002, Alexander 2002, Heumann 2001). But there are quite a few complicating factors.

A One-to-Many Mapping

The core of a Test Case is a simple and therefore deterministic sequence of actions, generally given a name, to be carried out by a test engineer on the system, supported as necessary by test equipment. Tests should be deterministic[2] to allow test engineers to know immediately whether a given test run has passed or failed—there should be no

---

[1] Automatic Teller Machine

[2] Statistical testing of processes that necessarily include non-deterministic elements, as with traffic flows on a network, is possible but is inherently more difficult.

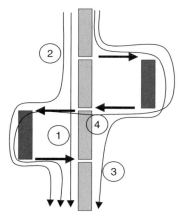

FIGURE 14.2   Multiple scenario paths in a use case with two recoverable exceptions

ifs and buts about it. A branching Use Case can generate many allowed sequences of actions (Scenarios), so there is a one-to-many relationship between Use Cases and Test Cases. Simple kinds of scenario such as User Stories (*see* Chapter 13, *User Stories in Agile Software Development*) often seem at first blush to map precisely one Test Case, but closer analysis often reveals several further possible Test Cases; complex Stories may have to be split to make them tractable.

The generated Scenarios are likely to be composed of a part of the main or happy day sequence, followed by a branch (Alternative or Exception), followed probably by another part of the main sequence. Therefore, we have to be careful to distinguish between the component sequences of actions (or 'courses of events') of a Use Case, which are often called 'Main Scenario' and so on, and generated Scenarios which are complete paths that might happen in practice and might need to be tested. A Use Case with two recoverable Exception sequences that do not overlap can generate at least four Scenarios (see Figure 14.2), and more when cycles are considered.

Slaying the Hydra

Where there are many variations possible, the number of Scenarios that can be generated grows combinatorially. This is especially serious if you have to consider several Use Cases at once. As soon as you have thought of one Test Case, you realise there are three other similar ones that you might need to include, rather as Hercules in Greek mythology sliced off one of the heads of the Hydra with his sword, only to find that three more heads grew in its place (Figure 14.3).

One traditional solution is to select a set of Test Cases that cover each branch at least once (every block of activities is executed in at least one test). Unfortunately, this is by no means the same thing: for instance, you could run a test of the Main Scenario, and then a cut-down test that merely started each Exception off and ended when the exception-handling steps had been run. This covers all the activities in the Use Case, but it completely fails to answer pressing questions like 'can normal activities resume successfully after this Exception?' It is only too easy for software to reset rather too well

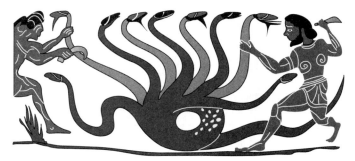

FIGURE 14.3   Hercules slaying the Hydra. Redrawn from a Greek Earthenware Vessel, about 525 BC

after an error; the error is apparently cleared, but the software fails to run the next normal case. So, as test engineers are well aware, Branch Coverage is a weak approximation to 'full' testing.

For simple Use Cases (those without too many combinations), the solution is to generate all possible combinations as Test Cases.

For larger Use Cases, we need to be more selective about which Test Cases to define. Starting from the principle that behaviour visible to users needs to be tested, and that the component sequences of Use Cases constitute such behaviours, we can state some rules for generating Test Cases,

- Every Normal (happy day) scenario should be run as a test from start to end. Since the goal of the Use Case cannot be achieved without the normal behaviour, this test is a precondition for all the other tests. If it fails, further testing may be nugatory until the normal scenario can be run successfully.
- Every Alternative and Exception should be run as part of a test, commencing at the start of the Normal sequence and ending as late as possible, that is,
  — at the end of the Normal sequence if this can be rejoined (recoverable Exception);
  — at the end of an irrecoverable Exception sequence.
- Every Exception that ends with rejoining the Normal sequence should also be run as part of a test that then executes the whole Normal sequence (again) from the start, to check that the error conditions have been correctly reset.

For a Use Case with two recoverable Exceptions as diagrammed above, this means that there will be at least five test cases, namely,

- the Normal Scenario
- Normal Start—Exception 1—Normal End
- Normal Start—Exception 2—Normal End
- Exception 1—Normal End—whole Normal sequence again
- Exception 2—Normal End—whole Normal sequence again

It is then a matter of judgement whether the additional Test Case containing both Exceptions are necessary. If there is any doubt whether handling the first exception could upset the handling of the other exception, then the test is necessary. It is not logically sufficient, as we would still not have tested whether running the second exception and then the first (on the next cycle) would work correctly. The Hydra has many heads and it is impossible to be sure that no possible faults remain in systems of any complexity. In practice, therefore, testers have to settle for some measure of reasonable coverage rather than anything close to complete coverage of all imaginable scenarios.

Prioritising the Tests

When there are many possible paths, it is sensible to prioritise them to help select which Test Cases to run. There are several possible selection criteria, such as

- paths most likely to fail in a test (most productive tests)
- paths most frequently followed by users (McGregor and Major 2000) (most needed tests)
- minimum number of paths to achieve branch coverage (most economical tests)
- paths asserted by stakeholders to be significant
- paths with high criticality to the mission
- paths that are highly related to safety.

Ahlowalia suggests computing a path factor by adding criticality and frequency, or possibly more complex metrics (Ahlowalia 2002). Different criteria may be right for different kinds of system.

The criteria for real-time, embedded, and safety-related systems are likely to differ from those for office software such as accounting and management information systems. For example, safety testing must comply with the verification plan set out in the system safety case. That will constitute an argument that the system is known to be acceptably safe because, amongst other evidence, the system has been tested against all major identified hazards. (*See* Chapter 7, *Negative Scenarios and Misuse Cases* for a discussion of hazard identification.) It would not be acceptable in a safety context to argue that because a path was rarely followed it need not be tested—on that basis, parachutes and fire extinguishers could be made cheap and unreliable.

McGregor & Major's focus is on business software, in which the number of possible paths is essentially infinite, and even achieving branch coverage is often difficult. In this context, a software system is imagined as a green field containing any number of untrodden paths. However, suppose the field has four gates and two stiles, and people usually walk between these points. Soon, paths appear in the grass, and the areas near the gates and stiles become trodden smooth, while areas far from these points remain lightly visited or unexplored. With this image in mind, McGregor & Major's approach is to make an operational profile of each class of user ('actor') and hence predict frequency of use, if not for each path then at least for each Use Case. Traditionally, operational profiles are created retrospectively; but Use Cases offer a way of predicting operational profiles in time for acceptance testing.

Tool Support

It is tempting to consider how the generation of Test Cases from Use Cases could be automated. A tool would require a representation of the Use Cases that could be traversed automatically, and a set of rules (such as those just given) for the traversal.

Any database that records the order of scenario steps is sufficient to allow a straight-line scenario to be traversed, and the task of copying and linking such a scenario to a Test Case is quite trivial.

Unfortunately, there are two major obstacles in the way of automating test generation,

- Naïve traversal generates enormous numbers of combinations, yielding an impractically large set of often very repetitive and unproductive Test Cases.
- Use Cases are structured for humans to read, not for test generators.

It is possible to make some reasonable assumptions to cut down on the number of pointless Test Cases, as we did in the rules given above. These do not guarantee perfect testing, but they do often give a sensible approximation to a workable set of tests.

The second obstacle is more challenging. Use Cases and scenarios in general are fundamentally stories told by people to people. They can be chatty, casual, allusive, and inconsistent. Branching can be indicated vaguely or not at all; branch positions can be indicated by numbering in 'come from' rather than 'go to' style, and so on. In short, people have ways that are infuriating to precise test engineers. The trouble is that the reason why engineers use scenarios in the first place is because they are informal enough and expressive enough to enable ordinary stakeholders to express and share their intentions. Formalising the Use Cases into something semantically tight and precise could make them much easier for engineering tools to traverse and impossible for non-technical people to cope with.

Where Use Cases have to be shared with ordinary stakeholders, a list of steps is probably as much formalisation as can readily be tolerated. Happily, a simple tool that can copy and link such a sequence to a Test Case fragment, together with simple editing tools allowing such fragments to be spliced together, can dramatically cut down the amount of work needed to prepare user-level tests. Essentially this is the approach taken in my Scenario Plus toolkit, in which support for testing is extremely simple—the test engineer selects a scenario and pushes a button to create and link a matching test case; refinements are then made "by hand" using link-preserving cut and paste (Scenario Plus 2003). In practice, this reduces the mechanical task of creating a test case to a few seconds; most of the effort is where it should be, in defining the test conditions and pass criteria.

Where Use Cases are essentially owned by engineers, as when they document interactions between sub-systems, it is possible to make them more analytical. Some engineers (*e.g.* Binder 1995, Gelperin 2003) as well as a persistent group of researchers (*see e.g.* Frappier and Habrias 2001 *for a range of approaches*) argue that Use Case specifications must be made more formal. It is a moot point—even if you concede that formal specifications are needed at some state of a project—whether Use Cases should be fully structured like program code (or pseudocode) with special syntax to express branching, looping, and so on, as Gelperin suggests. Binder proposes another approach, adding a decision table to the Use Case model to support systematic generation of test cases; otherwise 'the typical OMT[3] Specification is an untestable cartoon. The information is useful for human interpretation but cannot support automated test case generation.' (Binder 1995)

Such a structure makes it easy for a Test Case generator to traverse and analyse the cases; but since we know that even expertly written code contains an error every 1000 lines or so, such analytic scenario structures would be subject to subtle 'programming' errors. Given that this structure would drive the structure of system testing, any such errors would be magnified. In addition, analysis takes more time than simply writing down stories, so analytic Use Cases would be available only later in a project. However, for engineer-facing Use Cases these are no insurmountable objections.

Another approach is to develop models, such as swimlanes diagrams with activity/flow charts, state charts, and message sequence diagrams, that in their various ways express scenarios in more analytic forms. It is worth observing that sequence diagram representations are often called 'scenarios' (*e.g. Figure 14.5 in* Amyot and Mussbacher 2002). This use of models is of course the conventional software and systems engineering approach, gradually translating abstract stakeholder needs into concrete system designs. This view is echoed in the UML and associated processes like the Rational Unified Process (RUP) (Kruchten 2000; *see also* Peter Haumer's account in Chapter 12).

Any analytic model that correctly expresses the temporal and logical relationships of required activities can (in principle) be traversed to generate Test Cases. The diversity of types of model—both within and between projects—is an inconvenience for test case generation, but since the models are used directly to define the system, it has the merit that both the system and tests are generated from the same models.

For software, the logical outcome is a formal or semi-formal specification in, for example, Z or SDL (*see* Frappier and Habrias 2001), from which the code can be generated mechanically (if not yet necessarily automatically), and from which a systematic battery of test cases can be generated by rules such as those we have discussed.

Numerous research and industrial tools have been created to help construct such specifications, and then to translate them more or less automatically to sets of test cases. For example, Bell Labs have a free Message Sequence Chart (MSC) editor and Test Case generator (working from the MSC 'scenarios'), promising complete branch coverage and optimal performance, in the sense that the tests will be fewest in number and of the shortest length possible (UBET 2003).

Do Scenarios Yield Test Cases or Test Case Classes?

So far, we have effectively assumed that a (named) sequence of activities to be tested corresponds directly to a Test Case. However, this is not the whole story. Test conditions may need to be varied to take account of the range of possible operating environments. So, each Test Scenario generated from the Use Cases may need to be executed in not

---

[3] James Rumbaugh's OMT was a forerunner of UML. Rumbaugh was one of the 'three amigos' employed by Rational Software Corporation to develop their methods into a unified approach. Presumably, Binder would hold a similar view of UML Use Cases, though a full UML analysis would answer his objections.

just a single Test Case but also a whole Class of Test Cases, whose members differ in the environmental conditions in force.

For example, to test whether a CD player works in a car, a basic test scenario is to insert a CD, start the player, and then drive the car. The test passes if the CD is heard satisfactorily, whether the car is moving or not. This could be called the 'Journey Music' test. However, on reflection you can see that it could be important whether the car is driven gently on a smooth road, violently on a rough forest track, up and down steep hills, or accelerated and braked sharply. It could also matter whether the temperature is −40°C in arctic Norway, 11°C in rainy England, or 45°C in the dust of the Arabian Desert, if the car and the CD player are to be used in those places. How many Test Cases is that? Do we need an Arctic Forest-Track Rally-Driving Music Test?

The unpalatable answer might be that we need many more tests than scenarios. However, test engineers are used to making assumptions about environmental conditions, and combining results from different, fragmentary tests to predict overall performance. For instance, equipments are routinely tested by being vibrated and shaken to simulate being driven and dropped, and so on; they are separately tested by being heated and cooled repeatedly to simulate being used in different climates and when the weather changes. Passing those two tests does not actually prove that the equipment will work if shaken and heated at once, but unless there are reasons for supposing that the two factors would interact, much test effort is saved by not checking the combination.

In general, then, a Scenario identified as being worth testing corresponds to a Test Case Class, not a single Test Case as software engineers may assume: all really good disputes are founded on the simple fact that the world looks different from different places. It is a matter of judgement how many individual Test Cases are then generated, given the immense range of environmental conditions (temperature, noise, humidity, wind, pressure, electromagnetic radiation, magnetic fields, vibration...) that could apply. The default choice is just one—the ordinary 'room temperature' conditions of the test laboratory—but it is always possible that this is insufficient.

The possibilities for tool support in selecting appropriate combinations of environmental conditions are quite limited. The most useful guide is experience, perhaps encapsulated in a template derived from previous projects.

WORKED EXAMPLE

Let us continue with the simple example of Chapter 7, *Negative Scenarios and Misuse Cases*. Suppose that we have prepared Use Cases for a burglar alarm service, including installation, monitoring, and maintenance of household alarms (Figure 14.4).

Inputs

The principal inputs consist of the Use Cases. These tell the story of how the alarm service as a whole is to operate.

The householder protects the house with an alarm. This guards the house while the householder is out, and alerts the Control Centre if there seems to be an intrusion. The Control Centre handles the intrusion by trying to disconfirm it, and if that fails

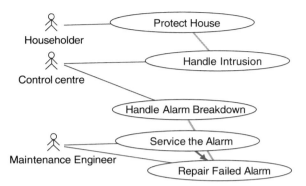

FIGURE 14.4   Use Case summary diagram for 'Provide Burglar Alarm Service'

by calling out a guard and notifying the police. The Control Centre also handles alarm breakdown as well as regular servicing, calling out a maintenance engineer to repair or service the alarm as appropriate. A service may, exceptionally, lead to the repair of an alarm. The Control Centre is also responsible for other tasks (not shown) including opening and maintaining customer accounts, taking payment for accounts, and arranging for new alarms to be installed.

Here is a summary of the Use Cases and their principal Exceptions.

> Protect House
>   *Alternative:* (Deluxe Model) Operate Alarm Remotely
> Handle Intrusion
>   *Exception:* Mistake: Handle False Alarm
>   *Exception:* Alarm Failed: Repair Failed Alarm
> Handle Alarm Breakdown
> Service the Alarm
>   *Exception:* Alarm Failed: Repair Failed Alarm
> Repair Failed Alarm
>   *Exception:* Alarm Irreparable: Install the Alarm
> Install the Alarm
> Open Customer Account
> Update Customer Account
> Collect Subscription Payment
>   *Exception:* Unpaid: Cancel Service, Chase Payment

Input Validation

Our first task is to validate these inputs: will these form good tests, and is the list complete?

It is important to test all aspects of the Use Cases. All of them will certainly be needed for the alarm service to work properly, and indeed for the company running the service to prosper. And they are reasonably discrete, end-to-end stories in their own right; of course we need to check the wording of the scenarios to see if they are adequately defined.

Notice, incidentally, that the cases are not all about exciting things at the sharp end of the stick, like activating the alarm or detecting intrusion. Many vital activities are about pedestrian details like recording that Mrs. Jones lives in 131 Acacia Avenue, that her phone number has just changed, and that she has paid her subscription for the year. Yet the address is critical to the burglar alarm service; if it is wrong, the guard and the police will be misdirected in the event of a burglary. Similarly, the phone number is needed—if it is wrong, the guard may be sent out to a false alarm, as the householder will not be reached to disconfirm intrusion. As for the subscription, the alarm service will work perfectly without it—until the alarm company goes bankrupt.

Completeness is inherently more difficult to validate. Stakeholders can tell, by playing through the stories in their minds, that these Use Cases would result in a working service. But what might be missing?

Thinking out what could go wrong, by analysing Exceptions and Misuse Cases (*see* Chapter 7), is one way to find out. A security breach, caused for instance by a corrupt employee in the Control Centre, could cause Handle Intrusion and perhaps Collect Subscription Payment to fail. This line of reasoning leads to the sort of requirements detailed in the Misuse Cases chapter, and suggests that there ought to be specific procedures (perhaps documented as Use Cases) to deal with security: for instance, monitoring of employee actions, analysis of patterns of burglaries, and false alarms. As test engineer, you might recommend Test Cases to cover such procedures even if the equivalent Use Cases were missing. You might also with some justification be a little suspicious about any cases with no documented Exceptions: is it really being claimed that nothing can go wrong? The ancient Greeks called that *hubris*, meaning 'tempting fate'.

Identifying Classes of Test Cases

We can now work out the full list of classes of functional Test Cases—we do not expect to cover all the non-functional requirements such as reliability here.

Firstly, there must be a normal course of events (happy day) test for each Use Case:

1. Protect House (from existing Use Cases)
2. Handle Intrusion
3. Handle Alarm Breakdown
4. Service the Alarm
5. Repair Failed Alarm
6. Collect Subscription Payment
7. Install the Alarm
8. Open Customer Account
9. Update Customer Account
10. Monitor Employee Actions (case added by Test Engineer)
11. Analyse Alarm Patterns (case added by Test Engineer)

Next, there must be a test for each documented Alternative or Exception. To minimise the number of tests, we can restrict ourselves to defining only the normal—Exception—repeat the normal test scenarios.

12. Protect House *Alternative:* (Deluxe Model) Operate Alarm Remotely
13. Handle Intrusion *Exception:* Mistake: Handle False Alarm, then Handle Intrusion normally
14. Handle Intrusion *Exception:* Alarm Failed: Repair Failed Alarm, then Handle Intrusion normally
15. Service the Alarm *Exception:* Alarm Failed: Repair Failed Alarm, then Handle Intrusion normally
16. Repair Failed Alarm *Exception:* Alarm Irreparable: Install the Alarm, then Handle Intrusion normally
17. Collect Subscription Payment *Exception*: Unpaid: Cancel Service, Chase Payment, then Collect Subscription Payment ("next year") normally

Notice that we have chosen to run the 'Handle Intrusion' scenario after servicing or repairing the alarm, even though this is structured as a separate Use Case (and would likely not be identified as necessary to these particular tests by a naïve test case generator). Our domain knowledge tells us that the alarm ought to be able to do this after maintenance. We could equally have chosen to run 'Protect the House', which is also a happy day scenario that could follow on from alarm maintenance. Another very economical choice would be to run 'Handle Intrusion' after one of the simulated repairs, and 'Protect House' after the other. That way we would at least have some evidence that both *can* work correctly after a repair. The more cautious but more costly test approach would be to run both follow-ons for both situations, creating two more test cases—not many in this small example, but in a large system it would represent a severe challenge: a combinatorial explosion in numbers of test cases, where many normal courses could be combined with many exception scenarios.

Then we have to consider whether to run combination tests, first within Use Cases that have two or more Exceptions, and then across Use Cases in case they interact.

Here, in this simplified story, we only have Handle Intrusion with two Exceptions. We might as well run all combinations within that Use Case,

18. Handle Intrusion—Handle False Alarm—Repair Failed Alarm—Handle Intrusion again.
19. Handle Intrusion—Repair Failed Alarm—Handle False Alarm—Handle Intrusion again.

Is that all the tests? By no means. Questions like whether the Control Centre can deal with the stress of multiple simultaneous alarms must be answered with convincing evidence, or the company's reputation may be irredeemably damaged. If you are lucky enough to have stories or scenarios covering what experts in the field think are the critical issues, then these are definitely worth converting into test cases—even though they probably will not be made into Use Cases.

Generating Classes of Test Cases

Given the decisions already made, it ought to be possible to generate Test Cases essentially automatically. This is easy for happy day tests—you just copy (and link if you want traces from test steps back to requirements, which you should) the Normal course from the Use Case in question.

If the requirements engineers have done their stuff, every step will have its own Acceptance (or 'Fit') Criteria (Alexander and Stevens 2002, Robertson and Robertson 1999), which you should be able to use directly to enable the person running the test to tell whether the step has passed or failed. If not, you have a bit of extra work to do.

Tests involving Alternatives or Exceptions are a little more tricky. Unfortunately, understanding text isn't something that computers are currently much good at, and so if the steps in your Use Cases are plain text, you will probably have to identify where Alternatives and Exceptions should branch off from the Normal sequence, and where (if anywhere) they rejoin it. That done, generation of test scenarios is simply a matter of copying and linking.

For example,

> 13. Handle Intrusion *Exception:* Mistake: Handle False Alarm, then Handle Intrusion normally

unpacks to form the rough test scenario

> (Intrusion simulated)
> —————————Normal:—————————
> Call Centre Operator studies details of *reported intrusion.*
> Call Centre Operator tries to disconfirm intrusion by calling Householder.
> Call Centre Operator authenticates Householder's identify.
> —————————Exception:—————————
> Householder admits Mistake.
> Call Centre Operator logs event.
> (*not including:* Call Centre Operator Calls out Guard.)
> (Intrusion simulated)
> —————————Normal:—————————
> Call Centre Operator studies details of *reported intrusion.*
> Call Centre Operator tries to disconfirm intrusion by calling Householder.
> Householder does not disconfirm.
> Call Centre Operator Calls out Guard.

This is only rough, because the person running the test does not want to know about people's job titles, but only which actions to take. So it may be necessary to tidy up the wording. It might be sensible to do this before generating test scenarios, if some Use Case sequences are going to be copied several times, as is likely.

Selecting Environmental Conditions for Test Cases

The final step in generation is to select which environmental conditions to test for each class of Test Cases, to create a set of fully defined individual Test Cases. For example, we might be concerned that the household alarm would not Protect the House correctly in stormy conditions, when wind, rain, hail, lightning, and rapid changes in temperature and humidity might either trigger false alarms, or might prevent real intrusions from being detected or reported. We might, therefore, create additional Test Cases in the Protect the House class

20. Protect House *in Electrical Storm*
21. Protect House *in Force 8 Wind*
22. Protect House *in Heavy Rain*

It might be considered necessary to create Test Cases for combinations of such conditions, including all of them at once.

Some environmental conditions can be set up quite readily, but simulating a full storm around a test house might be expensive, while the alternative of waiting for a real one would be unacceptable in most commercial situations.

Specialised test facilities such as wind generators (see photograph, Figure 14.5), temperature and humidity chambers, and 'shake, rattle, and roll' vibration generators are available in most developed nations, but they typically need to be booked or ordered far in advance.

FIGURE 14.5 The Proteus cross-wind blower. This machine simulates strong side-winds for testing jet engines. Courtesy of Rolls-Royce PLC

The effort required for thorough environmental testing provides a strong argument for writing scenarios that cover the whole life cycle (itself a scenario) from development through to disposal, and basing tests on them early in development. Well thought out scenarios make it possible to identify and plan for 'long poles in the tent' such as having to procure the use of test facilities, perhaps years before they will be needed.

COMPARISONS

It isn't very obvious as to what to compare scenario-based testing with: the unhappy truth is that without the sort of visibility of a system's intended uses that scenarios give naturally, test design is always somewhat in the dark, at least for end-to-end tests of whole systems. The problem is much less acute for white-box testing, where knowledge of the structure of the system is often (but definitely not always) enough to carry out a range of tests.

Testers' Domain Knowledge

In the absence of scenarios, testers have always used their personal knowledge of the domain to try to create realistic end-to-end black-box tests: in other words, they have been forced to invent plausible scenarios.

To give a somewhat extreme example, when consulting with a telecommunications company on the testing of a new accounting system, I made the uncomfortable discovery that while they had identified approximately 1500 test cases, there were no available requirements. The system was critical to their mission: if they didn't charge for phone calls, they didn't get paid. The company had bought and customised a commercial-off-the-shelf (COTS) package, and 'it did what it did' (Haim Kilov's phrase). The test team were given the job of showing that the software was all right, and they settled down to identify ways in which the thing might possibly be used. Since none of them seemed at all surprised at this part of their job, either this was the first time they had dealt with this kind of problem, or this was what usually happened on projects: a *Buy-Design-Guess the Test Cases* cycle.

This cycle might work well enough on small projects. After all, if you buy a set of COTS office automation software products, and develop a few small fragments of Visual Basic code to integrate a few office functions, you can to a large extent rely on the extensive testing done on the COTS products, and you only have to test the effect of the 'gluing' code you have added. This is attractive because it feels like wasted effort specifying something that already exists. Unfortunately, the lazy approach isn't safe, because it is always possible that while things may work locally, the system may break down on end-to-end scenarios. So a scenario-based testing approach looks suitable for COTS integrations. The whole question of how to specify COTS integrations is not surprisingly becoming a hot topic for requirements researchers (*see* Chapter 25, The Future of Scenarios).

Operational Scenarios

However, Use Cases are not the only basis for Scenario-based testing. Traditional Operational Scenarios, such as those listed in military/aerospace Concept of Operations (ConOps) documents also offer a workable approach. These are straightforward textual scenarios, sometimes classified into a hierarchy, for example

> *1. Flights.*
> *1.1 Takeoff.*
> *1.2 Flying.*
> *1.3 Landing.*

Plainly, these can be very useful for constructing end-to-end tests. Where they might not be as good as Use Cases for guiding test design is in their coverage of exceptions—which may be quite patchy.

User Stories

We have already mentioned the generation of Test Cases from User Stories, and it forms a central plank in agile methods (*see* Chapter 13, *User Stories in Agile Software Development*). Use Case and agile approaches share a strong emphasis on the importance of stakeholders, of story, and of verification (e.g. Cockburn 2001, Beck 2000). Agile methods are intended for software systems, though some of the practices—such as getting stakeholders to tell stories, and writing test cases early—are quite beneficial and could be applied to other types of system. Agile development seems to be most popular and is arguably most suitable for object-oriented, web-based and business software, where short development times and therefore repeated releases are favoured.

KEYWORDS

Use Case	Test Case Class	Test Script	Black-Box Test
Test Case	Test Step	Test Scenario	White-Box Test

REFERENCES

Alexander, I., Requirements and Testing: Two Sides of the Same Coin, Telelogic Innovate, September 2002. Available from http://easyweb.easynet.co.uk/~iany/consultancy/reqts_and_testing/reqts_and_testing.htm

Alexander, I. and Stevens, R., *Writing Better Requirements*, Addison-Wesley, 2002.

Ahlowalia, N., Testing from use cases using path analysis technique, *International Conference on Software Testing Analysis & Review (STAR)*, Anaheim, CA, November 4–8, 2002. Available from http://www.StickyMinds.com

Amyot, D. and Mussbacher, G., *URN: Towards a New Standard for the Visual Description of Requirements*, 2002, http://www.usecasemaps.org/pub/abstracts.shtml/sam02-URN.pdf

Beck, K., *Extreme Programming Explained, Embrace Change*, Addison-Wesley, 2000.

Binder, R., *TOOTSIE, A High-end OO Development Environment*, 1995, http://www.rbsc.com/pages/tootsie.html (revised 2001).

Cockburn, A., Writing Effective Use Cases, Addison-Wesley, 2001.

Frappier, M. and Habrias, H., *Software Specification Methods, An Overview Using a Case Study*, Springer, 2001.

Gelperin, D., Precise Use Cases, 2003, http://www.livespecs.com/downloads/LiveSpecs06V01_PreciseUseCases.pdf

Heumann, J., Generating Test Cases From Use Cases, The Rational Edge, June 2001, www.therationaledge.com

Kruchten, P., *The Rational Unified Process, An Introduction*, Addison-Wesley, 2000.

McGregor, J.D. and Major, M.L., Selecting Test Cases Based on User Priorities, SD Magazine, March 2000, http://www.sdmagazine.com/documents/s=815/sdm0003c/

Robertson, S. and Robertson, J., *Mastering the Requirements Process*, Addison-Wesley, 1999.

Scenario Plus, website (free Use Case templates, and a free Use/Misuse Case toolkit with Test Case generator for DOORS), 2003, http://www.scenarioplus.org.uk

UBET, website (free Message Sequence Chart editor / Test Case generator), 2003, http://cm.bell-labs.com/cm/cs/what/ubet/index.html

RECOMMENDED READING

Naresh Ahlowalia's paper at STAR 2002 is a practical approach from a software point of view to creating tests from use cases. There is an alarming subheading 'Determine all possible paths' but this is qualified, and the paper is one of the few published accounts of use-case-based testing.

Jim Heumann's article in The Rational Edge is a readable account from a leading software company.

CHAPTER 15

PROJECT STORIES: COMBINING LIFE-CYCLE PROCESS MODELS

Andrew Farncombe

John Boardman Associates Limited, Southampton, UK

THIS CHAPTER applies scenario thinking to the system development process itself. Projects succeed when their requirements are right and development is effectively managed to control risk. Both of these aspects often lead to iterative development life cycles (e.g. requirements are often gathered iteratively in a series of scenario workshops). The simplest life-cycle story is the single-pass 'waterfall'; in this chapter, the shortcomings of that story are examined, and an approach is developed that shows how to combine three kinds of life cycle to suit a wide range of project situations.

APPLICABILITY

The 'systems of interest' dealt with in this chapter should be not be thought of as implying any particular implementation technology. Systems comprising mechanical, electrical, electronic, software, and other solutions are all within the scope of the discussion. This requires a more general approach than, say, software development methods designed to be used within familiar implementation domains, possibly employing regularly occurring requirements and design 'patterns'.

Scenario use is almost by definition participative, and several authors in this volume explicitly involve stakeholders: for example, Suzanne Robertson in Chapter 3, Ellen Gottesdiener in Chapter 5, Karen Holtzblatt in Chapter 10. Stakeholder participation implies a willingness to listen to and accept changes as understanding develops. Hence, iteration is more or less mandatory. The applicability of the concepts in this chapter is not restricted to scenario-based development, but—along with the management of risk—the use of participative techniques such as scenarios makes the choice of more sophisticated life cycles essential.

POSITION IN THE LIFE CYCLE

Almost by definition, the ideas explored in this chapter relate to all the life-cycle elements shown in the table below. This is because we will be reasoning about the construction

Scenarios, Stories, Use Cases: Through the Systems Development Life-Cycle. Edited by Ian F Alexander and Neil Maiden
© 2004 John Wiley & Sons, Ltd. ISBN: 0-470-86194-0

and applicability of life-cycle processes in the most general sense. However, in what follows, we question explicitly whether the 'waterfall' life cycle depicted below (Royce 1970) is a sufficiently rich model to handle the wide range of project situations we typically encounter. Concluding that it is not, we use an enquiry-based approach to generate life-cycle models suitable for projects in different situations.

Requirements Discovery	Requirements Validation	System Specification	System Design	Coding, First of Class	Integration & Testing	Operations & Maintenance

KEY FEATURES

— The project life cycle is itself treated as a story.
— Composes project-specific life cycles from three basic life-cycle models.
— Adapts traditional thinking to suit risky projects, such as those with vague requirements and multiple stakeholders.

STRENGTHS

— Accommodates a very wide range of project scenarios.
— Not confined to computer-based or software systems.
— Can compose three basic life-cycle models to generate other life cycles.
— Offers a general enquiry-based framework for thinking about system development processes.
— Clearly distinguishes in-the-large iteration from in-the-small life-cycle sequence of activities.

WEAKNESSES

The ideas contained in this chapter challenge some basic assumptions, for example, that there is one perfect process model. Not everyone is receptive to this way of thinking and 'shooting the messenger' is a phrase that springs to mind when I think of my experiences trying to apply it. My advice therefore is that if you find the ideas expressed here attractive and/or useful, take care how you sell and use them.

TECHNIQUE

Introduction

This chapter may feel rather different from the others in this book.

Usually, we use scenario modelling or storytelling as a way of structuring what we know about some user domain. We do this to help us construct a system that will operate inside that domain and interact with the surrounding environment as required, providing some cost-effective benefit to the stakeholders in doing so.

By contrast, the ideas presented in this chapter apply storytelling not to constructing the system itself, but rather to the systems engineering processes used to direct the analysis and development activities involved. The story elements that we are concerned with are descriptions of parts of the development process; the resulting stories are composed for each project's situation according to a set of quite general rules.

Why do this?

From my experience, it seems that there is a lot of bad systems engineering process thinking 'out there', variously muddle-headed or inappropriate.

Bad process thinking can be worse than having no process at all. People lose the plot: *'Tell me again what I'm supposed to be doing'*. Paralysis sets in: *'Why am I doing what I'm doing? Where does it get me?'*. People feel cut off from common sense and what experience has taught them.

To be fair, people who write systems engineering processes have their hearts in the right place. They are attempting to encapsulate relevant wisdom and experience, and so lessen the chances that each project will have to learn project facts of life the hard way.

The trouble is that standardised process templates often suffer from the 'one size fits all' malaise. The institutionalised process model often does not fit individual projects. Projects have different shapes due to individual project circumstances and institutionalised process models fail to capture this variability.

To take a sideswipe at the life-cycle model used in the introduction to this chapter: to what extent is it realistic? Here it is again:

Requirements Discovery	Requirements Validation	System Specification	System Design	Coding, First of Class	Integration & Testing	Operations & Maintenance

To be sure, each of the stages in the 'waterfall' is necessary. Omit any one of them, and you have a distinctly dysfunctional project. Broadly, the sequencing is correct. It would be absurd to code the system before you have discovered what the requirements are (although there have been plenty of projects in which people have tried to do precisely that!). Furthermore, the approach, as introduced by Royce (1970) (who appreciated that iteration was necessary), and defined in popular standards such as Mazza et al. (1994), was certainly an improvement on unstructured development.

But let us constructively criticise it:

- There is a distinctly left to right, single-pass, do-it-all-in-one-go, 'big bang' feel about it. How do notions such as 'concept exploration', 'proof of concept', and 'phases' fit in?
- There seem to be firm walls between each stage stating which mode your brain is supposed to be in at any one time. Experience tells us that in practice, the engineer's mind jumps about from thinking about requirements, to thinking about solutions and how they might be implemented, and back again. This is not reflected in the model.

- There is the strong implication that we are starting with a clean sheet of paper (the 'green field' situation). What about 'brown field' situations in which we have to add some functionality to an existing system, or modify it in some way while it continues in service? How could it apply to the use of Commercial Off-The-Shelf (COTS) components and software?
- Iteration is not reflected at all. There is no sense of building prototypes and trying them out, feeding lessons learned back into the development process.
- Phasing of deliverables and incremental build-up of functionality and/or deployment is not represented. System upgrades and improvements are not dealt with.

So, although the story told by the model is in some senses correct, it also omits many project aspects that we all know to be a necessary part of project life. In fact, it is rather simplistic and inflexible. As a result, it may not be appropriate for many practical project situations.

Yet many organisations mandate exactly this sort of life cycle in their project standards, with high-level Gate or Phase Reviews punctuating the life-cycle stages.

If a project's life cycle itself fails to reflect the realities of the project's situation, a disconnect develops between organisational process mechanisms and the realities of the project. Management reviews can become meaningless.

Cultural factors within the organisation often inhibit resolution of this problem. From Management's point of view: developers and engineers need to be controlled and do what they are told. Many developers, on the other hand, feel that the process constrains creative and intellectual freedom and is imposed without consultation. In a business world characterised by 'initiative fatigue', an imposed process model is just another management fad *du jour*, and as a result, many of the people involved just go through the motions. In this situation, the benefits of all the cumulative experience of systems engineering fail to accrue and projects start out at a disadvantage.

This chapter is a plea from the heart against process rigidity. It looks at what can be done to provide useful process models that on the one hand support constructive systems engineering, while being flexible enough to reflect the needs of projects on the other.

However, it is one thing to criticise processes as being inflexible and simplistic. It is quite another to do something about it. On the basis, therefore, that to understand is to forgive, we look at why things are as they are.

It seems to be quite difficult to define effective systems engineering processes. Why is this? Several important factors seem to be at work:

- Muddled 'process levelling' (explained below).
- Insufficient attention paid to 'project characterisation' at the outset of a project.
- The concept of 'meta process' does not seem to have occurred to most people.
- Silly and false demarcations between management and technical issues when it comes to process definition.

Muddled Process Levelling

In any systems engineering process, there need to be two equally important levels working in concert, which we here refer to as SE 'in the large' and SE 'in the small'. However, the following situations are commonly encountered:

- Failing to recognise that these two levels even exist
- Muddling the two levels up
- Having insufficient variety or richness at either level
  Resultant problems include
- Inappropriate programme 'shapes' that lead to process rigidity as described above
- Inability to reduce risk systematically
- Inability to accommodate iteration

I should confess at the outset that I have had some difficulty in choosing names for these levels since there are many candidates available. There is also a danger of choosing a name that is overloaded by other concepts taken from closely related disciplines. This seems to be because of the great disparity between the number of concepts we have to give a name to in the modern world and the number of names available. So, let's make an accommodation: you as reader retain the right to disagree with my choice of name and suggest a better one.

The first level is about systems engineering 'in the large'. It is at this level that we find words like 'phase', 'concept exploration', 'proof of concept', 'feasibility study', 'project definition' 'full development', 'in-service maintenance', 'in-service upgrade', 'disposal' and so on. It can also be thought of as the macro picture of an entire project from cradle to grave, comprising a number of subprojects that make up the whole life cycle. It is at this level that risk can be managed most effectively. Budgets can be assessed on the best information available at the time and allocated in digestible portions. Sensible high-level review points can be inserted at which management takes stock of whether the overall project is proceeding as required and whether money is being well spent.

Other possible names for this level might be 'macro' systems engineering, as opposed to 'micro' systems engineering (*see* below). Actually, this is quite a good name. Unfortunately (and with no disrespect intended), Booch (1994) uses the term in the context of Object Orientated development with a somewhat different meaning. One could of course borrow the term and assign it the meaning described in this chapter, but that might cause confusion.

Another term might be 'Life-Cycle Level'. This suffers from the problem that it is too general; it is overused and overloaded with different meanings. For instance, the sequence of steps or activities that we started this chapter by discussing is itself referred to as a life cycle. As the reader will soon appreciate, it is precisely the need to distinguish between these activities and project phases 'in the large' that we are trying to emphasise. If we choose 'Life-Cycle Level' to mean 'in the large', there seems little to prevent people from saying 'Oh yes—I know what you mean. You mean the following sequence of steps:'

Requirements Discovery	Requirements Validation	System Specification	System Design	Coding, First of Class	Integration & Testing	Operations & Maintenance

Oh no we don't! We want to distinguish this sequence of steps from those 'in the large' and give a special label to them.

This brings us neatly to the point at which we introduce the second level of the systems engineering process. In fact, we have given the game away. The second level is broadly the sequence of activities shown in the table above.

We call this systems engineering 'in the small'. It concerns sequences of activities such as: user requirements, system requirements, architecture, system design, subsystem identification and specification, preliminary design, detailed design, implementation, test and integration, acceptance tests, certification, training, commissioning, and handover.

Why have we made this separation between 'in the large' and 'in the small'? Simply because 'in the small' is necessary but not sufficient for general systems development and project management. 'In the large' is needed to handle the sufficiency issue—that is, the bits that the 'in the small' process does not address.

At this stage, we should stress that we are not using the terms 'large' and 'small' in a pejorative sense. 'Large' does not mean more important than 'small'. To labour points already made:

- For any practical systems engineering/project management process model, you need to reflect and accommodate *both* levels explicitly.
- Focusing on one level at the expense of the other is a mistake, although both errors are encountered in practice.
- One often sees just one level depicted, with the other implicitly struggling to get out.
- There are a number of different 'in the large' models in use. Often one hears the claim that one particular model is the right one to use. Some people become almost religiously zealous when it comes to this. But this is inappropriate; there is no one correct 'in the large' model. To insist that this is the case is to invite and encourage process rigidity. 'Horses for courses' thinking should prevail. Choose the one that seems most appropriate for the project in question. This last point of course has an effect on people who write process standards. If there is process diversity in the large, what do you put in your process standard?

The answer seems to be that your process standard should instead be a meta process, or a process for generating a process. This seems to be a particularly powerful concept, since it seems to offer at a stroke full generality, flexibility and recycling of systems engineering good practice. It also requires you to have risk assessed the project and asked pertinent questions about how the project is likely to unfold (and having to do these cannot be considered a bad thing!). The ideas underlying meta processes are discussed in detail below.

Systems Engineering 'in the small'

We have already introduced and motivated systems engineering 'in the small' in the previous section. Most readers will recognise the activities, but for consistency and completeness we have tidied up the terminology used because reference is made to them extensively in the section on systems engineering 'in the large'. This is also the reason why we start our discussion 'in the small'.

Here are the 'in the small' activities

- User Requirements Definition (URD)
- System Requirements Definition (SRD)
- System Design/Architecture (SD/A)
- Preliminary Design (PD)
- Detailed Design (DD)
- Implementation (Imp)
- Test and Integration (T&I)
- Acceptance and Certification (A&C)

Note that we have consciously differentiated User Requirements from System Requirements as in Mazza et al. (1994). This is viewed as a contentious issue by some: they maintain that the distinction between User and System requirements is spurious and that in reality there are just 'requirements'. To be fair to this way of thinking, it is certainly true that requirements can at times be difficult to pigeonhole within this classification scheme. However, it seems equally obvious that there are two ends of a spectrum involved here, and that labelling the extreme points is a useful way of ensuring that a balanced requirements specification is produced.

User Requirements Definition (URD)

This activity is centred on the world of the *User*. 'User' is itself a troublesome word. Who is 'the user'? Very rarely is it just one person. Usually, the 'user' is a collection of stakeholders (i.e. identifiable individuals), some fulfilling more than one role. The essence of being a User is that the system is being built/procured <u>for them</u>. Without them, there would be no point in acquiring the system.

The stakeholder roles (*see* also the section on Stakeholders in Chapter 1, Introduction, of this volume) can be categorised, for example:

- Beneficiaries
  - ☐ Functional (i.e. whose jobs will the system make easier or more effective?)
  - ☐ Financial (i.e. which stakeholders will the system make richer?)
- Operational
  - ☐ Who is going to operate this system?
  - ☐ Which other systems have to interoperate with this system?
- Negative
  - ☐ Who has to be appeased/placated when building and operating this system?

This process of finding out the composition of the user community is often called 'stakeholder identification and analysis' and can be viewed as a subject in its own right.

The process of finding out what these stakeholders do and what their needs are is similarly a specialised topic. Indeed, it can be argued that this is what the rest of this book is about! Suzanne Robertson's approach to Requirements Discovery (Chapter 3) is a good example.

There are also categories of nonfunctional user requirements, such as:

- Cost
- Timescale
- Reliability
- Maintainability
- Availability
- Usability
- Safety
- Security
- Upgradability
- and so on. . . (the so-called 'ilities', or product qualities).

System Requirements Definition (SRD)

System Requirements, by contrast, have very little (if any) connection with the motivation for the system. Instead, they can be viewed as the constraints that have to be applied to the system acquisition process to obtain a fit-for-purpose result. Usually, system requirements are technical in nature and cover the following kinds of specialist areas:

- Detailed Functional Behaviour (including timing/performance)
- Legislation, Regulations and Standards
- Technical Interfaces
- Environmental
- Physical

System requirements are often the things that make system acquisition difficult. This is equivalent to saying that building the system would be straightforward if it were not for having to meet all the system requirements!

Peter Haumer's account in Chapter 12 of Use Case-Based Software Development and Alistair Mavin's description of Scenarios in Rail Rolling Stock in Chapter 20 give good examples of work in this phase.

System Design/Architecture (SD/A)

I hope it is obvious from the above discussion on requirements that both user **and** system requirements are needed for a successful system acquisition. Focusing on one to the detriment of the other will lead to disaster. Ignoring user requirements results in a system that fails to deliver benefit; ignoring system requirements will lead to inadequate definition of functionality or a mismatch with the intended environment.

Once requirements are understood, work can begin on designing a compliant solution. We call this process 'System Design/Architecture'. Many people use the terms 'Design' and 'Architecture' interchangeably. For this reason, we have incorporated both terms.

It is at this stage that the overall shape of a compliant solution is worked out. Principal subsystems are identified and their individual requirements flowed down and refined (sometimes called 'derived' requirements).

Often the SD/A will be multi-disciplinary and will have to embrace the engineering technologies applicable to the solution; for example, electronics, electrical, communications, mechanical, software, civil, and so on.

Preliminary Design (PD)

This activity is predominantly conducted at subsystem level. Its objective is to carry out sufficient design to provide confidence that the flowed-down system requirements are achievable at subsystem level. It is during this activity that a subsystem design authority commits to the flowed-down requirements. At system level, the system design authority needs to respond to the inevitable clarification requests and issues raised by the subsystem design authorities. It often concludes with a Preliminary Design Review (PDR).

Detailed Design (DD)

This activity is again conducted at subsystem level. Its purpose is to carry out sufficient design to support implementation. It should provide confidence that subsystem flowed-down requirements will be met. This activity should conclude with a Critical Design Review (CDR). This is an extremely important review. After this point, the spend rate incurs a step change increase as materials and labour are consumed. If there are any outstanding system uncertainties, it is better to sort them out at this point rather than leave it till later!

Implementation (Imp)

Here the subsystem designs are implemented using the relevant technologies, and tested at subsystem level. Testing should demonstrate that flowed-down requirements have been met.

Test and Integration (T&I)

During this activity, the individual components come together for testing as an integrated whole. Compliance with the user and system requirements should be demonstrated. If the requirements have been well-structured (e.g. by using scenarios and use cases), this activity is made a lot easier.

Ian Alexander's description of how to derive test cases from use cases in Chapter 14 illustrates some of the considerations necessary in this activity.

Acceptance and Certification (A&C)

This activity is when the user community or their representatives take a tested and integrated system and confirm that what has been built is indeed what was wanted. In highly regulated and/or high-integrity applications, this will involve approval by the appropriate certifying bodies.

Systems Engineering 'in the large'

As mentioned above, there are a number of representative process models operating 'in the large'. We now describe a selection of these in turn.

The point made above: that none of the following models have absolute superiority over the others, should be stressed. Rather, in a particular set of project circumstances, one model will be more relevant and therefore more appropriate.

Here is a list of some commonly encountered 'in the large' process models:

- Evolutionary model
- Incremental model
- US DoD model
- UK Ministry of Defence CADMID model
- RUP (Rational Unified Process)— (RUP 2003), and see Chapter 12 in this volume
- 'Agile Methods' (e.g. Extreme Programming (XP)—see Chapter 13 in this volume)

The basic process models are discussed in general terms in (Stevens et al. 1998, Conger 1994, Sommerville 2001).

It seems, however, that all of these can be built from a small number (three) of basic process models. Furthermore, variants and hybrids not found in the above list but which are encountered in practical situations can be constructed by composition of the three basic models.

In the above list, the evolutionary and incremental models are deemed to be in the basic set. To this we add another, which we have here called the 'High-Risk' model.

We will now discuss each of the three basic models in turn:

- Evolutionary model
- Incremental model
- High-Risk model

We will then proceed to examine their relationship to the commonly encountered process models listed above and ways in which they can be combined to form variants.

Evolutionary Model

Figure 15.1 shows this to be a particularly simple model—see Stevens et al. (1998). In essence, it consists of a sequence of successive versions of a product evolving over time, with feedback from version (n) into version $(n + 1)$. Inside each version cycle, we see the 'in the small' systems engineering activities embedded (note that for the sake of diagrammatic brevity, production, installation, in-service support, and disposal are not shown).

What scenario would suggest the evolutionary model? It would probably include:

- A rapid rate of technological evolution.
- A tacit acceptance from customers to accept the functionality that technology can offer in the short term, rather than waiting for perfection (whatever that means). It is probably sufficient for the offering to be competitive.
- The business need is to get the product to market in the shortest time possible.

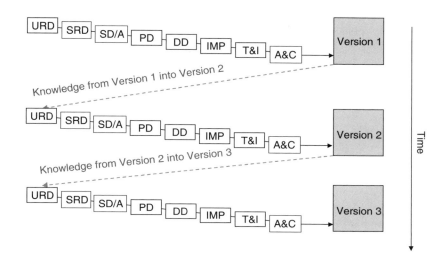

FIGURE 15.1 Evolutionary model

Markets using the evolutionary model include mass consumer products such as cars, personal computers, and PC software (i.e. operating systems and application packages).

Incremental Model

Figure 15.2 is subtly different from the evolutionary model—see (Stevens et al. 1998). In the incremental model, the system is specified and designed in broad architectural terms up front, and (in principle) the design stays unchanged thereafter. After the system specification and overall design are completed, an initial piece of functionality called Increment 1 is delivered. Some time later, some more functionality called Increment 2 is delivered, which fits together with Increment 1. Still later, Increment 3 is added, fitting together with Increments 1 and 2. And so on. (Note that as in the evolutionary model, production, installation, in-service support, and disposal are not shown. Note also that the inevitable change requests and associated configuration management activities are not shown explicitly.)

The 'in the small' systems engineering activities are embedded in the incremental deliveries, but notice the difference between this and the embedding used in the evolutionary model. In Figure 15.1 the complete cycle of activities is repeated for each version, whereas in Figure 15.2 the URD, SRD, and SD/A activities are factored out of the sequence of incremental deliveries and occur only once, at the outset of the project.

This distinction is important. It means that the sum of all increments represents the totality of a single system, which must be analysed and designed once at the start of the project. Thereafter, the physical increments are individually designed, tested, and delivered at successive points in time.

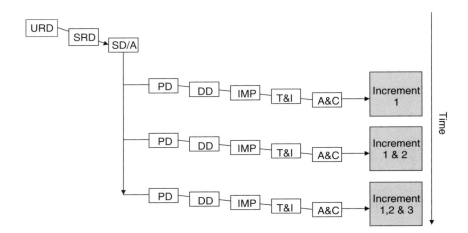

FIGURE 15.2 Incremental model

This aspect of requirements analysis and design once at the start of the project is not present in the evolutionary model in which the coupling between successive versions is much looser. Indeed, in the evolutionary model, compatibility between successive versions, although desirable, is by no means assured. In the incremental model, on the other hand, compatibility between successive increments is *de rigueur*.

So what project scenario would suggest use of the incremental model? The following factors will probably be present:

- The centrality of the understanding that there is <u>one</u> system under consideration.
- The inability to deliver total system functionality as one big bang for some reason. Time or financial constraints will probably be the chief factors here. The functionality contained in each increment will be decided on the basis of business or operational priority.
- The functionality of Increment 1 must deliver sufficient business or operational value to make it worthwhile.
- The freedom to phase system functionality sub-sets (i.e. increments) over time.
- The ability to impose top class configuration control between increments, thus preserving the integrity of interfaces between increments.

A variant of the Incremental model appears to be the 'Extreme Programming (XP)' approach put forward in Beck (2000) in which integrity of the system architecture across all increments is maintained by periodic design 'refactoring'.

High-Risk Model

The name of this model should not be misconstrued. It does not mean that use of this model will result in a high-risk project! It means the model is to be used with projects that are initially considered to be high risk. This model is particularly useful when contracting

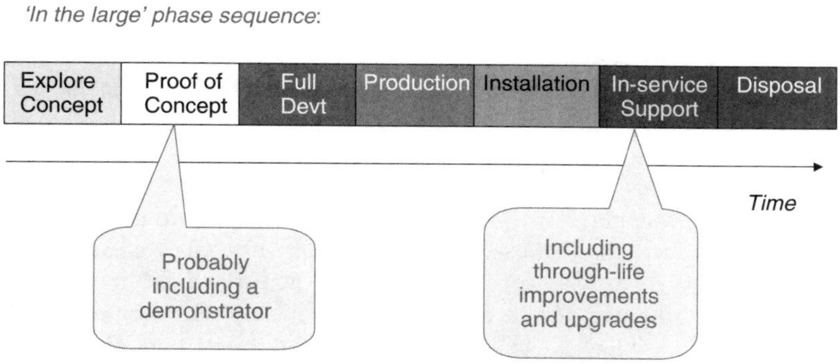

'In the large' phase sequence:

| Explore Concept | Proof of Concept | Full Devt | Production | Installation | In-service Support | Disposal |

Probably including a demonstrator

Including through-life improvements and upgrades

Time

FIGURE 15.3 High risk model

combined with potentially high financial risk is involved. By contracting for one phase at a time, both customer and supplier can keep contractual risk under control.

As can be seen, Figure 15.3 looks quite different from the preceding two models, and tells a more complicated story for reasons that will become clear.

We see that the 'in the large' level is divided into a number of phases:

- *Explore Concept*
  This phase is about exploring the business or operational needs. It asks questions like: what problems need to be brought into focus? Why is a system solution needed? What sort of solutions are possible? What benefits are to be expected from such a system?

- *Proof of Concept*
  In this phase, system ideas are taken further. Technology trials are conducted. Trade-off analyses of the different candidate solutions against each other are done ('optioneering'). Risk assessments are made. Detailed cost-models are built. One or more demonstrators may be designed, built, and formally assessed to judge whether the conclusions reached so far are valid. Demonstrators help answer the question: have we asked the right questions, and would a fully developed system incorporating the chief characteristics of the demonstrator solve the problems unearthed during the earlier phases.

- *Full Development*
  In this phase, a 'first of class' instance of the final system is built, tested against its specification (or 'verified'—to use the increasingly accepted meaning of this word), formally accepted, type-approved, and certified.

- *Production*
  The production line starts rolling.

- *Installation*
  Production units are delivered to operational units, installed, checked, and put into operation.

- *In-service support*

  Support facilities are made available. Stretching the meaning of the word 'support' somewhat, we could for the diagrammatic compactness imagine that 'mid-life' improvements and upgrades fit into this phase. Note that this phase represents the whole working life of the system.

- *Disposal*

  The overall cradle-to-grave aspect of the project ends with disposal of the system. This may seem an obvious thing to say, not adding very much. A moment's thought, however, should make it clear that in the case of some types of system, especially those using dangerous substances or components (such as nuclear reactors), disposal represents a non-trivial problem. If not thought about and planned for in advance, disposal of systems such as these becomes a major problem in its own right. Disposal issues may also in all likelihood affect the choice of solution.

Under what circumstances would this model be used?

As the name 'High-Risk Model' suggests, it seems particularly useful when one doesn't really know at the outset what the problem is, what the requirements are, what solutions might be relevant and/or feasible, or whether the stakeholders really know what they want. All one is really sure of is that a consensus exists that 'something needs to be done' and that (probably) some sort of improvement should be possible. To reduce the initial high risk, therefore, the 'in the large' sequence involves successive phases in which project risks (user need, requirements, technology and fitness for purpose) are reduced in a controlled, step-wise fashion.

Variants of this model are used by the US DoD and UK Ministry of Defence (in which they have a model referred to as 'CADMID' that stands for: Concept, Assessment, Demonstration, Manufacture, In-service, and Disposal).

What is less clear with this model is how the 'in the small' systems engineering activities fit into the 'in the large' phase structure. What should each of the 'in the large' phases contain in detailed systems engineering terms? This question is depicted in Figure 15.4.

It doesn't appear to make much sense simply to repeat identically the 'in the small' activities inside each 'in the large' phase. One the other hand, it does seem to be the case that the various 'in the small' activities such as user and system requirements, architecture and design, implementation, test and integration, and so on have individual relevance within each phase.

Is this a contradiction? No, it isn't.

What gets us out of this difficulty is the realisation that the scope, intensity, and objectives of each 'in the small' activity need to be interpreted in the context of each phase. In other words, the 'in the small' systems engineering activity sequence needs to be instantiated as a function of each 'in the large' phase.

For example, some element of architecting/design is needed in the Explore Concept phase, otherwise even a rudimentary meaningful cost/benefit case will be impossible to construct. Nevertheless, requirements-orientated activities will certainly predominate. Conversely, although it is certain that during Full Development design, implementation and testing activities will be dominant, there will still be requirements-orientated

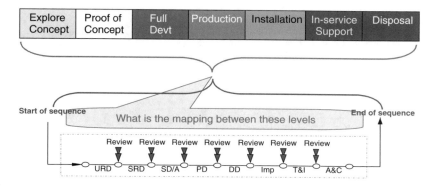

'In the large' phase sequence

'In the small' system engineering activity sequence

FIGURE 15.4   Mapping the levels

activities taking place to accommodate and assess requirements changes and refine any requirements not sufficiently defined during the earlier phases.

It seems therefore that something like Figure 15.5 helps to explain the mapping between the two levels.

In this diagram, the 'intensity' of each systems engineering activity is shown by the height of the respective bar column. Note further: there is one set of bar columns for three of the 'in the large' phases (i.e. Explore Concept, Proof of Concept, Full Development) and that within each set there is one bar column for each of the systems engineering activities (i.e. eight). It should be clear from this diagram that:

- the dominant activities during Explore Concept are User Requirements and System Requirements.
- the dominant activities during Proof of Concept are SD/A and PD.
- the dominant activities during Full Development are DD, imp, T&I and A&C.

However, it should be equally clear that most, if not all, of the systems engineering activities are of non-zero intensity in all 'in the large' phases.

Redrawing Figure 15.5 using the same information, we obtain the following in Figure 15.6:

This shows how the systems engineering activities in the context of each phase give rise to activity intensity levels that rise, peak, and fall over time. This gives us a useful insight into how skill mix on a project changes over time. Interestingly, it confirms that multi-disciplinary teams should be the order of the day, but that the specific skill ratios need to change over time.

This is instructive for project management and those concerned with organisational structure. For example, it is not unusual to find organisations in which different 'in the

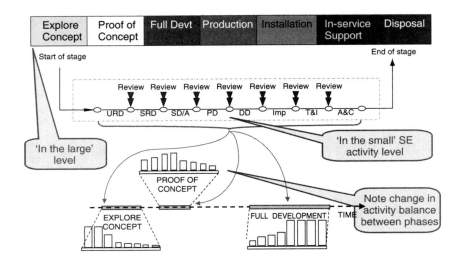

FIGURE 15.5   Changing activity balance between phases

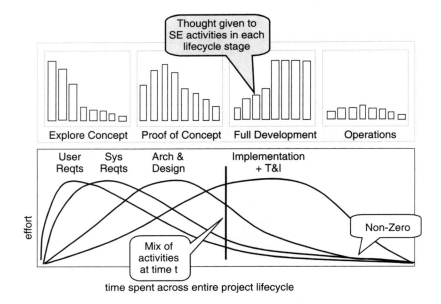

FIGURE 15.6   Changing activity skills mix over time

large' phases are 'owned' by different departments and staffed by their own people to the exclusion of the rest of the organisation. To continue the example, let us assume that:

- Projects of type 'Explore Concept' are the province of the Future Studies Group in Marketing and Strategic Planning;
- Projects of type 'Proof of Concept' are done by the Engineering Directorate;
- Full Developments are done by a Projects Directorate.

Now, even if we allow that the requisite skills exist in type and number within each part of the organisation (admittedly a big assumption!), not being allowed (for whatever reason) to use the right skills mix (because they exist only somewhere else in the organisation) will harm the project. If we just use business analysts and requirements specialists during Explore Concept (and it is not unknown for organisations to behave in precisely this way), the output from the Explore Concept phase will be decidedly lopsided. Business cases will not be worth the paper they're written on. Think about it: who constructed the cost side of the cost/benefit equation? What assumptions were used? Do they bear any relationship to engineering reality?

Combining Models

It is possible to combine different 'in the large' models as necessary. For example, it would be quite realistic to combine the High-Risk Model with the Incremental Model in some way, for example by extracting the system architectural aspects of the project and creating a phase after Proof of Concept called, say, Baseline Architecture (or something equivalent) and then repeating the relevant aspects of Full Development, Installation, and Production once per Increment, thus building up to full functionality in stages.

This combined model is similar to the *Rational Unified Process* (RUP 2003) which is normally described in terms of the following four phases:

- **Inception** (similar to Explore Concept)
- **Elaboration** (similar to Proof of Concept + System Level Architecture)
- **Construction** (N increments delivered either internally or externally)
- **Transition** (similar to aspects of In-Service Support e.g. handover and user training)

One could go further and suppose that during In-Service Support, there should be an accommodation for multiple successive in-service enhancements and upgrades. Adaptation and inclusion of the Evolutionary Model might be the preferred way of incorporating this extension.

Extending this extension even further, each evolutionary upgrade might itself be designed, constructed, and delivered incrementally.

On another tack, we could conceive of a situation in which we decide that the Evolutionary Model is combined with the Incremental Model. In this situation, each successive version (see Figure 15.1) is delivered in distinct increments i.e. embed Figure 15.2 inside each version within Figure 15.1.

And so on.

Meta-Process

The preceding sections have suggested that specific process models should not be institutionalised within an organisation's process manuals, since this leads to process rigidity and inappropriate project shapes.

Instead, we should 'go up' a level in our thinking and think about what sort of guidance we could write to help someone generate and tailor a process relevant to any specific project. This 'one level up' type of thinking can be considered as a Systems Engineering *Meta Process*.

It can be depicted in Figure 15.7, as follows:

A good way of constructing this meta process is to try and characterise the project in terms of the questions raised in the context of each 'in the large' phase model discussed above. This can be thought of as an application of 'storytelling' to the meta-level system context. Here are the questions and their implications:

- Is there a business need to get the product to market in the shortest time possible?
  □ Yes ⇒ Evolutionary Model
- Is there a very rapid rate of technological evolution relative to design and delivery lead-times (implying very short product lifetimes)?
  □ Yes ⇒ Evolutionary Model

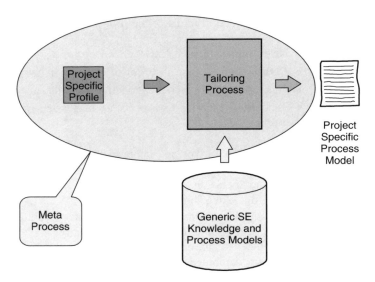

FIGURE 15.7 Systems engineering meta-process

- Are customers prepared to accept the functionality that you and technology can offer in the short term, rather than waiting longer for a better solution? Are they likely to pay for successive versions?

  ☐ Yes ⇒ Evolutionary Model

- Can you tolerate loose technical linkage between successive versions of a system/product?

  ☐ Yes ⇒ Evolutionary Model

- Is there some reason why it is impossible to deliver total system functionality in one chunk. Do time or financial constraints mean a 'salami slice' approach is required? Can functionality be prioritised? Do functionality sub-sets make operational and business sense? Do successive increments have to dovetail perfectly?

  ☐ Yes ⇒ Incremental Model

- Do you really know at the outset what exactly the problem is, what the requirements are, what solutions might be relevant, or whether the stakeholders really know what they want?

  ☐ No ⇒ High-Risk Model

- Is likely candidate technology proven?

  ☐ No ⇒ High-Risk Model

- How confident are you about the validity of the requirements discovery process?

  ☐ Not very confident ⇒ High-Risk Model

Alternatively, in tabular form:

Questions	Evolutionary	Incremental	High Risk
☐ Is there a business need to get the product to market in the shortest time possible?	**Yes**		
☐ Is there a very rapid rate of technological evolution relative to design and delivery lead-times (implying very short product lifetimes)?	**Yes**		
☐ Are customers prepared to accept the functionality that you and technology can offer in the short term, rather than waiting longer for a better solution? Are they likely to pay for successive versions?	**Yes**		
☐ Can you tolerate loose technical linkage between successive versions of a system/product?	**Yes**		

Questions	Evolutionary	Incremental	High Risk
☐ Is there some reason why it is impossible to deliver total system functionality in one chunk. Do time or financial constraints mean a 'salami slice' approach is required? Can functionality be prioritised? Do functionality sub-sets make operational and business sense? Do successive increments have to dovetail perfectly?		Yes	
☐ Do you really know at the outset what exactly the problem is, what the requirements are, what solutions might be relevant, or whether the stakeholders really know what they want?			No
☐ Is likely candidate technology proven?			No
☐ Do you have doubts about the validity of the requirements discovery process?			Yes

Things are relatively straightforward if this question-and-answer approach yields a single mutually exclusive solution, that is, all the answers indicate exactly one of the options Evolutionary, Incremental, or High Risk. But what happens if one of the four other possibilities arises, that is,

- Evolutionary and Incremental
- Evolutionary and High Risk
- Incremental and High Risk
- Evolutionary, Incremental and High Risk?

Evolutionary and Incremental

The combination of Evolutionary and Incremental probably means that the Evolutionary Model dominates but that due to timescale or resource constraints, the full functionality of a version cannot be delivered all at once. However, getting some critical and useful initial functionality into the field makes business and marketing sense. Once this is achieved, the remaining increment(s) can be added. Schematically, this would look something like this:

```
Version 1
      Increment 1.1
      Increment 1.2
      . . .
      Increment 1.N
Version 2
      Increment 2.1
      Increment 2.2
      . . .
      Increment 2.N
      . . .
Version M
      Increment M.1
      Increment M.2
      . . .
      Increment M.N
```

Interpreting it the other way round (i.e. Incremental dominating with Evolutionary contained inside) does not seem to make much sense. You should check your logic!

For example,

```
Increment 1
      Version 1.1
      Version 1.2
      . . .
      Version 1.N
Increment 2
      Version 2.1
      Version 2.2
      . . .
      Version 2.N
. . . Increment M
      Version M.1
      Version M.2
      . . .
      Version M.N
```

Evolutionary and High Risk

The combination of Evolutionary and High Risk only seems to make complete sense if the project falls predominantly into the High-Risk category and the evolutionary aspects relate to mid-life improvements and upgrades within In-Service Support. This would be implied by the following responses:

Questions	Answers
☐ Is there a business need to get the product to market in the shortest time possible?	**No**
☐ Is there a very rapid rate of technological evolution relative to design and delivery lead-times (implying very short product lifetimes)?	**No**
☐ Are customers prepared to accept the functionality that you and technology can offer in the short term, rather than waiting longer for a better solution? Are they likely to pay for successive versions?	**Yes**
☐ Can you tolerate loose technical linkage between successive versions of a system/product?	**Yes**
☐ Do you really know at the outset what exactly the problem is, what the requirements are, what solutions might be relevant, or whether the stakeholders really know what they want?	**No**
☐ Is likely candidate technology proven?	**No**
☐ Do you have doubts about the validity of the requirements discovery process?	**Yes**

The project structure would probably be as follows:

```
Concept exploration
Proof of Concept
Full Development
Production
Installation
In-Service Support:
        Version 2
        Version 3
        . . .
        Version N
```

However, suppose the responses are as follows:

Questions	Answers
☐ Is there a business need to get the product to market in the shortest time possible?	**Yes**
☐ Is there a very rapid rate of technological evolution relative to design and delivery lead-times (implying very short product lifetimes)?	**Yes**
☐ Do you really know at the outset what exactly the problem is, what the requirements are, what solutions might be relevant, or whether the stakeholders really know what they want?	**No**
☐ Is likely candidate technology proven?	**No**
☐ Do you have doubts about the validity of the requirements discovery process?	**Yes**

In this case you have a problem! You are faced with the challenge of designing, producing, and delivering a system in short order with high initial risks in the area of requirements and technology. This is very likely mission impossible and probably doomed to failure. You should ask yourself whether you are in the right business!

Incremental and High Risk

The combination of Incremental and High-Risk almost certainly means the High Risk model dominates with the Incremental aspect fitting inside it. So, you Explore Concept, do Proof of Concept and Baseline Architecture, then do Full Development, Installation, and Production *N* times on an Incremental basis. Doing it the other way round does not seem to make much sense. As already mentioned, RUP seems to be similar to this.

The project structure would be as follows:

```
Concept exploration
Proof of Concept
Baseline Architecture
Increment 1
        Full Development
        Production
        Installation
        In-Service Support
```

Increment 2
    Full Development
    Production
    Installation
    In-Service Support
. . .
Increment N
    Full Development
    Production
    Installation
    In-Service Support
Disposal

Evolutionary, Incremental and High Risk

The combination of Evolutionary, Incremental, and High Risk probably means that the situation as described in the previous section on Incremental and High Risk exists, but with the Evolutionary aspects confined to mid-life improvements and upgrades within In-Service Support. The project structure would be as follows:

Concept exploration
Proof of Concept
Baseline Architecture
Increment 1
    Full Development
    Production
    Installation
    In-Service Support
Increment 2
    Full Development
    Production
    Installation
    In-Service Support
. . .
Increment N
    Full Development
    Production
    Installation
    In-Service Support
Mid-life improvements and upgrades:
    Version 2
    Version 3
    . . .
    Version N

It could alternatively mean that:

- the project is predominantly High Risk;
- it has Evolutionary aspects confined to mid-life improvements and upgrades within In-Service Support;
- each mid-life improvement and upgrade is done Incrementally.

The project structure would probably be as follows:

```
Concept exploration
Proof of Concept
Full Development
Production
Installation
In-Service Support:
        Version 2
                Increment 2.1
                Increment 2.2
                . . .
                Increment 2.N
        Version 3
                Increment 3.1
                Increment 3.2
                . . .
                Increment 3.N
        . . .
        Version M
                Increment M.1
                Increment M.2
                . . .
                Increment M.N
```

But be careful, check that you are not in mission impossible mode again as described in the section on Evolutionary and High Risk!

CONCLUSION

This chapter has explored the idea of thinking about the system development life cycle in story form. Furthermore, it seems that a few simple stories can be composed in different ways to produce more complex process models.

The ideas discussed in this chapter started to form when I worked for a large UK company with a diverse assortment of projects employing a range of technologies. I had the job of trying to codify systems engineering knowledge and produce an in-house set of guidelines. The concept of separating the two levels of systems engineering process seemed to simplify things considerably, as did the realisation that there is no perfect 'one size fits all' process model. For those interested, the seeds of the thought processes contained here first saw light of day in Farncombe (1997).

KEYWORDS

Life cycle	Incremental (development)	Iteration	Tailoring
Evolutionary (development)	Risk Reduction	Systems Engineering	

REFERENCES

Beck, K., *Extreme Programming Explained*, Addison-Wesley, 2000.

Booch, G., *Object-Oriented Analysis and Design, with Applications*, The Benjamin/Cummings Publishing Company, 1994.

Conger, S., *The New Software Engineering*, Wadsworth, 1994.

Farncombe, A., Tayloring (sic) systems engineering processes to project management circumstances, *UK INCOSE Third Annual Symposium*, Luton, U.K., 1997.

Mazza, C., Fairclough, J., Melton, B., De Pablo, D., Scheffer, A., and Stevens, R., *Software Engineering Standards*, Prentice Hall, 1994. Formerly the European Space Agency's *PSS-05-0 Standards* (Issue 2, 1991; BSSC version 1984)

Royce, W.W., Managing the development of large software systems: concepts and techniques, *Proceedings of IEEE WESTCON*, Los Angeles, CA, Chapter 3, 1970.

RUP, *Rational Unified Process*, IBM Rational Software, RUP 2003.06, 2003.

Sommerville, I., *Software Engineering*, 6th ed. Addison-Wesley, 2001.

Stevens, R., Brook, P., Jackson, K., and Arnold, S., *Systems Engineering, Coping with Complexity*, Prentice Hall, 1998.

RECOMMENDED READING

Ian Sommerville's *Software Engineering* (Sommerville 2001) is a good general overview of the need to manage project life cycles and the basic need to control risk.

The (ESA) *Software Engineering Standards* (Mazza 1994) offer a plain and practical introduction to the life cycle. While on the surface they are framed as pure 'waterfall' terms, in truth the activities are the ingredients of all life cycles. The descriptions of the component processes and the supporting templates also provide a useful foundation.

PART III

SCENARIOS IN ACTION: CASE STUDIES

OVERVIEW OF PART 3—CASE STUDIES

INTRODUCTION

This part of the book consists of a set of case studies written by authors who have applied scenarios in their work. Each chapter can stand alone as an example of the use of scenarios; but the chapters follow a common framework, explained below, and authors have described some of the lessons learnt from their experience, which we hope will help you to identify approaches for your projects. Therefore, there are several ways of using this part of the book, other than simply reading it from start to end:

- find the chapters that describe the case studies closest to your projects, and study those in detail;
- read the Summaries of all the chapters to get an idea of how scenarios worked out in practice on a range of projects;
- skim through the chapters, especially the Roles Played by Scenarios, Strengths and Weaknesses, and Lessons Learnt sections, to get an appreciation of the relative merits of the various approaches.

STRUCTURE OF THE PART 3 CHAPTERS

Each chapter has the following framework:

Summary

A few paragraphs summarising the case study.

Type of Project

A brief factual statement of the type of project described in the case study.

Applicability

A brief statement of opinion about the types of project that could benefit from the approach that was followed in the case study.

Position in the Life Cycle

A diagram like the one below, showing the parts of the life cycle covered by the described approach.

Requirements Discovery	Requirements Validation	System Specification	System Design	Coding, First of Class	Integration & Testing	Operations & Maintenance

Roles Played by Scenarios

Explains in a short factual narrative the ways scenarios were used in the project and why. For example, were scenarios used to help to discover requirements? To give designers some context? To guide testing?

Strengths

A description of what worked well on the project because of its use of scenarios.

Weaknesses

A description of what did not work well and the limitations of the chosen approaches.

Case Study

A detailed stepwise account, telling the story of what was done in the project, what happened, what went well, and what went wrong or worked only with difficulty.

Lessons Learnt

A description of the lessons learnt during the project described in the case study.

Keywords

A list of terms for the main concepts used in the chapter.

TOPICS COVERED

The case studies are examples of industrial practice and consultancy from as diverse a set of projects as we were able to find. They vary greatly in scale—though without an example of the very largest projects, where scenario use is uncommon. They illustrate scenarios in the automotive, railway, aviation, telecommunications, and construction industries. We made a special effort to find examples that were not purely about software (to make the point that scenarios are more generally applicable), though it is no surprise that almost all the projects involved a significant element of software development.

CHAPTER 16

STORY USE AND REUSE IN AUTOMOTIVE SYSTEMS ENGINEERING

Frank Houdek[1] and Thomas Zink[2]

[1] *DaimlerChrysler, Ulm, Germany*
[2] *Nokia Mobile Phones, Ulm, Germany (formerly at DaimlerChrysler)*

THE SPECIFICATION volume needed to develop a premium car is amazing: The set of vehicle features and functions implemented in software now exceeds 10^4 pages. The countless requirements allocated to dozens of subsystems are described in intricate detail. They are influenced not only by market demands but also by technological opportunities and cost constraints.

Consequently, it is a non-trivial task to keep track of all the rationales behind individual requirements, or the interactions of all the functions. If new functions come into play or existing functions have to evolve because of changed constraints, it becomes hard not to get lost in detail.

In this context, we found scenarios to be beneficial in a range of activities supporting different stages of product definition and enhancement. They proved to be a good means of negotiating new product features, to provide meaningful rationales for requirements (without being too detailed), to provide a users' perspective on technological driven product features and to keep an overview in the chaos of detail.

To illustrate these benefits, the chapter gives first a brief overview of the characteristics of automotive software development. Then we sketch the benefits of scenarios for different activities in the specification area by typical examples.

TYPE OF PROJECT

Automotive software development (e.g. embedded systems, usually functionality distributed over various individual controllers).

APPLICABILITY

The approaches described in this chapter may be beneficial for many types of projects. Projects that could gain most from the approaches include:

Scenarios, Stories, Use Cases: Through the Systems Development Life-Cycle. Edited by Ian F Alexander and Neil Maiden
© 2004 John Wiley & Sons, Ltd. ISBN: 0-470-86194-0

- mass market products (i.e. no clear customer who really knows what he wants),
- complex systems with many (interacting) features and functions,
- projects whose stakeholders have (very) different backgrounds, and
- long-lasting projects (since rationales for requirements may be lost over time).

POSITION IN THE LIFE CYCLE

Requirements Discovery	Requirements Validation	System Specification	System Design	Coding, First of Class	Integration & Testing	Operations & Maintenance

ROLES PLAYED BY SCENARIOS

In our context, we used scenarios for

- communicating requirements from customers representatives to developers,
- identifying necessary interactions of available product features to maximise users benefit,
- providing an overview on detail-level specifications, and
- setting the context for individual requirements to increase understanding and reusability.

STRENGTHS

The strength of the chosen approach is its informality. Writing and reading stories is an everyday experience. It is an ideal means of communicating and documenting essential facts, both for non-specialists, and for engineers when they need to understand the 'bigger picture' around the software they are specifying.

WEAKNESSES

Informality has its shortcomings, too. There is no way of ensuring an informal description is complete. We use stories mainly in an 'opportunistic way', that is, where appropriate, but not throughout a project.

INTRODUCTION

Although cars do not look that different from how they looked 30 years ago (see Figure 16.1), they have changed dramatically underneath their steel surfaces. They are no longer just masterpieces of mechanical engineering—instead they have turned into

FIGURE 16.1   Some products of DaimlerChrysler (Courtesy of DaimlerChrysler AG)

complex computing devices embodying numerous processors and hundreds of thousands of lines of code. In the automotive domain, software has become the main driver of innovations and new functions. Of all upcoming innovations, 80% will be driven by electric/electronics systems, and of those, 90% are implemented in software (McKinsey, 2002).

Defining these new software functions, however, is a complex activity. As for all systems developed for the mass market, there is no really competent customer available in the sense that you can ask about the required features and functions and he can give precise answers. Instead, one has to triage potential new functions between technical feasibility, (potential) market demand, and cost (Davis, 2002). In this process, we found scenarios to be beneficial for various activities, as they helped us to focus on the essence of new or modified functions.

AUTOMOTIVE SOFTWARE DEVELOPMENT

In this section, we give a brief overview of automotive software development and its special characteristics. As Figure 16.2 illustrates, the volume (a), the contribution to the entire value chain (b) and the complexity (c) of automotive software has increased dramatically over the last three decades (DaimlerChrysler, 2002). Software started its success story in vehicles as a small supplement to classical electronic solutions, and has become a central part of today's complex distributed systems.

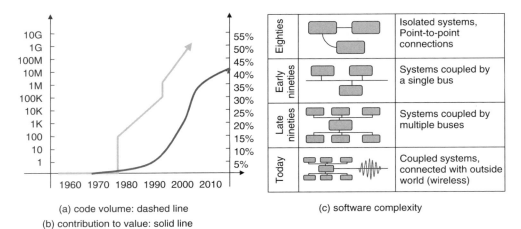

(a) code volume: dashed line

(b) contribution to value: solid line

(c) software complexity

FIGURE 16.2 Growing volume, contribution to value chain and complexity of automotive software over time

A recent medium to upper market segment vehicle typically embodies 40 to 100 electrical control units (ECUs, see e.g. Figure 16.3). The amount of software in all of these ECUs together has reached the order of 10^5 to 10^6 lines of code. In the recent Mercedes Benz S-class, for instance, there are more than 50 ECUs embodying more than 600,000 lines of code. The ECUs are connected by three buses with several hundred bus messages (Grimm, 2003). There are gateways between the buses, and functions are heavily interconnected. Via wireless interfaces, subsystems can connect to external systems, for instance, to receive traffic information or to report the car's position in an emergency.

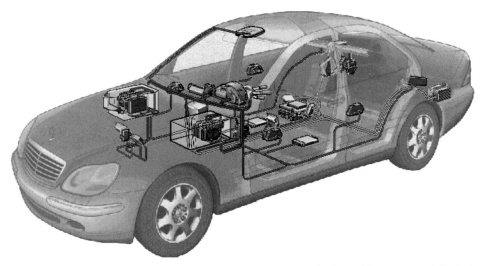

FIGURE 16.3 Sketch of ECU localisation in current S-class (Courtesy of Daimler-Chrysler AG)

The majority of the software is implemented by external suppliers, leaving us as a car manufacturer with the responsibility of specifying individual systems. ECUs are often purchased as 'black boxes' (thus incorporating both hardware and software). Of course, all rules have exceptions. Some parts of the software are developed in-house or by third-party software vendors.

This means that we as manufacturers have to orchestrate many different suppliers to realise one complete system. The specifications must ensure that the ECUs inter-operate properly. This means that the specifications have to define all ECU interfaces in detail, with requirements about interfaces, timing behaviour and error cases, described down to bits and bytes, protocols, and milliseconds. Otherwise, smooth integration of ECUs from different suppliers would not be possible (*see also* Weber and Weisbrod, 2002).

The period from initial requirements writing for a new vehicle model to the start of production ranges between three and six years in length. Given such a long period, changes are inevitable during development. There are many reasons for change:

- new features and functions released by competitors;
- technical feasibility and technological advance;
- changed legal regulations (e.g. fuel consumption and emission);
- expected savings in weight, space, or money.

The last of these, especially, makes the dependability and cost of hardware really important. Owing to the high number of units produced, savings in the region of a few cents per manufactured ECU may justify additional software development efforts in the range of several man-months. If, for example, there is a new sensor available that saves 10 cents per ECU compared to the old one, it may make perfect sense to switch to the new sensor even if a whole set of requirements has to be revised, causing additional down-stream development work.

Development of a new ECU is usually not 'green field': most often, there are comparable systems from earlier versions of the same model, or from sibling models. For example, the new S-class door control unit might be based on the E-class door control unit specified a year earlier. Consequently, the respective specifications are not created from scratch but by copying the relevant sections from existing documents. Having in mind that an individual specification document may consist of several hundred pages, consistent and complete copying and editing is a non-trivial task (Heumesser and Houdek, 2003; Alexander and Kiedaisch, 2002).

The specification of an individual ECU may be characterised as an extended negotiation process involving numerous stakeholders. The specification's author has to triage all the raised requirements, to detect conflicting requirements, and to initiate the necessary negotiations. The author is also the primary contact person for all questions and issues regarding the new ECU. Thus, a specification author usually does not consider himself a requirements engineer. Instead, he considers himself more as a domain expert. He sees solution finding as one of his primary activities. Writing a technical specification is a necessary step in this process. Aligned with the self-image of domain experts, the involved people are often electrical or mechanical engineers; they are rarely software specialists.

STORIES IN AUTOMOTIVE SOFTWARE DEVELOPMENT

Keeping up good communication is one of the most vital challenges for present day development projects in the automotive industry. Different roles inside and outside the organisation have to interact smoothly to create a product. Marketing and sales gather information about customer profiles and needs—which have to be communicated to development units. Developers responsible for particular functions have to communicate and reconcile their requirements with developers responsible for adjacent functions, with the architecture group, with the user interface design group, with marketing and with others.

Research efforts (e.g. Schank, 1990; IBM, 2001) show that stories are one means of managing knowledge, that is, of storing and spreading ('socialising') it. This observation can also be seen as a justification of the intensive use of story cards in XP projects, for example (see also Chapter 13, *User Stories in Agile Software Development*). Since requirements engineering is a special kind of knowledge management, stories can also be applied in this area. In our practical work on improving requirements-engineering processes at DaimlerChrysler, we found that stories could indeed help: we tried out stories in several pilot projects.

By 'stories' we mean narrative, sketchy, incomplete, example-like scenarios as opposed to fully analysed, comprehensive, generalised use case models. Alexander and Zink (2002) describe this range in more detail, and discuss where in the systems engineering process different scenario methods are best applied (see also Chapter 3, *Scenarios in Requirements Discovery*, and Chapter 4, *Scenarios for Innovation*).

In the following sections, we illustrate the use of stories in the specification of automotive software. As the technique of writing 'stories' is a natural one, we do not describe the approach in detail. Instead, we focus on the context in which stories were used, rationales for our decision to use stories, and the effects we observed.

The adoption of stories in DaimlerChrysler is proceeding gradually. Some groups have embraced the idea and apply stories regularly. Others are just starting to try them out, and yet others have not come in touch with stories at all.

Stories in Requirements Discovery, Negotiation and Communication

So let's take a closer look at typical tasks when developing embedded software systems in automotive industry, and see how stories can be applied.

One such task is defining actual user needs gathered by marketing or sales. How do you select features to include in a new product, or a new version of a product? The features should correspond to requirements—needs or wants of people who will buy and use the product. These people are different from the people who will develop and test the product, so there is a need for discovering and communicating the requirements in a form that can be understood by people with different backgrounds and roles.

One way of sharing such user needs is to tell stories. People immediately understand stories. A story begins with a first step, and continues to an ending. This means that stories are good at showing end-to-end sequences of interactions between users and the system. In particular, working with stories when discovering and negotiating requirements helps engineers focus on user benefits rather than on details of technical solutions.

> Stories enable people to share an understanding of user needs.
> Stories help people to focus on user benefits, instead of on technical solutions.

We wanted to bring two internal parties of our organisation closer together with respect to developing requirements—let's call the first 'Marketing' to indicate that this party has a good understanding of end-users. The second we'll call here 'Telematics Development' to show that these are technology experts responsible for defining and developing product features. The goal here is obvious: to transmit knowledge about users to Development, and to reach a shared understanding of wanted features. The basic idea was to conduct a joint story workshop, and to set up a process for handling the stories further.

The design of such a workshop should be as simple as possible. For our purposes, the following proved to be practical:

1. Set up workshop goals and introduce participants to the workshop design.
2. Present an example story to explain the method.
3. Divide the whole topic into several subtopics.
4. For each subtopic:

   — divide into groups of 2—4,

   — each group writes stories for a defined time span;

   — after that the groups rejoin together, each group presents a story to the whole workshop (rotationally, one story each group);

   — finally, participants make a coarse clustering of the stories.

A similar workshop pattern is described by Ellen Gottesdiener in Chapter 5 (*Running a Use Case Workshop*). Of course, the group of storywriters should always have members of both parties, to ensure that they share their different expertise and attain a common understanding of product usage.

To focus on the interactions between the user and the system, we used a simple paper template, as shown in Figure 16.4, to collect the stories. The example application is an intelligent weather forecast system that informs drivers about bad weather conditions on the planned route ahead.

Besides the story's name, the story writers told the story in the form "⟨role⟩ does ⟨some action⟩",
which forced workshop participants to focus on interactions. To illustrate this point further, we also invited the participants to actually 'play' the stories through: for example, one participant could play the driver, another the telematics system, a third the mobile phone system. Obviously, this feels unorthodox at first, but again helps focus on interactions and user goals rather than on internal system details and technology. Thus, we confirm Suzanne Robertson's suggestion for playing through scenarios (Chapter 3, *Scenarios in Requirements Discovery*) and Gottesdiener's role-play approach (Chapter 5, *Running a Use Case Workshop*).

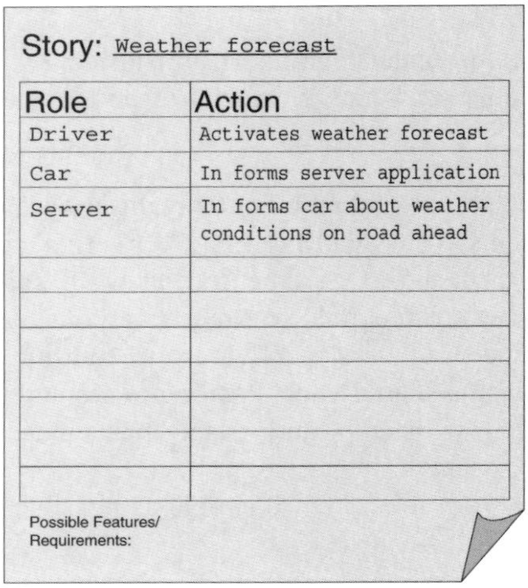

Story: Weather forecast	
Role	**Action**
Driver	Activates weather forecast
Car	In forms server application
Server	In forms car about weather conditions on road ahead

Possible Features/
Requirements:

FIGURE 16.4   A simple template for writing initial stories in a workshop

Nevertheless, if in a first discussion about a story, for example, 'Making a bank account transfer with the telematics system', some early technology requirements and features pop up already, like 'Secure Sockets Layer-Support', which shouldn't be forgotten, the workshop participants have a little space to note these at the bottom of the template.

Stories in Requirements Analysis

Many details of our specifications today already exist, because there are some real-world situations in which these details play a vital role. Consider for example the wiper system requirement (see also Figure 16.5):

> *req-0001: The washing function for the front wiper shall be put off, if both the car's speed is less than 5 km/h and one of the front doors is open.*

At first glance, the rationale for this requirement might not be too obvious. But thinking more about it, one concludes that this requirement does in fact protect the passengers from getting wet, if one of them were to get out while the washing function continues. On the other hand, why is there a speed condition there? Well, consider the following situation:

> *One of the front doors is not totally closed. The driver doesn't notice this and drives as usual. A lorry driving next to the driver's car runs through a huge mud slop and causes many mud splashes on the car's windscreen. Unfortunately, the sun is low, shining from the front, so that the driver can see almost nothing through the windscreen. In this dangerous situation, he immediately needs the wiper's washing functions to clear the windscreen.*

By reading the story it should be clear why the engineer has thought about the speed condition (less than 5 km/h) in the requirement req-0001. But now suppose that this first

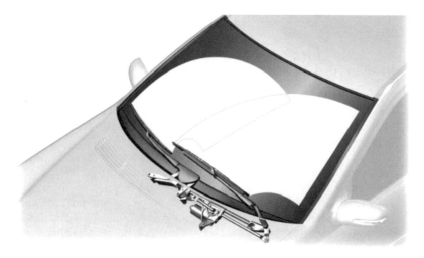

FIGURE 16.5   Wiping system of Mercedes C-class (Courtesy of DaimlerChrysler AG)

engineer takes other responsibilities, and somebody else takes over the specification of the wiper system for a new car model. The new engineer is young and dynamic, and always searches for improvements. When he reads the requirement req-0001, he might conclude—as we did—that this is to protect the passenger from getting wet. He thinks for a while, and concludes that in the document right now there isn't a requirement to stop washing if the sunroof is opened. So he includes such a requirement, but doesn't include the speed condition, as this isn't obvious to him. What he comes up with then is a wiper system, as in the story, which might not allow for washing the windscreen in a situation in which this is immediately needed (because of an open sunroof). He wouldn't have done so if he had been given the story mentioned above, as from this specific story everyone can easily generalise to similar situations.

> Stories help protect requirements from deletion or well-meaning editing.
> More generally, stories provide a pattern for new requirements (probably related to existing ones) to follow.

This tale is invented but quite close to industrial reality. Our experience suggests that by making these possible real-world situations explicit, they become much better thought through and serve as a basis for further requirements analysis (i.e. asking questions like: 'ah, but is 5 km/h a reasonable limit then? I could imagine the situation where [...]'). Obviously, stories cannot solve all the issues associated with requirements analysis, but they are an important piece in the puzzle.

This approach also brings us to the area of dealing with defects (e.g. a broken wiper) or system misuse (e.g. invoking a wiper cycle while the wiper is mechanically fixed). Defect detection and defect handling often represent more than 50% of the system's functionality. To our experience, stories are also beneficial in detecting 'what may go wrong'. Here, Ian Alexander's approach with misuse cases might provide some additional benefits (see Chapter 7, *Negative Scenarios & Misuse Cases*).

Identifying Feature Interactions and Conflicts

A car consists of several clusters of functionality: the body control (e.g. interior lights), the chassis control (e.g. ABS), power train (e.g. motor control) and telematics (e.g. navigation). Each of these coarse clusters has many functions, of which again each divides into several features and sub-features.

Different teams are responsible for different features, as different domain expertise is needed and work has to be divided. Historically, different features have usually been quite independent—the functionality can be specified in detail without too much knowledge of other features. However, in today's premium cars with highly integrated functions, complex kinds of interaction between features are nevertheless possible.

For example, suppose there is a feature in the telematics system that provides Traffic Warning Waiting: if a telephone call is in progress, a beep is heard and the Traffic Warning is delayed until the telephone call has ended. Now suppose that another caller tries to contact the driver, who has set up Call Waiting. The driver hangs up. Do the Traffic Warning and the Call Waiting collide? If so, what should happen?

Figure 16.6 shows the role of stories in this situation: the feature specifications can be thought of as columns, which are initially independent. A story can now involve several features in the steps of its narrative flow of events, such that the features involved are woven together by this story. The story then shows the interplay of the features, which might in the first iteration only be a question raised by one of the people responsible: 'What actually happens in this situation?' With a story, he has a means to point to a possible problem, and ask the other stakeholders what they think should happen. Together, they can rewrite the story to specify the wanted and agreed behaviour, and each of them can adjust the parts of the feature specifications to reflect this desired behaviour. One can view this as a pragmatic process to identify feature interactions, negotiate them, and document the reconciled solutions.

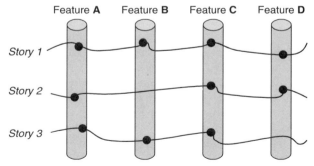

FIGURE 16.6 Features can be thought of as 'Specification Columns', and stories as means to weave features together, pointing to feature interactions or conflicts

> Stories help people identify and resolve feature interactions.

Since features that are the responsibility of different teams may interact, it is essential for the development of a good quality system that a system-wide vision is shared among all the teams. Formerly, the number of possible interactions between subsystems in a car was limited. As the sub-systems become more 'intelligent' and have more inputs and outputs, the likelihood of adverse interactions rises rapidly. The cost of resolving these interactions may become large if these are discovered late in development, or when the system is actually in service. Therefore, it is important to discover interactions early.

Relating Stories to Features

We have shown above how stories can be used to develop and communicate requirements, or to identify and document feature interactions and conflicts. By doing so, that is, by writing stories, you get a bunch of stories you have to incorporate somehow into your existing development process and requirements documentation. The best way of doing so is to put the stories logically 'before' traditional feature specification (see Figure 16.7).

In such a way, the stories become firstly a justification of features: they are rationales for the features being there or for the feature specification to be exactly as they are (e.g. in case of feature interactions). Secondly, the stories are an index to accessing and understanding the feature specifications and in turn the system requirements. System requirements might be seen as structured models, and as Karen Holzblatt argues in Chapter 10 (*Role of Scenarios in Contextual Design*), there has to be a relation between sequential scenarios and models. If feature specifications are already strongly solution-oriented, stories may help engineers to maintain an overview of stakeholder needs.

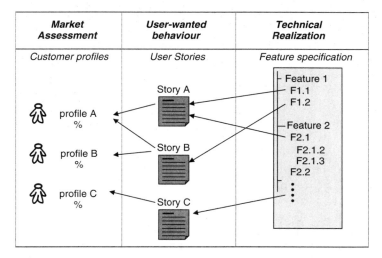

FIGURE 16.7 Relating stories to features

> Stories help justify proposed features and requirements.
> Stories help elicit requirements (that may have been assumed to be obvious).
> Stories can be used to index features and requirements.
> Stories provide engineers with an overview of stakeholder needs.

Stories describe wanted behaviour. But as Figure 16.7 depicts, we suggest that stories themselves need to be justified. Why do we think so? The reason is that products serve different market segments. In one such segment, the typical user (let's say that they are 80% of this product's users) might be business managers who need to have all kinds of communication channels with as many interfaces and options as technologically feasible—whereas in another product this kind of user might only make up 20% of all product users, but the user class of retired elderly ladies who need to have simple easy-to-use functionality might form a large group with 50% of all users. By relating such customer profiles to user stories (the relationship is many-to-many), the stories can be prioritised in terms of market needs.

> Stories describe wanted behaviour.
> Stories, being end-to-end descriptions at user level, are the right kind of structure to prioritise (all the requirements needed in a story must have at least that story's priority).

If, on the other hand, the development costs of features are assessed, product management can then weigh the benefits of 'giving the stories to the customer profiles' against the costs of developing the features needed to realise these stories. This should illustrate that keeping traceability between customer profiles, stories, and features eases feature prioritisation.

Requirements Recycling by Reusing Stories

In the common RE literature (Robertson and Robertson, 1999; Wiegers, 1999) the end user is thought of as the main source for requirements for a new product (see also Figure 16.7). Of course, this is in a way also true for the automotive area. However, we can distinguish two main types of embedded subsystems being developed for a new car model:

    a. innovative functions not available before,
    b. functions already being developed several times for existing car models.

In case (a), sub-system development is usually technology-driven, that is, domain experts try to figure out what is technologically feasible and at what development/production cost. To do so, they develop simulations and prototypes. In other words: the requirements there mainly come from the domain experts and not from users or business goals—although of course these are often implicitly there (e.g. 'the new innovation xyz will attract users by providing more safety; this will lead to higher sales").

In case (b), many requirements are taken over from an existing requirements document. For example, if a specification for a windscreen wiper-subsystem has to be written for a new car model (in order to contract this out to a supplier) the new specification usually will resemble that from an existing car model—after all, the basic functional requirements for wiping haven't changed for years. However, there might be differences in detail (e.g. a communication signal from another electronic control unit has changed, or for the new car model, the user should be able to choose between three wiping speeds, when up to now he was only able to choose from two wiping speeds). It's obvious that type (b) development happens more frequently, so it's a typical task for engineers to recycle existing requirements, which should be supported by the requirements-engineering methodology as much as possible.

Also in this situation, stories can be applied with benefit to foster reuse of existing requirements. This is because stories with their user-facing, narrative form are comparatively stable: for example, the story above describing that a hazard can arise if the wash functionality of the wiper system is not available for some reason, seems valid for as long as the windscreens and wiper systems we know today will exist. Of course, the underlying technology may change, communication signals may change, or sometimes even some functional details may change. But the stories are relatively unaffected by these changes as they shouldn't go into such detail if written properly.

What's more, if a domain expert needs to reuse existing detailed technical requirements, he first needs to have a good rough understanding of the basic situations that are important and from these he needs fast and easy access to the details. Now if the stories are connected to the technical specification by traceability links as, for example, shown in Figure 16.7, the story will serve as an index in the recycling process for existing requirements. This is because the domain expert can scan the stories (from which he gets a good initial understanding of the functionality, which might have been written by some other domain expert). He can then decide which stories are still valid, and for these he can follow the links to the technical details and see which of these details are also still valid, and copy them into the new specification. Also, if there are stories that aren't valid any more or that have to be adjusted or enhanced, he knows immediately by following the links which technical details might then be obsolete as well.[1]

Stories are conveniently stable units of requirement reuse, whereas individual (atomic) requirements are vulnerable to technological change.
If requirements are carefully (accurately and completely) traced back to stories, those stories form a means of recycling requirements in subsequent products.

If the stories are not totally stable, how do stories themselves get recycled and how does one start with such a recycling process? Figure 16.8 shows the simplest approach

---

[1] This is however an optimistic view, as it assumes sufficient quality (completeness and correctness) of links between scenarios and technical specifications.

to starting and living such a process: for the first product (car model A), initial stories are written only for new functions. Besides that, stories might also be written ('re-engineered') for existing functionality, if some situations are unclear and need to be analysed further. In this way, the quantity of stories grows while developing (sub-systems of) a new product. If a parallel development effort for another product (car model B) starts while the development of car model A is still in progress, the current set of existing stories can be reused by copying these together with the detailed technical specifications and the domain experts can start the recycling process as described above (by using the stories as an index).

Copying is extremely flexible—the new project can work independently from the other development, but it automatically creates redundancy, which can lead to inconsistencies. For example, if a story is revised during the development of model A, it ought also to be changed in model B. Of course, with tools and traceability links, this problem is mitigated. On the other hand, one might also strive to make the stories product-independent and manage the set of stories together for all product instantiations. Whether and how this can be done efficiently in practice is one of our current research topics.

LESSONS LEARNT

'Engineers think in solutions, not in problems'. Generally, this is a good thing because solutions are the driving force for innovations. But focusing on solutions means that the problem can be forgotten as soon as a solution is found. But problem situations put solutions in context. Without context, it is hard to judge the appropriateness of a solution, or to decide whether to search for another.

Let us recall the wash-wiping example. Is it relevant that we have the speed limit 5 km/h, or could it equally well be 4 km/h? The story tells us that we just need a threshold to differentiate a running car from a stationary one. If the speed limit is relevant, there may be another (technical) story that tells us problems with having too low a threshold (maybe caused by the resolution of the selected sensor).

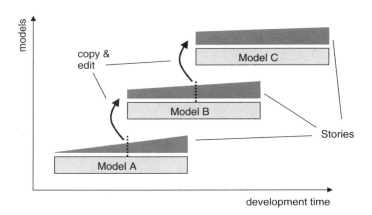

FIGURE 16.8 The simplest approach to recycling stories for different car models

Thinking in solutions does not only mean that the context is forgotten after a solution has been engineered. It also often means that the problem is not thought through thoroughly. Work may start from a rough idea such as a customer's suggestion, and a solution may be proposed—but the benefit to customers may not be evaluated. Using stories to document initial ideas automatically results in descriptions that combine user and real-world behaviour with system reactions. If stories are written down in a structured way (as sequences of situations and actions), they provide a good starting point for exploring alternatives; for example, 'what should happen, if wash-wiping is activated and the driver stops the car. Should washing stop?' Asking for alternatives and exceptions thus leads not only to more complete specifications but also immediately provides a set of test cases (see also Chapter 14, *Use Cases, Test Cases*).

So stories do help in many ways. But asked for our greatest lesson learnt we say frankly: 'be cautious!' Stories offer a method of describing dynamic behaviour informally. Their role is to improve communication, not to demonstrate completeness or consistency. Of course, they can be transferred into (or supplemented by) analytical, engineered use cases, which aim to be correct, consistent, complete, unambiguous, and so on. In other words, there is a continuum of methods available, ranging from the informal and concrete to the formal and abstract.

In our practical work, we experienced quite a few different project types with respect to stakeholders involved, complexity, innovation-grade, safety-relevance, system-level, and so on (compare e.g. Cockburn). What we discovered is that believing in just one of the methods and applying it blindly to different projects the same way is a great mistake. Only the opposite—analysing project type and needs beforehand and choosing from the variety—leads the way to more successful projects. The good news in this situation is that there are actually some project patterns that give hints on what methods to apply. We shortly present here two of them, which we believe are quite characteristic for the engineering of embedded systems:

The 'let's do it again'-project usually consists of a small team of engineers (a homogenous group of domain experts) responsible for some subsystem, for example, an ECU. Similar sub-systems, with some variations in functions and quality, have been developed by the team many times already. Team members understand each other well and they have an ongoing and deep discussion with their suppliers. Developing a new sub-system is mainly a matter of choosing the right features from the existing solutions, adding and changing some minor things to optimise the solution (e.g. altering some threshold) and putting this into a concise and consistent specification for development sub-contractors. As such 'let's do it again'-projects are strongly technology-oriented, and need a method of structuring the specification well to support intensive reuse. In this situation, a hierarchical feature-oriented approach serves well, and it's perfectly acceptable simply to supplement the feature specifications with stories or use cases in a few places to describe specific problems behind the specification, or to show and clarify some feature interactions.

A neat example is the development of instrument clusters, which are part of every vehicle. The basic behaviour of an instrument cluster is well known: there are precise specifications and competent suppliers available. Over time, the domain experts have built up their own 'domain model' with their own terminology and ways of express-ing particular information. But, as in every environment that has evolved naturally over time, it can happen that some requirements were stated by people who had left the group.

For instance, at some point in time, we faced the situation that we were negotiating warning messages that a new instrument cluster should cope with. So we went through the already specified ones and identified which are relevant for the new car and which are not (e.g. if the new vehicle does not embody a convertible top, we can omit the related warning messages). In this situation, we found a message that no one could explain immediately. It took the engineers sitting around quite a while to re-engineer the underlying real-world scenario behind this message from the precise (but completely technical) specification at hand. Of course, it is a wise idea to write down this re-engineered scenario as a story, a use case or whatever fits the audience, and to maintain it with the technical specification.

Stories can serve as a 'corporate memory' for design decisions.

On the other side, we face 'great innovation' projects, that is, projects that try to engineer a completely new system. These projects can be characterised as follows: The starting point is usually a rough idea—a vision—for a new functionality or service. Technical details as well as user benefits, however, are completely unclear and it is the duty of the involved experts to figure them out. The involved experts are usually from different disciplines with different backgrounds. Sometimes, they may have worked on systems that might become part of the new system (which means that they have a certain idea of their work, which might not be easily integrated in the new context).

In such projects, we found stories that try to draw 'holistic' pictures of new systems useful. As we said, engineers think in solutions, not in problems: they are often tempted to dive into technical details before the overall picture is clear. We advocate a layered approach. First, there should be an agreement on the vision and scope of the new system. Then, we need to document the high-level requirements as completely as possible (without thinking about any details). After that we need to write stories for all areas raised by the high-level requirements. These stories should not be analytic, in the sense that every alternative and exception is spelt out in detail. Instead, the stories should point to every region of the area of interest.

Let us consider the example of a driver monitoring and emergency braking system. The basic idea is to monitor the driver's attention with a video camera. If the system detects that the driver is not paying attention to traffic, the system first tries to wake-up the driver; if this does not work, the system stops the vehicle in a controlled manner. Such a project probably needs to bring together experts from vision recognition, safety analysis, driver behaviour analysis, psychology, vehicle electronics, and so on. Such a team will work in depth on recognising inattentive drivers or initiating emergency braking. But the team may well not think about an 'after-braking' scenario. What will happen after emergency braking has been initiated? What will happen if braking was initiated on a steep hill? Is the activated brake able to halt the car there for a prolonged period of time, or might the brake gradually release? Informal but concrete stories can effectively help in the exploration of such situations.

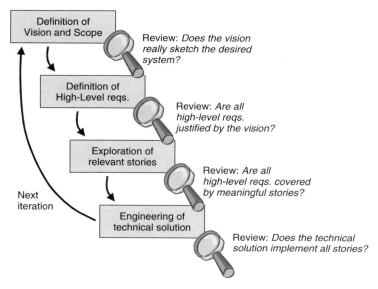

FIGURE 16.9   Iterative refinement

> Stories help explore side effects, consequences, and easily forgotten situations that need to be designed for.

Another characteristic element of such 'great innovation' projects is that they have to be iterative. It is unlikely to do the job right the first time. We might have to figure out that something that seemed simple at scenario level turned out to be more complicated (or impossible) at the technical level. It might also be that a solution at hand (e.g. a working prototype) causes new or changed visions. We found it essential to maintain traceability between the various levels of abstraction. This can be achieved with a rigid process of definition and analysis, as shown in Figure 16.9.

All in all, stories provide a useful vehicle for supporting the engineering of embedded automotive systems. But their application has to be justified by actual needs in development projects.

We should mention one last problem: Stories do not look like proper engineering artefacts. Stories are informal and imprecise—making them look completely unlike familiar artefacts such as state charts or pin descriptions. This can make engineers sceptical of stories when they first come into contact with them, so story workshops need to be properly facilitated.

KEYWORDS

Narrative	Embedded Systems	Feature Interaction	Requirements Documentation
Stories	Features	Requirements Negotiation	Automotive Industry

REFERENCES

Alexander, I. and Kiedaisch, F., Towards recyclable system requirements, *Proceedings of the 9th Annual IEEE International Conference and Workshop on the Engineering of Computer-Based Systems (ECBS 2002)*, Lund, Sweden, April 2002, pp. 9–16.

Alexander, I. and Zink, T., An introduction to systems engineering with use cases, *IEE Computing & Control Engineering Journal*, **13**(6), 289–297, 2002.

DaimlerChrysler, Soft and Safe, DaimlerChrysler Hightech Report, 1/2002. http://www.daimlerchrysler.com/research/htr2002/pdf_e/elektronik_6_e.pdf

Davis, A., Requirements Engineering, in J.J. Marciniak (Ed.), *Encyclopaedia on Software Engineering*, Vol. 2, 2nd ed., John Wiley & Sons, 2002, pp. 1145–1155.

Grimm, K., Software technology in an automotive company—major challenges, *Proceedings of the 25th International Conference on Software Engineering*, Portland, May 2003, pp. 498–503.

Heumesser, N. and Houdek, F., Towards systematic recycling of system requirements, *Proceedings of the 25th International Conference on Software Engineering*, Portland, May 2003, pp. 512–519.

IBM Research, Fostering the Collaborative Creation of Knowledge—A White Paper, John C. Thomas, IBM Research, Hawthorne, 2001, http://www.research.ibm.com/knowsoc/

McKinsey, Automotive Software: A Battle for Value, Preeti Bendele, Andreas Cornet, Guido Haak, Bernd Heid, Ulrich Näher, Klaus Richter, Auto Software, 2002, Vol. 11.

Robertson, J. and Robertson, S., *Mastering the Requirements Process*, Addison-Wesley, 1999.

Schank, R., *Tell me a Story: Narrative and Intelligence*, Northwestern University, Evanston, IL, 1990.

Weber, M. and Weisbrod, J., Requirements engineering in automotive development: experiences and challenges, *IEEE Software*, **20**(1), 16–24, 2003.

Wiegers, K., *Software Requirements*, Microsoft Press, 1999.

CHAPTER 17

USE AND MISUSE CASES IN RAILWAY SYSTEMS

Ian Alexander[1] and Andrew Farncombe[2]

[1]*Scenario Plus, London, UK*
[2]*John Boardman Associates Limited, Southampton, UK*

This chapter presents experiences with two radically different applications of scenario techniques in railway systems engineering, described separately.

A: Use Cases for Train Control Requirements Discovery

SCENARIO WORKSHOPS and interviews were used to check whether the functional requirements for a new version of a train control box were correct and complete. It quickly became clear that the described on-board functions were essentially correct, but that the requirements as written were very incomplete. The existing requirements focused on normal operations, and essentially ignored issues of testing and entry into service. By eliciting a whole-life-cycle scenario and then exploring each phase, the issues were quickly brought to the surface. These scenarios dictated the specification of a whole-journey simulator, which would otherwise have been missed, at the price of extensive delay and budget overrun. Enhancements to provide better control and easier maintenance were also agreed to be in scope.

TYPE OF PROJECT

This was a project to replace the Train Control Unit (TCU) on all the trains on a commuter railway line. Each TCU receives command codes from a safety unit. The TCU controls the speed of the train automatically. It is overridden by the safety units applying emergency braking whenever safety is threatened. The TCU is thus a safety-related (rather than a safety-critical) embedded control system.

Scenarios, Stories, Use Cases: Through the Systems Development Life-Cycle. Edited by Ian F Alexander and Neil Maiden
© 2004 John Wiley & Sons, Ltd. ISBN: 0-470-86194-0

APPLICABILITY

The approach taken did not depend on detailed knowledge of the rail environment. It could probably be applied to early requirements work—discovery and validation—in domains such as automotive, aerospace, process control, telecommunications, medical equipment, and so on. People in industry are well aware of the basic functionality of wanted systems, but may overlook 'big picture' issues such as how system are to be tested, brought into service, and maintained. Scenario workshops are good at surfacing such questions.

POSITION IN THE LIFE CYCLE

Requirements Discovery	Requirements Validation	System Specification	System Design	Coding, First of Class	Integration & Testing	Operations & Maintenance

ROLES PLAYED BY SCENARIOS

Scenarios were used initially to check whether an existing set of requirements adequately covered the project's real needs. They achieved this by helping to discover several missing requirements, especially the need for a complete simulation environment in addition to the control box itself. This is a noticeably different focus of attention from the usual role of Use Cases to document wanted 'system' interactions.

STRENGTHS

Scenarios were effective in this project in helping discover situations that were not catered for by the functional requirements. Since these situations included the process of bringing the system into service, it is certain that failure to discover the additional requirements would have caused severe cost and schedule overrun.

The form of scenarios used, Cockburn Use Cases, also proved effective at documenting constraints and other detailed requirements local to specific scenarios.

WEAKNESSES

The approach and the tools supporting it worked well, but in the circumstances of an existing set of functional requirements, there were diminishing returns from scenario approaches alone. Further work was carried out with analysis techniques such as state modelling.

With the exceptions of maintainability and verifiability, scenarios did not contribute significantly to improving the quality or completeness of 'non-functional requirements'.

Both maintenance and diagnosis/test are procedural activities, and it is not surprising that a scenario approach should be helpful in those cases.

We did in fact also apply other techniques, such as a template for non-functional requirements, an online glossary linked to the requirements, and conventional requirements database attributes for requirement justification, acceptance criteria, review status, and priority. These identified and helped fill further gaps in the specifications. There was no conflict between these and the use case approach, but there was a tendency to ignore the scenarios once they had 'done their work' and attention shifted to conventional specifications. The project provided no support for the extreme view that scenarios are all you need for elicitation and specification.

CASE STUDY

Background

The Train Control Unit (TCU), together with the Train Safety Unit (TSU), provides Automatic Train Operation on a commuter railway. Essentially, the TSU decides if the train is safe; if all is well, it allows the TCU to drive the train.

Component obsolescence led to the need to re-engineer the TCU to extend the operational life of trains. This provided the opportunity to specify smoother and faster braking, both improving passenger comfort and enabling trains to take less time between stations. Since braking can be later, trains travel faster on average, so the capacity of the line is increased.

This situation led to a divergence of viewpoints within the railway; some stakeholders took the view that this was a simple, like-for-like replacement, while others regarded it as new equipment with capabilities that were a superset of the old system's. To some extent, this split went along discipline boundaries.

Safety engineers, for instance, were more likely to believe that since the boxes had non-identical functionality and implementation, the new and old TCUs were not 'equivalent' and therefore, the safety case needed to be prepared afresh.

Most people on the project took a more relaxed view. They argued that the same basic functionality would be retained, making the Safety Case easier to establish, while permitting enhanced braking. The essence of the Safety Case from their point of view is that should the enhanced braking fail, old-style braking would continue to operate; and indeed, the separate Train Safety Unit would independently trip braking in an emergency. This viewpoint depends on several pieces of argumentation:

1. Systems can share a safety case if they are equivalent in function, even if different in physical implementation. (We created project dictionary definitions of two kinds of 'equivalence'—functional and physical—to make this point less contentious.)
2. The new box would be functionally equivalent to the old one, that is, the scenarios for old-style braking would be retained, even though the new implementation would probably use a modern programmable logic array in place of the discrete components in the old device.

3. Since the new box would have new braking functions not demonstrated before, safety would be ensured by guaranteeing that failure of the new 'enhanced' braking would be independent of the old-style braking, that is, it would be argued that it was very unlikely that the additional functions could cause the old-style functions to fail. Hence, there would be a fallback position exactly equivalent functionally to that covered by the old box's Safety Case.

This kind of behaviour is normally achieved by measuring whether the enhanced system is working, that is, whether the train is decelerating along the enhanced braking rate curve in this case. If it is not, a simple switch disconnects the enhanced functionality, leaving the fallback functionality of known reliability in place. This scenario effectively calls for an independent set of accelerometers and a switching device to control whether enhanced braking is to be overridden by fallback braking.

A second level of protection can be provided by incorporating a watchdog process that repeatedly checks that the processor responds normally; if the processor does not respond within a time-out period, it is assumed to have failed and emergency braking is applied (before the train actually passes a signal at danger and trips emergency braking that way).

The old specifications were incomplete, so an approach was selected to bridge gaps in the specifications to support a low-risk, 'right-first-time' procurement of the replacement unit. For example, the old specifications covered the system's behaviour with respect to the train's speed and track codes in detail, but did not cover issues of verification during development and maintenance; nor did they state explicitly the non-functional requirements such as reliability or conformance to existing interfaces.

METHODS AND TOOLS

Our basic approach was to run a series of workshops and interviews to elicit scenarios. We then organised the scenarios into Cockburn-style Use Cases with tool support, and played them back to the domain experts to validate them (Cockburn 2001).

The project managed its specifications with a combination of Microsoft Word and Telelogic DOORS, currently the market-leading requirements management tool. To enable DOORS to represent scenarios, we also installed Scenario Plus for Use Cases. This is an add-on that supports the capture, documentation, analysis, diagramming, navigation, and export as hypertext of Cockburn-style use cases (Scenario Plus 2003, Cockburn 2001) (Figure 17.1).

APPROACH

A series of workshops and interviews was held with railway experts to identify the stakeholders' viewpoints. The first workshop established that there was a need for a coherent set of scenarios to give an end-to-end overview of the system's context and required capabilities, and sketched out the shape of the largest scale scenarios involving the TCU.

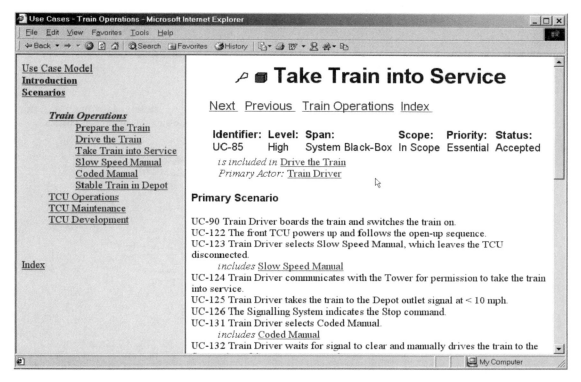

FIGURE 17.1 Use case model exported as a hypertext

Subsequent workshops discussed and agreed on operational scenarios not only for normal TCU operations but also for the testing, maintenance, and manual modes that had been omitted.

The scenario workshops discovered a key group of requirements for a Simulator, which would have been costly to add further downstream. Essentially, since the available track is in constant use, on-track test time is a scarce resource; new systems must be 'right first time'. Simulation must therefore cover not only the interfaces to the box, but must behave as if the box was in a train travelling the whole track, each station approach being unique.

The existing (partial) specifications were imported from Microsoft Word into the requirements tool. Attributes (database fields) were created to document test criteria, justifications, and other details not previously covered given the limitations of ordinary word-processed project documents.

The Specifications for the TCU, the Simulator, and other Test Equipment were checked against the use that would be made of these devices as described in the Scenarios.

The scenario structure consisted of operational goals (e.g. 'Drive the Train') and the sequences of steps these entailed. Additional information such as alternative possibilities within a scenario, exception conditions, the user roles involved, and any constraints (e.g. performance, braking accuracy, etc.) were developed and added in a systematic way.

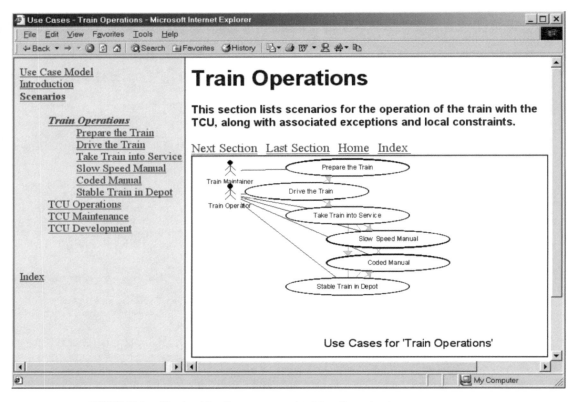

FIGURE 17.2   Navigable diagrams and table of contents

Results were exported as fully navigable hypertext available to the project team through a standard Web browser. Use Case diagrams were image-mapped to make the Use Case bubbles clickable; an equivalent hierarchical table of contents was constructed in text (Figure 17.2). This meant that no access to DOORS or skill in using it was required to review the scenarios.

A template of headings (similar to Appendix 1–4, NFR Template) was created to organise the system's non-functional requirements, including reliability, maintainability, physical and environmental constraints, and interfaces. Surprisingly, this led quite naturally to the identification of several more functional requirements, seen to be necessary to make the system maintainable. In other words, a template approach helpfully complemented the use of scenarios in discovering requirements.

LESSONS LEARNT

Scenarios are not necessarily better at defining the detailed functionality of a system than traditional requirements supported by suitable behaviour models (though Alistair Mavin describes a use of scenarios, persisting throughout the specification and design of another railway system in Chapter 20, alongside other modelling techniques). Once we had shown that scenarios were beneficial, some of the engineers involved displayed a tendency to try to force all the requirements into scenario form, in our view, to little benefit.

Other approaches that we used, including the use of a template (a hierarchy) of non-functional requirements, and a project glossary linked to the requirements, also helped to discover requirements and to clarify their meanings. Scenarios are useful but they need to be combined with other approaches, some of which are quite traditional.

The form of scenarios used, Cockburn Use Cases (Cockburn 2001), to some degree expects that there are human roles for each case, but in this instance most of the system's behaviour is automatic with little direct human involvement. It is sensible to be quite flexible about the amount of detail required for a use case; sometimes it helps to fill in a fully dressed template; sometimes a bare story is enough.

Some skill in facilitation was required initially for the workshops, given a team unused to such methods. A dogmatic or mechanical approach would not have worked.

Tool support worked perfectly in technical terms, but the human issues of getting busy engineers to take advantage of technology, rather than to simply continue working with familiar word-processed documents should not be underestimated. Under time pressure, people have a strong tendency to go back to the familiar—unless there are stronger reasons for using the new tools.

Overall, scenarios more than paid for themselves on this project, but most of the benefit was obtained quite quickly, with diminishing returns thereafter. Early gains do not necessarily imply much more benefit to come.

KEYWORDS

Use Case	Control System	Requirements Discovery
Scenario	Railway	Hypertext

B: Misuse Cases for a Seats Trade-Off

MISUSE CASES were applied to analyse Trade-Offs of design options against requirements for the construction of seats and armrests on a commuter railway.

In a Trade-Off workshop, a diagram was constructed showing Use Cases for goals held by system designers, and Misuse Cases for goals held by hostile agents. Relationships between these goals were elicited and documented on the diagram.

It seemed helpful to devise a simple set of relationships, specially suited to Trade-Off analysis: '*threatens*', '*mitigates*', '*aggravates*', and '*conflicts with*', to be used with the ordinary '*includes*'. The result is an easily appreciated diagram that makes clear to non-technical stakeholders such as railway maintenance engineers, managers, and seat designers how their requirements may conflict in the design domain. This clarity contributed to the success of the Trade-Off workshop.

TYPE OF PROJECT

Low-technology structural design complicated by previously unresolved stakeholder issues.

APPLICABILITY

This simple approach could be helpful in unravelling a range of stakeholder conflicts and design trade-offs in different settings.

POSITION IN THE LIFE CYCLE

Requirements Discovery	Requirements Validation	System Specification	System Design	Coding, First of Class	Integration & Testing	Operations & Maintenance

ROLES PLAYED BY SCENARIOS

Misuse Cases (*see* Chapter 7)

STRENGTHS

- The approach is simple and direct.
- The resulting diagrams are easy to understand intuitively.
- Just acknowledging issues is often enough to avert conflict.

WEAKNESSES

- The approach is essentially human and qualitative, so it is not suitable for complex risk-based trade-offs that should be handled with quantitative methods such as linear programming or Monte Carlo simulation.
- Diagrams can become cluttered if there are many interacting factors, though tool support can effectively mitigate this problem.

CASE STUDY

Scenarios can be helpful not only with difficult-looking problems in software and advanced systems, but with many apparently simple problems that lack software altogether. We were recently consulted by a railway company about the safety and comfort of the seats in their commuter trains (Figure 17.3). What looked at first like a trivial problem, turned out to be remarkably complex. This section presents part of the analysis of the requirements and design issues on the seats. It was a contribution to a participative workshop approach for a whole-day meeting of about 20 stakeholders from the railway company, including project management, design engineers, maintenance engineers, and quality assurance representatives.

The engineers on the seats project made it clear that they felt stuck, as long-standing discussions had reached deadlock. They were aware that there was a problem, but had not progressed beyond recording that different people in the company held differing views on the situation. Crucially, it appeared that Maintenance had not been involved in the discussions.

A suitable starting point for the workshop was the passenger's top-level goal for his or her seat, namely to sit comfortably and safely. This was threatened by numerous hostile agents, who adopted a variety of strategies. These are shown as Misuse Cases (*see* Chapter 7) in Figure 17.4, with threat arrows directed at the top-level goal. Some of the agents were literally hostile: Vandals armed with knives might slash seat covers; 'Pests' might seat themselves next to women, especially in seats that lacked dividing 'armrests'. Other metaphorically hostile agents included natural causes such as Fire, and Wear and Tear, or accidents like coffee or soft drinks being spilt on to seats, and trickling through the supposedly watertight box lid into the electronics below; engineers need not limit their thinking to literally hostile human agents.

FIGURE 17.3 Example seating on a commuter train   The illustration shows a different solution from the one discussed; in particular, high-level armrests are in place, fixed at a single point

Even apparently simple Misuse Cases like normal Wear and Tear of seats could be aggravated by design choices. The seat was locked into the sitting position after maintenance by an upward-pointing locking pin that was supposed to engage with a downward-opening bush on the underside of the seat. Unfortunately, this pin could be misaligned by maintenance staff, especially once it had started to wear and had some play in its mounting, and then protruded into the foam of the seat. This considerably aggravated the wear and tear on the seat caused by passenger movements.

The design engineers in the railway had considered various stratagems to mitigate these threats. They had become bogged down because they had found no clear way ahead: some of the proposed (and actually implemented) solutions aggravated some of the threats or conflicted with each other.

For example, the armrest had some years earlier been intentionally weakened so that in the event of a passenger being thrown against an armrest during an emergency stop, the armrest would snap off cleanly ('be frangible') at its base rather than cause injury to the passenger's abdomen. The railway company was aware of several problems that had been aggravated by this design change:

1. Vandals found it easier to break off the armrest intentionally, and the broken-off armrest formed an all-too-convenient weapon in the hands of such people.
2. The absence of an armrest—whether because it had been removed for safety or broken off—made female passengers uncomfortable as it increased the nuisance from 'pests'.
3. It reduced passenger comfort more generally, as in an undivided space, neighbours seem nearer and people accidentally sit on each others' coats, and so on.
4. The armrest was the only thing that maintenance engineers could hold on to, to lower the seat down to the locked (sitting) position after replacing the seat cover or accessing electronics subsystems in the boxes beneath the seats. It had been assumed that since armrests were mandatory, no other handgrip was required.

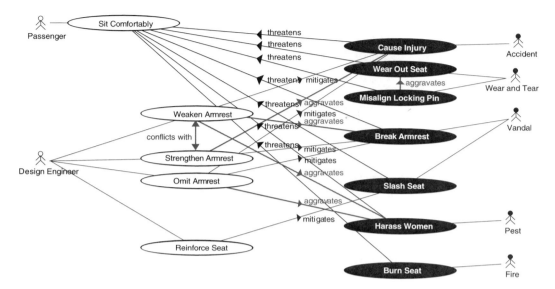

FIGURE 17.4   Misuse case-based trade-off analysis of railway seat issues ('*includes*' relationships omitted for clarity); normally presented in stages (see Figure 17.6)

Without any way of controlling the lowering of the 30-kilogram seat, it was allowed to fall, aggravating the wear and tear on the locking mechanism, and possibly presenting an increased risk of injury to maintenance staff.

The armrest was thus revealed to have numerous functions and to be safety related; its function was not just to provide a place for passengers to rest their arms.

The simplest solution perceived by the railway engineers was to strengthen the armrest, accepting the risk of injury this might cause. However, there was no agreement on this approach: there was evidently a conflict between the design goals of strengthening and weakening the armrest. For example, some engineers felt that a strengthened armrest could lead to structural damage to the seat frame itself in the event of a determined vandal attack, given a strong armrest firmly attached to the seat frame, and offering plenty of leverage. This would greatly increase the cost of an episode of armrest vandalism.

The undesired effects of weakening the armrest had not been considered when the decision to make the armrest frangible had been taken. It appears, therefore, that vandalism threats had not been taken into account in the decision-making process, despite the familiarity of vandalism to railway maintenance staff who daily make good a wide range of all kinds of deliberate damage, including graffiti, torn seat covers, burns, and breakages.

This suggests that stakeholders such as train maintainers had not been adequately involved in earlier decisions. In fact, one of the 'aha!' moments in the workshop occurred when the project managers and systems engineers present realised that maintainers had an important voice; the meeting tangibly relaxed as soon as the maintenance chief had explained his viewpoint.

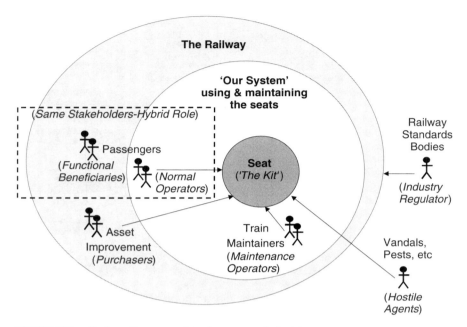

FIGURE 17.5 Onion diagram of train seat stakeholders

In general, inadequate attention to system scope leads to difficulties during system operations and maintenance. The scope of the train seat design is not passenger + seat, but includes the maintenance of the seat and the other scenarios already described. It is essential that the scenarios span the full range of the domain, and (as a corollary of that) that the viewpoints of all the stakeholders are considered. The Onion Diagram (Figure 17.5: *see* description in Chapter 1, under Stakeholders) shows that despite the apparent triviality of the problem—after all, 'using' the seat does not require an Operations Manual—the system of seats, people, maintenance procedures, and standards is wider than you might expect. In fact, the key role in daily use of the system is clearly seen from the diagram to be that of the train maintainers.

These and similar arguments were expressed simply and naturally in diagrammatic form with Misuse Cases, using the additional relationships '*aggravates*' and '*conflicts with*' already mentioned. The diagram was introduced in stages, presenting first the top-level goal and actors, then the Use Cases for the subsidiary goals, then the hostile actors and the seven Misuse Cases threatening the goals, and finally (with differently coloured arrows) the analysis of mitigations, aggravations and conflicts.

The Scenario Plus toolkit for Use/Misuse Case modelling makes such piece-by-piece presentation simple, by providing special-to-purpose filtering tools (Scenario Plus 2003) (Figure 17.6).

None of the stakeholders in the workshop challenged this analysis, though it was pointed out to them that the diagram was incomplete. Evidently, once the conflicts, threats, and aggravations were explicitly stated, much of the heat and confusion was

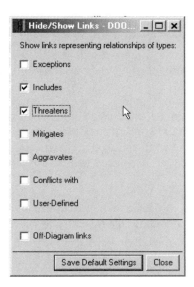

FIGURE 17.6   Special-to-purpose relationship filtering tool

taken out of the analysis. Further, the simple act of inviting the different stakeholders to a workshop itself made clear that different viewpoints could rightfully exist.

Faced with the challenge of resolving the problem with the armrest, the design engineers quickly pointed out that they could rethink the design of the armrest: it could be made strong, low, and curved, difficult to vandalise, protecting passengers and frustrating pests. They sketched a rough outline of a new 'armrest'—it had in effect become something new, something like a 'non-frangible vandal-resistant armrest/separator'—and promised full drawings for a week later. The sketch (Figure 17.7) is similar to what they drew.

As another example, the design engineers had previously considered that the seat-locking pin had to face upwards for two reasons.

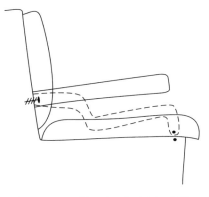

FIGURE 17.7   Sketch of old (solid) and new (dashed) armrest options

1. There was no room for a locking mechanism below the seat: electrical equipment was housed in the boxes under the passenger seats.
2. Since the equipment was electrical, the box lids had to be watertight, so that fluid such as a spilt drink could not cause a short-circuit.

However, the stakeholders in the workshop quickly ascertained by discussion amongst themselves that these fears were groundless; a simple blind-ended metal bush could be mounted in the box lid, requiring only a few millimetres of extra space, and offering no path for liquids to penetrate, so the locking pin could point downwards. There would then be nothing pointing upwards that could get misaligned and destroy the foam padding of the seat.

The Trade-Off Analysis had brought together the relevant facts for several inter-related issues, enabling the design to be reconsidered objectively in the light of the system requirements. Misuse Cases thus have a definite role in clarifying the interplay of system requirements and design, and indeed in addressing design issues and Trade-Offs during in-service operations and maintenance.

LESSONS LEARNT

In the examples discussed in detail—the armrest and the locking pin Trade-Offs—the problems were resolved by the combined domain knowledge and skill of the stake-holders, once the interactions (threats, mitigations, conflicts, aggravations) had been brought to their attention. The contribution made by consultancy, facilitation, and analysis techniques was purely to enable this resource of skill to be brought to bear on the problems.

Tool support is not essential for documenting and presenting such analyses, but it can be helpful. The Scenario Plus toolkit's Misuse Case and Trade-Off facilities proved to be effective in the railway case: the filters allow different types of relationship to be presented separately or together, so the presentation of threats, mitigations, and conflicts could be built up visually in stages, in a way that the stakeholders could understand.

Using any suitable tool encourages people to record the reasons for a design decision. A Trade-Off Analysis diagram automatically records much of the thinking embodied in a Trade-Off workshop. Scenario Plus also makes it easier to keep diagrams up to date. But more importantly, integration with an industrial-strength requirements engine, as with Scenario Plus' DOORS platform, enables design elements and tests to be traced back to (Use Case) requirements and (Misuse Case) justifications and Trade-Off arguments.

There are clear advantages in recording the justification for design decisions made in the presence of possibly conflicting viewpoints. If the reasons for a decision are not adequately documented and agreed, there is a danger of continual disputes in line with the shifting political fortunes of different stakeholder groups within an organisation. This can cause indefinite oscillation between conflicting outcomes ('paralysis by analysis'). Alternatively, if decisions are not discussed openly, they may be made excessively autocratically without adequate consideration. This can lead to shock discoveries of problems after decisions have been implemented. Trade-Off analysis, in contrast, provides a thorough cycle of stakeholder involvement, and leads to a shared and lasting decision. Simple graphics such as those illustrated here, which help people share their understanding of Trade-Offs, can contribute to this success.

To use a Misuse Case model in a workshop, it is obviously easiest if you can prepare a reasonably good model in advance using interview notes from one or two key stakeholders—this is what was done for the seats workshop. The facilitator then introduces the modelling approach and the model itself, explaining that the model is incomplete, and that participants are welcome to suggest additional items.

Scenario Plus makes it possible to edit quickly enough for an analyst to update a model while a facilitator obtains inputs from workshop participants using a whiteboard or flipcharts. This means that you can acknowledge a stakeholder's contribution by modifying the model, provided you don't divert stakeholders' attention from the workshop's business—analysing Trade-Offs—to optimising the model visually.

If you intend to create a model during a workshop, you certainly need a team of two people to manage simultaneous facilitation and modelling.

Whenever you build your model, you should allow opportunities for stakeholders to comment on the model, so that you can refine it with them. The essential thing is that the stakeholders should feel that the model describes their situation adequately.

Was the approach the right one? Without Misuse Cases, the seats workshop might still have been successful, but participants would have been less focussed on the nature of the conflicting forces. The workshop would probably have spent longer trying to analyse the existing situation. This might have put pressure on participants to reach a solution quickly. That is always unwise in a workshop as different participants work at different speeds, and people need time to express themselves, even if it is only to agree with what others are suggesting.

What benefit did identifying threats (as Misuse Cases) bring? It helped participants acknowledge that there were explicit choices confronting the design engineers, and that the approaches that had been thought of before the workshop were all problematic. Indeed, the temporary solution that had in fact been adopted, namely, removal of the armrests, was actually illegal. The Misuse Case model helped get the whole workshop to acknowledge that no pre-existing solution was acceptable and unproblematic. At that point, the workshop rapidly moved into a free space in which it could think creatively. It isn't easy to think of ways of measuring this effect, though with hindsight participants could have been asked to fill in feedback forms on the advantages and problems posed by the conflict analysis approach.

SUMMARY

This chapter has presented two quite different examples of railway projects in which scenario use, combined with other analyses and consultancy approaches, helped improve the quality of the systems engineering, and perhaps contributed to the safety, efficiency, and comfort of railway operations. As the conceptual tools used were quite independent of the domain, there seems every reason to believe that similar benefits could be gained by applying the same techniques elsewhere.

KEYWORDS

Railway	Design Trade-Off	Misuse Case

REFERENCES

Cockburn, A., *Writing Effective Use Cases*, Addison-Wesley, 2001.

Telelogic DOORS website, 2003, http://www.telelogic.com

Scenario Plus website, 2003, http://www.scenarioplus.org.uk

CHAPTER 18

SCENARIOS IN AIR TRAFFIC CONTROL (ATC)

Perminder Sahota
Praxis Critical Systems, London, UK

THE USE of scenarios to elicit and validate requirements as complete, correct, and testable is becoming increasingly popular. One of the few tested methods available for systematic and interactive scenario generation and walkthrough is CREWS-SAVRE (*Co-operative Requirements Engineering With Scenarios-Scenarios for Acquiring and Validating Requirements*).

CREWS-SAVRE is a process with supporting software tools. It was developed as part of the EU-funded Framework IV CREWS long-research project to support the systematic and domain-independent generation and walking through of scenarios described in Chapter 9. Design of the software scenario walkthrough tool was based on a cognitive principle familiar from prototyping—that people recognise items, such as events, better than they recall them with from memory. Therefore, CREWS-SAVRE automatically generates and presents candidate exceptions that stakeholders recognise as relevant and possible, helping people to generate new requirements and so reducing the risk of missing requirements.

This case study reports on an experience within Eurocontrol that used the CREWS-SAVRE walkthrough approach to help specifying the requirements for a state-of-the-art air traffic control system. The project was called CORA-2 (*COnflict Resolution Assistant*).

APPLICABILITY

The CREWS-SAVRE approach to scenario walkthroughs adopted for CORA-2 is part of the RESCUE process. This technique has been used in safety-critical domains such as warship development and air traffic control. We expect it to be suitable for safety-related projects in other domains.

Scenario walkthroughs are particularly useful for systems that have a large stakeholder involvement. The technique might be helpful in resolving the requirements for highly contentious projects even where safety is not a primary concern.

Scenarios, Stories, Use Cases: Through the Systems Development Life-Cycle. Edited by Ian F Alexander and Neil Maiden
© 2004 John Wiley & Sons, Ltd. ISBN: 0-470-86194-0

ROLES IN THE LIFE CYCLE

Requirements Discovery	Requirements Validation	System Specification	System Design	Coding, First of Class	Integration & Testing	Operations & Maintenance

Scenarios were used in facilitated workshops with stakeholders to walk through each scenario. The aim of these workshops was to elicit and validate correct, complete, and testable requirements.

For each normal course scenario of a use case, the CREWS-SAVRE software tool automatically generated and presented alternative course (candidate exception) scenarios, which stakeholders were able to identify as relevant and possible and to generate new requirements for them. A detailed overview of the CREWS-SAVRE tools is given in this volume, Chapter 9, Systematic Scenario Walkthroughs, by Neil Maiden.

We used the normal course scenario of each use case to structure and present the requirements. Each requirement was positioned according to the event in the scenario, which the requirement either enabled (e.g. functional requirements) or constrained (e.g. performance and reliability requirements). This traceability structure was mirrored in the supporting requirements management tool, Rational Requisite Pro.

Scenario walkthrough workshops provided the context for stakeholders to discuss, negotiate, and resolve information. The structure and natural language of the scenarios provided a solid focal point for stakeholders to resolve requirements conflicts.

KEY FEATURES

Key features of the CREWS-SAVRE scenarios walkthrough approach included

- Automatic generation of scenarios from use cases, using the CREWS-SAVRE automated generator tool. Each different possible ordering of normal course events is presented in a different scenario.
- Automatic generation of alternative courses specific to the Air Traffic Control (ATC) domain, using the CREWS-SAVRE generator tool. The tool's algorithm generates candidate possible alternative courses expressed as 'what-if' questions for each normal course event by querying a database that implements a simple model of abnormal behaviour and state in socio-technical systems.
- Specific domain exceptions from the ATC can be imported into the tool and used by the generation algorithm to generate domain-specific scenarios.
- Scenario walkthroughs are conducted with stakeholders to elicit and validate a set of complete, correct, and testable requirements.

STRENGTHS

The CREWS-SAVRE tool automatically generates alternative course scenarios from use cases.

The CREWS-SAVRE tool for automatic scenario generation can be configured to produce scenarios and exceptions that are more domain-specific, and hence more meaningful to stakeholders.

The CREWS-SAVRE scenario presenter tool allows requirements and domain assumptions to be presented (in context) to stakeholders, making it easier for stakeholders to understand why they are necessary. This in turn allows stakeholders to validate the requirements and assumptions.

The CREWS-SAVRE presenter tool allows requirements to be captured and recorded in the presence of stakeholders during scenario walkthroughs, allowing direct validation by stakeholders.

The CREWS-SAVRE presenter (using the interactive style of the scenario presenter tool) provides a virtual storyboard style simulation. This allows people to think and communicate in the real context, and highlights missing requirements.

Specific guidelines for writing use cases are provided, allowing a consistent and managed approach to developing complex use case models.

A process supported by detailed guidelines allows successful scenario walkthroughs to be conducted in a pragmatic and proven way. This provides the requirements team with added confidence to make scenario walkthroughs effective.

Information elicited during the walkthroughs can be managed and structured within use cases, allowing a direct dynamic traceable relationship between requirements and use cases.

Scenario walkthroughs elicit more requirements than other elicitation methods.

Using scenarios helps reduce system complexity by focusing stakeholders' attention on critical areas. The controlled and structured scenario walkthrough workshops provide the right environment to discuss such critical areas.

The natural language format of scenarios and the informal approach of the walkthroughs allow users to adapt quickly to the workshop techniques.

WEAKNESSES

Use cases need to be stable and formally signed off to allow the CREWS-SAVRE tool to generate accurate and useful scenarios. Changes in the use cases content after scenarios have been generated may require the scenario generation process to be repeated, causing delay and expense. However, one lesson learnt from the CORA-2 project is that obtaining formal agreement and sign-off of use cases can be difficult, especially when assumptions are made, and changes occur randomly as knowledge of the domain and system progresses during the course of the project.

Missing important stakeholders can affect the quality of output of the scenario walkthroughs and risk missing key requirements. For scenario walkthroughs to be successful in obtaining requirement completeness, relevant stakeholders are required to be available during the workshops. On the basis of the CORA-2 project experience, it is not easy to involve stakeholders, especially when they are widely dispersed geographically.

Running scenario walkthrough workshops using several scenarios can be difficult to do and time-consuming. The workshops need to be carefully designed to maximise efficiency, and encourage stakeholder involvement.

The CREWS-SAVRE generator tool needs to be fine-tuned to the project to control the generation of abnormal events and states in alternative course scenarios. Generating too many exceptions makes workshops difficult to run. Without historical data, it was difficult during the project to know which exceptions would be most useful and which were not applicable to the project.

BACKGROUND

The cora-2 Project

CORA-2 will provide computerised assistance to air traffic controllers to resolve potential conflicts between aircraft. This need is predicted to become critical as increases in the number of aircraft and conflicts lead to increased workload for controllers, and the need for more complex resolutions of conflicts.

The CORA-2 project requirements team was multinational and multi-disciplined. It consisted of system engineers, human factors experts, requirement engineers, and air traffic controllers. The team produced an Operational Requirements Document for the CORA-2 system with approximately 400 requirements structured as 22 use cases. The document also contained use case and i* models (Yu 1997), and some completed VOLERE requirement attributes (Robertson and Robertson 1999).

The rescue Process

Scenario walkthroughs were one particular stream of the RESCUE (Requirements Engineering with Scenarios for a User-Centred Environment) process, which was developed for Eurocontrol by multi-disciplinary researchers from the Centre for HCI Design at City University in London.

RESCUE supports a concurrent engineering process in which different modelling and analysis processes take place in parallel to support the generation of complete and correct use case models and descriptions and, ultimately, complete, correct, readable, and testable requirements (Maiden and Jones 2003, Maiden, Jones and Flynn 2003). The RESCUE process was divided into two phases: ELABORATION and ANALYSIS. The elaboration phase consists of eight distinct processes. The analysis phase consists of a further four distinct processes as shown in Figure 18.1.

Scenario Walkthroughs

The Use Case Modelling stage of the RESCUE process is made up by four key stages to conduct effective scenario walkthroughs, shown in Figure 18.2. The different roles and time-scales are shown for the stages in the CORA project.

The following sections explain each stage in further detail.

Use Case Modelling

The use case modelling involved the investigation and modelling of the different system boundaries. Context diagrams and i* modelling was used to directly inform the development of the use cases (Jacobson, Booch, and Rumbaugh 2000). During this stage the

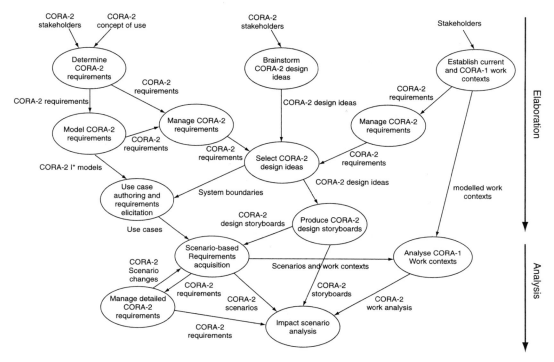

FIGURE 18.1 rescue process (2001)

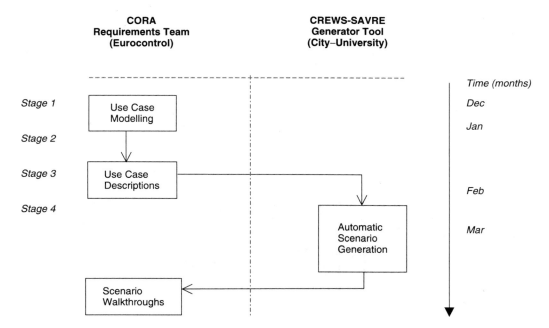

FIGURE 18.2 Stages for the scenario walkthrough process during the CORA project

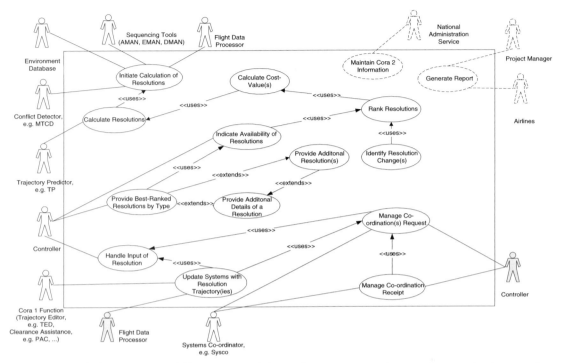

FIGURE 18.3 cora-2 Use case model supplies use cases; the crews-savre tool generates scenarios from these

team developed a use case model. The use case model consisted of 15 separate use cases with 13 actors. Figure 18.3 shows a snapshot of the final use case model.

Use Case Descriptions

The team wrote detailed use case descriptions in a structured template derived from industry-best practices (e.g. Cockburn 2000). This template encouraged consistency and completeness across the set of use cases. An actual use case from the CORA-2 project is illustrated in Figure 18.4.

Authoring was guided by

- use case style and content guidelines from the CREWS-L'ECRITOIRE method (Ben Achour, Rolland, Maiden, and Souveyet 1999); *see also* Chapter 8 of this volume on the *L'Ecritoire* guidelines by Camille Salinesi);
- temporal semantics expressed as action-ordering rules, and
- an extensive lexicon of domain-specific nouns and verbs elicited from ATC domain experts.

Each use case description was written using the work from the other steams in the RESCUE process (System Modelling and Creativity Workshops) and through structured interviews with domain experts.

Attribute	Purpose
Use Case Name	Goal of Use Case
Use Case ID	Unique ID for Use Case
Author	Name of author
Date	Date Use Case was written
Source	Source of Use Case
Actors	Actors involved in Use Case (from the Use Case Model)
Problem statement (now)	Description of current problem
Precis	Informal scenario description
Functional Requirement	Requirement that the use case **DECOMPOSES**
Non-Functional Requirement	Requirements that **CONSTRAINS** on the required behaviour in the use case
Added Value	Benefit of Use Case above and beyond the original scenario from the original system
Justification	Why is the Use Case needed?
Triggering event	Event or events that can trigger the Use Case
Preconditions	Necessary conditions for the Use Case to occur
Assumptions	Explicit statement of any assumptions made in writing the Use Case
Successful end states	Successful outcome(s) of the Use Case
Unsuccessful end states	Unsuccessful outcome(s) of the Use Case
Normal Course	Action 1 System requirement **ENABLES** Action 1 System requirement **CONSTRAINS** Action 1
	Action 2 System requirements **ENABLES** to Action 2 System requirement **CONSTRAINS** Action 2
Variations	1. If (condition) then (variation statement) (related to Action 1)
Alternatives	1. If (condition) then (alternative course statement) (related to Action 1)

FIGURE 18.4   cora-2 Use case template

Further richness was added to the use cases through investigating different contexts that use cases can be applied to (i.e. air traffic environments), and also possible variations of events in the use cases. This was not part of the original scenario walkthrough process, but proved to be an important piece of additional work.

During the walkthroughs, stakeholders raised different requirements and critical conflicts for the same use case, but for different contexts in which the use case's normal course (what Cockburn calls the main success scenario) can occur.

For example, air traffic controllers play different roles when dealing with conflicts in the sky. There is often a planning controller and a tactical controller, who together resolve conflicts. Each role has specific responsibilities. However, one air traffic controller can simultaneously play both roles whilst resolving conflicts. To capture this important domain knowledge, scenarios describing air traffic controller interactions in these different contexts were explored in the walkthroughs.

Other examples included scenario walkthroughs for the same use cases being conducted in the context of the different times of the day, that is, specific scenarios provided different requirements when assuming light air traffic on a Sunday morning, and heavy traffic on a Monday morning. By understanding the different contexts a particular use case can be applied to, important information was captured.

On completion of the use case descriptions, a use case specification was produced and parameterised to generate scenarios automatically using the CREWS-SAVRE software.

A key feature of the CREWS-SAVRE generator tool was that it had been tailored to generate scenarios with what-if alternative courses that were specific to the ATC domain, through the addition of 140 classes of abnormal behaviour and state. This allowed scenarios that are more specific to the domain to be generated. The domain-specific abnormal classes were elicited prior to scenario generation during a workshop with four air traffic controllers. The results were modelled in UML and extended with rules to generate alternative courses from an ATC lexicon used to define normal course actions in the use cases. The ATC lexicon consisted of 140 agents, objects and actions, and was further elicited from two controllers. During elicitation sessions, City University staff helped the controllers develop over 500 ATC-specific rules to generate ATC-specific alternative courses for different ATC actions.

Scenario Walkthroughs

The CORA team organised and facilitated a series of walkthrough workshops, involving key stakeholders. The generated scenarios were presented using the CREWS-SAVRE presenter tool; an example is shown in Figure 18.5.

There are four specific parts to a CREWS-SAVRE scenario. The left-hand menu provides different functions for viewing the scenario and comments and requirements

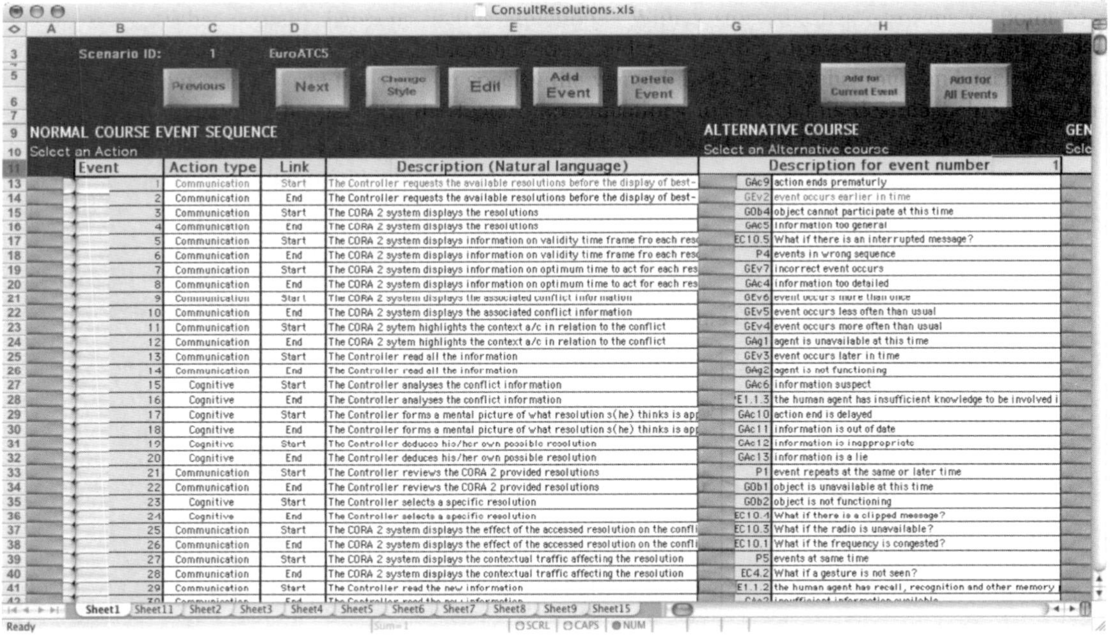

FIGURE 18.5 Scenario presenter tool

generated from it. The top-line buttons offer walkthrough functions (e.g. next or previous event, add/edit/delete event) and functions to add, edit, or delete comments and requirements (these functions were not available during the project). The left-hand main section describes the normal course event sequence for the scenario. Each event describes the start or end of an action, thus enabling a scenario to describe concurrent actions in this text-list form. The right-hand main section describes generated alternative courses for each normal course event, presented in the form of 'what-if' questions. Some generic requirement statements are provided on the Presenter for the team to reuse; during the workshops, these turned out to provide excellent triggers to start discussions, and helped to create actual requirements.

A series of walkthrough workshops were held, involving a wide variety of stakeholders. The scenarios were prioritised in order of importance. Depending on the type of scenario, specific stakeholders were invited (i.e. human factors stakeholders were invited to scenarios that occurred mostly of human-machine interactions). Each session lasted particularly two to three hours, and covered at least the scenarios for one use case (normal and alternative course). We used props (physical objects and artefacts) to encourage creative thinking amongst stakeholders and to help people think of different types of requirements (i.e. different requirement types and metrics, different ATC contexts).

Workshop Environment

The CREWS-SAVRE presenter tool encourages systematic requirement elicitation. It guides its users to walkthrough each normal course event, and each alternative course linked to that normal course event in turn. However, after the initial scenario walkthrough, the CORA team organised the workshops to take into account ergonomics issues about the style of facilitation, room layout, and so on. This is an important area for scenario workshops, and is not explicitly detailed in the process and guidelines provided. Workshops achieve more in less time if they are managed and facilitated properly (Cameron 2003).

The room layout chosen for the scenario workshops was structured according to RAD and JAD guidelines (Maiden and Jones 2003). Stakeholders sat around a U-shaped table with copies of the use case specification for the scenario being walked through. The facilitator stood inside this U-shaped table at the focal point of the interaction in the walkthrough; the layout is shown in Figure 18.6.

The facilitator controls the speed and focus of the walkthrough via the Scenario Presenter spreadsheet that is displayed permanently using a LCD projector. The screen is surrounded by prompts that encourage requirements discovery and creative thinking, and by a simple visual prompt of the repeating scenario walkthrough process that must be undertaken throughout the session. The prompts included ideas from earlier creativity workshops, different requirement types, and the ATC contexts that apply to the visible scenario.

To the left of the facilitator stands the scribe who records and manages information being stored on two large flipchart sheets. The first sheet records all requirements arising from the scenario walkthrough. It was divided into two parts—a description and rationale of the requirement, and the source of the requirement, in terms of the scenario event and alternative course ID that led to this requirement. To the right of the requirement flipchart

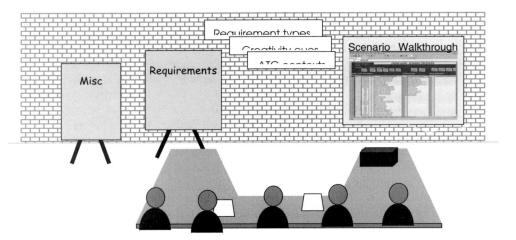

FIGURE 18.6 Sketch of the scenario workshops during the CORA Project

stands a prompt list of the different types of requirement that can be specified in the CORA-2 requirements specification. The second flipchart records information about information emerging from the walkthrough that are not requirements. Such information includes assumptions, problems, and even changes to the scenario. The scribe was responsible for the accuracy and clarity of the information being recorded on the flipcharts, as it is this information that later passes through the quality gateway (Robertson and Robertson 1999) into the requirements specification.

The walkthrough process causes requirements to emerge by being acquired, discovered, or invented. The main purpose of each session is to walk through the scenario, identifying, describing, and documenting the first-cut requirements. Therefore, the first-cut requirement description is recorded informally in paper-based form. The first-cut requirements were then formally recorded in the project requirement management tool (Rational RequisitePro). This maintained traceability and placed the requirements under change control. The requirements were then quality checked and those that were deemed to have passed check were marked as 'checked' and were ready for final approval.

Owing to project time constraints, stakeholder availability, and the time required to carry out scenario walkthroughs, the CORA team walked through 10 scenarios in total.

RESULTS

Requirements versus Time

Structured scenario walkthroughs were more effective for discovering requirements than the brainstorming and interview techniques applied earlier in the project. For the CORA project, more requirements were generated during the three-week period of the scenario walkthroughs, than the previous 10 months of the project requirements starting (Figure 18.7).

	Before scenario walkthroughs (Project ongoing for 10 months)	With scenario walkthroughs (over a 3-week period)
Number of new requirements generated	247	134
Average number of new requirements per week	6	45

FIGURE 18.7   Table showing the number of new requirements generated before and after the scenario walkthrough technique was introduced to the project

It is clear from these data that the scenario walkthroughs were more effective for requirement generation than whatever was done previously. However, it should be noted that the walkthrough workshops were intensive and lasted typically between three to five hours each. A more accurate measure of effectiveness would be obtained by comparing the actual time spent capturing requirements in the 10 months prior to the walkthroughs.

It may be suggested that if scenario walkthroughs are so cost-effective for requirement elicitation, then surely they should be introduced at the start of a project. But for the scenario walkthroughs to be successful, the generated scenarios must be accurate and relevant. This can only be achieved through solid engineering groundwork. The use cases in the CORA project were directly based on the work conducted during creativity workshops, as well as by system modelling using the i* methodology (Maiden, Jones and Flynn 2003).

Requirements Validation Using Use Cases

Scenario walkthrough interlinked the activities of eliciting and validating requirements.

During the scenario walkthroughs, existing requirements were incorporated into the scenario structures and paper copies were given to stakeholders during workshops. Stakeholders were then able to read requirements in the context of the underlying use case, making the requirements more readable and understandable. Requirements that were previously captured months ago from departed stakeholders could now be brought back to life and subsequently validated. Figure 18.8 shows a real snapshot of how requirements were integrated into scenarios.

Scenario walkthrough workshops provided the context for stakeholders to discuss, negotiate, and resolve information. The structure and natural language of the scenarios provided a solid focal point for stakeholders to resolve requirements conflicts.

Domain-Specific Scenarios

The experience of using CREWS-SAVRE scenarios in the CORA-2 project suggests that systematic walkthroughs of simple scenarios (not containing much domain knowledge) are more effective for discovering system requirements. The majority of the generated requirements were not associated with domain-specific alternative courses. The findings show that 33 of the 79 requirements linked with the domain-independent alternative courses were generated by just 5 of the 54 possible classes of ATC abnormal behaviour and state (Mavin and Maiden 2003).

Normal Course	**1. The CORA-2 system detects that a resolution is invalid.** FUN33. The CORA-2 system shall detect invalid resolutions. PRM12. The CORA-2 system shall detect invalid resolutions within 1 s of the resolution becoming invalid.
	2. The CORA-2 system removes the invalid resolution. FR34. The CORA-2 system shall only make available valid resolutions to the controller. USB12. The controller using the CORA-2 system shall only be able to access valid resolutions.

FIGURE 18.8 Snapshot of the use case specifications given to stakeholders during the scenario walkthroughs. Stakeholders and facilitators used this to validate the existing requirements and avoid duplicating requirements

However, a majority of the stakeholders stated that they reacted better to *seeing* ATC domain-specific scenarios, as these were described in their shared language, making it easier for them to communicate effectively. These conflicting views probably merit further testing for this finding.

Requirement Types

Most of the generated requirements were functional. Figure 18.9 shows the totals of requirements by type (Maiden and Mavin).

One reason for the greater number of functional requirements came from the walkthrough facilitators, who mentioned "due to time constraints the emphasis was often on functional rather than non-functional requirements". Non-functional requirements are more difficult to refine to a measurable level (*but see* Chapter 7 on Negative Scenarios by Ian Alexander in this volume) than functional requirements. During the time-boxed workshops, the majority of the non-functional requirements were elicited at high level only.

Requirement Type	Number of Requirements	Percentage (%)
Functional	95	70.9
Back-up	1	0.8
Performance	5	3.7
Reliability	16	11.9
Security	2	1.5
Training	3	2.2
Usability	12	9
Total	134	100

FIGURE 18.9 Totals of requirements by type discovered during the cora-2 scenario walkthroughs

Another possible factor contributing to the large proportion of functional requirements was the culture of the organisation, which relies on obtaining formal sign-off of functional specifications before proceeding with real life prototyping and simulation. Once the formal functional specifications are agreed, the organisation then reverse-engineers detailed non-functional requirements from the functional specification. There are obvious pros and cons with this approach, but we may simply note that whilst planning scenario walkthroughs, it is wise to take such issues into account.

Requirements Management

Scenario walkthroughs produce a mass of information, which needs to be managed to reap the benefits. The CORA team documented requirements within the scenarios themselves, and then reflected this structure in the supporting requirements management tool. This provided an effective method of analysing, documenting, and structuring the requirements in a format that all the different stakeholder groups (i.e. developers, testers, managers, and users) could understand.

Planning Workshops

It is important to be ready to act on unexpected events in any workshop. Most workshops achieve more in less time if they are managed and facilitated properly (Cameron 2003). An important lesson learnt from this case study is that it is not easy to generate or author the right use cases or scenarios first time. It is important for the stakeholders to familiarise themselves with the normal and alternative course scenarios *before* they are exposed to them during the walkthroughs. This will prevent long discussions, conflicting view, and confusion over some areas of the scenario during the time-boxed walkthroughs.

Formal review and change control process should be adhered to during scenario walkthrough process. The CREWS-SAVRE tool generated scenarios based on the normal course events of the use case. Changes to the use cases resulting from stakeholder discussion during the first walkthrough workshops resulted in the scenarios being regenerated.

How Many Scenarios Do We Need?

One issue for the CORA project was determining how many scenarios were needed to ensure that all the requirements had been captured or validated. This points to a dilemma underlying much of scenario-based RE:

- Scenarios are powerful because of the detail they contain, but "the devil lies in the detail", as you never know when you have captured everything that matters. This creates a pressure to explore yet more variations and exceptions to see if they are important.
- But since scenario workshops are costly in time and effort, it is essential to limit the number of scenarios used.

Other stakeholder-centred processes such as those described by Ellen Gottesdiener in Chapter 5 and Karen Holtzblatt in Chapter 10 of this volume can help provide confidence that a set of scenarios and requirements is reasonably complete.

The Way Forward with Scenario Walkthroughs

This case study helped show positive effectiveness that CREWS-SAVRE scenario walkthroughs has on a large-scale project. Important findings were captured, analysed, and implemented to improve the use of scenario walkthroughs.

From this case study and follow-on analysis work, the authors of the CREWS-SAVRE scenario walkthrough process have recommended five key lessons for using scenarios and use cases to discover requirements from stakeholders. These, along with other research findings, are currently being implemented in the next version of the process (Mavin and Maiden 2003).

- Make your walkthroughs domain-specific
- Impose structured walkthroughs
- Stakeholders own the scenarios
- Encourage exploration with scenarios
- Combine different walkthrough styles.

Work on CREWS-SAVRE's processes and tools is continuing. Details of the latest developments can be seen at www.soi.city.ac.uk/artscene.

KEYWORDS

Alternatives	Exceptions	Requirement Validation	Scenario Walkthroughs
CREWS-SAVRE	Requirement Elicitation	Scenarios	Use Cases

REFERENCES

Ben Achour, C., Rolland, C., Maiden, N.A.M., and Souveyet, C., Natural language studies on use case authoring, *Proceedings of the 4th IEEE Symposium on Requirements Engineering*, IEEE Computer Society Press, 1999, pp. 36–43.

Cameron, E., *Facilitation Made Easy*, Kogan Page Limited, 2003.

Cockburn, A., *Writing Effective Use Cases*, Addison-Wesley, 2001.

Jacobson, I., Booch, G., and Rumbaugh, J., *The Unified Software Development Process*, Addison-Wesley Longman, 2000.

Limbachia, N., *Scenario-based Requirements Engineering at Eurocontrol*, Final Year Project Thesis, City University, 2002

Maiden, N.A.M., SAVRE: Scenarios for acquiring and validating requirements, *Journal for Automated Software Engineering*, **5**, 419–446, 1998.

Maiden, N.A.M. and Jones, S., *An Integrated User-Centred Requirements Engineering Process*, Version 4, RESCUE Process Document, 2003.

Maiden, N.A.M. and Mavin, A., Determining socio-technical systems requirements: experiences with generating and walking through scenarios, *RE '03 Conference*, Monterey CA, IEEE Computer Society Press, 2003.

Maiden, N.A.M., Jones, S., and Flynn, M., *Innovative Requirements Techniques Applied to ATM (Air Traffic Management)*, Budapest, 23–27, 2003.

Robertson, S. and Robertson, J., *Mastering the Requirements Process*, Addison-Wesley, 1999.

Sutcliffe, A.G., Maiden, N.A.M., Minocha, S., and Manuel, D., Supporting scenario-based requirements engineering, *IEEE Transactions on Software Engineering*, **24**(12), 1072–1088, 1998.

Yu, E., Towards modelling and reasoning support for early-phase requirement engineering, *Proceedings of the 3rd IEEE International Symposium on Requirements Engineering (RE '97)*, Annapolis, USA, 1997, pp. 226–235.

CHAPTER 19

SCENARIOS AND QUALITY REQUIREMENTS IN TELECOMMUNICATIONS

Juha Savolainen
Nokia Research Center, Helsinki, Finland

THIS CHAPTER describes a practical approach in which scenarios are used together with (nonfunctional) quality requirements to design and document a high-quality telecommunications system. We investigate the connection between functional and nonfunctional requirements, and find ways to document our knowledge in a way that allows others to evaluate our design easily without going through hundreds of pages of different specifications. Our approach relies on describing design together with the key requirements that this design should fulfill. Finally, we will discuss the experiences gathered while using the approach in practical industrial projects.

TYPE OF PROJECT

This chapter describes the development of a base station in the telecommunications domain. The project involved a large number of developers working in multiple sites at several countries. In this case study, only one project is covered, although many parts of the approach have been used for other projects over the years. The experiences gathered from different projects and domains are collected as the Lessons Learnt.

APPLICABILITY

The approach represented in this chapter has been applied mainly to large telecommunications systems and to some embedded devices. The management of product quality in the telecommunications domain is a challenging task, where the work products of hundreds of engineers need to be assembled to create the final product release. Therefore, a careful and scalable way is needed to propagate quality characteristics from system level down to individual components. There is no major obstacle to using this approach

Scenarios, Stories, Use Cases: Through the Systems Development Life-Cycle. Edited by Ian F Alexander and Neil Maiden
© 2004 John Wiley & Sons, Ltd. ISBN: 0-470-86194-0

for smaller scale systems, but modifications may be needed to adapt it to other domains. Possible adaptations are discussed further in the Lessons Learnt section.

In this chapter, we will perform quality refinement using example scenarios to detect potential trouble spots in the software architecture. The assumption is that when the most demanding aspects of the software are produced to the desired quality, the system will most likely have the characteristics that the various stakeholders have expressed.

Our approach relies on the accurate choice of techniques for analyzing the characteristics of the solution. These techniques will presumably differ somewhat when operating in another domain. The selection of evaluation techniques that match the characteristics of the domain, as well as the needs and expectations of stakeholders, is crucial for the success of the quality management process.

POSITION IN THE LIFE CYCLE

Requirements Discovery	Requirements Validation	System Specification	System Design	Coding, First of Class	Integration & Testing	Operations & Maintenance

ROLES PLAYED BY SCENARIOS

Scenarios were applied to identify and specify (using a tabular format) the functional requirements of the system. The scenarios were also employed to assist and verify the refinement of quality requirements. A subset of the requirements was selected to form a set of architecturally significant requirements, which were used to validate the architecture. The validation is greatly assisted by using scenarios.

STRENGTHS

The main strengths of our approach come from improved understanding of the critical requirements of the system. Concentration on key requirements and then thorough investigation of their fulfillment allow you to gain confidence on the software architecture. The increased understanding of the key requirements for the system improves the architecture by aligning subsystem design better with overall objectives. When software designers know what is wanted from a product, they can design a system that has those properties.

WEAKNESSES

Besides bringing benefits, all practical methods have limitations. In our case, the approach does not guarantee that the system will ultimately satisfy the requirements of its stakeholders. By selecting just a few representative scenarios from the set of all possible scenarios, we favor practicality over the completeness of the approach. In this way, we are able to perform the analysis within the time constraints of a typical industrial project.

The approach relies heavily on the ability of the analyst and other experts to select effective scenarios—those that illustrate the key qualities wanted by stakeholders. If inappropriate scenarios are selected, the approach will not provide reliable results. Unfortunately, there is no formal way to select the right scenarios. The selection has to be made using the analyst's experience and the heuristics that guide the selection of architecturally significant requirements.

CASE STUDY

The telecommunications project described here developed a base station for third generation (3G) networks. The transition from previous GSM-based networks to WCDMA 3G-networks posed new challenges to the development organization. Next-generation base stations were to have much higher data transmission speeds, completely different algorithms, and potentially changed network layout.

The basic concept of the base station is simple. It interacts with a mobile device over the air interface, transmitting and receiving information using microwaves. The data is then sent to other network elements responsible for switching and routing the data to its final destination. The air interface is highly standardized and its functionality is well known. The real challenge for base station development is satisfying the quality requirements that apply to its operation.

This case study is used to demonstrate how scenarios can be used together with quality requirements to help create large-scale high-quality products. The diagrams, requirements, and designs have been modified to limit the complexity of the example, to increase the readability of the case study, and to prevent disclosure of company-specific information. The structure of this case study is shown in a sequential fashion, but this should not be read as implying that a classical waterfall process was used. On the contrary, the actual process was highly iterative, and multiple increments were used during the creation of the product. (Life-cycle process models are discussed by Andrew Farncombe in Chapter 15 of this volume.)

Software systems are specified by identifying what a system should do under specific circumstances. The specification of the system's behavior is done by describing functional requirements. The nonfunctional requirements define the constraints that the system should conform to while operating. Functional requirements are very effectively described by using scenarios, which pinpoint the actual required behavior. Defining the behavior as an interaction between the actor and the system makes scenarios intuitive, easy to understand, and very approachable by various stakeholders.

Nonfunctional requirements (including qualities such as security, dependability, interoperability, performance) typically affect many scenarios. If we are building a system that is supposed to be very secure, many aspects of the system's operation come into play. We must somehow be able to authenticate that the user is what she claims to be. In addition, we must provide services for access control and guarantee the protection of data from unauthorized disclosure. These are critical requirements in this context. These requirements typically affect every scenario that describes interactions between the system and the user.

Nonfunctional requirements can be specified with the help of scenarios. Despite their name, nonfunctional requirements are actually closely connected to system behaviour. Let us first consider performance.

Performance characteristics are very important for a telecommunications system. The speed of user data processing and the number of concurrent managed connections that the system allows are critical requirements for the success of the product. These qualities, however, attach to only a subset of base stations scenarios. For example, there is no extensive requirement for the number of concurrent users or for the high speed of the maintenance interface of a network device. Whether a network element responds within 60 ms or 500 ms to a maintenance mode change does not affect the user's perception of the system. Identifying which scenarios the quality requirements are attached to is a critical phase of specification. If we do not identify all the scenarios that are constrained by the specified qualities, we could easily design a product with inferior characteristics. Conversely, having strict quality requirements for unnecessary scenarios can make our task of designing the system much harder, and might lead to a product that is too complex and expensive for customers' needs.

Scenarios

Scenarios are created during the requirements specification phase. These scenarios form the basis on which the system is created. In this stage, scenarios are used to specify requirements for the system under development. They treat the system as a black box, describing only the interactions between the system and the actor. (The concept of the actor in the Unified Modeling Language is explained by Peter Haumer in Chapter 12 of this volume—see for example his Figure 19.2.) Later, we will define realizations of the scenarios that define the collaboration of architectural elements when performing the scenario. Each scenario is defined within a scope where it applies.

Our initial list included scenarios like

Transmit user data,
Transmit voice call,
Transmit high-speed data, and
Accept new user.

All these scenarios see the systems from the mobile user's perspective, treating the system as a black box.

The software architecture documentation focuses on how the system will satisfy the key requirements. The properties of the architecture can be made concrete by describing how the scenario is performed by the collaborating architectural elements. These inter-actions clearly take place within the system boundary and, therefore, are out of reach of the black-box scenarios. This is the reason why the software architecture can only be described by using white-box scenarios. We cannot easily discuss the properties of the architecture unless we allow ourselves to define the scenarios in the context of the pieces of which the architecture is formed. This does not mean that scenarios that do not uncover the architectural pieces are without merit. On the contrary, black-box scenarios allow us to easily define the requirements for the architecture without prematurely diving into design. Restricting yourself to only discussing interaction between the environment and the system limits the ways in which you might accidentally start designing the various components of the system while doing requirements.

Quality Requirements

The structure of the software architecture is strongly affected by the quality requirements that the system has to satisfy. A system designed for maximum reliability using highly redundant hardware and advanced software techniques typically has a very different structure than a system aimed at low-cost, mass product markets. For us to be successful in developing systems with strict quality requirements, we must understand correctly the key user requirements for all the wanted characteristics. Naturally, the system must also realize its functional requirements, but those only drive the architectural choices when they are attached to major quality constraints.

Quality Models — Defining What We Want

A quality model defines the main quality requirements that the system should fulfill. The quality model is a refinement hierarchy that makes general quality requirements more concrete and easier to measure.

The need for such a model is real. Most requirement documents, which I have read during my professional career, specify many wonderful properties of the future products. All these systems shall be extremely fast, very reliable, and highly usable. But what does it mean to have a fast system? Does it move quickly or does it have the fastest user interface ever? Or can it process calculations faster than the latest supercomputers? Inability to connect a quality requirement to the corresponding functionality renders a specification worthless. The requirement specifications should be always as concrete and measurable as possible.

Even if we manage to do a good job with the initial requirements, we may lose sight of them during the development project. The high-level goals are forgotten and they fail to guide the development work of the various subsystems and components that are created. The most common problem is that initial requirements remain at the system level and they are not sufficiently taken into account during subsystem design. Correct subsystem design requires that the high-level requirements be transformed into subsystem-specific requirements.

A basic quality model is typically created at the first stage of product development. The model is formed after initial workshops among the most critical stakeholders of the project. Initially, it contains only vague hopes for the system's characteristics. To prevent ambiguity in the specifications, these definitions must be made more concrete without delay. The easiest way to do this is to create a scenario that defines the quality requirement in the context of system functionality.

Many quality requirements can be derived from domain properties. Systems that belong to the same domain typically share many characteristics. For telecommunications systems, these domain requirements often include high reliability and good performance. Since network elements handle between hundreds to tens of thousands of calls, a failure in such a device can have major consequences. The performance of the system should be adequate to handle the high load associated with the number of concurrent calls. In addition to that, the reliability of the system must be very high to guarantee service to

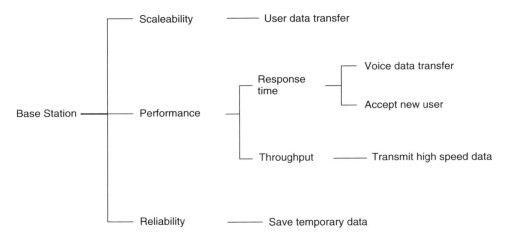

FIGURE 19.1 A quality tree for a base station

mobile network users. Figure 19.1 describes the quality tree for our base station case study. For a real base station, the number of quality requirements is naturally much higher than shown in the figure.

Figure 19.1 shows the qualities initially considered important for our case study. The leaf nodes (such as '*User data transfer*') describe concrete scenarios for which the defined quality is important. Scenarios are added early to make qualities concrete. Typically, only most relevant scenario is added, but nothing prevents the listing of additional ones if this is felt important. Most of the scenarios presented were invented in the previous phase, but some may emerge while creating the quality tree. In any case, the resulting tree is not considered to be a complete mapping of scenarios to qualities. Nor are the scenarios themselves completely specified. Initially, only small narratives are recorded, focusing on interplay between the functionality and related quality constraints.

The Architecture Trade-off Analysis Method (ATAM) was created by the Software Engineering Institute (SEI) to evaluate software architectures (Kazman, Klein and Clements 2000). This method uses scenarios to assess the architecture against the identified quality characteristics. It matches quality attributes to scenarios in the same way that is demonstrated here. In fact, many architecture analysis methods are of great help when applying our approach for software architecture specification. All these architecture evaluation methods provide guidance and examples how to match together specifications on the wanted characteristics and the realization of the architecture.

Organizing quality requirements into hierarchies is nothing new. Besides using the approach for single products it can be also adapted to a case when you are building a family of systems. Quality refinement for product families has been demonstrated in an earlier paper by the author (Kuusela and Savolainen 2000).

Architecturally Significant Requirements (ASRs)

A large system may have a huge number of requirements. Nobody is able to handle all the requirements simultaneously while architecting the system. Development of the software architecture relies on identifying the critical requirements that the system should satisfy. These requirements are said to be architecturally significant. Unfortunately, there is no simple way to identify architecturally significant requirements (ASRs) from the set of all possible requirements. There are, however, some general guidelines for identifying ASRs (Jazayeri, Ran, and van der Linden 2000). According to Alexander Ran, ASRs include

- Characteristics that give the reason for building a new product
- Aspects of the product that crosscutting most of the system
- Requirements that impact the coordination or management of the subsystems

In our case, requirements emerging from the transition to 3G are the main source of ASRs. Many ASRs are recorded in the list of key scenarios together with a quality model. They are also recorded in tabular format. Typically, ASRs reflect the needs of all the stakeholders of the project. Therefore, some ASRs are added to restrict the choices of product development on how to develop the system. An example of such an ASR is

ASR.1 *Base station shall be easily configured.*

Refinement of ASRs

Earlier we identified a major problem—that a critical system-level requirement may be forgotten during the development. To fight this problem, we try to create component requirements from those defined for the whole system. Again both scenarios and quality requirements are tackled.

The basic process for ASR refinement is easy. First, identify architecturally significant requirements at system level. For each ASR, decide whether it is relevant for every subsystem of the architecture. Record the subsystems that are affected by the ASR. This is typically done together with chief and subsystem architects.

Then refine the ASRs for each subsystem where that requirement was relevant. Ideally, subsystem ASRs should describe concrete requirements for that subsystem. That is, the requirement should not apply system-wide. Rather it should describe some concrete characteristics of the subsystem. It should be easy to check whether the ASR is fulfilled in the subsystem architecture. This is assisted by explicitly demonstrating how the ASRs are fulfilled, by tying them to the architectural solutions at each level of architectural documentation.

In our case study, we divided up the ASRs according to the components in the architecture, and created new requirements for the corresponding components. For example, to match

ASR.1 *Base station shall be easily configured,*
we can now add a requirement

ASR.ANT.1 *Adapt to different antenna configurations*
to the Antenna component. For the data processor component the requirement becomes

ASR.DP.1 *Easy changeability of data processing algorithms.*
The structure of the software architecture is described in the following section.

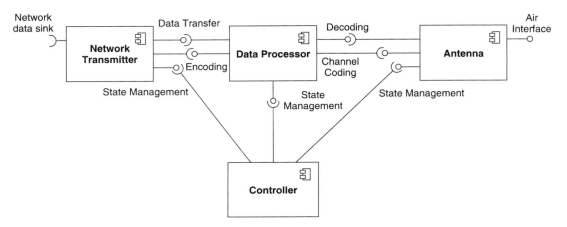

FIGURE 19.2   Simplified component architecture

Software Architecture

For a large project it is impractical to have the software specified, designed, and documented in one document or by one person. It is necessary to have different scopes where each of those phases can be done semi-independently. On the basis of our knowledge of the required functionality and qualities, an initial architectural model is created. In this section, we introduce a partial component architecture of the base station.

Figure 19.2 shows the component architecture of the base station. Our example consists of four major components. The basic operation of the system can be described by extending the basic scenario to cover the collaboration of individual components.

Documentation of the software architecture serves many purposes. It describes the key concepts and principles on which the architecture is designed. It defines the main architectural styles, and lays down the fundamental building blocks of the software. This documentation gives the rationale for key decisions such as division of the architecture into subsystems, selected communication mechanisms, and the hardware deployment of the software.

Despite that, many traditional architecture methods apply a very structure-oriented view; but the behavioral aspects are equally important. Ignoring behavioral characteristics of the architecture reduces the focus on satisfying the main functionality of the system, and thus may easily lead to overly complex solutions that wrongly emphasize flexibility. Excess flexibility may reduce performance because of higher processing power requirements, and may adversely affect maintainability by making the architecture more complicated.

Other approaches such as Jan Bosch's architecture transformation (Bosch 2000) rely on late introduction of quality characteristics. Architecture is first designed using the functionality of the system, and then evaluated against the wanted quality requirements. If the characteristics of the system do not match the requirements, the architecture is transformed. During the transformation, architectural patterns and styles are injected into the design to provide the wanted properties. For systems that operate in very constrained domains this may result in major overhauls of the system design, making such process unlikely to be a success when taking into account the economic constraints.

In these domains, systems must be designed considering both functional and quality aspects simultaneously. Unfortunately, it is very difficult to define a formal process that would take both of these aspects into account simultaneously. Until software engineering matures enough to provide us tools to do so, architecting will remain a process that is largely guided by heuristics and intuition (Maier and Rechtin 2000) in addition to theoretical models. But you can still at least specify and document the wanted characteristics in a way that allows you to describe functional and quality characteristics together in the context of the software architecture.

What kind of scenarios should be documented? Clearly having all possible scenarios described in the architecture document would be overkill for a large system. We have to be able to select those scenarios that greatly contribute to the understanding of the software architecture. In our approach, those scenarios come from two categories. In the first category belong scenarios that represent the basic functionality of the system. For a mobile phone, it would be the ability to place a call and send an SMS message. In the context of the architecture, these scenarios would describe how the architectural elements collaborate to produce this functionality. That lays the foundation for improving architectural understanding.

Scenarios that are related to the architecturally significant requirements form the second category. Again, for a mobile phone these could include the ability to send high-speed data and perform a video playback. Here, the first scenario would test the speed of the encoding and compression functionality by measuring the throughput of the system, and the latter would evaluate the efficiency of the video codecs, determining if enough processing power exists to perform this operation.

Examples in Documenting Specific Quality Characteristics

Typically, when the architecture document is created, the document is used to communicate the intent of the high-level design to the subsystem architects. Naturally, the architecture specification by itself is not enough to establish a common vision, so close collaboration among chief architects and subsystem architects is required. But this process is greatly facilitated by suitable architecture documentation. Ideally, the document describes aspects of the system design that are meaningful for the subsystem architects and developers.

As discussed before, some scenarios are selected to be part of the architecture documentation because they contribute to some important quality characteristics. In this section, we provide examples on how to document those scenarios for the selected quality attributes, and how to use scenarios to validate that the selected architectural choices were correct.

Documenting Performance Characteristics

Achieving the performance characteristics is important for most embedded systems. In our case, we identified the scenario *transmit high-speed data* as the most challenging one from the performance perspective. For the performance characteristics this means defining the time budgets for the subsystems and possibly exposing the rationale behind the decisions by including the preliminary performance analysis results.

The time budgets can be easily created with the help of the white-box scenario. After identifying the collaboration of architectural elements for the scenario, maximum execution times for each element can be listed. The sum of the execution times of the elements in the collaboration should be less than the time allowed for the scenario. This way of creating the time budgets is very easy, but unfortunately it is not enough to completely verify the response time characteristics for a complex embedded device with multiple, different interactions running concurrently in the system.

As with any quality attribute, there are many methods and techniques for evaluating and validating system properties. In the case of performance, our initial approach for dividing the allowed response time into time budgets of the architectural elements does not take account the effect of shared resources. Such sharing happens in almost all systems, since hardware resources are typically used by more than one entity. Therefore, some processes must wait for access to needed resources. This means that for accurate performance estimation, the possible blocking of shared resources must be considered. Many different methods allow analysis at various level of detail: for example, queuing network analysis (Smith and Williams 2002) (Menasce, Almeida, and Dowdy 2004); rate monotonic analysis (Klein et al. 1993, Briand and Roy 1999).

It is important to notice that execution times are not the only performance-related parameters that need to be specified. Defining the constraints on memory usage, available communication links, and process creation is equally important.

Documenting Modifiability Characteristics

In our initial scenario list, we did not identify any scenarios for validating the modifiability of the architecture. This is because modifiability does not attach to current functionality. Rather, it explores the amount of change needed when the current functionality is changed or new functions appear.

Ideally, we could change any requirement we like and still be able to make this change quickly with minimal adaptation of other assets. This requires that any change would always nicely localize in the architecture, either by having a single module that realizes the requirement or by having explicit points that provide places where additional functionality can be easily attached. In real life, no architecture allows flexibility for all imaginable changes. All modularizations of the architecture leave many changes that do not localize into a small set of software modules; and excess flexibility has potentially a large negative impact on other qualities such as understandability of the system, development cost, maintainability, and performance. This all means that the modifiability of the system can only be analyzed against an identified change.

For our project, this means listing the possible changes in form of scenarios that briefly describes the change in the context of the system. For these kinds of scenarios it is better to be too concrete than too abstract. This is because you want to have a way to test the architecture and demonstrate its properties. One scenario for our case could be

Add new ABCD antenna to the base station without changing the software, where ABCD is the actual type of the future antenna. This type of scenario is clearly superior to an alternative scenario

Add new hardware to the base station.

The latter scenario is too generic to be easily analyzed, and it cannot be fulfilled by almost any system, because the scenario does not state which piece of hardware is to be added to the base station. It is not possible to integrate a hair dryer or a toaster into the base station, and it is hard to see that this kind of requirement would ever emerge.

The change of antenna type fortunately localizes into the module *HW Drivers*. The layered architecture view covering the module structure is shown in Figure 19.3.The scenario claims that the addition of the future antenna should happen without any changes to the software. This means that either a driver for the future antenna already exists in the module or that a compatible driver can be used. In real life, this means that at least the driver interface—if not the actual code—must be investigated for compatibility.

LESSONS LEARNT

Describing and documenting the satisfaction of quality requirements was more difficult than initially estimated. Varying quality requirements, different architectural views and evolving solutions make universally applicable guidelines difficult to give. Lack of books,

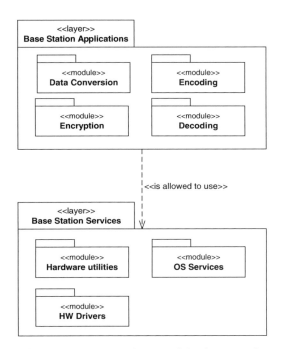

FIGURE 19.3   Layered view of the base station

scientific articles, or tutorial material on how to combine different techniques makes this particularly challenging. But even if the design solutions are documented in an imperfect way, our approach promotes subsystem architects and developers to think about the key requirements and create solutions that, more often than not, satisfy the identified needs.

Good practical examples are needed that clearly demonstrate how scenarios can be described in different architectural views. This collection of examples should be large enough to cover many different circumstances. Depending on the abstraction level, a quality requirement can be most easily described in a view that matches the level of detail. For example, when describing a performance critical scenario at high level, the most appropriate method would be to show that scenario as a collaboration of architectural elements. However, better estimations can be made when the scenario is mapped to the process structure. Since for large systems, at high level, the process structure may not exist, the preferred representation of the performance critical scenario, and its location in the architecture description, may depend on whether the documentation is describing large subsystems or individual components. Describing quality scenarios in complex industrial projects is not easy, and it requires much more hands-on training than we initially anticipated.

The major benefit of our approach is the concretization of the key requirements that guide the development of the software architecture. Refining the needed quality characteristics down to subsystems seems to improve the resulting system considerably. Defining subsystem requirements exposes the hidden assumptions that people make when interpreting system-level requirements.

The duality of scenarios and quality requirements makes one wonder what comes first. Which is more important? Should I specify my scenarios first or start from the quality requirements? The only right answer is that both are equally important. However, the order in which you should specify the requirements is dominated by your domain.

Suggestions for Well-Understood Domains

In a well-understood domain, the choice among competing products can be based on required qualities. For example; how light the product is, how often it has to be recharged, and whether the measurements of the device can be trusted to determine whether the device will be commercially successful. Typically, all the competing products in a market offer very similar functionality. In this case, I suggest that you start by defining those critical qualities that your product should possess. Then identify which scenarios contribute for the qualities that you just discovered. Especially, try to identify new scenarios that might provide the user added value. These discoveries might allow your product to be differentiated from the other products in the market place. Additionally, your existing assets may become handy. You may be able to also reuse existing scenario descriptions from your the previous products.

Suggestions for Emerging Markets

For emerging markets things are different. If the concept of the product is vague, inventing good, measurable quality requirements is a daunting task. Then, concentrating on user scenarios is most likely the best approach. Concentrating on what the system should do and the most valuable scenarios for the user of the system builds a basis on which the first prototypes can be built. When you have managed to identify the exact user goals in terms of scenarios—discovering the quality requirements becomes much easier.

These are just suggestions for some possible circumstances that you may encounter while trying to apply these ideas. You should first understand your problem and then adapt the ideas presented in this book to fit your problem. There is no such thing as one size fits all.

ACKNOWLEDGEMENTS

I would like to thank all the people working for the base station domain without whom this chapter would not have been possible. Especially I would like to thank (in no particular order) Aki Nyyssönen, Ari Evisalmi, Pekka Rusi, Eero Lähde, Aapo Rautiainen, Tuomo Vehkomäki, and Tanya Widen for their commitment throughout the project.

KEYWORDS

System Specification Quality Requirements Software Design Software Architecture

REFERENCES

Bosch, J., *Design and Use of Software Architectures: Adopting and Evolving a Product-Line Approach*, Addison-Wesley, 2000.

Briand, L. and Roy, D., *Meeting Deadlines in Hard Real-Time Systems—The Rate Monotonic Approach*, IEEE Computer Society Press, 1999.

Jazayeri, M., Ran, A., and van der Linder, F., *Software Architecture in Practice*, Addison-Wesley, 2000.

Kazman, R., Klein, M., and Clements, P., *ATAM: Method for Architecture Evaluation*, Technical Report CMU/SEI-2000-TR-004, Software Engineering Institute, Carnegie Mellon University, Pittsburgh, PA, August 2000.

Klein, M., Ralya, T., Pollak, B., Obenza, R., and Harbour, M., *A Practioner's Handbook for Real-Time Analysis: Guide to Rate Monotonic Analysis for Real-Time Systems*, Kluwer Academic Publishers, 1993.

Kuusela, J. and Savolainen, J., requirements engineering for product lines, *International Conference on Software Engineering (ICSE2000)*, IEEE, 2000, pp. 61–69.

Maier, M. and Rechtin, E., *The Art of Systems Architecting*, CRC Press, 2000 (based on Systems Architecting by E. Rectin, Prentice Hall, 1990).

Smith, C. and Williams, L., *Performance Solutions—A Practical Guide to Creating Responsive*, Scalable Software, Addison-Wesley, 2002.

CHAPTER 20

SCENARIOS IN RAIL ROLLING STOCK WITH REVEAL

Alistair Mavin

Praxis Critical Systems Limited, London, UK

THIS CASE Study chapter reports on a project with a major international rail rolling stock manufacturer during requirements elicitation and system specification for new metro Trains. The project used the Praxis REVEAL[1] requirements engineering method.

Scenarios were used to analyse Train requirements to derive specifications and domain knowledge. The same scenarios were then used as the contextual glue to show that the requirements had been satisfied by the specifications, given the domain assumptions. The scenarios were, therefore, a key part of the Satisfaction Argument used to show that the solution will satisfy the requirement. Similarly, scenarios were used in the analysis of Train specifications to derive requirements for the sub-systems, which also uncovered further domain knowledge.

The process produced Train specifications that were written at the right level of granularity. During the development of activity diagrams, engineers tended to write simple descriptions of the external behaviour of the system as a black box. Previously, they had tended to go into the detail of specifications too early.

The scenarios explicitly showed dependencies on domain assumptions, as well as dependencies between different sub-systems. This visibility helped sub-system suppliers to understand the environment in which their products would be used. Using this process, the sub-system requirements contained *all* relevant information, and *only* relevant information. This made it easier for sub-system suppliers to respond, and for the client to assess their responses.

APPLICABILITY

The client designs Trains to satisfy both high-level customer requirements and rigorous rail standards. The new Train is a complex system of systems. Train sub-systems such as Car bodies, Bogies, and Bodyside Doors are specified and procured from third-party suppliers located all over the world. The client is responsible for ensuring that the systems can be built into a working Train.

---

[1] REVEAL® is a registered trade mark of Praxis Critical Systems Limited.

Scenarios, Stories, Use Cases: Through the Systems Development Life-Cycle. Edited by Ian F Alexander and Neil Maiden
© 2004 John Wiley & Sons, Ltd. ISBN: 0-470-86194-0

REVEAL has been applied widely in the Rail, Aerospace, Defence, Telecomms, Finance, Nuclear, and other industries, mainly for real time control applications. REVEAL has also been applied to business requirements, to help define product strategy and during the analysis and assessment of bids. Scenarios are not a mandatory part of the REVEAL method, but are often used to explore operational and maintenance requirements.

POSITION IN THE LIFE CYCLE

Requirements Discovery	Requirements Validation	System Specification	System Design	Coding, First of Class	Integration & Testing	Operations & Maintenance

KEY FEATURES

Scenarios were used to situate the requirements, specifications, and domain knowledge within the context of use of the system being developed. Scenarios were used to address requirements for discrete events such as starting and stopping Trains in a range of operating modes. One scenario was written for each requirement. Each scenario consisted of a set of End-to-End conditions and an activity diagram.

Each event in the Train swimlane was represented in the requirements database as a Train specification (to be further elaborated into requirements on Train sub-systems). Each event in any other swimlane corresponded with a domain knowledge statement in the database about that domain entity (such as Train Driver, Passenger, Automatic Train Control).

All statements are categorised as being Requirement, Specification, or Domain Knowledge. In REVEAL this is called the *Separation of Concerns*.

A central feature of the REVEAL method is the notion of the Satisfaction Argument. A Satisfaction Argument is written to show that the system specifications are sufficient to satisfy the system requirement, as long as the domain statements hold true. For a good introduction to the principles of REVEAL, see the *Will it work?* paper (Hammond, Rawlings and Hall 2001).

Failure conditions for each scenario were not formally considered as part of this project. However, a checklist of *What-if* questions was used to investigate any possible breaks in the scenario thread. This was a simple application of the concepts used in the ART-SCENE Scenario Presenter (Mavin and Maiden 2003).

STRENGTHS

Scenarios are easy to understand and easy for engineers to write, without the need to learn a complex new notation. This helps with getting projects off to a strong start, as scenarios can be used on day one.

Scenarios are written in the language of the engineers, who are experts in the domain. This focuses the analysis on realistic situations and encourages buy-in from stakeholders.

Scenarios help with scoping the system. Only domain entities included on the Rich Context Diagram can be included in the activity diagrams. The rigour that this brings promotes the consistent use of terminology.

Train specifications, sub-system requirements, and domain knowledge are contextualised by the scenario. By embedding them in a scenario, it is easier to see why they are necessary and why they take a particular form. The activity diagram provides an easy to understand single-page representation of how the system will operate in a particular set of circumstances. It also documents how the environment around the system is expected to behave. The activity diagram thus provides a coherent description of the expected interaction between the system and its environment.

This approach helps drive out issues of ownership of data and functions between sub-systems and therefore between different suppliers. The demarcation between sub-systems is clearly defined by the use of swimlanes to show which entity carries out any particular activity.

The scenario model supports the Satisfaction Argument, and as such is a simple one-page proof that the requirement will be satisfied. The Satisfaction Argument states that the Specifications will be sufficient to satisfy the Requirement so long as the Domain Statements hold true. The scenario shows how these statements are related and therefore proves that the requirement will be satisfied.

The Satisfaction Argument is automatically built as the activity diagram is being developed during elicitation. The activity diagram explains how the specifications and domain statements fit together to satisfy the requirement.

The Rich Traceability afforded by Satisfaction Arguments allows for easy impact analysis of requirement changes. When any statement changes, the effects can be traced through Satisfaction Arguments to investigate which other statements are affected. Should a specification change, it can be traced upwards to see if the Satisfaction Arguments to which it contributes still hold true. It can also be traced downwards to see if sub-system requirements below it are still sufficient to satisfy the changed specification.

WEAKNESSES

The technique can highlight so many issues; there is a danger that circular discussions take over and analysis descends into a talking shop. This is an issue for the management of the elicitation sessions, which can be minimised by effective facilitation skills.

The process is not suitable for the analysis of continuous functional requirements. Since scenarios are essentially linear, they do not tend to accommodate feedback loops easily.

Detailed scenario analysis can be unnecessary for trivial scenarios—engineering judgement is necessary to determine which scenarios require this level of analysis.

There is a tendency for engineers to treat activity diagrams as an end in themselves and to polish them repeatedly. Engineers usually understand that the accuracy of the scenario content is very important. However, they may need to be reminded that the layout and visual appeal of the activity diagram are not particularly important.

Ensuring consistency between activity diagrams, Rich Context Diagrams and statements in the requirements database is likely to be a manual process, although traceability tools can help with this. Developing automated consistency is likely to require a large development effort, which may be uneconomic.

CASE STUDY

Background

The project took place in a complex contractual environment. The client company is part of a consortium of companies, from whom the work was sub-contracted to our client. In addition to the rolling stock (the metro Trains), the contract also included requirements for associated signalling, and the maintenance of the rolling stock, but these were outside the scope of the project reported here. The national government and other authorities were also involved. Since the project was commercially sensitive, some of the specific details have not been included in this chapter. An example scenario, anonymised from a real scenario used during the system development, is included later in this section.

The client builds Trains to satisfy customer requirements. However, in this case the customer was not a single organisation—requirements came from a variety of sources. Some requirements were assumed and not stated anywhere (e.g. there was no documented requirement stated by the customer to be able to start the Train).

Basic customer requirements were expressed as high-level capabilities such as 'Transport X thousand people per hour between Y and Z'. The Trains also had to satisfy more detailed requirements from a number of sources, such as rigorous rail standards, a variety of other national and international standards, and the schedules of contractual documents. Requirements contained in these documents were written to different levels of precision and included many conflicts. The content of these documents typically included informative text (this is effectively filler), contextual information (domain knowledge), and features of the expected solution (specifications), in addition to requirements.

The client intended to develop some of the metro Train sub-systems itself, but the majority of the sub-systems and components were sourced from third parties. The client works closely with a small set of suppliers, and usually builds Trains from known existing components. Suppliers typically provide detailed specifications of the products and components that they intend to supply. However, these documents do not show whether the specifications will satisfy the requirements. When the specifications *do* satisfy the requirements, it is unlikely to be clear *how* they are satisfied. The responsibility for integration of these sub-systems is entirely with the client.

Figure 20.1 below shows how the Train requirements were allocated to the various sub-systems of the Train prior to our involvement in the project. The process relied heavily on the expert knowledge and experience of the systems engineers. They used their knowledge of the domain, along with a high-level vision of the Train (the *Train Concept*) to decide which requirements impacted on which sub-systems.

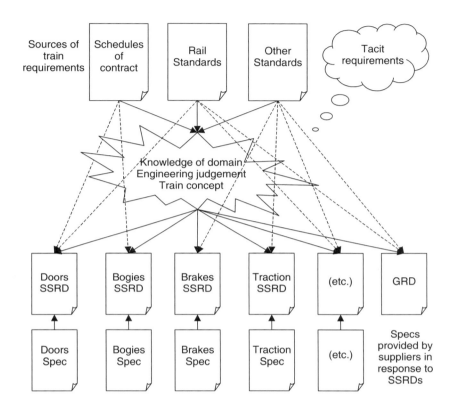

FIGURE 20.1   The requirements process before praxis was involved, showing the relationships between requirements, tacit requirements, and Sub-System Requirements Documents (SSRDs), against which suppliers provided specifications

In some cases, whole standards applied to the Train or to particular sub-systems and would therefore be flowed directly to the appropriate sub-system(s). In other cases, only parts of a standard would apply to all or part of the Train, and engineering judgement would be needed to decide which parts of the standard applied to which sub-system. This process was unsystematic and decisions (and the reasons for them) tended to be undocumented.

Performance requirements such as those concerning reliability would usually be apportioned to the relevant sub-systems, so that the aggregated reliability of all the sub-systems would satisfy the Train-level requirement.

Inevitably, engineers made assumptions about the system and its context whilst allocating requirements to sub-systems, but there was little formal mechanism for recording these. These unrecorded tacit assumptions represented a significant risk to the project and the organisation more widely.

Concurrently with this 'top-down' analysis of Train requirements, the client would also work 'bottom-up' through close liaison with suppliers. Each sub-system of the Train was the responsibility of a systems engineer, who worked closely with suppliers, and was familiar with the available products and components.

The systems engineers wrote a Sub-System Requirements Document (SSRD) for each sub-system, to which the suppliers responded. In practice, these responses tended to be product specifications, which gave little indication as to which requirements would be met, and *how* they would be met.

The systems engineers' knowledge of the suppliers' products informed the generation and contents of the SSRD. This meant that often the requirements for the sub-system were driven by the specifications. It could also mean that the *Train Concept* that drove the proposed solution was focussed on the solution rather than the need.

The SSRD typically contained some high-level requirements and complete Standards that were copied verbatim from the source document. These often included large numbers of clauses that were irrelevant to the sub-system in question. Along with the SSRD, suppliers were also sent a General Requirements Document (GRD), which listed requirements and other information considered relevant to all (or at least most) subsystems.

The superfluous requirements in these documents meant that suppliers had to analyse and interpret the contents of the SSRD and the GRD to determine which parts they had to address. This analysis added a significant overhead to the work of the supplier. It also made assessment of supplier responses time-consuming and difficult.

Our Approach to the Project

Praxis Critical Systems Limited was engaged by the client to help them to bridge the gap between the high-level needs of their customers and the detailed specifications that they received from suppliers. The project also sought to document domain knowledge and facilitate the reuse of requirements, specifications, and even Satisfaction Arguments. The work included tailoring the REVEAL process, training the client's engineers, and onsite coaching to embed the new process into the organisation.

Scenarios were used during the analysis of some of the Train requirements. These were mainly non-trivial operational requirements. Some requirements were flowed down directly to a sub-system or were understood well enough by the client not to warrant this level of analysis. Scenarios were used to analyse the selected requirements to create Specifications and to support the central REVEAL concept of the Satisfaction Argument. Such arguments are necessary, as Specifications alone are rarely sufficient to satisfy requirements: we almost always also rely on some properties of the domain holding true. A Satisfaction Argument is written for every requirement, and is the formal means by which we show that the proposed solution will satisfy the requirement, given the assumptions we have made about the domain. The general form of a Satisfaction Argument, supported by a Scenario, is shown in Figure 20.2.

Using the highest-level requirement (*'Transport X thousand people per hour between Y and Z'*) as a starting point, a Rich Context Diagram was developed, showing all the domain entities that are influenced by or have some influence over the operation of the Train. In REVEAL, we use 'Rich Context Diagrams' including second-order entities that do not interact directly with the system under consideration. An example Rich Context Diagram is shown in Figure 20.3.

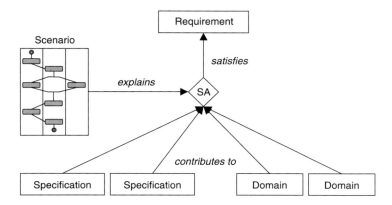

FIGURE 20.2 Satisfaction argument (SA) explained by a scenario. The scenario illustrates how the contributing statements will be sufficient to satisfy the requirement, as explained by the satisfaction argument text

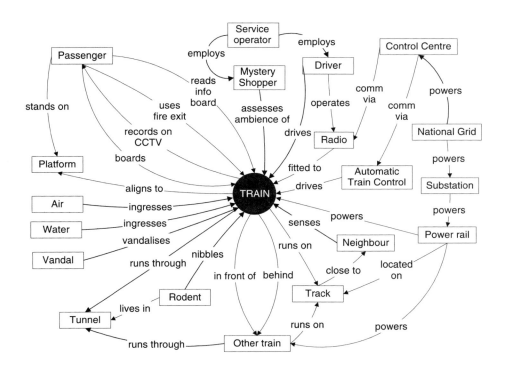

FIGURE 20.3 Rich context diagram for the train, showing second-order entities (not directly interfacing with the train) and relationships between domain entities. Only entities included on the rich context diagram appeared in scenarios

The Rich Context Diagram was a living document that was referred to throughout the project, and was modified as understanding grew and decisions were made. Entities on the Rich Context Diagram became important in our later use of scenarios, since any entity participating in a scenario must be included on the Rich Context Diagram.

The disparate requirements were refined into a coherent set of Train requirements. These requirements were further analysed to the Train specification level, and then on into sub-system requirements. At each level, relevant domain knowledge was recorded as it appeared. Figure 20.4 gives an overview of the process used, and highlights where scenarios featured during the analysis.

The source documents (contractual documents and standards) were imported into the requirements management tool, and a Compliance Argument was developed with the help of special tool, the Compliance Argument Editor. A Compliance Argument is

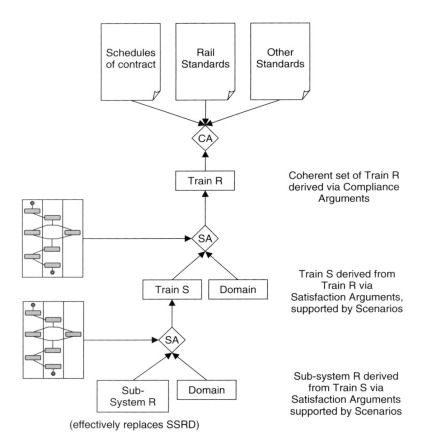

FIGURE 20.4   Compliance arguments (CA) were used to show compliance against each clause of contractual documents, resulting in a single set of train requirements. Scenarios were used to derive train specifications and domain statements from train requirements, and to explain the Satisfaction Argument (SA). Similarly, scenarios were used to derive sub-system requirements from train specifications

similar to a Satisfaction Argument, and is the mechanism for showing compliance against each clause of a contractual document. The source documents typically contained a rich mixture of requirements, specifications, domain knowledge, and informative text. The client's engineers analysed each document clause-by-clause and statements were written in the requirements database for each clause that contained a requirement, specification, or relevant domain assumption.

Each Train requirement was then analysed, Train specifications and further domain statements were written and a Satisfaction Argument was formulated. Where appropriate, scenarios were used for this analysis, and also to support the Satisfaction Argument.

Using the Separation of Concerns, each clause (or part of one) corresponded with a statement in the requirements database. Statements from more than one document could be traced to the same statement in the database. Hence, we could derive a single set of statements that complied with a large number of documentary sources. The term 'statement' is used deliberately, since many of the statements were specifications of the proposed solution, or contextual information (which in REVEAL is called *Domain Knowledge*).

How Scenarios were Used

One scenario was written for each Train requirement that was suitable for such analysis. These were essentially *operational* requirements, which led to linear, deterministic interactions with other entities. These included requirements for discrete events such as starting, stopping, door control, and change of Train operating mode, as well as various maintenance, depot, and emergency procedures. Each scenario was used as the basis for deriving Train specifications, and the domain knowledge required to show that the requirement was satisfied. Scenarios were also used to further analyse Train specifications, deriving sub-system requirements and additional domain knowledge. The scenario acts as the contextual glue that shows *how* satisfaction will be achieved. In REVEAL, a scenario consists of a set of End-to-End Conditions and an activity diagram.

In each elicitation session, a facilitator led a group of two to four client engineers in the analysis of a single Train-level requirement. This was a two-stage process that firstly involved eliciting information to complete the End-to-End Conditions using a simple tabular template. Secondly, it involved facilitating the development of an activity diagram for the scenario. The main purpose was to elicit the system specifications and domain knowledge needed to address the requirement. A useful side effect of the method was that the Satisfaction Argument was developed automatically as the activity diagram was built. This was because the activity diagram showed the relationships and dependencies between the system being developed and the entities with which it would interact. The activity diagram explained *how* each activity related to the preceding and subsequent activities by other participating entities.

The End-to-End Conditions include attributes such as the *Stimulus* that initiates the scenario, the *Goal*, and the *Success End Conditions* (the required conditions at the successful completion of the scenario). They also include any *Assumptions* (pre-conditions) that must hold for the scenario to occur and *Possible Failure Conditions* (acceptable circumstances that may prevent the scenario from reaching its intended Goal). The *Frequency* of occurrence and any *Constraints* on the scenario are recorded, and there is

Scenario Name	Emergency Alarm in Automatic Mode
Stimulus	Any situation that causes a Passenger to operate the emergency alarm.
Goal	Stop the Train safely. (This will be in the station if any part of the Train is in a station when the alarm is raised. If no part of the Train is in a station, the Train continues to the next station, unless the Driver decides to intervene and stop the Train in the tunnel).
Assumptions	Automatic Train Control will determine whether any part of the Train is in the station. At any point after the Driver receives the indication that the Emergency Alarm has been operated, the Driver may intervene and stop the Train manually if the Driver feels it is necessary.
Success End Conditions	Train stopped. Train in a safe mode. Emergency Alarm reset to allow the Train to continue when appropriate.
Possible Failure Conditions	(not explored in detail)
Constraints	Train operating under Automatic Train Control.
Rationale	(Not needed in this case: used to explain why the particular conditions have been used for the analysis of the scenario)
Frequency	(not explored, but would be based on past data available)

FIGURE 20.5 Scenario end-to-end conditions completed in a simple tabular template, which provides slots for useful information about the scenario and collectively defines the scope of the scenario

an optional *Rationale* to explain why the scenario has been written in a particular way. Together, these attributes define the scope of the scenario.

A set of End-to-End conditions for an example scenario is shown in Figure 20.5, and the corresponding activity diagram is described below. The scenario addresses the Train-level requirement for 'Emergency Alarm in Automatic Mode'.

In this case, the *Stimulus* was not very specific, but this reflects the reality of the situation. It is not possible to predict the circumstances that will lead to a passenger operating the alarm. Indeed, it is not particularly important *why* the alarm was raised. For the development of the scenario, it was more important to document the desired behaviour of the Train as a result of the alarm being raised.

The *Goal* was more clear-cut: to stop the Train safely. However, even this needs some qualification, as it depends upon where the Train is when the alarm is raised. This point raised an important (and contentious) issue during the development of this scenario. There was disagreement among the client's engineers as to how the position of the Train would be determined. Specifically, it had not yet been decided whether the Train itself, or the Automatic Train Control (ATC) would determine the position of the Train. This was important, not only because the ATC was outside the scope of the system being built, but also because there would be significant cost implications if the Train itself had to determine its position. A domain statement was written stating that the ATC would determine the position of the Train, and an assumption was included in the End-to-End conditions.

The End-to-End Conditions template provided placeholders for recording useful information, to help contextualise the scenario. For example, note the assumption that the driver could actually stop the Train *at any point* in the scenario. While this was considered to be the likely reality, the scenario model was nonetheless developed to show what would happen if the driver didn't intervene, or if the driver intervened only at particular points in the scenario. Note also the Constraint that the Train must be operating under ATC. It is necessary to record this, since the scenario could only occur when this is the case.

The main part of each facilitated session consisted of developing the activity diagram, written using basic UML notation. This was recorded on a flipchart, using sticky notes for each activity, so that the model could be easily changed. In addition, one of the client's engineers documented the attributes of any specifications that were written, while another would document the domain statements. The activity diagram was then drawn in Visio, tailored with UML templates, and the statements entered into the requirements database. The development of the example activity diagram is shown in Figures 20.6 to 20.8 and is described below.

Swimlanes were used to partition the activities into those carried by each entity. Initially, a swimlane was always put on the activity diagram for the system being considered (in this case, the Train). Then a decision was made about which domain entities had a role in the scenario (though more may be added during development of the scenario). A swimlane was added to the activity diagram for each participating domain entity. These were then cross-referenced with the Rich Context Diagram. Figure 20.6 shows that the swimlanes for the example scenario are *Passenger*, *Driver*, *Train*, and *Automatic Train Control*.

To begin populating the activity diagram, the first question was always '*What is the stimulus?*'. The details of the Stimulus appeared in the scenario End-to-End conditions, in this case the Stimulus was '*Any situation that causes a Passenger to operate the emergency alarm*'. When developing the activity diagram, the Stimulus was always challenged, as the true start of a scenario is not always easy to determine. The Stimulus was shown on the activity diagram as a solid black circle. Having determined the Stimulus, we would then consider '*What happens in response to the Stimulus?*', that is, '*what is the first event on the activity diagram?*'

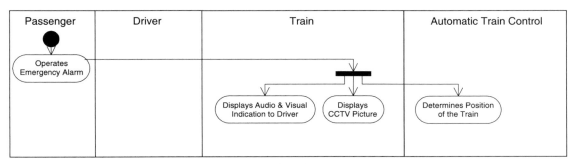

FIGURE 20.6   Swimlanes and initial activities for example scenario showing a synchronisation point: the completion of the activity before the solid horizontal bar causes all the subsequent activities to begin

The first activity was carried out by the Passenger; it was *'Operates Emergency Alarm'*. A domain statement was written to give more detail about this, but on the activity diagram we included only this simple description. We would then consider the question *'When this activity ends, what happens next?'*

The activity diagram shows a synchronisation point, where two or more activities were initiated by the completion of the preceding activity. In this case, the operation of the alarm by the Passenger initiated the Train activities: *Displays Audio and Visual Indication to Driver* and *Displays CCTV Picture*. Simultaneously, the Automatic Train Control (ATC) *Determines Position of the Train*.

Any event in the 'system' (Train) swimlane was recorded on a card as a Train specification, and was subsequently entered into the requirements management database. Specifications were given attributes, such as *Name, Source, Approval Status, Content, Confidence, Stability, Rationale, Guidance, Priority*, and various attributes associated with *Risk*. For example, the Train activity *Displays CCTV Picture* was written as

Name	S.Train.EmergencyAlarmCCTVDisplay
Source	(stakeholder name)
Approv Status	Not Approved
Content	When the Emergency Alarm has been operated, the CCTV image from the appropriate camera will be displayed in the active cab of the Train
Confidence	75%
Stability	High
Rationale	Driver needs to be aware of the situation in the car in which the alarm has been operated
Guidance	(guidance from engineers' experience on how this might be achieved—none was given in this case)
Priority	High

Statements were tagged rather than numbered, so that the *Name* was meaningful. Each statement was labelled R (requirement), S (specification), or D (domain) to indicate the statement type. The next part of the name was always the entity that was the subject of the statement. The rest of the *Name* was used to inform the reader what the statement was about.

Any event in a domain entity swimlane was recorded as a domain statement about the appropriate entity. Each domain statement was given a *Name, Text, Source,* (a document or an individual) and a level of *Confidence*. Statements with a low confidence would be checked and, when resolved, given a higher level of confidence.

For example, the ATC activity *Determines Position of the Train* was written as

Name	D.ATC.TrainPosition
Text	ATC will determine the position of the Train
Source	(stakeholder name)
Confidence	50%

Note that in this case, the *Confidence* is quite low, as the statement was an assumption at the time of writing.

Notice that even in this immature form, the activity diagram was already starting to show how the activities related to one another. This started to make explicit which activities in the domain we relied on (e.g. the scenario would not even begin if the Passenger did not operate the alarm). In this way, we facilitated the building of the *story* of the expected system behaviour in response to the known (or assumed) behaviour of domain entities.

Figure 20.7 shows a more advanced version of the developing activity diagram, including decision points and a re-synchronisation point. Following the ATC activity *Determines Position of the Train*, the ATC carried out a different activity dependent upon the answer to the question *Is any part of the Train in a Station?* This is called a decision point. If the answer to the question was *Yes*, the ATC *Demands Application of Emergency Brake* (which then led to a series of activities starting with an activity carried by the Train; see the complete model Figure 20.8). If the answer was *No*, the ATC *Drives the Train*.

Meanwhile, the two activities previously carried out by the Train result in certain expected behaviour by the Driver. At this point the Driver entity must react to the Train Specifications detailed in *Displays Audio and Visual Indication to Driver*, and *Displays CCTV Picture*. Here, the scenario relied on the fact that the Driver *Observes Audio Visual Indication*, and *Observes CCTV Picture*. The Driver was outside the scope of the system being built, but the system relied on his behaviour. This shows how the activity diagram helped to show causality between actions by different entities, and how it acted to support the Satisfaction Argument for the Train Requirement.

Next there was a re-synchronisation point, followed by another decision point. This time the Driver made a decision, based on the information available, whether or not to

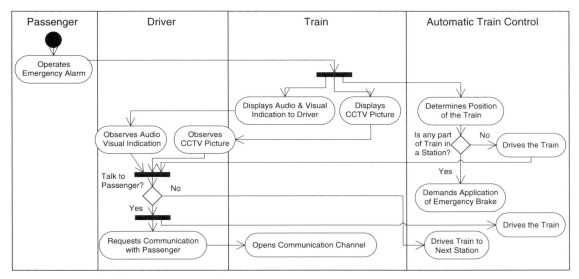

FIGURE 20.7   Activity diagram showing decision points and re-synchronisation point. The re-synchronisation shows that the subsequent activity cannot commence until all of the preceding activities have completed

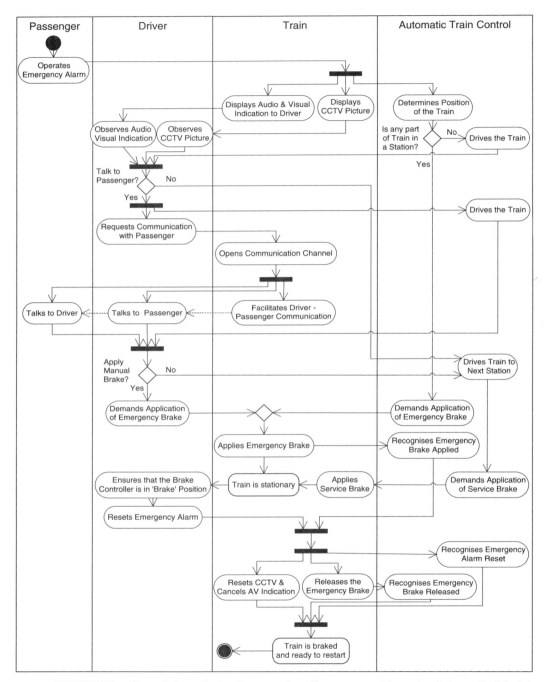

FIGURE 20.8 Complete activity diagram for 'Emergency Alarm in Automatic Mode'. Note that 'Train is Stationary' and 'Train is Braked and Ready to Start' in the Train swimlane are not activities, but states that result from the preceding activities

Talk to Passenger? If the answer was *No*, then the ATC *Drives Train to Next Station*. If the answer was *Yes*, the Driver then *Requests Communication with Passenger*, which in turn leads to the Train Specification *Opens Communication Channel*.

Using the basic rules of UML, the rest of the activity diagram was built up in this way, as shown by the complete diagram in Figure 20.8.

The scenario (End-to-End Conditions and activity diagram) was tagged as *Sc.EmergencyAlarmAuto* and entered into the requirements management database. It was then linked by an *Explains* link to the Satisfaction Argument for the Train requirement. The Satisfaction Argument was typically output from the tool in tabular form for review, as shown in Figure 20.9.

The Rich Traceability provided by Satisfaction Arguments does far more than provide a simple link between specifications and the requirements that they address. The *Contributes to* links show which specifications and domain statements contribute to the satisfaction of the requirement. The *Satisfaction Argument Text* explains in simple terms why the specifications will satisfy the requirement, as long as the domain statements hold true. The scenario is linked to the Satisfaction Argument by an *Explains* link, and

Requirement	Satisfaction Argument Text	Contributing Statements
R.Train.EmergencyAlarmAuto	Whenever the Emergency Alarm is operated, the Train provides various indications to the Driver. The Driver can decide to intervene and stop the Train using emergency braking. If the Driver does not intervene, ATC continues to drive the Train to the next station.	D.Passenger.EmergencyAlarmOperate D.Passenger.EmergencyAlarmTalkToDriver D.Driver.AVObserve D.Driver.CCTVObserve D.Driver.RequestCommWith Passenger D.Driver.TalkToPassenger D.Driver.EmergencyBrakeDemand D.Driver.BrakeControllerBrakePosition D.Driver.EmergencyAlarmReset S.Train.EmergencyAlarmAVDisplay S.Train.EmergencyAlarmCCTVDisplay S.Train.CommChannelOpen S.Train.FacilitateComm S.Train.EmergencyBrakeApply S.Train.ServiceBrakeApply S.Train.AV&CCTVReset S.Train.EmergencyBrakeRelease D.ATC.TrainPosition D.ATC.DriveTrain D.ATC.DriveToNextStation D.ATC.EmergencyBrakeDemand D.ATC.EmergencyBrakeRecognise D.ATC.ServiceBrakeDemand D.ATC.EmergencyAlarmResetRecognise D.ATC.EmergencyBrakeReleaseRecognise Sc.EmergencyAlarmAuto

FIGURE 20.9   Satisfaction Argument (SA) for the example scenario in tabular form. The *Satisfaction Argument Text* gave a simple explanation of how the contributing statements were sufficient to satisfy the requirement. The *Contributing Statements* listed all of the statements attached to the SA by *Contributes to* or *Explains* links

shows how the contributing statements combine to provide the capability expressed in the requirement.

A similar scenario-based approach was used to analyse Train Specifications so as to derive sub-system requirements. In this case, the activity diagram included a separate swimlane for each Train sub-system, and each activity corresponded with a requirement on that sub-system. For each sub-system supplier, the requirements on other sub-systems were effectively domain knowledge. For example, the supplier of the *Brakes* sub-system considered any requirements on the *Traction* sub-system to be Domain Statements, since these were outside the scope of the system for which they had responsibility.

Postscript to Case Study

Towards the end of our involvement in this project, we carried out some analysis of the *Possible Failure Conditions* for the example scenario, using a simple checklist of *What if?* questions. We used a list of about 25 questions based on the generic exception classes used in the RESCUE process (Mavin and Maiden 2003). The session involved walking through the scenario with a group of four stakeholders, asking appropriate *What if?* questions for each activity. This was always a subset of the full list of questions based on the entities involved in the activity.

The checklist included questions about activities such as '*What if the activity does not occur?*', '*What if the activity occurs earlier or later in time?*', and '*What if the activity does not complete?*'. It also included questions about human agents such as '*What if the human agent makes a cognitive mistake?*', and '*What if the human agent is physically incapable of being involved in the activity?*'. There were also generic questions relating to machine agents, objects, information, communication, organisational, and environmental exceptions.

This session was quite slow getting started, but once the stakeholders were warmed up, some useful information was elicited. Initially, the walkthrough was very systematic, with all applicable exceptions considered for each activity in turn. A few additional requirements were uncovered and several issues were raised for clarification. Several activity-exception pairs were seen by the stakeholders as 'showstoppers' that would effectively terminate the scenario. For example, if some activities did not occur, this would result in a total break in the scenario thread.

Many more activity-exceptions pairs were considered to be quite trivial—even if the exception occurred, the scenario would continue relatively unaffected. For example, if the Train failed to display the CCTV image, the Driver would make a decision based on the audio and visual indication only, and the scenario would continue. The less clear-cut activity-exception pairs led to more discussion, and as the session progressed, the effort was concentrated on these areas.

LESSONS LEARNT

The process resulted in Train specifications that were written at the right level of granularity. When created during the development of an activity diagram, engineers wrote simple statements about each specification, offering an external or black box view of the system. In doing so, they documented what the effects of a specification should be, where previously they tended to go into the detail of the specification too early.

Suppliers of components and sub-systems had a better understanding of what the need was and how their product would be used within the system as a whole. The scenarios explicitly showed dependencies on domain assumptions, and between different sub-systems. This visibility helped sub-system suppliers to understand the environment in which their products and components would be used. In turn, this made it easier for them to demonstrate *how* their responses would meet the requirements placed on them.

Domain knowledge was recorded explicitly. There was only one statement of each domain assumption, which everyone used. This led to a single, common understanding of the system's context. The documentation of domain assumptions whilst writing activity diagrams enabled us to resolve issues early, and helped us reach a consensus. Where there was uncertainty about domain statements, the best guess was recorded, and assigned a low level of confidence. Unresolved issues were flagged and assigned to an issue owner, who was responsible for their resolution. This allowed progress to be made until a more concrete resolution was reached.

As a result of this process, the SSRD contained *only* relevant information—so it was easier for suppliers to respond. The SSRD also contained *all* relevant information (e.g. Domain Statements & possibly even Satisfaction Arguments)—so suppliers understood the wider picture and context of use of the products and components that they supplied. Since supplier responses were better matched to the requirements placed upon them, it was easier for the client to assess their responses.

KEYWORDS

Activity Diagram	System Context	Satisfaction Argument	Rail
Requirements Elicitation	System Specification	REVEAL	Real Time
System of Systems	Domain Knowledge	Scenario	

REFERENCES

Hammond, J., Rawlings, R., and Hall, A., Will it work? *Proceedings of RE01, the 5th IEEE International Symposium on Requirements Engineering*, IEEE Computer Society Press, 2001, pp. 102–109.

Mavin, Alistair and Maiden, Neil, Determining socio-technical systems requirements: experiences with generating and walking through scenarios, *Proceedings of RE03, the 11th IEEE International Requirements Engineering Conference*, IEEE Computer Society Press, 2003, pp. 213–222.

CHAPTER 21

EVALUATING SCENARIOS BY SIMULATION

Professor Pericles Loucopoulos

Chair of Information Systems Engineering, Manchester, UK

THIS CHAPTER is about the use of simulation in developing scenarios to validate requirements from stakeholders. These requirements were for the design of venue operations for the Athens 2004 Olympic Games. In early 2001, the Organising Committee for the Athens 2004 Olympic Games (ATHOC) began a project to define system requirements for venue operations of the Olympic Games. This project activity has always formed part of the planning activities of recent Olympic Organising Committees. However, ATHOC departed from the traditional approach of using only peer-to-peer knowledge transfer, facilitated by expert consultants. Instead, it adopted a systematic method for discovering, defining, negotiating, and agreeing the requirements for systems to support venue operations.

The Athens 2004 Olympic Games, will last 16 days, during which time 16,000 athletes from 36 different sports will take part in 300 events across 28 venues located in the Greater Athens area. They will be watched by an estimated 5 million ticketed spectators, together with over 20,000 journalists and broadcasters, and 2500 members of international committees. ATHOC has a budget of $5 billion, and a workforce of over 175,000 for the duration of the Games. ATHOC's task is to ensure the efficient and effective running of the Games in all competition venues, fully co-ordinated with non-competition venues (e.g. airport, Olympic village, etc) and the city's infrastructure (transportation, city operations, etc).

Systems to support venue functions are developed by contractors from ATHOC's requirements specifications. Specifying each venue, by consensus among stakeholders from all ATHOC's functional areas, is critical to system delivery. The approach uses a Requirements Engineering (RE) framework in which scenario generation plays an essential role. It helps provide confidence in the modelled system, and enables stakeholders to articulate and test assumptions about system properties.

TYPE OF PROJECT

Organisational planning systems. The business context is that of *Enterprise Integration* to co-ordinate decisions and actions among subcontractors, individuals, and systems. The

Scenarios, Stories, Use Cases: Through the Systems Development Life-Cycle. Edited by Ian F Alexander and Neil Maiden
© 2004 John Wiley & Sons, Ltd. ISBN: 0-470-86194-0

integration is along a process dimension. This implies a need to understand task-level interactions between people, departments, services, and companies to deliver appropriate system interconnectivity.

APPLICABILITY

The approach adopted in this project has general applicability. The modelling approach, using well-known principles and the simulation techniques related to these models, is suitable for most projects and particularly those that adopt a process-oriented, customer-driven philosophy.

POSITION IN THE LIFE CYCLE

Requirements Discovery	Requirements Validation	System Specification	System Design	Coding, First of Class	Integration & Testing	Operations & Maintenance

ROLES PLAYED BY SCENARIOS

Scenarios were used extensively in stakeholder workshops. These workshops ranged from small, functional area-specific (typically 2–3 people) to participants from all functional areas (typically 30–50 people). The greatest contribution of scenarios was in identifying key factors influencing the performance of system components and of the overall system. Scenarios were used

- in validating stakeholders' assumptions relating to their requirements and
- in testing alternative realisations of system functionality.

STRENGTHS

Scenarios through simulation proved to be the only technique that worked satisfactorily in engaging all stakeholders to discuss and agree a complete set of requirements for each venue. Two other techniques, peer-to-peer knowledge transfer facilitated by expert consultants and business process modelling, were also tried but proved to be problematic.

WEAKNESSES

The approach required a careful construction of system models, prior to simulation, with the inclusion of relevant parameters to control system behaviour. Experts from different areas (e.g. security, accreditation etc) need to be involved in the modelling process and in defining these critical parameters. During scenario evaluation, the participation of such experts is critical in gaining confidence in the model and in defining realistic sets of requirements.

CASE STUDY

Background to the Case Study

The purpose of the RE project was for ATHOC to develop specifications for Venue Operations that would then serve as the basis for the delivery of systems by external contractors. *Venue operations* concerns the support components that need to be put in place at each venue so that it can function according to the specifications set by the International Olympic Committee. Therefore, the term *venue operations system* is defined as being composed of hardware, software, people, rules, and procedures or any combination of these components, interacting in space and time reflecting the dynamic behaviour of its underlying structure. The design of this system needs to address both its functional requirements (the resources and procedures for their management) and its non-functional requirements (the quality of service provision). Specifying the requirements prior to the design is the concern of stakeholders from 27 functional areas, the primary ones being accreditation, security, technology, transportation, spectator services, venue staffing, logistics, catering, sponsors, ticketing, and broadcasting.

As a general rule, Organising Committees for the staging of the Olympic Games are established a few years prior to the staging of the Games. Whilst at the outset the structure of an Organising Committee is strictly hierarchical and centred around individual functional areas, this has to be gradually transformed, as the Games approach, to a venue-based process orientation in order to shift the emphasis away from internal organisational efficiency towards venue operation efficiency. While designing venue operations, members of the Organising Committee from different functional areas form teams whose function is to manage the way that venues are run during the Games. This completes the transformation from a fully hierarchical, centralised structure to a venue-based, process-oriented, and distributed organisation.

Traditionally, the problem of designing venue operation specifications was approached by organising workshops, with the participation of representatives from various functional areas and experts from organising committees of previous Olympiads. These workshops were based on brainstorming sessions and focus group discussions, and the major information management tools used were text documents and architectural diagrams of the various venues. These workshops undeniably facilitated the exchange of knowledge among the functional area representatives involved, as well as the transfer of experience from one host city to the other. However, they were not sufficient for developing a common understanding among all participants, due to the lack of a common reference model and the significant variations in experience and background among the participants. The whole process under this approach is far too informal.

The closest substitutes for a common reference model available involved the use of architectural plans and representations of venue physical layouts. This practice imposed various constraints on the effectiveness of the workshops, the most important being the exclusive focus on specific operations taking place at specific venues. This fact prevented the participants from fully understanding the implications of service specifications in terms of resource requirements and resulting levels of service.

These shortcomings were overcome by adopting a *systematic* and *systemic* approach to requirements elicitation, definition, and validation. This approach was adopted in seven different applications within the broad area of venue operations, as shown in Table 21.1. The effort for these projects involved approximately 160 person/months effort from dedicated Requirements Modellers and Domain Experts.

The RE process was motivated by a desire to elicit, to model, and to reason about early requirements, requirements that exhibited the following characteristics:

- They focused on many co-operating systems rather than a single system.
- They were not confined to just software requirements.
- They were driven by a need to meet certain levels of desirable service to 'customer groups'.
- They were owned by multiple stakeholders who set the levels of service and need to reach an agreed set of functionality due to limited resources and therefore inability to meet every single individual desirable level of service.

The applications shown in Table 21.1 focused on specific problems areas, such as printing and distribution of competition results, or athletes' transportation, but also on broader problem areas such as the dynamic profiling of an entire venue for the duration of a whole day. These applications ranged from simple processes involving a small set of actors and resources to complicated ones involving venues with multiple stadiums and many thousands of 'customers'. Customers may be spectators, athletes, Games staff, Olympic family, broadcasters, journalists, and many others.

TABLE 21.1 RE Projects at ATHOC

Project	Description
Accreditation	Verification of accredited personnel during their arrival at various sites.
Venue staff arrival	Arrival of venue staff at site, security check, and check-in.
Results distribution	generation of competition results (hardcopy) and distribution within a venue.
Athletes' transport	Transportation of athletes from the Olympic village to and from various other venues.
Simple venue profile	Systems for a single venue for an entire Games day.
Complex venue profile	Systems for a multiple venue, including common areas, for an entire Games day.
City operations	Control of pedestrian flow around major venue sites during arrival and departure of spectators.

The RE Framework

The particular characteristics of the Olympic Games as a large-scale project and the overall complexity of designing venue operations create a number of issues in terms of both methodology and practice. Such issues included the systematic and reliable representation of a system of this magnitude, the ability for rapid exploration of multiple scenarios to test different hypotheses, and the cooperative and multifaceted environment in which these activities are to take place.

To support the process of RE, an approach that involved four interrelated activities, as shown in Figure 21.1, was adopted.

These activities were bound together by the use of a single generic approach capable of dealing with dynamic complexity of systems in order to understand the implications of interconnected components of venue operations. The approach was based on System Dynamics (Andersen, Richardson and Vennix 1997, Forrester 1961, Richmond 1997, Sterman 2000, Vennix 1999) as the underlying theoretical baseline. An advantage of the chosen paradigm is that the structure of a model of a system defines the system's behaviour that can be used to show how a change in any stage of the process can propagate to all subsequent stages. The language based on stocks and flows (Mass 1980, Richmond 1985, 1998), offered the possibility to develop maps that represented interdependent factors, causality, non-instantaneous impacts, and non-linear impacts. Furthermore, the models thus developed provided the ability to develop graphs of behaviour over time. The time frame for a single venue was a competition day and these were aggregated for the control system into a time frame spanning the entire duration of the Games.

Application Ontology Modelling

The basic concepts found in venue operations were grouped in the following four categories:

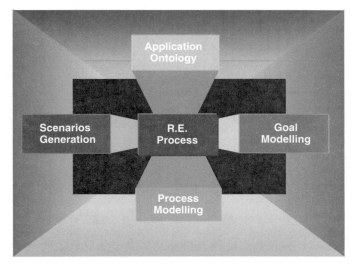

FIGURE 21.1 A requirements engineering framework

- *Events:* Events represent the *temporal* aspect of the ontology but also the one around which all the others revolve, as it is the trigger and the point of reference for the entire Games system.
- *Venues:* Venues represent the *spatial* aspect of the application. Venue knowledge is critical because topology heavily influences the way in which Games-related processes operate but also because planning traditionally revolves around architectural designs.
- *Customers:* There are 15 different customer groups that are involved in the venue operations system. A clear definition of each customer group and of its characteristics is necessary for understanding the different requirements that need to be satisfied by the organisers.
- *Services:* The services aspect details the functional areas involved and the resources required to support the various customer activities.

Application ontology modelling addressed the following questions:

1. What is the boundary of the system?
2. Who are the 'beneficiaries' of the system? In other words, who uses the system and for what purpose?
3. What are the different types of support that these users need in order to achieve their goals?

The answer to the first question defined the RE project space, which is presented as a conceptual model in Figure 21.2. This model defines the processes that the various functional areas will have to establish (lower shaded rectangle). These processes will manage resources established in order to provide a level of service previously agreed and that the implementation will have to achieve (middle shaded rectangle). The purpose of these resources is in supporting customer processes (upper shaded rectangle).

This brings forth the second question, namely defining the 'beneficiaries' of the system, the different customer groups of venue operations. A *customer group* is a specific category of Games participants, with a well-identified role and, therefore, characteristics that distinguish them from any other group. One such group is that of spectators, by far the largest and with a wide variety of needs, ranging from transportation to/from a venue to the ability for on-site purchase of tickets, food, and memorabilia. Another important customer group is of course that of athletes and team officials, a group that is at the focus of attention during the Games, and whose needs have a very high priority. There are 15 customer groups in total, including among others broadcasters, paid staff, volunteers, international federations, and the International Olympic Committee.

The answer to the third question defines the various *types of service* that ATHOC must put in place so that each customer group can successfully complete its mission in the Games. These services vary depending on the customer group for which they are intended, the time and location at which they are provided, and so on. One such service is security checking, which all customer groups must undergo before they can access any venue area. Because of the importance accorded by ATHOC to security issues, this is considered to be a key service and its successful implementation essential for the smooth functioning of the venue operations system. While security checking is uniformly

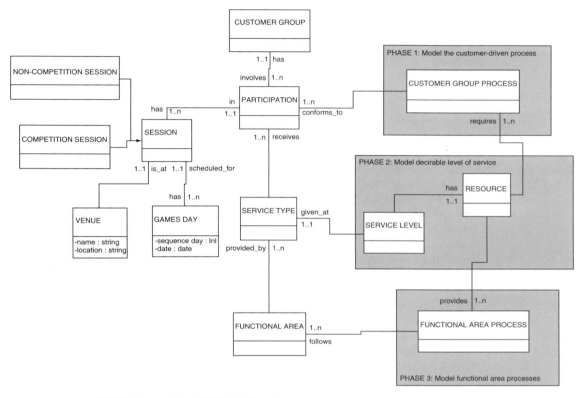

FIGURE 21.2   The ATHOC RE project boundary

provided to all customer groups, there are services that can be specific to one group only. The check-in of paid staff upon their arrival at a venue is such a service; it enables the implementation of the defined shift schedule and is therefore necessary for venue staff, yet it is invisible by all other customer groups.

The notions of customer group and service type are closely interlinked because *one helps define the other*. Each customer group is primarily characterised by its needs and by the services that satisfy these needs, while the requirements (both functional and non-functional) of each service type are defined with reference to the respective customer group. The notion of customer, in particular, should not be perceived as purely passive. As all categories of Games participants are by definition involved in various activities, it is possible for a customer group to be a service receiver at a specific instant and subsequently become a service provider. Paid staff, for example, are *serviced* during their check-in, while later on they *service* spectators at various points inside the venue.

Stakeholders' Goal Elicitation

Goal modelling is about describing the causal structure of a system (be it a business system, or a software system, etc.), in terms of the *goals-means* relations from the "intentional" objectives that control and govern the system functions to the actual "physical" processes and activities available for achieving these objectives. Goal modelling aims at providing the means for describing the *purpose* of the system under consideration, why it came into being (Dardenne, Lamsweerde and Fickas 1993, van Lamsweerde 2001).

In eliciting the goals for the venue operations system, the aim was to understand what determined the successful operation of the system. This involved helping the various stakeholders externalise the (sometimes implicit) goals that they had, capturing these goals, and synthesising that knowledge with information from other sources, such as existing documentation, abstract descriptions of various systems and procedures, and so forth. Stakeholders' goals were thus an initial, high-level expression of system requirements viewed from the perspective of ATHOC, that is, the *service provider* (as opposed to that of the *user*).

With respect to goal categorisation, it was found that it was often relatively straightforward to capture goals about the functions that the system should provide (i.e. the functional requirements), while in most cases it was difficult to accurately define goals regarding the quality of venue operations. In both cases, the multitude of stakeholders (i.e. functional areas) involved in the requirements specification often resulted to competing, and sometimes clearly conflicting, goals about the system. Furthermore, it was especially difficult for stakeholders to express their goals in specific (i.e. measurable) terms. Indeed, while each functional area found it relatively easy to identify distinct functional/quality aspects of the system, it was much more difficult to quantify each of these aspects. This difficulty unfailingly complicated subsequent stages of system design because it had a decisive influence on the type and amount of resources required, and by extension on the final cost of the system.

To deal with the complex situation of goal elicitation a stepwise, cyclical approach was adopted, starting from high-level, sometimes fuzzy, goals. These goals were refined with the help of the affected functional areas. By modelling venue operations system processes, and by testing different scenarios on how quality goals can be implemented in each of these processes, we identified different ways of refining goals into specific quality requirements.

An example of a high-level goal that all functional areas expressed, irrespective of customer group and service type, was

'Minimise the time that a customer has to wait to get serviced'.

This translates into goals such as

'Minimise the time that a spectator has to wait in to go through security checking' or
'Minimise the time that a staff member has to wait in to check in upon arrival at the venue'.

This type of goal does not translate very well into operational terms, because it does not specify a concrete target for the waiting time. To complicate matters further, there is not a single acceptable waiting time as that depends on the service type and the customer group for which it is intended. What is acceptable for spectators or staff, for instance, may not be acceptable for members of the Olympic family or for athletes. Therefore, the first question that had to be address in order to refine this goal was:

> **"If we can't provide enough resources so that nobody ever has to wait in a queue, what is an acceptable waiting time?"**

In other words, what is the *level of service* that each functional area is aiming to offer to the customers that will service? Will the functional area be happy with 30 seconds waiting time or with 15 minutes? In some cases even that answer was not ready, so it had to be negotiated.

A different type of high-level goal was expressed with respect to the overall presence of spectators in a venue. Given that a venue may hold more than one event (e.g. competition session) during a day, at any time there may be spectators arriving at the venue area for one of the upcoming sessions, spectators leaving the venue from one of the past sessions, and spectators participating in a current session. The total number of spectators present has to be somehow controlled for practical reasons such as the availability of resources (e.g. space), but also due to safety concerns. This translates into the goal

> **'Manage the total presence of spectators in the venue area'.**

Again this is an abstract goal that needs to be made more specific; to refine it, the stakeholders examined the factors influencing the presence of spectators in the venue and their distribution in the various areas of which it consists. These factors included the competition schedule at each venue, the transportation capabilities to/from the venue, the availability of open spaces and/or service areas within the venue, and so forth. Addressing issues such as those concerning these two high-level goals was the first step towards visualising an operational system.

Process Modelling

During the RE stage, process modelling concerns the analysis of high-level goals into operational requirements. In our approach, this analysis engages the use of System Dynamics in describing the business processes and relating them to the stakeholder goals (Loucopoulos 2003).

To demonstrate the approach, consider again the example application.

There was a wide range of process-related problems to be studied while addressing the issue of venue operations. At one end of the spectrum, there were problems with 'local' impact, that is, affecting a single customer group, a small area of the venue, and a small part of venue resources (workforce, machinery, consumables). At the other end of the spectrum, there was the problem of the 'behaviour' of an entire venue as a complex, interconnected system. This corresponds to process models focusing on the dynamic profiling of all venue components, over an extended time frame (e.g. an entire day of the Games), possibly with respect to the needs of more than one customer group.

A distinguishing feature of this type of situation is the large number of different service types that the model must represent, since the behaviour of the venue operations system is affected by each of these service sub-components. As a result, the degree of complexity in the resulting process model rises dramatically.

Examples of the problems studied include

- Staff arrival at venue site and check-in
- Verification of accredited personnel at various sites
- Printing and distribution of competition results
- Transportation of athletes from the Olympic Village to various venue sites
- Spectator profiling at the main Olympic Complex.

The first facet of the venue operations system, that is, the behaviour of specific components of the system is examined by model components like the one presented in Figure 21.3. This fragment is about the various types of service facilities that are available to the spectators' customer group inside the Olympic Complex. These facilities service needs such as buying food or memorabilia, withdrawing money from an ATM, and so on.

The behaviour of the services component is determined by two issues, the *demand* for each type of service and the *supply* offered by the service provider. The demand is determined in part through the **'pct of specs per service type'** variable, which expresses the number of customers expected at each type of service facility per unit of time as a percentage of total spectator presence. Total spectator presence depends on overall spectators' behaviour in the venue area, which interacts with this model fragment through a number of feedback loops (not shown here due to the complexity of the complete model).

The supply is determined by two parameters: the number of **'Service Points'** available (e.g. 10 stands selling food), and the **'specs per channel per minute'** service rate (e.g. two spectators serviced per service point per minute). According to this representation, spectators arrive at the service facility (**'going to facilities'**), queue there for a while if no service point is available (**'Specs Queue at Facilities'**), and eventually get serviced (**'servicing'**).

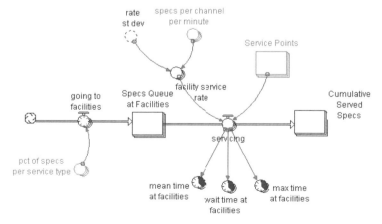

FIGURE 21.3 Model fragment describing spectators' service facilities

Using this model fragment it is possible to elaborate on the way that stakeholder goals were refined through the use of process modelling. As stated already the high-level goal was to

> **'Minimise the time that a customer has to wait in order to get serviced'.**

The realisation of this goal for a given type of service facility, and for a given demand, depends on the availability of supply for that facility. Supply is composed of two independent factors, the number of service points and the service rate. Therefore, the initial goal was decomposed into two complementary (i.e. non-competing) goals,

> **'Maximise the number of service points' and**
> **'Maximise the service rate'.**

These goals are more accurate than the initial one, however, they need to be analysed further in order to become quantifiable.

The second facet of the venue operations system, that is, the overall behaviour of the system, is the result of composing smaller system components (such as the services component) so as to build the complete system model. For instance, a summarised version of the model describing spectators' behaviour at the Olympic Complex is presented in Figure 21.4. The full version of the model contains a significant number of feedback loops and its behaviour is controlled by about 600 equations.

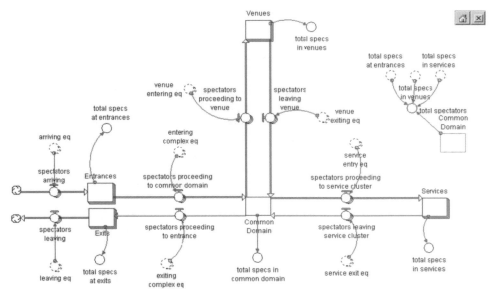

FIGURE 21.4   Model regarding overall spectators' behaviour in the Olympic Complex (summary)

Each of the main stages of the process ('**Entrances**', '**Venues**', '**Services**' etc.) corresponds to a detailed model component like the one presented in Figure 21.3, describing the sub-processes taking place at the respective venue area. One can see the interactions between these sub-processes. The behaviour of the '**Services**' component, for instance, (i.e. its servicing capacity) influences the system as it determines the number of people that are queuing there and thus not participating in activities elsewhere. As another example, it is clear from the model that spectator arrival rate at the '**Entrances**' and departure rate at the '**Exits**', determines the number of people circulating in the common domain of the complex. Moreover, these rates affect the availability of spectators to fill the venues, and they also affect the demand at the service facilities. Therefore, the high-level goal

> '**Manage the total presence of spectators in the venue area**'

could be achieved (partly at least) through the more specific goal

> '**Manage the arrival and departure of spectators in the venue area**'.

Scenario Generation

The generation of different scenarios concerning each problem studied, and the simulation of these scenarios with the help of the process models developed, is an essential part of requirements definition. In the ATHOC case study, scenarios are an indispensable tool for truly understanding the implications of stakeholders in their deliberation of requirements. As the models were being developed and the stakeholders were becoming more aware of the different factors influencing each problem, the range of possible values for each of these factors became more evident, thus creating the initial ideas for different scenarios.

In the model of Figure 21.3, for example, scenario formulation focused on the three variables defining demand and supply for each service facility, namely the percentage of spectators expected for each type of service (demand), the number of service points per service type and the respective service rate (supply). Other relevant factors, such as spectators' arrival and departure patterns, were taken into account. The stakeholders involved in scenario generation investigated the range of probable values for each of these parameters, as well as some 'extreme' values that were less probable but worth investigating nonetheless. Each scenario was characterised by the values of *all* independent variables; the number of possible scenarios thus depended on the number of their feasible combinations.

Figure 21.5 presents the results of the simulation for a scenario concerning the '**Merchandising**' service in one of the four areas of the Olympic Complex. The demand is set at **15% of spectators** using merchandising services, while supply is provided by **32 points of service**, and a service rate of **1.5 minutes per customer**. Graphical results include total spectators waiting to be serviced at each moment (blue curve), and the corresponding waiting time (red curve), while numerical results include the mean and maximum waiting times, as well as the number of spectators served throughout the day. In this particular scenario, a total of **8526 spectators** were serviced, with **a mean waiting**

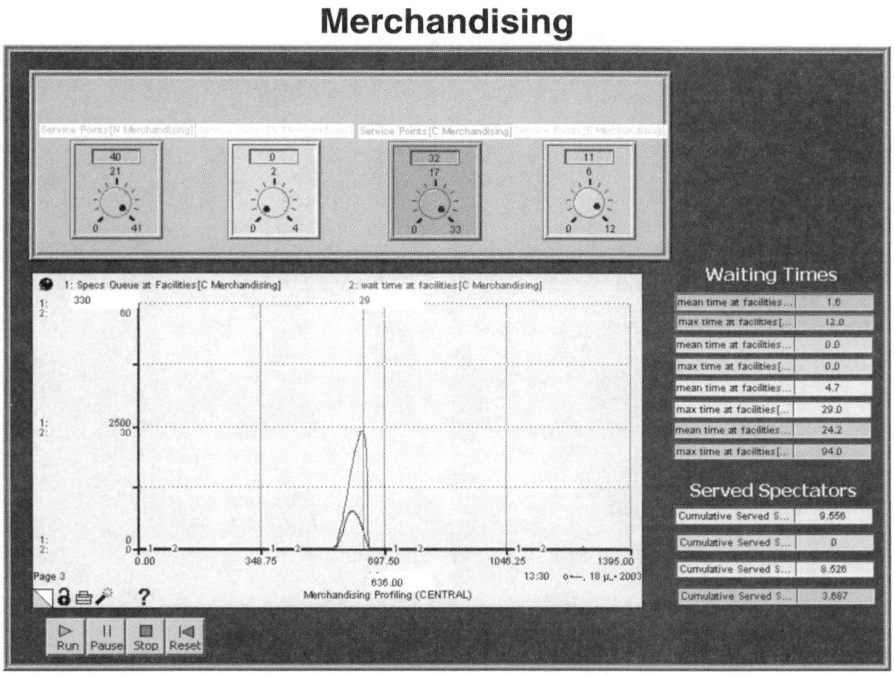

Merchandising

FIGURE 21.5   Simulation results for the 'merchandising' service

time **of 4.7 minutes** and **a maximum waiting time of 29 minutes** (numbers shown in the green numerical indicators).

The results of scenario simulation helped the stakeholders realise the implications of their design choices in terms of the service level provided to customers. This realisation in turn contributed to a quantification of the goals that each functional area set for the final system, for example,

> 'Achieve a total of 85 service points for merchandising in the Olympic Complex' or
> 'Achieve a service rate of one customer per minute'.

Simulating the behaviour of the venue operations system overall yields results like those presented in Figure 21.6. The screenshot shows the profile of spectators' behaviour for the entire day at four key points of the complex: arrival, presence in the common area, presence inside venues and, finally, departure. According to the scenario presented here, spectators arrive to the Olympic Complex during the **two hours preceding** each competition session and leave the complex during the **two hours following** the session. This gives spectators time to stroll in the common domain of the complex, to visit service facilities, to be at a specified venue in time for the corresponding session, and to leave the complex in an orderly fashion. At the same time, a key goal was to ensure that the

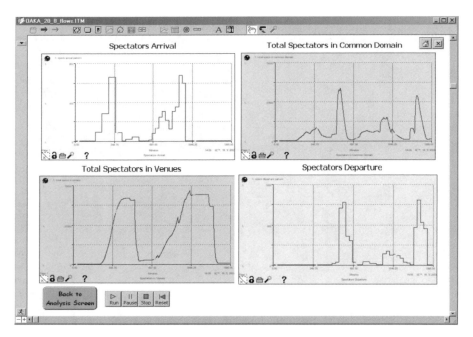

FIGURE 21.6 Overall spectator profiling at the Olympic Complex

total number of spectators in the common domain of the complex was kept at a relatively comfortable level. In other words, the goal

'Manage the arrival and departure of spectators in the venue area'

was quantified in terms of the two goals

'Distribute spectator arrival in the two hours preceding each session' and
'Distribute spectator departure in the two hours following each session'.

The models were subjected to testing through simulation sessions, in workshops involving from 5 to as many as 40 participants. In all workshops, the models were presented to project stakeholders together with the corresponding scenarios and simulated runs. As most of the participants were not familiar either with RE methodologies or with the system dynamics way-of-thinking, their initial reactions ranged from excitement to disbelief. However, even sceptical participants soon realised the advantages of a visual yet operating model consisting of interacting components, and the power of rapid scenario development and simulation.

These features enabled stakeholders to reach a consensus about the underlying processes and the implications that each choice would have on overall system behaviour. The first type of result, that is, results concerning specific components of the system, helped to answer operational questions concerning the rational allocation of resources and the resulting service provision capabilities of the system. The second type of result proved useful for understanding the overall behaviour of a venue, thus answering higher-level, management questions concerning customer presence and distribution, arrival and departure patterns, and so on.

LESSONS LEARNT

Requirements engineering is considered by many as the most critical of all development activities for socio-technical systems. In most cases, different stakeholders are involved with different experiences, backgrounds, goals for the system, and so on.

Venue operations was a typical planning and design problem of a class of problems that has been termed "ill-structured problems" (Reitman 1965, Rittel and Webber 1984, Simon 1984). The problem state is not a-priori specified and there is no definitive formulation. Formulating the problem amounts, in large part, to solving it. While each group of stakeholders from each functional area at ATHOC had a general idea of their individual tasks, complexity arose from the need to coordinate activities across all the functional areas in a venue.

Initially, stakeholder workshops, facilitated on the basis of past experience, were only partially helpful. Architectural and topological designs imposed constraints on thinking about customer-oriented service provision. Textual requirements specification resulted in voluminous documentation with little chance for proper agreement, estimation of resources and planning for a coordinated implementation.

The advantages of a conceptual modelling language for representing system structures and behaviour over informal, natural language descriptions are well documented (Bubenko 1979, Loucopoulos 1992, Mylopoulos 1992). The goal of developing conceptual models of venue operations was to gain insights into the problem and through this to arrive at an agreed set of requirements. This was in the context of an organisational setting that, as well as the usual facets of time constraints, interpersonal conflicts, organisational politics, ambiguities, and so on, had the almost unique characteristic that the organisation itself was transient.

However, eliciting and developing maps of stakeholders' mental models were not sufficient by themselves for achieving stakeholders' agreement. Models needed to be subjected to 'testing' in order to understand the implications of changes to a system component on the overall behaviour of the system. Such a testing was achieved through simulation activities. Simulation of models was a necessary component for developing scenarios, and this way of working proved to be invaluable in experimenting with alternative solutions and to encourage cooperative design in multiple workshop sessions.

The field of *scenarios* has been a fertile one for many types of application, from industrial decision-making (Chindemi et al. 1998) to medical applications (Dangerfield, Fang and Roberts 2001, Georgantzas, Batista, Demos and Ames 2000), finance

(LaRoche and Kohn 2000), human computer interaction (Carroll 2000), software development (Abdel-Hamid and Madnick 1991), and requirements engineering (Carroll 2002, Filippidou and Loucopoulos 1997, Potts, Takahashi and Anton 1994). A common feature of scenarios in all these domains is their use in examining alternative future situations. (*See also* the discussion of 'Situation, Alternative World' by Ian Alexander in Chapter 1, Introduction—Scenarios in System Development, this volume; and David Bush's account of Requirement Stability through Alternative Scenarios in Chapter 6 of this volume.)

According to Carroll, scenarios support the way experts work on ill-structured problem settings such as planning and design (Carroll 2002). In our application, scenarios encouraged group brainstorming through which participants could focus on alternative solutions and envision system behaviour prior to its implementation. Scenarios helped us define and agree desirable levels of service for venue operations, following much experimentation. This confirmed the findings of several empirical studies on the cognitive nature of design, that have shown that expert designers develop sub-solutions to help understand large problems (Darke 1978, Malhotra, Thomas, Carroll and Miller 1980, Rowe 1987). Our stakeholders first defined what they thought might be important aspects of the problem. They subsequently developed tentative designs in scenario analysis sessions to find out whether more could be discovered about the problem. The design paradigm resembled the 'generator-conjecture-analysis' paradigm (Hillier, Musgrove and O'Sullivan 1984).

This caused a fundamental change in the way stakeholders were working. The gradual shift of emphasis from informal to reflective was based on the realisation that there is no well-founded route from problem setting to problem solving, but there is a continuous interaction between the two.

Methodologically, the framework adopted in this project supports a 'solution-first strategy' (Carroll 2002) to requirements definition. Analysis guides design and design guides analysis—and all in an effort to gain an understanding of the problem, of the situation in hand.

KEYWORDS

Early Requirements	Quantitative Models	Behavioural Scenarios.	Alternative Future Situations
Simulation	Dynamic System Modelling	Alternative Scenarios	

REFERENCES

Abdel-Hamid, T.K. and Madnick, S.E., *Software Project Dynamics: An Integrated Approach*, Prentice Hall, Englewood Cliffs, NJ, 1991.

Andersen, D.F., Richardson, G.P., and Vennix, J.A.M., Group model building: adding more science to the craft, *System Dynamics Review*, **13**(2), 187–201, 1997.

Bubenko, J.A. Jr, On the role of understanding models in conceptual schema design, *Proceedings of 5th International Conference on Very Large Data Bases (VLDB)*, Morgan Kaufmann, Rio de Janeiro, Brazil, 1979.

Carroll, J.M., *Making Use: Scenario-Based Design of Human-Computer Interactions*, MIT Press, Cambridge, MA, 2000.

Carroll, J.M., Scenarios and design cognition, in E. Dubois and K. Pohl (Ed.), *Proceedings of IEEE Joint International Conference on Requirements Engineering (RE'02)*, IEEE Computer Society, Essen, Germany, September 9–13, 2002, pp. 3–5.

Chindemi, M., Manca, S., Marcello, G., Turatto, R., and Ventola, N., Evolutionary scenarios in power generation. Modeling competitive effects in the Italian electricity market, *Proceedings of 16th International Conference of the System Dynamics Society, Quebec '98*, System Dynamics Society, Quebec City, Canada, 1998, pp. 25.

Dangerfield, B.C., Fang, Y., nd Roberts, C.A., Model-based scenarios for the epidemiology of HIV/AIDS : the consequences of highly active antiretroviral therapy, *System Dynamics Review*, **17**(2), 119–150, 2001.

Dardenne, A., van Lamsweerde, A., and Fickas, S., Goal-directed requirements acquisition, *Science of Computer Programming*, **20** (1-2), 3–50, 1993.

Darke, J., The primary generator and the design process, in W.E. Rogers and W.H. Ittelson (Eds.), *Proceedings of New Directions in Environmental Design Research (EDRA9)*, EDRA, Washington, DC, 1978, pp. 325–337.

Filippidou, D. and Loucopoulos, P., Using scenarios to validate requirements in a plausibility-centred approach, in A. Olive (Ed.), *Proceedings of 9th International Conference on Advanced Information Systems Engineering (CaiSE '97)*, Springer-Verlag, Barcelona, June 16–20, 1997.

Forrester, J.W., *Industrial Dynamics*, Productivity Press, Cambridge, MA, 1961.

Georgantzas, N.C., Batista, A., Demos, D., and Ames, T., Renal care dynamics, *Proceedings of 18th International Conference of the System Dynamics Society*, System Dynamics Society, Bergen, Norway, August 6–10, 2000, p. 78.

Hillier, B., Musgrove, J., and O'Sullivan, P., Knowledge and design, in N. Cross (Ed.), *Developments in Design Methodology*, John Wiley & Sons, 1984, pp. 245–264.

LaRoche, U. and Kohn, L., Prediction of exchange rates, *Proceedings of 18th International Conference of the System Dynamics Society*, System Dynamics Society, Bergen, Norway, August 6–10, 2000, pp. 123–124.

Loucopoulos, P., Conceptual modelling, in P. Loucopoulos and R. Zicari (Eds.), *Conceptual Modelling, Databases and CASE: An Integrated View of Information Systems Development*, John Wiley & Sons, New York, 1992, pp. 1–26.

Loucopoulos, P., The S3 (strategy-service-support) framework for business process modelling, in J. Eder, R. Mittermeir, and B. Pernici (Eds.), *Proceedings of Workshop on Requirements Engineering for Business Process Support (REBPS '03)*, Klagenfurt/Velden, Austria, June 17, 2003, pp. 378–382.

Malhotra, A., Thomas, J.C., Carroll, J.M., and Miller, L.A., Cognitive processes in design, *International Journal of Man-Machine Studies*, **12** (2), 119–140, 1980.

Mass, N.J., Stock and flow variables and the dynamics of supply and demand, in J. Randers (Ed.), *Elements of the System Dynamics Method*, Productivity Press, Cambridge, MA, 1980, pp. 95–112.

Mylopoulos, J. Conceptual modelling and telos, in P. Loucopoulos and R. Zicari (Ed.), *Conceptual Modelling, Databases and CASE: An Integrated View of Information Systems Development*, John Wiley & Sons, New York, 1992, pp. 49–68.

Potts, C., Takahashi, K., and Anton, A., *Inquiry-Based Scenario Analysis of System Requirements*, Technical Report GIT-CC-94/14, College of Computing, Georgia Institute of Technology, Atlanta, GA, January 1994.

Reitman, W.R., *Cognition and Thought: An Information Processing Approach*, John Wiley & Sons, New York, 1965.

Richmond, B.M., STELLA: Software for bringing system dynamics to the other 98%, *Proceedings of the 1985 International Conference of the Systems Dynamics Society*, Keystone, Colorado, 1985, pp. 706–718.

Richmond, B., The strategic forum: aligning objectives, strategy and process, *System Dynamics Review*, **13**(2), 131–148, 1997.

Richmond, B., Operational thinking, *The Systems Thinker*, **9**(2), 6–7, 1998.

Rittel, H.W. and Webber, M.M., Planning problems are wicked problems, in N. Cross (Ed.), *Developments in Design Methodology*, John Wiley & Sons, 1984, pp. 135–144.

Rowe, P.G., *Design Thinking*, MIT Press, Cambridge, MA, 1987.

Simon, H.A., The structure of ill-structured problems, in N. Cross (Ed.), *Developments in Design Methodology*, John Wiley & Sons, 1984, pp. 146–166.

Sterman, J.D., *Business Dynamics: Systems Thinking and Modeling for a Complex World*, Irwin/McGraw-Hill, Boston, MA, 2000.

van Lamsweerde, A., Goal-oriented requirements engineering: a guided tour, *Proceedings of 5th IEEE International Symposium on Requirements Engineering, RE '01*, Springer, Toronto, Canada, 2001, pp. 249–263.

Vennix, J.A.M., Group model-building: tackling messy problems, *System Dynamics Review*, **15**(4), 379–401, 1999.

PART IV

THE WAY AHEAD

CHAPTER 22

PUTTING SCENARIOS INTO PRACTICE

Ian Alexander[1] and Ramin Tavakoli Kolagari[2]

[1]*Scenario Plus, London, UK*
[2]*DaimlerChrysler Research & Technology, Ulm, Germany*

SCENARIOS ARE being applied in an increasingly rich and inventive way to a wide range of different types of problem in almost all areas of systems and software engineering. Scenarios in general are applicable throughout the life cycles of software and system developments, and indeed those of development programmes such as of whole product families. They are useful—in different forms—across the entire spectrum of domains and scales of project.

Perhaps it is becoming possible to see roughly which kinds of scenario are most likely to be helpful in different situations. We will try to draw some broad conclusions about how to put scenarios into practice—some may appear to be common sense; others may seem more surprising.

WHICH KIND OF SCENARIO, WHEN?

As the contributions from our chapter authors show in Parts 2 and 3 of this book, scenarios can be represented in many forms and can be applied to essentially any programme and project life-cycle activity (Figure 22.1). Engineers from different disciplines see scenarios differently, and they work in domains as varied as telecommunications, software, aerospace, human–computer interaction, transportation, and civil engineering.

But development engineers are neither the only group who may write scenarios, requirements, and specifications, nor the only group who may read them. Stakeholders (see discussion in Chapter 1) can include test engineers, trainers, skilled, and unskilled operators—including mass-market consumers and the general public, system maintainers, and almost anyone involved in procuring systems. Scenarios can help these people to define and to see what results their systems should deliver, and hence also how to test, operate, and maintain these systems, and to train people in their use. To say the least, this is a tremendously wide scope (Figure 22.1).

Scenarios, Stories, Use Cases: Through the Systems Development Life-Cycle. Edited by Ian F Alexander and Neil Maiden
© 2004 John Wiley & Sons, Ltd. ISBN: 0-470-86194-0

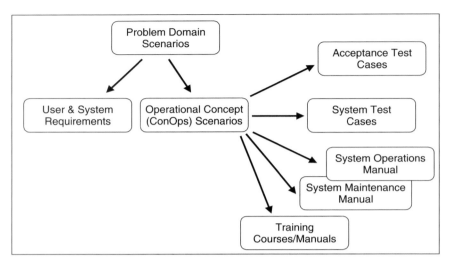

FIGURE 22.1 Some applications of scenarios in system development

WHICH SCENARIO TECHNIQUE, WHEN? CONCLUSIONS FROM PART 2

Is it possible to give any meaningful guidance about which kind of scenario is appropriate across such a wide range of circumstances? Questions of applicability are shades of grey—hard and fast rules are unlikely to be correct. But perhaps humour can come to our aid here. I well remember the reaction of an experienced system development team in a requirements course I was teaching, when after a presentation of alternative elicitation methods I asked what would be the most suitable way of explaining requirements to their managers. "With puppets" was the unanimous reply.

In Part 2 of this book, various scenario techniques were presented. Let us briefly recapitulate the messages of the chapters in Part 2.

Chapter 3: Suzanne Robertson emphasises the human aspect to requirements engineering. Scenarios help people to come up with creative and inventive ideas for systems; they help with requirements discovery.

Chapter 4: Joy van Helvert and Chris Fowler describe their method of analysing user needs. They study 'a day in the life of' scenarios, which are mined in a workshop to identify user needs. These are organised into a needs hierarchy. This is evaluated in a further workshop. The output is a high-level service specification.

Chapter 5: Ellen Gottesdiener describes a range of workshops, guided with skilled facilitation, in which participants are vigorously engaged to shape scenarios and requirements rapidly, and to sketch out the design of wanted systems. Workshop retrospectives are held to review both deliverable artefacts and process.

Chapter 6: David Bush describes the use of imagined future worlds (the oil industry's meaning for 'scenario') to evaluate the stability of goals. Essentially, if a goal is required in all imagined worlds, then it has a good chance of remaining stable for many years to come, and is therefore a good candidate for implementation in one or more systems.

Chapter 7: Ian Alexander describes negative scenarios and misuse cases, and shows how these can help to elicit and document requirements, in particular to handle exceptions that might otherwise be missed. Descriptions of threats from misuse cases help to justify the existence of requirements for security and other qualities, which in turn can lead to requirements for additional system functions.

Chapter 8: Camille Salinesi presents a set of guidelines developed in the CREWS project. The guidelines cover goals and attributes of scenarios, including the recommended style for writing scenario steps, and the contents of use cases.

Chapter 9: Neil Maiden describes how to use the CREWS-SAVRE tool and approach to carry out systematic scenario walkthroughs based (critically) on well-crafted use cases. Walkthroughs can exploit both generic and domain-specific questions based on known classes of exception.

Chapter 10: Karen Holtzblatt describes her Contextual Design method, which is a proven way of developing systems participatively from vision and storyboards through to user interface design, full use case specification and object modelling, and including continued inquiry throughout implementation and testing.

Chapter 11: David Benyon and Catriona Macaulay describe how they use four kinds of scenario, namely user stories, conceptual scenarios, concrete scenarios, and use cases, to design system interactions.

Chapter 12: Peter Haumer describes how scenarios are used in the Rational Unified Process. He takes the story from use cases and goals through various Unified Modeling Language analysis and design models, showing how it deals with both business and system analysis.

Chapter 13: Kent Beck and David West describe the place of user stories in agile approaches. These stories are strongly focused on the user's point of view and person-to-person communication: artefacts are secondary to the essential process. Stories can be categorised as interrogatory, delegation, composite, collaborative, or fuzzy.

Chapter 14: Ian Alexander describes the intimate relationship of use cases and test cases, showing that these are different kinds of scenario, and that test cases can logically and in practice be generated from use cases according to some simple rules.

Chapter 15: Andrew Farncombe looks at the stories behind the development life cycles chosen for individual projects. He shows that while there are only a few basic stories, these can be combined to form many individual life cycles suitable for different kinds of projects.

The authors have indicated how they believe their scenario techniques apply to a basic life cycle. That life cycle (as Farncombe persuasively argues) is of course a fiction, a helpful but over-simplified linear scenario in a world of iterative projects. Indeed, a key message of this book is that development is often better when it is story-driven, which means that stakeholders participate throughout—which means in turn that iteration is inevitable and desirable. Figure 22.2 gathers up these suggested applicabilities into a synoptic linear view.

Project Phase Author & Technique	Requirements Discovery	Requirements Validation	System Specification	System Design	Coding, 1st of Class	Integration & Testing	Operations & Maintenance
Salinesi, Authoring Use Cases	Templates, Guidelines						
Van Helvert & Fowler, User Needs Analysis	Storytelling, Workshops						
Bush, Requirement Stability		evaluate use in imagined worlds					
Alexander, Misuse Cases	identify hostile agents, threats Workshops, Diagrams					Identify hazards, etc	
Alexander, Use Cases, Test Cases		identify test approaches				Identify paths	
Robertson, Discovery	Business Event Responses, Sketches, What-if Stories					?	
Holtzblatt, Contextual Design	Observe, make Models	*	User Interface Prototyping, Use Cases, Object Models			Continued Inquiry	
Benyon & Macaulay, HCI Design	Workshops for User Stories	Conceptual Scenarios, Claims	Use Cases, Object/Data Model, HCI Design				
Maiden, Walkthroughs	Scenario Walkthroughs with exception-based questions						
Gottesdiener, Use Case Workshops	Facilitator works with team to create and validate various scenario artefacts						
Haumer, Use Cases			Analysts document and develop a disciplined sequence of use- case based models as defined in an industry-standard process				
Beck & West, User Stories	Story-on-a-Card, Dialogue about the stories		...	...	Story Cards as guidance	...	Continued iteration

FIGURE 22.2 Scenario techniques (from Part 2) across the life cycle, by phase
*Contextual design has an extra phase here. *Work practice redesign*, using visioning and storyboarding

Farncombe's chapter on management, which discusses all phases of the life cycle, naturally applies across the board; but equally, it is not a technique for any particular phase of development. Rather, it is a way of thinking that is applicable to project planning, and to the setting-up of intelligent company rules governing the planning of projects. These activities take place outside the frame of reference of Figure 22.2.

The remaining techniques are sorted in Figure 22.2 to indicate that there are broadly two groups of techniques: those that mainly apply in the early requirements phases, and those that apply more or less throughout the development life cycle. In other words, the matrix consists mainly of a column on the left for the 'early' techniques, and a row at the bottom for the 'throughout' techniques; most of the rest of the matrix is unpopulated.

The traditional view of scenarios—as something useful in getting a general overview of a domain and of the way a system will be used—suggests that scenarios should mainly be used early in the life cycle. However, several of the 'early' techniques here are quite new and radical, involving workshops, storytelling, and automated walkthroughs amongst other things.

The 'throughout' techniques correspond broadly to more participative methods, along with an increased emphasis on iteration. These techniques include both documentation-intensive methods like the RUP (described by Peter Haumer), and agile methods like XP (described by Kent Beck and David West). So, again, the early/throughout split does not correspond to traditional versus modern. As discussed below (see Figure 22.4) it may relate to size of project—rapid iteration and agility are mainly for smaller projects, just as the movements of ants are more rapid than those of elephants.

Some trends are apparent from these chapters, as summarised in these notes and in Figure 22.2.

- Requirements discovery and validation are the places where engineers instinctively feel that scenarios belong, so it is not surprising that several techniques apply especially to these activities.
- Scenarios can be applied right across the life cycle, but while it is possible to find examples of both theoretical approaches and practical projects applying scenarios in any life-cycle phase, their explicit use in the later phases is rare, and few conventional projects seem to use scenarios continuously. Explicitly iterative methods including inquiry cycles, contextual design and agile methods are more consistent and continuous in their scenario usage. Earlier participative methods (not illustrated here) such as RAD and DSDM (*e.g.* RAD Advisor 2003, DSDM 2003) also often made good if informal use of scenario thinking.

WHO, AND WHY?

The kinds of scenario that may be useful vary with life-cycle activity, and consequently also with the roles of the people creating and reading the scenarios (Figure 22.3).

Figure 22.3 tries to suggest, for a typical domain, that there is more or less a simple gradient from representations like stories and acted-out scenes that non-specialists can readily understand, through to analytic diagrams that have meaning mainly for engineers. But any such naïve view is at best both right and wrong. Seemingly simple representations like stories and role-play in workshops are certainly valuable among engineers, while complex representations like simulations are extremely valuable among business managers and other non-technical stakeholders when they provide or illustrate results that could not be obtained any other way.

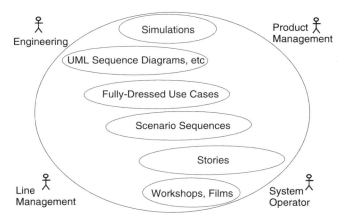

FIGURE 22.3   Scenario types for different people and purposes

Therefore, we should be cautious about assuming that a sophisticated-looking technique would be too difficult for a particular group of stakeholders. As long as the information is presented in a clear and appropriate way, it doesn't matter how elaborate the mechanism is behind the scenes. For example, stakeholders do not have to understand that a Markov simulation was run so many times to give a result; it is sufficient to show the results clearly, in the language of the domain—everyone understands the meaning of a two-hour wait for a hamburger, as Peri Loucopoulos argues in Chapter 21, even if they have never heard of queuing theory.

Note also that more technology to present scenario results better is not necessarily the answer. It might be appropriate to make an animation as a front end for a simulation model; or it might be enough just to explain the results and to answer questions in a workshop session.

Scenarios are used by people in many different professional disciplines; and unlike almost all other techniques, they are suitable for people who are not systems developers. This does not imply that scenarios by themselves are sufficient for good systems or software engineering, even in those life-cycle activities where they are most useful—indeed, none of our authors suggest this. Some of the presented approaches are scenario-based or scenario-centred, but that always leaves room for a 'mix and match' development style in which scenario use is combined with other techniques such as the use of templates, brainstorming, reviews, prototyping, simulation, and analysis to suit the needs of the project.

Such embedding of scenarios in other engineering methods is reasonable, as the discovered knowledge can be passed on to later phases of the development process, for example in short informal scenario-sketches.

SCENARIOS EVERYWHERE?

The scenario representations that seem to be most generally useful are the unspecialised kinds, namely stories and sequences of events. Perhaps with hindsight this seems predictable: specialised creatures like anteaters and orchids live in precisely defined habitats, whereas generalists like rats, cockroaches, and man live nearly anywhere. Story is arguably the most natural form of a scenario: everyone understands without training or explanation what a story is and what it means. Sequence is also essentially universal, at least to engineers and probably more widely than that: everyone knows that a numbered list of instructions means start at step 1 and continue to the end.

The only other form of scenario that can make a plausible claim to being universal is the use case, and it is the new kid on the block—story has been around for hundreds of thousands of years, sequence since the invention of counting, and the use case for only a dozen years or so. Jacobson himself claims,

> "Use cases have been universally adopted for requirements specification."

(Jacobson 2003), but as we will argue below (in 'Diversity of Scale'), this is something of an exaggeration: use cases as currently applied cover neither the largest and most complex system developments, nor the smallest and most agile software projects. The use case is however certainly fashionable, which brings both costs and benefits.

On the plus side, the fame of the use case has brought scenario thinking into many areas of engineering where it was sorely needed, and it has helped to encourage cooperative development in some very traditional domains.

Against that, there is a marked bandwagon effect, illustrated by the fact that people are inventing hybrid terms like fully dressed use case, precise use case, executable use case (and indeed abuse case, misuse case). Some of these will find niches for themselves while others will fade away. The danger is that what began as a powerful general medium for sharing requirements will be hijacked by the technically minded, and converted into yet more complicated and specialised technical notations, accessible only to a few.

That over-emphasis in turn will lead—indeed, is already leading—to a backlash, with people arguing that scenarios and episode-based descriptions of behaviour are inadequate, or worse, inappropriate on their projects.

We believe that scenarios are essential but not sufficient—there is much more to a good specification and to a successful project than simply writing scenarios. Scenarios are essential, as it is hard to see how any project that does not have a clear story of what it is trying to do can succeed.

It is also a happy accident that the term use case recalls the idea of case-based reasoning, or Casuistry to give it its proper if now pejorative name. The failure of the rule-based approach to Artificial Intelligence in the 1980s demonstrated that human beings are not very good at reasoning with explicit rules (Graubard 1988, Dreyfus 1992). Tacit knowledge (Polanyi 1966), for instance of tasks requiring skill, is better handled by giving examples of concrete cases—scenario instances—that people can see are relevant to their work, and that they can reason about accurately and without effort. Casuistry got itself a bad name for the same reason that Sophistry did: you can invent cases and scenarios to support any claim, if you have enough money and a clever enough lawyer. But, genuine descriptions by stakeholders of the results and behaviour that they want are poles apart from casuistry. Such scenarios are simple, direct, practical, and concrete statements of need, and they have a good chance of being far more down-to-earth than long lists of so-called requirements framed as '*shall*' statements.

Scenarios are not everything: they do not, contrary to some extreme claims, replace system models, and they plainly do not cover all 'non-functional' requirements and constraints. Scenarios make sense when used together with data models, behaviour and timing models, simulations, prototypes, quality and configuration plans, and a host of other project documents (or 'artifacts').

We believe that there are already good notations—not least in UML—for describing system behaviour in analytic detail, just as there is a place for simulation and animation of computer models to explore and illustrate scenarios. The use case is a powerful tool but it should not be made to do everything. So a key theme of this book is the value of diversity: different problems do often demand different solutions.

HOW DOES PROJECT SCALE AFFECT SCENARIO USAGE?

A crucial aspect of project diversity is scale, closely linked to complexity. Barry Boehm has argued that much present confusion is caused by people from different backgrounds failing to see where other people are coming from. Most software projects (60% of them) are quite small and can be completed by a team of no more than 10 programmers in a year or so (Boehm 2003, *quoting* Highsmith 2002). A similar statement could be made about systems that are not mainly software. But, and this is Boehm's point, those small projects only produce 17% of the world's software output. Eighty-three percent of the world's software is developed by the few very large projects that require teams of thousands of engineers (Figure 22.4). Smaller projects enthusiastically report success after success with XP and other agile methods; larger projects respond with scepticism—they have to have more sharply defined procedures and interfaces. Both are justified in their own contexts: what is not justified is over-generalisation. In short, most projects could benefit from more agility, but most software cannot.

Small projects can and probably should adopt a participative life cycle—possibly an agile one, and the requirements can be allowed to evolve as the project proceeds. Early product releases can be explored and tested as prototypes, and new requirements can be captured in scenarios. Chapter 13 on User Stories by Kent Beck and David West illustrates this kind of approach admirably.

Very large projects can certainly make use of stakeholder participation, but their interfaces and contractual structures cannot change radically from day to day. That world is described by Andrew Farncombe in Chapter 15 on Stories and Life-Cycle Process Models. Such projects must have agreed requirements and interfaces between subsystems, kept under efficient configuration control. Scenarios can illustrate the required end-to-end behaviour of the whole system, to explain to sub-sub-subsystem makers how their component fits in and how it will be used. Participation tends to take forms such as 'Integrated Project Teams', containing a carefully planned assemblage of representatives of different stakeholder roles. For example, a military logistics project would typically include a skilled mechanic and a transport specialist to take ownership of key requirements within the development team. Chapter 20 on Scenarios in Rail Rolling Stock by Alistair Mavin perfectly encapsulates the careful use of stories to justify and explain requirements in a 'system of systems' setting—a Passenger Emergency Alarm is of course a small system inside some much larger ones.

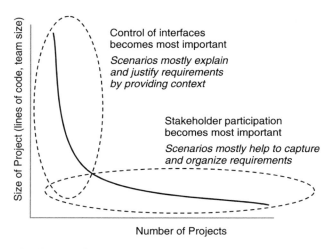

FIGURE 22.4   Dominant concerns related to scales of projects

Medium-scale projects may be able to benefit from an intermediate approach, applying scenarios in a disciplined sequence of steps to gain some of the benefits of iteration and the advantages of careful modelling. Peter Haumer shows how use cases serve these purposes in the Rational Unified Process, in chapter 12, Use Case–Based Software Development.

We hope that with such an understanding of the inevitable diversity of projects, engineers and project managers (as well as researchers and industry gurus) will come to accept that scenarios are useful throughout every project, but in ways that depend on the size and type of project, and alongside a wealth of other techniques in different project phases.

INTO PRACTICE: CONCLUSIONS FROM THE PART 3 CASE STUDIES

Let us now briefly summarise the messages of the case study chapters in Part 3.

Chapter 16: Thomas Zink and Frank Houdek describe the benefits of introducing scenarios into automotive software development. They found that scenarios were good in product feature negotiation, for providing requirement rationales, and for giving the user perspective on product subsystem features.

Chapter 17: Ian Alexander and Andrew Farncombe describe two examples of scenario usage from the railway domain.

- One is a straight use of scenarios (in the form of use cases) to capture the context of a system and hence to discover requirements that would have been missed, notably for a whole-line simulator.
- The other applied misuse cases to document design trade-offs for a seemingly trivial problem that turned out to be more complex than expected, but which was resolved quite readily given the appropriate presentation of facts to the appropriate collection of stakeholders in a workshop.

Chapter 18: Perminder Sahota describes a use of CREWS-SAVRE to manage scenario walkthroughs in air traffic control. The tool was extended to handle domain-specific scenarios. These helped to elicit and to validate the requirements.

Chapter 19: Juha Savolainen describes how scenarios and quality requirements are used in telecommunications to elicit and document functional requirements, to locate problem areas in the software architecture, and to validate the architecture.

Chapter 20: Alistair Mavin describes the use of scenarios in a railway project with the REVEAL method. A scenario was written for each goal or event. Train-level scenarios were used to derive subsystem requirements. Scenarios also formed key elements in satisfaction arguments.

Chapter 21: Peri Loucopoulos shows how simulation can explore the concrete meaning of proposed requirements. In the case of the 2004 Olympic Games at Athens, modelling of venues' ability to handle the expected crowds showed that innocent-sounding assumptions

Author & Technique	Project Phase Requirements Discovery	Requirements Validation	System Specification	System Design	Coding, 1st of Class	Integration & Testing	Operations & Maintenance
Loucopoulos, Simulation	Using the results of simulation to push for workable requirements						
Sahota, Air Traffic Control	Walking through scenarios to elicit and validate requirements						
Mavin, Railway	Swimlanes / Activity Diagram per event-handling requirement						
Houdek & Zink, Automotive	Informal Stories, Role / Action tables		Use Cases to justify reqts				
Alexander & Farncombe, Railway	Use Cases, Workshops			Misuse Cases (for trade-offs)			
Savolainen, Telecommunications			Tabular Scenarios	Subset of Scenarios			
Rosson & Carroll, Teaching Usability				Scenarios & Claims			

FIGURE 22.5 Scenario usage by phase and technique in the case studies (in Part 3)

can have serious consequences. Feeding these back to stakeholders can rapidly improve the consistency and realism of specifications.

Chapter 23: Mary Beth Rosson and John Carroll present their view, based on many years of experience, of how students can be taught to use scenarios in usability engineering.

Figure 22.5 collects up how the case studies and experiences described in Part 3 made use of scenarios; as in Figure 22.2, the case study rows are sorted by the phases to which they apply. It isn't possible to conclude anything statistically from such a small sample—essentially one in each domain—though the Strengths and Weaknesses discussions in each chapter provide qualitative guidance. But this book does demonstrate that there is a rich variety of ways in which people use scenarios on their projects.

This is clearly a diverse picture, not least in the range of topics addressed. However, it is worth observing that scenarios seem in practice (at least in this small sample) to be applied mainly on the left-hand-side of the table (and the V-model). That is to say, the experience of the authors of this book suggests that industrial practice mostly makes relatively conservative use of scenarios. It seems, incidentally, to be hard to find instances both of very large projects and of very agile ones. Late life-cycle phases such as testing, operations, and maintenance are not represented in our sample. This may be no big surprise, but it does suggest that there is scope for encouraging people to use scenarios more adventurously to guide testing, maintenance and operations procedures, training, and so on.

DO SCENARIOS REPLACE REQUIREMENTS?

A vexed question is whether projects need both scenarios and requirements, or whether scenarios can serve as specifications on their own. As for most such questions, there is probably no single right answer.

Small projects with a team of less than a dozen people and a client who is closely and personally involved in the development can get by with very little in the way of written specifications. A robust architecture and an agreed but evolving set of scenarios may be sufficient (and test cases can be written from the scenarios). An agile approach might be appropriate. This might be the situation in a small custom financial software project.

Large projects involving contracts let to suppliers and development subcontractors inevitably demand much greater stability in their specifications. This generally means written requirements with contractual force. In such projects, scenarios are needed to give the big picture, to generate, explain and justify the requirements, and to guide acceptance testing. A formally defined process for the life cycle is necessary—changes to contracts are costly, so planning is essential (see Chapter 15, Stories and Life-Cycle Process Models by Andrew Farncombe). This situation is typical of mass-market product developments in the automotive, telecommunications and consumer electronics industries, and also in bespoke developments in the defence and aerospace industries. In such a context, it is easy to understand why Raymond Jorgensen thinks 'Use Case Requirements' an 'Oxymoron'[1] (Jorgensen 2001).

Systems engineers like Jorgensen see the place of scenarios as being in early scene-setting documents such as the 'Operational Concept', which applies to a large system (say, a warship) as a whole. Scenarios illustrate how systems will be used operationally; they are valuable for checking that the system does the right thing (in end-to-end operational trials). Requirements, on the other hand, apply to systems, subsystems, and sub-subsystems all the way down to individual components. They are valuable both for driving design, and for verifying that the system complies with each wanted thing, that is, each requirement. From this world-viewpoint, it is indeed oxymoronic to combine Use Cases and Requirements:

> "Terms are being combined inappropriately to describe concepts; . . . Examples include 'design requirements' and 'use case requirements'. . .

> I personally must object to the notion introduced by many UML proponents that a 'Use Case' is equivalent to or expresses a 'Requirement'. . . A Use Case can be effectively used to help more concisely define a requirement, but use cases do not substitute for requirements. . . The Use Case does help to discover which functions are needed. . . " (Jorgensen 2001)

From the point of view of agile methods on manageably sized projects, on the other hand, the merging of scenario and requirement looks perfectly reasonable. Kent Beck writes:

> "The first iteration puts the architecture in place. Pick stories for the first iteration that will force you to create 'the whole system', even if it is in skeletal form.

> Picking stories for subsequent iterations is entirely at the discretion of the customer. The question to ask is, 'What is the most valuable thing for us to be working on in this iteration?'" (Beck 2000, page 134)

---

[1] A juxtaposition of seemingly incompatible elements, as in 'wise fool'.

Beck implies that a set of stories describes system behaviour sufficiently for design and coding—no more detailed specifications are needed. What is more, concepts such as release planning and incremental development are subsumed into the choice of stories for each iteration; iterations are stated to be rapid, for example, taking 'three weeks'. (See Chapter 13 for a description, by Kent Beck and David West, of User Stories in Agile Software Development.)

Between the positions of Jorgensen and Beck, Alistair Cockburn writes:

> "If you are writing use cases as requirements, keep two things in mind:
>
> They really are requirements. You shouldn't have to convert them into some other form of behavioral requirements. Properly written, they accurately detail what the system must do.
>
> They are not all of the requirements. They don't detail external interfaces, data formats, business rules, and complex formulae..." (Cockburn 2001, page 13)

In other words, the functional requirements are all expressed in use cases. They are relatively formally defined, but scenarios and requirements are not separate documents (See Chapter 12 for an account of Use Case-Based Software Development, by Peter Haumer).

A resolution to this argument can be sketched in terms of the concepts depicted in Figure 22.4, which illustrates the few large projects/many small projects divide. Figure 22.6 suggests that the largest projects (a la Jorgensen) may prefer separate scenarios and requirements, applying scenarios mainly 'up front' to give an overall picture and help discover requirements. Medium-sized projects may prefer use cases (a la Cockburn) to organise their requirements. Smaller, more agile projects may find informal user stories (a la Beck) sufficient documentation for their purposes—indeed, they would be encumbered by more formal documentation and control processes. Project size, iteration

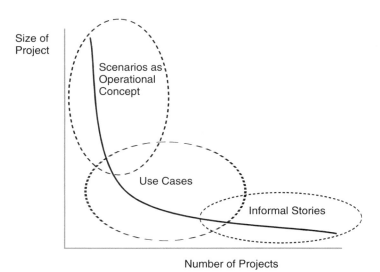

FIGURE 22.6　Scenario structures related to scales of projects

time, formality of life cycle, and organisation of documents all correlate with the divisions suggested by the graph. Who was right? Everybody, but we need to be careful not to over-generalise from our experience.

GETTING STARTED

How, given this diversity, should you get started with scenarios? It's hard to give much guidance when projects and stakeholders vary so widely, but here are some general suggestions.

- Create the right life-cycle approach for your project (*see* Chapter 15, Stories and Life-Cycle Process Models, by Andrew Farncombe). Decide how much iteration you need, based on how many stakeholders there are, how well-defined the requirements are, and how risky the project is given its size, cost, timescale, technological innovation, experience of staff, and other factors. Iteration becomes essential when risk is high, when requirements are poorly understood, and when there are many stakeholders. (If you think that means most projects, we won't disagree with you.) If you need plenty of iteration, then a scenario approach like Contextual Inquiry or an agile method may be appropriate. If you need less iteration, then a more conventional approach may be suitable.
- Choose scenario techniques to fit your project. If you are trying out a scenario technique for the first time in a project, it should be a well-established technique described in the literature and already in use in similar projects and situations (in other organisations, at least). Since scenarios are very "soft" you might expect that there are no rules to be followed—but this is not the case. Skill and experience are needed.
- Try out new approaches in a small way, when their success is not critical.
- Play with the approaches to see what they do well in your own situation, and where they start to struggle. Play is the best way of learning a skill; it isn't an accident that we humans have a ridiculously lengthened infantile-play stage of 20 years or so. That is either an unbelievable luxury or clear evidence that play is extremely important[2]. Perhaps there is another general principle here: that every technique has a comfort zone (or a tennis racket's sweet spot) where it works effortlessly. This comes with the implied warning that if a technique is proving difficult, it is probably the wrong one for your situation.
- Have the courage of your convictions. If a combination of techniques works well for your project, then however unorthodox or naïve it may seem, it is right for your situation. There isn't and can't be any higher authority than a team of skilled practitioners doing a job effectively. Researchers can theorise, study, observe,

---

[2] Zoologists call the retention of early-stage features into adulthood 'neoteny'. For example, newts keep their tails and gills, whereas frogs only have these features at the tadpole larva stage. The change clearly had value in fitting newts for an all-aquatic lifestyle. Humans seem to be adapted by neotenous playfulness to a learning lifestyle.

and possibly even predict, but it's the practical outworking of knowledge and skill that gets projects done.

That does not mean that once you have managed to get one scenario technique to work on one project, you know everything about the subject. We're all just learning too. Practice makes perfect only if you observe the effects of what you are doing, reflect on it, and work out how to improve on your local 'state of the art'. In that inquiry cycle, discussion, experienced colleagues, and other people's suggestions in the form of books and articles can contribute.

Where this is leading is that systems engineering with scenarios is a set of practical skills that need to be learnt (*see* Chapter 23, Teaching Computer Scientists to Make Use). These skills are collaborative, so learning them requires practice on projects and in teams, with a variety of stakeholders. We hope that this book helps to get you thinking about scenarios, and that it may encourage you to try out and benefit from the wealth of new approaches that it describes.

KEYWORDS

Scenario Technique	Use Case	Software	Manuals
Story	Life cycle	Project	Training
User Story	System	Stakeholder Participation	

REFERENCES

Beck, K., *Extreme Programming Explained, Embrace Change*, Addison-Wesley, 2000.

Boehm, B. and Beck, K., Agility through discipline: a debate, *IEEE Computer*, **36**(6) 44–46, 2003.

Cockburn, A., *Writing Effective Use Cases*, Addison-Wesley, 2001.

Dreyfus, H., *What Computers Still Can't Do: A Critique of Artificial Reason*, MIT Press, 1992.

DSDM, the Dynamic Systems Development Method consortium website, 1997–2003, http://www.dsdm.org

Graubard, S., *The Artificial Intelligence Debate: False Starts, Real Foundations*, MIT Press, 1988.

Highsmith, J., *Agile Software Development Ecosystems*, Addison-Wesley, 2003, p. 358.

Jacobson, I., Use cases and aspects - working seamlessly together, *Journal of Object Technology*, **2**(2), 7–28, 2003, http://www.jot.fm/issues/issue_2003_07/column1

Jorgensen, R., *The Oxymoron of Use Case Requirements*, INCOSE Insight, July 2001, pp. 21–22. Available from http://www.incose.org

Polanyi, M., *The Tacit Dimension*, Peter Smith, Gloucester, MA, 1983; first published by Doubleday, 1966.

RAD Advisor, *Rapid Application Development*, 2003, http://www.rad-advisor.com

CHAPTER 23

TEACHING COMPUTER SCIENTISTS TO MAKE USE

Mary Beth Rosson, John M. Carroll, and Con Rodi

School of Information Sciences and Technology, Pennsylvania State University, USA

SCENARIO-BASED DESIGN is a family of techniques in which the *use* of a future system is concretely described at an early point in the development process. Narrative descriptions of envisioned usage episodes are then employed in a variety of ways to guide the development of the system that will enable these use experiences. Scenarios are stories of users and their behavior, which makes them an excellent medium for discovering, addressing, refining, and managing usage concerns in the design of software systems.

In this chapter, we present a scenario-based approach to teach computer science students to make use—that is to design and build software with use as the goal. Our audience is computer science students who have been trained in programming and software engineering methods. Few, if any have taken classes that study human behavior. Thus as instructors, we must convey the concepts of *human–computer interaction* (e.g., human perception, interpretation, and social interaction with computing systems) at the same time that we teach a suite of methods for *usability engineering* (e.g., scenario analysis and development, prototyping, usability evaluation). We describe how we are using case-based learning techniques to integrate these two complementary aspects of making use.

CHALLENGES IN TEACHING STUDENTS TO MAKE USE

Design is an ill-structured problem, and the art of design is a complex skill regardless of the domain (Simon 1972). Designing software systems with use in mind is no exception. Starting conditions and design options are never completely specified; any given design problem has many possible solutions that present a variety of competing trade-offs (Brooks 1995, Reitman 1965). To recognize and address these trade-offs, designers must recruit many different perspectives and values, meaning that an individual designer rarely holds all the expertise relevant to a design problem. For interactive software system

Scenarios, Stories, Use Cases: Through the Systems Development Life-Cycle. Edited by Ian F Alexander and Neil Maiden
© 2004 John Wiley & Sons, Ltd. ISBN: 0-470-86194-0

design, the impact that a designed artifact will have on people—both at an individual level and at a cultural or societal level—are an essential and pervasive concern that few software designers are equipped to consider.

When human–computer interaction (HCI) first emerged as a scientific discipline, it borrowed heavily from existing theories of psychology (Carroll 1997). Attention focused on the mechanisms of perception and attention, interpretation of visual displays, and relatively low-level planning and actions (Card, Moran and Newell 1983, Carroll and Thomas 1982, Norman 1996). More recently, HCI has developed into a highly interdisciplinary field, integrating the concerns and methods of disciplines as diverse as anthropology, sociology, artificial intelligence, ethics, and policy analysis (Carroll 2000).

Through the past two decades, HCI has also increasingly focused on science-based design, integrating its interdisciplinary scientific roots with the engineering goal of improving the *usability* of computer systems and applications. Thus the practice of HCI is often referred to as *usability engineering* (Nielsen 1993, Mayhew 1999, Rosson and Carroll 2002), pointing to the important role of establishing usability targets early in design, and using evaluation results to iterate toward these targets.

These twin bodies of knowledge—diverse perspectives on humans and their use of information technology, and user-centered methods for analyzing and ensuring the design of effective systems—present a major challenge for undergraduate education. Many American universities are just beginning to integrate HCI within their curricula and offer students a single introductory course. Educators may provide a comprehensive survey of the field, ensuring that students encounter a large number of concepts and theories relevant to HCI, but at a fairly high level. An alternative—and the one that we have adopted in our own teaching—is to provide a more eclectic survey of HCI topics and methods, but ensure that exposure is deep enough that students can be expected to apply it as they continue their education and professional work.

COMPARISONS – SCENARIOS FOR MAKING USE

Scenario-Based Design (SBD) methods have become pervasive in HCI research and practice (Carroll 1995, 2000, Cooper 1999, Rosson and Carroll 2002). Scenarios are increasingly recognized as a promising representation for raising and integrating the concerns of diverse stakeholders (Benyon and Macaulay, Chapter 11 in this volume; Carroll 1995; Holtzblatt, Chapter 10 in this volume; Rosson and Carroll 2000).

Scenarios are an excellent medium for teaching a user-centered perspective on design. They are concrete stories, which make them easy for HCI novices to develop and share; at the same time are flexible, quickly elaborated, or revised. A scenario can be rendered in many forms, from a lightweight text description to an elaborate and realistic scenario-machine (Kyng 1995, Nielsen 1995, Rosson and Carroll 2002; *see also* Chapter 1 of this volume). Because scenarios are stories about use, they maintain a central focus on use as the goal of design. Scenarios narrate one more users' experience during an activity, which helps designers to empathize with and analyze the factors that are causing different aspects of the usage experience.

In thinking about how best to teach SBD to computer scientists, we began with the software-engineering perspective that pervades computer science curricula—software development is largely about writing code, and writing code involves an iterative cycle of design and implementation, with testing and debugging guiding progressive refinement of the software. To support our education goals, we developed a usability engineering life cycle for SBD that elaborates and systematizes the *task-artifact cycle* (Carroll, Kellogg and Rosson 1991, Carroll and Rosson 1992). The task-artifact cycle describes how usage analyses and visions continually point to new opportunities for system design, while users' reactions to and adaptations of software systems establish new forms of activity.

In scenario-based usability engineering, scenarios represent users' activities and a broad range of scenario analysis and design techniques are used to guide the transition from use to artifact and back again (Figure 23.1). The critical step from current practice to design is inspired by metaphor, available technologies, and theory, but design possibilities are also considered in a more systematic fashion by examining associated design rationale—the likely consequences a specific design move might have for users (Moran and Carroll, 1996). When one or more scenarios are implemented as a system, the system in use is analyzed in terms of the new scenarios it now supports or evokes. These new scenarios describe how the artifact is used but are grounded in a rich context of system stakeholders, their needs, and their evolving work practices.

The usability engineering life cycle we teach to undergraduates is similar in many respects to the software engineering perspective conveyed by Boehm's spiral model (1988). Prototyping and testing of ideas is a crucial element at all phases of the design, with many opportunities to revisit and refine earlier analyses and design products. However, we teach students usability engineering methods that emphasize a forward progression of scenario representations and associated design rationale. They work with scenarios that originate in the problem domain and learn to continuously analyze and incrementally transform these scenarios into a design that better meet the needs and preferences of system stakeholders.

A complete description of the scenario-based process we teach to students is beyond the scope of this chapter, but the diagram in Figure 23.2 summarizes key concepts (for more detailed descriptions, see Rosson and Carroll 2002, 2003). *Problem scenarios* are written to synthesize observations and other field data gathered during **requirements analysis**. These scenarios are iteratively refined through *claims analysis*, which identifies

FIGURE 23.1   Scenarios as a central representation in the task-artifact cycle

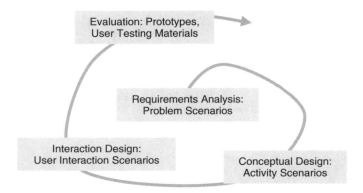

FIGURE 23.2 Phases in scenario-based usability engineering

features of current practice that have important positive and negative consequences for users, particularly consequences that may be addressed by information technology. During **conceptual design**, the problem scenarios are transformed into *activity scenarios* that envision future practices; this crucial design step is guided by analyses of existing technologies, conceptual metaphors, user profiles, and HCI theory and guidelines. The trade-offs documented through claims analysis also play a critical role, as designers seek to enhance the design's positive impacts on usage and minimize its negative impacts.

During **detailed design**, the activity scenarios (which are deliberately neutral with respect to technology details) are progressively elaborated as *information scenarios* and later as *interaction scenarios*, that specify in detail how technology will be used to present and manipulate the software objects and procedures needed to support the envisioned activity. Again, claims analyses are developed in a continuing fashion to identify and reason about important trade-offs in the emerging design. As soon as possible, **implementation** and **testing** begins, supported by a range of low- and high-fidelity prototypes that instantiate some or all of the design scenarios. The evaluation materials and criteria are based on the scenarios and claims analyses created during design.

With respect to undergraduate education, placing SBD within a usability engineering process of this sort accomplishes several aims,

- Articulates the ideas and methods of SBD by decomposing the overall process into phases;
- Assumes and leverages students' prior knowledge of methods for phased software development; and
- Offers a concrete SBD process model, including analysis and design techniques and representations, for completing a class project in several phases.

Importantly, the phased approach also provides a natural structure within which to introduce HCI concepts and theories. For example, we teach students about the subtleties of work practice, tacit and explicit knowledge, artifact analysis, and so on, during the problem scenario analysis. Mental models and metaphorical reasoning are covered during activity design, while the psychological process of perception, interpretation, learning, and action are considered during information and interaction design.

USING CASES TO TEACH SCENARIO-BASED USABILITY ENGINEERING

All HCI educators recognize the crucial role of realistic examples and projects in teaching the concepts and methods of user-centered design (Hewitt et al. 1990, Strong et al. 1994). However, it is a constant challenge to meet these pedagogical goals—many convenient examples are generic or piecemeal, and projects are often simplified to fit within the time constraints of a conventional course (e.g., three hours of credit over a 15-week period). Given our scenario-based usability engineering, we also have a requirement to introduce (and practice) an SBD life-cycle approach while simultaneously conveying the aspects of HCI most critical for supporting students' analysis and design projects. A *case study* is a narrative description of a specific and realistic instance of a process. Case studies invariably evoke trade-offs—often trade-offs that have no simple solution—and thus are an excellent vehicle for illustrating complex processes like usability engineering.

Why Case-Based?

Case-based learning enjoys status as favored pedagogy in many disciplines, but is most firmly entrenched and adopted in professional schools. Many law, business, and medical schools use cases to scaffold the experience of students as they acquire discipline-specific skills and expertise. The transition from neophyte to practitioner is not simple, and in many ways learners' exposure to "real world" issues through case analysis and discussion provides a surrogate for the experience set necessary to make expert-level decisions and judgments. The classroom becomes more than a place to learn facts and theories; it becomes a sort of simulated world in which students learn about "being in the trenches" without having to go there first.

What is it about cases and case-based learning that allows educators achieve such lofty ambitions? To understand this, it's important to fix a few characteristics of the cases themselves. While cases may appear to be isolated examples extracted from specific experiences, they are, in fact, interconnected through the principles they exemplify. To present a case argues that the present example is an instance of a broader category (Shulman 1992). A case study integrates the concepts and criteria for making decisions with the decision-making process itself. Thus we are able to construct "pedagogical case studies" for SBD that illustrate how the theories and concepts of HCI (e.g., visual perception, planning for action) can be applied through the methods of usability engineering (e.g., prototyping and user testing).

Case-based learning involves learning by doing, the development of analytical and decision-making skills, internalization of learning, and learning how to grapple with messy real-life problems. Indeed it is the messy and real-world character of case studies that leads to one their greatest strengths—providing persuasive evidence to novice designers that trade-offs are inevitable and pervasive in design, that there is never a single "right" answer, and that being able to compare the strengths and weaknesses of different solutions is evidence of a successful design process.

The Usability Case Study Library

In the course of developing a textbook for our usability engineering course, we documented a case study from our own development work—a virtual science fair within the MOOsburg environment, where students could exhibit their science projects and family and friends could visit, ask questions, and so on (Carroll 2000). In developing this textbook example, we were careful to document the case completely, from problem scenario analysis through prototyping and evaluation (see Chapters 2–8 in Rosson and Carroll 2002). However, from the start we also intended to complement this case with others drawn from commercial organizations; we obtained support from the U.S. National Science Foundation to develop a prototype library and browser for several usability case studies.

Table 23.1 summarizes three cases documented for our use in teaching scenario-based usability engineering (*see also* http://ucs.cs.vt.edu, which includes the virtual science fair and several other partial examples). The cases were selected to cover a range of problem domains and usability interaction techniques—a fairly conventional e-Commerce site for browsing and purchasing gardening supplies; a banking application for palmtop computers; and a telephony project. As the figure suggests, the analysis and design work for each case are organized by the main "phases" of our scenario-based usability engineering life cycle, beginning with requirements analysis and continuing through design and evaluation.

Table 23.2 provides a more detailed view of the most comprehensive case study (Garden.com), expanding each phase to reveal the individual documents in a category.

TABLE 23.1 Usability engineering case studies

Case Study	Case Documents
Garden.com: a virtual store offering comprehensive services for researching and purchasing garden and lawn supplies. Customers were given personalized treatment after registering for the store. It also included community-building support, for example advice from experts, chat, and so on.	Requirements Analysis: 25 Activity Design: 9 Information Design: 12 Interaction Design: 12 Documentation: 0 Usability Testing: 24
m-Banking: an extension to existing e-banking services (Web-based) that allows mobile users to access and manipulate their bank accounts and stock portfolios using a handheld mobile device (Palm VII). Eventually the services were available for both PDAs and WAP phones, but the case study chronicles the early phases of development for PDAs.	Requirements Analysis: 11 Activity Design: 4 Information Design: 12 Interaction Design: 9 Documentation: 4 Usability Testing: 6
PhoneWriter: a proof-of-concept telephony project that explored the contributions of various user input technologies (e.g., pen-based input, voice recognition) on the note-taking, form completion and other tasks common in telephony interactions. Collaboration based on documents transferred among telephony partners is also supported.	Requirements Analysis: 9 Activity Design: 4 Information Design: 6 Interaction Design: 0 Documentation: 2 Usability Testing: 7

TABLE 23.2   Detailed content for the Garden.com case study

Requirements Analysis

Planning: initial brainstorming session; market research; root concept

Methods and Materials: script for interviewing nursery workers; script for interviewing customers; focus group agenda; focus group recruiting ad; screening survey questions

Information Gathering: photo of highway entrance sign; photo of nursery exterior; photo of nursery interior; photo of nursery main retail display; photo of outside covered retail display; photo of outside open retail display; photo of superstore outdoor display; photo of indoor superstore display; photo of gardening customer; garden sketch; plant hardiness map; catalog index; catalog order form; interview excerpt-nursery workers; interview excerpt-customers.

Synthesis: problem claims; problem scenarios

Activity Design

Exploration: summary of proposed activities; conceptual metaphors; system technology

Envisionment: activity scenarios; shopping model; sequence analysis; point-of-view analysis

Rationale: activity claims

Information Design

Exploration: department information requirements; product page information requirements; summary of proposed information offerings; information metaphors; information technology options

Envisionment: sketch of map metaphor; sketch of catalog metaphor; sketch of homepage; sketch of search results; sketch of product page; information scenarios

Rationale: information claims

Interaction Design

Exploration: interaction metaphors; interaction technology

Envisionment: online shopping script; functional study; design revision #1; design revision #2

Rationale: before/after main page; before/after department page; before/after product list page; before/after product information page; before/after wheelbarrow page; usability study #2 report

Usability Testing

Planning: operational definition; usability specifications

Methods and Materials: user background survey; gardening quiz; attitudes toward the Internet survey; session script; usability testing scenarios; post-scenario ease of use assessment; usability report card; strategy questions; debriefing questions; equipment list

Data Collection: notes on sessions; notes on participants; post-subtask comments; post-session comments; usability report card scores

Interpretation: gardening quiz scores; attitudes toward the Internet; time on task; lostness ratings; number of mouse clicks; post-subtask ratings

Synthesis: design recommendations

As this expansion suggests, one way to view each of our prototype case studies is as a mini library of analysis and design documents, interconnected with a narrative that describes the role and consequences of each document within the project life cycle. The Garden.com case study is particularly rich in the Information Gathering portion of Requirements Analysis, providing a total of nine photographs of nursery and/or garden shopping settings. These concrete field study artifacts are effective probes for interactive class discussion, prompting questions like

"What is the role of that Sale sign?"
"Could we accomplish that same effect online?"
"Would we want to?"

The Garden.com case also includes a large number of usability testing documents. These are particularly useful to computer science undergraduates who have never conducted a behavioral study before and thus have little insight into the kinds of questions one might ask, behavioral measures one might collect, interpretations warranted from a set of data, how to draw recommendations for redesign, and so on.

In sum, the library of case studies provide a wealth of examples that illustrate different aspects of the *process* of usability engineering—the preparatory analysis activities, the design and user studies, and the more formal evaluation of progress. As a pedagogical device, case studies rely on reasoning from examples, a well-studied phenomenon in psychology and cognitive science (Kolodner 1993, Leake 1998). As examples, each case varies in the amount of detail provided for each phase, and on the related HCI content, but across the set of cases the overall process of usability engineering and the concepts and theories of HCI receive broad coverage.

Browsing the Usability Cases

The usability case studies consist of analysis and design documents threaded together with a narrative of how the problem was analyzed and a solution developed. As the summary of Garden.com suggests, the amount of material comprising a case will often be large (Garden.com case includes 82 documents), so it was important to provide a tool that would facilitate students' browsing and analysis of the cases. Our general approach was to build a hypermedia browser that presented the cases in a canonical fashion (organized by the usability engineering phases) but also included linkages among related design documents and issues.

Figure 23.3 contains a screenshot of the case browser as it is being used to compare and contrast the *activity design scenarios* and *activity design claims* in the m-Banking case study. As summarized in Figure 23.2, scenarios play a central integrating role in SBD, by emphasizing the experiences and trade-offs of use. A *claim* is a feature of the usage scenario (typically a designed feature) that has positive and negative consequences (identified as plus and minus signs in the figure) for the users in this or related scenarios Claims are addressed in design by finding ways to maintain or enhance positive consequences while minimizing or removing negative. The browser simplifies learners' analysis of scenarios and claims by providing direct links from the scenario text to an associated claim and vice versa.

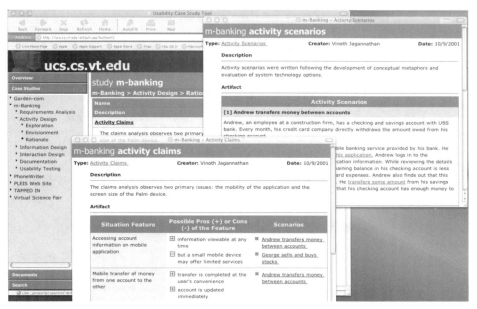

FIGURE 23.3   Case study browser being used to investigate relations between a scenario and its claims analysis

Although the canonical use of the case browser is to start at the "beginning" of a case (i.e., at the beginning of Requirements Analysis) and work through it sequentially, the tool supports more focused and/or piecemeal investigations as well. For instance, there is a glossary of terms useful to learners unfamiliar with SBD or usability engineering in general. Students can also traverse a case study by following links from document to document; the hierarchical, phased exploration of the case study is only suggested, not required.

The tool also supports a document-type view of the case library. In this mode, learners see a classification of different analysis or design documents (e.g., a "root concept" as used in Requirements Analysis, "conceptual metaphors" as used in Activity Design, the "information scenarios" developed during Information Design). We created this document-type view to encourage learners to compare and contrast *across* case studies, for instance noting how metaphors are used to shape the design of two rather different products. We have found this organization to be particularly useful to students preparing to do some phase of their own project, where they can benefit from examining multiple examples of a usability engineering method or concept.

Finally, learners can use a search dialog to construct a custom list of design documents related to a specific topic of interest. For instance, if a learner types "agent" as a search string, the system would return a list of all documents that use the word agent in any way. The search mechanism supports ad hoc tasks not anticipated by the phase-based document hierarchy. The search can be restricted to a single case study (e.g., suppose the viewer wants to study the role of "George" as a stakeholder in m-Banking), or it can be applied across all of the case studies.

Case-Based Learning Activities

Applying cases in the teaching usability engineering requires more than a tool to examine the body of case material. Students need direction, challenges, and focus, in order systematically approach the body of experience represented in the case library. These cases are each extensive, spanning the scenario-based usability engineering process from beginning to end. Portions of each case are applicable, in sequence, as the SBD process unfolds throughout the semester or quarter. To better leverage the case studies, we have developed series of *activities* that guide students to read and analyze case materials in support of specific pedagogical goals.

The case library as it exists can support a broad range of activities for students in their first exposure to usability engineering. Most of our case-based learning activities focus on one phase of scenario-based development or on the transition between the phases. Activities can be implemented as written homework assignments, in-class discussions, and small group discussions. Some typical activities we have used include:

> **Modeling:**   Refer to a segment of the SBD process as implemented in one of the case studies and use it as a model in developing another instance. For example, study the problem scenarios of Garden.com case and create another example that would be consistent with the field data, stakeholder analyses, and so on.
>
> **Perturbation:**   Given some point in the SBD process illustrated by a case study, make a change to the conditions leading up to this point and redevelop the succeeding steps and implications. For example, consider the new problem scenarios that might arise if the requirements for m-Banking focus exclusively on international clients.
>
> **Summarizing:**   Study a phase of SBD in a case study and explain how a specific SBD technique facilitated the usability engineering process. For example, summarize how metaphors were used to clarify requirements for Garden.com.
>
> **Tracing:**   Follow the progress of a case while assessing subsequent impacts of earlier decisions. For example, trace a claim from m-Banking Requirements Analysis to determine whether or how it was addressed during Activity or Interaction Design. Answer questions such as *Did they do what they said they would?"* while checking for internal consistency.
>
> **Contrasting:**   Contrast two different cases with respect to how they implement a phase of scenario-based usability engineering. For instance, contrast how prototyping was used to make progress in the Virtual Science Fair and in Garden.com.
>
> **Analyzing:**   This is similar to the summarize activities but includes student evaluation and reflection on how well the process was implemented and whether it was the best process at this stage. By analyzing Interaction Design trade-offs in Garden.com, students probe how well the designers addressed the issues they set for themselves.

These activities vary in the degree of cognitive effort demanded, and we tend to assign the least demanding activities early in the class and make more demanding assignments later on. For instance, modeling and summarization are relatively simple example-based learning activities, but are good ways to encounter and reflect on the "lingo" of SBD (scenarios, claims, etc.). However, contrasting two cases with respect to a phase is a more challenging and open-ended assignment, because each case addresses rather different HCI issues and techniques.

We have used activities based on this taxonomy in several iterations of our courses in usability engineering. Most activities are specified as homework assignments, with written solutions (the case browser currently provides no specific support for learning activities). The case-based homework facilitates two important pedagogical goals,

(1) the students contemplate the issues in depth and on their own before in-class discussions; and

(2) the level of in-class discussion is more active and insightful because of this preparation.

Student Performance and Reactions

Measuring the learning impacts of case study activities is difficult; gathering quantifiable data is particularly challenging. In our first iterations with case study assignments, we gathered general subjective reactions and comments. As Figure 23.4 suggests, early student reactions were generally quite positive. Most students (61%) agreed that overall the case-based learning assignments were either "Excellent" or "Very Good". No students rated them as "Below Average" or "Poor". Table 23.3 elaborates on these general ratings

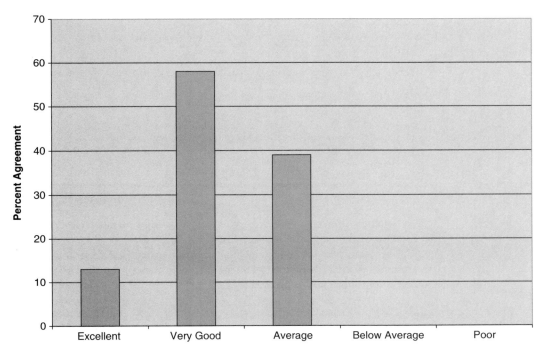

FIGURE 23.4 Students' general reactions to case-based learning activities

TABLE 23.3   Feedback received from students

Sample responses to "What did you like best about the case study activities?"
"Gave me an opportunity to use concepts in class in a hands-on environment that helped a lot when transitioning to the group projects."
"I liked the brainstorming activities because they were a lot of fun to do in teams. It was interesting to find out what other people could come up with."
"It was interesting to see how the strategies we learned in class are applied in a real prototype. Real life examples always make learning more interesting."
"I liked working in groups a lot, it allowed us to combine different ideas and approaches. I also thought it gave us a window into real-life applications. Definitely continues these types of activities."
Sample responses to "What did you like least about the case study activities?"
"Not everyone was always prepared to contribute."
"Sometimes the questions asked were like pulling teeth. It was a stretch sometimes to answer the question."
"I am not too fond of speaking in public, so I did not like the talking part."
"Some of the classroom assignments were ambiguous and too open-ended to be productive. We often spent a large portion of our time trying to figure out what the assignment was, leaving only minutes to actually brainstorm on the topic."
Sample responses to "What could we do to improve the case study activities?"
"I would conduct the activities with the entire class as a whole and not in small groups. When each group gets to share their thoughts many of the ideas are repeated."
"Make the requirements and timing more clear and stick to the times assigned for each part."
"Perhaps allow students to participate with other people in the class. We were always put in our pre-assigned groups."
"Maybe interact with laptops more in class?"

with comments offered in response to questions asking students what they liked the most, the least, and what suggestions they had for improvement.

A problem with these early evaluative efforts was their generality. Although learners' comments sometimes mentioned specific activities or features of the cases, most of their reactions were to the general idea of case-based learning. In more recent iterations of the course, we have explored the use of more specific evaluation instruments. We have adapted the concepts of perceived self-efficacy (Bandura 1993) to construct two to three "usability engineering self-efficacy" probes for each activity assigned. Table 23.4 summarizes student responses to a set of such items, where reactions were gathered on a Likert scale (from 1 = Strongly Disagree to 5 = Strongly Agree).

TABLE 23.4   Self-efficacy judgments for six case-based learning activities

Activities and Associated Efficacy Probes	Mean
Model Garden.com by creating an original problem scenario and claim.	
Even if a requirements analysis was thought to be complete, I could extend it with an original scenario	4.15
If presented with a scenario in an unfamiliar problem domain, I could identify legitimate usability claims.	3.81
Overall mean for *Model* activity	**3.98**
Summarize how metaphors clarified requirements; suggest starting points for activity design.	
Even though I only studied examples of metaphors, I could generate new metaphors useful for activity design.	4.18
I could use a conceptual metaphor to clarify design requirements even though some parts of the metaphor are irrelevant.	3.89
Overall mean for *Summarize* activity	**4.04**
Trace claims through activity design, information design, and interaction design phases.	
Even when a design develops over a number of phases, I can identify design issues and trace how they were managed in the design process	3.85
Although problem scenarios may be very different from design scenarios, I can map problem claims onto corresponding design claims.	3.85
Even though the PhoneWriter design process was presented to me within the limits of a case study, I am confident I could investigate and report on a similar design effort in the real world.	4.15
Overall mean for *Trace* activity	**3.95**
Contrast Virtual Science Fair and Garden.com use of prototyping.	
Though design and interaction prototyping can be done in a variety of ways, I could select an appropriate prototyping strategy even if I was the sole usability engineer on a project.	4.16
If I joined a project team midstream, I could generate an interaction prototyping strategy even if this required digging up or backfilling some of the information design details.	4.03
Even though there are many project-specific reasons for choosing prototyping techniques, I could compare the effectiveness of prototyping approaches in different projects.	4.10
Overall mean for *Contrast* activity	**4.10**

(*continued overleaf*)

TABLE 23.4 (*continued*)

Activities and Associated Efficacy Probes	Mean
Analyze design trade-offs in Garden.com's interaction design	
Even though I only studied interaction design issues for Garden.com, I could analyze trade-offs for other interaction designs	3.95
I could evaluate how trade-offs were resolved in an interaction design even when the design documentation did not discuss each trade-off in detail.	3.72
Overall mean for first *Analyze* activity	**3.84**
Analyze m-Banking.com with respect to a choice of models	
Even in a case where documentation design blends minimalism and the systems approach, I can identify which documentation features correspond to each model	3.83
Even without any empirical data evaluating a set of documentation, I can use analytic methods to judge how well the documentation implements minimalism or the systems approach.	3.82
Overall mean for second *Analyze* activity	**3.83**

As the table conveys, students' reactions were again generally positive. The modal response for each probe was "Agree", with more ratings of "Strongly Agree" than "Neutral". We were surprised that the differences between activities were rather small. For example, even at the beginning of the course, students seemed to be fairly confident about their abilities to model and summarize parts of case studies. Later on in the course, when they attempted more ambitious assignments, they continued to express confidence, even for the more cognitively demanding activities of contrasting and analyzing cases.

Although self-efficacy ratings are known to be a good predictor of achievement (Bandura 1976), at this point we can only speculate about the relation of our self-efficacy probes to students' actual comprehension and facility with usability engineering concepts and methods. However, we are able to report that during the same course in which the Table 23.4 data were gathered, the instructor wrote exams that in the past had yielded quite varied scores, and was pleasantly surprised to find what appeared to be a ceiling effect in this class—it seems that either students were highly motivated to prepare for the exam or they had genuinely learned the material thoroughly.

STRENGTHS AND WEAKNESSES

Case-based discussions in class can be, and often are, lively and interesting. As the previous section shows, students seem to appreciate the "real worldness" of case-based activities and seem to get a lot out of them. And while the cost of creating case studies, and designing effective case-based learning activities is high, once such materials are in place, the cost to educators of conducting these activities is rather low. Each of the activities in Table 23.4 required students to spend considerable time reading and synthesizing case documents but resulted in relatively short and pointed assignments for review and grading.

Case-based methods of learning intentionally create contextualized appreciation. This can deepen processing of information and aid learning, but it is not clear that all learners will reach the same level of understanding on their own. Written homework assignments may be used to "force" learners to receive similar exposure to the underlying principles, whereas in class discussions some students may become passive and not participate in the exchange. We believe that by combining these teaching methods, we can ensure a basic level of exposure and increase the likelihood of participation in group discussion.

Initially, instructors may find it more difficult to use case-based teaching methods than lecturing on a topic. Case-based instruction requires more effort to select or design an effective case and to understand it thoroughly before interacting with students. It also requires discussion-facilitation skills that not all academic faculty possess. Owing to the dynamic nature of discussions, instructors must be flexible and let the learners take the lead in determining the direction for the discussion. This may mean that conversations may not go exactly where the instructor wants it to go. It takes considerable classroom presence to provide appropriate interjections that guide the discussion without stifling it.

Evaluating student learning based on case methods is also a challenge that requires careful consideration and planning. Teaching assistants who grade homework based on case methods may need extra guidance, as there is often no single answer and design arguments may need subjective evaluation. A graduate assistant asked to evaluate an undergraduate's level of understanding will need extra guidance in how to attend to the "thought process" more than the "solution" provided.

Overall, case-based learning activities seem to be quite appropriate for teaching a complex process like usability engineering. By grounding learners' exposure to HCI principles in real-world contexts, students used to the concrete world of programming and software development begin to appreciate the fuzziness that accompanies software system design. For many students, their first HCI class provides their initial exposure to the nuances introduced when considering real people doing real things in real settings. The credibility contained in cases is significant and important. Learning to reason about trade-offs when the grounds for decision-making are unclear and incomplete is a crucial skill that is often only learned on the job.

DISCUSSION AND FUTURE DIRECTIONS

Over the past 20 years, considerable effort and resources have been directed to the development and application of case studies in engineering education (Kardos 1979, Smith and Kardos 2000). One of the most refined products of this work is the NEEDS (National Engineering Education Delivery System) project (http://www.needs.org). This digital library project presents online materials collected and refined through the collaborative efforts of many engineering schools over many years; detailed case studies are an important element in the library. Our prototype project is an initial step toward analogous resources for HCI education.

While our current case studies cover a range of problem domains, we are currently working to identify and develop examples from other domains of interest to the HCI community. For example, HCI professionals have recently become heavily involved in collaborative computing, studying user interface mechanisms that promote the development of online communities. Another attractive domain is scientific computing (e.g., "problem-solving environments"), where users are likely to be considerably more sophisticated than those for the average application. Two other domains of current interest in HCI are medical informatics and entertainment.

In addition to expanding the case library, we are developing new requirements for the case-browsing tool. For example, students in usability engineering typically carry out a semester project, from requirements through evaluation. These group projects might benefit from authoring support in the tool, so that each student project can itself be documented (and shared) as a mini-case. We also hope to better integrate the learning activities with the tool support; for example, an activity that requires analysis of how metaphors are used to move from problem to design scenarios might encapsulate or index into the library to make the relevant material more evident and convenient for learners.

Our ongoing work with case studies for teaching usability engineering continues to evolve from merely including interesting cases in an HCI course to using the case method as a pedagogy for the entire course. As we have refined our usability-engineering course, it has come to rely more extensively on case-based activities as *the* paradigm for exposing students to key HCI concepts. We have found ourselves moving from the use of cases as illustrations of usability engineering to using them to let students experience "vicariously" the complexities and trade-offs endemic to user-centered design. We are learning how the study of cases can be, in some ways, comparable to partaking in the experience narrated by the case study. Moreover, we believe that careful and systematic exposure to meaningful case studies may yield broader and more well-founded expertise than what is obtained through the more random experience of real world projects.

At the same time we are making contact with other HCI educators to share and further explore case-based learning of scenario-based usability engineering. For example, we have recently conducted a workshop involving a dozen HCI educators from universities in the United States and Canada. Preliminary results from the workshop include

- General agreement that the case method is effective in teaching usability engineering as a process.
- Observation that student projects could be and often were formatted in a manner akin to the structure found in the case study browser.
- Acknowledgement that additional cases would be useful and that student produced cases based on their projects would be particularly interesting.
- Identification of further requirements to extend and improve the case study browser.
- Agreement to participate in and share case study exercises and evaluation of their effectiveness.

We will continue to facilitate discussion and sharing among this group of educators, as well as to begin disseminating and evaluating the cases and associated learning activities more generally.

The scenario-based case studies we have developed are comprehensive, comprising many different documents woven together via text summaries for each phase of the project. Another direction for future work is the editing of a full case to tell the story of just one or two key issues addressed in a design project. Such a treatment would remove much of the real world context that makes the overall case complex, but might serve the pedagogical goal of helping students to understand how a particular HCI concern was raised and addressed (to some extent, this is what the Trace activity was designed to do; see the section titled "Using Cases to Teach Scenario-Based Usability Engineering". These "brief cases" might be particularly useful in teaching agile development skills (Beck and West, Chapter 13), where getting to the heart of an issue quickly is essential to making progress. Alternatively, if we collected user stories as they evolved in an extreme programming project, perhaps annotated with connections to design ideas and trade-offs, we could construct a scenario-based case study of an agile development project.

Case studies have a long and successful history in learning and education. But case studies are more than examples. Cases illustrate the *process* of solving a problem; exploration of case studies is particularly important in disciplines where the problems are ill-defined and complex, where solutions rely on understanding and addressing the details of a situation, where there is usually more than one right answer, and where it is impossible to crystallize an expert's problem-solving abilities into a set of guidelines or principles. In many ways, case studies can be a surrogate for joining the workforce and gaining actual project experience. Computer science students who grasp the usage complexities and trade-offs in real world usability engineering cases are well on their way to making use.

ACKNOWLEDGEMENTS

Development of the case studies and browser was supported by The National Science Foundation (DUE-0088396 and DUE-0231111)h. We thank Jennifer Thompson, Richard Bowman, Wesley Lloyd, Jiunwei Chen, and Vinoth Jagannathan for their help with the case study content, activities, tools, and evaluations. An abbreviated version of this curriculum project was presented in March 2004 at ACM SIGCSE in Richmond VA (Rosson, Carroll & Rodi, 2004).

KEYWORDS

Usability Engineering	Undergraduate Education	Case Studies
Human–Computer Interaction (HCI)	Scenario-Based Design (SBD)	Active Learning

REFERENCES

Bandura, A., Perceived self-efficacy in cognitive development and functioning, *Educational Psychologist*, **28**, 117–148, 1993.

Bandura, A, *Self-efficacy: The exercise of control*, W.H. Freeman and Company, 1997.

Boehm, B., The spiral model of software development and enhancement, *IEEE Computer*, **21**(5), 61–72, 1988.

Brooks, F., *The Mythical Man-Month: Essays on Software Engineering*, Addison-Wesley, 1995.

Card, S.K., Moran, T.P., and Newell, A., *The Psychology of Human-Computer Interaction*, Lawrence Erlbaum Associates, 1983.

Carroll, J.M. (Ed.), *Scenario-Based Design: Envisioning Work and Technology in System Development*, John Wiley & Sons, 1995.

Carroll, J.M, Human-Computer Interaction: Psychology as a science of design, *International Journal of Human-Computer Studies*, **46**, 501–522, 1997.

Carroll, J.M., *Making Use: Scenario-Based Design of Human-Computer Interactions*, MIT Press, 2000.

Carroll, J.M. and Rosson, M.B., Getting around the task-artifact cycle: How to make claims and design by scenario, *ACM Transactions on Information Systems*, **10**(2), 181–212, 1992.

Carroll, J.M. and Thomas, J.C., Metaphors and the cognitive representation of computing systems, *IEEE Transactions on Systems, Man, and Cybernetics*, **12**(2), 107–116, 1983.

Hewitt, T. Baecker, R., Card, S., Carey, T., Gasen J., Mantei, M., Perlman, G., Strong G., Verplank, W., *ACM SIGCHI Curricula for Human-Computer Interaction*, ACM Press, 1992.

Carroll, J.M., Kellogg, W.A., and Rosson, M.B., The task-artifact cycle, in J.M. Carroll (Ed.), *Designing Interaction: Psychology at the Human-Computer Interface*, Cambridge University Press, 1991, 74–102.

Cooper, A., *The Inmates are Running the Asylum: Why High Tech Products Drive Us Crazy and How to Restore the Sanity*, SAMS Press, 1999.

Kardos, G., *Engineering Cases in the Classroom*, Online paper available from Carleton University, 1979, http://www.civeng.carleton.ca/ECL/cclas.html

Kolodner, J., *Case-Based Reasoning*, Morgan Kaufmann, 1993.

Kyng, M., Creating contexts for design, in J. Carroll (Ed.), *Scenario-Based Design: Envisioning Work and Technology in System Development*, John Wiley & Sons, 1995, pp. 85–108.

Leake, D.B. (Ed.), *Case-Based Reasoning: Experiences, Lessons, and Future Directions*, AAAI Press, 1998.

Mayhew, D.J., *The Usability Engineering Lifecycle: A Practioner's Handbook for User Interface Design*, Morgan Kaufmann, 1999.

Moran, T. and Carroll, J.M. (Eds.), *Design Rationale: Concepts, Methods and Techniques*, Lawrence Erlbaum Associates, 1996.

NEEDS, National Engineering Education Delivery System, 2004, http://www.needs.org/

Nielsen, J., *Usability Engineering*, Academic Press, 1993.

Norman, D.A., Cognitive engineering, in D.A. Norman and S.D. Draper (Eds.), *User Centered System Design*, Lawrence Erlbaum Associates, 1986, pp. 31–61.

Reitman, W.R., *Cognition and thought.: An information processing approach*, John Wiley and Sons, New York, 1965.

Rosson, M.B. and Carroll, J.M., *Usability Engineering: Scenario-Based Development of Human-Computer Interaction*, Morgan Kaufmann, 2002.

Rosson, M.B. and Carroll, J.M., Scenario-based design, *The Human-Computer Interaction Handbook*, Lawrence Erlbaum Associates, 2003.

Rosson, M.B., Carroll, J.M., Rodi, C.M, Case studies for teaching usability engineering, Proceedings of Technical Symposium on Computer Science Education , 36–40, 2004.

Shulman, J.H. (Ed.), *Case methods in teacher education*, Teachers College Press, New York, 1992.

Simon, H.A, The structure of ill-structured problems, *Artificial Intelligence*, **4**, 181–201, 1973

Smith, C.O. and Kardos, G., *Design in Materials Courses? Naturally!* Online paper available from Carleton University, 2000, http://www.civeng.carleton.ca/ECL/dsngmat.html

Strong, G. et al., *New Directions in Human-Computer Interaction Education, Research, and Practice*, NSF-ISP, NSF-AATP, and ARPA-SIST, 1994.

RECOMMENDED READINGS

Carroll, J.M., *Making Use: Scenario-Based Design of Human-Computer Interactions*, MIT Press, 2000. This monograph presents theoretical arguments for scenario-based analysis and design of interactive systems, as well as a number of examples of these techniques applied to projects involving education, design, and software development.

Harvard Business School, *Teaching and the Case Method*, 3rd ed, McGraw-Hill, 1994. This is one of the classic texts on case-based methods that has been revised and updated over many years. The book introduces a variety of techniques for case-based teaching that can be applied to fields as diverse as medicine and business administration. It also includes an Instructor's Guide with teaching notes and suggestions for starting and running case-based teaching seminars.

Rosson, M.B. and Carroll, J.M., *Usability Engineering: Scenario-Based Development of Human-Computer Interaction*, Morgan Kaufmann, 2002. This textbook provides a comprehensive introduction to the SBD framework summarized in the section titled "Comparisons—Scenarios for Making Use". It integrates coverage of key concepts and theories in human-computer interaction with the phases of an SBD project, and illustrates the entire lifecycle with an extended case study.

CHAPTER 24

WHAT SCENARIOS (STILL) AREN'T GOOD FOR

Ian Alexander[1] and Neil Maiden[2]

[1] *Scenario Plus, London, UK*
[2] *Centre for HCI Design, City University, London, UK*

Scenarios are extremely versatile and useful in systems development—and in other places, but they do not offer help in every situation, and may even be misleading if over-enthusiastically applied. This short chapter suggests some possible limits to scenario use—at least until we gain a better understanding. We hope this may restrain the over-enthusiastic, give readers a better feel for what scenarios really can do well, and perhaps indicate some open areas where researchers and innovative practitioners can explore and develop new techniques.

CONTINUOUS BEHAVIOUR

Scenario modelling assumes that behaviour can be divided up into meaningful episodes or chunks, such as transactions: you go and get some cash from the teller machine. But some systems provide continuous behaviour that just doesn't fall into that pattern. As Michael Jackson writes, possibly damning with faint praise,

> The use case view can work quite well when it makes sense to think of the machine as a facility offering discrete services that are used in clearly delimited episodes. (Jackson 2001)

Consider a couple of examples:

- System A is a message router for a large organisation. A huge stream of traffic of all kinds arrives from all over the world, is split into its components, and sent on to the addressees of the individual messages. Another stream travels in the other direction all the time.
- System B is a weather forecasting model. A huge mass of reports pour in from weather ships, coastal stations, and satellites. The data are fed into the model,

and the system simulates the weather up to several days ahead. Forecasts are sent to customers.

Now, even in these intentionally awkward examples, you can identify more or less standard situations to consider separately as scenarios. In Systems A and B, you still need to cope with cases like failure, diagnosis, repair, test, restart, upgrade, statistics, and logging, although the main case is just one enormous routing or forecasting algorithm. In System B, you also have some stories to tell about customers who ask for rapid delivery of high definition video pictures for their TV channels, or faxed weather maps of The Lake District to print out in monochrome at a fuzzy 60 dots per inch for hillwalkers. Scenarios will therefore be of some help, but they probably cannot address the core elements of the system in any detail.

VERY LARGE SYSTEMS

Scenarios seem to be rather ineffective when applied top-down on large system hierarchies. We simply don't know how to apply scenarios consistently throughout the many years and across all the contractual boundaries of the biggest system engineering projects. It would be nice to claim that a new aircraft carrier could be specified, designed, built, and tested entirely (*pace* the many non-functional requirements and constraints) on the basis of scenarios, but it wouldn't be true. The huge search space implied by the set of all the end-to-end scenarios for such a system, multiplied up by all the details, exceptions, and combinations that would be created by all the subsystems and sub-subsystems, would today be utterly unmanageable. That is not even to mention the complexity of navigating the many contractual interfaces other than via traditional lists of textual requirements.

In practice (therefore), such big systems do not yet use scenarios wholeheartedly.

FRAGMENTARY MODELS

Another issue for large projects is that we do not yet have what a jet engine maker would call 'whole engine model' understanding. There are CAD/CAM models, static thermodynamic models, noise models, partial models of what happens in the high-pressure turbine when the pilot moves the throttle—but putting all these pieces together is another matter.

A complete system scenario model would enable us to inject any set of conditions, and get a simulated or animated set of results. Ultimately (not at the start of a project), such a model would be completely mathematical; but a complete model even at high level and expressed in text or diagrammatic form would be very useful also.

The power and convenience of a tool like David Harel and Rami Marelly's Live Sequence Chart engine as described in *Come, Let's Play* (Harel and Marelly 2003; see also the discussion in Chapter 1 of this volume, in the section on Simulation) for small interactive software developments might one day be available to explore all aspects of system behaviour, performance, and reliability for systems of all kinds and sizes.

EPISODIC, ALLUSORY

As hinted above, scenarios are inherently episodic and allusory. They try to grasp the essence of complex situations and systems by giving examples, by describing significant cases, and by hinting at important aspects of system behaviour. They lead to system design by induction, rather than by defining rules; they are in a word not very specification-like. Theorists like Michael Jackson who believe that systems should be specified as a whole with some kind of comprehensive model are inevitably uncomfortable with the use of scenarios as specifications: they must feel that the RUP (see Peter Haumer's account in Chapter 12) is a serious mistake, and its popularity one of the stranger vagaries of fashion.

DOMAIN-SPECIFIC?

Are scenarios domain-specific? Do you need (much) domain knowledge in scenarios? The answer may be yes, at least in Work and Business Models. If you try to proceed directly to system usage scenarios without making any such models, trouble may ensue. On the other hand, there is certainly a school of thought that scenarios are simple human things that can be described and understood regardless of the domain. Perhaps the truth is somewhere between these extremes. Scenarios do help bridge the gap between domain specialists and developers; but they may not be totally successful in this attempt.

WHICH REPRESENTATION?

If the range of approaches described in this book makes anything clear, it must be that there are many possible scenario representations. We do not today know how to select the best representation (storyboard, video, simulation, use case, user story, acting out, etc.) for a specific project. In practice, most current usage is of textual scenarios—stories or sequences of steps described in words—but it is far from certain that this is optimal in all cases.

Interestingly, there are some applicable rules from other domains. For example, psychology theory says that errors are best found when expressed in the third-person form (the operator does X, somebody else does Y, then a third person does Z) as this form results in unthreatening statements that people can evaluate more objectively.

We can at present only wonder whether there are equivalent rules governing the use of graphics, animations, and other more colourful ways of presenting scenarios. It's tempting to suppose that the use of non-technical and non-exclusively verbal scenarios might help with the specification of systems, especially where stakeholders are from widely varying backgrounds with different cultures and languages. There is some evidence that analytic models are poorly understood by non-engineers. Psychologists joke that business executives treat all diagrams as flowcharts. If there is any truth in that, there is plenty of room for research into the applicability of different scenario representations.

OPEN-ENDED

Scenarios give less guidance to developers than many more prescriptive sorts of models or ways of writing requirements. Conversely, scenarios often imply that a specific time-ordering is mandatory where a goal or task model might be vague about time constraints—or might state them explicitly (this must be synchronised with that, those can be performed in any order). When several concrete scenarios overlap, or when a Use Case documents numerous alternatives, it may be a moot point which is the 'right' modelling approach. Scenario use increases uncertainty by giving many choices, so people may be left not knowing what they should explore. This is so even when scenarios and Use Cases are analytic and supposedly generic. When scenarios illustrate concrete situations as examples of what a system might possibly do, different developers could take quite different solution approaches.

TACIT KNOWLEDGE

Scenarios only capture knowledge that people can consciously express, or at least work out by stepping through operational tasks with the help of a requirements engineer. Some kinds of knowledge, such as recognising faces or doing skilled work, are inherently tacit: 'we know more than we can tell' (Polanyi 1966, page 4). It is indeed possible to build facial recognition systems, but as Polanyi himself said, that just gives us something else to point at. We can't hope to make all tacit knowledge explicit, but 'we can communicate . . . provided we are given adequate means of expressing ourselves' (Polanyi 1966, page 5). The development of such means of expression may encompass facilitation techniques, new types of model, diagram, and animation, and may well include domain-specific techniques.

NON-FUNCTIONAL REQUIREMENTS (NFRs)

Scenarios can, with some effort (see Chapter 7, Negative Scenarios and Misuse Cases by Ian Alexander, in this volumes) be used to capture and at least indirectly document some kinds of requirements other than those directly describing system functions. But we ourselves document and indeed discover most of our NFRs by populating templates (e.g. Scenario Plus 2004, Volere 2004) and applying other conventional requirements approaches. When you know a system constraint or required quality, you simply don't need to go to the trouble of writing scenarios about it: it's quicker and more sensible just to write it as a requirement.

SUMMARY

We don't mean to sound negative—we think scenarios are wonderful and indispensable in process modelling and system development. But scenarios don't do everything—certainly not now; and there are some things they will never do. Of course all these limitations are part of the challenge for scenario researchers, and opportunities for the future.

REFERENCES

Harel, D. and Marelly, R., *Come, Let's Play: Scenario-Based Programming Using LSCs and the Play-Engine*, Springer-Verlag, 2003

Jackson, M., *Problem Frames: Analyzing and Structuring Software Development Problems*, Addison-Wesley, 2001.

Polanyi, M., *The Tacit Dimension*, Doubleday & Co, 1966; Reprinted Peter Smith, Gloucester, MA, 1983.

Scenario Plus: templates from website at http://www.scenarioplus.org.uk, 2004.

Volere: templates from website at http://www.volere.co.uk, 2004.

CHAPTER 25

THE FUTURE OF SCENARIOS

Ian Alexander[1] and Neil Maiden[2]

[1]*Scenario Plus, London, UK*
[2]*Centre for HCI Design, City University, London, UK*

INTRODUCTION: HORSES FOR COURSES

The previous chapter, *What Scenarios (Still) Aren't Good For*, toured some of the issues that beset scenarios, and suggested some elements of an agenda for research into scenario applications in system development.

Today we have an idea of how useful scenarios can be, but we certainly do not have a complete picture of how all the different possible scenario techniques might fit together with each other and with other specification techniques. The key questions that we have tried to address in this book are what scenario approaches there are, and what they are good for. A racing man might say 'there's a horse for every course'; the trick, naturally, is knowing which one it is before you place your bet.

The question that arises for researchers is of course how one would know, and hence what guidance one could give to a project trying to select the best techniques for its circumstances. This brief chapter peers over the horizon at what a future version of this book might contain.

TOWARDS A FRAMEWORK

Researchers would like to have a comprehensive framework encompassing all scenario techniques, all domains, and all contexts of use—describing access to stakeholders, issues of how fixed or flexible scenarios should be to permit innovation, and so on. Clearly, this is a huge challenge, and it has many dimensions, some of which are mentioned below.

REPRESENTATION

Scenarios are today mainly represented as more or less highly structured text. They are also sometimes represented as storyboards, sequence diagrams and flowcharts, and

Scenarios, Stories, Use Cases: Through the Systems Development Life-Cycle. Edited by Ian F Alexander and Neil Maiden
© 2004 John Wiley & Sons, Ltd. ISBN: 0-470-86194-0

less often as films, acted scenes, tape recordings, sequences of maps, and other audio-visual forms.

There is a broad scope of possible investigations that could help show how we should be using scenarios in different circumstances. How should we tailor our choice of representation according to domain? to stakeholders? to project type? We simply don't know, and we'd like to.

A wider issue revolves around incompatibility of models of different aspects of a wanted system: if you draw a flowchart to define a scenario of interaction, a state-chart to define the corresponding internal system states, a message sequence diagram to define the timing and nature of messages between software objects, and a class diagram to define the relationships of those objects, how do you check that the definitions represented in these diverse ways are consistent, or even use them together to generate code? As a footnote to those questions, if scenarios are to be represented more analytically to suit such development purposes, can they remain useful for communication with stakeholders?

PROCESS

There are several mutually incompatible scenario-based system development processes described in this book, and several other techniques that might fit into a range of different business processes. We do not today know how scenarios can best support processes of innovation, of negotiation, of validation, or of management of product families. For that matter, how well do they support business processes themselves, and all the modelling, improvement, and re-engineering activities beloved of business analysts and process improvement people?

We have a hunch—supported by preliminary findings and experiences—that scenarios might be very useful in all these areas.

For instance, scenarios might be used to index features or requirements for reuse across a product line. They permit a suitable end-to-end description of problems, and they have the potential to remain stable while technologies come and go. We hope that the reuse of requirements will soon advance well beyond the rudimentary steps that have been taken so far.

As another example, it's already clear that a scenario-directed search for exceptions is easier to conduct and more effective than a relatively undifferentiated analysis based on requirements (Alexander 2000). The same seems to apply in more specialised areas such as safety, where Functional Hazard Analysis, pioneered by Karen Allenby and Tim Kelly, promises to extend the power of traditional Failure Modes and Effects Analysis (FMEA) and similar techniques (Allenby and Kelly 2001).

Similarly, scenario modelling in the form of misuse case analysis may be a useful addition to the tool chest of facilitators of trade-off and negotiation workshops (see Ian Alexander's description of this technique and a case study of its application in Chapters 7 and 18). The technique may also be helpful in identifying threat-handling business processes, such as security checks to combat money-laundering and fraud, controls on credit, and monitoring of transactions (Regev, Alexander and Wegmann 2004). But there is very little evidence for this as yet.

There are probably many other ways in which scenarios may turn out to be useful in business and system development process work.

DOMAIN KNOWLEDGE

Numerous 'different' disciplines today work on modelling business domains: operational analysis, business process modelling, business analysis, requirements engineering, contextual design, knowledge management—to name just a few. All of these must (if they are doing anything useful at all) be constructing more or less standardised scenarios describing what people (need to) do in different domains.

How can these diverse and conflicting approaches be unified, if at all? How should scenarios best be applied in different domains? How far can techniques be generalised? We do not know. In this book, we have asked chapter authors to try to say how domain-specific or generally applicable they believe their techniques to be, and why. They have all been admirably frank in their replies, but there is clearly still much to learn.

COTS

It is no secret that Commercial-Off-The-Shelf (COTS) software and hardware products are steadily encroaching on the preserves of custom development. Today, no one in their right mind would develop their own database or network protocol, yet it is only in the last decade that these things have become universally accepted (and cheap) commodities.

COTS products solve some problems (like record indexing and sharing, transaction handling, file transfer) essentially perfectly; but they raise many more. Developers are familiar with the practical issues of wrestling with imperfect documentation, software bugs, and arrogant manufacturers. The challenges for requirements and specification are just as acute. For instance, it seems pointless to write requirements that you know will be handled by COTS products ('*The spreadsheet shall be able to multiply two 32-bit floating point numbers*'), but equally it could be disastrous not to specify what facilities you need. Can scenarios be used conveniently to describe overall behaviour without going into too much detail on the obvious, while giving enough detail on the problematic parts and interfaces to guide design and testing? How should COTS-integration projects be specified? One of the few pieces of published work on the subject (Gregor, Hutson and Oresky 2002) describes using Storyboards to define requirements for COTS integration. Its focus on the user interface is natural and helpful but is clearly useful mostly for software products, and leaves many interesting questions unanswered.

DISSEMINATION

We are very glad to be able to include an account written specially for this volume (Chapter 23) by Mary Beth Rosson and John Carroll on teaching students how to use scenarios well. But there are wider issues such as of the dissemination of scenario knowledge gathered by researchers, of training and certification in scenario usage and in special skills such as facilitation (see Ellen Gottesdiener's description of her Use Case workshop technique in Chapter 5).

The UML with its Use Cases, sequence charts, and activity diagrams (to name just one example—and three different scenario notations) has a strong industrial bias, and probably a software bias too. We have worked hard to give this book some sort of balance between research and industry, between large and small applications, between domains, and between hardware and software. Needless to say, this was only partially possible. There is a clear need for practitioners who know the field in a cross-disciplinary way. Few such people exist today, for several reasons: the current 'heads-down, no books, no courses, no conferences' attitude in industry, and the equivalent pressure on academics to secure reliable sources of funding rather than risking cross-disciplinary approaches, leaves no vehicle for dissemination of good practice. Scenarios are taught as part of software engineering or as part of human–machine interaction studies. They are used in process modelling and rapid/agile development methods in industry. But they are rarely seen as something bigger, understood as something more than the preserve of technicians, and applied consistently in problem solving at all levels. It will take far more than technical research programmes, no matter how elegant, to make scenarios as well understood and as widely applied as they ought to be.

SUMMARY

Any reader who imagined that this book, long as it is, might contain definitive answers and rules for scenario usage will have been sadly disappointed. We hope we have succeeded in painting a picture of the current state of the art of scenario-based engineering and system development. But many exciting challenges remain, both for academic researchers and for adventurous industrial practitioners. Perhaps this book, and these concluding chapters, may help to guide and stimulate some readers to investigate further. There is much to be done, and any well-planned and practical investigations or trials are almost bound to be interesting and useful.

REFERENCES

Alexander, I., Scenario-driven search finds more exceptions, *Requirements Engineering Process Workshop (REP 2000)*, Greenwich; *Proceedings of the 11th International Workshop on Database and Expert System Applications*, IEEE, September 4–8, 2000, pp. 991–994.

Allenby, K. and Kelly, T., Deriving safety requirements using scenarios, *Proceedings of the 5th International Symposium on Requirements Engineering*, Toronto, Canada, August 27–31, 2001, pp. 228–235.

Gregor, S., Hutson, J., and Oresky, C., Storyboard process to assist in requirements verification and adaptation to capabilities inherent in COTS, in J. Dean and A. Gravel (Eds.), *COTS-Based Software Systems*, Lecture Notes in Computer Science, Springer; *Proceedings of the First International Conference, ICCBSS 2002*, Orlando, FL, February 4–6, 2002.

Regev, G., Alexander, I., and Wegmann, A., Modelling the regulative role of business processes with use and misuse cases, *Business Process Management Journal*, 2005; to appear.

SCENARIO-BASED SYSTEM DEVELOPMENT TEMPLATES

Ian Alexander

This Appendix provides document templates for:

1. Mission and Objectives
2. Stakeholder Analysis
3. Use Cases
4. Non-Functional Requirements
5. Test Cases

The templates may freely be copied and applied on projects, provided they are used as instructed, and provided that the copyright and source are acknowledged on each copy. They must not be sold or hired out.

The templates are believed to be suitable as a basis for simple projects, but they may need to be adapted for specialised projects and development approaches.

They are provided for free download at http://www.scenarioplus.org.uk

Scenarios, Stories, Use Cases: Through the Systems Development Life-Cycle. Edited by Ian F Alexander and Neil Maiden
© 2004 John Wiley & Sons, Ltd. ISBN: 0-470-86194-0

Appendix 1.1: Mission and Objectives Template

Ian Alexander

This document provides a standardised set of headings to document the top-level goals, often called the Project Mission and Objectives, in any style of project documentation.

Use of Copyright Material

This template may freely be copied and applied on projects, provided it is used as instructed, and provided that its copyright and source are acknowledged. It must not be sold or hired out.

1.   Project Mission

1.1   Project Sponsor / Champion

Identify the person, probably in a position of power, who has openly stated that he/she intends to champion the project right through to completion. The sponsor / champion need not be involved in day-to-day management of the project, but must be determined that it shall succeed, be willing to fight for it when necessary, and have the ability to obtain the necessary resources (e.g. money, staff, test facilities, etc) to ensure its success. They must also be likely to stay in the organisation for the duration of the project.

The Project Sponsor / Champion is ....

(name, job title, department, contact details)

1.2   Mission Statement

Write a sentence defining the single central thing that the project, system, or product in question must accomplish. This is also the basic criterion as to whether the project has been successful.
    For example,

> *"The mission of the RuriSportBike project is:"*
> *"To become the market leader in sporting bicycles in Ruritania."*

 The mission must be brief, clear, and realistic. It must be verifiable, that is, you would know if you had achieved it (e.g. you know have 31% of the Ruritanian bicycle market).

The mission of the .... **project is:**

To ....

2.   Business Objectives

Write one sentence for each business objective, that is, each key purpose of the project, system, or product in question. A high-level requirement is only an objective if it is a defining feature, that is, that a successful result could not exist without it. Only a few of a project's mandatory requirements are really central to its being.

It is allowed to have more than one objective, but if there are multiple objectives they must not conflict. However, there should not be too many objectives or focus will be lost.

For example,

"To develop an attractive sporting bicycle that we can produce locally."
"To set up an effective bicycle production facility."
"To set up an effective national bicycle sales & distribution network."

Objectives must be brief, clear, and realistic (within the limits of budget, time, skill, geography and other relevant resources). Objectives must be verifiable, that is, it must be possible to know whether or not you have attained each objective.

Each objective should be owned by a named stakeholder, who will be responsible for achieving it within the framework of the project.

2.1   Objective 1

To ....

Owner: .... *(name, contact details)*

2.2   Objective 2

To ....

Owner: .... *(name, contact details)*

2.3   Objective 3

To ....

Owner: .... *(name, contact details)*

3.   Initial SWOT Analysis

Briefly and honestly list the main factors that will affect the success of the project, under the following headings.

3.1   Strengths

List the factors favouring the project compared to its rivals, past projects, and so on.

3.2   Weakness Analysis

3.2.1   Weaknesses

List the internal factors such as shortage of funding, staff turnover, skill shortage, and so on, working against the project.

3.2.2   Remedies

State for each identified weakness how you intend to remedy the weakness so that the project can succeed. Remedies must be realistic, that is, they must be capable of resolving the problems and they must be achievable within the resources of the project.

3.3   Opportunities

List the external factors such as the state of the market that would be beneficial if the project were to succeed.

3.4   Threat Analysis

3.4.1   Threats

List the external factors such as changing technology, rivals, internal opposition, and so on, that could threaten the success of the project.

3.4.2   Mitigations

State for each identified threat how you intend to mitigate or prevent the threat from causing harm. Mitigations must be realistic, that is, they must be capable of neutralising the threats and they must be achievable within the budget, timescale, skill and the other actual resources to hand.

Appendix 1.2: A Stakeholder Template

Ian Alexander

1. Project Stakeholders

This document provides a standardised set of headings for use when analysing stakeholders in any style of project documentation. This first section illustrates the structure and gives an example of its use. The second section offers some guidelines. The third section is the template.

1.1 Example 'Onion-Rings' Stakeholder Diagram

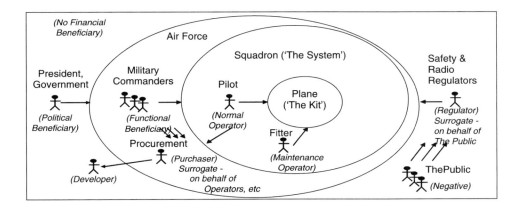

A Typical Set of Stakeholder Roles

The Onion-Rings Diagram offers a simple way of visualising a set of stakeholder roles on a project. A free tool to create and manage onion diagrams and associated stakeholder information in the DOORS requirements tool environment is available from http://www.scenarioplus.org.uk

The centre is always the equipment ('kit', 'product') in question.

The system or 'work' is always larger than the equipment—in particular, it includes the people who play operational roles, such as the pilots and fitters who carry out normal and maintenance operations on an aircraft. Systems also normally include operational procedures, training manuals and other information as well as the equipment.

Many systems also include maintenance and training kit, such as simulators and automated test equipment, and it is important to determine whether these are inside or outside the work boundary.

Outside the work boundary lie the direct beneficiaries of the work. These include those who immediately benefit from the functions carried out by the system (including the operators and the kit). Usually these beneficiaries are different from the operators, but sometimes these roles can be combined, as with home entertainment products such as music players where the operator is also often the person benefiting from using the product.

Further out still are people who are affected indirectly, either deriving benefits such as political gains or financial rewards (e.g. through shareholdings), or suffering harm (having negative stakes) such as the impact of noise, pollution, electromagnetic radiation, loss of amenity, or loss of work.

Roles often involve an element of surrogacy. For example,

- Regulators are typically appointed by government or industry to act as informed surrogates for the public. For example, a health and safety authority monitors and controls industry to ensure practice conforms to standards, and hence minimises risk to both operators and the public. As another example, the international radio regulator creates a framework of rules and assigns radio frequencies to different purposes, so as to minimise electromagnetic interference.
- Purchasing / procurement is generally carried out by a department distinct from operations, and essentially on behalf of both operational and beneficiary roles, whether or not those roles exist at the time the procurement is made.

Surrogate opinions are important, but they are not necessarily equivalent to the views of the people they claim to represent. For instance, it is dangerous for requirements engineers to assume that the viewpoint of a manager corresponds to those of the people—for example maintenance operators—being managed.

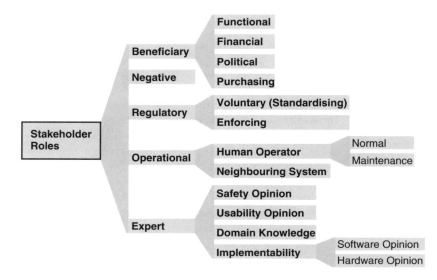

A Simple Classification of Stakeholder Roles

1.2   An Extensible Hierarchy

The purpose of this approach to stakeholder analysis is to help projects pay more effective attention to the roles and viewpoints involved. All domains are different, but some features of stakeholder structure are essentially similar everywhere.

This hierarchy is meant to be extended on specific projects and in specific domains, by splitting (i.e. specialising) the categories to make them easy to understand and to apply.

For example, in the Railway domain, Normal Operators include Train Driver, Line Controller, Station Controller (depending on the specific system you are considering), while Maintenance Operator in general means Asset Maintainer, which can be specialised into Train Maintainer, Track Maintainer, Lift/Escalator Maintainer, and so on.

2.   Guidelines

2.1   Stakeholder Analysis

Fill in the template for your project, using it as a set of general hints to help you discover the key roles and individuals playing those roles. Add table rows for additional stakeholders. Document stakeholders' actual names and their personal viewpoints on the project; if need be, document their roles in more detail, and record their job titles, departments and other clues to their involvement on the project.

Pay special attention to anomalies:

- if any positive role is filled by more than one stakeholder or group of stakeholders, there may be conflicting viewpoints on your project. Take care to discover the different viewpoints, and plan for conflict resolution workshops or other preventative measures. For example, if the Purchasing role is split (procurement is split across more than one agency) then you must ensure there will not be constant debate on acceptance criteria, and so on.

- if any role is unfilled on your project, there may be hidden requirements that will not be discovered until late in the project.

- if people are reluctant to discuss an area, this may be because it is known to be dangerous within the organisation. Take care to understand the cause, and find out what kinds of risk it poses to your project.

- if some people say a role is important and some say it is not, this is always significant. Acknowledge the different viewpoints, remain neutral, and make clear that you are collecting viewpoints from all affected stakeholders.

If you find the template does not exactly match the needs of your project—as is likely—then add roles or otherwise modify the template to reflect reality more accurately.

2.2   Tool Support

The template can be used directly to analyse stakeholder roles and viewpoints using only a word processing tool, and this immediately provides benefit through increased clarity and reduced risk to the project.

However, where there are many requirements, frequent changes, large or distributed teams, and long projects, word processing alone is not sufficient to manage all the project information, and especially not the traces or links between items such as goals, viewpoints, requirements, and tests essential to ensure that stakeholders get what they need.

Such projects should select a requirements management tool (such as DOORS, Slate, Cradle, Requisite Pro, etc) to enable project engineers to create, maintain, and receive the benefit of a complete and consistent view of project information.

2.3 Use of Copyright Material

This template may freely be copied and applied on projects, provided it is used as instructed, and provided that its copyright and source are acknowledged. It must not be sold or hired out.

3. Stakeholder Roles

3.1 Beneficiary

3.1.1 Functional Beneficiary

Stakeholder:	Viewpoint:
John Smith	*wants to see accurate weekly and monthly sales figures and forecasts*

3.1.2 Financial Beneficiary

Stakeholder:	Viewpoint:

3.1.3 Political Beneficiary

Stakeholder:	Viewpoint:

3.1.4 Purchasing

Stakeholder:	Viewpoint:

3.2 Negative

Stakeholder:	Viewpoint:

3.3 Regulatory

3.3.1 Voluntary (Standardising)

Stakeholder:	Viewpoint:

3.3.2 Enforcing

Stakeholder:	Viewpoint:

3.4 Operational Roles

3.4.1 Human Operators

3.4.1.1 Normal

Stakeholder:	Viewpoint:

3.4.1.2 Maintenance

Stakeholder:	Viewpoint:

3.4.2 Neighbouring Systems

Stakeholder:	Viewpoint:

3.5 Expert

3.5.1 Safety Opinion

Stakeholder:	Viewpoint:

3.5.2 Usability Opinion

Stakeholder:	Viewpoint:

3.5.3 Domain Knowledge *(divide this into sub-domains if appropriate)*

Stakeholder:	Viewpoint:

3.5.4 Implementability

3.5.4.1 Software Opinion

Stakeholder:	Viewpoint:

3.5.4.2 Hardware Opinion

Stakeholder:	Viewpoint:

Appendix 1.3: Use Case Templates

Ian Alexander

This appendix is a set of templates for different styles of Use Case. Similar templates can be generated automatically by Scenario Plus (http://www.scenarioplus.org.uk) in a DOORS environment; online versions of the templates are provided in a range of file formats on the Scenario Plus website for free downloading. The templates can be used in essentially any software tool that provides document, spreadsheet, or database-like facilities. Paradoxically the most limiting tools for the purpose are those mainly graphical tools that are intended for editing use case and other software specification models.

The values that each attribute can take in columns 4 to 7 are listed in the Introduction. Values are expected only once per Use Case.

Use of Copyright Material

This template may freely be copied and applied on projects, provided it is used as instructed, and provided that its copyright and source are acknowledged. It must not be sold or hired out.

ID	Use Case Headings & Text	Actor	Use Case Level	Use Case Span	Use Case Scope	Review Status
UC-1	**1. 1 Introduction** This document contains requirements organised as use cases.		*Overview*	*Organisation Black-Box*	*Out of Scope*	*Draft*
UC-2	**1.1 Actors** This section lists human and other actors with roles in the use cases.		*High*	*Organisation White-Box*	*In Scope*	*Proposed*
UC-3	**1.1.1 Unnamed Actor**		*Surface*	*System Black-Box*		*Accepted*
UC-4	**1.2 Definitions**		*Low*	*System White-Box*		*Rejected*
UC-5	**1.2.1 Unnamed Term to be defined**		*Too Detailed*	*Component*		*On Hold*
UC-6	**1.3 References**			—		*Completed*
UC-7	**1.3.1 Unnamed Document**			—		

ID	Use Case Headings & Text	Actor	Use Case Level	Use Case Span	Use Case Scope	Review Status
UC-8	**2. Requirements (Use Cases)** This chapter lists use cases, grouped into diagrams. Included Use Case names are underlined.			—		
UC-9	**2.1 Unnamed Use Case Diagram** This section represents one use case diagram. It lists use cases with associated information.			—		
UC-11	**2.1.1 'Minimal Sketch' Use Case**		Surface	System Black-Box	In Scope	Draft
UC-12	**2.1.1.1 Primary Scenario**			—		
UC-13	Undefined Step			—		
UC-14	Undefined Step			—		
UC-15	Undefined Step			—		
UC-16	**2.1.2 'Branching Paths' Use Case**		Surface	System Black-Box	In Scope	Draft
UC-17	**2.1.2.1 Primary Scenario**			—		
UC-18	Undefined Step			—		
UC-26	Undefined Step			—		
UC-19	**2.1.2.2 Alternative Paths**			—		
UC-20	2.1.2.2.1 Unnamed Alternative Path			—		
UC-21	Undefined Step			—		
UC-28	Undefined Step			—		
UC-32	Undefined Step			—		
UC-22	**2.1.2.3 Exceptions**			—		
UC-23	2.1.2.3.1 Unnamed Exception			—		
UC-24	Undefined Step			—		
UC-30	Undefined Step			—		
UC-34	Undefined Step			—		
UC-35	**2.1.3 'Fully-Dressed' Use Case**		Surface	System Black-Box	In Scope	Draft

ID	Use Case Headings & Text	Actor	Use Case Level	Use Case Span	Use Case Scope	Review Status
UC-36	**2.1.3.1 Primary Scenario**			—		
UC-37	Undefined Step			—		
UC-64	Undefined Step			—		
UC-63	Undefined Step			—		
UC-38	**2.1.3.2 Alternative Paths**			—		
UC-39	2.1.3.2.1 Unnamed Alternative Path			—		
UC-40	Undefined Step			—		
UC-66	Undefined Step			—		
UC-65	Undefined Step			—		
UC-41	**2.1.3.3 Exceptions**			—		
UC-42	2.1.3.3.1 Unnamed Exception			—		
UC-43	Undefined Step			—		
UC-68	Undefined Step			—		
UC-67	Undefined Step			—		
UC-44	**2.1.3.4 Trigger**			—		
UC-45	—			—		
UC-46	**2.1.3.5 Preconditions**			—		
UC-47	—			—		
UC-69	—			—		
UC-48	**2.1.3.6 Stakeholders and Interests**			—		
UC-49	—			—		
UC-71	—			—		
UC-70	—			—		
UC-50	**2.1.3.7 Minimal Guarantees**			—		
UC-51	—			—		
UC-72	—			—		
UC-52	**2.1.3.8 Success Guarantees**			—		
UC-53	—			—		
UC-73	—			—		
UC-54	**2.1.3.9 Constraints**			—		

ID	Use Case Headings & Text	Actor	Use Case Level	Use Case Span	Use Case Scope	Review Status
UC-55	—			—		
UC-74	—			—		
UC-56	**2.1.3.10 Non-Functional Requirements**			—		
UC-57	—			—		
UC-76	—			—		
UC-75	—			—		
UC-78	**2.1.4 'Conflict Analysis' Use Case**		Surface	System Black-Box	In Scope	Draft
UC-79	**2.1.4.1 Primary Scenario**			—		
UC-80	Undefined Step			—		
UC-87	Undefined Step			—		
UC-86	Undefined Step			—		
UC-81	**2.1.4.2 Relationships** *(these are in addition to the normal Includes and Has Exception relationships, which should be documented in the main body of the Use Case)*			—		
UC-82	2.1.4.2.1 Conflicts With			—		
UC-94	*(this Use Case makes it impossible or more difficult to achieve the goal of the named Use Case)*			—		
UC-83	—			—		
UC-84	2.1.4.2.2 Aggravates			—		
UC-95	*(this Use Case makes more serious (or more likely to succeed) the hostile goal of the named Misuse Case)*			—		
UC-85	—			—		
UC-88	2.1.4.2.3 Threatens			—		
UC-96	*(this Misuse Case makes it more difficult to achieve the goal of the named Use Case)*			—		
UC-89	—			—		

ID	Use Case Headings & Text	Actor	Use Case Level	Use Case Span	Use Case Scope	Review Status
UC-90	2.1.4.2.4 Mitigates			—		
UC-97	*(this Use Case prevents or makes less serious the hostile goal of the named Misuse Case)*			—		
UC-91	—					
UC-92	2.1.4.2.5 Supports			—		
UC-98	*(this Use Case has the side-effect of enhancing the beneficial effects of the goal of the named Use Case) (Note: where a Use Case simply contributes to achieving another Use Case, use the ordinary Includes relationship)*			—		
UC-93	—					
UC-10	### 3. Global Non-Functional Requirements This chapter lists NFRs and constraints that apply to the entire system.			—		
UC-77	*Note: see the NFR Template for guidance on how to structure this chapter.*			—		

Appendix 1.4: Non-Functional Requirements Template

Introduction

Non-Functional Requirements Template

This template is a hierarchy of headings that we find helpfully suggestive of questions to ask our clients when putting specifications together, annotated with suggestions as to how each category of Non-Functional Requirements (NFRs) may be verified—for many NFRs are difficult to test, and testing is often an inappropriate verification approach for them.

You will certainly need to customise both the list of NFRs and the associated Verification Approach to suit your kind of system. However, it may be a useful antidote to software-only thinking: even software houses have to ensure their computers and networks have compatible connectors.

The Verification Approach in particular must be thought through for each specific project as the effort necessary is a function of the criticality of the system to your business, whether safety is involved, and not least the particular characteristics of your domain. The suggestions are meant to be generally applicable but this cannot be guaranteed.

For many engineering systems, the NFRs form a much larger part of the specifications than the behaviour (functions and performance) does. Once you have customised the template you will find that it saves you a lot of effort when you start a project.

Acknowledgements

This template was originally developed for project use in discussions with Andrew Farncombe. It has been revised in the light of work done by Don Firesmith at the SEI, and of course it is part of a wider body of work to make NFRs more tractable by INCOSE, the RESG and others.

Use of Copyright Material

This template may freely be copied and applied on projects, provided it is used as instructed, and provided that its copyright and source are acknowledged. It must not be sold or hired out.

1. **Non-Functional Requirements** (suggestions for a typical engineering project)	**Verification Approach** (suggestions for a typical project)
1.1 Interfaces	Interfaces are generally verifiable by direct test, preferably fully automated.
1.1.1 Incoming	Functional Test
1.1.2 Outgoing	Functional Test

1.1.3	**Physical Connectors**	Inspection
1.2	**Constraints on Design and Implementation**	
1.2.1	**Hardware & Software Design Constraints**	
1.2.1.1	**Software**	Inspection; automated check of headers, syntax, and so on
1.2.1.2	**Hardware**	Inspection; Manufacturer's product datasheets
1.2.1.3	**Electronic Components**	Inspection; Manufacturer's product datasheets
1.2.1.4	**Construction**	Inspection
1.2.2	**Regulations**	Certificate of Compliance from Regulatory Authorities; Legal Opinion
1.2.3	**Human Factors**	*Human factors are notoriously variable and subjective; test is possible but may need to use a statistical sample of users.*
1.2.3.1	**Operator Interface**	Design Review; Statement of Compliance (to standards); Inspection; Functional Test
1.2.3.2	**Maintenance Training**	Inspection of Training Materials / Plans; Demonstration.
1.2.3.3	**Documentation**	Inspection of User Manual, Reference Manual, Operating Procedures, and so on.
1.2.4	**Environmental**	
1.2.4.1	**Mechanical Environment**	
1.2.4.1.1	Shock & Vibration	Laboratory Test; Field Trials
1.2.4.1.2	Transportation and Packaging	Inspection; Laboratory Test; Packaging Manufacturer's product certificate; Field Trials
1.2.4.1.3	Dirt and Contamination	Laboratory Test; Inspection
1.2.4.1.4	Temperature Range	Laboratory Test; Field Trials
1.2.4.1.5	Water Resistance	Laboratory Test; Field Trials
1.2.4.1.6	Corrosion Resistance	Laboratory Test; Field Trials
1.2.4.2	**Electrical Environment**	
1.2.4.2.1	Power Supply	Inspection; Manufacturer's product certificate

1.2.4.2.2 ElectroMagnetic Compatibility	
1.2.4.2.2.1 ElectroMagnetic Susceptibility	Design Review; Laboratory Test
1.2.4.2.2.2 ElectroMagnetic Emissions	Certificate from Regulatory Authorities
1.2.4.3 Physical Emissions	
1.2.4.3.1 Noise	Test
1.2.4.3.2 Polluting Materials	Test
1.2.4.3.3 Other Emissions for example Heat, Vibration	Test
1.2.5 Physical	
1.2.5.1 Mechanical Construction	Design Review; Inspection
1.2.5.2 Material Safety	Design Review; Laboratory Test
1.2.5.3 Size and Dimensions	Design Review; Inspection
1.2.5.4 Weight	Design Review (Mass Budget); Inspection
1.2.5.5 Finish, Colour, and Labelling	
1.2.5.5.1 Finish	Inspection; Laboratory Test
1.2.5.5.2 Colour	Inspection
1.2.5.5.3 Identification Labelling/Signage	Inspection
1.3 Development Qualities Support for Initial and Ongoing Development	
1.3.1 Reusability	
1.3.1.1 Compliance with Standards Standardisation of interfaces, protocols, etc	Design Review; Functional Test; Certificates from Regulatory Authorities
1.3.1.2 Commonality Use of components shared across product line, Commercial Off The Shelf (COTS) components, and so on	Design Review
1.3.2 Upgradability	Design Review
1.3.3 Scalability	Design Review
1.3.4 Modifiability	Design Review
1.3.5 Portability	Design Review
1.3.6 Testability	Design Review; Functional Test

1.4 Usage Qualities	Qualities are especially difficult to test. Careful planning is vital for adequate verification.
1.4.1 Dependability During Operational Life	Analysis of results of verification of Availability, Security, Safety
1.4.1.1 Availability	Design Review; Analysis of results of verification of Reliability, Maintainability, and so on
1.4.1.1.1 Reliability	Design Review; Reliability Analysis (using manufacturer's product datasheets); Reliability History; Accelerated Testing
1.4.1.1.2 Maintainability (Hardware)	
1.4.1.1.2.1 Supportability & Integrated Logistic Support	Design Review
1.4.1.1.2.2 Accessibility	Design Review; Functional Test
1.4.1.1.2.3 Self-Diagnosability	Design Review; Functional Test
1.4.1.1.3 Storage & Shelf Life	Design Review; Test where appropriate
1.4.1.2 Safety	Safety Case; Functional Test where appropriate; Certificate from Standards Body / Industry Regulator
1.4.1.2.1 Safety to Health	,,
1.4.1.2.2 Safety to Property	,,
1.4.1.2.3 Safety to Environment for example Toxicity and Disposability	,,
1.4.1.3 Security	Design Review; Functional Test where appropriate; Red Team Trials
1.4.1.4 Survivability	Design Review; Simulation; Functional Test where appropriate.
1.4.2 Performance	
1.4.2.1 Capacity	Design Review; Test
1.4.2.2 Rate (Speed)	Statistical Test
1.4.2.3 Endurance	Statistical Test
1.4.2.4 Accuracy	Statistical Test
1.4.2.5 Latency and Response Time	Statistical Test
1.4.2.6 Efficiency Minimisation of consumption of resources	Test

1.4.3 **Operational Qualities**	
1.4.3.1 **Installability**	Design Review; Inspection of Installation Instructions; Functional Test
1.4.3.2 **Configurability**	Design Review; Functional Test
1.4.3.3 **Operability**	Design Review; Functional Test
1.4.3.4 **Tolerance of Human Variability**	
1.4.3.4.1 Accessibility to the Disabled	Design Review; Functional Test
1.4.3.4.2 Adjustability For people of different sizes, preferences, etc	Design Review; Functional Test
1.4.3.4.3 Internationalisability Configurability to different languages, character sets	Design Review; Functional Test
1.4.3.4.4 Adaptivity Ability to adapt to the human operator.	Design Review; Functional Test
1.4.3.5 **Transportability**	Design Review; Functional Test
1.5 **Programme Requirements**	
1.5.1 **Development Requirements**	Review
1.5.2 **Test Requirements**	
1.5.2.1 **Test Approach**	Review
1.5.2.2 **Special to Purpose Test Equipment**	Review; Test
1.5.2.3 **Simulators**	Review; Test
1.5.2.4 **Trials & Parallel Operations**	Review
1.5.3 **Programme Constraints**	
1.5.3.1 **Costs**	Review
1.5.3.2 **Timescales**	Review
1.5.3.3 **Other Resources**	Review

Appendix 1.5: Test Case Templates

Ian Alexander

This is a set of templates for a range of common kinds of test case, based rather directly on use cases (see Appendix 1-3 Use Case Templates).

They are simple, frequently occurring patterns or idioms in scenario-based systems engineering. They are not all necessarily required on all projects, but it is likely that most projects will need to use most of them.

In the (simple) view taken here, test cases are purely sequential, straight-line scenarios. It is true that some software test tools, for example, can automatically navigate a tree structure and test all the paths it defines. But firstly, doing so is equivalent to running a set of simple sequential test cases; and secondly, the automated rules for navigating such a tree need to cater for the test case patterns described here, because sometimes you need to do things twice to be reasonably sure the system is working properly. (Issues of concurrency and non-determinism due to multi-threading are another matter entirely.)

The test case structures can act as hints as to the kinds of test that you should be constructing, based on the pattern of use cases that you have in your projects. They effectively ask you certain questions about the completeness of your verification approach, such as 'do you know whether such-and-such a function would be restored after a reset?'

Use of Copyright Material

This set of templates may freely be copied and applied on projects, provided it is used as instructed, and provided that its copyright and source are acknowledged. It must not be sold or hired out.

1. Functional / Performance Tests

For each Use Case:

a) Set up the required preconditions

   (Note: this may mean creating a set of similar tests, varying one environmental condition e.g. temperature, vibration, or humidity at a time.)

b) Set up any needed performance monitoring equipment

c) Run the entire normal course / 'happy day' scenario

d) Check that the expected normal result is obtained

e) Check that the performance target is met.

2. Stress Tests

For each Use Case that can be run as a transaction (or group of such Use Cases that can form a mix of transactions) to be performed many times / in parallel within the system:

a) Set up the required preconditions

b) Set up any needed performance monitoring equipment

c) Set up any needed stress-load simulator / equipment

d) Run the entire normal course / 'happy day' scenario as many times / in parallel as required to stress the system

e) Check that the stress target is met.

3. Stopping Tests (for Faults, Security Threats, Safety Hazards)

For each System Fault, Security Threat or Misuse Case, or Safety-related Hazard corresponding to an Exception Event which should cause the system to Stop safely:

a) Set up the required preconditions

b) Set up the required test equipment, simulator, fault injector, and so on

c) Run the normal course / 'happy day' scenario starting from its beginning

d) Inject the threatened event / fault condition (or simulate it)

e) Check that the correct Exception-handling scenario is executed

f) Check that the system stops safely.

If appropriate:

g) Reset the system manually in accordance with standard operating procedure

h) Run the entire normal course / 'happy day' scenario again

i) Check that the normal result is obtained.

4. Recovery Tests (for Faults, Security Threats, Safety Hazards)

For each System Fault, Security Threat or Misuse Case, or Safety-related Hazard corresponding to an Exception Event from which the system is expected to Recover:

a) Set up the required preconditions

b) Set up the required test equipment, simulator, fault injector, and so on

c) Run the normal course / 'happy day' scenario starting from its beginning

d) Inject the threatened event / fault condition (or simulate it)

e) Check that the correct Exception-handling scenario is executed
f) Run the rest of the normal course to completion
g) Check that the normal result is obtained
h) Run the entire normal course / 'happy day' scenario again
i) Check that the normal result is again obtained.

EXERCISES

Ian Alexander

*These exercises are provided to enable readers to get started on their own with a little prac-
tice in simple scenario-based development techniques. They use the Templates supplied in
Appendix 1 (available online at* http://www.scenarioplus.org.uk). *Suggested answers are
provided in Appendix 3. Academic institutions are welcome to copy these exercises for
students' use, provided the source and copyright are acknowledged on each copy.*

1. Context

*You are developing a new Wash-Wipe system to be used in a range of medium to large
passenger cars including a saloon, an estate, a jeep and a cabriolet version. The cars
will be sold all over the world including regions such as Scandinavia, mainland Europe,
the Arabian Gulf, and South-East Asia. The environment in these regions includes arctic
(winter temperatures down to −40°C), desert (summer temperatures up to 50°C; winter
sandstorms), and monsoon (100% humidity; temperatures up to 35°C; precipitation up
to 50 mm/hour) climates. Both left- and right-hand drive versions are required to cater
for the countries involved. The jeep and the estate will be used on- and off-road, are
subjected to intense vibration off-road, and may become very muddy. In all the versions,
driver comfort and simplicity of operation have high priority, second only to safety.*

2. Mission

Write a Mission Statement for the Wash-Wipe System, using the Mission and Objectives
Template (Appendix 1-1).

3. Stakeholders

List the Stakeholders for the Wash-Wipe System, using the Stakeholders Template as a
guide (Appendix 1-2).

Scenarios, Stories, Use Cases: Through the Systems Development Life-Cycle. Edited by Ian F Alexander and Neil Maiden
© 2004 John Wiley & Sons, Ltd. ISBN: 0-470-86194-0

4. Use Case Sketches

Document the main Use Cases for the Wash-Wipe System using the 'Minimal Sketch' Use Case Template (Appendix 1-3).

5. Exceptions

List the main Exceptions for the Wash-Wipe System, using the 'Branching Paths' Use Case Template (also in Appendix 1-3).

6. NFRs

List the key Interfaces and Usage Qualities for the Wash-Wipe System, using the relevant parts of the NFR Template as a guide (Appendix 1-4).

7. Test Approach Sketch

Sketch the structure of your test approach for the Wash-Wipe System using the Test Case Template as a guide (Appendix 1-5). Limit the detail you provide to naming the Test Cases and indicating briefly any special resources (such as simulators or test equipment) you would need to run the tests.

Additional Project: Revisit your Use Cases and Exceptions, and document additional branches suggested by considering your Test Approach.

ANSWERS TO EXERCISES

Ian Alexander

This appendix offers some possible answers to the Exercises of Appendix 2. Given the very brief sketch of the system context, these can be no more than plausible suggestions—they are certainly not definitive. If you study the problems carefully you should be able to refine these answers and add more detail.

1. Mission

To maintain safe visibility through the windscreen(s).

More specifically: to clear rain, drizzle, snow, hail, or mud from the windscreen, quickly and reliably enough to maintain visibility, for all the car versions in all the expected climates.

2. Stakeholders

Beneficiary

Functional Beneficiary

Stakeholder:	Viewpoint:
Driver	wants comfortable, safe, impressive car
Other Road User	wants not to be injured (by drivers who can't see clearly)

Financial Beneficiary

Stakeholder:	Viewpoint:
Board, Shareholder	want to minimise risk; want good Return on Investment (RoI).

Scenarios, Stories, Use Cases: Through the Systems Development Life-Cycle. Edited by Ian F Alexander and Neil Maiden
© 2004 John Wiley & Sons, Ltd. ISBN: 0-470-86194-0

Political Beneficiary

Stakeholder:	Viewpoint:
Global Marketing Director	wants to show other board members that Global Marketing understands the market and deserves high position on board

Purchasing

Stakeholder:	Viewpoint:
Product Manager	wants new car versions rolled out on time, to budget

Negative

Stakeholder:	Viewpoint:
Other Directors	doubtful about Global Marketing
Environmental Activist	wants to reduce pollution, off-road driving

Regulatory

Voluntary (Standardising)

Stakeholder:	Viewpoint:
Auto Industry Standards body	wants to promote high standards of manufacture

Enforcing

Stakeholder:	Viewpoint:
EU / other safety regulators	want cars to comply with national laws

Operational Roles

Human Operators

Normal

Stakeholder:	Viewpoint:
Driver	wants operation to be intuitive, similar to other cars (of the same make), and effective

Maintenance

Stakeholder:	Viewpoint:
Mechanic	wants system to be quick to diagnose and to fix

Neighbouring Systems

Stakeholder:	Viewpoint:
Door/Window Management	not soak passengers
Power Management	conserve battery power for critical functions

3. Use Case Sketches

Clear Windscreen of Rain

Primary Scenario

It starts to rain. The windscreen is wiped regularly until the rain stops.

Clear Windscreen of Drizzle

Primary Scenario

It starts to rain lightly. The windscreen is wiped intermittently until the rain stops.

Alternative Path

It starts to rain very lightly. The driver commands the windscreen to be cleared of drizzle.

The windscreen is wiped intermittently.

The drizzle stops. The driver cancels the command to clear the windscreen of drizzle.

Clear Windscreen of Mud Splash

Primary Scenario

The car drives through a puddle or goes past a dirty truck. Muddy water splashes on to the windscreen. The driver commands the windscreen to be cleared of mud splash.

The windscreen is simultaneously washed and wiped five times.

Maintain Windscreen Cleaning Subsystem

Primary Scenario

The mechanic refills the WCS with correctly diluted windscreen washing fluid.

The mechanic connects the WCS test equipment and commands a test.

The WCS test equipment commands a sequence of tests (Clear Mud Splash, Clear Drizzle, Clear Rain). The mechanic observes the test operation.

4. Exceptions

Clear Windscreen of Rain

Exceptions:

Wiping fails to start in rain: The driver commands the windscreen to be cleared of rain.

Clear Windscreen of Drizzle

Exceptions:

Wiping fails to start in drizzle: the driver commands the windscreen to be cleared of drizzle. The windscreen is wiped intermittently. The drizzle stops. The driver cancels the command to clear the windscreen of drizzle.

Maintain Windscreen Cleaning Subsystem

Exceptions:

WCS test equipment reports a fault: Mechanic reads the fault report and cleans, replaces, or fastens the affected components as necessary. Mechanic reruns the automated test sequence.

Mechanic observes a fault: Mechanic cleans, replaces, or fastens the affected components as necessary. Mechanic reruns the automated test sequence.

Did you think of other exceptions?—good. There are many other possibilities.

5. NFRs

Interfaces

Incoming

NFR-1: 12 Volt nominal DC power supply
NFR-2: Driver commands on CAN bus

Outgoing

NFR-3: Fault Message to Fault Handler on CAN bus

Physical Connectors

NFR-4: 12 V DC 2-pin power connector
NFR-5: CAN bus connector

Usage Qualities

Reliability

NFR-6: The WCS shall fail less than once per 10,000 hours of operation.

Maintainability

NFR-7: The WCS shall be composed entirely of Line Replaceable Units (LRUs).
NFR-8: A trained mechanic shall be able to replace any WCS LRU within 5 minutes.

Supportability & Integrated Logistic Support

NFR-9: The WCS test equipment shall enable 1st-level diagnosis to the affected LRU.
NFR-10: The packaging of each WCS LRU shall be bar-coded with its manufacturer's ID and manufacturer's part number.

Safety

Note: windscreen visibility is safety-related but must remain the responsibility of the driver. A caution to this effect is needed in the Driver's Manual.

Self-Diagnosability

NFR-11: The WCS shall be able to report pump failure.
NFR-12: The WCS shall be able to report washing fluid pipe blockage.

Commonality / Interoperability

NFR-13: The same WCS shall be used on the saloon, cabriolet, and estate versions.
Did you think of other qualities?—well done. There are many other possibilities.

Upgradability

NFR-14: The WCS control functionality shall be upgradable by replacement of a single Control Unit.*(Note: this will be in an LRU)*

Toxicity & Disposability

NFR-15: The WCS shall comply with Standard 123-456-789 Use of Toxic Materials.

Storage & Shelf Life

NFR-16: WCS parts, stored without washing fluid, shall have a shelf life of at least 5 years.

6. Test Approach Sketch

Rain Test
Stress (continuous heavy rain) Test
Drizzle Test
Drizzle (manual start) Test
The rain and drizzle tests call for a Rain/Drizzle generator capable of working continuously for 24 hours.

Mud Splash Test

The Splash Test requires a test area that can tolerate hundreds of litres of muddy water.

Fault Diagnosis (standard Test Equipment) Test

The Diagnosis test requires a test car and a standard garage-issue WCS Test Equipment.

Rough Track (vibration, mud splash) Test

The Rough Track Test requires use of a test car on a vibration / mud splash test track.

Icing Test

The Icing Test requires a refrigerated test room.

GLOSSARY

Glossary writers generally try to produce a single, complete, consistent, and universally-acceptable set of definitions of terms for their books' domains. In the case of scenarios, this isn't possible as key terms are frequently used in different ways. Indeed, one of the aims of this book is to explore the range of uses of scenarios, and that inevitably means that the word has multiple meanings. So, instead, this glossary tries to point out where words are slippery, where they overlap, and how they are typically used—with synonyms and examples where necessary. Defined terms are indicated in **Boldface**.

Actor: UML term for **Role**. Note that officially the term does not imply either human agency or an individual agent. Human Actors are **Operators**. 'Role' is preferable to 'Actor' for discussions with **Stakeholders**.

Agile Methods: Software development approaches that emphasise user involvement and rapid iteration. *See also* **User Story**.

Alternative Course (Path, Scenario, Branch): Sequence of **Steps** that branches off from a **Normal Course** in a **Use Case**; typically represents the handling of an Exception. *Note that* 'Alternative' is ambiguous, meaning either **Exception** or **Variation**.

Alternative World: (= **Situation, Snapshot**) A **Scenario** that describes a more or less static picture of an imagined future situation, often parameterised in a **Simulation** model to explore and compare system options.

Atomic: (Something, e.g. a requirement) that cannot be cut up or sub-divided.

Black-Box Test: A **Test (Case)** that does not make use of knowledge of the construction of a **System** (*compare* **White-Box Test**).

Business Event: **Event** that is significant at the business level, i.e. in the world, as opposed to some (sub)system level. For example, arrival of a sales order, rather than a key-click.

Business Use Case: **Use Case** describing **Goals** and **Events** at the business level, that is, in a way that defines the work to be done without reference to the system to be built. *Compare* **System Use Case**.

Collaborative (Method, Workshop): A style of development that involves a group of **Stakeholders** as well as developers. Collaborative methods are usually iterative and are based on **Scenarios** or other shared artefacts (**Requirements**, prototypes...) that the whole team understands.
A collaborative **Workshop** implies facilitation (Gottesdiener).

Concept of Operations : *See* **Operational Concept**

Condition: a) Something that must be true before a **Scenario** can begin (a **Pre-condition** [Cockburn], Assumption [REVEAL]). Includes as a special case **Trigger** conditions.
b) Something that is **Required** to become true when a scenario has completed (a **Post-condition**), whether with success (Success Guarantees [Cockburn]) or failure (Failure Conditions [REVEAL], Minimal Guarantees [Cockburn]).

Constraint: A **Requirement** that imposes a limit on a development project, e.g. its overall budget and timescale.
A Requirement that imposes a limit on a product's design or construction, for example the non-use of toxic materials, the selection of programming languages, compliance with an existing interface design or communications protocol. *Compare* **Non-Functional Requirement**.

Contextual Design: A full customer-centred design process for system and product design, providing explicit steps and deliverables from initial discovery through system specification (Karen Holtzblatt).

Scenarios, Stories, Use Cases: Through the Systems Development Life-Cycle.   Edited by Ian F Alexander and Neil Maiden
© 2004 John Wiley & Sons, Ltd.   ISBN: 0-470-86194-0

Contextual Inquiry: Iterative ethnographic technique for obtaining reliable knowledge about what people do and what they care about, within **Contextual Design**.

Course (of Events):   A **Sequence** of **Steps** forming a part of a **Use Case**; that is a partial **Scenario**. **See also Normal Course**, **Alternative Course**, **Exception Course**.

CRC (card):   Class- Responsibility-Collaborator definition, traditionally on a white index card, describing the expected behaviour of a software object. Adapted by Kent Beck to capture **User Stories**.

Domain (Knowledge):   The part of the world in which the **System** operates, for example, railway, insurance, or banking. Knowledge of the domain is often tacit—skilled people know more than they can tell. Statements about a domain are complementary to **Requirements**, providing context—statements that are always true, whereas requirements are statements that will have to be made to come true by the behaviour of the system. Requirements that contradict truths about the domain (e.g. Newton's laws of motion) are not **valid**.

Elicitation: The discovery, gathering, or 'capture' of **Requirements**, often by developing **Scenarios**. *See also* **Validation**.

Embedded System: A **System** that controls its own behaviour in real time by using software that it contains (often in ROM chips, etc.).

Event: Discrete change (in the World for a **Business Event**, or in a **System** for a System Event) occurring in time. Significant Events trigger **Event Responses** in the form of **Scenarios**, **Exception Scenarios**, or entire **Use Cases**. *See also* **Business Event**, **Exception**.
Note the ambiguity of grammatical mood: in the *indicative*, we describe things that just happen as events; in the *optative*, we specify things we require to be made to happen, as actions. Scenarios can be either descriptions or specifications. For example, when we say '. . . course of events' we may accidentally imply that the scenario just happens.

Event Response: **Scenario** or partial scenario (**Course**) that deals with an **Event**. In event-driven approaches, the response to an incoming event may combine with one or more needed event-generating scenarios for outgoing events to form a complete end-to-end scenario.

Exception: Undesired **Event** that disturbs progress towards a **Goal**. In a **Use Case**, Exception Events are handled by **Exception Courses** (**Alternative Courses**).
"[Business process] exceptions are not 'errors' as they would be in a computer program; they are important—often business critical—variants on the use cases" (Ian Graham)

Exception Course (Path, Scenario, Branch):   Branches from the Normal (Main, Primary, Success) **Course**; such branches are weakly called **Alternative Courses** by software people, but are perhaps more naturally called Exception Paths by system people.

Feature: Item of **System** behaviour or structure used as a shorthand for a set of related **Requirements**. Often corresponds to a subsystem, for example 'antilock braking'.

Feature Interaction: Undesired and often unpredicted side-effects when two **Features** are included in a **System**.

Functional: (**Goal** or **Requirement**) that describes a desired result from a business process or **System**. **Scenarios** typically describe sequences of such functional results.

Goal: The effect that a Scenario is desired to have, typically by a primary **Role/Actor**. **Use Case** titles should be **Functional** goals, e.g. (To) Order a Chequebook. Goals can also be modelled separately; **UML** provides a 'target' icon to which use cases can be linked; **i*** (and the related GRL) provides a rich notation for hard and soft (i.e. **Non-Functional**) goals held by different agents.

Guarantee: *see* **Condition**.

i*:   **Goal** modelling language (from University of Toronto) that distinguishes hard and soft goals held by different agents, and represents items such as tasks as well as relationships between goals and these items. The implied approach with a network of simultaneously held AND/OR-related goals is non-procedural (i.e. it is a complement to time-based **Scenario** modelling).

Live Sequence Chart: An extended kind of **Sequence Chart** introduced by David Harel and Werner Damm (*see* Chapter 1), enabling behaviour to be specified unambiguously in graphical form, for example, whether an action is optional or mandatory. The notation is highly analytic and unsuitable for stakeholders, but it permits **Simulation**.

Misuse Case: **Negative Scenario** represented analogously to a **Use Case** with a hostile **Role/Actor**, a threatening **Goal** and possibly a brief sequence of **Events**. Other details are usually not needed.
In a Misuse Case Model (*see* Chapter 7), each misuse case *threatens* one or more use cases, and there should be at least one use case that *mitigates* it (the italicised relationships being drawn as arrows on the use case diagram).

Negative Scenario: **Scenario** desired not to happen by system owners and other stakeholders; possibly documented in **Misuse Cases**, and resolved by a mitigating **Use Case** or **Exception**-handling scenario.

Non-Functional: (**Goal** or **Requirement**) that describes a desired quality such as safety, security, reliability, and so on, *in contrast to* a **Functional** goal or requirement.
Sometimes used to include **Constraints** as well as qualities.

Normal Course: The (main, primary, 'happy day', or success) **Course** forming the trunk of a **Use Case**, from which all other Courses branch off. *See also* **Alternative Course**, **Exception Course**.

Object-Oriented Analysis and Design (OOAD): An approach to software **System** development centred on conceptual objects (which will be represented as active software structures containing both code and data), contrasted with older approaches centred on either system data or system functions. Functions delivered to users are represented as **Use Cases**.

Operational Concept: (= Concept of Operations) A set of **Scenarios** describing in more or less design-independent terms how a (typically large, military) **System** is expected to be used in practice. Such a document typically precedes the writing of **Requirements**. *See also* **Schedule of Manoeuvre**.

Operator: Person, part of a **System**, who operates the machine part of the System via (any subset of) its controls and displays. For example a driver operates a car, but so does a mechanic who views diagnostics and sends signals to the control boxes, and so on. The Operator is part of the System because it would not function otherwise. *See also* **User**, **Stakeholder**.

Path: A complete sequence of actions (a **Scenario**) representing one way through a **Use Case**. When Use Cases have several **Variations** and **Exceptions**, the number of Paths increases combinatorially (*See* Chapter 14, Figure 2).

Playthrough: (= **Roleplay**) The process of acting out a **Scenario** in a **Workshop**. Participants take on human and machine **Roles**
a) in a dramatic, playful, or humorous Scene, with "an element of fun or silliness" to bring it to life and encourage **Stakeholders** to suggest changes and additional requirements. (*See* Chapter 3)
b) in 'play-reading' style in which seated participants, for example, throw a soft ball to indicate the flow of actions in a **Scenario**, while saying what they are doing, for example, 'I'm the Customer and I'm pressing the "Request Statement" button now'. (*See* Chapter 5).
Playthroughs are effective for getting Stakeholders involved, checking Scenarios and exploring **Exceptions** and **Negative Scenarios**. Players might use props such as flipcharts or other simple **Prototypes**. *Compare* **Walkthrough**.

Pre-Condition, Post-Condition: *see* **Condition**.

Prototype: An early form of a **System** constructed of any materials (wood, clay, paper, software, etc) to illustrate any aspect (user interface, size, shape, market acceptability, behaviour, etc) to **Stakeholders**. Software Prototypes that exhibit actual behaviour may be useful in **Simulating** performance by stepping through **Scenarios**. Almost any Prototype can be used in an acted-out **Scene** to help identify **Requirements** and **Exceptions**.

Requirement: A statement that a **System** is to satisfy, whether
a) by providing a desired **Functional** result such as may be delivered by a **Scenario** or **Scenario Step**;
b) by having a desired quality such as a given measure of performance or reliability (a **Non-Functional Requirement** or '-ility');
c) satisfying some external **Constraint** such as an interface definition or a physical size, power consumption, and so on.

Role: a) (System Role): a class of **Stakeholders**, possibly but not necessarily a Scenario Role (*see* (b)). For example, a Maintenance Operator appears in some Scenarios (those dealing with system maintenance), but a Financial Beneficiary, while having a stake in the System, does not play a part in any operational Scenario.
b) (Scenario Role, **Actor**): a class of agents responsible for initiating, and often also carrying out, a **Scenario** or Use Case. Roles are often but not always fulfilled by human **Operators**; subsystem-level Use Cases will have most Roles

played by other sub-systems (possibly modelled as Objects). Role responsibility demands sufficient active 'intelligence' to make all necessary decisions; a Role cannot be played by a purely passive device or component.

Roleplay: *see* **Playthrough.**

Rational Unified Process (RUP): An industry-standard model of the software development life cycle, favouring **Object-Oriented Analysis and Design.** It makes use of **Scenarios** in the form of **UML Use Cases.**

Scenario: Primary sense of Scenario used in this book is a **Script** or "**Sequence** of **Steps** that defines a task performed to achieve an intent" (Karen Holtzblatt). This is typically stated in generalized abstract terms, so that a documented scenario is effectively a class, covering any number of concrete instances. For example, 'Withdraw Cash' generalises from concrete scenarios like 'Anna Hussein withdraws $100 on Main St on Jan 1st in driving rain', and so on. "A Scenario describes the **System**'s behavior as a unique flow of interactions taking place under given conditions with its users who try to achieve their **Goal. Alternative Scenarios** describe different ways to achieve the same goal. Whether with a normal ending or exceptional, Alternative scenarios should be described separately" (Camille Salinesi; *see also his definition of* **Use Case**).

A **Use Case** represents several such sequences (courses of events), condensed into a branching tree with allowed **Variations** and **Exceptions**; hence from a Use Case perspective, a Scenario is a **Path** through a Use Case. *See also* **Goal.**

Other types of Scenario including **Stories** and **Alternative Worlds** are defined in Chapters 1 and 2, and discussed throughout the book.

Scenario Step: *see* **Step.**

Scene: *see* **Playthrough.**

Schedule of Manoeuvre: A military **Scenario** defining how a mission or goal is to be achieved by the forces under command. It is written as a **Script,** usually accompanied by a sequence of maps. It typically includes a **Synchronisation Matrix,** and an analysis of likely **Negative Scenarios** in the form of enemy actions, with planned counter-measures should these occur. It thus combines textual, graphical, and time-based scenario presentations.

Script: A **Sequence** of **Steps** (i.e. a **Scenario** in our primary sense) described in text, interpreted procedurally to mean '(you are expected to) do this,

then do that, . . . ' as defined by Roger Schank (e.g. his customer-in-restaurant script).

A **Test Case** is a Script in this sense, but note that "test script" generally means specifically an automatically executable scenario.

Scripted Sequence Diagram: An analytic representation of a **Scenario,** using a UML **Sequence Diagram,** typically with a pair of timelines for a human **Actor** and the **System** under design. Such a diagram is a suitable first step to designing a system to realise (part of) a **System Use Case.** The system timeline's activities are connected by incoming stimuli and outgoing responses to the actor's timeline. Each such round-trip **Transaction** is annotated with the text from one or more **Steps** of the System Use Case. (*see* Chapter 12 by Peter Haumer). *Compare* **Swimlanes Diagram.**

Sequence: A simple (straight-line) list of items ordered by time, possibly numbered. Where the items are **Steps** the sequence represents a **Scenario,** or a **Course** of **Events.**

Sequence Diagram: An analytic UML **Scenario** notation with a timeline for each **Actor.** Activities are shown as unlabelled boxes on timelines. Messages are shown as labelled arrows between timelines. Other symbols can be added. The notation does not indicate whether paths are optional and is thus not in itself suitable for example, a **Walkthrough** of **Scenarios** with **Stakeholders** (a flowchart with **Swimlanes** is better), *but see* **Live Sequence Chart.**

Simulation: A concrete representation of a **Scenario,** playing it out repeatedly on a machine of some kind—now almost always a digital computer, sometimes with specialised user interface hardware (e.g. to **Prototype** a cockpit or control room).

Situation: *see* **Alternative World.**

Snapshot: *see* **Alternative World.**

Stakeholder: An individual or an organisation having a legitimate interest in a system, including possibly a negative interest. Stakeholders include both system Operators (*see* **Actor, Role**) and a range of less directly involved classes of people such as functional, political and financial beneficiaries, regulators, purchasers, owners of interfacing systems, developers, and so on.

Step: An action or **Event** representing an atomic component of a **Scenario.** In a **Use Case,** each Step is normally described in a separate paragraph of text; in a **Storyboard**, an image.

Stimulus: *see* **Trigger**.

Story: A text that narrates a **Scenario**, possibly with little or no formal structure.

Storyboard: A sequence of diagrams or other images that narrates a **Scenario**. Each such image or frame represents a **Step**.

Synchronisation Matrix: A table whose rows are for military units or **Roles**, and whose columns are for a sequence of time-periods (not necessarily of equal length). The cells in the matrix describe activities to be carried out by each unit or role at the stated time; hence, the matrix as a whole defines a many-threaded **Scenario**. The Synchronisation Matrix is the textual/tabular equivalent of a **Swimlanes Diagram**. It is the analytic part of a **Schedule of Manoeuvre**.

System: A set of interacting components that together provide behaviours not provided by any of the components alone. For example, powered flight can be provided by an aircraft, that is, a socio-technical system of {pilot, airframe, motor, avionics, flight rules}. Systems can act as components for larger systems, for example, a train is part of a railway line, which is part of a railway network, which is part of a transport network. Hence, 'system' is relative to the context and scope, which must be stated.
The **RUP** definition (see chapter 12) is: "A *system*, which may contain hardware (computational and non-computational), software and human workers, delivers some needed operational capability to its users. A system is composed of sub-systems, which collaborate to yield the behaviour and characteristics of the system."
See also **Operator**, **User**.

Swimlanes Diagram: A diagram such as a flowchart or UML activity diagram, arranged with a 'swimming pool lane' usually vertically down the page for each **Role**, showing a **Use Case** with both the actions of each Role (including decisions) and interactions between Roles over time. Both concurrency (actions in parallel) and alternatives can be shown. One of the few analytic formats suitable for validation by **Stakeholders**. *Compare* **Scripted Sequence Diagram**.

System Use Case: **Use Case** describing **Goals** and **Events** at a system level, that is, in a way that defines activities to be carried out by the system to be built. This is close to the original meaning of Use Case. *Compare* **Business Use Case**.

Template: A more or less generally agreed and standardised structure or pattern for a (component of a) document, such as a **Use Case**.

Test Case: A **Test Case Scenario** used to test repeatedly whether a **System** meets its **Requirements**, annotated with preconditions to make it into a reliable **Verification** procedure. A **Use Case** that contains branches (**Exceptions**, **Alternatives**) requires several overlapping Test Cases to provide complete or even reasonable coverage. *See also* **Test Case Class**.

Test Case Class: A set of **Test Cases**, sharing the same **Test Case Scenario**, but differing in their environmental conditions. For example, the '*Clear the Windscreen*' Test Case Class may consist of '*Press the Wipe switch; Wiper clears the screen*'; but Test Cases may include conditions such as heavy rain, rain + wind, snow, and so on.

Test Case Scenario: A deterministic **Scenario**, generally a single thread of actions, each described as a brief textual command (e.g. '*Log in to the database*'), forming the body of a **Test Case**. Test Case Scenarios may be translated into automatically-executable **Test Scripts**.

Test Script: An executable **Scenario** based on a **Test Case** with a specific set of preconditions. Test Scripts are often fully automated.

Test Step: One of the sequences of steps composing a **Test Case**.

Transaction: A **Scenario** involving at least two **Roles**, one often human, and consisting of a stimulus-response cycle or round-trip between these roles. For example, a human requests a balance statement from a bank, and the bank supplies the statement. In practice, Scenarios often contain a series of Transactions—*see* **Scripted Sequence Diagram**.

Trigger (condition): **Event** such as a human action that causes a **Scenario** to begin. Triggers [Cockburn] are a subclass of pre-**Conditions**. Also called 'Stimuli' (the singular is 'Stimulus') [REVEAL].

Unhappy Scenario: *See* **Negative Scenario**.

Unified Modeling Language (UML): Set of notations for **Use Case** Models, Sequence Diagrams, and Activity Diagrams (all of which are representations of **Scenarios**) and various **OOAD** diagram types. *See also* **RUP**.

Use Case: The **Scenario** format used in UML, consisting of an **Actor**, a **Goal**, and a text which is typically a detailed structure, for example, in Alistair Cockburn's "Fully-Dressed" style, allowing for a set of related scenarios (**Courses**, **Sequences**) of the Use Case, depending on **Events**. There is no universally agreed definition or structure of Use Case.
"A Use Case is composed of a collection of Scenarios describing: (i) alternative ways of achieving a goal, (ii) unwanted endings, and (iii) the reaction to potential exceptions that could arise at different times during otherwise normal scenarios" (Camille Salinesi, see Chapter 8).
See also **Business Use Case, System Use Case**.

User: A **Stakeholder** who plays a hybrid **Role**, as both an **Operator** and a **Functional Beneficiary** of a product; for example, a person operating the controls of and listening to the music played by a hand-held device.

User Story: A **Scenario** format used in some **Agile Methods** (see Chapter 13), consisting of a brief and often informal narrative text (a **Story**) that typically mentions an **Actor** and the actor's **Goal**, with a description, possibly by example, of how the goal can be achieved.

Validation: Showing that a **System**'s **Requirements** make sense in the **Domain**, that is, that they are indeed what **Stakeholders** want, that they are realistic (e.g. can be afforded, do not contradict laws of nature) and consistent with domain constraints (e.g. existing interfaces and protocols). Scenario **Walkthrough** is an effective means of validation.

Compare **Verification**; *note that the two terms are often interchanged or confused.*

Variation: A way of reaching a **Goal** in normal circumstances, different from the **Normal Course** (but such non-determinism is inconvenient for software). Where a Variation differs in only a few **Steps**, it is customary to document only those, and to indicate as for an **Exception Course** where it departs from and where it rejoins the Normal Course. *Compare* **Alternative Course, Exception Course**.

Verification: Showing or proving that a **System**'s implementation conforms to its **Requirements**. **Test** is the most common means of verification. *Compare* **Validation**.

Walkthrough: A meeting in which **Stakeholders** step through **Scenarios** to discover errors, omissions, **Exceptions**, and **Requirements**. Often run as a facilitated **Workshop**.

White-Box Test: A **Test (Case)** that makes use of knowledge of the construction of a **System** (*compare* **Black-Box Test**). With respect to the system as a whole, a user trial is white-box. With respect to sub-systems, an integration test that only makes use of the defined in and out sub-system interfaces is white-box.

Workshop: Facilitated interactive session, typically of one or a few days, in which **Stakeholders** work out **Scenarios, Requirements**, Models, or other pieces of project information, possibly acting in **Playthroughs**, running **Walkthroughs**, commenting on **Prototypes**, and so on.

INDEX

A

Abuse cases, 134
Activity diagram, 393, 395, 401, 403, 404
Actor, 8, 14, 31, 67, 68, 88, 94, 96, 119, 247, 263
  goals, 241
  key, 67
  See also Role; Stakeholders
Affinity diagram, 190
Agile, 9, 83, 266–268
  methods, 206, 207, 297, 435
  See also User stories
Air Traffic Control (ATC), 364
Alternative courses, 161–164, 166, 168, 169, 174, 364, 370, 373
  See also Use case scenarios
Alternative scenarios, 103–116, 146
  applicability, 103
  features, 104
  strengths, 104
  technique, 105
  weaknesses, 104
Alternative world, 10
  See also Situation
Alternative world scenarios, 106
Analysis, 4, 228, 249, 250, 252, 254
  bottom-up, 397
  object/action, 224
  top-down, 397
Anti-scenarios, 136
Architecturally Significant Requirements (ASR), 384, 385
Architecture Trade-off Analysis Method (ATAM), 384
ART-SCENE, 161, 166
  applicability, 161
  approach, 164
  comparisons, 176

features, 162
process and environment, 162
research, 163
software environment, 166
strengths, 162
structure and representation, 164
weaknesses, 162
worked example, 173
ASR. *See* Architecturally Significant Requirements
Assumptions, 77, 105–110, 215, 300, 365, 393, 401, 409, 411
ATHOC, 411
Attribute, 26, 219
Automatic Teller Machine (ATM), 284
Automatic Train Control (ATC), 402, 404
Automotive industry, 334
Automotive software development, 331, 334
  strengths, 330
  weaknesses, 330

B

Bayesian Belief Networks (BBNs), 176
Black-Box Test, 296
British Telecom (BT), 61
Business event, 40
  identification, 44
Business Use Cases, 40, 49
  alternative case scenario, 50
  identification, 44

C

Claims analysis, 447
Class-Responsibility-Collaborator (CRC), 278

Collaboration patterns, 90
Collaborative (or facilitated) requirements workshop, 85, 90, 99
Combining process models
  evolutionary and high risk, 319
  evolutionary and incremental, 318
  evolutionary, incremental and high risk, 322
  incremental and high risk, 321
Commercial-Off-The-Shelf (COTS), 296, 302, 473
Compliance Arguments (CA), 400
Concept of Operations. *See* Operational concept
Concept, Assessment, Demonstration, Manufacture, In-service, and Disposal (CADMID), 312
Conceptual Design (CD), 222, 229, 448
Conceptual scenarios, 153, 211, 215, 223, 226
Concrete scenarios, 211, 214, 215, 217, 223
Condition, 76, 146, 189, 281, 286, 289, 290, 295, 336
  pre-conditions, 61, 154, 204, 401
  trigger, 189
COnflict Resolution Assistant. *See* CORA-2
Constraints, 51, 61, 66, 68, 351, 401, 413
  cost, 329
  design, 110, 221
  economic, 387
  explicit, 157
  financial, 310
  implicit, 157

Scenarios, Stories, Use Cases: Through the Systems Development Life-Cycle. Edited by Ian F Alexander and Neil Maiden
© 2004 John Wiley & Sons, Ltd. ISBN: 0-470-86194-0

Use Case Guidelines

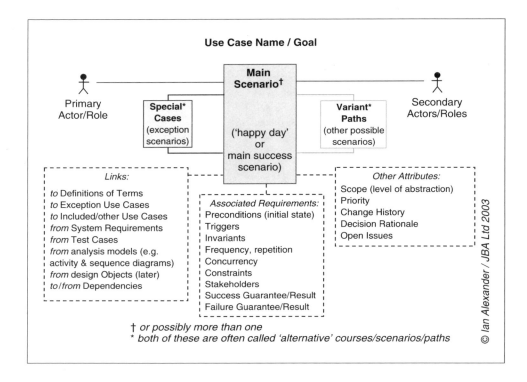

abbreviated from CREWS-L'ECRITOIRE *(see Chapter 8 for full details)*

General Guidelines

GG_1: Name each Use Case as an active goal (e.g. 'Publish a Report', 'Service the Car', 'Buy a Gift').
GG_2: Fill out a Use Case template (e.g. Templates in Appendix 1-3)—scenarios alone are not enough.
GG_3: In each Use Case, write a set of scenarios describing alternative ways to achieve the goal.
GG_4: Write all the scenarios of a Use Case in consistent terminology, style, and content.
GG_5: Validate your Use Cases with a checklist (e.g. these guidelines).

Style Guidelines

Style of scenario interactions:

SG_1: Describe scenario interactions in action clauses, e.g. 'The cook puts the prepared pizza into the oven.'
SG_2: Do not include circumstances, e.g. 'in the morning', 'at the office', 'quickly'.
SG_3: Describe what should occur; avoid negation (e.g. 'not', 'never') and modal verbs (e.g. 'could', 'may').

Style of scenario flows of actions:

SG_4: Describe sequences of interactions to tell a story; avoid flashbacks and forward references.
SG_5: Make explicit when repetitions and concurrency are needed.
SG_6: Avoid describing alternatives (e.g. 'if', 'else') within a scenario—describe alternatives separately.